Chevrolet Lumina Monte Carlo
& Front-wheel Drive
Impala
Automotive
Repair
Manual

**by Jeff Kibler, Jay Storer
and John H Haynes**

Member of the Guild of Motoring Writers

Models covered:
All Chevrolet Lumina, Monte Carlo and
Front-wheel Drive Impala models
1995 through 2005

(3M10 - 24048)

ABCDE
FGHIJ
K

2

Haynes Publishing Group
Sparkford Nr Yeovil
Somerset BA22 7JJ England

Haynes North America, Inc
861 Lawrence Drive
Newbury Park
California 91320 USA

About this manual

Its purpose

The purpose of this manual is to help you get the best value from your vehicle. It can do so in several ways. It can help you decide what work must be done, even if you choose to have it done by a dealer service department or a repair shop; it provides information and procedures for routine maintenance and servicing; and it offers diagnostic and repair procedures to follow when trouble occurs.

We hope you use the manual to tackle the work yourself. For many simpler jobs, doing it yourself may be quicker than arranging an appointment to get the vehicle into a shop and making the trips to leave it and pick it up. More importantly, a lot of money can be saved by avoiding the expense the shop must pass on to you to cover its labor and overhead costs. An added benefit is the sense of satisfaction and accomplishment that you feel after doing the job yourself.

Using the manual

The manual is divided into Chapters. Each Chapter is divided into numbered Sections, which are headed in bold type between horizontal lines. Each Section consists of consecutively numbered paragraphs.

At the beginning of each numbered Section you will be referred to any illustrations which apply to the procedures in that Section. The reference numbers used in illustration captions pinpoint the pertinent Section and the Step within that Section. That is, illustration 3.2 means the illustration refers to Section 3 and Step (or paragraph) 2 within that Section.

Procedures, once described in the text, are not normally repeated. When it's necessary to refer to another Chapter, the reference will be given as Chapter and Section number. Cross references given without use of the word "Chapter" apply to Sections and/or paragraphs in the same Chapter. For example, "see Section 8" means in the same Chapter.

References to the left or right side of the vehicle assume you are sitting in the driver's seat, facing forward.

Even though we have prepared this manual with extreme care, neither the publisher nor the author can accept responsibility for any errors in, or omissions from, the information given.

NOTE

A **Note** provides information necessary to properly complete a procedure or information which will make the procedure easier to understand.

CAUTION

A **Caution** provides a special procedure or special steps which must be taken while completing the procedure where the Caution is found. Not heeding a Caution can result in damage to the assembly being worked on.

WARNING

A **Warning** provides a special procedure or special steps which must be taken while completing the procedure where the Warning is found. Not heeding a Warning can result in personal injury.

Acknowledgements

Wiring diagrams provided exclusively for Haynes North America, Inc. by Valley Forge Technical Communications.

© **Haynes North America, Inc. 1998, 1999, 2000, 2001, 2005, 2006**

With permission from J.H. Haynes & Co. Ltd.

A book in the Haynes Automotive Repair Manual Series

Printed in the U.S.A.

ISBN-13: 978-1-56392-632-7
ISBN-10: 1-56392-632-6

Library of Congress Control Number: 2006928003

Contents

Haynes photographer, mechanic and author with 1997 Chevrolet Monte Carlo

Introduction to the Chevrolet Lumina, Monte Carlo and front-wheel drive Impala

The models covered by this manual are available in two and four-door sedan body styles.

Engines used in these vehicles include the 3.1 and 3.4 liter OHV, 3.4 liter DOHC and a 3.8 liter (3800) V6 engine. All models are equipped with Multi-port fuel injection (MPFI). 1996 and later models are equipped with the On Board Diagnostic Second Generation (OBDII) computerized engine management system that controls virtually every aspect of engine operation. OBDII is designed to keep the emissions system operating at the federally specified level for the life of the vehicle. OBDII monitors emissions system components for signs of degradation and engine operation for any malfunction that could affect emissions, turning on the Service Engine Soon light if any faults are detected.

The transversely mounted engine transmits power to the front wheels through an electronically controlled four-speed automatic transaxle via independent driveaxles.

Suspension is independent in the front, utilizing coil springs with struts and lower control arms to locate the knuckle assembly at each wheel. The rear suspension features strut/coil spring assemblies, trailing arms and lateral link rods.

The rack-and-pinion steering unit is mounted behind the engine with power-assist as standard equipment.

The brakes are disc at the front and disc or drums at the rear, with power assist standard. An Anti-lock Braking System (ABS) is standard on most models.

VIN engine and model year codes

Two particularly important pieces of information found in the VIN are the engine code and the model year code. Counting from the left, the engine code letter designation is the 8th digit and the model year code letter or number designation is the 10th digit.

On the models covered by this manual the engine codes are:

M .... 3.1L OHV V6
E .... 3.4L OHV V6
X 3.4L DOHCV6
K 3.8L (3800) V6

On the models covered by this manual the model year codes are:

S 1995
T 1996
V 1997
W 1998
X 1999
Y 2000
1 2001
2 2002
3 2003
4 2004
5 2005

Engine identification numbers

The engine identification number(s) are found on a pad on the left side of engine block by the transmission bellhousing **(see illustration)**.

Automatic transaxle identification number

The transaxle ID number on 3T40 models is stamped into the top of the casting by the shift lever **(see illustration)**. The transaxle ID number on 4T60-E and 4T65-E models is stamped onto a plate that is riveted to the right rear corner of the transaxle housing.

Vehicle Emissions Control Information label

This label is found in the engine compartment. See Chapter 6 for more information on this label.

The Vehicle Identification Number (VIN) is visible through the driver's side of the windshield

V6 engine identification number locations

A   Engine ID number   B   VIN number

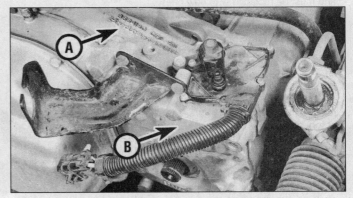

Transaxle identification number locations

A   VIN number   B   Transaxle ID number

Buying parts

Replacement parts are available from many sources, which generally fall into one of two categories - authorized dealer parts departments and independent retail auto parts stores. Our advice concerning these parts is as follows:

Retail auto parts stores: Good auto parts stores will stock frequently needed components which wear out relatively fast, such as clutch components, exhaust systems, brake parts, tune-up parts, etc. These stores often supply new or reconditioned parts on an exchange basis, which can save a considerable amount of money. Discount auto parts stores are often very good places to buy materials and parts needed for general vehicle maintenance such as oil, grease, filters, spark plugs, belts, touch-up paint, bulbs, etc. They also usually sell tools and general accessories, have convenient hours, charge lower prices and can often be found not far from home.

Authorized dealer parts department: This is the best source for parts which are unique to the vehicle and not generally available elsewhere (such as major engine parts, transmission parts, trim pieces, etc.).

Warranty information: If the vehicle is still covered under warranty, be sure that any replacement parts purchased - regardless of the source - do not invalidate the warranty!

To be sure of obtaining the correct parts, have engine and chassis numbers available and, if possible, take the old parts along for positive identification.

Maintenance techniques, tools and working facilities

Maintenance techniques

There are a number of techniques involved in maintenance and repair that will be referred to throughout this manual. Application of these techniques will enable the home mechanic to be more efficient, better organized and capable of performing the various tasks properly, which will ensure that the repair job is thorough and complete.

Fasteners

Fasteners are nuts, bolts, studs and screws used to hold two or more parts together. There are a few things to keep in mind when working with fasteners. Almost all of them use a locking device of some type, either a lockwasher, locknut, locking tab or thread adhesive. All threaded fasteners should be clean and straight, with undamaged threads and undamaged corners on the hex head where the wrench fits. Develop the habit of replacing all damaged nuts and bolts with new ones. Special locknuts with nylon or fiber inserts can only be used once. If they are removed, they lose their locking ability and must be replaced with new ones.

Rusted nuts and bolts should be treated with a penetrating fluid to ease removal and prevent breakage. Some mechanics use turpentine in a spout-type oil can, which works quite well. After applying the rust penetrant, let it work for a few minutes before trying to loosen the nut or bolt. Badly rusted fasteners may have to be chiseled or sawed off or removed with a special nut breaker, available at tool stores.

If a bolt or stud breaks off in an assembly, it can be drilled and removed with a special tool commonly available for this purpose. Most automotive machine shops can perform this task, as well as other repair procedures, such as the repair of threaded holes that have been stripped out.

Flat washers and lockwashers, when removed from an assembly, should always be replaced exactly as removed. Replace any damaged washers with new ones. Never use a lockwasher on any soft metal surface (such as aluminum), thin sheet metal or plastic.

Fastener sizes

For a number of reasons, automobile manufacturers are making wider and wider use of metric fasteners. Therefore, it is important to be able to tell the difference between standard (sometimes called U.S. or SAE) and metric hardware, since they cannot be interchanged.

All bolts, whether standard or metric, are sized according to diameter, thread pitch and length. For example, a standard 1/2 - 13 x 1 bolt is 1/2 inch in diameter, has 13 threads per inch and is 1 inch long. An M12 - 1.75 x 25 metric bolt is 12 mm in diameter, has a thread pitch of 1.75 mm (the distance between threads) and is 25 mm long. The two bolts are nearly identical, and easily confused, but they are not interchangeable.

In addition to the differences in diameter, thread pitch and length, metric and standard bolts can also be distinguished by examining the bolt heads. To begin with, the distance across the flats on a standard bolt head is measured in inches, while the same dimension on a metric bolt is sized in millimeters (the same is true for nuts). As a result, a standard wrench should not be used on a metric bolt and a metric wrench should not be used on a standard bolt. Also, most standard bolts have slashes radiating out from the center of the head to denote the grade or strength of the bolt, which is an indication of the amount of torque that can be applied to it. The greater the number of slashes, the greater the strength of the bolt. Grades 0 through 5 are commonly used on automobiles. Metric bolts have a property class (grade) number, rather than a slash, molded into their heads to indicate bolt strength. In this case, the higher the number, the stronger the bolt. Property class numbers 8.8, 9.8 and 10.9 are commonly used on automobiles.

Strength markings can also be used to distinguish standard hex nuts from metric hex nuts. Many standard nuts have dots stamped into one side, while metric nuts are marked with a number. The greater the number of dots, or the higher the number, the greater the strength of the nut.

Metric studs are also marked on their ends according to property class (grade). Larger studs are numbered (the same as metric bolts), while smaller studs carry a geometric code to denote grade.

It should be noted that many fasteners, especially Grades 0 through 2, have no dis-

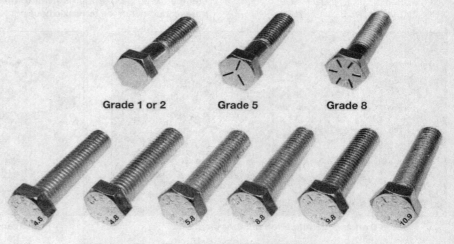

Bolt strength marking (standard/SAE/USS; bottom - metric)

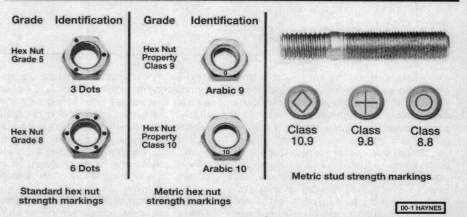

Grade	Identification	Grade	Identification
Hex Nut Grade 5	3 Dots	Hex Nut Property Class 9	Arabic 9
Hex Nut Grade 8	6 Dots	Hex Nut Property Class 10	Arabic 10

Standard hex nut strength markings

Metric hex nut strength markings

Class 10.9   Class 9.8   Class 8.8

Metric stud strength markings

tinguishing marks on them. When such is the case, the only way to determine whether it is standard or metric is to measure the thread pitch or compare it to a known fastener of the same size.

Standard fasteners are often referred to as SAE, as opposed to metric. However, it should be noted that SAE technically refers to a non-metric fine thread fastener only. Coarse thread non-metric fasteners are referred to as USS sizes.

Since fasteners of the same size (both standard and metric) may have different strength ratings, be sure to reinstall any bolts, studs or nuts removed from your vehicle in their original locations. Also, when replacing a fastener with a new one, make sure that the new one has a strength rating equal to or greater than the original.

Tightening sequences and procedures

Most threaded fasteners should be tightened to a specific torque value (torque is the twisting force applied to a threaded component such as a nut or bolt). Overtightening the fastener can weaken it and cause it to break, while undertightening can cause it to eventually come loose. Bolts, screws and studs, depending on the material they are made of and their thread diameters, have specific torque values, many of which are noted in the Specifications at the beginning of each Chapter. Be sure to follow the torque recommendations closely. For fasteners not assigned a specific torque, a general torque value chart is presented here as a guide. These torque values are for dry (unlubricated) fasteners threaded into steel or cast iron (not aluminum). As was previously mentioned, the size and grade of a fastener determine the amount of torque that can safely be applied to it. The figures listed here are approximate for Grade 2 and Grade 3 fasteners. Higher grades can tolerate higher torque values.

Fasteners laid out in a pattern, such as cylinder head bolts, oil pan bolts, differential cover bolts, etc., must be loosened or tightened in sequence to avoid warping the component. This sequence will normally be shown in the appropriate Chapter. If a specific pattern is not given, the following procedures can be used to prevent warping.

Initially, the bolts or nuts should be assembled finger-tight only. Next, they should be tightened one full turn each, in a criss-cross or diagonal pattern. After each one has been tightened one full turn, return to the first one and tighten them all one-half turn, following the same pattern. Finally, tighten each of them one-quarter turn at a time until each fastener has been tightened to the proper torque. To loosen and remove the fasteners, the procedure would be reversed.

Component disassembly

Component disassembly should be done with care and purpose to help ensure that the parts go back together properly. Always keep track of the sequence in which parts are removed. Make note of special characteristics or marks on parts that can be installed more than one way, such as a grooved thrust washer on a shaft. It is a good idea to lay the disassembled parts out on a clean surface in the order that they were removed. It may also be helpful to make sketches or take instant photos of components before removal.

When removing fasteners from a component, keep track of their locations. Sometimes threading a bolt back in a part, or putting the washers and nut back on a stud, can prevent mix-ups later. If nuts and bolts cannot be returned to their original locations, they should be kept in a compartmented box or a series of small boxes. A cupcake or muffin tin is ideal for this purpose, since each cavity can hold the bolts and nuts from a particular area (i.e. oil pan bolts, valve cover bolts, engine mount bolts, etc.). A pan of this type is especially helpful when working on assemblies with very small parts, such as the carburetor, alternator, valve train or interior dash and trim pieces. The cavities can be marked with paint or tape to identify the contents.

Whenever wiring looms, harnesses or connectors are separated, it is a good idea to identify the two halves with numbered pieces of masking tape so they can be easily reconnected.

Gasket sealing surfaces

Throughout any vehicle, gaskets are used to seal the mating surfaces between two parts and keep lubricants, fluids, vacuum or pressure contained in an assembly.

Metric thread sizes	Ft-lbs	Nm
M-6	6 to 9	9 to 12
M-8	14 to 21	19 to 28
M-10	28 to 40	38 to 54
M-12	50 to 71	68 to 96
M-14	80 to 140	109 to 154

Pipe thread sizes		
1/8	5 to 8	7 to 10
1/4	12 to 18	17 to 24
3/8	22 to 33	30 to 44
1/2	25 to 35	34 to 47

U.S. thread sizes		
1/4 - 20	6 to 9	9 to 12
5/16 - 18	12 to 18	17 to 24
5/16 - 24	14 to 20	19 to 27
3/8 - 16	22 to 32	30 to 43
3/8 - 24	27 to 38	37 to 51
7/16 - 14	40 to 55	55 to 74
7/16 - 20	40 to 60	55 to 81
1/2 - 13	55 to 80	75 to 108

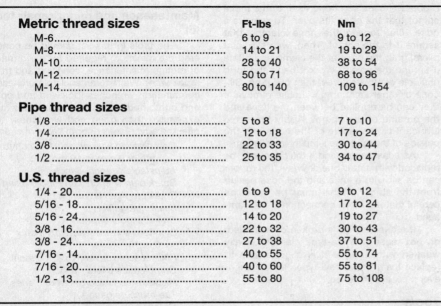

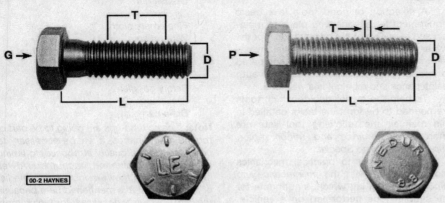

00-2 HAYNES

Standard (SAE and USS) bolt dimensions/grade marks

G   Grade marks (bolt strength)
L   Length (in inches)
T   Thread pitch (number of threads per inch)
D   Nominal diameter (in inches)

Metric bolt dimensions/grade marks

P   Property class (bolt strength)
L   Length (in millimeters)
T   Thread pitch (distance between threads in millimeters)
D   Diameter

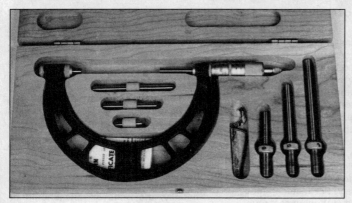

Micrometer set

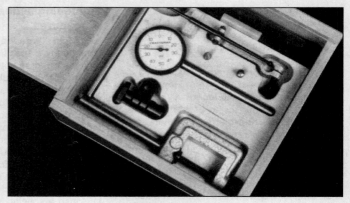

Dial indicator set

Many times these gaskets are coated with a liquid or paste-type gasket sealing compound before assembly. Age, heat and pressure can sometimes cause the two parts to stick together so tightly that they are very difficult to separate. Often, the assembly can be loosened by striking it with a soft-face hammer near the mating surfaces. A regular hammer can be used if a block of wood is placed between the hammer and the part. Do not hammer on cast parts or parts that could be easily damaged. With any particularly stubborn part, always recheck to make sure that every fastener has been removed.

Avoid using a screwdriver or bar to pry apart an assembly, as they can easily mar the gasket sealing surfaces of the parts, which must remain smooth. If prying is absolutely necessary, use an old broom handle, but keep in mind that extra clean up will be necessary if the wood splinters.

After the parts are separated, the old gasket must be carefully scraped off and the gasket surfaces cleaned. Stubborn gasket material can be soaked with rust penetrant or treated with a special chemical to soften it so it can be easily scraped off. A scraper can be fashioned from a piece of copper tubing by flattening and sharpening one end. Copper is recommended because it is usually softer than the surfaces to be scraped, which reduces the chance of gouging the part. Some gaskets can be removed with a wire brush, but regardless of the method used, the mating surfaces must be left clean and smooth. If for some reason the gasket surface is gouged, then a gasket sealer thick enough to fill scratches will have to be used during reassembly of the components. For most applications, a non-drying (or semi-drying) gasket sealer should be used.

Hose removal tips

Warning: *If the vehicle is equipped with air conditioning, do not disconnect any of the A/C hoses without first having the system depressurized by a dealer service department or a service station.*

Hose removal precautions closely parallel gasket removal precautions. Avoid scratching or gouging the surface that the hose mates against or the connection may leak. This is especially true for radiator hoses. Because of various chemical reactions, the rubber in hoses can bond itself to the metal spigot that the hose fits over. To remove a hose, first loosen the hose clamps that secure it to the spigot. Then, with slip-joint pliers, grab the hose at the clamp and rotate it around the spigot. Work it back and forth until it is completely free, then pull it off. Silicone or other lubricants will ease removal if they can be applied between the hose and the outside of the spigot. Apply the same lubricant to the inside of the hose and the outside of the spigot to simplify installation.

As a last resort (and if the hose is to be replaced with a new one anyway), the rubber can be slit with a knife and the hose peeled from the spigot. If this must be done, be careful that the metal connection is not damaged.

If a hose clamp is broken or damaged, do not reuse it. Wire-type clamps usually weaken with age, so it is a good idea to replace them with screw-type clamps whenever a hose is removed.

Tools

A selection of good tools is a basic requirement for anyone who plans to maintain and repair his or her own vehicle. For the owner who has few tools, the initial investment might seem high, but when compared to the spiraling costs of professional auto maintenance and repair, it is a wise one.

To help the owner decide which tools are needed to perform the tasks detailed in this manual, the following tool lists are offered: *Maintenance and minor repair, Repair/overhaul* and *Special*.

The newcomer to practical mechanics should start off with the *maintenance and minor repair* tool kit, which is adequate for the simpler jobs performed on a vehicle. Then, as confidence and experience grow, the owner can tackle more difficult tasks, buying additional tools as they are needed. Eventually the basic kit will be expanded into the *repair and overhaul* tool set. Over a period of time, the experienced do-it-yourselfer will assemble a tool set complete enough for most repair and overhaul procedures and will add tools from the special category when it is felt that the expense is justified by the frequency of use.

Maintenance and minor repair tool kit

The tools in this list should be considered the minimum required for performance of routine maintenance, servicing and minor repair work. We recommend the purchase of combination wrenches (box-end and open-end combined in one wrench). While more expensive than open end wrenches, they offer the advantages of both types of wrench.

Combination wrench set (1/4-inch to 1 inch or 6 mm to 19 mm)
Adjustable wrench, 8 inch
Spark plug wrench with rubber insert
Spark plug gap adjusting tool
Feeler gauge set
Brake bleeder wrench
Standard screwdriver (5/16-inch x 6 inch)
Phillips screwdriver (No. 2 x 6 inch)
Combination pliers - 6 inch
Hacksaw and assortment of blades
Tire pressure gauge
Grease gun
Oil can
Fine emery cloth
Wire brush
Battery post and cable cleaning tool
Oil filter wrench
Funnel (medium size)
Safety goggles
Jackstands (2)
Drain pan

Note: *If basic tune-ups are going to be part of routine maintenance, it will be necessary to purchase a good quality stroboscopic timing light and combination tachometer/dwell meter. Although they are included in the list of special tools, it is mentioned here because they are absolutely necessary for tuning most vehicles properly.*

Repair and overhaul tool set

These tools are essential for anyone who plans to perform major repairs and are in addition to those in the maintenance and minor repair tool kit. Included is a comprehensive set of sockets which, though expensive, are invaluable because of their versatil-

Dial caliper

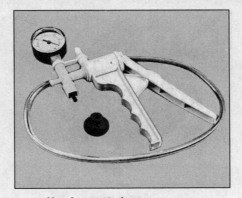

Hand-operated vacuum pump

Timing light

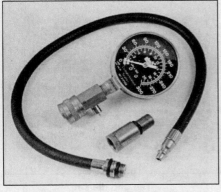

Compression gauge with spark plug hole adapter

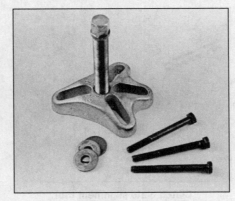

Damper/steering wheel puller

General purpose puller

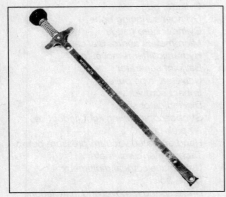

Hydraulic lifter removal tool

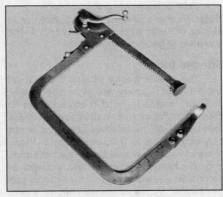

Valve spring compressor

Valve spring compressor

Ridge reamer

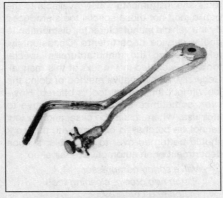

Piston ring groove cleaning tool

Ring removal/installation tool

Ring compressor

Cylinder hone

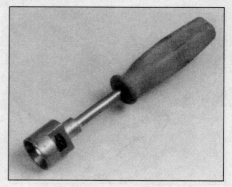

Brake hold-down spring tool

Torque angle gauge

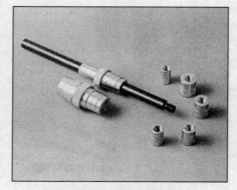

Clutch plate alignment tool

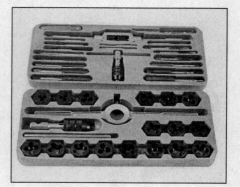

Tap and die set

ity, especially when various extensions and drives are available. We recommend the 1/2-inch drive over the 3/8-inch drive. Although the larger drive is bulky and more expensive, it has the capacity of accepting a very wide range of large sockets. Ideally, however, the mechanic should have a 3/8-inch drive set and a 1/2-inch drive set.

Socket set(s)
Reversible ratchet
Extension - 10 inch
Universal joint
Torque wrench (same size drive as
*   sockets)*
Ball peen hammer - 8 ounce
Soft-face hammer (plastic/rubber)
Standard screwdriver (1/4-inch x 6 inch)
Standard screwdriver (stubby -
*   5/16-inch)*
Phillips screwdriver (No. 3 x 8 inch)
Phillips screwdriver (stubby - No. 2)
Pliers - vise grip
Pliers - lineman's
Pliers - needle nose
Pliers - snap-ring (internal and external)
Cold chisel - 1/2-inch
Scribe
Scraper (made from flattened copper
*   tubing)*
Centerpunch
Pin punches (1/16, 1/8, 3/16-inch)
Steel rule/straightedge - 12 inch
Allen wrench set (1/8 to 3/8-inch or
*   4 mm to 10 mm)*
A selection of files
Wire brush (large)

Jackstands (second set)
Jack (scissor or hydraulic type)

Note: *Another tool which is often useful is an electric drill with a chuck capacity of 3/8-inch and a set of good quality drill bits.*

Special tools

The tools in this list include those which are not used regularly, are expensive to buy, or which need to be used in accordance with their manufacturer's instructions. Unless these tools will be used frequently, it is not very economical to purchase many of them. A consideration would be to split the cost and use between yourself and a friend or friends. In addition, most of these tools can be obtained from a tool rental shop on a temporary basis.

This list primarily contains only those tools and instruments widely available to the public, and not those special tools produced by the vehicle manufacturer for distribution to dealer service departments. Occasionally, references to the manufacturer's special tools are included in the text of this manual. Generally, an alternative method of doing the job without the special tool is offered. However, sometimes there is no alternative to their use. Where this is the case, and the tool cannot be purchased or borrowed, the work should be turned over to the dealer service department or an automotive repair shop.

Valve spring compressor
Piston ring groove cleaning tool
Piston ring compressor
Piston ring installation tool

Cylinder compression gauge
Cylinder ridge reamer
Cylinder surfacing hone
Cylinder bore gauge
Micrometers and/or dial calipers
Hydraulic lifter removal tool
Balljoint separator
Universal-type puller
Impact screwdriver
Dial indicator set
Stroboscopic timing light (inductive
*   pick-up)*
Hand operated vacuum/pressure pump
Tachometer/dwell meter
Universal electrical multimeter
Cable hoist
Brake spring removal and installation
*   tools*
Floor jack

Buying tools

For the do-it-yourselfer who is just starting to get involved in vehicle maintenance and repair, there are a number of options available when purchasing tools. If maintenance and minor repair is the extent of the work to be done, the purchase of individual tools is satisfactory. If, on the other hand, extensive work is planned, it would be a good idea to purchase a modest tool set from one of the large retail chain stores. A set can usually be bought at a substantial savings over the individual tool prices, and they often come with a tool box. As additional tools are needed, add-on sets, individual tools and a larger tool box can be purchased to expand the tool selection. Building a tool set gradually allows the cost of the tools to be spread over a longer period of time and gives the mechanic the freedom to choose only those tools that will actually be used.

Tool stores will often be the only source of some of the special tools that are needed, but regardless of where tools are bought, try to avoid cheap ones, especially when buying screwdrivers and sockets, because they won't last very long. The expense involved in replacing cheap tools will eventually be greater than the initial cost of quality tools.

Care and maintenance of tools

Good tools are expensive, so it makes sense to treat them with respect. Keep them clean and in usable condition and store them properly when not in use. Always wipe off any dirt, grease or metal chips before putting them away. Never leave tools lying around in the work area. Upon completion of a job, always check closely under the hood for tools that may have been left there so they won't get lost during a test drive.

Some tools, such as screwdrivers, pliers, wrenches and sockets, can be hung on a panel mounted on the garage or workshop wall, while others should be kept in a tool box or tray. Measuring instruments, gauges, meters, etc. must be carefully stored where they cannot be damaged by weather or impact from other tools.

When tools are used with care and stored properly, they will last a very long time. Even with the best of care, though, tools will wear out if used frequently. When a tool is damaged or worn out, replace it. Subsequent jobs will be safer and more enjoyable if you do.

How to repair damaged threads

Sometimes, the internal threads of a nut or bolt hole can become stripped, usually from overtightening. Stripping threads is an all-too-common occurrence, especially when working with aluminum parts, because aluminum is so soft that it easily strips out.

Usually, external or internal threads are only partially stripped. After they've been cleaned up with a tap or die, they'll still work. Sometimes, however, threads are badly damaged. When this happens, you've got three choices:

1) *Drill and tap the hole to the next suitable oversize and install a larger diameter bolt, screw or stud.*

2) *Drill and tap the hole to accept a threaded plug, then drill and tap the plug to the original screw size. You can also buy a plug already threaded to the original size. Then you simply drill a hole to the specified size, then run the threaded plug into the hole with a bolt and jam nut. Once the plug is fully seated, remove the jam nut and bolt.*

3) *The third method uses a patented thread repair kit like Heli-Coil or Slimsert. These easy-to-use kits are designed to repair damaged threads in straight-through holes and blind holes. Both are available as kits which can handle a variety of sizes and thread patterns. Drill the hole, then tap it with the special included tap. Install the Heli-Coil and the hole is back to its original diameter and thread pitch.*

Regardless of which method you use, be sure to proceed calmly and carefully. A little impatience or carelessness during one of these relatively simple procedures can ruin your whole day's work and cost you a bundle if you wreck an expensive part.

Working facilities

Not to be overlooked when discussing tools is the workshop. If anything more than routine maintenance is to be carried out, some sort of suitable work area is essential.

It is understood, and appreciated, that many home mechanics do not have a good workshop or garage available, and end up removing an engine or doing major repairs outside. It is recommended, however, that the overhaul or repair be completed under the cover of a roof.

A clean, flat workbench or table of comfortable working height is an absolute necessity. The workbench should be equipped with a vise that has a jaw opening of at least four inches.

As mentioned previously, some clean, dry storage space is also required for tools, as well as the lubricants, fluids, cleaning solvents, etc. which soon become necessary.

Sometimes waste oil and fluids, drained from the engine or cooling system during normal maintenance or repairs, present a disposal problem. To avoid pouring them on the ground or into a sewage system, pour the used fluids into large containers, seal them with caps and take them to an authorized disposal site or recycling center. Plastic jugs, such as old antifreeze containers, are ideal for this purpose.

Always keep a supply of old newspapers and clean rags available. Old towels are excellent for mopping up spills. Many mechanics use rolls of paper towels for most work because they are readily available and disposable. To help keep the area under the vehicle clean, a large cardboard box can be cut open and flattened to protect the garage or shop floor.

Whenever working over a painted surface, such as when leaning over a fender to service something under the hood, always cover it with an old blanket or bedspread to protect the finish. Vinyl covered pads, made especially for this purpose, are available at auto parts stores.

Anti-theft audio system

General information

1   Some of these models are equipped with THEFTLOCK audio systems, which include an anti-theft feature that will render the stereo inoperative if stolen. If the power source to the stereo is cut with the anti-theft feature activated, the stereo will be inoperative. Even if the power source is immediately re-connected, the stereo will not function.

2   If your vehicle is equipped with this anti-theft system, do not disconnect the battery, remove the stereo or disconnect related components unless you have either turned off the feature or have the individual ID (code) number for the stereo.

Disabling the anti-theft feature

3   Press the stereo's 1 and 4 buttons at the same time for five seconds with the ignition on and the radio power off. The display will show SEC, indicating the unit is in the secure mode (anti-theft feature enabled).

4   Press the MIN button. The display will show "000".

5   Press the MIN button to make the last two numbers appear.

6   Press HR to display the first one or two numbers of your code. The numbers will be displayed as entered.

7   Press AM/FM. If the display shows "_ _" you have successfully disabled the anti-theft feature. If SEC is displayed, the code you entered was incorrect and the anti-theft feature is still enabled.

Unlocking the stereo after a power loss

8   When power is restored to the stereo, the stereo won't turn on and LOC will appear on the display. Enter your ID code as follows; pause no more than 15 seconds between Steps.

9   Turn the ignition switch to ON, but leave the stereo off.

10   Press the MIN button. "000" should display.

11   Press the HR button to make the last two numbers appear, then release the button.

12   Press the HR button until the first one or two numbers appear.

13   Press AM/FM. SEC should appear, indicating the stereo is unlocked. If LOC appears, the numbers you entered were not correct and the stereo is still inoperative.

Jacking and towing

Jacking

Warning: *The jack supplied with the vehicle should only be used for raising the vehicle when changing a tire or placing jackstands under the frame. Never work under the vehicle or start the engine while the jack is being used as the only means of support.*

The vehicle must be on a level surface with the wheels blocked and the transmission in Park. Apply the parking brake if the front of the vehicle must be raised. Make sure no one is in the vehicle as it's being raised with the jack.

The head of the jack should fit squarely in the notch on the rocker flange at either the front or rear of the vehicle

Remove the jack, lug nut wrench and spare tire from the trunk compartment.

To replace the tire, use the tapered end of the lug wrench to pry loose the wheel cover. **Note:** *If the vehicle is equipped with aluminum wheels, it may be necessary to pry out the special lug nut covers. Also, aluminum wheels normally have anti-theft lug nuts (one per wheel) which require using a special "key" between the lug wrench and lug nut. The key is usually in the glove compartment.* Loosen the lug nuts one-half turn, but leave them in place until the tire is raised off the ground.

Position the jack under the side of the vehicle at the indicated jacking points. There's a front and rear jacking point on each side of the vehicle **(see illustration)**.

Turn the jack handle clockwise (the lug wrench also serves as the jack handle) until the tire clears the ground. Remove the lug nuts and pull the tire off. Clean the mating surfaces of the hub and wheel, then install the spare. Replace the lug nuts with the beveled edges facing in and tighten them snugly. Don't attempt to tighten them completely until the vehicle is lowered or it could slip off the jack.

Turn the jack handle counterclockwise to lower the vehicle. Remove the jack and tighten the lug nuts in a criss-cross pattern. If possible, tighten the nuts with a torque wrench (see Chapter 1 for the torque values). If you don't have access to a torque wrench,

have the nuts checked by a service station or repair shop as soon as possible. **Caution:** *The compact spare included with these vehicles is intended for temporary use only. Have the tire repaired and reinstall it on the vehicle at the earliest opportunity and don't exceed 50 mph with the spare tire on the car.*

Install the wheel cover, then stow the tire, jack and wrench and unblock the wheels.

Towing

We recommend these vehicles be towed from the front, with the front wheels off the ground. If it's absolutely necessary, these vehicles can be towed from the rear with the front wheels on the ground, provided that speeds don't exceed 35 mph and the distance is less than 50 miles; the transaxle can be damaged if these mileage/speed limitations are exceeded.

Equipment specifically designed for towing should be used. It must be attached to the main structural members of the vehicle, not the bumpers or brackets.

Safety is a major consideration when towing and all applicable state and local laws must be obeyed. A safety chain must be used at all times.

The parking brake must be released and the transaxle must be in Neutral. The steering must be unlocked (ignition switch in the Off position). Remember that power steering and power brakes won't work with the engine off.

Booster battery (jump) starting

Observe these precautions when using a booster battery to start a vehicle:

a) *Before connecting the booster battery, make sure the ignition switch is in the Off position.*

b) *Turn off the lights, heater and other electrical loads.*

c) *Your eyes should be shielded. Safety goggles are a good idea.*

d) *Make sure the booster battery is the same voltage as the dead one in the vehicle.*

e) *The two vehicles MUST NOT TOUCH each other!*

f) *Make sure the transaxle is in Neutral (manual) or Park (automatic).*

g) *If the booster battery is not a maintenance-free type, remove the vent caps and lay a cloth over the vent holes.*

Connect the red jumper cable to the positive (+) terminals of each battery. **Note:** *The vehicles covered in this manual are equipped with a remote positive terminal. This terminal is located in the left (driver's) side of the engine compartment, covered by a red plastic cap* **(see illustration)**.

Connect one end of the black jumper cable to the negative (-) terminal of the

booster battery. The other end of this cable should be connected to a good ground on the vehicle to be started, such as a bolt or bracket on the body.

Start the engine using the booster battery, then, with the engine running at idle speed, disconnect the jumper cables in the reverse order of connection.

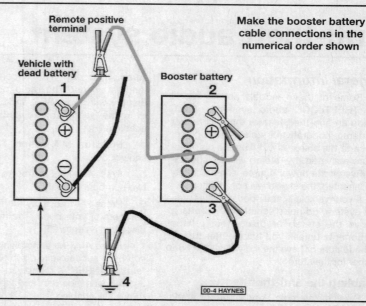

Make the booster battery cable connections in the numerical order shown

00-4 HAYNES

Automotive chemicals and lubricants

A number of automotive chemicals and lubricants are available for use during vehicle maintenance and repair. They include a wide variety of products ranging from cleaning solvents and degreasers to lubricants and protective sprays for rubber, plastic and vinyl.

Cleaners

Carburetor cleaner and choke cleaner is a strong solvent for gum, varnish and carbon. Most carburetor cleaners leave a dry-type lubricant film which will not harden or gum up. Because of this film it is not recommended for use on electrical components.

Brake system cleaner is used to remove brake dust, grease and brake fluid from the brake system, where clean surfaces are absolutely necessary. It leaves no residue and often eliminates brake squeal caused by contaminants.

Electrical cleaner removes oxidation, corrosion and carbon deposits from electrical contacts, restoring full current flow. It can also be used to clean spark plugs, carburetor jets, voltage regulators and other parts where an oil-free surface is desired.

Demoisturants remove water and moisture from electrical components such as alternators, voltage regulators, electrical connectors and fuse blocks. They are non-conductive and non-corrosive.

Degreasers are heavy-duty solvents used to remove grease from the outside of the engine and from chassis components. They can be sprayed or brushed on and, depending on the type, are rinsed off either with water or solvent.

Lubricants

Motor oil is the lubricant formulated for use in engines. It normally contains a wide variety of additives to prevent corrosion and reduce foaming and wear. Motor oil comes in various weights (viscosity ratings) from 0 to 50. The recommended weight of the oil depends on the season, temperature and the demands on the engine. Light oil is used in cold climates and under light load conditions. Heavy oil is used in hot climates and where high loads are encountered. Multi-viscosity oils are designed to have characteristics of both light and heavy oils and are available in a number of weights from 5W-20 to 20W-50.

Gear oil is designed to be used in differentials, manual transmissions and other areas where high-temperature lubrication is required.

Chassis and wheel bearing grease is a heavy grease used where increased loads and friction are encountered, such as for wheel bearings, balljoints, tie-rod ends and universal joints.

High-temperature wheel bearing grease is designed to withstand the extreme temperatures encountered by wheel bearings in disc brake equipped vehicles. It usually contains molybdenum disulfide (moly), which is a dry-type lubricant.

White grease is a heavy grease for metal-to-metal applications where water is a problem. White grease stays soft under both low and high temperatures (usually from -100 to +190-degrees F), and will not wash off or dilute in the presence of water.

Assembly lube is a special extreme pressure lubricant, usually containing moly, used to lubricate high-load parts (such as main and rod bearings and cam lobes) for initial start-up of a new engine. The assembly lube lubricates the parts without being squeezed out or washed away until the engine oiling system begins to function.

Silicone lubricants are used to protect rubber, plastic, vinyl and nylon parts.

Graphite lubricants are used where oils cannot be used due to contamination problems, such as in locks. The dry graphite will lubricate metal parts while remaining uncontaminated by dirt, water, oil or acids. It is electrically conductive and will not foul electrical contacts in locks such as the ignition switch.

Moly penetrants loosen and lubricate frozen, rusted and corroded fasteners and prevent future rusting or freezing.

Heat-sink grease is a special electrically non-conductive grease that is used for mounting electronic ignition modules where it is essential that heat is transferred away from the module.

Sealants

RTV sealant is one of the most widely used gasket compounds. Made from silicone, RTV is air curing, it seals, bonds, waterproofs, fills surface irregularities, remains flexible, doesn't shrink, is relatively easy to remove, and is used as a supplementary sealer with almost all low and medium temperature gaskets.

Anaerobic sealant is much like RTV in that it can be used either to seal gaskets or to form gaskets by itself. It remains flexible, is solvent resistant and fills surface imperfections. The difference between an anaerobic sealant and an RTV-type sealant is in the curing. RTV cures when exposed to air, while an anaerobic sealant cures only in the absence of air. This means that an anaerobic sealant cures only after the assembly of parts, sealing them together.

Thread and pipe sealant is used for sealing hydraulic and pneumatic fittings and vacuum lines. It is usually made from a Teflon compound, and comes in a spray, a paint-on liquid and as a wrap-around tape.

Chemicals

Anti-seize compound prevents seizing, galling, cold welding, rust and corrosion in fasteners. High-temperature ant-seize, usually made with copper and graphite lubricants, is used for exhaust system and exhaust manifold bolts.

Anaerobic locking compounds are used to keep fasteners from vibrating or working loose and cure only after installation, in the absence of air. Medium strength locking compound is used for small nuts, bolts and screws that may be removed later. High-strength locking compound is for large nuts, bolts and studs which aren't removed on a regular basis.

Oil additives range from viscosity index improvers to chemical treatments that claim to reduce internal engine friction. It should be noted that most oil manufacturers caution against using additives with their oils.

Gas additives perform several functions, depending on their chemical makeup. They usually contain solvents that help dissolve gum and varnish that build up on carburetor, fuel injection and intake parts. They also serve to break down carbon deposits that form on the inside surfaces of the combustion chambers. Some additives contain upper cylinder lubricants for valves and piston rings, and others contain chemicals to remove condensation from the gas tank.

Miscellaneous

Brake fluid is specially formulated hydraulic fluid that can withstand the heat and pressure encountered in brake systems. Care must be taken so this fluid does not come in contact with painted surfaces or plastics. An opened container should always be resealed to prevent contamination by water or dirt.

Weatherstrip adhesive is used to bond weatherstripping around doors, windows and trunk lids. It is sometimes used to attach trim pieces.

Undercoating is a petroleum-based, tar-like substance that is designed to protect metal surfaces on the underside of the vehicle from corrosion. It also acts as a sound-deadening agent by insulating the bottom of the vehicle.

Waxes and polishes are used to help protect painted and plated surfaces from the weather. Different types of paint may require the use of different types of wax and polish. Some polishes utilize a chemical or abrasive cleaner to help remove the top layer of oxidized (dull) paint on older vehicles. In recent years many non-wax polishes that contain a wide variety of chemicals such as polymers and silicones have been introduced. These non-wax polishes are usually easier to apply and last longer than conventional waxes and polishes.

Conversion factors

Length (distance)

Inches (in)	X	25.4	= Millimeters (mm)	X	0.0394	= Inches (in)
Feet (ft)	X	0.305	= Meters (m)	X	3.281	= Feet (ft)
Miles	X	1.609	= Kilometers (km)	X	0.621	= Miles

Volume (capacity)

Cubic inches (cu in; in³)	X	16.387	= Cubic centimeters (cc; cm³)	X	0.061	= Cubic inches (cu in; in³)
Imperial pints (Imp pt)	X	0.568	= Liters (l)	X	1.76	= Imperial pints (Imp pt)
Imperial quarts (Imp qt)	X	1.137	= Liters (l)	X	0.88	= Imperial quarts (Imp qt)
Imperial quarts (Imp qt)	X	1.201	= US quarts (US qt)	X	0.833	= Imperial quarts (Imp qt)
US quarts (US qt)	X	0.946	= Liters (l)	X	1.057	= US quarts (US qt)
Imperial gallons (Imp gal)	X	4.546	= Liters (l)	X	0.22	= Imperial gallons (Imp gal)
Imperial gallons (Imp gal)	X	1.201	= US gallons (US gal)	X	0.833	= Imperial gallons (Imp gal)
US gallons (US gal)	X	3.785	= Liters (l)	X	0.264	= US gallons (US gal)

Mass (weight)

Ounces (oz)	X	28.35	= Grams (g)	X	0.035	= Ounces (oz)
Pounds (lb)	X	0.454	= Kilograms (kg)	X	2.205	= Pounds (lb)

Force

Ounces-force (ozf; oz)	X	0.278	= Newtons (N)	X	3.6	= Ounces-force (ozf; oz)
Pounds-force (lbf; lb)	X	4.448	= Newtons (N)	X	0.225	= Pounds-force (lbf; lb)
Newtons (N)	X	0.1	= Kilograms-force (kgf; kg)	X	9.81	= Newtons (N)

Pressure

Pounds-force per square inch (psi; lbf/in²; lb/in²)	X	0.070	= Kilograms-force per square centimeter (kgf/cm²; kg/cm²)	X	14.223	= Pounds-force per square inch (psi; lbf/in²; lb/in²)
Pounds-force per square inch (psi; lbf/in²; lb/in²)	X	0.068	= Atmospheres (atm)	X	14.696	= Pounds-force per square inch (psi; lbf/in²; lb/in²)
Pounds-force per square inch (psi; lbf/in²; lb/in²)	X	0.069	= Bars	X	14.5	= Pounds-force per square inch (psi; lbf/in²; lb/in²)
Pounds-force per square inch (psi; lbf/in²; lb/in²)	X	6.895	= Kilopascals (kPa)	X	0.145	= Pounds-force per square inch (psi; lbf/in²; lb/in²)
Kilopascals (kPa)	X	0.01	= Kilograms-force per square centimeter (kgf/cm²; kg/cm²)	X	98.1	= Kilopascals (kPa)

Torque (moment of force)

Pounds-force inches (lbf in; lb in)	X	1.152	= Kilograms-force centimeter (kgf cm; kg cm)	X	0.868	= Pounds-force inches (lbf in; lb in)
Pounds-force inches (lbf in; lb in)	X	0.113	= Newton meters (Nm)	X	8.85	= Pounds-force inches (lbf in; lb in)
Pounds-force inches (lbf in; lb in)	X	0.083	= Pounds-force feet (lbf ft; lb ft)	X	12	= Pounds-force inches (lbf in; lb in)
Pounds-force feet (lbf ft; lb ft)	X	0.138	= Kilograms-force meters (kgf m; kg m)	X	7.233	= Pounds-force feet (lbf ft; lb ft)
Pounds-force feet (lbf ft; lb ft)	X	1.356	= Newton meters (Nm)	X	0.738	= Pounds-force feet (lbf ft; lb ft)
Newton meters (Nm)	X	0.102	= Kilograms-force meters (kgf m; kg m)	X	9.804	= Newton meters (Nm)

Vacuum

Inches mercury (in. Hg)	X	3.377	= Kilopascals (kPa)	X	0.2961	= Inches mercury
Inches mercury (in. Hg)	X	25.4	= Millimeters mercury (mm Hg)	X	0.0394	= Inches mercury

Power

Horsepower (hp)	X	745.7	= Watts (W)	X	0.0013	= Horsepower (hp)

Velocity (speed)

Miles per hour (miles/hr; mph)	X	1.609	= Kilometers per hour (km/hr; kph)	X	0.621	= Miles per hour (miles/hr; mph)

Fuel consumption*

Miles per gallon, Imperial (mpg)	X	0.354	= Kilometers per liter (km/l)	X	2.825	= Miles per gallon, Imperial (mpg)
Miles per gallon, US (mpg)	X	0.425	= Kilometers per liter (km/l)	X	2.352	= Miles per gallon, US (mpg)

Temperature

Degrees Fahrenheit = (°C x 1.8) + 32

Degrees Celsius (Degrees Centigrade; °C) = (°F - 32) x 0.56

*It is common practice to convert from miles per gallon (mpg) to liters/100 kilometers (l/100km), where mpg (Imperial) x l/100 km = 282 and mpg (US) x l/100 km = 235

DECIMALS to MILLIMETERS

Decimal	mm	Decimal	mm
0.001	0.0254	0.500	12.7000
0.002	0.0508	0.510	12.9540
0.003	0.0762	0.520	13.2080
0.004	0.1016	0.530	13.4620
0.005	0.1270	0.540	13.7160
0.006	0.1524	0.550	13.9700
0.007	0.1778	0.560	14.2240
0.008	0.2032	0.570	14.4780
0.009	0.2286	0.580	14.7320
		0.590	14.9860
0.010	0.2540		
0.020	0.5080		
0.030	0.7620		
0.040	1.0160	0.600	15.2400
0.050	1.2700	0.610	15.4940
0.060	1.5240	0.620	15.7480
0.070	1.7780	0.630	16.0020
0.080	2.0320	0.640	16.2560
0.090	2.2860	0.650	16.5100
		0.660	16.7640
0.100	2.5400	0.670	17.0180
0.110	2.7940	0.680	17.2720
0.120	3.0480	0.690	17.5260
0.130	3.3020		
0.140	3.5560		
0.150	3.8100		
0.160	4.0640	0.700	17.7800
0.170	4.3180	0.710	18.0340
0.180	4.5720	0.720	18.2880
0.190	4.8260	0.730	18.5420
		0.740	18.7960
0.200	5.0800	0.750	19.0500
0.210	5.3340	0.760	19.3040
0.220	5.5880	0.770	19.5580
0.230	5.8420	0.780	19.8120
0.240	6.0960	0.790	20.0660
0.250	6.3500		
0.260	6.6040		
0.270	6.8580	0.800	20.3200
0.280	7.1120	0.810	20.5740
0.290	7.3660	0.820	21.8280
		0.830	21.0820
0.300	7.6200	0.840	21.3360
0.310	7.8740	0.850	21.5900
0.320	8.1280	0.860	21.8440
0.330	8.3820	0.870	22.0980
0.340	8.6360	0.880	22.3520
0.350	8.9000	0.890	22.6060
0.360	9.1440		
0.370	9.3980		
0.380	9.6520		
0.390	9.9060		
		0.900	22.8600
0.400	10.1600	0.910	23.1140
0.410	10.4140	0.920	23.3680
0.420	10.6680	0.930	23.6220
0.430	10.9220	0.940	23.8760
0.440	11.1760	0.950	24.1300
0.450	11.4300	0.960	24.3840
0.460	11.6840	0.970	24.6380
0.470	11.9380	0.980	24.8920
0.480	12.1920	0.990	25.1460
0.490	12.4460	1.000	25.4000

FRACTIONS to DECIMALS to MILLIMETERS

Fraction	Decimal	mm	Fraction	Decimal	mm
1/64	0.0156	0.3969	33/64	0.5156	13.0969
1/32	0.0312	0.7938	17/32	0.5312	13.4938
3/64	0.0469	1.1906	35/64	0.5469	13.8906
1/16	0.0625	1.5875	9/16	0.5625	14.2875
5/64	0.0781	1.9844	37/64	0.5781	14.6844
3/32	0.0938	2.3812	19/32	0.5938	15.0812
7/64	0.1094	2.7781	39/64	0.6094	15.4781
1/8	0.1250	3.1750	5/8	0.6250	15.8750
9/64	0.1406	3.5719	41/64	0.6406	16.2719
5/32	0.1562	3.9688	21/32	0.6562	16.6688
11/64	0.1719	4.3656	43/64	0.6719	17.0656
3/16	0.1875	4.7625	11/16	0.6875	17.4625
13/64	0.2031	5.1594	45/64	0.7031	17.8594
7/32	0.2188	5.5562	23/32	0.7188	18.2562
15/64	0.2344	5.9531	47/64	0.7344	18.6531
1/4	0.2500	6.3500	3/4	0.7500	19.0500
17/64	0.2656	6.7469	49/64	0.7656	19.4469
9/32	0.2812	7.1438	25/32	0.7812	19.8438
19/64	0.2969	7.5406	51/64	0.7969	20.2406
5/16	0.3125	7.9375	13/16	0.8125	20.6375
21/64	0.3281	8.3344	53/64	0.8281	21.0344
11/32	0.3438	8.7312	27/32	0.8438	21.4312
23/64	0.3594	9.1281	55/64	0.8594	21.8281
3/8	0.3750	9.5250	7/8	0.8750	22.2250
25/64	0.3906	9.9219	57/64	0.8906	22.6219
13/32	0.4062	10.3188	29/32	0.9062	23.0188
27/64	0.4219	10.7156	59/64	0.9219	23.4156
7/16	0.4375	11.1125	15/16	0.9375	23.8125
29/64	0.4531	11.5094	61/64	0.9531	24.2094
15/32	0.4688	11.9062	31/32	0.9688	24.6062
31/64	0.4844	12.3031	63/64	0.9844	25.0031
1/2	0.5000	12.7000	1	1.0000	25.4000

Safety first!

Regardless of how enthusiastic you may be about getting on with the job at hand, take the time to ensure that your safety is not jeopardized. A moment's lack of attention can result in an accident, as can failure to observe certain simple safety precautions. The possibility of an accident will always exist, and the following points should not be considered a comprehensive list of all dangers. Rather, they are intended to make you aware of the risks and to encourage a safety conscious approach to all work you carry out on your vehicle.

Essential DOs and DON'Ts

DON'T rely on a jack when working under the vehicle. Always use approved jackstands to support the weight of the vehicle and place them under the recommended lift or support points.

DON'T attempt to loosen extremely tight fasteners (i.e. wheel lug nuts) while the vehicle is on a jack - it may fall.

DON'T start the engine without first making sure that the transmission is in Neutral (or Park where applicable) and the parking brake is set.

DON'T remove the radiator cap from a hot cooling system - let it cool or cover it with a cloth and release the pressure gradually.

DON'T attempt to drain the engine oil until you are sure it has cooled to the point that it will not burn you.

DON'T touch any part of the engine or exhaust system until it has cooled sufficiently to avoid burns.

DON'T siphon toxic liquids such as gasoline, antifreeze and brake fluid by mouth, or allow them to remain on your skin.

DON'T inhale brake lining dust - it is potentially hazardous (see *Asbestos* below).

DON'T allow spilled oil or grease to remain on the floor - wipe it up before someone slips on it.

DON'T use loose fitting wrenches or other tools which may slip and cause injury.

DON'T push on wrenches when loosening or tightening nuts or bolts. Always try to pull the wrench toward you. If the situation calls for pushing the wrench away, push with an open hand to avoid scraped knuckles if the wrench should slip.

DON'T attempt to lift a heavy component alone - get someone to help you.

DON'T rush or take unsafe shortcuts to finish a job.

DON'T allow children or animals in or around the vehicle while you are working on it.

DO wear eye protection when using power tools such as a drill, sander, bench grinder, etc. and when working under a vehicle.

DO keep loose clothing and long hair well out of the way of moving parts.

DO make sure that any hoist used has a safe working load rating adequate for the job.

DO get someone to check on you periodically when working alone on a vehicle.

DO carry out work in a logical sequence and make sure that everything is correctly assembled and tightened.

DO keep chemicals and fluids tightly capped and out of the reach of children and pets.

DO remember that your vehicle's safety affects that of yourself and others. If in doubt on any point, get professional advice.

Asbestos

Certain friction, insulating, sealing, and other products - such as brake linings, brake bands, clutch linings, torque converters, gaskets, etc. - may contain asbestos. Extreme care must be taken to avoid inhalation of dust from such products, since it is hazardous to health. If in doubt, assume that they do contain asbestos.

Fire

Remember at all times that gasoline is highly flammable. Never smoke or have any kind of open flame around when working on a vehicle. But the risk does not end there. A spark caused by an electrical short circuit, by two metal surfaces contacting each other, or even by static electricity built up in your body under certain conditions, can ignite gasoline vapors, which in a confined space are highly explosive. Do not, under any circumstances, use gasoline for cleaning parts. Use an approved safety solvent.

Always disconnect the battery ground (-) cable at the battery before working on any part of the fuel system or electrical system. Never risk spilling fuel on a hot engine or exhaust component. It is strongly recommended that a fire extinguisher suitable for use on fuel and electrical fires be kept handy in the garage or workshop at all times. Never try to extinguish a fuel or electrical fire with water.

Fumes

Certain fumes are highly toxic and can quickly cause unconsciousness and even death if inhaled to any extent. Gasoline vapor falls into this category, as do the vapors from some cleaning solvents. Any draining or pouring of such volatile fluids should be done in a well ventilated area.

When using cleaning fluids and solvents, read the instructions on the container carefully. Never use materials from unmarked containers.

Never run the engine in an enclosed space, such as a garage. Exhaust fumes contain carbon monoxide, which is extremely poisonous. If you need to run the engine, always do so in the open air, or at least have the rear of the vehicle outside the work area.

If you are fortunate enough to have the use of an inspection pit, never drain or pour gasoline and never run the engine while the vehicle is over the pit. The fumes, being heavier than air, will concentrate in the pit with possibly lethal results.

The battery

Never create a spark or allow a bare light bulb near a battery. They normally give off a certain amount of hydrogen gas, which is highly explosive.

Always disconnect the battery ground (-) cable at the battery before working on the fuel or electrical systems.

If possible, loosen the filler caps or cover when charging the battery from an external source (this does not apply to sealed or maintenance-free batteries). Do not charge at an excessive rate or the battery may burst.

Take care when adding water to a non maintenance-free battery and when carrying a battery. The electrolyte, even when diluted, is very corrosive and should not be allowed to contact clothing or skin.

Always wear eye protection when cleaning the battery to prevent the caustic deposits from entering your eyes.

Household current

When using an electric power tool, inspection light, etc., which operates on household current, always make sure that the tool is correctly connected to its plug and that, where necessary, it is properly grounded. Do not use such items in damp conditions and, again, do not create a spark or apply excessive heat in the vicinity of fuel or fuel vapor.

Secondary ignition system voltage

A severe electric shock can result from touching certain parts of the ignition system (such as the spark plug wires) when the engine is running or being cranked, particularly if components are damp or the insulation is defective. In the case of an electronic ignition system, the secondary system voltage is much higher and could prove fatal.

Troubleshooting

Contents

Engine and performance

1   Engine will not rotate when attempting to start

1   Battery terminal connections loose or corroded. Check the cable terminals at the battery; tighten cable clamp and/or clean off corrosion as necessary (see Chapter 1).
2   Battery discharged or faulty. If the cable ends are clean and tight on the battery posts, turn the key to the On position and switch on the headlights or windshield wipers. If they won't run, the battery is discharged.
3   Automatic transaxle not engaged in park (P) or Neutral (N).
4   Broken, loose or disconnected wires in the starting circuit. Inspect all wires and connectors at the battery, starter solenoid and ignition switch (on steering column).
5   Starter motor pinion jammed in driveplate ring gear. Remove starter (Chapter 5) and inspect pinion and driveplate (Chapter 2) at earliest convenience.
6   Starter solenoid faulty (Chapter 5).
7   Starter motor faulty (Chapter 5).
8   Ignition switch faulty (Chapter 12).
9   Engine seized. Try to turn the crankshaft with a large socket and breaker bar on the pulley bolt.

2   Engine rotates but will not start

1   Fuel tank empty.
2   Battery discharged (engine rotates slowly). Check the operation of electrical components as described in previous Section.
3   Battery terminal connections loose or corroded. See previous Section.
4   Fuel not reaching fuel injectors. Check for clogged fuel filter or lines and defective fuel pump. Also make sure the tank vent lines aren't clogged (Chapter 4).
5   Faulty ignition module. (Chapter 5).
6   Low cylinder compression. Check as described in Chapter 2.
7   Water in fuel. Drain tank and fill with new fuel.
8   Dirty or clogged fuel injectors.
9   Faulty idle control system (Chapter 4).
10   Faulty emissions or engine control systems (Chapter 6).
11   Wet or damaged ignition components (Chapters 1 and 5).
12   Worn, faulty or incorrectly gapped spark plugs (Chapter 1).
13   Broken, loose or disconnected wires in the ignition circuit.
14   Broken, loose or disconnected wires at the ignition coil(s) or faulty coil(s) (Chapter 5).
15   Timing chain or belt failure or wear affecting valve timing (Chapter 2).

3   Starter motor operates without turning engine

1   Starter pinion sticking. Remove the starter (Chapter 5) and inspect.
2   Starter pinion or driveplate teeth worn or broken. Remove the inspection cover on the left side of the engine and inspect.

4   Engine hard to start when cold

1   Battery discharged or low. Check as described in Chapter 1.
2   Fuel not reaching the fuel injectors. Check the fuel filter and lines (Chapters 1 and 4).
3   Defective spark plugs (Chapter 1).
4   Intake manifold vacuum leaks. Make sure all mounting bolts/nuts are tight and all vacuum hoses connected to the manifold are attached properly and in good condition.
5   Faulty idle control system (Chapter 4).
4   Faulty emissions or engine control systems (Chapter 6).

5   Engine hard to start when hot

1   Air filter dirty (Chapter 1).
2   Bad engine ground connection.
3   Fuel not reaching the injectors (Chapter 4).
4   Loose connection in the ignition system (Chapter 5).
5   Faulty idle control system (Chapter 4).
6   Faulty emissions or engine control systems (Chapter 6).

6   Starter motor noisy or engages roughly

1   Pinion or flywheel/driveplate teeth worn or broken. Remove the inspection cover and inspect.
2   Starter motor mounting bolts loose or missing.

7   Engine starts but stops immediately

1   Loose or damaged wiring in the ignition system.
2   Intake manifold vacuum leaks. Make sure all mounting bolts/nuts are tight and all vacuum hoses connected to the manifold are attached properly and in good condition.
5   Faulty idle control system (Chapter 4).
4   Faulty emissions or engine control systems (Chapter 6).

8   Engine 'lopes' while idling or idles erratically

1   Vacuum leaks. Check mounting bolts at the intake manifold or plenum for tightness. Make sure that all vacuum hoses are connected and in good condition. Use a stethoscope or a length of fuel hose held against your ear to listen for vacuum leaks while the engine is running. A hissing sound will be heard. A soapy water solution will also detect leaks. Check the intake manifold or plenum gasket surfaces.
2   Leaking EGR valve or plugged PCV valve (Chapter 6).
3   Air filter clogged (Chapter 1).
4   Leaking head gasket. Perform a cylinder compression check (Chapter 2).
5   Worn timing chain or belt (Chapter 2).
6   Camshaft lobes worn (Chapter 2).
7   Valves burned or otherwise leaking (Chapter 2).
8   Ignition system not operating properly (Chapters 1 and 5).
9   Dirty or clogged injectors (Chapter 4).
10   Faulty idle control system (Chapter 4).
11   Faulty emissions or engine control systems (Chapter 6).

9   Engine misses at idle speed

1   Spark plugs faulty or not gapped properly (Chapter 1).
2   Faulty spark plug wires (Chapter 1).
3   Wet or damaged ignition components (Chapter 1).
4   Short circuits in ignition, coil(s) or spark plug wires.
5   Faulty emissions or engine control systems (Chapter 6).
6   Clogged fuel filter and/or foreign matter in fuel. Replace the fuel filter (Chapter 1).
7   Vacuum leaks at intake manifold or plenum or hose connections. Check as described in Section 8.
8   Low or uneven cylinder compression. Check as described in Chapter 2.
9   Clogged or dirty fuel injectors (Chapter 4).
10   Leaky EGR valve (Chapter 6).
11   Faulty emissions or engine control systems (Chapter 6).

10   Excessively high idle speed

1   Sticking throttle linkage (Chapter 4).
2   Idle speed incorrect (Chapter 4).
3   Faulty idle control system (Chapter 4).
4   Faulty emissions or engine control systems (Chapter 6).

11   Battery will not hold a charge

1   Drivebelt defective or not adjusted properly (Chapter 1).

2 Battery cables loose or corroded (Chapter 1).
3 Alternator not charging properly (Chapter 5).
4 Loose, broken or faulty wires in the charging circuit (Chapter 5).
5 Short circuit causing a continuous drain on the battery (Chapter 12).
6 Battery defective internally.
7 Faulty regulator (Chapter 5).

12 Alternator light stays on

1 Fault in alternator or charging circuit (Chapter 5).
2 Drivebelt defective or not properly adjusted (Chapter 1).

13 Alternator light fails to come on when key is turned on

1 Faulty bulb (Chapter 12).
2 Defective alternator (Chapter 5).
3 Fault in the printed circuit, dash wiring or bulb holder (Chapter 12).

14 Engine misses throughout driving speed range

1 Fuel filter clogged and/or impurities in the fuel system. Check fuel filter (Chapter 1) or clean system (Chapter 4).
2 Faulty or incorrectly gapped spark plugs (Chapter 1).
3 Incorrect ignition timing (Chapter 5).
4 Disconnected ignition system wires or damaged ignition system components (Chapter 1).
5 Defective spark plug wires (Chapter 1).
6 Emissions or engine control system components faulty (Chapter 6).
7 Low or uneven cylinder compression pressures. Check as described in Chapter 2.
8 Weak or faulty ignition coil(s) (Chapter 5).
9 Weak or faulty ignition system (Chapter 5).
10 Vacuum leaks at intake manifold or plenum or vacuum hoses (see Section 8).
11 Dirty or clogged fuel injector (Chapter 4).

15 Hesitation or stumble during acceleration

1 Ignition timing incorrect (Chapter 5).
2 Ignition system not operating properly (Chapter 5).
3 Dirty or clogged fuel injectors (Chapter 4).
4 Low fuel pressure. Check for proper operation of the fuel pump and for restrictions in the fuel filter and lines (Chapter 4).
5 Emissions or engine control system components faulty (Chapter 6).

16 Engine stalls

1 Faulty idle air control valve (Chapter 4).
2 Fuel filter clogged and/or water and impurities in the fuel system (Chapter 1).
3 Damaged or wet ignition system wires or components.
4 Faulty idle control system (Chapter 4).
5 Emissions or engine control system components faulty (Chapter 6).
6 Faulty or incorrectly gapped spark plugs (Chapter 1). Also check the spark plug wires (Chapter 1).
7 Vacuum leak at the intake manifold or plenum or vacuum hoses. Check as described in Section 8.

17 Engine lacks power

1 Incorrect ignition timing (Chapter 5).
2 Check for faulty ignition wires, etc. (Chapter 1).
3 Faulty or incorrectly gapped spark plugs (Chapter 1).
4 Air filter dirty (Chapter 1).
5 Spark timing control system not operating properly (Chapter 5).
6 Faulty ignition coil(s) (Chapter 5).
7 Brakes binding (Chapters 1 and 9).
8 Automatic transaxle fluid level incorrect, causing slippage (Chapter 1).
9 Fuel filter clogged and/or impurities in the fuel system (Chapters 1 and 4).
10 EGR system not functioning properly (Chapter 6).
11 Use of sub-standard fuel. Fill tank with proper octane fuel.
12 Low or uneven cylinder compression pressures. Check as described in Chapter 2.
13 Air (vacuum) leak at intake manifold or plenum (check as described in Section 8).

18 Engine backfires

1 EGR system not functioning properly (Chapter 6).
2 Ignition timing incorrect (Chapter 5).
3 Vacuum leak (refer to Section 8).
4 Damaged valve springs or sticking valves (Chapter 2).
5 Intake air (vacuum) leak (see Section 8).

19 Engine surges while holding accelerator steady

1 Intake air (vacuum) leak (see Section 8).
2 Fuel pump not working properly.
3 Faulty idle air control system (Chapter 4).
4 Emissions or engine control system components faulty (Chapter 6).

20 Pinging or knocking engine sounds when engine is under load

1 Incorrect grade of fuel. Fill tank with fuel of the proper octane rating.
2 Ignition timing incorrect (Chapter 5) or problem in the ignition system (Chapter 5).
3 Carbon build-up in combustion chambers. Remove cylinder head(s) and clean combustion chambers (Chapter 2).
4 Incorrect spark plugs (Chapter 1).
5 Knock sensor system not functioning properly (Chapter 6).

21 Engine diesels (continues to run) after being turned off

1 Idle speed too high (Chapter 4).
2 Ignition timing incorrect (Chapter 5).
3 Incorrect spark plug heat range (Chapter 1).
4 Intake air (vacuum) leak (see Section 8).
5 Carbon build-up in combustion chambers. Remove the cylinder head and clean the combustion chambers (Chapter 2).
6 Valves sticking (Chapter 2).
7 Valve clearance incorrect (Chapter 1).
8 EGR system not operating properly (Chapter 6).
9 Leaking fuel injector(s) (Chapter 4).
10 Check for causes of overheating (Section 27).

22 Low oil pressure

1 Improper grade of oil.
2 Oil pump regulator valve not operating properly (Chapter 2).
3 Oil pump worn or damaged (Chapter 2).
4 Engine overheating (refer to Section 27).
5 Clogged oil filter (Chapter 1).
6 Clogged oil strainer (Chapter 2).
7 Oil pressure gauge not working properly (Chapter 2).

23 Excessive oil consumption

1 Loose oil drain plug.
2 Loose bolts or damaged oil pan gasket (Chapter 2).
3 Loose bolts or damaged front cover gasket (Chapter 2).
4 Front or rear crankshaft oil seal leaking (Chapter 2).
5 Loose bolts or damaged valve cover gasket (Chapter 2).
6 Loose oil filter (Chapter 1).
7 Loose or damaged oil pressure switch (Chapter 2).
8 Pistons and cylinders excessively worn (Chapter 2).
9 Piston rings not installed correctly on pistons (Chapter 2).

10   Worn or damaged piston rings (Chapter 2).
11   Intake and/or exhaust valve oil seals worn or damaged (Chapter 2).
12   Worn valve stems.
13   Worn or damaged valves/guides (Chapter 2).

24   Excessive fuel consumption

1   Dirty or clogged air filter element (Chapter 1).
2   Incorrect ignition timing (Chapter 5).
3   Incorrect idle speed (Chapter 4).
4   Low tire pressure or incorrect tire size (Chapter 10).
5   Fuel leakage. Check all connections, lines and components in the fuel system (Chapter 4).
6   Dirty or clogged fuel injectors (Chapter 4).
7   Problem in the fuel injection system (Chapter 4).

25   Fuel odor

1   Fuel leakage. Check all connections, lines and components in the fuel system (Chapter 4).
2   Fuel tank overfilled. Fill only to automatic shut-off.
3   Charcoal canister filter in Evaporative Emissions Control system clogged (Chapter 6).
4   Vapor leaks from Evaporative Emissions Control system lines (Chapter 6).

26   Miscellaneous engine noises

1   A strong dull noise that becomes more rapid as the engine accelerates indicates worn or damaged crankshaft bearings or an unevenly worn crankshaft. To pinpoint the trouble spot, remove the spark plug wire from one plug at a time and crank the engine over. If the noise stops, the cylinder with the removed plug wire indicates the problem area. Replace the bearing and/or service or replace the crankshaft (Chapter 2).
2   A similar (yet slightly higher pitched) noise to the crankshaft knocking described in the previous paragraph, that becomes more rapid as the engine accelerates, indicates worn or damaged connecting rod bearings (Chapter 2). The procedure for locating the problem cylinder is the same as described in Paragraph 1.
3   An overlapping metallic noise that increases in intensity as the engine speed increases, yet diminishes as the engine warms up indicates abnormal piston and cylinder wear (Chapter 2).To locate the problem cylinder, use the procedure described in Paragraph 1.
4   A rapid clicking noise that becomes

faster as the engine accelerates indicates a worn piston pin or piston pin hole. This sound will happen each time the piston hits the highest and lowest points in the stroke (Chapter 2). The procedure for locating the problem piston is described in Paragraph 1.
5   A metallic clicking noise coming from the water pump indicates worn or damaged water pump bearings or pump. Replace the water pump with a new one (Chapter 3).
6   A rapid tapping sound or clicking sound that becomes faster as the engine speed increases indicates "valve tapping" or stuck valve lifters. This can be identified by holding one end of a section of hose to your ear and placing the other end at different spots along the rocker arm cover. The point where the sound is loudest indicates the problem valve. Adjust the valve clearance (Chapter 1).
7   A steady metallic rattling or rapping sound coming from the area of the timing chain cover indicates a worn, damaged or out-of-adjustment timing chain. Service or replace the chain and related components (Chapter 2).

27   Overheating

1   Insufficient coolant in system (Chapter 1).
2   Water pump drivebelt defective or out of adjustment (Chapter 1).
3   Radiator core blocked or grille restricted (Chapter 3).
4   Thermostat faulty (Chapter 3).
5   Electric cooling fan blades broken or cracked (Chapter 3).
6   Radiator cap not maintaining proper pressure (Chapter 3).

28   Overcooling

Faulty thermostat (Chapter 3).

29   External coolant leakage

1   Deteriorated/damaged hoses or loose clamps (Chapters 1 and 3).
2   Water pump seal defective (Chapters 1 and 3).
3   Leakage from radiator core or header tank (Chapter 3).
4   Engine drain or water jacket core plugs leaking (Chapter 2).
5   Leak at engine oil cooler (Chapter 3).

30   Internal coolant leakage

1   Leaking cylinder head gasket (Chapter 2).
2   Cracked cylinder bore or cylinder head (Chapter 2).

31   Coolant loss

1   Too much coolant in system (Chapter 1).
2   Coolant boiling away because of overheating (Chapter 3).
3   Internal or external leakage (Chapter 3).
4   Faulty radiator cap (Chapter 3).

32   Poor coolant circulation

1   Inoperative water pump (Chapter 3).
2   Restriction in cooling system (Chapters 1 and 3).
3   Water pump drivebelt defective or out of adjustment (Chapter 1).
4   Thermostat sticking (Chapter 3).

Automatic transaxle

Note: *Due to the complexity of the automatic transaxle, it's difficult for the home mechanic to properly diagnose and service this component. For problems other than the following, the vehicle should be taken to a dealer service department or a transmission shop.*

33   Fluid leakage

1   Automatic transmission fluid is a deep red color. Fluid leaks should not be confused with engine oil, which can easily be blown by air flow to the transaxle.
2   To pinpoint a leak, first remove all built-up dirt and grime from the transaxle housing with degreasing agents and/or steam cleaning. Drive the vehicle at low speeds so air flow will not blow the leak far from its source. Raise the vehicle and determine where the leak is coming from. Common areas of leakage are:

   a) *Pan (Chapters 1 and 7)*
   b) *Filler pipe (Chapter 7)*
   c) *Transaxle oil lines (Chapter 7)*
   d) *Speedometer gear or sensor (Chapter 7)*
   e) *Vacuum modulator (Chapter 7)*

34   Transaxle fluid brown or has a burned smell

Transaxle overheated. Change the fluid (Chapter 1).

35   General shift mechanism problems

1   Chapter 7 deals with checking and adjusting the shift linkage on automatic transaxles. Common problems which may be attributed to poorly adjusted linkage are:

   a) *Engine starting in gears other than Park or Neutral.*
   b) *Indicator on shifter pointing to a gear other than the one actually being used.*
   c) *Vehicle moves when in Park.*
2   Refer to Chapter 7 for the shift linkage adjustment procedure.

36 Transaxle will not downshift with accelerator pedal pressed to the floor

Throttle Valve (TV) cable out of adjustment (Chapter 7).

37 Engine will start in gears other than Park or Neutral

Park/Neutral switch malfunctioning (Chapter 7).

38 Transaxle slips, shifts roughly, is noisy or has no drive in forward or reverse gears

There are many probable causes for the above problems, but the home mechanic should be concerned with only one possibility - fluid level. Before taking the vehicle to a repair shop, check the level and condition of the fluid as described in Chapter 1.

Correct the fluid level as necessary or change the fluid and filter if needed. If the problem persists, have a professional diagnose the probable cause.

Driveaxles

39 Clicking noise in turns

Worn or damaged outer CV joint. Check for cut or damaged boots (Chapter 1). Repair as necessary (Chapter 8).

40 Knock or clunk when accelerating after coasting

Worn or damaged CV joint. Check for cut or damaged boots (Chapter 1). Repair as necessary (Chapter 8).

41 Shudder or vibration during acceleration

1 Excessive inner CV joint angle. Check and correct as necessary (Chapter 8).
2 Worn or damaged CV joints. Repair or replace as necessary (Chapter 8).
3 Sticking inboard joint assembly. Correct or replace as necessary (Chapter 8).

Brakes

Note: *Before assuming that a brake problem exists, make sure . . .*
 a) The tires are in good condition and properly inflated (Chapter 1).
 b) The front end alignment is correct (Chapter 10).
 c) The vehicle isn't loaded with weight in an unequal manner.

42 Vehicle pulls to one side during braking

1 Incorrect tire pressures (Chapter 1).
2 Front end out of line (have the front end aligned).
3 Unmatched tires on same axle.
4 Restricted brake lines or hoses (Chapter 9).
5 Malfunctioning brake assembly (Chapter 9).
6 Loose suspension parts (Chapter 10).
7 Loose brake calipers (Chapter 9).
8 Contaminated brake linings (Chapters 1 and 9).

43 Noise (high-pitched squeal when the brakes are applied)

Front disc brake pads worn out. The noise comes from the wear sensor rubbing against the disc. Replace pads with new ones immediately (Chapter 9).

44 Brake roughness or chatter (pedal pulsates)

Note: *Brake pedal pulsation during operation of the Anti-Lock Brake System (ABS) is normal.*
1 Excessive front brake disc lateral runout (Chapter 9).
2 Parallelism not within specifications (Chapter 9).
3 Uneven pad wear caused by caliper not sliding due to improper clearance or dirt (Chapter 9).
4 Defective brake disc (Chapter 9).

45 Excessive pedal effort required to stop vehicle

1 Malfunctioning power brake booster (Chapter 9).
2 Partial system failure (Chapter 9).
3 Excessively worn pads (Chapter 9).
4 One or more caliper pistons or wheel cylinders seized or sticking (Chapter 9).
5 Brake pads contaminated with oil or grease (Chapter 9).
6 New pads installed and not yet seated. It will take a while for the new material to seat.

46 Excessive brake pedal travel

1 Partial brake system failure (Chapter 9).
2 Insufficient fluid in master cylinder (Chapters 1 and 9).
3 Air trapped in system (Chapters 1 and 9).
4 Excessively worn rear shoes (Chapter 9).

47 Dragging brakes

1 Master cylinder pistons not returning correctly (Chapter 9).
2 Restricted brakes lines or hoses (Chapters 1 and 9).
3 Incorrect parking brake adjustment (Chapter 9).
4 Sticking pistons in calipers (Chapter 9).

48 Grabbing or uneven braking action

1 Malfunction of proportioner valves (Chapter 9).
2 Malfunction of power brake booster unit (Chapter 9).
3 Binding brake pedal mechanism (Chapter 9).
4 Sticking pistons in calipers (Chapter 9).

49 Brake pedal feels spongy when depressed

1 Air in hydraulic lines (Chapter 9).
2 Master cylinder mounting bolts loose (Chapter 9).
3 Master cylinder defective (Chapter 9).

50 Brake pedal travels to the floor with little resistance

Little or no fluid in the master cylinder reservoir caused by leaking caliper or wheel cylinder pistons, loose, damaged or disconnected brake lines (Chapter 9).

51 Parking brake does not hold

Check the parking brake (Chapter 9).

Suspension and steering systems

Note: *Before attempting to diagnose the suspension and steering systems, perform the following preliminary checks:*
 a) Check the tire pressures and look for uneven wear.
 b) Check the steering universal joints or coupling from the column to the steering gear for loose fasteners and wear.
 c) Check the front and rear suspension and the steering gear assembly for loose and damaged parts.

d) Look for out-of-round or out-of-balance tires, bent rims and loose and/or rough wheel bearings.

52 Vehicle pulls to one side

1   Mismatched or uneven tires (Chapter 10).
2   Broken or sagging springs (Chapter 10).
3   Front wheel alignment incorrect (Chapter 10).
4   Front brakes dragging (Chapter 9).

53 Abnormal or excessive tire wear

1   Front wheel alignment incorrect (Chapter 10).
2   Sagging or broken springs (Chapter 10).
3   Tire out-of-balance (Chapter 10).
4   Worn shock absorber (Chapter 10).
5   Overloaded vehicle.
6   Tires not rotated regularly.

54 Wheel makes a "thumping" noise

1   Blister or bump on tire (Chapter 1).
2   Improper shock absorber action (Chapter 10).

55 Shimmy, shake or vibration

1   Tire or wheel out-of-balance or out-of-round (Chapter 10).
2   Loose or worn wheel bearings (Chapter 10).
3   Worn tie-rod ends (Chapter 10).
4   Worn balljoints (Chapter 10).
5   Excessive wheel runout (Chapter 10).
6   Blister or bump on tire (Chapter 1).

56 Hard steering

1   Lack of lubrication at balljoints, tie-rod ends and steering gear assembly (Chapter 10).
2   Front wheel alignment incorrect (Chapter 10).
3   Low tire pressure (Chapter 1).

57 Steering wheel does not return to center position correctly

1   Lack of lubrication at balljoints and tie-rod ends (Chapter 10).
2   Binding in steering column (Chapter 10).
3   Defective rack-and-pinion assembly (Chapter 10).

4   Front wheel alignment problem (Chapter 10).

58 Abnormal noise at the front end

1   Lack of lubrication at balljoints and tie-rod ends (Chapter 1).
2   Loose upper strut mount (Chapter 10).
3   Worn tie-rod ends (Chapter 10).
4   Loose stabilizer bar (Chapter 10).
5   Loose wheel lug nuts (Chapter 1).
6   Loose suspension bolts (Chapter 10).

59 Wander or poor steering stability

1   Mismatched or uneven tires (Chapter 10).
2   Lack of lubrication at balljoints or tie-rod ends (Chapters 1 and 10).
3   Worn shock absorbers (Chapter 10).
4   Loose stabilizer bar (Chapter 10).
5   Broken or sagging springs (Chapter 10).
6   Front wheel alignment incorrect (Chapter 10).
7   Worn steering gear clamp bushings (Chapter 10).

60 Erratic steering when braking

1   Wheel bearings worn (Chapters 8 and 10).
2   Broken or sagging springs (Chapter 10).
3   Leaking wheel cylinder or caliper (Chapter 9).
4   Warped brake discs (Chapter 9).
5   Worn steering gear clamp bushings (Chapter 10).

61 Excessive pitching and/or rolling around corners or during braking

1   Loose stabilizer bar (Chapter 10).
2   Worn shock absorbers or mounts (Chapter 10).
3   Broken or sagging springs (Chapter 10).
4   Overloaded vehicle.

62 Suspension bottoms

1   Overloaded vehicle.
2   Worn shock absorbers (Chapter 10).
3   Incorrect, broken or sagging springs (Chapter 10).

63 Cupped tires

1   Front wheel alignment incorrect (Chapter 10).
2   Worn shock absorbers (Chapter 10).
3   Wheel bearings worn (Chapters 8 and 10).
4   Excessive tire or wheel runout (Chapter 10).
5   Worn balljoints (Chapter 10).

64 Excessive tire wear on outside edge

1   Inflation pressures incorrect (Chapter 1).
2   Excessive speed in turns.
3   Front end alignment incorrect (excessive toe-in or positive camber). Have professionally aligned.
4   Suspension arm bent or twisted (Chapter 10).

65 Excessive tire wear on inside edge

1   Inflation pressures incorrect (Chapter 1).
2   Front end alignment incorrect (toe-out or excessive negative camber). Have professionally aligned.
3   Loose or damaged steering components (Chapter 10).

66 Tire tread worn in one place

1   Tires out-of-balance.
2   Damaged or buckled wheel. Inspect and replace if necessary.
3   Defective tire (Chapter 1).

67 Excessive play or looseness in steering system

1   Wheel bearings worn (Chapter 10).
2   Tie-rod end loose or worn (Chapter 10).
3   Steering gear loose (Chapter 10).

68 Rattling or clicking noise in rack and pinion

Steering gear clamps loose (Chapter 10).

Chapter 1
Tune-up and routine maintenance

Contents

Specifications

Recommended lubricants and fluids

Note: *Listed here are manufacturer recommendations at the time this manual was written. Manufacturers occasionally upgrade their fluid and lubricant specifications, so check with your local auto parts store for current recommendations.*

Engine oil
  Type ... API "certified for gasoline engines"
  Viscosity ... See accompanying chart
Automatic transmission fluid ... Dexron III Automatic Transmission Fluid (ATF)
Engine coolant ... 50/50 mixture of water and the specified ethylene glycol-based (green color) antifreeze or "DEX-COOL", silicate-free (orange-color) coolant - DO NOT mix the two types (refer to Sections 4, 11 and 27)
Brake fluid ... DOT 3 brake fluid
Power steering fluid ... GM power steering fluid or equivalent
Chassis grease ... SAE NLGI no. 2 chassis grease

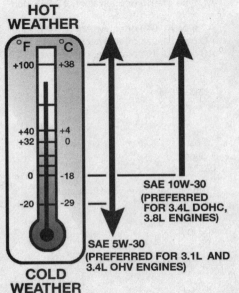

Engine oil viscosity chart - For best fuel economy and cold starting, select the lowest SAE viscosity grade for the expected temperature range

LOOK FOR ONE OF THESE LABELS

1-a3 HAYNES

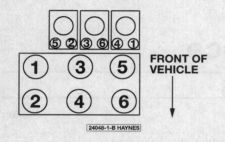

Cylinder location and coil terminal identification diagram - 3.1L and 3.4L OHV engine

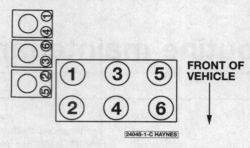

Cylinder location and coil terminal identification diagram - 3.4L DOHC engine

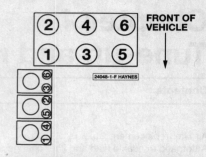

Cylinder location and coil terminal identification diagram - 3.8L engine

Capacities*

Engine oil (with filter change)	
3.1L and 3.4L OHV	4.0 to 5.0 qts
3.4L DOHC	5.5 to 6.0 qts
3.8L	4.5 to 5.0 qts
Fuel tank	
All (except 3.1L)...	17.1 gallons
3.1L	16.1 gallons
Cooling system	
1995 through 1996	
3.1L (with 3T40 transmission)......................................	12.7 qts
3.1L (with 4T60-E transmission)...................................	12.5 qts
3.4L DOHC (with 4T60-E transmission).........................	12.7 qts
1997 on	
3.1L and 3.4L OHV	11.6 qts
3.4L DOHC	12.3 qts
3.8L	11.6 qts
Automatic transmission (fluid and filter replacement)	7.4 to 10 qts

All capacities approximate. Add as necessary to bring to appropriate level.

Ignition system

Spark plug type and gap	
1995	
3.1L	AC type R44LTSM or equivalent @ 0.060 inch
3.4L	AC type R42LTSM or equivalent @ 0.045 inch
1996 through 1997	
3.1L	AC type 41-940 or equivalent @ 0.060 inch
3.4L	AC type 41-919 or equivalent @ 0.045 inch
1998 through 2002	
3.1L and 3.4L OHV	AC type 41-940 or equivalent @ 0.060 inch
3.8L	AC type 41-921 or equivalent @ 0.060 inch
2003 and later (all engines)	AC type 41-101 platinum, or equivalent @ 0.060 inch
Firing order	
3.1L and 3.4L OHV	1-2-3-4-5-6
3.4L DOHC	1-2-3-4-5-6
3.8L	1-6-5-4-3-2

General

Radiator cap pressure rating	15 psi
Brake pad lining wear limit	1/8 inch
Brake shoe lining wear limit..	3/32 inch

Torque specifications

	Ft-lbs (unless otherwise indicated)
Automatic transmission pan bolts	90 to 100 in-lbs
Engine oil drain plug	15 to 20
Spark plugs..	132 in-lbs
Wheel lug nuts	100

**Typical engine
compartment components
- 3.1L engine (3.4L similar)**

1   Ignition coil pack and
    spark plug wires
2   Automatic transmission
    fluid dipstick
3   Brake master cylinder
    reservoir
4   Engine compartment fuse
    block No. 2
5   Battery (not visible)
6   Windshield washer fluid
    reservoir
7   Upper radiator hose
8   Air filter housing
9   PCV valve
10 Engine oil dipstick
11 Engine oil filler cap
12 Spark plugs (front side)
13 Lower radiator hose
14 Radiator cap
15 Engine compartment fuse
    block No. 1
16 Power steering fluid
    reservoir
17 Engine coolant reservoir
18 Drivebelt

**Typical engine
compartment components
- 3800 engine**

1   Automatic transmission
    fluid dipstick
2   Brake master cylinder
    reservoir
3   Engine compartment fuse
    block No. 2
4   Battery (not visible)
5   Windshield washer fluid
    reservoir
6   Air filter housing
7   Upper radiator hose
8   Spark plugs (front side)
9   Engine oil filler cap
10 Engine oil dipstick
11 Lower radiator hose
12 Radiator cap
13 Engine compartment fuse
    block No. 1
14 Ignition coil pack and
    spark plug wires
15 PCV valve
16 Engine coolant reservoir
17 Drivebelt
18 Power steering fluid
    reservoir (not visible in
    photo; below alternator)

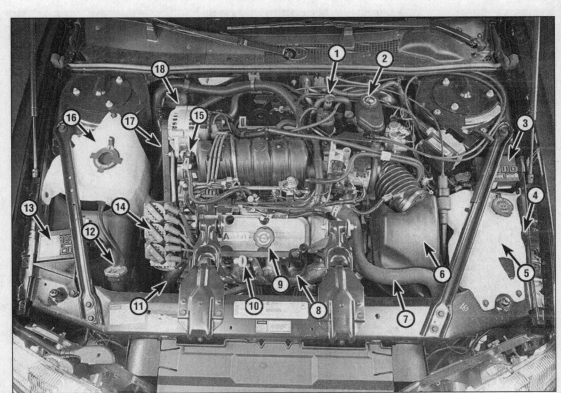

Typical front underside components

1 Radiator drain plug (not visible)
2 Front brake caliper
3 Lower control arm bushing
4 Fuel lines
5 Automatic transaxle fluid pan
6 Engine oil drain plug
7 Steering gear
8 Tie-rod end
9 Driveaxle

Typical rear underside components

1 Fuel filler pipe and hose assembly
2 Exhaust hanger
3 Muffler
4 Rear brake hose
5 Trailing arm bushing
6 Fuel tank
7 Lateral link rod
8 Shock/strut assembly
9 Stabilizer bar bushing

1 Chevrolet Lumina, Monte Carlo and front-wheel drive Impala Maintenance schedule

The following maintenance intervals are based on the assumption that the vehicle owner will be doing the maintenance or service work, as opposed to having a dealer service department do the work. Although the time/mileage intervals are loosely based on factory recommendations, most have been shortened to ensure, for example, that such items as lubricants and fluids are checked/changed at intervals that promote maximum engine/driveline service life. Also, subject to the preference of the individual owner interested in keeping his or her vehicle in peak condition at all times, and with the vehicle's ultimate resale in mind, many of the maintenance procedures may be performed more often than recommended in the following schedule. We encourage such owner initiative.

When the vehicle is new it should be serviced initially by a factory authorized dealer service department to protect the factory warranty. In many cases the initial maintenance check is done at no cost to the owner (check with your dealer service department for more information).

Every 250 miles or weekly, whichever comes first

Check the engine oil level (Section 4)
Check the engine coolant level (Section 4)
Check the windshield washer fluid level (Section 4)
Check the brake fluid level (Section 4)
Check the tires and tire pressures (Section 5)

Every 3000 miles or 3 months, whichever comes first

All items listed above plus:
Check the power steering fluid level (Section 6)
Check the automatic transmission fluid level (Section 7)
Change the engine oil and filter (Section 8)
Lubricate the chassis (Section 9)

Every 6000 miles or 6 months, whichever comes first

All items listed above plus:
Check and service the battery (Section 10)
Check the cooling system (Section 11)
Inspect and replace, if necessary, all underhood hoses (Section 12)
Check the engine drivebelt (Section 13)
Inspect the suspension and steering components and the driveaxle boots (Section 14)
Check the brakes (Section 15)*
Rotate the tires (Section 16)
Inspect the exhaust system (Section 17)

Every 12,000 miles or 12 months, whichever comes first

Inspect the throttle linkage (Section 18)
Inspect and replace, if necessary, the windshield wiper blades (Section 19)
Inspect the seat belts (Section 20)
Replace the air filter (Section 21)
Replace the interior ventilation filter (2000 and later models) (Section 30)

Every 30,000 miles or 24 months, whichever comes first

All items listed above plus:
Inspect and replace, if necessary, the PCV valve (Section 22)
Inspect and replace, if necessary the spark plug wires (Section 23)
Replace the spark plugs (conventional [non-platinum] spark plugs) (Section 24)
Replace the fuel filter (Section 25)
Inspect the fuel system (Section 26)
Service the cooling system (drain, flush and refill) (green-colored ethylene glycol anti-freeze only) (Section 27)

Every 60,000 miles or 48 months, whichever comes first

Change the automatic transaxle fluid and filter (Section 28)**
Inspect and replace, if necessary the timing belt (3.4L DOHC V6 engines) (Chapter 2B). **Note:** *After 60,000 miles, the timing belt should be inspected every 15,000 miles.*

Every 100,000 miles or 5 years, whichever comes first

Replace the spark plugs (platinum-tipped spark plugs) (Section 24)
Service the cooling system (drain, flush and refill) (orange-colored "DEX-COOL" silicate-free coolant only) (Section 27)

*If the vehicle frequently tows a trailer, is operated primarily in stop-and-go conditions or its brakes receive severe usage for any other reason, check the brakes every 3000 miles or three months.
**If operated under one or more of the following conditions, change the automatic transmission fluid every 30,000 miles:
In heavy city traffic where the outside temperature regularly reaches 90-degrees F (32-degrees C) or higher
In hilly or mountainous terrain
Frequent trailer pulling

4.2 The engine oil dipstick (arrow) is located on the front side of the engine on all models

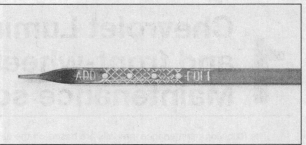

4.4 The oil level should be at or near the upper hole or in the cross-hatched area on the dipstick - if it's below the ADD line, add enough oil to bring the level into the upper hole or top of the cross-hatched area

2   Introduction

This Chapter is designed to help the home mechanic maintain the Chevrolet Lumina, Monte Carlo and front-wheel drive Impala models with the goals of maximum performance, economy, safety and reliability in mind.

Included is a master maintenance schedule, followed by procedures dealing specifically with each item on the schedule. Visual checks, adjustments, component replacement and other helpful items are included. Refer to the **accompanying illustrations** of the engine compartment and the underside of the vehicle for the locations of various components.

Servicing your vehicle in accordance with the mileage/time maintenance schedule and the step-by-step procedures will result in a planned maintenance program that should produce a long and reliable service life. Keep in mind that it's a comprehensive plan, so maintaining some items but not others at the specified intervals will not produce the same results.

As you service your vehicle, you'll discover that many of the procedures can - and should - be grouped together because of the nature of the particular procedure you're performing or because of the close proximity of two otherwise unrelated components to one another.

For example, if the vehicle is raised, you should inspect the exhaust, suspension, steering and fuel systems while you're under the vehicle. When you're rotating the tires, it makes good sense to check the brakes since the wheels are already removed. Finally, let's suppose you have to borrow or rent a torque wrench. Even if you only need it to tighten the spark plugs, you might as well check the torque of as many critical fasteners as time allows.

The first step in this maintenance program is to prepare yourself before the actual work begins. Read through all the procedures you're planning to do, then gather up all the parts and tools needed. If it looks like you might run into problems during a particular job, seek advice from a mechanic or an experienced do-it-yourselfer. **Caution:** *The stereo in your vehicle may be equipped with an anti-theft system. Refer to the information at the front of this manual before performing any procedure which requires disconnecting the battery cable.*

3   Tune-up general information

The term tune-up is used in this manual to represent a combination of individual operations rather than one specific procedure.

If, from the time the vehicle is new, the routine maintenance schedule is followed closely and frequent checks are made of fluid levels and high wear items, as suggested throughout this manual, the engine will be kept in relatively good running condition and the need for additional work will be minimized due to lack of regular maintenance. This is even more likely if a used vehicle, which has not received regular and frequent maintenance checks, is purchased. In such cases, an engine tune-up will be needed outside of the regular routine maintenance intervals.

The first step in any tune-up or diagnostic procedure to help correct a poor running engine is a cylinder compression check. A compression check (see Chapter 2, Part B) will help determine the condition of internal engine components and should be used as a guide for tune-up and repair procedures. If, for instance, a compression check indicates serious internal engine wear, a conventional tune-up won't improve the performance of the engine and would be a waste of time and money. Because of its importance, the compression check should be done by someone with the right equipment and the knowledge to use it properly.

The following procedures are those most often needed to bring a generally poor running engine back into a proper state of tune.

Minor tune-up

Check all engine related fluids (Section 4)
Clean, inspect and test the battery (Section 10)
Check the cooling system (Section 11)
Check all underhood hoses (Section 12)
Check and adjust the drivebelts (Section 13)
Check the air filter (Section 21)
Check the PCV valve (Section 22)
Inspect the spark plug wires (Section 23)
Replace the spark plugs (Section 24)

Major tune-up

All items listed under Minor tune-up plus . . .

Replace the air filter (Section 21)
Replace the spark plug wires (Section 23)
Replace the fuel filter (Section 25)
Check the fuel system (Section 26)
Check the ignition timing (Chapter 5)
Check the charging system (Chapter 5)
Check the EGR system (Chapter 6)

4   Fluid level checks (every 250 miles or weekly)

Note: *The following are fluid level checks to be done on a 250 mile or weekly basis. Additional fluid level checks can be found in specific maintenance procedures which follow. Regardless of intervals, be alert to fluid leaks under the vehicle which would indicate a problem to be corrected immediately.*

1   Fluids are an essential part of the lubrication, cooling, brake and windshield washer systems. Because the fluids gradually become depleted and/or contaminated during normal operation of the vehicle, they must be periodically replenished. See *Recommended lubricants and fluids* at the beginning of this Chapter before adding fluid to any of the following components. **Note:** *The vehicle must be on level ground when fluid levels are checked.*

Engine oil

Refer to illustrations 4.2, 4.4 and 4.6

2   The engine oil level is checked with a dipstick **(see illustration)**. The dipstick extends through a metal tube down into the oil pan.
3   The oil level should be checked before the vehicle has been driven, or about 15 minutes after the engine has been shut off. If the oil is checked immediately after driving the vehicle, some of the oil will remain in the upper part of the engine, resulting in an inaccurate reading on the dipstick.
4   Pull the dipstick from the tube and wipe all the oil from the end with a clean rag or paper towel. Insert the clean dipstick all the way back into the tube and pull it out again. Note the oil at the end of the dipstick. Add oil as necessary to keep the level above the ADD mark in the cross hatched area of the dipstick **(see illustration)**.

4.6 The engine oil filler cap (arrow) is clearly marked and threads into the tube on the valve cover - turn it counterclockwise to remove it

4.9 The coolant reservoir is located on the right (passenger's) side of the engine compartment - the coolant level can be checked by observing it through the translucent reservoir

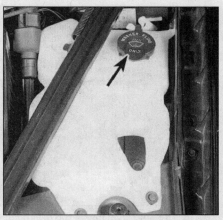

4.14 Flip the windshield washer fluid cap (arrow) up to add fluid

5   Do not overfill the engine by adding too much oil since this may result in oil fouled spark plugs, oil leaks or oil seal failures.

6   Oil is added to the engine after removing a twist-off cap located on the valve cover **(see illustration)**. A funnel may help to reduce spills.

7   Checking the oil level is an important preventive maintenance step. A consistently low oil level indicates oil leakage through damaged seals, defective gaskets or past worn rings or valve guides. If the oil looks milky in color or has water droplets in it, the cylinder head gasket may be blown or the head or block may be cracked. The engine should be checked immediately. The condition of the oil should also be checked. Whenever you check the oil level, slide your thumb and index finger up the dipstick before wiping off the oil. If you see small dirt or metal particles clinging to the dipstick, the oil should be changed (see Section 8).

Engine coolant

Refer to illustration 4.9

Warning: *Do not allow antifreeze to come in contact with your skin or painted surfaces of the vehicle. Flush contaminated areas immediately with plenty of water. Do not store new coolant or leave old coolant lying around where it's accessible to children or pets - they're attracted by its sweet smell. Ingestion of even a small amount of coolant can be fatal! Wipe up garage floor and drip pan coolant spills immediately. Keep antifreeze containers covered and repair leaks in the cooling system immediately.*

Caution: *Never mix green-colored ethylene glycol anti-freeze and orange-colored "DEX-COOL" silicate-free coolant because doing so will destroy the efficiency of the "DEX-COOL" coolant which is designed to last for 100,000 miles or five years.*

8   All vehicles covered by this manual are equipped with a pressurized coolant recovery system. A plastic coolant reservoir located at the front of the engine compartment is connected by a hose to the radiator assembly. As the engine warms up and the coolant expands, it escapes through a valve in the radiator cap and travels through the hose into the reservoir. As the engine cools, the coolant is automatically drawn back into the cooling system to maintain the correct level.

9   The coolant level in the reservoir should be checked regularly. **Warning:** *Do not remove the radiator cap or the reservoir cap to check the coolant level when the engine is warm.* The level of coolant in the reservoir varies with the temperature of the engine. When the engine is cold, the coolant level should be at or slightly above the COLD mark on the reservoir **(see illustration)**. Once the engine has warmed up, the level should be at or near the HOT mark. If it isn't, add coolant to the reservoir. To add coolant simply flip up the cap and add a 50/50 mixture of ethylene glycol based green-colored antifreeze or orange-colored "DEX-COOL" silicate-free coolant and water (see **Caution** above).

10   Drive the vehicle and recheck the coolant level. If only a small amount of coolant is required to bring the system up to the proper level, water can be used. However, repeated additions of water will dilute the antifreeze and water solution. In order to maintain the proper ratio of antifreeze and water, always top up the coolant level with the correct mixture. An empty plastic milk jug or bleach bottle makes an excellent container for mixing coolant. Do not use rust inhibitors or additives.

11   If the coolant level drops consistently, there may be a leak in the system. Inspect the radiator, hoses, filler cap, drain plugs and water pump (see Section 11). If no leaks are noted, have the radiator cap or coolant reservoir cap pressure tested by a service station.

12   If you have to remove the radiator cap, wait until the engine has cooled completely, then wrap a thick cloth around the cap and turn it to the first stop. If coolant or steam escapes, let the engine cool down longer, then remove the cap.

13   Check the condition of the coolant as well. It should be relatively clear. If it is brown or rust colored, the system should be drained, flushed and refilled. Even if the coolant appears to be normal, the corrosion inhibitors wear out, so it must be replaced at the specified intervals.

Windshield washer fluid

Refer to illustration 4.14

14   Fluid for the windshield washer system is located in a plastic reservoir on the left side (driver's side) of the engine compartment **(see illustration)**. In milder climates, plain water can be used in the reservoir, but it should be kept no more than two-thirds full to allow for expansion if the water freezes. In colder climates, use windshield washer system antifreeze, available at any auto parts store, to lower the freezing point of the fluid. Mix the antifreeze with water in accordance with the manufacturer's directions on the container. **Caution:** *Do not use cooling system antifreeze - it will damage the vehicle's paint.*

15   To help prevent icing in cold weather, warm the windshield with the defroster before using the washer.

Battery electrolyte

16   All vehicles covered by this manual are equipped with a battery which is permanently sealed (except for vent holes) and has no filler caps. Water does not have to be added to these batteries at any time.

Brake fluid

Refer to illustration 4.18

17   The brake fluid level is checked by looking through the plastic reservoir mounted on the master cylinder. The master cylinder is mounted on the front of the power booster unit in the left (driver's side) rear corner of the engine compartment.

18   The fluid level should be at or near the

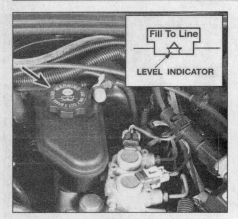

4.18 The fluid level inside the brake fluid reservoir can easily be checked by observing the level after unscrewing the cap - if necessary, add additional fluid until it reaches the top of the level indicator - DO NOT OVERFILL

base of the reservoir filler neck **(see illustration)**. If the fluid level is low, wipe the top of the reservoir and the lid with a clean rag to prevent contamination of the system as the lid is pried off.

19   When adding fluid, pour it carefully into the reservoir to avoid spilling it on surrounding painted surfaces. Be sure the specified fluid is used, since mixing different types of brake fluid can cause damage to the system. See *Recommended lubricants and fluids* at the front of this Chapter or your

5.2 Use a tire tread depth gauge to monitor tire wear - they are available at auto parts stores and service stations and cost very little

owner's manual. **Warning:** *Brake fluid can harm your eyes and damage painted surfaces, so use extreme caution when handling or pouring it. Do not use brake fluid that has been standing open or is more than one year old. Brake fluid absorbs moisture from the air. Excess moisture can cause a dangerous loss of braking effectiveness.*

20   At this time the fluid and master cylinder can be inspected for contamination. The system should be drained and refilled if deposits, dirt particles or water droplets are seen in the fluid.

21   After filling the reservoir to the proper level, make sure the lid completely snaps in

place to prevent fluid leakage.

22   The brake fluid level in the master cylinder will drop slightly as the pads at each wheel wear down during normal operation. If the master cylinder requires repeated replenishing to keep it at the proper level, this is an indication of leakage in the brake system, which should be corrected immediately. Check all brake lines and connections (see Section 15 for more information).

23   If, when checking the master cylinder fluid level, you discover one or both reservoirs empty or nearly empty, the brake system should be bled (see Chapter 9).

5   Tire and tire pressure checks (every 250 miles or weekly)

Refer to illustrations 5.2, 5.3, 5.4a, 5.4b and 5.8

1   Periodic inspection of the tires may spare you the inconvenience of being stranded with a flat tire. It can also provide you with vital information regarding possible problems in the steering and suspension systems before major damage occurs.

2   The original tires on this vehicle are equipped with 1/2-inch wide bands that appear when tread depth reaches 1/16-inch, indicating the tires are worn out. Tread wear can be monitored with a simple, inexpensive device known as a tread depth indicator **(see illustration)**.

3   Note any abnormal tread wear **(see illustration)**. Tread pattern irregularities such as cupping, flat spots and more wear on one

UNDERINFLATION

CUPPING

Cupping may be caused by:
- Underinflation and/or mechanical irregularities such as out-of-balance condition of wheel and/or tire, and bent or damaged wheel.
- Loose or worn steering tie-rod or steering idler arm.
- Loose, damaged or worn front suspension parts.

OVERINFLATION

INCORRECT TOE-IN OR EXTREME CAMBER

FEATHERING DUE TO MISALIGNMENT

5.3 This chart will help you determine the condition of the tires, the probable cause(s) of abnormal wear and the corrective action necessary

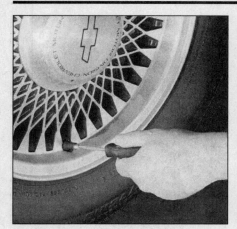

5.4a If a tire loses air on a steady basis, check the valve core first to make sure it's snug (special inexpensive wrenches are commonly available at auto parts stores)

5.4b If the valve core is tight, raise the corner of the vehicle with the low tire and spray a soapy water solution onto the tread as the tire is turned slowly - leaks will cause small bubbles to appear

5.8 To extend the life of the tires, check the air pressure at least once a week with an accurate gauge (don't forget the spare)

side than the other are indications of front end alignment and/or balance problems. If any of these conditions are noted, take the vehicle to a tire shop or service station to correct the problem.

4 Look closely for cuts, punctures and embedded nails or tacks. Sometimes a tire will hold air pressure for short time or leak down very slowly after a nail has embedded itself in the tread. If a slow leak persists, check the valve stem core to make sure it's tight **(see illustration)**. Examine the tread for an object that may have embedded itself in the tire or for a "plug" that may have begun to leak (radial tire punctures are repaired with a plug that's installed in a puncture). If a puncture is suspected, it can be easily verified by spraying a solution of soapy water onto the suspected area **(see illustration)**. The soapy solution will bubble if there's a leak. Unless the puncture is unusually large, a tire shop or service station can usually repair the tire.

5 Carefully inspect the inner sidewall of each tire for evidence of brake fluid. If you see any, inspect the brakes immediately.

6 Correct air pressure adds miles to the lifespan of the tires, improves mileage and enhances overall ride quality. Tire pressure cannot be accurately estimated by looking at a tire, especially if it's a radial. A tire pressure gauge is essential. Keep an accurate gauge in the vehicle. The pressure gauges attached to the nozzles of air hoses at gas stations are often inaccurate.

7 Always check tire pressure when the tires are cold. Cold, in this case, means the vehicle has not been driven over a mile in the three hours preceding a tire pressure check. A pressure rise of four to eight pounds is not uncommon once the tires are warm.

8 Unscrew the valve cap protruding from the wheel or hubcap and push the gauge firmly onto the valve stem **(see illustration)**. Note the reading on the gauge and compare the figure to the recommended tire pressure shown on the label attached to the inside of

6.2 The power steering fluid reservoir (arrow) is located on the right (passenger's) side of the engine compartment - turn the cap counterclockwise for removal (3.1L and 3.4L location shown)

the glove compartment door. Be sure to reinstall the valve cap to keep dirt and moisture out of the valve stem mechanism. Check all four tires and, if necessary, add enough air to bring them up to the recommended pressure.

9 Don't forget to keep the spare tire inflated to the specified pressure (refer to your owner's manual or the tire sidewall).

6 Power steering fluid level check (every 3000 miles or 3 months)

Refer to illustrations 6.2 and 6.6

1 The power steering system relies on fluid which may, over a period of time, require replenishing.

2 The fluid reservoir for the power steering

6.6 The marks on the dipstick indicate the safe fluid range

pump is mounted on the front of the engine by the engine drivebelt **(see illustration)**.

3 For the check, the front wheels should be pointed straight ahead and the engine should be off.

4 Use a clean rag to wipe off the reservoir cap and the area around the cap. This will help prevent any foreign matter from entering the reservoir during the check.

5 Twist off the cap and check the temperature of the fluid at the end of the dipstick with your finger.

6 Wipe off the fluid with a clean rag, reinsert it, then withdraw it and read the fluid level. The level should be at the HOT mark if the fluid was hot to the touch **(see illustration)**. It should be at the COLD mark if the fluid was cool to the touch.

7 If additional fluid is required, pour the specified type directly into the reservoir, using a funnel to prevent spills.

8 If the reservoir requires frequent fluid additions, all power steering hoses, hose connections, the power steering pump and the rack and pinion assembly should be carefully checked for leaks.

7.3 The automatic transmission fluid dipstick (arrow) is located at the rear of the engine compartment on all models

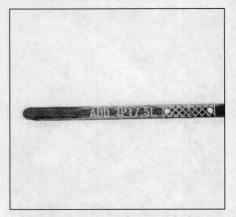

7.6 With the automatic transmission at normal operating temperature, the fluid level must be maintained within the cross-hatched area on the dipstick, between the upper and lower holes

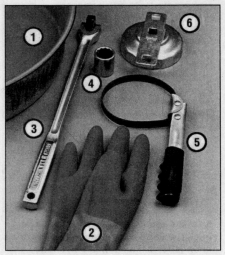

8.2 These tools are required when changing the engine oil and filter

1   **Drain pan** - *It should be fairly shallow in depth, but wide to prevent spills*
2   **Rubber gloves** - *When removing the drain plug and filter, you will get oil on your hands (the gloves will prevent burns)*
3   **Breaker bar** - *Sometimes the oil drain plug is tight, and a long breaker bar is needed to loosen it*
4   **Socket** - *To be used with the breaker bar or a ratchet (must be the correct size to fit the drain plug)*
5   **Filter wrench** - *This is a metal band-type wrench, which requires clearance around the filter to be effective*
6   **Filter wrench** - *This type fits on the bottom of the filter and can be turned with a ratchet or breaker bar (different-size wrenches are available for different types of filters)*

7   Automatic transaxle fluid level check (every 3000 miles or 3 months)

Refer to illustrations 7.3 and 7.6

1   The automatic transmission fluid level should be carefully maintained. Low fluid level can lead to slipping or loss of drive, while overfilling can cause foaming and loss of fluid.
2   With the parking brake set, start the engine, then move the shift lever through all the gear ranges, ending in Park. The fluid level must be checked with the vehicle level and the engine running at idle. **Note:** *Incorrect fluid level readings will result if the vehicle has just been driven at high speeds for an extended period, in hot weather in city traffic, or if it has been pulling a trailer. If any of these conditions apply, wait until the fluid has cooled (about 30 minutes).*
3   With the transmission at normal operating temperature, remove the dipstick from the filler tube. The dipstick is located at the rear of the engine compartment **(see illustration)**.
4   Carefully touch the fluid at the end of the dipstick to determine if the fluid is cool, warm or hot. Wipe the fluid from the dipstick with a clean rag and push it back into the filler tube until the cap seats.
5   Pull the dipstick out again and note the fluid level.
6   If the fluid felt cool, the level should be within the lower marks on the dipstick **(see illustration)**. If it felt warm or hot, the level should be within the cross-hatched upper areas on the dipstick. If additional fluid is required, pour it directly into the tube using a funnel. It takes about one pint to raise the level from the lower mark to the upper edge of the cross-hatched area with a hot transmission, so add the fluid a little at a time and keep checking the level until it's correct.
7   The condition of the fluid should also be checked along with the level. If the fluid at the end of the dipstick is a dark reddish-brown color, or if the fluid has a burned smell, the

fluid should be changed. If you're in doubt about the condition of the fluid, purchase some new fluid and compare the two for color and smell.

8   Engine oil and filter change (every 3000 miles or 3 months)

Refer to illustrations 8.2, 8.7, 8.12 and 8.14

1   Frequent oil changes are the best preventive maintenance the home mechanic can give the engine, because aging oil becomes diluted and contaminated, which leads to premature engine wear.
2   Make sure you have all the necessary tools before you begin this procedure **(see illustration)**. You should also have plenty of rags or newspapers handy for mopping up any spills.
3   Access to the underside of the vehicle is greatly improved if the vehicle can be lifted on a hoist, driven onto ramps or supported by jackstands. **Warning:** *Do not work under a vehicle which is supported only by a hydraulic or scissors-type jack.*
4   If this is your first oil change, get under

8.7 The engine oil drain plug is located at the rear of the oil pan - it is usually very tight, so use a socket or box-end wrench to avoid rounding off the hex

the vehicle and familiarize yourself with the locations of the oil drain plug and the oil filter. The engine and exhaust components will be warm during the actual work, so try to anticipate any potential problems before the engine and accessories are hot.
5   Park the vehicle on a level spot. Start the engine and allow it to reach its normal operating temperature. Warm oil and sludge will flow out more easily. Turn off the engine when it's warmed up. Remove the filler cap from the valve cover.
6   Raise the vehicle and support it securely on jackstands. **Warning:** *Never get beneath the vehicle when it is supported only by a jack. The jack provided with your vehicle is designed solely for raising the vehicle to remove and replace the wheels. Always use jackstands to support the vehicle when it becomes necessary to place your body underneath the vehicle.*
7   Being careful not to touch the hot exhaust components, place the drain pan under the drain plug in the bottom of the pan and remove the plug **(see illustration)**. You may want to wear gloves while unscrewing the plug the final few turns if the engine is hot.

8.12 The oil filter is usually on very tight as well and will require a special wrench for removal - DO NOT use the wrench to tighten the new filter!

8.14 Lubricate the oil filter gasket with clean engine oil before installing the filter on the engine

9.1 Materials required for chassis and body lubrication

1 *Engine oil* - Light engine oil in a can like this can be used for door and hood hinges
2 *Graphite spray* - Used to lubricate lock cylinders
3 *Grease* - Grease, in a variety of types and weights, is available for use in a grease gun. Check the Specification for your requirements
4 *Grease gun* - A common grease gun, shown here with a detachable hose and nozzle, is needed for chassis lubrication. After use, clean it thoroughly!

8   Allow the old oil to drain into the pan. It may be necessary to move the pan farther under the engine as the oil flow slows to a trickle. Inspect the old oil for the presence of metal shavings and chips.

9   After all the oil has drained, wipe off the drain plug with a clean rag. Even minute metal particles clinging to the plug would immediately contaminate the new oil.

10   Clean the area around the drain plug opening, reinstall the plug and tighten it to the specifications listed at the beginning of this Chapter.

11   Move the drain pan into position under the oil filter.

12   Loosen the oil filter **(see illustration)** by turning it counterclockwise with the filter wrench. **Note:** *Oil filters on 3.1L and 3.4L engines are located on the front side of the engine block, while the oil filter on 3.8L engines is located on the rear side of the engine block next the crankshaft pulley.* Use a quality filter wrench of the correct size and be careful not to collapse the canister as you apply pressure. Once the filter is loose, use your hands to unscrew it from the block. Just as the filter is detached from the block, immediately tilt the open end up to prevent the oil inside the filter from spilling out. **Warning:** *The exhaust system may still be hot, so be careful.*

13   With a clean rag, wipe off the mounting surface on the block. If a residue of old oil is allowed to remain, it will smoke when the block is heated up. Also make sure that none of the old gasket remains stuck to the mounting surface. It can be removed with a scraper if necessary.

14   Compare the old filter with the new one to make sure they are the same type. Smear some clean engine oil on the rubber gasket of the new filter and screw it into place **(see illustration)**. Because overtightening the filter will damage the gasket, do not use a filter wrench to tighten the filter. Tighten it by hand until the gasket contacts the seating surface. Then seat the filter by giving it an additional 3/4-turn.

15   Remove all tools, rags, etc. from under the vehicle, being careful not to spill the oil in

the drain pan, then lower the vehicle.

16   Add new oil to the engine through the oil filler cap in the valve cover. Use a funnel, if necessary, to prevent oil from spilling onto the top of the engine. Pour three quarts of fresh oil into the engine. Wait a few minutes to allow the oil to drain into the pan, then check the level on the oil dipstick (see Section 4 if necessary). If the oil level is at or near the upper hole on the dipstick, install the filler cap hand tight, start the engine and allow the new oil to circulate.

17   Allow the engine to run for about a minute. While the engine is running, look under the vehicle and check for leaks at the oil pan drain plug and around the oil filter. If either is leaking, stop the engine and tighten the plug or filter.

18   Wait a few minutes to allow the oil to trickle down into the pan, then recheck the level on the dipstick and, if necessary, add enough oil to bring the level to the upper hole.

19   During the first few trips after an oil change, make it a point to check frequently for leaks and proper oil level.

20   The old oil drained from the engine cannot be re-used in its present state and should be discarded. Check with your local refuse disposal company, disposal facility or environmental agency to see whether they will accept the oil for recycling. Don't pour used oil into drains or onto the ground. After the oil has cooled, it can be drained into a suitable container (capped plastic jugs, topped bottles, milk cartons, etc.) for transport to one of these disposal sites.

9   Chassis lubrication (every 3000 miles or 3 months)

Refer to illustrations 9.1 and 9.6

1   All suspension and steering joints are factory sealed and DO NOT require lubrication, however other various chassis components such as hood and door hinges, door locks, parking brake cable guides and transaxle shift linkage require regularly scheduled lubrication. Specific materials and equipment are needed to perform these tasks

(see illustration).

2   Open the hood and smear a little chassis grease on the hood latch mechanism. Have an assistant pull the hood release lever from inside the vehicle as you lubricate the cable at the latch.

3   Lubricate all the hinges (door, hood, etc.) with engine oil to keep them in proper working order.

4   The key lock cylinders can be lubricated with spray graphite or silicone lubricant, which is available at auto parts stores.

5   Lubricate the door weatherstripping with silicone spray. This will reduce chafing and retard wear.

6   For easier access under the vehicle, raise it with a jack and place jackstands under the frame. Make sure it's safely supported by the stands. Then clean and lubricate the transaxle shift linkage with engine oil **(see illustration)**.

9.6 Lubricate the transaxle shift linkage (arrow) with clean engine oil

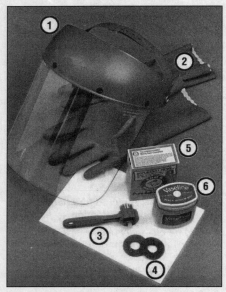

10.1 Tools and materials required for battery maintenance

1   **Face shield/safety goggles** - *When removing corrosion with a brush, the acidic particles can easily fly up into your eyes*
2   **Rubber gloves** - *Another safety item to consider when servicing the battery - remember that's acid inside the battery!*
3   **Battery terminal/cable cleaner** - *This wire brush cleaning tool will remove all traces of corrosion from the battery and cable*
4   **Treated felt washers** - *Placing one of these on each terminal, directly under the cable end, will help prevent corrosion (be sure to get the correct type for side-terminal batteries)*
5   **Baking soda** - *A solution of baking soda and water can be used to neutralize corrosion*
6   **Petroleum jelly** - *A layer of this on the battery terminal bolts will help prevent corrosion*

7   Clean and lubricate the parking brake cable guides and levers. This can be done by using a grease gun. **Note:** *DO NOT lubricate the parking brake cables, as this will deteriorate the plastic coating used to prevent the cables from rusting.*

10   Battery check, maintenance and charging (every 6000 miles or 6 months)

Refer to illustrations 10.1, 10.4, 10.5a, 10.5b and 10.5c
Warning: *Hydrogen gas is produced by the battery, so keep open flames and lighted tobacco away from it at all times. Always wear eye protection when working around the battery. Rinse off spilled electrolyte immedi-*

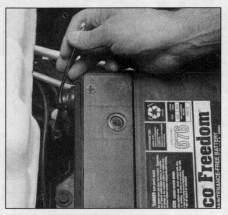

10.4 Check the tightness of the battery cable terminal bolts

10.5b Use the brush to finish the cleaning job

ately with large amounts of water. When removing the battery cables, always detach the negative cable first and hook it up last!
Caution: *If the radio in your vehicle is equipped with an anti-theft system, make sure you have the correct activation code before disconnecting the battery.*
1   Battery maintenance is an important procedure which will help ensure you aren't stranded because of a dead battery. Several tools are required for this procedure **(see illustration)**.
2   A sealed battery is standard equipment on all vehicles covered by this manual. Although this type of battery has many advantages over the older, capped cell type, and never requires the addition of water, it should still be routinely maintained according to the procedures which follow.

Check

3   The battery is located in the left front corner of the engine compartment beneath the windshield washer fluid reservoir. To access the battery, first remove the engine compartment support brace and the windshield washer fluid reservoir as described in the battery removal procedure in Chapter 5.

10.5a A tool like this one (available at auto parts stores) is used to clean the side terminal type battery contact area

10.5c The result should be a clean, shiny terminal area

4   Check the tightness of the battery cable terminals and connections to ensure good electrical connections and check the entire length of each cable for cracks and frayed conductors **(see illustration)**.
5   If corrosion (visible as white, fluffy deposits) is evident, remove the cables from the terminals, clean them with a battery brush and reinstall the cables **(see illustrations)**. Corrosion can be kept to a minimum by using special treated fiber washers available at auto parts stores or by applying a layer of petroleum jelly to the terminals and cables after they are assembled.
6   Make sure that the battery tray is in good condition and the hold-down clamp bolt is tight. If the battery is removed from the tray, make sure no parts remain in the bottom of the tray when the battery is reinstalled. When reinstalling the hold-down clamp bolt, do not overtighten it.
7   Information on removing and installing the battery can be found in Chapter 5. Information on jump starting can be found at the front of this manual. For more detailed battery checking procedures, refer to the *Haynes Automotive Electrical Manual*.

Cleaning

8   Corrosion on the hold-down components, battery case and surrounding areas can be removed with a solution of water and baking soda. Thoroughly rinse all cleaned areas with plain water.

9   Any metal parts of the vehicle damaged by corrosion should be covered with a zinc-based primer, then painted.

Charging

Warning: *When batteries are being charged, hydrogen gas, which is very explosive and flammable, is produced. Do not smoke or allow open flames near a charging or a recently charged battery. Wear eye protection when near the battery during charging. Also, make sure the charger is unplugged before connecting or disconnecting the battery from the charger.*

10   Slow-rate charging is the best way to restore a battery that's discharged to the point where it will not start the engine. It's also a good way to maintain the battery charge in a vehicle that's only driven a few miles between starts. Maintaining the battery charge is particularly important in the winter when the battery must work harder to start the engine and electrical accessories that drain the battery are in greater use.

11   It's best to use a one or two-amp battery charger (sometimes called a "trickle" charger). They are the safest and put the least strain on the battery. They are also the least expensive. For a faster charge, you can use a higher amperage charger, but don't use one rated more than 1/10th the amp/hour rating of the battery. Rapid boost charges that claim to restore the power of the battery in one to two hours are hardest on the battery and can damage batteries that aren't in good condition. This type of charging should only be used in emergency situations.

12   The average time necessary to charge a battery should be listed in the instructions that come with the charger. As a general rule, a trickle charger will charge a battery in 12 to 16 hours.

13   Remove all of the cell caps (if equipped) and cover the holes with a clean cloth to prevent spattering electrolyte. Disconnect the negative battery cable and hook the battery charger leads to the battery posts (positive to positive, negative to negative), then plug in the charger. Make sure it is set at 12-volts if it has a selector switch.

14   If you're using a charger with a rate higher than two amps, check the battery regularly during charging to make sure it doesn't overheat. If you're using a trickle charger, you can safely let the battery charge overnight after you've checked it regularly for the first couple of hours.

15   If the battery has removable cell caps, measure the specific gravity with a hydrometer every hour during the last few hours of the charging cycle. Hydrometers are available inexpensively from auto parts stores - follow the instructions that come with the

hydrometer. Consider the battery charged when there's no change in the specific gravity reading for two hours and the electrolyte in the cells is gassing (bubbling) freely. The specific gravity reading from each cell should be very close to the others. If not, the battery probably has a bad cell(s).

16   Some batteries with sealed tops have built-in hydrometers on the top that indicate the state of charge by the color displayed in the hydrometer window. Normally, a bright-colored hydrometer indicates a full charge and a dark hydrometer indicates the battery still needs charging. Check the battery manufacturer's instructions to be sure you know what the colors mean.

17   If the battery has a sealed top and no built-in hydrometer, you can hook up a digital voltmeter across the battery terminals to check the charge. A fully charged battery should read 12.5-volts or higher.

---

11   Cooling system check (every 6000 miles or 6 months)

Refer to illustration 11.4
Caution: *Never mix green-colored ethylene glycol anti-freeze and orange-colored "DEX-COOL" silicate-free coolant because doing so will destroy the efficiency of the "DEX-COOL" coolant which is designed to last for 100,000 miles or five years.*

1   Many major engine failures can be attributed to a faulty cooling system. If the vehicle is equipped with an automatic transmission, the cooling system also cools the transmission fluid and plays an important role in prolonging transmission life.

2   The cooling system should be checked with the engine cold. Do this before the vehicle is driven for the day or after the engine has been shut off for at least three hours.

3   Remove the radiator cap by turning it to the left until it reaches a stop. If you hear any hissing sounds (indicating there is still pressure in the system), wait until it stops. Now press down on the cap with the palm of your hand and continue turning to the left until the cap can be removed. Thoroughly clean the cap, inside and out, with clean water. Also clean the filler neck on the radiator. All traces of corrosion should be removed. The coolant inside the radiator should be relatively transparent. If it is rust colored, the system should be drained and refilled (see Section 27). If the coolant level is not up to the top, add additional antifreeze/coolant mixture (see Section 4).

4   Carefully check the large upper and lower radiator hoses along with any smaller diameter heater hoses which run from the engine to the firewall. Inspect each hose along its entire length, replacing any hose which is cracked, swollen or shows signs of deterioration. Cracks may become more apparent if the hose is squeezed **(see illustration)**.

5   Make sure all hose connections are

Check for a chafed area that could fail prematurely.

Check for a soft area indicating the hose has deteriorated inside.

Overtightening the clamp on a hardened hose will damage the hose and cause a leak.

Check each hose for swelling and oil-soaked ends. Cracks and breaks can be located by squeezing the hose.

11.4 Hoses, like drivebelts, have a habit of failing at the worst possible time - to prevent the inconvenience of a blown radiator or heater hose, inspect them carefully as shown here

---

tight. A leak in the cooling system will usually show up as white or rust colored deposits on the areas adjoining the leak. If wire-type clamps are used at the ends of the hoses, it may be wise to replace them with more secure screw-type clamps.

6   Use compressed air or a soft brush to remove bugs, leaves, etc. from the front of the radiator or air conditioning condenser. Be careful not to damage the delicate cooling fins or cut yourself on them.

7   Every other inspection, or at the first indication of cooling system problems, have the cap and system pressure tested. If you don't have a pressure tester, most gas stations and repair shops will do this for a minimal charge.

12   Underhood hose check and replacement (every 6000 miles or 6 months)

General

1   **Warning:** *Replacement of air conditioning hoses must be left to a dealer service department or air conditioning shop that has the equipment to depressurize the system safely. Never remove air conditioning components or hoses until the system has been depressurized.*

2   High temperatures under the hood can cause the deterioration of the rubber and plastic hoses used for engine, accessory and emission systems operation. Periodic inspection should be made for cracks, loose clamps, material hardening and leaks. Information specific to the cooling system hoses can be found in Section 11.

3   Some, but not all, hoses are secured to the fittings with clamps. Where clamps are used, check to be sure they haven't lost their tension, allowing the hose to leak. If clamps aren't used, make sure the hose hasn't expanded and/or hardened where it slips over the fitting, allowing it to leak.

Vacuum hoses

4   It's quite common for vacuum hoses, especially those in the emissions system, to be color coded or identified by colored stripes molded into each hose. Various systems require hoses with different wall thicknesses, collapse resistance and temperature resistance. When replacing hoses, be sure the new ones are made of the same material.

5   Often the only effective way to check a hose is to remove it completely from the vehicle. If more than one hose is removed, be sure to label the hoses and fittings to ensure correct installation.

6   When checking vacuum hoses, be sure to include any plastic T-fittings in the check. Inspect the fittings for cracks and the hose where it fits over the fitting for distortion, which could cause leakage.

7   A small piece of vacuum hose (1/4-inch inside diameter) can be used as a stethoscope to detect vacuum leaks. Hold one end of the hose to your ear and probe around vacuum hoses and fittings, listening for the "hissing" sound characteristic of a vacuum leak. **Warning:** *When probing with the vacuum hose stethoscope, be careful not to allow your body or the hose to come into contact with moving engine components such as the drivebelt, cooling fan, etc.*

Fuel hose

Warning: *Gasoline is extremely flammable, so take extra precautions when you work on any part of the fuel system. Don't smoke or allow open flames or bare light bulbs near the work area, and don't work in a garage where a gas-type appliance (such as a water heater or clothes dryer) is present. Since gasoline is carcinogenic, wear latex gloves when there's a*

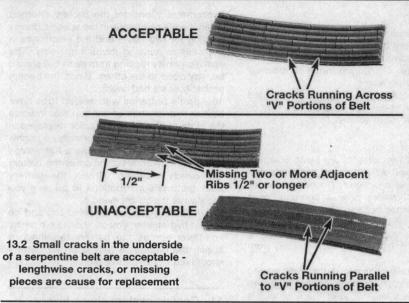

ACCEPTABLE

Cracks Running Across "V" Portions of Belt

1/2"   Missing Two or More Adjacent Ribs 1/2" or longer

UNACCEPTABLE

Cracks Running Parallel to "V" Portions of Belt

13.2 Small cracks in the underside of a serpentine belt are acceptable - lengthwise cracks, or missing pieces are cause for replacement

possibility of being exposed to fuel, and, if you spill any fuel on your skin, rinse it off immediately with soap and water. Mop up any spills immediately and do not store fuel-soaked rags where they could ignite. When you perform any kind of work on the fuel system, wear safety glasses and have a Class B type fire extinguisher on hand. The fuel system is under pressure, so if any lines must be disconnected, the pressure in the system must be relieved first (see Chapter 4 for more information).

8   Check all rubber fuel lines for deterioration and chafing. Check especially for cracks in areas where the hose bends and just before fittings, such as where a hose attaches to the fuel filter and fuel injection unit.

9   High quality fuel line, specifically designed for high-pressure fuel injection applications, must be used for fuel line replacement. Never, under any circumstances, use regular fuel line, unreinforced vacuum line, clear plastic tubing or water hose for fuel lines.

10   Spring-type clamps are commonly used on fuel lines. These clamps often lose their tension over a period of time, and can be "sprung" during the removal process. As a result spring-type clamps should be replaced with screw-type clamps whenever a hose is replaced.

Metal lines

11   Sections of steel tubing often used for fuel line between the fuel pump and fuel injection unit. Check carefully for cracks, kinks and flat spots in the line.

12   If a section of metal fuel line must be replaced, only seamless steel tubing should be used, since copper and aluminum tubing do not have the strength necessary to withstand normal engine vibration.

13   Check the metal brake lines where they enter the master cylinder and brake proportioning unit (if used) for cracks in the lines and loose fittings. Any sign of brake fluid leakage

calls for an immediate thorough inspection of the brake system.

13   Drivebelt and tensioner check and replacement (every 6000 miles or 6 months)

Drivebelt

Refer to illustrations 13.2, 13.5a and 13.5b

1   A single serpentine drivebelt is located at the front of the engine and plays an important role in the overall operation of the engine and its components. Due to its function and material make up, the belt is prone to wear and should be periodically inspected. The serpentine belt drives the alternator, power steering pump, water pump and air conditioning compressor.

2   With the engine off, open the hood and use your fingers (and a flashlight, if necessary), to move along the belt checking for cracks and separation of the belt plies. Also check for fraying and glazing, which gives the belt a shiny appearance **(see illustration)**. Both sides of the belt should be inspected, which means you will have to twist the belt to check the underside.

3   Check the ribs on the underside of the belt. They should all be the same depth, with none of the surface uneven.

4   The tension of the belt is maintained by the tensioner assembly and isn't adjustable. The belt should be checked at the mileage specified in the maintenance schedule at the front of this Chapter, if the belt shows noticeable damage or wear during these checks it should be replaced.

5   To replace the belt on 3.1L, 3.4L OHV and 3.8L engines, rotate the tensioner counterclockwise to release belt tension **(see illustration)**. To replace the belt on 3.4L DOHC engines, rotate the tensioner clockwise to release belt tension. Note the routing of the belt before removing it. **Note:**

13.5a On 3.1L and 3.8L engines rotate the drivebelt tensioner (arrow) counter-clockwise to remove or install the belt

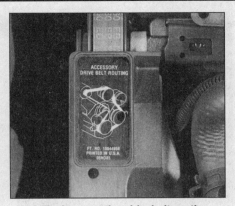

13.5b A serpentine drivebelt routing diagram is located on the engine (3.1L V6 shown)

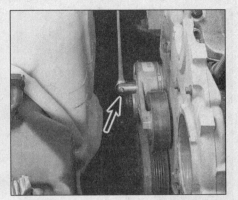

13.9 Remove the retaining bolt (arrow) located at the center of the tensioner assembly

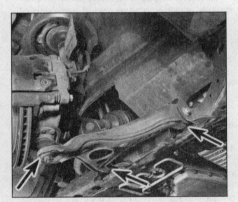

14.3a Inspect the lower control arm bushings and balljoint . . .

14.3b . . . the front and rear stabilizer bar bushings . . .

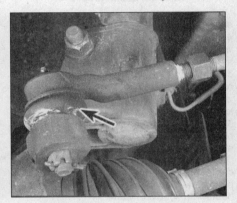

14.3c . . . and the tie rod ends for deteriorated bushings and torn grease seals

These models have a drivebelt routing decal on the engine to help during drivebelt installation **(see illustration)**. *If the decal is missing, make a sketch.*

6   Remove the belt from the auxiliary components and slowly release the tensioner.

7   Route the new belt over the various pulleys, again rotating the tensioner to allow the belt to be installed, then release the belt tensioner.

Tensioner

8   Remove the engine drivebelt as described above in Steps 5 and 6.

3.1L and 3.4L engines

Refer to illustration 13.9

9   On 3.1L and 3.4L engines, simply remove the tensioner retaining bolt **(see illustration)** and detach the tensioner assembly from the front of the engine. **Note:** *It may be necessary to detach and position the coolant recovery reservoir aside (see Chapter 3) to allow access to the tensioner retaining bolt.* Installation is the reverse of the removal procedure.

3.8L engine

Warning: *If you're removing the tensioner from a 3.8L engine, wait until the engine has cooled completely before beginning the job.*

10   Disconnect the negative battery cable

from the battery. **Caution:** *On models equipped with a Delco Theftlock audio system, be sure the lockout feature is turned off before performing any procedure which requires disconnecting the battery.*

11   Drain the engine coolant (see Section 27), and if necessary, remove the coolant reservoir (see Chapter 3).

12   On 1999 and later models (or where necessary), remove the alternator.

13   Move a large container under the front of the engine to catch the coolant and remove the heater hose adapters with the heater hoses attached from the drivebelt tensioner assembly.

14   Detach the drivebelt tensioner retaining bolts and remove the tensioner assembly from the vehicle. Installation is the reverse of the removal procedure.

15   Refill the cooling system (see Section 27), start the engine and check for leaks.

---

14 Steering, suspension and driveaxle boot check (every 6000 miles or 6 months)

Refer to illustrations 14.3a, 14.3b, 14.3c, 14.3d and 14.6

1   Indications of a fault in these systems are excessive play in the steering wheel before the front wheels react, excessive sway

14.3d Check the steering gear boots for cracks and leaking steering fluid

around corners, body movement over rough roads or binding at some point as the steering wheel is turned.

2   Raise the front of the vehicle periodically and visually check the suspension and steering components for wear. Because of the work to be done, make sure the vehicle cannot fall from the stands.

3   From under the vehicle check for loose bolts, broken or disconnected parts and deteriorated rubber bushings on all suspension and steering components **(see illustrations)**. Check the power steering hoses and connections for leaks. Check the

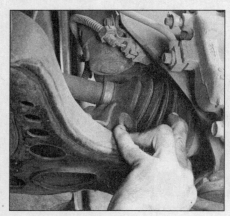

14.6 Check the driveaxle boots for cracks and/or leaking grease

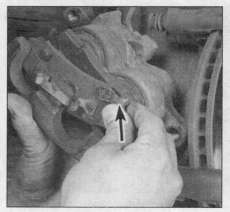

15.3 The disc brake pads are equipped with wear indicators that contact the disc and make a squealing sound when the pad has worn to its limit

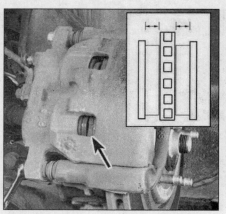

15.5 With the wheels removed, the brake pad lining can be inspected through the caliper window (arrow) and at each end of the caliper - if the pad is bonded to the metal backing plate, measure the pad thickness from the outer surface to the metal backing plate, as shown here; if the pad is riveted to the metal backing plate, measure from the pad outer surface to the rivet head

shock absorbers or leaking fluid or damage.

4   Have an assistant turn the steering wheel from side-to-side and check the steering components for free movement, chafing and binding. If the steering doesn't react with the movement of the steering wheel, try to determine where the slack is located.

5   The driveaxle boots are very important because they prevent dirt, water and foreign material from entering and damaging the constant velocity (CV) joints. Oil and grease can cause the boot material to deteriorate prematurely, so it's a good idea to wash the boots with soap and water.

6   Inspect the boots for tears and cracks as well as loose clamps **(see illustration)**. If there is any evidence of cracks or leaking lubricant, they must be replaced as described in Chapter 8.

15   Brake check (every 6000 miles or 6 months)

Note: *For detailed information of the brake system, refer to Chapter 9.*
Warning: *Brake system dust is hazardous to your health. DO NOT blow it out with compressed air, inhale it or use gasoline or solvents to remove it. Use brake system cleaner only.*

1   In addition to the specified intervals, the brakes should be inspected every time the wheels are removed or whenever a defect is suspected. Raise the vehicle and place it securely on jackstands. Remove the wheels (see *Jacking and towing* at the front of the manual, if necessary).

Disc brakes

Refer to illustrations 15.3, 15.5 and 15.7

2   Disc brakes can be checked without removing any parts except the wheels. Extensive disc damage can occur if the pads are not replaced when needed.

3   The disc brake pads have built-in wear indicators **(see illustration)** which make a high-pitched squealing sound when the pads

are worn. **Caution:** *Expensive damage to the disc can result if the pads are not replaced soon after the wear indicators start squealing.*

4   The disc brake calipers, which contain the brake pads, have an inner pad and outer pad in each caliper. All pads should be inspected.

5   Each caliper has a "window" to inspect the pads **(see illustration)**. If the pad material has worn to about 1/8-inch thick or less, the pads should be replaced.

6   If you're unsure about the exact thickness of the remaining lining material, remove the pads for further inspection or replacement (see Chapter 9).

7   Before installing the wheels, check for leakage and/or damage at the brake hoses and connections **(see illustration)**. Replace the hose or fittings as necessary, (see Chapter 9).

8   Check the condition of the brake disc. Look for score marks, deep scratches and overheated areas (they will appear blue or discolored). If damage or wear is noted, the disc can be removed and resurfaced by an automotive machine shop or replaced with a new one. See Chapter 9 for more detailed inspection and repair procedures.

Drum brakes

Refer to illustrations 15.14 and 15.16

9   Raise the vehicle and support it securely on jackstands. Block the front tires to prevent the vehicle from rolling; however, don't apply the parking brake or it will lock the drums in place.

10   Remove the wheels, referring to *Jacking and towing* at the front of this manual if necessary.

11   Mark the hub so it can be reinstalled in the same position. Use a scribe, chalk, etc. on the drum, hub and backing plate.

12   Remove the brake drum (see Chapter 9 if necessary).

13   With the drum removed, carefully clean the brake assembly with brake system cleaner. **Warning:** *Don't blow the dust out*

with compressed air and don't inhale any of it *(it is harmful to your health).*

14   Note the thickness of the lining material on both front and rear brake shoes. If the material has worn away to within 3/32-inch of the recessed rivets or metal backing, the shoes should be replaced **(see illustration)**. The shoes should also be replaced if they're cracked, glazed (shiny areas), or covered with brake fluid.

15   Make sure all the brake assembly springs are connected and in good condition.

16   Check the brake components for signs of fluid leakage. With your finger or a small screwdriver, carefully pry back the rubber boots on the wheel cylinder located at the top of the brake shoes **(see illustration)**. Any leakage here is an indication that the wheel cylinders should be overhauled immediately (see Chapter 9). Also, check all hoses and connections for signs of leakage.

15.7 Check for any sign of brake fluid leakage at the line fittings (arrow) and the brake hoses

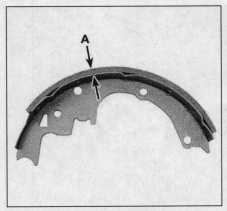

15.14 If the lining is bonded to the brake shoe, measure the lining thickness from the outer surface to the metal shoe, as shown here; if the lining is riveted to the shoe, measure from the lining outer surface to the rivet head

15.16 Check for fluid leakage at both ends of the wheel cylinder dust boots

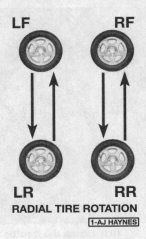

16.2 Tire rotation diagram

17   Wipe the inside of the drum with a clean rag and denatured alcohol or brake cleaner. Again, be careful not to breathe the dangerous dust.

18   Check the inside of the drum for cracks, score marks, deep scratches and "hard spots" which will appear as small discolored areas. If imperfections cannot be removed with fine emery cloth, the drum must be taken to an automotive machine shop for resurfacing.

19   Repeat the procedure for the remaining wheel. If the inspection reveals that all parts are in good condition, reinstall the brake drums, install the wheels and lower the vehicle to the ground.

Parking brake

20   The parking brake is operated by a foot pedal and locks the rear brake system. The easiest, and perhaps most obvious, method of periodically checking the operation of the parking brake assembly is to park the vehicle on a steep hill with the parking brake set and the transmission in Neutral (be sure to stay in the vehicle during this check!). If the parking brake cannot prevent the vehicle from rolling, it needs service (see Chapter 9).

16   Tire rotation (every 6000 miles or 6 months)

Refer to illustration 16.2

1   The tires should be rotated at the specified intervals and whenever uneven wear is noticed.

2   Refer to the **accompanying illustration** for the preferred tire rotation pattern.

3   Refer to the information in *Jacking and towing* at the front of this manual for the proper procedures to follow when raising the vehicle and changing a tire. If the brakes are to be checked, don't apply the parking brake

as stated. Make sure the tires are blocked to prevent the vehicle from rolling as it's raised.

4   Preferably, the entire vehicle should be raised at the same time. This can be done on a hoist or by jacking up each corner and then lowering the vehicle onto jackstands placed under the frame rails. Always use four jackstands and make sure the vehicle is safely supported.

5   After rotation, check and adjust the tire pressures as necessary and be sure to properly tighten the lug nuts.

17   Exhaust system check (every 6000 miles or 6 months)

Refer to illustrations 17.2a and 17.2b

1   With the engine cold (at least three hours after the vehicle has been driven), check the complete exhaust system from the engine to the end of the tailpipe. Ideally, the inspection should be done with the vehicle on a hoist to permit unrestricted access. If a hoist is not available, raise the vehicle and support it securely on jackstands.

2   Check the exhaust pipes and connec-

tions for evidence of leaks, severe corrosion and damage. Make sure that all brackets and hangers are in good condition and tight (**see illustrations**).

3   At the same time, inspect the underside of the body for holes, corrosion, open seams, etc. which may allow exhaust gases to enter the interior. Seal all body openings with silicone or body putty.

4   Rattles and other noises can often be traced to the exhaust system, especially the mounts and hangers. Try to move the pipes, muffler and catalytic converter. If the components can come in contact with the body or suspension parts, secure the exhaust system with new mounts.

18   Throttle linkage check (every 12,000 miles or 12 months)

Refer to illustration 18.2

1   At the specified intervals the throttle linkage should be inspected for kinks, binding and misalignment.

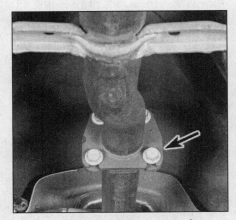

17.2a Check the flange connections (arrow) for exhaust leaks - also check that the retaining nuts are securely tightened

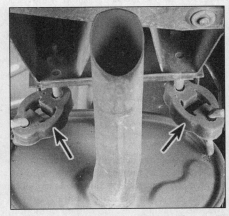

17.2b Check the exhaust system hangers (arrows) for damage and cracks

18.2 Check the throttle linkage for binding

19.3 Gently pry off the trim cap and check the tightness of the wiper arm retaining nut

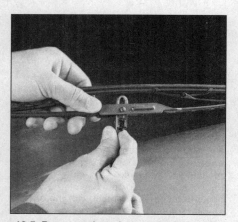

19.5 Press on the release tab, then push the blade assembly down and out of the hook in the arm

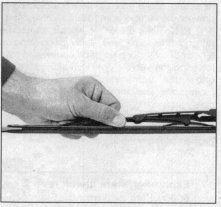

19.6 Use needle-nose pliers to compress the rubber element, then slide the element out - slide the new element in and lock the blade assembly fingers into the notches of the wiper element

6   Use needle-nose pliers to compress the blade element, then slide the element out of the frame (claws) and discard it **(see illustration)**.
7   Compare the new element with the old for length, design, etc.
8   Slide the new element into the frame (claws), notched end last and secure the claw into the notches of the blade element.
9   Reinstall the blade assembly on the arm, wet the windshield and test for proper operation.

20 Seat belt check (every 12,000 miles or 12 months)

1   Check the seat belts, buckles, latch plates and guide loops for obvious damage and signs of wear.
2   See if the seat belt reminder light comes on when the key is turned to the Run or Start position. A chime should also sound.
3   The seat belts are designed to lock up during a sudden stop or impact, yet allow free movement during normal driving. Make sure the retractors return the belt against your chest while driving and rewind the belt fully when the buckle is unlatched.
4   If any of the above checks reveal problems with the seat belt system, replace parts as necessary.

21 Air filter replacement (every 12,000 miles or 12 months)

Refer to illustration 21.1a and 21.1b
1   The air filter is located inside the air cleaner housing at the left (driver's) side of the engine compartment. To remove the air filter, release the screws **(see illustration)** that secure the two halves of the air cleaner housing together, then separate the cover halves and remove the air filter element **(see illustration)**.
2   Inspect the outer surface of the filter element. If it is dirty, replace it. If it is only moderately dusty, it can be reused by blowing it clean from the back to the front surface with

2   Starting at the throttle body in the engine compartment, with the engine OFF, grasp the throttle lever and open it to the full throttle position **(see illustration)**. Quickly release your hand from the throttle lever and note the amount of time it takes the throttle lever to return to the idle position. If the lever returns quickly to the idle position the throttle linkage is in proper working order. If the lever returns slowly to the idle position, inspect the accelerator cable or cruise control cable for kinks or signs of binding. Also check the cable retaining brackets for missing retaining clips. **Note:** *Never lubricate the accelerator or cruise control cable as this will destroy the protective plastic coating on the outside of the cable.* If signs of kinks or binding exist in the cable assembly, replace the cable as described in Chapter 4.
3   If there's no evidence of binding in the cable assembly, remove the cables from the throttle lever and repeat the test described in Step 2. If the throttle lever returns slowly to the idle position with the cables detached, the problem lies in the throttle body assembly. See Chapter 4 for further inspection of the throttle body assembly.

19 Wiper blade inspection and replacement (every 12,000 miles or 12 months)

Refer to illustrations 19.3, 19.5 and 19.6
1   The windshield wiper and blade assemblies should be inspected periodically for damage, loose components and cracked or worn blade elements.
2   Road film can build up on the wiper blades and affect their efficiency, so they should be washed regularly with a mild detergent solution.
3   The action of the wiping mechanism can loosen the bolts, nuts and fasteners, so they should be checked and tightened, as necessary, at the same time the wiper blades are checked **(see illustration)**.
4   If the wiper blade elements (sometimes called inserts) are cracked, worn or warped, they should be replaced with new ones.
5   Lift the arm assembly away from the glass for clearance, press on the release lever, then slide the wiper blade assembly out of the hook in the end of the arm **(see illustration)**.

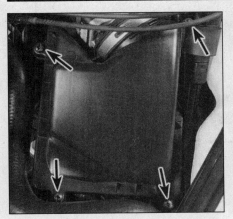

21.1a Remove the screws and separate the cover from the air cleaner housing

21.1b Lift the cover up and slide the element out of the housing

22.1 The PCV valve on 3.1L and later 3.4L OHV engines is located in the valve cover

22.5 The PCV valve on 3.8L engines is located at the front of the intake manifold below the MAP sensor (arrow)

22.13 Disconnect the electrical connector and unclip the MAP sensor from the PCV valve access cover

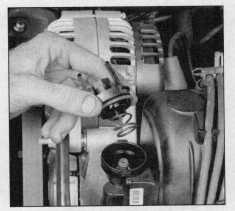

22.14 Press down on the PCV valve access cover, rotate it counterclockwise then pull up to remove it (be sure to check the O-ring and replace it if necessary)

compressed air. Because it is a pleated paper type filter, it cannot be washed or oiled. If it cannot be cleaned satisfactorily with compressed air, discard and replace it. While the cover is off, be careful not to drop anything down into the housing. **Caution:** *Never drive the vehicle with the air cleaner removed. Excessive engine wear could result and backfiring could even cause a fire under the hood.*

3   Wipe out the inside of the air cleaner housing.

4   Place the new filter into the air cleaner housing, making sure it seats properly.

5   Installation of the housing is the reverse of removal.

22   Positive Crankcase Ventilation (PCV) valve check and replacement (every 30,000 miles or 24 months)

Check

3.1L and 3.4L engine
Refer to illustration 22.1

1   On 3.1L and later 3.4L OHV engines, the PCV valve is located in the forward valve cover **(see illustration)**. On earlier 3.4L engines, the PCV valve is located in the

intake manifold just behind the throttle body assembly.

2   With the engine idling at normal operating temperature, pull the valve (with hose attached) out of the rubber grommet in the intake plenum or valve cover.

3   Place your finger over the end of the valve. If there is no vacuum at the valve, check for a plugged hose, manifold port, or the valve itself. Replace any plugged or deteriorated hoses.

4   Turn off the engine and shake the PCV valve, listening for a rattle. If the valve doesn't rattle, replace it with a new one.

3.8L engine
Refer to illustration 22.5

5   On 3.8L engines the PCV valve is located in the intake manifold under the MAP sensor at the front (passenger side) of the engine **(see illustration)**.

6   To check the valve it must first be removed (see Step 12). Then shake the PCV valve, listening for a rattle. If the valve doesn't rattle, replace it with a new one.

Replacement

3.1L and 3.4L engine

7   To replace the valve, pull it out of the

end of the hose, noting its installed position and direction.

8   When purchasing a replacement PCV valve, make sure it's for your particular vehicle, model year and engine size. Compare the old valve with the new one to make sure they are the same.

9   Push the valve into the end of the hose until it's seated.

10   Inspect the rubber grommet for damage and replace it with a new one if necessary.

11   Push the PCV valve and hose securely into position.

3.8L engine
Refer to illustration 22.13, 22.14 and 22.15

12   Detach the fuel injector cover (see Chapter 4).

13   Disconnect the electrical connector from the MAP sensor and unclip the MAP sensor from the PCV valve access cover **(see illustration)**.

14   Press downward on the PCV valve access cover and rotate it counterclockwise to remove it **(see illustration)**.

15   To replace the valve, pull the PCV valve and O-ring assembly from the intake

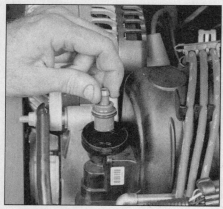

22.15 Remove the PCV valve and the O-ring from the intake manifold

manifold noting its installed position and direction **(see illustration)**.

16 When purchasing a replacement PCV valve, make sure it's for your particular vehicle, model year and engine size. Compare the old valve with the new one to make sure they are the same.

17 Installation of the valve is the reverse of removal.

23 Spark plug wire check and replacement (every 30,000 miles or 24 months)

Refer to illustrations 23.4 and 23.8

Note 1: *On 3.1L and some 3.4L OHV engines the engine must be rotated forward (towards the front of the car) to allow access to the right side (rear) spark plugs or plug wires.*

Note 2: *On 3.4L engines the upper intake manifold must be removed first to allow access to the right side (rear) spark plugs or plug wires. See Chapter 2B for the intake manifold removal procedure.*

Note 3: *On 3.8L engines the fuel injector cover must be removed first to access the right side (rear) spark plugs or plug wires.*

1 The spark plug wires should be checked

23.8 Remove each spark plug wire from the ignition coil packs - check for corrosion and a tight fit

and, if necessary, replaced at the same time new spark plugs are installed.

2 The easiest way to identify bad wires is to make a visual check while the engine is running. In a dark, well-ventilated garage, start the engine and look at each plug wire. Be careful not to come into contact with any moving engine parts. If there is a break in the wire, you will see arcing or a small spark at the damaged area. If arcing is noticed, make a note to obtain new wires.

3 The spark plug wires should be inspected one at a time, beginning with the spark plug for the number one cylinder, (see the specifications section at the beginning of this Chapter), to prevent confusion. Clearly label each plug wire with a piece of tape marked with the correct number. The plug wires must be reinstalled in the correct order to ensure proper engine operation.

4 Disconnect the plug wire from the first spark plug. A removal tool can be used, or you can grab the wire boot, twist it slightly and pull the wire free. Do not pull on the wire itself, only on the rubber boot **(see illustration)**.

5 Push the wire and boot back onto the end of the spark plug. It should fit snugly. If it doesn't, detach the wire and boot once more and use a pair of pliers to carefully crimp the metal connector inside the wire boot until it does.

6 Using a clean rag, wipe the entire length of the wire to remove built-up dirt and grease.

7 Once the wire is clean, check for burns, cracks and other damage. Do not bend the wire sharply or you might break the conductor.

8 Disconnect the wire from the coil pack. Pull only on the rubber boot. Check for corrosion and a tight fit **(see illustration)**. Reinstall the wire.

9 Inspect each of the remaining spark plug wires, making sure that each one is securely fastened on each end.

10 If new spark plug wires are required, purchase a set for your specific engine model. Pre-cut wire sets with the boots already installed are available. Remove and replace the wires one at a time to avoid mixups in the firing order. Should a mix up occur refer to the Specifications at the beginning of this Chapter.

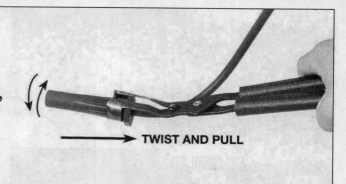

23.4 Using a spark plug boot puller tool like this one will make the job of removing the spark plug boots much easier

TWIST AND PULL

24 Spark plug check and replacement (see maintenance schedule for service intervals)

Refer to illustrations 24.2, 24.5a, 24.5b, 24.8, 24.9 and 24.10

Note 1: *On 3.1L and some 3.4L OHV engines, the engine must be rotated to allow access to the right side (rear) spark plugs or plug wires, as outlined in Section 29.*

Note 2: *On 3.4L engines the upper intake manifold must be removed first to allow access to the right side (rear) spark plugs or plug wires. See Chapter 2B for the intake manifold removal procedure.*

Note 3: *On 3.8L engines the fuel injector cover must be removed first to access the right side (rear) spark plugs or plug wires.*

1 All vehicles covered by this manual are equipped with transversely mounted V6 engines which locate the spark plugs on the side of the engine at the front and the rear of the engine compartment. The left side (front) spark plugs can be reached from the front of the vehicle while the right side (rear) spark plugs are located between the engine and the firewall. Removal of the right side (rear) spark plugs requires special removal procedures (as noted above) to be performed first to allow access to the right side (rear) spark plugs or plug wires.

2 In most cases, the tools necessary for spark plug replacement include a spark plug socket which fits onto a ratchet (spark plug sockets are padded inside to prevent damage to the porcelain insulators on the new plugs), various extensions and a gap gauge to check and adjust the gaps on the new plugs **(see illustration)**. A special plug wire removal tool is available for separating the wire boots from the spark plugs, and is a good idea on these models because the boots fit very tightly. A torque wrench should be used to tighten the new plugs. It is a good idea to allow the engine to cool before removing or installing the spark plugs.

3 The best approach when replacing the spark plugs is to purchase the new ones in advance, adjust them to the proper gap and replace the plugs one at a time. When buying the new spark plugs, be sure to obtain the correct plug type for your particular engine. The plug type can be found in the Specifica-

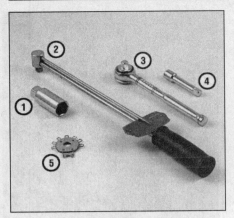

24.2 Tools required for changing spark plugs

1 *Spark plug socket - This will have special padding inside to protect the spark plug's porcelain insulator*
2 *Torque wrench - Although not mandatory, using this tool is the best way to ensure the plugs are tightened properly*
3 *Ratchet - Standard hand tool to fit the spark plug socket*
4 *Extension - Depending on model and accessories, you may need special extensions and universal joints to reach one or more of the plugs*
5 *Spark plug gap gauge - This gauge for checking the gap comes in a variety of styles. Make sure the gap for your engine is included*

tions at the front of this Chapter and on the Emission Control Information label located under the hood. If these two sources list different plug types, consider the emission control label correct.

4 Allow the engine to cool completely before attempting to remove any of the plugs. While you are waiting for the engine to cool, check the new plugs for defects and adjust the gaps.

5 Check the gap by inserting the proper thickness gauge between the electrodes at the tip of the plug **(see illustration)**. The gap between the electrodes should be the same as the one specified on the Emissions Control Information label or as listed in this Chapter's Specifications. The gauge should slide between the electrodes with a slight amount of drag. If the gap is incorrect, use the adjuster on the gauge body to bend the curved side electrode slightly until the proper gap is obtained **(see illustration)**. If the side electrode is not exactly over the center electrode, bend it with the adjuster until it is. Check for cracks in the porcelain insulator (if any are found, the plug should not be used). **Note:** *Manufacturers recommend using a tapered thickness gauge when checking platinum-type spark plugs. Other types of gauges may scrape the thin platinum coating from the electrodes, thus dramatically shortening the life of the plugs.*

6 With the engine cool, remove the spark plug wire as described in Section 23 from

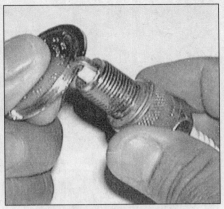

24.5a Spark plug manufacturers recommend using a tapered thickness gauge when checking the gap - slide the thin side into the gap and turn until the gauge just fills the gap, then read the thickness on the gauge - do not force the tool into the gap or use the tapered portion to widen a gap

24.8 Use a special spark plug socket with a long extension to unscrew the spark plugs

one spark plug. Pull only on the boot at the end of the wire - do not pull on the wire. A plug wire removal tool should be used if available.

7 If compressed air is available, use it to blow any dirt or foreign material away from the spark plug hole. A common bicycle pump will also work. The idea here is to eliminate the possibility of debris falling into the cylinder as the spark plug is removed.

8 The spark plugs on these models are, for the most part, difficult to reach so a spark plug socket incorporating a universal joint will be necessary. Place the spark plug socket over the plug and remove it from the engine by turning it in a counterclockwise direction **(see illustration)**.

9 Compare the spark plug with the chart shown on the inside back cover of this manual to get an indication of the general running condition of the engine. Before installing the new plugs, it is a good idea to apply a thin coat of anti-seize compound to the threads **(see illustration)**.

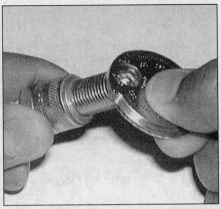

24.5b To change the gap, bend the side electrode only, using the adjuster hole in the tool, and be very careful not to crack or chip the porcelain insulator surrounding the center electrode

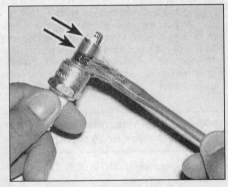

24.9 Apply a thin coat of anti-seize compound to the spark plug threads, being careful not to get any near the lower threads (arrows)

10 Thread one of the new plugs into the hole until you can no longer turn it with your fingers, then tighten it with a torque wrench (if available) or the ratchet. It's a good idea to slip a short length of rubber hose over the end of the plug to use as a tool to thread it into place **(see illustration)**. The hose will grip the plug well enough to turn it, but will start to slip if the plug begins to cross-thread in the hole - this will prevent damaged threads and the accompanying repair costs.

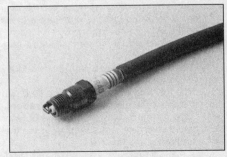

24.10 A length of snug-fitting rubber hose will save time and prevent damaged threads when installing the spark plugs

25.3 The fuel filter (arrow) is located underneath the vehicle in front of the gas tank

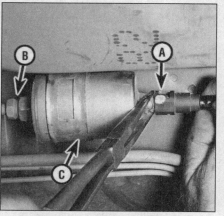

25.5 Squeeze the white plastic quick-disconnect tabs together and pull the inlet line (A) away from the filter, then detach the outlet line (B) from the fuel filter - unbolt the filter mounting bracket (C) to remove the fuel filter

26.4 Check the fuel filler lines (arrows) for cracks and deterioration and the hose clamps for tightness

11   Before pushing the spark plug wire onto the end of the plug, inspect it following the procedures outlined in Section 23

12   Attach the plug wire to the new spark plug, again using a twisting motion on the boot until it's seated on the spark plug.

13   Repeat the procedure for the remaining spark plugs, replacing them one at a time to prevent mixing up the spark plug wires.

25   Fuel filter replacement (every 30,000 miles or 24 months)

Refer to illustrations 25.3 and 25.5

Warning: *Gasoline is extremely flammable, so take extra precautions when you work on any part of the fuel system. Don't smoke or allow open flames or bare light bulbs near the work area, and don't work in a garage where a gas-type appliance (such as a water heater or clothes dryer) is present. Since gasoline is carcinogenic, wear latex gloves when there's a possibility of being exposed to fuel, and, if you spill any fuel on your skin, rinse it off immediately with soap and water. Mop up any spills immediately and do not store fuel-soaked rags where they could ignite. The fuel system is under constant pressure, so, if any fuel lines are to be disconnected, the fuel pressure in the system must be relieved first (see Chapter 4 for more information). When you perform any kind of work on the fuel system, wear safety glasses and have a Class B type fire extinguisher on hand.*

1   Relieve the fuel system pressure (see Chapter 4).

2   Raise the vehicle and support it securely on jackstands.

3   The fuel filter is mounted to the floor pan just in front of the fuel tank **(see illustration)**.

4   Use compressed air or carburetor cleaner to clean any dirt surrounding the fuel inlet and outlet line fittings.

5   Once all the dirt has been removed, depress the white plastic quick-disconnect tabs and detach the inlet line from the fuel filter **(see illustration)**. **Note:** *Have spare rags or a*

small container to catch or wipe up extra gasoline which will spill from the filter assembly.

6   Use an open end wrench to steady the outlet side of the filter and a flare nut wrench to unscrew the fuel line nut, then separate the outlet line from the filter while noting the installed position of the O-ring. Using a flare nut wrench will help to avoid rounding the corners off of the fuel line nut.

7   Detach the fuel filter mounting bracket bolt and remove the fuel filter.

8   Installation is the reverse of removal. **Note:** *Be sure to install a new O-ring on the outlet line before reassembling.*

26   Fuel system check (every 30,000 miles or 24 months)

Refer to illustration 26.4

Warning: *Gasoline is extremely flammable, so take extra precautions when you work on any part of the fuel system. Don't smoke or allow open flames or bare light bulbs near the work area, and don't work in a garage where a gas-type appliance (such as a water heater or clothes dryer) is present. Since gasoline is carcinogenic, wear latex gloves when there's a possibility of being exposed to fuel, and, if you spill any fuel on your skin, rinse it off immediately with soap and water. Mop up any spills immediately and do not store fuel-soaked rags where they could ignite. The fuel system is under constant pressure, so, if any fuel lines are to be disconnected, the fuel pressure in the system must be relieved first (see Chapter 4 for more information). When you perform any kind of work on the fuel system, wear safety glasses and have a Class B type fire extinguisher on hand.*

1   The fuel system is most easily checked with the vehicle raised on a hoist so the components underneath the vehicle are readily visible and accessible.

2   If the smell of gasoline is noticed while driving or after the vehicle has been in the sun, the system should be thoroughly inspected immediately.

3   Remove the fuel filler cap and check for damage, corrosion and an unbroken sealing imprint on the gasket. Replace the cap with a new one if necessary.

4   With the vehicle raised, inspect the fuel tank and filler neck for cracks and other damage **(see illustration)**. The connection between the filler neck and tank is especially critical. Sometimes a filler neck will leak due to cracks, problems a home mechanic can't repair. **Warning:** *Do not, under any circumstances, try to repair a fuel tank yourself (except rubber components). A welding torch or any open flame can easily cause the fuel vapors to explode if the proper precautions are not taken.*

5   Carefully check all rubber hoses and metal lines leading away from the fuel tank. Check for loose connections, deteriorated hoses, crimped lines and other damage. Follow the lines to the front of the vehicle, carefully inspecting them all the way. Repair or replace damaged sections as necessary.

27   Cooling system servicing (draining, flushing and refilling) (see maintenance schedule for service intervals)

Refer to illustrations 27.4a, 27.4b and 27.6

Warning: *Make sure the engine is completely cool before performing this procedure.*

Caution: *Never mix green-colored ethylene glycol anti-freeze and orange-colored "DEX-COOL" silicate-free coolant because doing so will destroy the efficiency of the "DEX-COOL" coolant which is designed to last for 100,000 miles or five years.*

Note: *A back flush kit, available at auto parts stores, may be a preferable alternative to the following method. It involves installing a fitting in the heater inlet hose to which a garden*

27.4a Remove the radiator cap (arrow) by pushing downward and rotating it counterclockwise

27.4b Use a screwdriver to open the bleeder screw (arrow) on the thermostat housing, two or three turns

27.6 The drain plug (arrow) is located at the lower left corner of the radiator

hose can be attached. *This permits back flushing the entire cooling system without removing the thermostat.*

1   Periodically, the cooling system should be drained, flushed and refilled to replenish the antifreeze mixture and prevent formation of rust and corrosion, which can impair the performance of the cooling system and cause engine damage.

2   At the same time the cooling system is serviced, all hoses and the radiator cap should be inspected and replaced if defective (see Section 11).

3   Since antifreeze is a corrosive and poisonous solution, be careful not to spill any of the coolant mixture on the vehicle's paint or your skin. If this happens, rinse it off immediately with plenty of clean water. Consult local authorities about the dumping of antifreeze before draining the cooling system. In many areas, reclamation centers have been set up to collect automobile oil and drained antifreeze/water mixtures, rather than allowing them to be added to the sewage system.

4   With the engine cold, remove the radiator cap, reservoir cap and the air bleed screws (if equipped) **(see illustrations)**.

5   Move a large container under the radiator to catch the coolant as it's drained.

6   Drain the radiator by opening the drain plug at the bottom of the radiator **(see illus-tration)**. If the drain plug is corroded and can't be turned easily, or if the radiator isn't equipped with a plug, disconnect the lower radiator hose to allow the coolant to drain. Be careful not to get antifreeze on your skin or in your eyes.

7   After the coolant stops flowing out of the radiator, remove the lower radiator hose and allow the remaining fluid in the upper half of the engine block to drain.

8   While the coolant is draining from the engine block, disconnect the hose from the coolant reservoir and remove the reservoir (see Chapter 3 if necessary). Flush the reservoir out with water until it's clean,

9   Remove the thermostat from the engine (see Chapter 3). Then reinstall the thermostat housing without the thermostat. This will allow the system to be back flushed.

10   Reinstall the lower radiator hose and tighten the radiator drain plug.

11   Disconnect the upper radiator hose, then place a garden hose in the upper radiator inlet and flush the system until the water runs clear at the upper radiator hose.

12   Many deposits can be removed by the chemical action of a cleaner available at auto parts stores. Follow the procedure outlined in the manufacturer's instructions.

13   In severe cases of contamination or clogging of the radiator, remove the radiator (see Chapter 3) and have a radiator repair facility clean and repair it if necessary.

14   To refill the system, install the thermostat, reconnect any radiator hoses and install the reservoir and the overflow hose.

15   Be sure to use the proper coolant (see **Caution** above). The manufacturer recommends adding GM cooling system sealer part number 3634621 any time the coolant is changed. Slowly fill the radiator with the recommended mixture of antifreeze and water to the base of the filler neck. On models without a radiator cap, add coolant to the coolant reservoir. Wait two minutes and recheck the coolant level, adding if necessary. Close the bleed screws (if equipped) when the coolant issuing from them is free of bubbles. **Note:** *The low coolant light may illuminate after the draining and flushing procedure has been completed. Start the engine and let it run until it reaches normal operating temperature, then let it completely cool down. Repeat this procedure two more times until the light goes out.*

16   Keep a close watch on the coolant level and the cooling system hoses during the first few miles of driving. Tighten the hose clamps and/or add more coolant as necessary. The coolant level should be a little above the HOT mark on the reservoir with the engine at normal operating temperature.

28   Automatic transaxle fluid and filter change (every 50,000 miles)

Refer to illustrations 28.7, 28.10a, 28.10b and 28.12

1   At the specified time intervals, the transaxle fluid should be drained and replaced. Since the fluid will remain hot long after driving, perform this procedure only after everything has cooled down completely.

2   Before beginning work, purchase the specified transaxle fluid (see *Recommended lubricants and fluids* at the front of this Chapter) and a new filter.

3   Other tools necessary for this job include jackstands to support the vehicle in a raised position, a drain pan capable of holding several quarts, newspapers and clean rags.

4   Raise and support the vehicle on jackstands.

5   With a drain pan in place, remove the front and side transaxle pan mounting bolts.

6   Loosen the rear pan bolts one turn.

7   Carefully pry the transaxle pan loose

28.7 After removing the front and side pan bolts, loosen the rear bolts and allow the fluid to drain, then remove the bolts and lower the pan from the vehicle

28.10a Pull the filter straight down to remove it

28.10b Pry out the old seal

28.12 After cleaning the pan, place the magnet in position and install the gasket

29.3 To reach the rear spark plugs, remove the strut bolts (arrows) and rotate the engine forward

with a screwdriver, allowing the fluid to drain **(see illustration).**

8   Remove the remaining bolts, pan and gasket. Carefully clean the gasket surface of the transaxle to remove all traces of the old gasket and sealant.

9   Drain the fluid from the transaxle pan, clean the pan with solvent and dry it with compressed air. Be careful not to lose the magnet.

10   Remove the filter and pry out the seal **(see illustrations).**

11   Push a new filter seal fully into its bore, using a socket of the appropriate size and a soft-faced hammer, if necessary, to tap it into place. Then install the new filter.

12   Make sure the gasket surface on the transaxle pan is clean, then install the magnet and a new gasket **(see illustration).** Put the pan in place against the transaxle and install the bolts. Working around the pan, tighten each bolt a little at a time until the final torque figure is reached.

13   Lower the vehicle and add the specified amount of automatic transmission fluid through the filler tube (see Section 7).

14   With the shift lever in Park and the

parking brake set, run the engine at a fast idle, but don't race it.

15   Move the shift lever through each gear and back to Park. Check the fluid level.

16   Check under the vehicle for leaks during the first few trips.

29   Rotating the engine

Refer to illustration 29.3

1   Block the wheels, place the transaxle in "Neutral," and disconnect the negative battery cable.

2   Disconnect the air cleaner intake duct.

3   Remove the torque strut to engine bracket bolts **(see illustration),** and swing the struts aside. Place the bolt back into the passenger side bracket.

4   Using a pry bar in the passenger side bracket, rotate the engine forward and secure it in this position. To secure the engine in the forward (rotated) position, it will require connecting a ratchet strap to the engine and to the frame or radiator core support.

5   Reverse the procedure when you have completed the task that required rotating the engine. Place the transaxle in "Park," and torque the strut to engine bracket bolts to 35 ft-lbs.

30   Interior ventilation filter replacement (every 12,000 miles or 12 months)

1   2000 and later models are equipped with an air filter in a housing in the passenger's side cowl area that cleans the air before it enters the passenger compartment.

2   Turn the ignition key to the ON position and turn the windshield wipers on, allow the wiper to travel to the top of the windshield, then turn the ignition OFF.

3   Open the hood and remove the weather-strip from the back of the engine compartment at the cowl.

4   Remove the right side of the air inlet and remove the filter.

5   Install the filter and the air inlet back into the cowl, then reinstall the weatherstrip.

Chapter 2 Part A   3.1L and 3.4L OHV V6 engines

Contents

Specifications

General

Displacement	
3.1L OHV V6	191 cubic inches
3.4L OHV V6	204 cubic inches
Bore and stroke	
3.1L OHV V6	3.50 x 3.31 inches
3.4L OHV V6	3.62 x 3.31 inches
Cylinder numbers (drivebelt end-to-transaxle end)	
Front bank (radiator side)	2-4-6
Rear bank	1-3-5
Firing order	1-2-3-4-5-6

Cylinder location and coil terminal identification diagram

Torque specifications

Ft-lbs (unless otherwise indicated)

Camshaft sprocket bolt	
1995	74
1996 and 1997	81
1998 and later	103
Cylinder head bolts	
Step 1	
1997 and earlier	33
1998 through 2001	37
2002 and later	44
Step 2	
1995 through 2001	Rotate an additional 90 degrees
2002 and later	Rotate an additional 95 degrees
Exhaust manifold retaining nuts	
1996 and earlier	89 in-lbs
1998 and later	144 in-lbs
Exhaust heat shield bolts	89 in-lbs
Exhaust crossover pipe nuts	18
Flywheel/Driveplate-to-crankshaft bolts	
1995	59
1996 and 1997	61
1998 and later	52
Intake manifold bolts (lower)	
Step 1	115 in-lbs
Step 2	115 in-lbs

Torque specifications (continued)

	Ft-lbs (unless otherwise indicated)
Intake manifold bolts/studs (upper)	18
Oil pan bolts/nuts	
To block	18
Side bolts	37
Oil pump mounting bolt	30
Rocker arm bolts	
1995	18
1996 and 1997	
Step 1	89 in-lbs
Step 2	Rotate an additional 30 degrees
1998 through 2004	
Step 1	168 in-lbs
Step 2	Rotate an additional 30 degrees
2005 and later	24
Timing chain cover bolts	
1995	
Small	18
Large	41
1996 and 1997	
Small	15
Large	35
1998 and 1999	
Small	15
Medium	35
Large	41
2000 and later	
Small	20
Medium	41
Large	41
Timing chain damper bolts	15
Valve cover-to-cylinder head bolts	89 in-lbs
Crankshaft balancer-to-crankshaft bolt	
1995 through 2000	76
2001	
Step 1	52
Step 2	Tighten an additional 85 degrees
2002 and later	
Step 1	52
Step 2	Tighten an additional 72 degrees
Front engine mount	
Bracket-to-oil pan bolts	43
Mount-to-bracket nuts	35
Mount-to-chassis nuts	35
Rear engine mount	
Bracket-to-transaxle bolts	70
Mount-to-bracket nuts	35
Mount-to-chassis nuts	46
Engine/transaxle brace	
Brace-to-engine bolts	46
Brace-to-transaxle bolts	32
Torque strut through-bolt nuts	35
Left strut mount-to-cylinder head bolts	52
Right strut mount-to-block bolt	37
Radiator strut mount-to-chassis bolts	21

1 General information

This Part of Chapter 2 is devoted to in-vehicle repair procedures for the 3.1L and 3.4L OHV (Overhead Valve) V6 engines. These engines utilize cast-iron blocks with six cylinders arranged in a "V" shape at a 60-degree angle between the two banks. The overhead valve aluminum cylinder heads are equipped with replaceable valve guides and seats. Hydraulic lifters actuate the valves through tubular pushrods.

The engines are easily identified by looking for the designations printed directly on top of the upper intake plenum.

All information concerning engine removal and installation and engine block and cylinder head overhaul can be found in Part D of this Chapter. The following repair proce-dures are based on the assumption that the engine is installed in the vehicle. If the engine has been removed from the vehicle and mounted on a stand, many of the steps outlined in this Part of Chapter 2 will not apply.

The Specifications included in this Part of Chapter 2 apply only to the procedures contained in this Part. Part D of Chapter 2 contains the Specifications necessary for cylinder head and engine block rebuilding.

2 Repair operations possible with the engine in the vehicle

Many major repair operations can be accomplished without removing the engine from the vehicle.

Clean the engine compartment and the exterior of the engine with some type of degreaser before any work is done. It'll make the job easier and help keep dirt out of the internal areas of the engine.

Depending on the components involved, it may be helpful to remove the hood to improve access to the engine as repairs are performed (refer to Chapter 11 if necessary). Cover the fenders to prevent damage to the paint. Special pads are available, but an old bedspread or blanket will also work.

If vacuum, exhaust, oil or coolant leaks develop, indicating a need for gasket or seal replacement, the repairs can generally be done with the engine in the vehicle. The intake and exhaust manifold gaskets, timing chain cover gasket, oil pan gasket, crankshaft oil seals and cylinder head gaskets are all accessible with the engine in place.

Exterior engine components, such as the intake and exhaust manifolds, the oil pan (and the oil pump), the water pump, the starter motor, the alternator and the fuel system components can be removed for repair with the engine in place.

Since the cylinder heads can be removed without pulling the engine, valve component servicing can also be accomplished with the engine in the vehicle. Replacement of the timing chain and sprockets is also possible with the engine in the vehicle, although camshaft removal can not be performed with the engine in the chassis (see Part D of this Chapter).

In extreme cases caused by a lack of necessary equipment, repair or replacement of piston rings, pistons, connecting rods and rod bearings is possible with the engine in the vehicle. However, this practice is not recommended because of the cleaning and preparation work that must be done to the components involved.

3 Top Dead Center (TDC) - locating

Refer to illustration 3.8

1 Top Dead Center (TDC) is the highest point in the cylinder each piston reaches as it travels up-and-down when the crankshaft turns. Each piston reaches TDC on the compression stroke and again on the exhaust stroke, but TDC generally refers to piston position on the compression stroke.

2 Positioning the piston(s) at TDC is an essential part of certain procedures such as timing chain/sprocket removal and camshaft removal.

3 Before beginning this procedure, be sure to place the transaxle in Park, apply the parking brake and block the rear wheels. Raise the front of the vehicle and support it

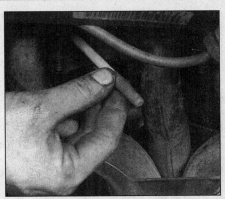

3.8 A plastic object inserted in the number one spark plug hole can be used to determine the highest point reached by that piston

securely on jackstands.

4 Remove the spark plugs (see Chapter 1).

5 When looking at the drivebelt end of the engine, normal crankshaft rotation is clockwise. In order to bring any piston to TDC, the crankshaft must be turned with a socket and ratchet attached to the bolt threaded into the center of the vibration damper on the crankshaft.

6 Have an assistant turn the crankshaft with a socket and ratchet as described above while you hold a finger over the number one spark plug hole. **Note:** *See the cylinder numbering diagram in the specifications for this Chapter.*

7 When the piston approaches TDC, air pressure will be felt at the spark plug hole. Instruct your assistant to turn the crankshaft slowly.

8 Insert a long blunt object into the spark plug hole **(see illustration)**. As the piston rises the object will be pushed out. Note the point where the object stops moving out - this is TDC. **Note:** *It is preferred that a long plastic object be used during this procedure to ensure that object won't fall into the cylinder and will not scratch the cylinder walls. Always hold the object upright while the engine is being rotated so that the object will not get wedged as the piston travels upward.*

9 After the number one piston has been positioned at TDC on the compression stroke, TDC for any of the remaining pistons can be located by repeating the procedure described above and following the firing order.

4 Valve covers - removal and installation

Removal

1 Disconnect the cable from the negative terminal of the battery. **Caution:** *On models equipped with the Theftlock audio system, be sure the lockout feature is turned off before performing any procedure which requires disconnecting the battery (see the front of this manual).*

4.7 Loosen the valve cover mounting bolts (arrows indicate three) - the bolts will stay with the cover

Front cover

Refer to illustration 4.7

2 Remove the air cleaner assembly (see Chapter 4).

3 Remove the spark plug wires from the spark plugs (see Chapter 1). Be sure each wire is labeled before removal to ensure correct reinstallation.

4 Detach the spark plug wire harness clamps from the coolant tube.

5 Remove the PCV tube from the valve cover. If the vehicle is equipped with Secondary Air Injection (AIR), the front AIR check valve and solenoid will be bolted to a bracket below the oil filler cap. Disconnect the vacuum line to the valve and the electrical connector to the solenoid and remove the two nuts from the AIR pipe below the valve. Remove the bracket with the valve and solenoid attached.

6 Drain the coolant (see Chapter 1), and disconnect the coolant bypass pipe (see Chapter 3). **Note:** *If necessary, remove the passenger-side engine torque strut (connecting the engine to the radiator support) at the engine.*

7 Loosen the valve cover mounting bolts **(see illustration)**. **Note:** *Some models are equipped with Torx type bolts. Remove them with a Torx driver.*

8 Detach the valve cover. **Note:** *If the cover sticks to the cylinder head, use a block of wood and a hammer to dislodge it. If the cover still won't come loose, pry on it carefully, but don't distort the sealing flange.*

Rear cover

Refer to illustration 4.14

9 Remove the spark plug wires from the spark plugs (see Chapter 1). Be sure each wire is labeled before removal to ensure correct reinstallation.

10 If the vehicle is equipped with Secondary Air Injection (AIR), the rear AIR check valve and solenoid will be bolted to a bracket below the ignition coil pack. Disconnect the vacuum line to the valve and the electrical connector to the solenoid and remove the two nuts from the AIR pipe below the valve. Remove the bracket with the valve and

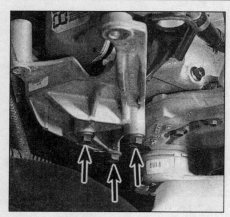

4.14 Remove the bolts (arrows) and detach the alternator support bracket

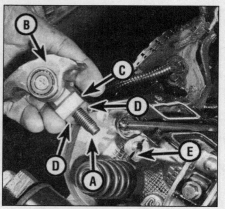

5.3 Rocker arm installation details - the rocker arms are kept as an assembly by a small sleeve between the bolt and the pedestal - note the projections on the pedestal; they fit into grooves in the head

A   Rocker arm bolt
B   Rocker arm
C   Rocker arm pedestal
D   Pedestal projections
E   Grooves in the head

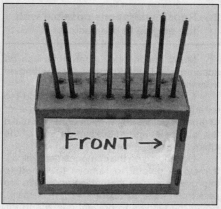

5.4 A perforated cardboard box can be used to store the pushrods to ensure they are reinstalled in their original locations - note the label indicating the front end of the engine

solenoid attached.

11   Remove the ignition coil assembly (see Chapter 5), which also includes the solenoids for the EVAP canister purge control (if equipped). Tag all disconnected wires and hoses.

12   Detach the brake booster vacuum hose from the upper intake manifold.

13   Remove the serpentine drivebelt (see Chapter 1).

14   Remove the alternator (see Chapter 5) and the alternator support bracket **(see illustration)**.

15   Loosen the valve cover mounting bolts. **Note:** *Some models are equipped with Torx-head type bolts. Remove them with a Torx driver.*

16   Detach the valve cover. **Note:** *If the cover sticks to the cylinder head, use a block of wood and a hammer to dislodge it. If the cover still won't come loose, pry on it carefully, but don't distort the sealing flange.*

Installation

17   The mating surfaces of each cylinder head and valve cover must be perfectly clean when the covers are installed. Use a gasket scraper to remove all traces of sealant or old gasket material, then clean the mating surfaces with lacquer thinner or acetone (if there's sealant or oil on the mating surfaces when the cover is installed, oil leaks may develop). The valve covers are made of aluminum, so be extra careful not to nick or gouge the mating surfaces with the scraper.

18   Clean the mounting bolt threads with a die if necessary to remove any corrosion and restore damaged threads. Use a tap to clean the threaded holes in the heads.

19   Apply a dab of RTV sealant to the two joints where the intake manifold and cylinder head meet.

20   Place the valve cover and new gasket in position, then install the bolts. Tighten the bolts in several steps to the torque listed in this Chapter's Specifications.

21   Complete the installation by reversing the removal procedure. Start the engine and check carefully for oil leaks at the valve cover-to-head joints.

5   Rocker arms and pushrods - removal, inspection and installation

Refer to illustrations 5.3 and 5.4

Removal

1   Disconnect the cable from the negative terminal of the battery. **Caution:** *On models equipped with the Theftlock audio system, be sure the lockout feature is turned off before performing any procedure which requires disconnecting the battery (see the front of this manual).*

2   Remove the valve cover(s) (see Section 4).

3   Beginning at the drivebelt end of one cylinder head, remove the rocker arm mounting bolts one at a time and detach the rocker arms, pivot balls and pedestals **(see illustration)**. Store each set of rocker arm components separately in a marked plastic bag to ensure they're reinstalled in their original locations. **Note:** *The rocker arms have the pedestal mount "captured" on the rocker arm bolt by a metal sleeve inside. The components can be separated if necessary by tapping the bolt out of the pedestal, but normally all components for a particular valve will stay as an assembly.*

4   Remove the pushrods and store them separately to make sure they don't get mixed up during installation **(see illustration)**. **Note:** *Intake and exhaust pushrods are different lengths. Intake pushrods are approximately 5-3/4 inches long, while exhausts are 6.0 inches long. They may also have color codes to easily tell them apart.*

Inspection

5   Inspect each rocker arm for wear, cracks and other damage, especially where

the pushrods and valve stems make contact.

6   Make sure the rollers operate freely as well.

7   Make sure the hole at the pushrod end of each rocker arm is open.

8   Inspect the pushrods for cracks and excessive wear at the ends. Roll each pushrod across a piece of plate glass to see if it's bent (if it wobbles, it's bent).

Installation

9   Lubricate the lower end of each pushrod with clean engine oil or moly-base grease and install them in their original locations. Make sure each pushrod seats completely in the lifter socket.

10   Apply moly-base grease to the ends of the valve stems and the upper ends of the pushrods.

11   Apply clean engine oil to the pivot balls and to the bearing surfaces of each rocker arm to prevent damage to the mating surfaces before engine oil pressure builds up. Install the rocker arms, pivot balls, pedestals and bolts and tighten them to the torque listed in this Chapter's Specifications. As the bolts are tightened, make sure the pushrods engage properly in the rocker arms and that the projections on the bottom of the pedestals fit into the grooves on the head before tightening the bolts **(see illustration 5.3)**.

12   Install the valve covers. Start and run the engine, then check for oil leaks and unusual sounds coming from the valve cover area.

6   Valve springs, retainers and seals - replacement

Refer to illustrations 6.4, 6.6, 6.12 and 6.14
Note: *Broken valve springs and defective valve stem seals can be replaced without removing the cylinder head. Two special tools and a compressed air source are normally required to perform this operation, so read through this Section carefully and rent or buy the tools before beginning the job.*

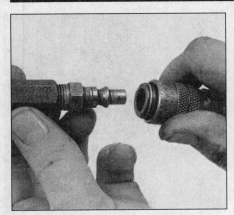

6.4 This is what the typical air hose adapter that threads into the spark plug hole looks like - they're commonly available at auto parts stores

6.6 While the valve spring tool is compressing the spring, remove the keepers with a small magnet or pliers

6.12 Tap the new seal in place on the guide with a socket

1   Remove the valve cover (see Section 4).

2   Remove the spark plugs from the cylinders which have the defective components. If all of the valve stem seals are being replaced, all of the spark plugs should be removed.

3   Turn the crankshaft until the piston in the affected cylinder is at top dead center (see Section 3). If you're replacing all of the valve stem seals, begin with cylinder number one and work on the valves for one cylinder at a time. Move from cylinder-to-cylinder following the firing order sequence (see this Chapter's Specifications).

4   Thread an adapter into the spark plug hole **(see illustration)** and connect an air hose from a compressed air source to it. Most auto parts stores can supply the air hose adapter. **Note:** *Many cylinder compression gauges utilize a screw-in fitting that may work with your air hose quick-disconnect fitting.*

5   Apply compressed air to the cylinder. **Warning:** *The piston may be forced down by compressed air, causing the crankshaft to turn suddenly. If the wrench used when positioning the number one piston at TDC is still attached to the bolt in the crankshaft nose, it could cause damage or injury when the crankshaft moves. The valves should be held in place by the air pressure. If the valve faces or seats are in poor condition, leaks may prevent air pressure from retaining the valves - a "valve job" is necessary to correct this problem.*

6   Stuff shop rags into the cylinder head holes above and below the valves to prevent parts and tools from falling into the engine, then use a valve spring compressor to compress the spring. Remove the keepers **(see illustration)** with small needle-nose pliers or a magnet.

7   Remove the spring retainer and valve spring, then remove the valve guide seal.

8   Wrap a rubber band or tape around the top of the valve stem so the valve won't fall into the combustion chamber, then release the air pressure.

9   Inspect the valve stem for damage. Rotate the valve in the guide and check the end for eccentric movement, which would indicate the valve stem is bent.

10   Move the valve up-and-down in the guide and make sure it doesn't bind. If the valve stem binds, either the valve is bent or the guide is damaged. In either case, the head will have to be removed for repair.

11   Reapply air pressure to the cylinder to retain the valve in the closed position, then remove the tape or rubber band from the valve stem.

12   Lubricate the valve stem with engine oil and install a new valve guide seal. An appropriate-size socket can be used to install the new seal, just don't force it once it bottoms **(see illustration)**.

13   Install the spring in position over the valve. **Note:** *The large end of the spring goes toward the cylinder head.*

14   Install the valve spring retainer. Compress the valve spring and carefully install the keepers in the groove. Apply a small dab of grease to the inside of each keeper to hold it in place if necessary **(see illustration)**. Remove the pressure from the spring tool and make sure the keepers are seated.

15   Disconnect the air hose and remove the adapter from the spark plug hole.

16   Install the spark plug(s) and hook up the wire(s).

17   Install the valve cover(s).

18   Start and run the engine, then check for oil leaks and unusual sounds coming from the valve cover area.

7   Intake manifold - removal and installation

Upper intake manifold (plenum)

Refer to illustration 7.8

1   Disconnect the cable from the negative terminal of the battery. **Caution:** *On models equipped with the Theftlock audio system, be sure the lockout feature is turned off before performing any procedure which requires disconnecting the battery (see the front of this manual).*

2   Refer to Chapter 4 and relieve the fuel

system pressure, then remove the air intake duct and detach the throttle cable and the cruise control cable from the throttle body.

3   Label and disconnect the hoses and electrical connectors attached to the plenum and throttle body. If the throttle body has coolant hose connections to the thermostat bypass pipe, it will be necessary to drain the cooling system (see Chapter 1) before removing these connections.

4   Refer to Chapter 6 and remove the EGR valve-to-plenum bolts. On some models it may also be necessary to remove the alternator (see Chapter 5).

5   Remove the spark plug wires and the ignition coil and module assembly (see Chapter 5).

6   Loosen the upper intake manifold bolts/studs in the reverse order of the tightening sequence **(see illustration 7.8)** and remove the upper plenum with the throttle body attached. Later models have only six fasteners (five bolts and a stud, which goes at the rear corner on the passenger side) and no specific tightening sequence. Start with the center bolts and work out.

7   To install the upper manifold, clean the mounting surfaces of the lower intake manifold and the upper plenum with lacquer thinner and remove all traces of the old gasket material or sealant.

6.14 Keepers don't always stay in place, so apply a small dab of grease to each one as shown here before installation - the grease will hold the keepers in place on the valve stem

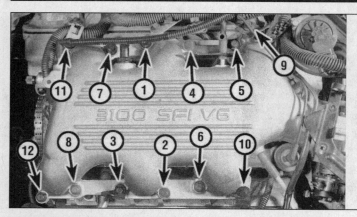

7.8 Upper intake manifold TIGHTENING sequence (earlier models). Later models have only six fasteners

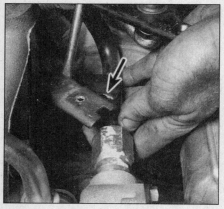

7.13b ... then remove bolt securing the heater pipe bracket to the cylinder head and pull it out the (arrow) from the lower intake manifold - use a screwdriver under the bracket to twist the pipe until it comes out of the fitting

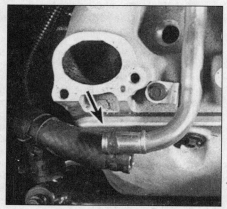

7.14 Disconnect the thermostat bypass hose (arrow) from the pipe

7.13a Loosen the heater pipe fitting from the thermostat housing/lower intake manifold ...

8   Install the new gasket over the lower intake manifold, then install the upper plenum onto the lower intake manifold and tighten the bolts in the recommended tightening sequence (see illustration) to the torque listed in this Chapter's Specifications. The remainder of the installation is the reverse of removal.

Lower intake manifold

Refer to illustrations 7.13a, 7.13b, 7.14, 7.16, 7.20, 7.21 and 7.23

9   Remove the upper intake manifold (see Steps 1 through 6). Drain the cooling system (see Chapter 1).
10   Label and disconnect any remaining wires, fuel and vacuum lines from the lower intake manifold.
11   Refer to Chapter 4 and remove the fuel rail and injectors from the lower intake manifold.

12   Remove the valve covers (see Section 4). Remove the power steering pump without disconnecting the hoses and set it aside (see Chapter 10).
13   Remove the heater pipe from the transaxle end of the lower intake manifold (see illustrations).
14   Disconnect the thermostat bypass hose from the bypass pipe (see illustration).
15   Loosen the manifold mounting bolts/nuts in 1/4-turn increments until they can be removed by hand.
16   The manifold will probably be stuck to the cylinder heads and force may be required to break the gasket seal (see illustration). Caution: *Don't pry between the manifold and the heads or damage to the gasket sealing surfaces may occur, leading to vacuum leaks.*
17   Loosen the rocker arm bolts, rotate the rocker arms out of the way and remove the pushrods that go through the manifold gaskets (see Section 5).
18   Lift the old gaskets off. Use a gasket scraper to remove all traces of sealant and old gasket material, then clean the mating surfaces with lacquer thinner or acetone. Note: *The mating surfaces of the cylinder heads, block and manifold must be perfectly clean when the manifold is installed. Gasket*

7.16 Pry the manifold loose at a casting boss (arrow) - don't pry between the gasket surfaces!

7.20 Install the intake gaskets (arrows) against each cylinder head

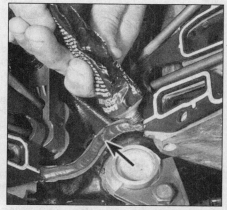

7.21 Apply a bead of sealant to the end ridges between the heads (arrow indicates ridge at transaxle end)

7.23 Intake manifold TIGHTENING sequence - make sure the bolts in the center (1 through 4) are completely tightened before tightening the end bolts (5 through 8)

8.4 Remove the screws (A) and the exhaust manifold heat shield, then remove the exhaust crossover heat shield (B indicates the two front bolts, others are at the rear manifold)

removal solvents are available at most auto parts stores and may be helpful when removing old gasket material that's stuck to the heads and manifold (since the manifold is made of aluminum, aggressive scraping can cause damage). Be sure to follow the directions printed on the container. If there's old sealant or oil on the mating surfaces when the manifold is installed, oil or vacuum leaks may develop. Use a vacuum cleaner to remove any gasket material that falls into the intake ports or the lifter valley.

19   Use a tap of the correct size to chase the threads in the bolt holes, if necessary, then use compressed air (if available) to remove the debris from the holes. **Warning:** *Wear safety glasses or a face shield to protect your eyes when using compressed air!*

20   Place the intake manifold gaskets in position on the heads **(see illustration)**. Then install the pushrods and rocker arms (see Section 4).

21   Apply a 3/16-inch (5 mm) bead of RTV sealant to the front and rear ridges of the engine block between the heads **(see illustration)**.

22   Carefully lower the manifold into place and install the mounting bolts/nuts finger tight. **Note:** *Coat the bolt threads with pipe sealant before installing them.*

23   Tighten the four vertical bolts (1 through 4) at the center of the manifold in the recommended tightening sequence **(see illustration)** to the torque listed in this Chapter's Specifications.

24   Tighten the four angled bolts (5 through 8) at the ends of the manifold in the recommended tightening sequence to the torque listed in this Chapter's Specifications. **Caution:** *To prevent oil leaks, tighten the vertical bolts first to ensure that the lower manifold stays centered on the gaskets, then tighten the angled bolts.*

25   Install the remaining components in the reverse order of removal.

26   Change the oil and filter and refill the cooling system (see Chapter 1). Start the engine and check for leaks.

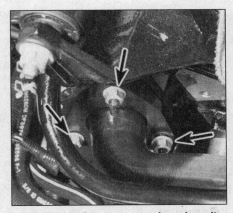

8.5 Unbolt the crossover pipe where it joins the front manifold (arrows)

8   Exhaust manifolds - removal and installation

Removal

1   Disconnect the cable from the negative terminal of the battery. **Caution:** *On models equipped with the Theftlock audio system, be sure the lockout feature is turned off before performing any procedure which requires disconnecting the battery (see the front of this manual).*

2   Remove the air cleaner assembly and duct (see Chapter 4).

Front manifold

Refer to illustrations 8.4, 8.5 and 8.6

3   Disconnect the coolant bypass pipe from the front exhaust manifold and the water pump (see Chapter 3).

4   Remove the crossover pipe heat shield. Remove the passenger-side engine mount strut bracket and the manifold heat shield **(see illustration)**.

5   Unbolt the crossover pipe where it joins the front manifold **(see illustration)**. You should first apply penetrating oil to the fas-

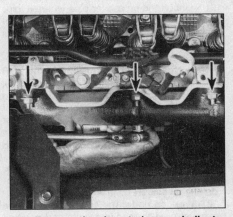

8.6 Remove the six nuts (arrows indicate the upper three) from the exhaust manifold studs

tener threads - they're usually rusted. **Note:** *After removing the three nuts, pull the crossover pipe back (the flexible joint toward the rear will allow some movement) and remove the three studs. There are hex portions on the studs. If the studs are not removed from the manifold, it is difficult to pull the manifold from the cylinder head because the manifold is also mounted on studs.*

6   Remove the mounting nuts and detach the manifold from the cylinder head **(see illustration)**.

Rear manifold

Refer to illustration 8.12

7   On later models:

a) *Detach the throttle cable and cruise control cable (if equipped) and bracket from the throttle body.*

b) *Rotate the engine for access.*

c) *Remove the spark plug wires from the rear spark plugs.*

d) *Remove the ignition coil module and bracket.*

e) *Remove the EVAP purge valve bracket (see Chapter 6).*

8.12 Remove the nuts (arrows) holding the exhaust pipe to the rear manifold

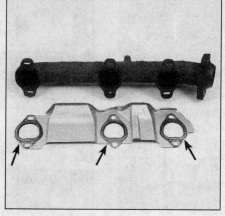

8.16 Examine the gasket areas (arrows) of both sides of the inner heat shield - if bad, the whole shield must be replaced

9.3 Remove the bolt (arrow) holding the oil dipstick tube to the front cylinder head

9.11 Remove the old gasket and carefully scrape off all old gasket material and sealant

8   Remove the crossover pipe heat shield and the manifold heat shield, if equipped.

9   Unbolt the crossover pipe where it joins the rear manifold. You should first apply penetrating oil to the fastener threads - they're usually rusted.

10   Disconnect the electrical connector from oxygen sensor(s) and remove the EGR tube from the rear manifold (see Chapter 6). **Note:** *To help prevent possible damage to the oxygen sensor(s) it is recommended that the sensor(s) be removed from the exhaust manifold before the manifold is removed from the engine (see Chapter 6).* Remove the MAP sensor (see Chapter 6).

11   Set the parking brake, block the rear wheels and raise the front of the vehicle, supporting it securely on jackstands.

12   Working under the vehicle, remove the exhaust pipe-to-manifold bolts and position the front exhaust pipe aside **(see illustration)**. **Note:** *You may have to apply penetrating oil to the fastener threads - they're usually corroded.*

13   On early models remove the bracket bolt on the automatic transaxle dipstick tube and move the tube aside.

14   Unbolt and remove the rear exhaust manifold.

Installation (front or rear)

Refer to illustration 8.16

15   Clean the mating surfaces to remove all traces of old gasket material, then inspect the manifold for distortion and cracks. Warpage can be checked with a precision straightedge held against the mating flange. If a feeler gauge thicker than 0.030-inch can be inserted between the straightedge and flange surface, take the manifold to an automotive machine shop for resurfacing.

16   Remove the exhaust manifold inner heat shield (the gasket material is part of the inner heat shield) and examine the gasket areas for signs of corrosion or leakage **(see illustration)**. If the shield/gasket seems reusable, reinstall it, place the manifold in position and install the mounting bolts finger tight.

17   Starting in the middle and working out toward the ends, tighten the mounting bolts a little at a time until all of them are at the torque listed in this Chapter's Specifications.

18   Install the remaining components in the reverse order of removal.

19   Start the engine and check for exhaust leaks between the manifold and cylinder head and between the manifold and exhaust pipe.

9   Cylinder heads - removal and installation

Refer to illustrations 9.3, 9.11, 9.14a, 9.14b and 9.17

Removal

1   Disconnect the cable from the negative terminal of the battery. **Caution:** *On models equipped with the Theftlock audio system, be sure the lockout feature is turned off before performing any procedure which requires disconnecting the battery (see the front of this manual).*

2   Remove the air cleaner assembly (see Chapter 4) and then remove the upper and lower intake manifold as described in Section 7. If not already done, remove both engine torque struts (connecting the engine to the radiator support).

3   If you're removing the front cylinder head, remove the oil dipstick tube mounting bolt **(see illustration)**.

4   Disconnect all wires and vacuum hoses from the cylinder head(s). Be sure to label them to simplify reinstallation. Remove the spark plugs. **Note:** *Removing the rear spark plugs, exhaust manifold (next step), and cylinder head will require rotating the engine for access (see Chapter 1).*

5   Detach the exhaust manifold from the cylinder head being removed (see Section 8).

6   Remove the rocker arms and pushrods (see Section 5).

7   Using the new head gasket, outline the cylinders and bolt pattern on a piece of cardboard. Be sure to indicate the front (drivebelt end) of the engine for reference. Punch holes at the bolt locations. Loosen each of the cylinder head mounting bolts 1/4-turn at a time until they can be removed by hand - work from bolt-to-bolt in a pattern that's the *reverse* of the tightening sequence **(see illustration 9.17)**. **Caution:** *The engine must be completely cool before loosening the cylinder head bolts.* Store the bolts in the cardboard holder as they're removed - this will ensure they are reinstalled in their original locations, which is absolutely essential. Note which ones are studs and their location.

8   Lift the head(s) off the engine. If resistance is felt, don't pry between the head and block as damage to the mating surfaces will result. Recheck for head bolts that may have been overlooked, then use a hammer and block of wood to tap up on the head and break the gasket seal. Be careful because there are locating dowels in the block which position each head. As a last resort, pry each head up at the rear corner only and be careful not to damage anything. After removal, place the head on blocks of wood to prevent damage to the gasket surfaces.

9   Refer to Chapter 2, Part D, for cylinder head disassembly, inspection and valve service procedures.

9.14a Position the new gasket over the dowel pins (arrows) . . .

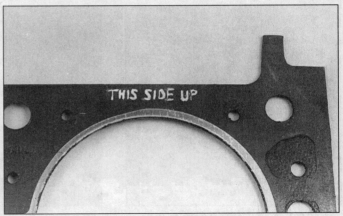

9.14b . . . with the correct side facing up

9.17a Cylinder head bolt TIGHTENING sequence
(2001 and earlier models)

9.17b Cylinder head bolt TIGHTENING sequence
(2002 and later models)

Installation

10   The mating surfaces of each cylinder head and block must be perfectly clean when the head is installed.

11   Use a gasket scraper to remove all traces of carbon and old gasket material **(see illustration)**, then clean the mating surfaces with lacquer thinner or acetone. If there's oil on the mating surfaces when the head is installed, the gasket may not seal correctly and leaks may develop. When working on the block, it's a good idea to cover the lifter valley with shop rags to keep debris out of the engine. Use a shop rag or vacuum cleaner to remove any debris that falls into the cylinders.

12   Check the block and head mating surfaces for nicks, deep scratches and other damage. If damage is slight, it can be removed with a file; if it's excessive, machining may be the only alternative.

13   Use a tap of the correct size to chase the threads in the head bolt holes. Dirt, corrosion, sealant and damaged threads will affect torque readings.

14   Position the new gasket over the dowel pins in the block. Some gaskets are marked TOP or THIS SIDE UP to ensure correct installation **(see illustrations)**.

15   Carefully position the head on the block

without disturbing the gasket.

16   Clean the bolt threads and install the bolts in the correct locations - two different lengths are used. Here's where the cardboard holder comes in handy.

17   Tighten the bolts, using the recommended sequence **(see illustrations)**, to the torque listed in this Chapter's Specifications. Then, using the same sequence, turn each bolt the amount of angle listed in this Chapter's Specifications.

18   The remaining installation steps are the reverse of removal.

19   Change the engine oil and filter (see Chapter 1).

10   Crankshaft pulley - removal and installation

Refer to illustrations 10.5, 10.6, and 10.7

1   Disconnect the cable from the negative terminal of the battery. **Caution:** *On models equipped with the Theftlock audio system, be sure the lockout feature is turned off before performing any procedure which requires disconnecting the battery (see the front of this manual).*

2   With the parking brake applied and the

shifter in Park (automatic) or in gear (manual), loosen the lugnuts from the right front wheel, then raise the front of the vehicle and support it securely on jackstands.

3   Remove the right front wheel and the right splash shield from the wheelwell.

4   Remove the drivebelt (see Chapter 1).

5   Remove the bolt from the front of the crankshaft **(see illustration)**. The bolt is normally very tight, so use a large breaker bar

10.5 Remove the crankshaft bolt (arrow) - it's very tight, so use a six-point socket and a breaker bar

10.6 Use a puller that bolts to the crankshaft pulley hub; jaw-type pullers will damage the crankshaft pulley

10.7 The pulley keyway must be aligned with the Woodruff key (arrow) in the crankshaft nose

11.2 Carefully pry the old seal out of the timing chain cover - don't damage the crankshaft in the process

and a six-point socket to remove it. **Note 1:** *On automatic transaxle equipped models, remove the driveplate cover and position a large screwdriver in the ring gear teeth to keep the crankshaft from turning while an assistant removes the crankshaft pulley bolt.* **Note 2:** *On some models it will be necessary to remove the engine torque struts, then support the right side of the engine crossmember frame with a floor jack. Remove the right side crossmember bolts and loosen the left side bolts (DO NOT REMOVE THEM!) Lower the right side of the crossmember frame to allow clearance for the removal of the crankshaft pulley and the pulley bolt.*

6   Using a puller that bolts to the crankshaft hub, remove the crankshaft pulley/balancer from the crankshaft **(see illustration)**. **Caution:** *On these engines a rubber sleeve connects the inertia weight to the balancer hub. Take care when working on the crankshaft pulley/balancer that you do not accidentally shift the inertia weight's position relative to the sleeve or balancer hub, as this will upset the tuning of the balancer.*

7   Position the crankshaft pulley/balancer on the crankshaft and slide it on as far as it will go. Note that the slot (keyway) in the hub must be aligned with the Woodruff key in the end of the crankshaft **(see illustration)**.

8   Using a crankshaft balancer installation tool, press the crankshaft pulley/balancer onto the crankshaft. Note that the crankshaft bolt can also be used to press the crankshaft balancer into position, but when doing so, use a liberal amount of clean engine oil on the bolt threads to prevent galling.

9   Tighten the crankshaft bolt to the torque listed in this Chapter's Specifications.

10   The remaining installation steps are the reverse of removal.

11   Crankshaft front oil seal - removal and installation

Refer to illustrations 11.2, 11.3 and 11.4

1   Remove the crankshaft pulley (see Section 10).

11.3 Drive the new seal into place with a large socket and hammer

2   Note how the seal is installed - the new one must be installed to the same depth and facing the same way. Carefully pry the oil seal out of the cover with a seal puller or a large screwdriver **(see illustration)**. Be very careful not to distort the cover or scratch the crankshaft! Wrap electrician's tape around the tip of the screwdriver to avoid damage to the crankshaft.

3   Apply clean engine oil or multi-purpose grease to the outer edge of the new seal, then install it in the cover with the lip (spring side) facing IN. Drive the seal into place **(see illustration)** with a large socket and a hammer (if a large socket isn't available, a piece of pipe will also work). Make sure the seal enters the bore squarely and stop when the front face is at the proper depth.

4   Check the surface on the pulley hub that the oil seal rides on. if the surface has been grooved from long time contact with the seal, a press on sleeve may be available to renew the sealing surface **(see illustration)**. This sleeve is pressed into place with a hammer and a block of wood and is commonly available at auto parts stores for various applications.

5   Lubricate the pulley hub with clean engine oil and reinstall the crankshaft pulley.

11.4 If the sealing surface of the pulley hub has a wear groove from contact with the seal, repair sleeves are available at most auto parts stores

Use a vibration damper installation tool to press the pulley onto the crankshaft.

6   Install the crankshaft pulley retaining bolt and tighten it to the torque listed in this Chapter's Specifications.

7   The remainder of installation is the reverse of the removal.

12   Timing chain and sprockets - removal, inspection and installation

Removal

Refer to illustrations 12.5, 12.11, 12.15a, 12.15b, 12.18a, 12.18b and 12.20

1   Disconnect the cable from the negative terminal of the battery. **Caution:** *On models equipped with the Theftlock audio system, be sure the lockout feature is turned off before performing any procedure which requires disconnecting the battery (see the front of this manual).*

2   Loosen, but do not remove, the water pump pulley bolts, then remove the serpentine drivebelt (see Chapter 1).

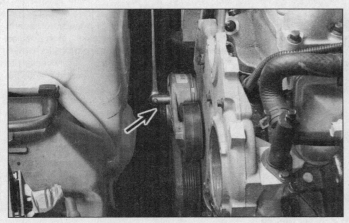

12.5 The drivebelt tensioner is secured to the timing chain cover by a bolt (arrow)

12.11 Support the engine with an engine support fixture and chains to the front and rear engine lifting eyes (arrows)

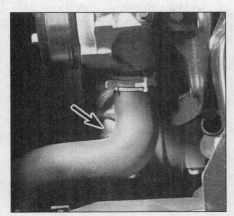

12.15a Disconnect the radiator hose (arrow) from the water pump housing

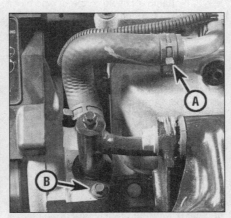

12.15b Disconnect the hose at the intake manifold pipe (A), then remove the bolt (B) at the bypass and pull the bypass from the front cover

12.18a Timing chain cover bolt locations (arrows), upper . . .

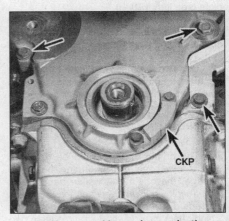

12.18b . . . and lower (arrows) - the crankshaft position sensor (CKP) should be unbolted and laid aside

3   Remove the water pump pulley (see Chapter 3).

4   Remove the crankshaft pulley (see Section 10).

5   Unbolt the drivebelt tensioner **(see illustration)** and idler, if equipped.

6   Drain the coolant and engine oil (see Chapter 1).

7   On 1995 through 2000 models, remove the alternator and loosen the mounting bracket (see Chapter 5).

8   Unbolt the power steering pump (if equipped) and tie it aside (see Chapter 10). Leave the hoses connected.

9   On 1995 through 2000 models, unbolt the flywheel/driveplate cover below the transaxle.

10   On 1995 through 2000 models, remove the starter (see Chapter 5).

11   Remove the passenger side upper engine mount and the mount support bracket from the front of the timing chain cover (see Section 18). **Note:** *This procedure requires an engine support fixture* **(see illustration)** *to secure the engine from above when the mounts are removed. Make sure you have these tools or rent them before beginning the procedure.* On 1995 through 2000 models,

refer to Chapter 3 and remove the engine cooling fan assembly, unbolt the air-conditioning compressor and set it aside without disconnecting the refrigerant lines, then remove the compressor mounting bracket.

12   On 1995 through 2000 models, remove the front exhaust manifold (see Section 8).

13   On 1995 through 2000 models, remove the hood (see Chapter 11).

14   Remove the oil pan (see Section 14). **Note:** *The front cover can be removed with the oil pan in place, but the pan must be removed for a good installation to seal against the bottom of the front cover.*

15   Disconnect the coolant hoses from the bypass pipe and water pump, and remove the coolant bypass pipe from the front cover **(see illustrations)** (see Chapter 3).

16   Disconnect the electrical connector at the crankshaft position sensor (see Chapter 6).

17   On 1995 through 2000 models, remove the right side ball joint and the lower control arm, then remove the suspension support (see Chapter 10).

18   Remove the timing chain cover-to-engine block bolts **(see illustrations)**.

19   Separate the cover from the engine. If it's stuck, tap it with a soft-face hammer, but don't try to pry it off.

20   Temporarily install the crankshaft pulley bolt and turn the crankshaft with the bolt to align the timing marks on the crankshaft and camshaft sprockets. When aligned at TDC for number 1 piston, the crankshaft sprocket

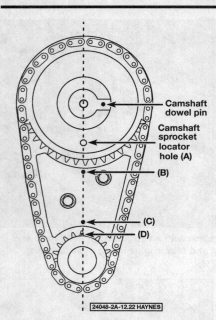

12.24 The timing chain damper (guide) is retained by two bolts (arrows)

12.20 The timing marks on the sprockets should align as shown - a straight line should pass through the center of the camshaft, camshaft sprocket timing hole (A), the upper mark on the tensioner (B), the lower mark on the tensioner (C), the crankshaft sprocket timing mark (D) and the center of the crankshaft

timing mark should align with the mark on the bottom of the chain tensioner plate, and the small hole in the camshaft sprocket should be at the 6 o'clock position, aligned with the timing mark in the top of the chain tensioner plate **(see illustration)**.

21   Remove the camshaft sprocket bolt. Do not turn the camshaft in the process (if you do, realign the timing marks before the bolt is removed).

22   Use two large screwdrivers to carefully pry the camshaft sprocket off the camshaft dowel pin. Slip the timing chain and camshaft sprocket off the engine.

Inspection

Refer to illustration 12.24

23   The timing chain should be replaced with a new one if the engine has high mileage, the chain has visible damage, or total freeplay midway between the sprockets exceeds one-inch. Failure to replace a worn timing chain may result in erratic engine performance, loss of power and decreased fuel mileage. Loose chains can "jump" timing. In the worst case, chain "jumping" or breakage will result in severe engine damage. Always replace the timing chain and sprockets in sets. If you intend to install a new timing chain, remove the crankshaft sprocket with a puller and install a new one. Be sure to align the key in the crankshaft with the keyway in the sprocket during installation.

24   Inspect the timing chain damper (guide) for cracks and wear and replace it if neces-

sary. The damper is held to the engine block by two bolts **(see illustration)**. The damper should be reinstalled before installing the new timing chain and sprockets.

25   Clean the timing chain and sprockets with solvent and dry them with compressed air (if available). **Warning:** *Wear eye protection when using compressed air.*

26   Inspect the components for wear and damage. Look for teeth that are deformed, chipped, pitted and cracked.

Installation

27   If the camshaft has turned at all since removal of the sprocket, turn the camshaft to position the dowel pin at 3 o'clock. Mesh the timing chain with the camshaft sprocket, then engage it with the crankshaft sprocket. The timing marks should be aligned as shown in **illustration 12.20. Note:** *If the crankshaft has been disturbed, turn it until the "O" stamped on the crankshaft sprocket is exactly at the top.*

28   Install the camshaft sprocket bolt (make sure the dowel hole in the sprocket is aligned with the dowel pin in the camshaft) and tighten to the torque listed in this Chapter's Specifications.

29   Lubricate the chain and sprocket with clean engine oil.

30   Use a gasket scraper to remove all traces of old gasket material and sealant from the cover and engine block. The cover is made of aluminum, so be careful not to nick or gouge it. Clean the gasket sealing surfaces

with lacquer thinner or acetone.

31   Apply a thin layer of anaerobic sealant to both sides of the new gasket, then position the gasket on the engine block (the dowel pins should keep it in place). Apply sealant to the bottom of the gasket, where it meets the oil pan.

32   Attach the cover to the engine and install the bolts. Follow a criss-cross pattern when tightening the fasteners and work up to the torque listed in this Chapter's Specifications in three steps.

33   The remainder of installation is the reverse of removal. Refer to Section 14 for oil pan installation.

34   Add oil and coolant, start the engine and check for leaks.

13   Valve lifters - removal, inspection and installation

1   A noisy valve lifter can be isolated when the engine is idling. Hold a mechanic's stethoscope or a length of hose near the location of each valve while listening at the other end. Another method is to remove the valve cover and, with the engine idling, touch each of the valve spring retainers, one at a time. If a valve lifter is defective, it'll be evident from the shock felt at the retainer each time the valve seats.

2   The most likely causes of noisy valve lifters are dirt trapped inside the lifter and lack of oil flow, viscosity or pressure. Before condemning the lifters, check the oil for fuel contamination, correct level, cleanliness and correct viscosity.

Removal

Refer to illustrations 13.5, 13.6a, 13.6b and 13.7

3   Remove the valve cover(s) and intake manifold as described in Sections 4 and 7.

4   Remove the rocker arms and pushrods (see Section 5).

5   Remove the bolts holding the roller lifter guide to the block, and remove the two roller lifter guides **(see illustration)**. Mark the guides as to which side they came from.

6   There are several ways to extract the lifters from the bores. A special tool designed to grip and remove lifters is manufactured by

13.5 Remove the bolts (A) and pull up the roller lifter guides (B)

13.6a A magnetic pick-up tool . . .

13.6b . . . or a scribe can be used to remove the lifters

13.7 Store the lifters in order to ensure installation in their original locations

many tool companies and is widely available, but it may not be required in every case. On newer engines without a lot of varnish buildup, the lifters can often be removed with a small magnet or even with your fingers. A machinist's scribe with a bent end can be used to pull the lifters out by positioning the point under the retainer ring in the top of each lifter **(see illustrations)**. **Caution:** *Don't use pliers to remove the lifters unless you intend to replace them with new ones (along with the camshaft). The pliers may damage the precision machined and hardened lifters, rendering them useless.*

7   Before removing the lifters, arrange to store them in a clearly labeled box to ensure they're reinstalled in their original locations. Remove the lifters and store them where they won't get dirty **(see illustration)**.

Inspection and installation

Refer to illustrations 13.10a and 13.10b

8   Parts for valve lifters are not available separately. The work required to remove them from the engine again if cleaning is unsuccessful outweighs any potential savings from repairing them.

9   Clean the lifters thoroughly with solvent and dry them thoroughly, without mixing them up.

10   Check each lifter wall and plunger seat for scuffing, score marks or uneven wear **(see illustration)**. Check the rollers carefully for wear or damage and make sure they turn freely without excessive play **(see illustration)**. If the lifters walls are worn (not very likely), inspect the lifter bores in the block. If the pushrod seats are worn, inspect the pushrods also.

11   When reinstalling used lifters, make sure they're replaced in their original bores. Soak new lifters in oil to remove trapped air. Coat all lifters with moly-base grease or engine assembly lube prior to installation.

12   Install the push rods and the rocker arms (see Section 5).

13   The remaining installation steps are the reverse of removal.

14   Run the engine and check for oil leaks.

---

14   Oil pan - removal and installation

Removal

Refer to illustrations 14.3, 14.15, 14.16a, 14.16b and 14.17

1   Disconnect the cable from the negative terminal of the battery. **Caution:** *On models*

equipped with the Theftlock audio system, be sure the lockout feature is turned off before performing any procedure which requires disconnecting the battery (see the front of this manual).

2   Remove the serpentine drivebelt (see Chapter 1) and the belt tensioner **(see illustration 12.5)**.

3   Raise the front of the vehicle and place it securely on jackstands. Apply the parking brake and block the rear wheels to keep it from rolling off the stands. Remove the lower splash pan and drain the engine oil (refer to Chapter 1 if necessary). Disconnect the oil-level sensor connector from the sensor **(see illustration)**.

4   Refer to Chapter 3 and unbolt the air conditioning compressor and set it aside without disconnecting the refrigerant lines. On some models it may be necessary to remove the A/C line at the accumulator. **Warning:** *The air conditioning system is under high pressure. Do not loosen any hose fittings or remove any components until after the system has been discharged by a dealer service department or service station. Always wear eye protection when disconnecting air conditioning system fittings.*

5   Remove the right side ball joint. Remove

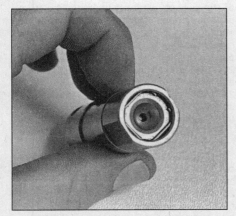

13.10a Check the pushrod seat in the top of each lifter for wear

13.10b The roller on the roller lifters must turn freely - check for wear and excessive play as well

14.3 Disconnect the oil level sensor connector (arrow) if equipped

14.15 Remove these bolts (arrows) at the pan and transmission, then remove the transmission-to-engine brace if equipped

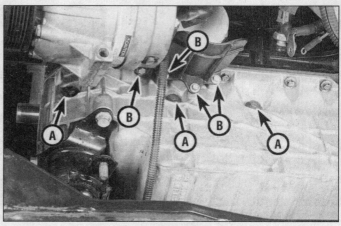

14.16a Remove the oil pan side bolts (arrows A indicate three on the radiator side) - also remove the oil filter shield bolts (B)

14.16b The side bolts on the rear side of the oil pan are more difficult to remove, but a box wrench with an offset bend in it can remove them

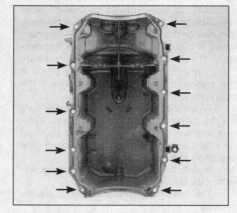

14.17 Remove the 12 oil pan-to-block bolts (arrows) - pan removed for clarity

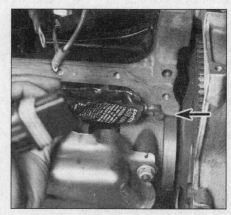

14.19 Apply a bead of RTV sealant on either side of the rear main cap, where the pan gasket will meet it (arrow)

the lower control arm, then remove the suspension support (see Chapter 10). On 2001 and later models (or where necessary), remove the right outer tie rod from the steering knuckle and remove the right stabilizer link nut and bolt.

6   Remove the front exhaust pipe.
7   Remove the steering gear pinch bolt (see Chapter 10). **Caution:** *Be sure to separate the steering gear from the rack and pinion stub shaft to avoid damage to the steering gear and intermediate shaft.*
8   Remove the flywheel/driveplate lower cover.
9   Remove the starter (see Chapter 5).
10   Remove the hood (see Chapter 11) and support the engine with a support fixture **(see illustration 12.11).**
11   On 1995 through 2000 models, refer to Section 18 and remove the engine torque struts, then remove the passenger side lower mount and bracket if equipped. Remove the through bolt/nuts holding the driver's side transaxle mount to the frame, then remove the retaining bolts/nuts securing the mount to transaxle.
12   Place a floor jack under the frame front

center crossmember.
13   Loosen the left side frame bolts - DO NOT REMOVE THEM!
14   Remove the right side frame bolts and lower the right side of the frame. On 1995 through 2000 models, remove the crankshaft pulley. On 2000 and later models (or where necessary), remove the passenger side engine mount and bracket from the oil pan.
15   At the rear side of the oil pan, remove the bolts and the brace (if equipped) from transaxle to engine **(see illustration)**.
16   Remove the three side bolts (connecting the sides of the cast oil pan to the main cap supports) on each side of the oil pan **(see illustrations)**. Also remove the oil filter shield bolted to the top front of the pan.
17   Remove the remaining 12 oil pan-to-block bolts, then carefully separate the oil pan from the block **(see illustration)**. Don't pry between the block and the pan or damage to the sealing surfaces could occur and oil leaks may develop. Instead, tap the pan with a soft-face hammer to break the gasket seal.

Installation
Refer to illustration 14.19
18   Clean the pan with solvent and remove

all old sealant and gasket material from the block and pan mating surfaces. Clean the mating surfaces with lacquer thinner or acetone and make sure the bolt holes in the block are clear.
19   Apply a bead of RTV sealant to the front of the gasket, where it contacts the front cover, and a short bead (9/32-inch wide) to either side of the rear main cap where it meets the block, then install the new one-piece oil pan gasket **(see illustration)**.
20   Place the oil pan in position on the block and install the nuts/bolts.
21   After the pan-to-block fasteners are installed, tighten them to the torque listed in this Chapter's Specifications. Starting at the center, follow a criss-cross pattern and work up to the final torque in three steps.
22   After all the pan-to-block bolts have been torqued, install the oil pan side bolts and tighten them to Specifications.
23   The remaining steps are the reverse of the removal procedure.
24   Refill the engine with oil, run it until normal operating temperature is reached and check for leaks.

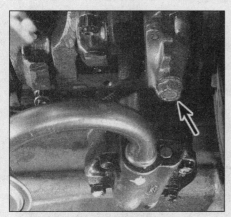

15.2 Oil pump mounting bolt location (arrow)

16.2a Most flywheels/driveplates have locating dowels (arrow) - if the one you're working on doesn't have one, make some marks to ensure proper alignment on reassembly

16.2b A large screwdriver wedged in one of the holes in the flywheel/driveplate can be used to keep the flywheel/driveplate from turning as the mounting bolts are removed

15   Oil pump - removal and installation

Refer to illustration 15.2

1   Remove the oil pan (see Section 14).
2   Unbolt the oil pump and lower it from the engine **(see illustration)**. **Note:** *The oil pump driveshaft will come out with the pump as you lower it. It's a rod with a flat-sided portion at each end*.
3   If the pump is defective, replace it with a new one - don't reuse the original or attempt to rebuild it. Inspect the ends of the oil pump driveshaft and the plastic collar that retains the driveshaft to the oil pump. If there are signs of wear on the shaft or if the plastic collar is cracked or missing, replace the shaft with a new one. **Note:** *The plastic collar centers the oil pump driveshaft over the oil pump shaft. If the collar is not used or is missing, damage to the oil pump driveshaft and the oil pump will occur. A new plastic collar is usually included with a new oil pump or driveshaft*.
4   Prime the pump by pouring clean engine oil into the pick-up screen while turning the pump driveshaft.
5   To install the pump, turn the flat on the driveshaft so it mates with the slot in the oil pump shaft. Make sure the plastic collar is fitted over the oil pump-to-oil pump driveshaft joint, then install the oil pump and driveshaft assembly into the block while engaging the upper end of the oil pump driveshaft into the oil pump drive.
6   Install the pump mounting bolt and tighten it to the torque listed in this Chapter's Specifications.
7   The remainder of assembly is the reverse of the removal procedure.

16   Flywheel/driveplate - removal and installation

Removal

Refer to illustrations 16.2a and 16.2b

1   Raise the vehicle and support it securely on jackstands, then refer to Chapter 7 and remove the transaxle. If the vehicle is equipped with a manual transaxle, remove the clutch components (see Chapter 8).
2   Remove the bolts that secure the flywheel/driveplate to the crankshaft **(see illustration)**. If the crankshaft turns, wedge a screwdriver in the ring gear teeth to jam the flywheel/driveplate **(see illustration)**. **Note:** *If there is a retaining ring between the bolts and the driveplate, note which side faces the driveplate when removing it*.
3   Remove the flywheel/driveplate from the crankshaft. Since the flywheel/driveplate is fairly heavy, be sure to support it while removing the last bolt. **Caution:** *When removing a flywheel, wear gloves to protect your fingers - the edges of the ring gear teeth may be sharp*.
4   Clean the flywheel/driveplate to remove grease and oil. Inspect the surface for cracks, and check for cracked and broken ring gear teeth. Lay the driveplate on a flat surface to check for warpage.
5   Clean and inspect the mating surfaces of the flywheel/driveplate and the crankshaft. If the crankshaft rear seal is leaking, replace it before reinstalling the driveplate (see Section 17).

Installation

6   Position the flywheel/driveplate against the crankshaft. Be sure to align the marks made during removal. Note that some engines have an alignment dowel or staggered bolt holes to ensure correct installation. Before installing the bolts, apply thread locking compound to the threads and place the retaining ring in position on the flywheel/driveplate.
7   Wedge a screwdriver through the ring gear teeth to keep the flywheel/driveplate from turning as you tighten the bolts to the torque listed in this Chapter's Specifications. On vehicles equipped with automatic transaxles, if the front pump seal/O-ring is leaking, now would be a very good time to replace it.
8   The remainder of installation is the reverse of the removal procedure.

17   Rear main oil seal - replacement

Refer to illustration 17.4

1   Remove the transaxle (see Chapter 7).
2   Remove the flywheel/driveplate (see Section 16).
3   Inspect the oil seal, as well as the oil pan and engine block surface for signs of leakage. Sometimes an oil pan gasket leak can appear to be a rear oil seal leak.
4   Pry the oil seal from the block with a screwdriver **(see illustration)**. Be careful not to nick or scratch the crankshaft or the seal bore. Thoroughly clean the seal bore in the block with a shop towel. Remove all traces of oil and dirt.
5   Lubricate the lips of the new seal with engine oil or multi-purpose grease. Install the seal over the end of the crankshaft (make sure the lips of the seal point toward the engine) and carefully tap it into place. A special aftermarket tool may be available at your local auto parts store. The tool just fits the diameter of the seal and, used with a hammer, drives the seal in. **Note:** *Do not drive it in any further than the original seal was installed*.
6   Install the flywheel/driveplate (see Section 16).
7   Install the transaxle (see Chapter 7).

17.4 Carefully pry the old seal out

18.9a The passenger side lower engine mount (A) is between the front of the oil pan and the chassis - with the engine supported from above remove the bolts (arrows) holding the bracket to the oil pan . . .

18.9b . . . and from below remove the nuts (arrows) on the crossmember, then unbolt the mount from the engine bracket and install the new mount

18   Powertrain mounts - check and replacement

1   There are two mounts that connect the powertrain to the chassis, one at the timing chain end and one at the transaxle end (see Chapter 7), and two upper mounts connecting the engine torque struts to the body near the top of the radiator. There is also a brace that connects the engine's oil pan to the transaxle **(see illustration 14.16a)**.

2   Engine mounts seldom require attention, but broken or deteriorated mounts should be replaced immediately or the added strain placed on the powertrain components may cause damage or wear.

Check

3   During the check, the engine must be raised slightly to remove the weight from the mounts.

4   Raise the vehicle and support it securely on jackstands, then position a jack under the engine oil pan. Place a large block of wood between the jack head and the oil pan, then carefully raise the engine just enough to take the weight off the mounts. **Warning:** *DO NOT place any part of your body under the engine when it's supported only by a jack!*

5   Check the mount insulators (the rubber part between the engine and the chassis brackets) to see if the rubber is cracked, hardened or separated from the metal plates. Sometimes the rubber will split right down the center.

6   Check for relative movement between the mount plates and the engine or frame (use a large screwdriver or prybar to attempt to move the mounts). If movement is noted, lower the engine and tighten the mount fasteners.

7   Rubber preservative should be applied to the insulators to slow deterioration.

Replacement

Refer to illustrations 18.9a and 18.9b

8   Disconnect the negative battery cable from the battery, then raise the vehicle and support it securely on jackstands (if not already done). **Note:** *On models equipped with the Theftlock audio system, be sure the lockout feature is turned off before performing any procedure which requires disconnecting the battery.*

9   Raise the engine slightly with a jack or hoist. Remove the bolts/nuts holding the mount to the engine and to the chassis brackets, then raise the engine more until you can remove the mount **(see illustrations)**.

10   Installation is the reverse of removal. Use thread-locking compound on the mount bolts and be sure to tighten them securely to this Chapter's Specifications.

Chapter 2 Part B
3.4L DOHC V6 engine

Contents

Specifications

General

Cylinder numbers (drivebelt end-to-transaxle end)	
Front bank (radiator side)	2-4-6
Rear bank	1-3-5
Firing order	1-2-3-4-5-6

Cylinder location and coil terminal identification diagram - 3.4L DOHC engine

```
  1   3   5
  2   4   6     FRONT OF VEHICLE →
24048-1-C HAYNES
```

Camshafts

Lobe lift	
Intake	0.370 inch (9.398 mm)
Exhaust	0.370 inch (9.398 mm)
Journal diameter	2.1643 to 2.1654 inches (54.973 to 55.001 mm)
Journal clearance	0.0019 to 0.0040 inch (0.049 to 0.102 mm)

Oil pump

Gear backlash	0.0037 to 0.00771 inch (0.094 to 0.195 mm)
Gear length	1.199 to 1.200 inches (30.45 to 30.48 mm)
Gear diameter	1.498 to 1.500 inches (38.05 to 38.10 mm)
Gear housing depth	1.202 to 1.205 inches (30.53 to 30.61 mm)
Gear housing inner diameter	1.504 to 1.506 inches (38.202 to 38.252 mm)
Gear side clearance	0.003 to 0.004 inch (0.08 to 0.10 mm)
Gear end clearance	0.002 to 0.006 inch (0.05 to 0.152 mm)
Pressure valve-to-bore clearance	0.0015 to 0.0035 inch (0.038 to 0.089 mm)

Torque specifications

Ft-lbs (unless otherwise indicated)

Camshaft carrier cover bolts	97 in-lbs
Camshaft carrier-to-cylinder head bolts	20
Camshaft sprocket bolts	96
Cylinder head bolts	
First step	44
Second step	Tighten an additional 90-degrees

Torque specifications (continued)   Ft-lbs (unless otherwise indicated)

Exhaust manifold-to-cylinder head	
Nut	
1995	18
1996 and 1997	116 in-lbs
Stud	13
Flywheel/driveplate-to-crankshaft bolts	60
Intake manifold-to-cylinder head bolts/nuts	
1995	22
1996 and 1997	116 in-lbs
Intake plenum-to-intake manifold bolts	
1995	22
1996 and 1997	19
Intermediate shaft belt sprocket bolt	96
Oil pan bolts/nuts	
Pan bolt (rear)	20
Others	97 in-lbs
Oil pump	
Mounting bolt	40
Drive bolt	27
Cover bolt	89 in-lbs
Engine front cover bolts	
Small	20
Large	35
Timing chain tensioner bolts	18
Crankshaft damper bolt	79
Crankshaft pulley-to-damper bolts	44

1   General information

Refer to illustration 1.4
Note: *On models equipped with the Theftlock audio system, be sure the lockout feature is turned off before performing any procedure which requires disconnecting the battery.*

This Part of Chapter 2 is devoted to in-vehicle repair procedures for the 3.4 DOHC liter V6 engine. This engine utilizes a cast-iron block with six cylinders arranged in a "V" shape at a 60-degree angle between the two banks.

The overhead camshaft aluminum cylinder heads have two exhaust valves and two intake valves for each cylinder, and have pressed-in valve guides and valve seats.

The camshafts are located inside aluminum camshaft carrier housings that are located on top of each cylinder head. Each camshaft carrier contains two camshafts, one for the exhaust valves and one for the intake valves. The camshaft thrust plates are at rear

1.4 3.4 liter Double Overhead Camshaft (DOHC) V6 engine

of the carriers. The aluminum of the carriers serves as the bearing surface for the camshafts.

The engine is easily identified by looking at the designation printed on the fuel rail cover **(see illustration)**.

All information concerning engine removal and installation and engine block and cylinder head overhaul can be found in Part D of this Chapter. The following repair procedures are based on the assumption the engine is installed in the vehicle. If the engine has been removed from the vehicle and mounted on a stand, many of the steps outlined in this Part of Chapter 2 will not apply.

The Specifications included in this Part of Chapter 2 apply only to the procedures contained in this Part. Part D of Chapter 2 contains the Specifications necessary for cylinder head and engine block rebuilding.

2   Repair operations possible with the engine in the vehicle

Many major repair operations can be accomplished without removing the engine from the vehicle.

Clean the engine compartment and the exterior of the engine with some type of degreaser before any work is done. It'll make the job easier and help keep dirt out of the internal areas of the engine.

Depending on the components involved, it may be helpful to remove the hood to improve access to the engine as repairs are performed (refer to Chapter 11 if necessary). Cover the fenders to prevent damage to the paint. Special pads are available, but an old bedspread or blanket will also work.

If vacuum, exhaust, oil or coolant leaks develop, indicating a need for gasket or seal replacement, the repairs can generally be done with the engine in the vehicle. The intake and exhaust manifold gaskets, timing chain cover gasket, oil pan gasket, crankshaft oil seals and cylinder head gaskets are all accessible with the engine in place.

Exterior engine components, such as the intake and exhaust manifolds, the oil pan (and the oil pump), the water pump, the starter motor, the alternator and the fuel system components can be removed for repair with the engine in place.

Since the cylinder heads can be removed without pulling the engine, valve component servicing can also be accomplished with the engine in the vehicle. Replacement of the camshaft timing belts and intermediate shaft chain and sprockets is also possible with the engine in the vehicle.

In extreme cases caused by a lack of necessary equipment, repair or replacement of piston rings, pistons, connecting rods and rod bearings is possible with the engine in the vehicle. However, this practice is not recommended because of the cleaning and preparation work that must be done to the components involved.

3   Top Dead Center (TDC) for number one position - locating

This procedure is essentially the same as that for the 3.1L/3.4L OHV V6 engine. Refer to Part A and follow the procedure outlined there.

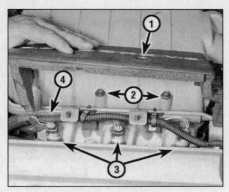

4.4 3.4L V6 plenum installation details

1. Engine identification cover
2. Plenum mounting bolts (front side shown)
3. Fuel injectors
4. Fuel rail

4 Intake manifold - removal and installation

Removal

Refer to illustrations 4.4 and 4.5

1 Disconnect the negative battery cable from the battery. **Caution:** *On models equipped with a Delco Theftlock audio system, be sure the lockout feature is turned off before performing any procedure which requires disconnecting the battery.*

2 Relieve the fuel system pressure (see Chapter 4).

3 Remove the fuel rail and disconnect any hoses or wires attached to the throttle body (see Chapter 4). **Note:** *When disconnecting fuel line fittings, be prepared to catch some fuel with a rag, then cap the fittings to prevent contamination.*

4 Raise the engine identification covers for access, then remove the plenum mounting bolts and lift off the plenum with the throttle body attached **(see illustration)**.

5 Remove the radiator hose from the thermostat housing **(see illustration)**.

6 Remove the connector from the coolant temperature sensor.

7 Remove the heater pipe nut at the throttle body.

8 Remove the manifold mounting bolts and nuts, then separate the manifold from the engine. Don't pry between the manifold and heads, as damage to the soft aluminum gasket sealing surfaces may result. If you're installing a new manifold, transfer all fittings and sensors to the new manifold.

Installation

Note: *The mating surfaces of the cylinder heads, block and manifold must be perfectly clean when the manifold is installed. Gasket removal solvents are available at most auto parts stores and may be helpful when removing old gasket material that's stuck to the heads and manifold (since the manifold is made of aluminum, aggressive scraping can*

4.5 Thermostat housing outlet (arrow)

cause damage). Be sure to follow the directions printed on the container.

9 Lift the old gaskets off. Use a gasket scraper to remove all traces of sealant and old gasket material, then clean the mating surfaces with lacquer thinner or acetone. If there's old sealant or oil on the mating surfaces when the manifold is installed, oil or vacuum leaks may develop. Use a vacuum cleaner to remove any gasket material that falls into the intake ports or the lifter valley.

10 Use a tap of the correct size to chase the threads in the bolt holes, if necessary, then use compressed air (if available) to remove the debris from the holes. **Warning:** *Wear safety glasses or a face shield to protect your eyes when using compressed air!*

11 Install the intake manifold gaskets.

12 Carefully lower the manifold into place and install the mounting bolts/nuts finger tight. **Note:** *To ease reassembly, you can temporarily install two M8 x 1.25 x 50 mm bolts, with washers, in the vertical holes in the intake manifold. This will help align the intake bolt grommet bores with the threaded holes in the cylinder heads.*

13 Tighten the mounting bolts/nuts in two steps, working from the center out, in a circular pattern, until they're all at the torque listed in this Chapter's Specifications. Then remove the two bolts from the vertical holes in the intake manifold.

14 Install the remaining components in the reverse order of removal. Use a new gasket between the lower intake manifold and the plenum.

15 Change the oil and filter and refill the cooling system (see Chapter 1). Start the engine and check for leaks.

5 Exhaust manifolds - removal and installation

Front Manifold

Refer to illustration 5.3

1 Disconnect the negative battery cable from the battery. **Caution:** *On models equipped with a Delco Theftlock audio system, be sure the lockout feature is turned off before performing any procedure which*

5.3 Remove the exhaust crossover pipe from the manifold

1. Front exhaust manifold
2. Exhaust crossover pipe
3. Engine torque strut

requires disconnecting the battery.

2 Remove the air cleaner assembly (see Chapter 4).

3 Remove the exhaust crossover pipe from the manifolds **(see illustration)**. **Note:** *The fasteners will be rusty; soak them with penetrating oil for 15 minutes before beginning removal.*

4 Remove the cooling fans (see Chapter 3).

5 Remove the mounting nuts, then remove the front exhaust manifold from the cylinder head. **Note:** *The heat shield will come off with the manifold.*

6 Clean the mating surfaces to remove all traces of old gasket material, then inspect the manifold for distortion and cracks. Warpage can be checked with a precision straightedge held against the mating flange. If a feeler gauge thicker than 0.030-inch can be inserted between the straightedge and flange surface, take the manifold to an automotive machine shop for resurfacing.

7 Place the manifold in position with a new gasket and install the mounting nuts finger tight. Make sure the heat shield is in its original position.

8 Starting in the middle and working out toward the ends, tighten the mounting nuts a little at a time until all of them are at the torque listed in this Chapter's Specifications.

9 Install the remaining components in the reverse order of removal.

10 Start the engine and check for exhaust leaks between the manifold and cylinder head and between the manifold and exhaust pipe.

Rear manifold

Refer to illustration 5.13

11 Disconnect the negative battery cable from the battery. **Caution:** *On models equipped with a Delco Theftlock audio system, be sure the lockout feature is turned off before performing any procedure which requires disconnecting the battery.*

12 Remove the air cleaner and duct assembly.

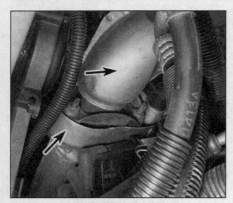

5.13 Remove the exhaust crossover pipe from the manifold (arrows)

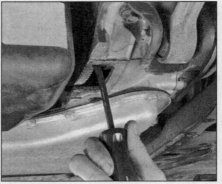

6.7 Have an assistant hold the ring gear with a large screwdriver as the damper-to-crankshaft bolt is loosened/tightened

6.9 Use a puller to remove the damper - use only the type that pulls on the hub of the damper (a puller that pulls on the outer circumference of the damper may cause damage)

13   Remove the exhaust crossover pipe from the manifold **(see illustration)**.
14   Remove the EGR tube from the exhaust manifold (see Chapter 4).
15   Set the parking brake, block the rear wheels and raise the front of the vehicle supporting it securely on jackstands.
16   Remove the front exhaust pipe and catalytic converter assembly.
17   Remove the oxygen sensor.
18   If necessary, remove the rear alternator bracket.
19   Remove the transmission fluid dipstick tube.
20   Remove the steering gear intermediate shaft (see Chapter 10).
21   Remove the exhaust manifold nuts.
22   With the front of the vehicle on jackstands (not under the front engine/suspension "cradle") remove the rear cradle bolts, then lower the cradle with a hydraulic floorjack and remove the steering gear heat shield (see Chapter 10). **Warning:** *Make sure you have sturdy backup support materials (lengths of 4x4 or larger lumber, etc.) under the cradle just in case the hydraulic jack should fail.*
23   Remove the exhaust manifold heat shield, manifold and gasket.
24   Clean the mating surfaces to remove all traces of old gasket material, then inspect the manifold for distortion and cracks. Warpage can be checked with a precision straightedge held against the mating flange. If a feeler gauge thicker than 0.030-inch can be inserted between the straightedge and flange surface, take the manifold to an automotive machine shop for resurfacing.
25   Place the manifold in position with a new gasket and install the mounting nuts finger tight. Install the heat shield as it was installed originally.
26   Starting in the middle and working out toward the ends, tighten the mounting nuts a little at a time until all of them are at the torque listed in this Chapter's Specifications.
27   Install the remaining components in the reverse order of removal.
28   Start the engine and check for exhaust leaks between the manifold and cylinder head and between the manifold and exhaust pipe.

6   Crankshaft front oil seal - replacement

Refer to illustrations 6.7, 6.9, 6.10 and 6.11

1   Disconnect the negative battery cable from the battery. **Caution:** *On models equipped with a Delco Theftlock audio system, be sure the lockout feature is turned off before performing any procedure which requires disconnecting the battery.*
2   Loosen the lug nuts on the right front wheel.
3   Raise the vehicle and support it securely on jackstands.
4   Remove the right front wheel.
5   Remove the right front inner fender splash shield.
6   Remove the serpentine drivebelt (see Chapter 1).
7   Remove the driveplate cover and position a large screwdriver in the ring gear teeth to keep the crankshaft from turning while an assistant removes the crankshaft (center) bolt **(see illustration)**. **Note:** *The bolt is normally very tight, so use a large breaker bar and a six-point socket.*
8   Remove the pulley-to-damper bolts, then remove the pulley from the damper.
9   Pull the damper off the crankshaft with a bolt-type puller **(see illustration)**. Leave the

Woodruff key in place in the end of the crankshaft.
10   Note how the seal is installed - the new one must be installed to the same depth and facing the same way. Carefully pry the oil seal out of the cover with a seal puller **(see illustration)** or a large screwdriver. Be very careful not to distort the cover or scratch the crankshaft! Wrap electrician's tape around the tip of the screwdriver to avoid damage to the crankshaft.
11   Apply clean engine oil or multi-purpose grease to the outer edge of the new seal, then install it in the cover with the lip (spring side) facing IN. Drive the seal into place **(see illustration)** with a large socket and a hammer (if a large socket isn't available, a piece of pipe will also work). Make sure the seal enters the bore squarely; stop when the front face is at the proper depth.
12   Be sure to apply moly-base grease to the seal contact surface of the damper hub (if it isn't lubricated, the seal lip could be damaged and oil leakage would result). Apply a dab of RTV sealant to the keyway before tapping the damper in place with a block of wood, aligning the hub keyway with the Woodruff key in the crankshaft.
13   Install the pulley and tighten the bolts to the torque listed in this Chapter's Specifications.

6.10 Carefully pry the old seal out with a seal removal tool (shown) or a large screwdriver

6.11 Drive the new seal into place with a large socket and hammer

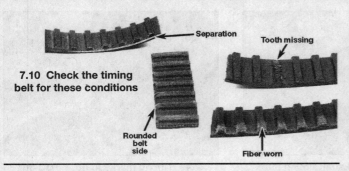

7.10 Check the timing belt for these conditions

Separation

Tooth missing

Rounded belt side

Fiber worn

7.11 To check the camshaft timing belt length, insert a small ruler between the tensioner pulley and the front cover flange (arrow), and measure the depth

14   Install and tighten the damper-to-crankshaft bolt to the torque listed in this Chapter's Specifications.

15   Reinstall the remaining parts in the reverse order of removal.

7   Timing belt, belt tensioner and pulleys - removal, inspection and installation

Note: *This procedure is complicated, time-consuming and requires several special factory tools. Read through this entire section and acquire the necessary tools before beginning.*

Timing belt cover removal

1   Disconnect the negative battery cable. **Caution:** *On models equipped with a Delco Theftlock audio system, be sure the lockout feature is turned off before performing any procedure which requires disconnecting the battery.*

2   Remove the bolts retaining the front cover to the camshaft carrier.

3   Remove the cover.

4   Refer to Chapter 5 and remove the ignition coil pack and its mounting bracket.

5   Remove the bolts and take off the rear cover.

6   Remove the ECM harness cover.

7   Remove the serpentine belt (see Chapter 1) and the serpentine belt tensioner.

8   Remove the clip holding the power steering line at the alternator stud.

9   Remove the cover bolts, then the center cover.

Timing belt inspection

Refer to illustrations 7.10a, 7.10b, 7.10c and 7.11

10   Inspect the timing belt for signs of wear, such as cracks or tears, and for oil contamination. Make sure the belt's teeth are in good condition. Check also for fraying or for wear around one edge of the belt, which would indicate misalignment of camshaft/belt drive components **(see illustrations)**. Replace the belt as necessary.

11   Check the timing belt length. Insert a very thin, narrow ruler under the tensioner pulley until it contacts the tensioner base **(see illustration)**. If the belt is too long, the ruler will drop into the groove in the tensioner bracket. Check this by recording the length indicated on the ruler. If the depth from the edge of the pulley to

the base of the tensioner measures 1.62 inches (41.1 mm) or less, the length of the belt is OK. If the ruler shows 1.75 inches (45.1 mm) or more, it means it dropped into the groove in the tensioner bracket, indicating that the belt is too long and must be replaced. **Note:** *If you are doing a repair procedure which requires you to remove the timing belts and you are close to the mileage or time schedule (see Chapter 1) for belt replacement, replace the belt.*

Timing belt removal

> **✱✱ CAUTION ✱✱**
>
> The timing system is complex. Severe engine damage will occur if you make any mistakes. Do not attempt this procedure unless you are highly experienced with this type of repair. If you are at all unsure of your abilities, consult an expert. Double-check all your work and be sure everything is correct before you attempt to start the engine.

Refer to illustrations 7.20 and 7.22

12   Remove the upper intake manifold (plenum) (see Chapter 4).

13   Remove the serpentine belt (see Chapter 1), and the coolant recovery tank (see Chapter 3).

14   If necessary, move the ECM aside, then remove its mounting bracket.

15   Remove the timing belt covers (see Steps 1 through 9).

16   Refer to Chapter 10 and unbolt the power steering pump and set it aside without disconnecting the fluid hoses.

17   Remove the camshaft carrier covers (see Section 8).

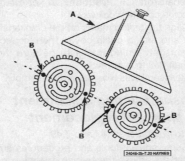

7.20 Align the original timing marks on the camshaft sprockets (B) or make new marks - the factory holding tool (A) locks the camshafts from turning

18   Remove the plastic cover over the wiring harness on the right strut tower.

19   Align the timing marks, by rotating the engine (clockwise only!) until the mark on the crankshaft damper is aligned with the arrow on the front cover.

20   Loosely clamp the two camshaft sprockets on each side of the engine together using clamping pliers or equivalent. The marks on the camshaft sprocket pairs should be aligned with a straight line through the center of the sprockets. If the old marks do not align, wipe the old marks off and make new marks **(see illustration)**. Do not allow the camshafts to move until after the tensioner and new timing belt are in place. If you have access to the factory camshaft-holding tools (Kent-Moore J-38613-A), insert one through the slot in each camshaft carrier (at the timing belt end of the front cylinder head, at the flywheel end of the rear cylinder head). Make sure the camshaft flats are aligned with the tool and bolt the tool in place to keep the camshafts from turning.

21   If the timing belt is not going to be removed (just the tensioner is going to be removed), use a C-clamp and a protective cloth to hold the belt in position on the rear exhaust camshaft sprocket. **Note:** *Make sure there is no deflection in the sprocket. If there is, set up your clamp again.*

22   Remove the retaining bolts from the tensioner side plate, then remove the side plate **(see illustration)**.

23   Remove the tensioner actuator from its base with a rotating motion. **Note:** *When you do this the tensioner will extend to its maximum travel.* **Caution:** *A tapered bushing is positioned between the actuator and the mounting base; be careful not to lose it when removing the actuator.*

24   If you're going to reuse the belt, mark

7.22 Timing belt tensioner side plate

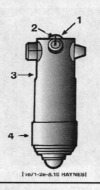

7.26 Timing belt tensioner actuator

1. *Rubber end plug*
2. *Paper clip (installation tool)*
3. *Rubber boot*
4. *Rod tip*

the direction of rotation on the belt.

25   Remove the belt by sliding it carefully off the sprockets and pulleys. **Caution:** *Do not kink, fold, twist or pry on the belt or you will cause damage.* **Note:** *If the sprockets are to be removed for replacement, see Camshaft timing Steps.*

Installation

> ## ** CAUTION **
>
> Before starting the engine, carefully rotate the crankshaft by hand through at least two full revolutions (use a socket and breaker bar on the crankshaft pulley center bolt). If you feel any resistance, STOP! There is something wrong - most likely, valves are contacting the pistons. You must find the problem before proceeding. Check your work and see if any updated repair information is available.

Refer to illustration 7.26
Note: *When the camshaft timing procedure is complete, the position of the timing flats on the front bank of camshafts should differ from those of the rear bank camshafts by 180 degrees, i.e. the flats should be UP on one set while the flats on the other set are DOWN.*

26   Lightly clamp the body of the tensioner actuator in a vise with its rod tip facing down **(see illustration)**. **Caution:** *Do not position the actuator in a manner that will cause damage to the rod tip or the rubber boot.*

27   Leave the actuator in this position for at least five minutes to allow the oil to drain into the boot end.

28   Find a standard paper clip - one with no serrations - and straighten it out so that you have a straight length of about two inches. Form the remaining portion of the paper clip into a loop.

29   Remove the rubber end plug from the rear of the actuator **(see illustration 8.10).** Do not remove the vent plug.

30   Push your paper clip through the center hole in the vent plug, and on into the pilot hole.

31   Retract the tensioner plunger by pushing the rod tip against a table top while turning the screw at the rear of the actuator clockwise.

32   When the tensioner plunger is fully retracted, align the screw slot with the vent hole and push the paper clip into the slot to retain the plunger.

7.47 Align the crankshaft timing mark with the pointer on the front cover (A) - The mark on the intermediate shaft sprocket should align with the mark on the front cover (B)

33   If oil was lost from the tensioner, fill it to the bottom of the plug hole with a synthetic 5W-30 engine oil. **Note:** *Fill the tensioner only when it is fully retracted and the paper clip is installed.*

34   Install the rubber end plug; be sure it is snapped fully into place and fits flush against the body of the tensioner.

35   Check to be sure that all bushings and the holes they fit into are in good condition and properly installed, then fit the actuator onto its base. Be sure the actuator is free and can rotate under its own weight. **Note:** *Do not oil the bushings.* **Caution:** *Make sure the tensioner's tapered fulcrum is properly seated in its bushing.*

36   Install the tensioner plate assembly and tighten the bolts to the torque listed in this Chapter's Specifications.

37   Make sure the actuator rod tip is seated in the tensioner pulley socket, then remove the paper clip; this will allow the actuator to extend to its normal position.

38   Install the new timing belt by routing it counterclockwise around all the sprockets, staring with the intermediate shaft sprocket. Keep the belt firmly into the teeth of each sprocket and do not let slack develop.

39   Remove the clamps from the sprockets and rotate the tensioner pivot pulley (11 ft-lbs) to make sure the actuator engages the socket on the back of the pulley.

40   Seat the belt by rotating the engine three full turns clockwise (the direction of crankshaft rotation). **Caution:** *Do not rotate the engine counterclockwise.*

41   Align the timing marks on the crankshaft pulley and timing chain cover, then inspect the camshaft timing marks to be sure the camshaft timing is correct.

42   Reassembly is reverse of disassembly.

Camshaft timing adjustment and sprocket replacement

Refer to illustrations 7.47 and 7.49
43   Some special tools and procedures are required to adjust the camshaft timing or replace the sprockets. If you suspect that the camshaft timing is out of adjustment, check to see if the timing marks on the camshaft sprockets are properly aligned when the

7.49 Timing marks at no. 1 TDC on exhaust stroke

1. *Camshaft sprocket timing marks (front bank shown). Make sure the camshafts are aligned this way*
2. *Intermediate shaft sprocket timing mark*

engine is at Top Dead Center (TDC) on the number 1 cylinder's exhaust stroke. When at #1 TDC exhaust, the timing marks should be aligned **(see illustration 7.20)**. If the timing marks are not aligned as shown, first try to determine if the cause is a slipped timing belt. If the belt has slipped, find the cause and replace the belt as required. If the belt is good (or new) and you suspect the camshafts are out of time, they will have to checked and/or adjusted as follows.

44   Turn the camshafts so the "flats" are facing up, then install the factory camshaft holders (refer to Step 20).

45   Loosen and remove the camshaft sprockets bolts so the sprockets can be pulled off for inspection or replacement. It might take a few light taps with a plastic hammer to free the sprockets. **Note:** *Do not lose the tapered lock rings for the sprocket bolts.*

46   Install the sprockets (new ones if they are being replaced) finger-tight.

47   Position the crankshaft timing mark at the TDC position **(see illustration).**

48   Install the timing belt as in Step 38.

49   If necessary, scribe new timing marks on the camshaft sprockets using a straight-edge and a scribe, and remove the old timing marks. Slight movement of the camshaft sprockets may be necessary to align the marks **(see illustration).**

50   Tighten the sprocket bolts at the rear bank camshafts and remove the timing clamp. **Note:** *The "running torque" (the torque required to turn the bolt before it is seated) should be 44 to 66 ft-lbs. If the running torque is either more or less than this specification, replace the shim ring and lock ring and inspect the camshaft for brinelling or damaged threads. The sprocket bolt is fully seated when the edge of the lock ring is flush with the sprocket.*

51   Turn the crankshaft 360 degrees and realign the crankshaft timing mark. **Note:** *The camshafts on the rear bank should now turn with the crankshaft, while the camshafts sprockets on the front bank should still freewheel.*

52   Repeat steps 49 and 50 on the front bank. **Note:** *When the camshaft timing*

procedure is complete, the position of the timing flats on the front bank of camshafts should differ from those of the rear bank camshafts by 180 degrees, i.e. the flats should be UP on one set while the flats on the other set are DOWN.

53 The remainder of the procedure is the reverse of the disassembly process. When installing a new belt, rotate the engine three turns clockwise to seat the belt and recheck the timing marks.

8 Camshaft carriers - removal and installation

Note: *This procedure is complicated, time-consuming and requires several special factory tools. Read through this entire Section and acquire the necessary tools before beginning.*

Removal

Front carrier

Refer to illustrations 8.3, 8.12 and 8.13

1 Remove the breather hose from the front camshaft carrier cover.

2 Remove the spark plug wires from the spark plugs. **Note:** *Be sure each wire is labeled before removal to ensure correct reinstallation.*

3 Remove the carrier cover bolts **(see illustration)**, then remove the cover. **Note:** *If the cover sticks to the cylinder head, use a block of wood and a hammer to dislodge it. If the cover still won't come loose, pry on it carefully, but don't distort the sealing flange.*

4 Remove the gasket and O-rings from the cover.

5 Remove the timing belt (see Section 7).

6 Remove the exhaust crossover pipe (see Section 5).

7 Drain the coolant and remove the upper radiator hose.

8 Remove the heater pipe hose at the plenum.

9 Remove the front exhaust manifold (see Section 5).

10 Remove the engine torque strut (see Section 19).

11 Remove the front engine coolant pipe and the front engine lift bracket from the cylinder head.

12 Install fuel line hoses under the camshafts and between the lifters to hold the lifters in place when the carrier is removed **(see illustration). Note:** *You will need 6 lengths of hose. On the exhaust side the hose dimensions should be 6 x 3/16 inch. On the intake side the hose dimensions should be 3 x 5/32 inch.*

13 Remove the camshaft carrier mounting bolts, then remove the camshaft carrier **(see illustration).**

Rear carrier

14 Remove the upper intake plenum (see Chapter 4).

15 Remove the rear timing belt cover (see Section 7).

8.3 Remove the camshaft carrier cover bolts with a socket, ratchet and extension

16 Remove the spark plug wires from the spark plugs (see Chapter 1). **Note:** *Be sure each wire is labeled before removal to ensure correct reinstallation.*

17 Remove the breather hose from the cover.

18 Remove the carrier cover bolts, then remove the cover. **Note:** *If the cover sticks to the cylinder head, use a block of wood and a hammer to dislodge it. If the cover still won't come loose, pry on it carefully, but don't distort the sealing flange.*

19 Remove the gasket and O-rings from the cover.

20 Remove the timing belt (see Section 7).

21 Install fuel line hoses under the camshafts and between the lifters to hold the lifters in place when the carrier is removed **(see illustration 8.12). Note:** *You will need 6 lengths of hose. On the exhaust side the hose dimensions should be 6 x 3/16 inch. On the intake side the hose dimensions should be 3 x 5/32 inch.*

22 Remove the camshaft carrier mounting bolts, then remove the camshaft carrier **(see illustration 8.13).**

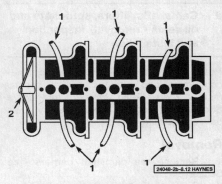

8.12 Install fuel line hoses under the camshafts and between the lifters to hold the lifters in place when the carrier is removed

1 Fuel hoses   2 Timing clamp

Installation

Refer to illustration 11.24

23 Installation is the reverse of removal, using new gaskets under the carriers and covers. **Note 1:** *Remove any accumulated oil from the lower (closest to exhaust) carrier-to-cylinder head bolt holes before installing the carriers.* **Note 2:** *The rubber hoses should keep the lifters in place, but while the carriers are off the engine, coat each lifter (bore surfaces) with petroleum jelly to further insure they stay in place during carrier installation. Remove the rubber hoses after carrier installation is complete.*

24 Refer to Section 7 for installation and timing of the camshaft timing belt. When installing the cover retaining bolts, be sure the bolt isolators **(see illustration)** are fully seated in the cover, then tighten the bolts to the torque listed in this Chapter's Specifications.

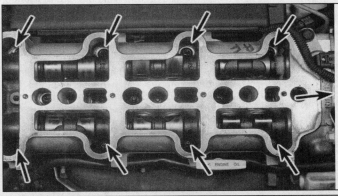

8.13 Camshaft carrier bolt locations (arrows) - arrow at right indicates location of the camshaft thrust plate cover

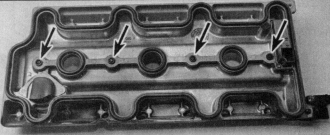

8.24 Make sure the bolt isolators (arrows) are fully seated before installing the cover

9   Camshafts, lifters, sprockets and oil seals - removal, inspection and installation

Note: *This procedure is complicated, time-consuming and requires several special factory tools. Read through this entire Section and acquire the necessary tools before beginning.*

Removal

1   Remove the camshaft carriers (see Section 8).

2   Remove the lifters from the camshaft carrier housing. **Note:** *Keep the lifters in order so that they can be replaced in their original positions.*

3   Turn the camshafts so the "flats" are facing up, then lock the camshafts in position with the special tool, or equivalent (see Section 7).

4   Remove the camshaft sprocket bolts. Fabricate a special tool, to hold the sprockets while you loosen the bolts.

5   Using a soft-faced hammer, gently tap the sprockets off the camshafts or use a puller, if necessary. Remove the flat ring from the sprocket bore.

6   Remove the camshaft thrust plate cover and gasket (at the flywheel end of the carriers), then the thrust plate **(see illustration 8.13)**.

7   Remove the timing clamp, then remove the camshafts by carefully withdrawing them through the back of the camshaft carrier. **Caution:** *Be sure you don't damage the camshaft journals inside the carrier when you remove the camshafts.*

8   Remove the seals from the carrier by carefully prying them it out with a screwdriver. **Caution:** *The aluminum seal seating surface in the carrier is easily damaged.*

Inspection

Refer to illustration 9.9

9   Check for damage or pitting on the camshaft lobes. Check the nose of the camshaft for brinelling. Check the camshaft journals inside the carrier for wear or damage. For camshaft lobe lift inspection and journal diameter inspection, refer to Chapter 2 Part D. Visually inspect the lifters for wear, galling, score marks or discolorations from overheating **(see illustration)**.

Installation

10   Install the camshaft seal using a hammer and large socket or section of pipe the exact diameter of the seal. Make sure the seal enters the bore squarely; stop when the front face is at the same depth as the original seal. **Note:** *Coat the seal with clean engine oil or multi-purpose grease prior to installation.*

11   The remainder of installation is the reverse of removal paying particular attention to the following points:

a) *Coat the camshaft lobes and journals with moly-base grease or engine assembly lube prior to installation.*

b) *When installing the camshaft, exercise care to avoid damaging the seal.*

c) *When installing the thrust plate, be sure the arrow points up.*

d) *Be sure to check camshaft timing after reassembly and before starting the engine (see Sections 7 and 8).*

10   Valve springs, retainers and seals - replacement

This procedure is essentially the same as that described for the 3.1L/3.4L OHV engine. Refer to Part A of this Chapter and follow the procedure outlined there. The camshaft carriers must be removed for access to the valve springs (see Section 8).

11   Cylinder head - removal and installation

Caution: *Allow the engine to cool completely before loosening the cylinder head bolts.*
Note: *This procedure is complicated, time-consuming and requires several special factory tools. Read through this entire section and acquire the necessary tools before beginning.*

Removal

1   Remove the intake upper plenum (see Chapter 4) and lower intake manifold (see Section 4).

2   Remove the camshaft carrier (see Section 8).

3   If you're removing the front cylinder head, remove the oil dipstick tube mounting bolt and the electrical connector for the temperature sender. If you're removing the rear cylinder head, remove the electrical connector for the oxygen sensor.

4   If you're removing the front cylinder head, remove the exhaust manifold (see Section 5). If you're removing the rear cylinder head, remove the exhaust crossover

pipe, separate the exhaust pipe at the exhaust manifold.

5   If you're removing the rear cylinder head, remove the timing belt tensioner bracket (see Section 7), and the rear exhaust manifold (see Section 5).

6   Lift the head off the engine. If resistance is felt, don't pry between the head and block as damage to the mating surfaces will result. Recheck for head bolts that may have been overlooked, then use a hammer and block of wood to tap up on the head and break the gasket seal. Be careful because there are locating dowels in the block which position each head. As a last resort, pry each head up at the rear corner only and be careful not to damage anything. After removal, place the head on blocks of wood to prevent damage to the gasket surfaces.

7   Refer to Part D for cylinder head disassembly, inspection and valve service procedures.

Installation

Refer to illustrations 11.12 and 11.14

8   The mating surfaces of each cylinder head and block must be perfectly clean when the head is installed.

9   Use a gasket scraper to remove all traces of carbon and old gasket material, then clean the mating surfaces with lacquer thinner or acetone. If there's oil on the mating surfaces when the head is installed, the gasket may not seal correctly and leaks may develop. When working on the block, it's a good idea to cover any holes with shop rags to keep debris out of the engine. Use a shop rag or vacuum cleaner to remove any debris that falls into the cylinders.

10   Check the block and head mating surfaces for nicks, deep scratches and other damage. If damage is slight, it can be removed with a file; if it's excessive, machining may be the only alternative.

11   Use a tap of the correct size to chase the threads in the head bolt holes. Dirt, corrosion, sealant and damaged threads will affect torque readings.

12   Position the new gasket over the dowel pins in the block **(see illustration)**. Be sure the metal tabs between the cylinders are facing up.

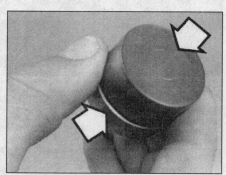

9.9   Check the lifters for signs of wear on the camshaft surface, valve surface and bore surface

11.12   Position the new gasket over the dowel pins (arrows)

Tightening Sequence

24048-2b-11.14 HAYNES

11.14 Cylinder head bolt tightening sequence

13   Carefully position the head on the block without disturbing the gasket.

14   Install the bolts and tighten them in the sequence shown **(see illustration)** to the torque listed in this Chapter's Specifications. Then, using the same sequence, further tighten each bolt the required angle listed in this Chapter's Specifications. Special torque-angle tools are available at most automotive parts stores. They are used with a standard torque wrench to achieve the desired angle and are highly recommended. If the tool is not available, mark the cylinder head bolt with paint to keep track of how far it has been turned.

15   The remaining installation steps are the reverse of removal.

16   Change the engine oil and filter (see Chapter 1).

12   Intermediate shaft belt sprocket and oil seal - removal and installation

Note: *This procedure is complicated, time-consuming and requires several special factory tools. Read through this entire Section and acquire the necessary tools before beginning.*

Removal

Refer to illustration 12.4

1   Align the camshaft timing marks, then remove the timing belt (see Section 7).

2   Raise the car and support it on jackstands.

3   Remove the flywheel inspection cover.

4   Position a large screwdriver in the ring gear teeth to keep the crankshaft from turning

while an assistant removes the intermediate shaft timing belt sprocket bolt **(see illustration)**. **Note:** *The intermediate shaft timing belt sprocket bolt is normally very tight, so use a large breaker bar and a six-point socket.*

5   Note the relationship of the sprocket's timing mark to the timing chain cover, then remove the sprocket with a puller. **Caution:** *Avoid pounding on the intermediate shaft or prying on the sprocket as these actions can damage the thrust bearing.*

6   Note how the oil seal is installed - the new one must be installed to the same depth and facing the same way. Carefully pry the oil seal out of the cover with a seal puller or a large screwdriver **(see illustration 6.10)**. Be very careful not to distort the cover or scratch the intermediate shaft! Wrap electrician's tape around the tip of the screwdriver to avoid damage to the intermediate shaft.

Installation

7   Apply clean engine oil or multi-purpose grease to the outer edge of the new seal, then install it in the cover with the lip (spring side) facing IN. Drive the seal into place with a hammer and large socket or section of pipe the exact diameter of the seal. **(see illustration 6.11)**. Make sure the seal enters the bore squarely and stop when the front face is at the proper depth.

8   Lubricate the seal "running surface" of the sprocket, then carefully fit the sprocket onto the intermediate shaft, through the seal and into the timing chain cover. **Note:** *Be sure the locating tangs of the intermediate shaft timing belt sprocket align with those on the timing chain sprocket (hidden behind the timing chain cover). To be sure the tangs are aligned, measure the distance from the front of the intermediate shaft sprocket to the timing chain cover. If the distance is more than 1.65 inches (42 mm), the tangs are not aligned.*

9   Check that the timing mark on the sprocket is aligned with the reference mark on the timing chain cover **(see illustration 7.49)**. If necessary, reposition the sprocket.

10   Lubricate the intermediate shaft O-ring with clean engine oil, then carefully place it into position on the end of the shaft.

11   Apply clean engine oil on the threads of the sprocket bolt, then install the sprocket bolt and washer. Tighten the bolt to the

torque listed in this Chapter's Specifications while an assistant prevents the crankshaft from turning.

12   The remainder of installation is the reverse of removal.

13   Engine front cover - removal and installation

Note: *This procedure is complicated, time-consuming and requires several special factory tools. Read through this entire Section and acquire the necessary tools before beginning.*

Removal

Refer to illustrations 13.5 and 13.15

1   Disconnect the negative battery cable, drain the engine oil and the coolant (see Chapter 1). **Caution:** *On models equipped with a Delco Theftlock audio system, be sure the lockout feature is turned off before performing any procedure which requires disconnecting the battery.*

2   Remove the serpentine drivebelt (see Chapter 1).

3   Remove the camshaft timing belt tensioner and it's bracket (see Section 7).

4   Remove the timing belt (see Section 7) and the timing belt idler pulleys. **Note:** *Mark the direction of rotation on the timing belt before removing it.*

5   Remove the front engine lift bracket **(see illustration)**.

6   Remove the cooling fans.

7   Disconnect the coolant hoses from the water pump.

8   Remove the heater pipe retaining screws from the frame.

9   Remove the starter (see Chapter 5).

10   Remove the crankshaft damper (see Section 6).

11   Remove the alternator (see Chapter 5).

12   Remove the oil filter.

13   Remove the oil cooler assembly, if equipped (see Chapter 3).

14   Remove the oil pan front nuts and bolts, and loosen the remaining oil pan fasteners.

15   Remove the air conditioning compressor and lay it aside without disconnecting the refrigerant lines **(see illustration)**.

12.4 Remove the bolt from the intermediate shaft sprocket (arrow)

13.5 Engine lift bracket (arrow)

13.15 Unbolt the air conditioning compressor and lay it aside, but DO NOT disconnect the refrigerant lines (arrow)

16   Remove the lower front cover bolts.

17   Remove the intermediate shaft timing belt sprocket (see Section 12).

18   Remove the water pump pulley.

19   Remove any wiring or relays that will interfere with removal of the cover. Remove the screws and position the forward lamp relay center aside (see Chapter 12).

20   Remove the front cover-to-engine block bolts.

21   Separate the cover from the engine. If it's stuck, tap it with a soft-face hammer, but don't try to pry it off.

22   Use a gasket scraper to remove all traces of old gasket material and sealant from the cover and engine block. The cover is made of aluminum, so be careful not to nick or gouge it. Clean the gasket sealing surfaces with lacquer thinner or acetone.

Installation

23   Install the new gasket.

24   Apply a thin layer of RTV sealant to the lower edges of the timing chain cover, then install the cover.

25   Apply thread sealant to the upper timing chain cover bolts then install them. Draw the timing chain cover against the block by tightening the bolts in a criss-cross pattern. Tighten the bolts to the torque listed in this Chapter's Specifications.

26   The remainder of installation is the reverse of removal.

27   Add oil and coolant, start the engine and check for leaks.

14   Intermediate shaft chain and sprockets - removal, inspection and installation

Note: *This procedure is complicated, time-consuming and requires several special factory tools. Read through this entire Section and acquire the necessary tools before beginning.*

Removal

1   Remove the engine front cover (see Section 13).

2   Mark the positions of the sprockets to the chain.

3   Remove the intermediate shaft chain tensioner bolts.

4   Remove the chain and sprockets as an assembly using a puller to pull the crankshaft sprocket off the crankshaft.

5   Remove the intermediate shaft chain tensioner. **Note:** *Replacement of the intermediate shaft itself requires engine removal, but this shaft is seldom replaced except during a complete engine overhaul.*

Inspection

6   The intermediate shaft chain should be replaced with a new one if the engine has high mileage, the chain has visible damage, or has too much freeplay. Failure to replace a worn intermediate shaft chain may result in erratic engine performance, loss of power and decreased fuel mileage. A worn, damaged or loose chain can break or "jump" time. In the worst case, chain breakage or "jumping" will result in severe engine damage.

7   The intermediate shaft chain tensioner should be replaced if it is worn, cracked, or displays other damage.

Installation

Refer to illustration 14.11

8   Install the tensioner on the block. **Note:** *Use the upper attaching bolt as the primary locator.*

9   Thread the remaining tensioner bolts into their holes finger tight.

10   Tighten the bolt in the slotted hole in the tensioner first, then tighten the remaining bolts to the torque listed in this Chapter's Specifications.

11   Fabricate a tool from a one-foot length of 1/8-inch welding rod or a coat hanger bent into a U-shape and formed into a hand grip at the end away from the bend. Retract the tensioner shoe using the special tool and insert an appropriately-sized drill bit or nail into the spring pin hole in the tensioner to hold it in position **(see illustration). Caution:** *Avoid using any type of tool that will damage the tensioner or mar the surface of the tensioner shoe.* **Note:** *Be sure the rivet or nail is stout enough to maintain the shoe in it's retracted position.*

12   Apply a light coating of clean engine oil to the tensioner's chain contact surfaces

13   Carefully install the intermediate shaft chain and sprockets assembly. **Note:** *Try to keep the two sprockets parallel as you install them on their respective shafts.* The crankshaft sprocket should be installed with it's large chamfer and counterbore toward the crankshaft. The intermediate shaft sprocket should be installed with it's splines facing away from the block. The crankshaft sprocket will need to be pressed on for the

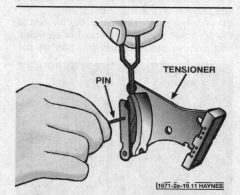

14.11 Retract the tensioner shoe using a special tool fabricated from a coat hanger or welding rod, and insert an appropriately-sized drill bit or nail into the spring pin hole in the tensioner

last 5/16-inch (8 mm) of it's travel; fabricate a special installer using a section of pipe and several washers and press it on using the crankshaft damper bolt. Finally, be sure the timing marks are aligned after installation. **Caution:** *Be sure the tensioner shoe and guide do not become dislodged or damaged during installation of the sprocket and chain assembly.*

14   When the sprockets and chain assembly are in place and properly timed, remove the retaining pin from the tensioner.

15   Install the intermediate shaft chain cover in the reverse order of removal (see Section 14).

15   Oil pan - removal and installation

Note: *On vehicles equipped with an automatic transaxle, it may be necessary to remove the transaxle (see Chapter 7) to provide additional clearance for the oil pan.*

Removal

Refer to illustrations 15.16a and 15.16b

1   Disconnect the cable from the negative battery terminal. Remove the air cleaner duct (see Chapter 4). **Caution:** *On models equipped with a Delco Theftlock audio system, be sure the lockout feature is turned off before performing any procedure which requires disconnecting the battery.*

2   Support the engine from above with a three-bar fixture hooked to the engine lifting brackets on the engine (see Chapter 2 Part A, Section 12).

3   Raise the front of the vehicle and place it securely on jackstands. Apply the parking brake and block the rear wheels to keep it from rolling off the stands.

4   Remove the front wheels and remove the lower splash pan.

5   Drain the engine oil (see Chapter 1) and remove the oil filter, the oil cooler assembly, and the oil level sensor.

6   Drain the coolant (see Chapter 1) and remove the coolant recovery tank.

7   Remove the steering gear mounting bolts and use a section of wire to hang the steering gear from the body (see Chapter 10).

8   Remove the right and left lower ball joint nuts, then separate the ball joints from the control arms (see Chapter 10).

9   Disconnect the power steering cooler line clamps at the frame.

10   Remove the engine mount nuts at the frame (see Section 19).

11   If necessary, remove the driveplate lower cover.

12   Remove the starter (see Chapter 5).

13   Place a floor jack under the frame front center crossmember.

14   Loosen the rear frame bolts - DO NOT REMOVE THEM!

15   Remove the front frame bolts and lower the front of the frame.

16   Remove the bolts and nuts, then carefully separate the oil pan from the block

15.16a Remove the bolts and nuts from around the perimeter of the oil pan . . .

15.16b . . . then carefully separate the oil pan from the block

(see illustrations). Don't pry between the block and the pan or damage to the sealing surfaces could occur and oil leaks may develop. Instead, tap the pan with a soft-face hammer to break the gasket seal.

Installation

17   Clean the pan with solvent and remove all old sealant and gasket material from the block and pan mating surfaces. Clean the mating surfaces with lacquer thinner or acetone and make sure the bolt holes in the block are clear. Check the oil pan flange for distortion, particularly around the bolt holes. If necessary, place the pan on a block of wood and use a hammer to flatten and restore the gasket surface.

18   Always use a new gasket whenever the oil pan is installed. Apply a bead of RTV sealant to the front of the one-piece gasket, where it contacts the timing chain cover, and to the two tabs at the rear that fit where the rear main cap meets the block.

19   Place the oil pan in position on the block and install the nuts/bolts.

20   After the fasteners are installed, tighten them to the torque listed in this Chapter's Specifications. Starting at the center, follow a criss-cross pattern and work up to the final torque in three steps.

21   The remaining steps are the reverse of the removal procedure.

22   Refill the engine with oil, run it until normal operating temperature is reached and check for leaks.

16   Oil pump - removal, inspection and installation

This procedure is essentially the same as for the 3.1L/3.4L OHV V6 engine. Refer to Part A and follow the procedure outlined there. However, use the bolt torque listed in this Chapter's Specifications.

17   Driveplate - removal and installation

This procedure is essentially the same as for the 3.1L/3.4L OHV V6 engine. Refer to Part A and follow the procedure outlined there. However, use the bolt torque listed in this Chapter's Specifications.

18   Rear main oil seal - replacement

This procedure is essentially the same as that for the 3.1L/3.4L OHV V6 engine. Refer to Part A and follow the procedure outlined there.

19   Engine mounts - check and replacement

1   There are four mounts that connect the drivetrain to the chassis, two at the timing chain end (a front and a rear), one at the transaxle end, and one upper mount connecting the engine torque strut to the body near the top of the radiator.

2   Engine mounts seldom require attention, but broken or deteriorated mounts should be replaced immediately or the added strain placed on the driveline components may cause damage or wear.

Check

3   During the check, the engine must be raised slightly to remove the weight from the mounts.

4   Raise the vehicle and support it securely on jackstands, then position a jack under the engine oil pan. Place a large block of wood between the jack head and the oil pan, then carefully raise the engine just enough to take the weight off the mounts. **Warning:** *DO NOT place*

any part of your body under the engine when it's supported only by a jack!

5   Check the mount insulators (the rubber part between the engine and the chassis brackets) to see if the rubber is cracked, hardened or separated from the metal plates. Sometimes the rubber will split right down the center.

6   Check for relative movement between the mount plates and the engine or frame (use a large screwdriver or prybar to attempt to move the mounts). If movement is noted, lower the engine and tighten the mount fasteners.

7   Rubber preservative should be applied to the insulators to slow deterioration.

Replacement

8   Disconnect the negative battery cable from the battery, then raise the vehicle and support it securely on jackstands (if not already done). **Caution:** *On models equipped with a Delco Theftlock audio system, be sure the lockout feature is turned off before performing any procedure which requires disconnecting the battery.*

All except the right (rear) engine mount

9   Raise the engine slightly with a jack or hoist. Remove the bolts/nuts holding the mount to the engine and to the chassis brackets, then raise the engine more until you can remove the mount nuts, remove the old mount and insert the new one, then lower the engine and tighten the nuts to Specifications.

Right (rear) engine mount

10   The procedure for replacing the rear engine mount is more involved. The hood must be removed and a three-bar engine support must be used to support the engine from above. Raise and support the front of the vehicle on jackstands.

11   Refer to Chapter 3 and remove the engine cooling fan.

12   Disconnect the engine torque strut from its mount.

13   Refer to Chapter 8 and remove the right driveaxle, then refer to Chapter 10 and disconnect the right balljoint at the control arm.

14   Remove the nuts from the right engine mount (it attaches the transaxle-to-engine brace to the front subframe), raise the engine and replace the mount.

15   Installation is the reverse of removal. Use thread-locking compound on the mount bolts and be sure to tighten them securely to this Chapter's Specifications.

Notes

Chapter 2 Part C 3800 V6 Engine

Contents

Specifications

General

Cylinder numbers (drivebelt end-to-transaxle end)
- Front bank (radiator side) 1-3-5
- Rear bank 2-4-6

Firing order 1-6-5-4-3-2
Displacement .... 3.8 liters (231 cubic inches)

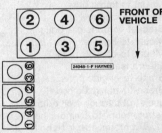

Cylinder location and coil terminal identification diagram - 3.8L engine

Camshaft

Lobe lift
- Intake .... 0.258 inch (6.55 mm)
- Exhaust
  - 1995 through 2001 .... 0.255 inch (6.48 mm)
  - 2002 and later .... 0.258 inch (6.55 mm)

Oil pump

- Outer gear-to-housing clearance .... 0.008 to 0.015 inch (0.20 to 0.38 mm)
- Inner gear tip-to-outer gear tip clearance .... 0.006 inch (0.15 mm)
- Gear end clearance .... 0.001 to 0.0035 inch (0.026 to 0.089 mm)
- Pump cover warpage limit .... 0.002 inch (0.05 mm)
- Relief valve-to-bore clearance .... 0.0015 to 0.003 inch (0.038 to 0.076 mm)

Torque specifications

Ft-lbs (unless otherwise indicated)

Camshaft sprocket bolts
- Step one 74
- Step two .... Tighten an additional 90-degrees

Cylinder head bolts
- Step one 37
- Step two .... Tighten an additional 120-degrees

Driveplate-to-crankshaft bolts
- Step one 11
- Step two .... Tighten an additional 50-degrees

Exhaust manifold-to-cylinder head bolts/nuts 22
Exhaust crossover bolts/studs 15
Upper intake manifold-to-lower manifold bolts/stud .... 89 in-lbs
Lower intake manifold-to-cylinder head bolts/nuts .... 132 in-lbs
Oil pan bolts .... 124 in-lbs

Oil filter adapter-to-timing chain cover bolts
- 1995 through 1999 22
- 2000 and later
  - Step 1 11
  - Step 2 .... Tighten an additional 50-degrees

Oil pump
- Cover-to-timing chain cover bolts .... 97 in-lbs
- Pickup tube and screen assembly bolts .... 132 in-lbs

Torque specifications (continued)

Ft-lbs (unless otherwise indicated)

Rocker arm pivot bolts	
Step one	11
Step two	Tighten an additional 90-degrees
Timing chain cover bolts	
1995 and 1996	
Large bolts	35
Small bolts	15
1997	
Large bolts	41
Small bolts	18
1998	
Step one	133 in-lbs
Step two	Tighten an additional 40-degrees
1999	
Step one	177 in-lbs
Step two	Tighten an additional 40-degrees
Timing chain damper bolt	16
Valve cover nuts/bolts	88 in-lbs
Crankshaft balancer-to-crankshaft bolt	
Step one	111
Step two	Tighten an additional 76-degrees
Front engine mount	
Mount to engine bracket nuts	32
Bracket to engine bolts	75
Mount to frame nuts	32
Rear engine mount	
Bracket-to-transaxle bolts	70
Mount-to-bracket nuts	35
Mount-to-chassis nuts	46
Engine/transaxle brace	
Brace-to-engine bolts	46
Brace-to-transaxle bolts	32
Torque strut through-bolt nuts	35
Left strut mount-to-cylinder-head bolts	37
Right strut mount-to-block bolt	37
Radiator strut mount-to-chassis bolts	21

1   General information

Caution: *On models equipped with the Theftlock audio system, be sure the lockout feature is turned off before performing any procedure which requires disconnecting the battery.*

This Part of Chapter 2 is devoted to in-vehicle repair procedures for the "3800" V6 engine (VIN code K).

Information concerning camshaft, balance shaft and engine removal and installation, as well as engine block and cylinder head overhaul, is in Part D of this Chapter.

The following repair procedures are based on the assumption the engine is installed in the vehicle. If the engine has been removed from the vehicle and mounted on a stand, many of the steps included in this Part of Chapter 2 will not apply.

The Specifications included in this Part of Chapter 2 apply only to the procedures in this Part. The Specifications necessary for rebuilding the block and cylinder heads are found in Part D.

2   Repair operations possible with the engine in the vehicle

Many major repair operations can be accomplished without removing the engine from the vehicle.

Clean the engine compartment and the exterior of the engine with some type of pressure washer before any work is done. A clean engine will make the job easier and will help keep dirt out of the internal areas of the engine.

Depending on the components involved, it may be a good idea to remove the hood to improve access to the engine as repairs are performed (refer to Chapter 11 if necessary).

If vacuum, exhaust, oil or coolant leaks develop, indicating a need for gasket or seal replacement, the repairs can generally be made with the engine in the vehicle. The intake and exhaust manifold gaskets, oil pan gasket and cylinder head gaskets are all accessible with the engine in place.

Exterior engine components such as the intake and exhaust manifolds, the oil pan, the oil pump, the water pump, the starter motor, the alternator and the fuel injection system can be removed for repair with the engine in place. The timing chain and sprockets can also be replaced with the engine in the vehicle, but the camshaft and balance shaft cannot be removed with the engine in place.

Since the cylinder heads can be removed without pulling the engine, valve component servicing can also be accomplished with the engine in the vehicle.

In extreme cases caused by a lack of necessary equipment, repair or replacement of piston rings, pistons, connecting rods and rod bearings is possible with the engine in the vehicle. However, this practice is not recommended because of the cleaning and preparation work that must be done to the components involved.

3   Top Dead Center (TDC) for number one piston - locating

This procedure is essentially the same as that for the 3.1L V6 engine. Refer to Part A and follow the procedure outlined there.

4   Valve covers - removal and installation

Front cover removal

Refer to illustrations 4.4, 4.7a and 4.7b

1   Disconnect the negative battery cable from the battery. **Caution:** *On models equipped with the Theftlock audio system, be sure the lockout feature is turned off before performing any procedure which requires disconnecting the battery.*

4.4 Remove the acoustic cover by twisting out the oil filler neck, then pulling up and forward on the cover

4.7a Remove the plastic cover (arrow) if equipped . . .

4.7b . . . then remove the valve cover bolts (arrows)

2   Remove the spark plug wires from the spark plugs and remove the harness cover. Number each wire before removal to ensure correct reinstallation.

3   On 1995 through 2000 models (or where necessary), remove the serpentine drivebelt (see Chapter 1) and the alternator brace (see Chapter 5).

4   Remove the oil filler cap, then lift off and remove the acoustic trim cover (see illustration).

5   Remove the passenger-side engine torque strut bracket (upper and lower sections), then remove the engine lift bracket from the front exhaust manifold.

6   Remove the fuel injector sight shield, if equipped.

7   Remove the valve cover mounting bolts/nuts (see illustrations). Detach the valve cover. **Note:** *If the cover sticks to the cylinder head, use a soft-face hammer to dislodge it.*

Rear cover removal

8   Remove the spark plug wires from the spark plugs and remove the harness cover. Number each wire before removal to ensure correct reinstallation.

9   Remove the serpentine drivebelt (see Chapter 1).

10   Remove the coolant reservoir (see Chapter 3).

11   On 1999 and later models (or where necessary), remove the alternator (see Chapter 5).

12   Remove the power steering pump, if necessary (see Chapter 10).

13   Remove the fuel injection system trim cover bracket from the rear exhaust manifold. Remove the engine lift bracket.

2000 through 2002 models

14   Disconnect the intake air temperature (IAT) sensor electrical connector (see Chapter 6) and remove the air inlet duct from the throttle body (see Chapter 4).

15   Remove the serpentine drivebelt and drivebelt tensioner (see Chapter 1).

16   Remove both engine torque struts (connecting the engine to the radiator support).

17   Rotate the engine for access (see Chapter 1).

18   Remove the spark plug wires from the spark plugs and remove the harness cover. Number each wire before removal to ensure correct reinstallation.

19   Remove the fuel injection system trim cover bracket from the rear exhaust manifold. If the vehicle is equipped with Secondary Air Injection (AIR), the AIR check valve and solenoid will be bolted to the trim cover bracket. Disconnect the vacuum line to the valve and the electrical connector to the solenoid and remove the two bolts from the AIR pipe coupling below the valve. Remove the bracket with the valve and solenoid attached.

20   Remove the engine lift bracket.

2003 and later models

21   Remove the serpentine drivebelt and drivebelt tensioner (see Chapter 1).

22   Remove the alternator (see Chapter 5).

23   Remove the spark plug wires from the spark plugs and remove the harness cover. Number each wire before removal to ensure correct reinstallation.

24   Remove the fuel injection system trim cover bracket from the rear exhaust manifold. Remove the engine lift bracket.

All models

25   Remove the valve cover mounting bolts/nuts. Detach the valve cover. **Note:** *If the cover sticks to the cylinder head, use a soft-face hammer to dislodge it.*

Installation

26   The mating surfaces of the cylinder head and valve cover must be perfectly clean when the covers are installed. Use a gasket scraper to remove all traces of sealant or old gasket, then clean the mating surfaces with lacquer thinner or acetone (if there's sealant or oil on the mating surfaces when the cover is installed, oil leaks may develop). The valve covers are made of soft material, so be extra careful not to nick or gouge the mating surfaces with the scraper.

27   Apply thread locking compound to the mounting bolt threads. Place the valve cover and new gasket in position, then install the bolts.

5.3 If more than one pushrod is being removed, store them in a perforated cardboard box to prevent mix-ups during installation - note the label indicating the front of the engine

28   Tighten the bolts/nuts in several steps to the torque listed in this Chapter's specifications.

29   Complete the installation by reversing the removal procedure. Be sure to add coolant if it was drained.

30   Start the engine and check for oil leaks at the valve cover-to-cylinder head joints.

---

5   Rocker arms and pushrods - removal, inspection and installation

Removal

Refer to illustration 5.3

1   Refer to Section 4 and detach the valve covers from the cylinder heads.

2   Loosen the rocker arm pivot bolts one at a time and detach the rocker arms, bolts, pivots and pivot retainers. Keep track of the rocker arm positions, since they must be returned to the same location. Store each set of rocker components separately in a marked plastic bag to ensure that they're reinstalled in their original locations.

3   Remove the pushrods and store them separately to make sure they don't get mixed up during installation (see illustration).

7.9a Remove the mounting bolts (not seen in this view) for the
upper intake manifold (arrow)

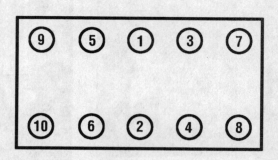

7.9b Upper intake manifold bolt/stud TIGHTENING sequence.
Earlier models have only nine fasteners

Inspection

4   Check each rocker arm for wear, cracks and other damage, especially where the pushrods and valve stems contact the rocker arm.

5   Check the pivot seat in each rocker arm and the pivot faces. Look for galling, stress cracks and unusual wear patterns. If the rocker arms are worn or damaged, replace them with new ones and install new pivots or shafts as well.

6   Make sure the hole at the pushrod end of each rocker arm is open.

7   Inspect the pushrods for cracks and excessive wear at the ends. Roll each pushrod across a piece of plate glass to see if it's bent (if it wobbles, it's bent).

Installation

8   Lubricate the lower end of each pushrod with clean engine oil or moly-base grease and install them in their original locations. Make sure each pushrod seats completely in the lifter socket.

9   Apply moly-base grease to the ends of the valve stems, the upper ends of the pushrods and to the pivot faces to prevent damage to the mating surfaces before engine oil pressure builds up.

10   Coat the rocker arm pivot bolts with moly-base grease. Install the rocker arms, pivots and pivot retainers. Tighten the bolts to the torque listed in this Chapter's Specifications. As the bolts are tightened, make sure the pushrods seat properly in the rocker arms.

11   Install the valve covers (see Section 4).

6   Valve springs, retainers and seals - replacement

This procedure is essentially the same as that described for the 3.1L engine. Refer to Part A of this Chapter and follow the procedure outlined there.

7   Intake manifold - removal and installation

Refer to illustrations 7.9a and 7.9b

Upper intake manifold (plenum)
Removal

1   Disconnect the negative battery cable from the battery. Remove the acoustic cover over the plenum (see illustration 4.4). **Caution:** *On models equipped with the Theftlock audio system, be sure the lockout feature is turned off before performing any procedure which requires disconnecting the battery.*

2   Refer to Chapter 4 and relieve the fuel system pressure.

3   Label and disconnect the hoses and electrical connectors attached to the upper intake manifold, throttle body and air intake duct. Remove the air intake duct.

4   Detach the throttle cable and cruise control cable (if equipped) and bracket from the throttle body.

5   Drain the cooling system.

6   Remove the spark plug wires for the rear bank of spark plugs (2, 4 and 6) from the ignition coil module (see Chapter 1) and move them aside.

7   Remove the fuel rail assembly (see Chapter 4).

8   Remove the heat shield from the EGR valve (at the rear of the upper intake manifold, on the driver's side). Remove the upper bolt from the throttle body support bracket (on the front of the throttle body).

9   Remove the upper intake manifold mounting bolts (and one stud) and the upper

7.19 Carefully pry up on a casting boss - don't pry between gasket surfaces

7.20 Remove all traces of gasket material, but don't gouge the mating surfaces

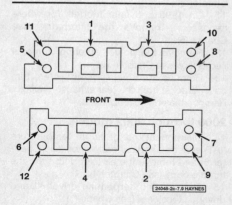

7.24 Lower intake manifold bolt TIGHTENING sequence

8.5 Remove the nuts and take off the engine lift bracket (arrow)

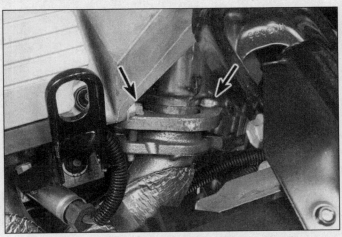

8.9 Remove the exhaust crossover pipe heat shield and remove the nuts (arrows) holding the crossover pipe to the manifold

intake manifold **(see illustrations)** with the throttle body attached.

Installation

10   Clean the mounting surfaces of the lower and upper intake manifolds with lacquer thinner and remove all traces of the old gasket material or sealant.

11   Install the new gasket over the lower intake manifold, then install the upper manifold onto the lower and tighten the bolts in the recommended tightening sequence **(see illustration 7.9b)** to the torque listed in this Chapter's Specifications. The remainder of the installation is the reverse of removal.

Lower intake manifold

Removal

Refer to illustration 7.19

12   Remove the upper intake manifold (see Steps 1 through 9). **Note:** *The upper intake manifold must be removed to access two of the lower intake manifold bolts.*

13   Remove the EGR valve (and pipes, if necessary) (see Chapter 6).

14   Remove the alternator and the brackets and braces necessary for clearance (see Chapter 5).

15   Remove the drivebelt tensioner assembly, if necessary (see Chapter 1).

16   Label and disconnect the hoses and electrical connectors attached to the lower intake manifold.

17   Remove the passenger-side engine torque strut upper bracket.

18   Loosen the manifold mounting bolts in 1/4-turn increments, in the reverse order of the tightening sequence, until they can be removed by hand.

19   The manifold will probably be stuck to the cylinder heads, and force may be required to break the gasket seal **(see illustration). Caution:** *Don't pry between the manifold and the heads or damage to the gasket sealing surfaces may occur, leading to vacuum leaks.*

Installation

Refer to illustrations 7.20 and 7.24

Note: *The mating surfaces of the cylinder heads, block and manifold must be perfectly clean when the manifold is installed. Gasket removal solvents in aerosol cans are available at most auto parts stores and may be helpful when removing old gasket material that's stuck to the heads and manifold (since the manifold is made of aluminum, aggressive scraping can cause damage). Be sure to follow the directions printed on the container.*

20   Before cleaning the old manifold, remove all fittings and sensors. If you're installing a new manifold, clean it before installing the fittings and sensors on it. Use a gasket scraper to remove all traces of sealant and old gasket material **(see illustration)**, then clean the mating surfaces with lacquer thinner or acetone. If there's old sealant or oil on the mating surfaces when the manifold is installed, oil or vacuum leaks may develop. Use shop towels to protect the lifter valley during gasket removal and a vacuum cleaner to remove any final debris.

21   Use a tap of the correct size to chase the threads in the bolt holes, then use compressed air (if available) to remove the debris from the holes. **Warning:** *Wear safety glasses or a face shield to protect your eyes when using compressed air.*

22   Install the new manifold gasket(s) and seals, if applicable. Apply RTV sealant to the four corners where the manifold, head and block come together and to the ends of the seals, if applicable.

23   Carefully lower the manifold into place. Apply thread locking compound to the mounting bolt threads and install the bolts finger tight.

24   Tighten the mounting bolts, following the recommended sequence **(see illustration)**, to the torque listed in this Chapter's specifications, including the two hidden bolts.

25   Install the remaining components in the reverse order of removal. Install a new plenum-to-lower intake manifold gasket

when installing the plenum.

26   Change the oil and filter and fill the cooling system (see Chapter 1). Start the engine and check for oil and vacuum leaks.

8   Exhaust manifolds - removal and installation

Warning: *Allow the engine to cool completely before beginning this procedure.* **Note:** *Exhaust system fasteners are frequently difficult to remove - they get frozen in place because of the heating/cooling cycle to which they're constantly exposed. To ease removal, apply penetrating oil to the threads of all exhaust manifold and exhaust pipe fasteners and allow it to soak in.*

Removal

Front manifold

Refer to illustrations 8.5, 8.9 and 8.11

1   Disconnect the negative battery cable, and drain the cooling system (see Chapter 1). **Caution:** *On models equipped with the Theftlock audio system, be sure the lockout feature is turned off before performing any procedure which requires disconnecting the battery.*

2   If necessary for clearance, remove the cooling fan for access (see Chapter 3).

3   If necessary for clearance, remove the EGR valve adapter and pipe (see Chapter 6).

4   Remove the engine torque struts and the passenger-side engine torque strut lower bracket (see Section 17).

5   Remove the engine lifting bracket **(see illustration)**.

6   Remove the acoustic cover over the intake manifold **(see illustration 4.4)**.

7   Remove the dipstick tube hold-down nut and work the dipstick tube out of the block.

8   Detach the spark plug wires from the front spark plugs, then remove the spark plugs (see Chapter 1).

9   Unbolt the crossover pipe and heat shield from the manifold **(see illustration)**.

8.11 Remove the front exhaust manifold bolts/studs (arrows indicate three)

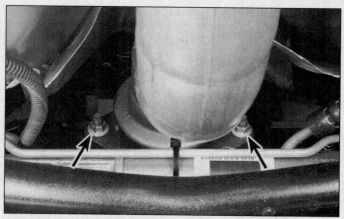

8.20 Remove the nuts (arrows) to separate the exhaust pipe from the rear manifold, just above the steering rack

10 Remove the manifold heat shield.
11 Unbolt and remove the exhaust manifold **(see illustration)**.

Rear manifold

Refer to illustration 8.20
12 Disconnect the negative battery cable. **Caution:** *On models equipped with the Theftlock audio system, be sure the lockout feature is turned off before performing any procedure which requires disconnecting the battery.*

1999 and earlier models

13 Drain the coolant from the radiator (see Chapter 1).
14 Remove the two nuts attaching the crossover pipe to the rear exhaust manifold. On 1998 models, remove the heat shield at the brake booster.
15 Disconnect the spark plug wires from the rear spark plugs and remove the spark plugs (see Chapter 1).
16 Remove the EGR pipe and transaxle dipstick tube if it's in the way (see Chapters 6 and 7).
17 Remove the acoustic cover **(see illustration 4.4)** and the cover bracket. **Note:** *Disconnect the oxygen sensor electrical connector to allow the bracket to be removed.*
18 Remove the rear engine lifting bracket from the studs on the rear manifold.
19 Set the parking brake, block the rear wheels and raise the front of the vehicle, supporting it securely on jackstands.
20 Working under the vehicle, remove the two exhaust pipe-to-manifold nuts, then lower the vehicle **(see illustration)**. **Note:** *Soak the nuts with penetrating oil before attempting removal.*
21 Remove the right-rear engine mount-to-frame nuts (see Section 17) and raise the engine slightly with a floorjack to provide extra working room around the rear manifold.
22 Remove the bolts/studs and detach the manifold from the head. Note the location of the studs for later reference.

2000 and later models

23 Remove the cross-vehicle brace (see Chapter 11).
24 Remove the oil cap and the engine trim cover.
25 Remove the exhaust crossover heat shield and the two studs attaching the crossover pipe to the rear exhaust manifold.
26 Set the parking brake, block the rear wheels and raise the front of the vehicle, supporting it securely on jackstands.
27 Working under the vehicle, remove the two exhaust pipe-to-manifold nuts **(see illustration 8.20)** and detach the exhaust pipe from the studs. **Note:** *Soak the nuts with penetrating oil before attempting removal.* Lower the vehicle.
28 Rotate the engine for access (see Chapter 1).
29 Remove the EGR inlet pipe bolt from the driver's side of the exhaust manifold.
30 Disconnect the oxygen sensor electrical connector, remove it from the fuel injection system trim cover bracket, and remove the trim cover bracket. Remove the engine lift bracket.
31 Disconnect the spark plug wires from the rear spark plugs and remove the spark plugs (see Chapter 1).
32 Remove the nuts/studs and detach the exhaust manifold and gasket from the head.

Installation (front or rear)

33 Clean the mating surfaces of the manifold and cylinder head to remove all traces of old gasket material, then check the manifold for warpage and cracks. If the manifold gasket was blown, take the manifold to an automotive machine shop for resurfacing.
34 Place the manifold in position with a new gasket and install the bolts finger tight.
35 Starting in the middle and working out toward the ends, tighten the mounting bolts a little at a time until all of them are at the specified torque.
36 Install the remaining components in the reverse order of removal.
37 Start the engine and check for exhaust leaks between the manifold and cylinder

head, between the manifold and exhaust pipe, between the manifolds and the crossover pipe, and at the EGR pipe connections.

---

9   Cylinder heads - removal and installation

Removal

Refer to illustrations 9.4a, 9.4b, 9.5 and 9.10
1 Disconnect the negative battery cable at the battery. Refer to Chapter 1 and drain the cooling system. **Caution:** *On models equipped with the Theftlock audio system, be sure the lockout feature is turned off before performing any procedure which requires disconnecting the battery.*
2 Disconnect the spark plug wires and remove the spark plugs (see Chapter 1). Be sure to label the plug wires to simplify reinstallation.
3 Remove the intake manifold as described in Section 7.
4 Refer to Chapter 5 and remove the ignition coil-pack, then refer to Section 17 and remove the torque struts from their brackets. One is mounted at each end of the front cylinder head. Remove the nuts/bolts holding the torque strut brackets to the cylinder head **(see illustrations)**.
5 Disconnect all wires and hoses from the cylinder head(s). Be sure to label them to simplify reinstallation. If removing the rear cylinder head, remove the alternator (see Chapter 5), then remove the water bypass hoses from the belt tensioner and remove the belt tensioner **(see illustration)**. When removing the rear cylinder head on later models, it may be necessary to remove the power steering pump. Set it aside without disconnecting the lines.
6 Detach the exhaust manifold(s) from the cylinder head(s) being removed (see Section 8).
7 Remove the valve cover(s) (see Section 4).
8 Remove the rocker arms and pushrods (see Section 5). **Caution:** *Keep the rocker*

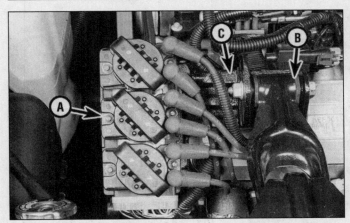

9.4a Remove the ignition coil-pack (A) and the torque strut (B) from the right torque strut mounting bracket (C) - left torque strut similar

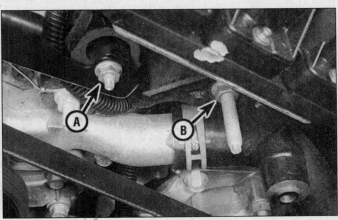

9.4b Under the coil-pack, remove the alternator brace bolt (A) and the torque strut mount-to-head nut (B)

arm components for each cylinder identified and together. They must go back in their original locations.

9 Loosen the head bolts in 1/4-turn increments until they can be removed by hand. Work from the ends of the cylinder head to the center.

10 Lift the cylinder head off the engine. If resistance is felt, don't pry between the cylinder head and block as damage to the mating surfaces will result. Recheck for cylinder head bolts that may have been overlooked, then use a hammer and block of wood to tap the cylinder head and break the gasket seal. Be careful because there are locating dowels in the block which position each cylinder head. As a last resort, pry each cylinder head up at the rear corner only and be careful not to damage anything (see illustration). After removal, place the cylinder head on blocks of wood to prevent damage to the gasket surfaces.

11 Refer to Chapter 2, Part D, for cylinder head disassembly, inspection and valve service procedures.

Installation
Refer to illustrations 9.13, 9.16 and 9.19

12 The mating surfaces of the cylinder heads and block must be perfectly clean when the heads are installed.

13 Use a gasket scraper to remove all traces of carbon and old gasket material (see illustration), then clean the mating surfaces with lacquer thinner or acetone. If there's oil on the mating surfaces when the heads are installed, the gaskets may not seal correctly and leaks may develop. When working on the block, it's a good idea to cover the lifter valley with shop rags to keep debris out of the engine. Use a shop rag or vacuum cleaner to remove any debris that falls into the cylinders.

14 Check the block and head mating surfaces for nicks, deep scratches and other damage. If damage is slight, it can be removed with a file; if it's excessive, machining may be the only alternative.

15 Use a tap of the correct size to chase the threads in the head bolt holes. Dirt, corrosion, sealant and damaged threads will affect torque readings.

16 Position the new gaskets over the dowel pins in the block. Install "non-retorquing" type gaskets dry (no sealant), unless the manufacturer states otherwise. Most gaskets are marked UP or TOP (see illustration) because they must be installed a certain way and they have an arrow that must point to the

9.5 Remove the bolts holding the water bypass hoses to the belt tensioner (A indicates one of the hoses and its bolt), then remove the tensioner bolts (B indicates two)

front (timing chain end) of the engine. The left gasket may have an "L" near the arrow.

17 Carefully position the heads on the block without disturbing the gaskets.

18 Use NEW head bolts of the correct part number, as these are a torque-to-yield design and the old ones must not be reused.

9.10 Pry carefully - don't force a tool between the gasket surfaces

9.13 Carefully remove all traces of old gasket material

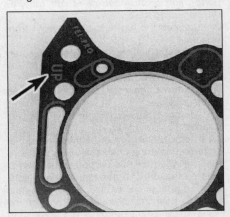

9.16 Look for gasket marks (arrow) to ensure correct installation

9.19 Cylinder head bolt TIGHTENING sequence

10.1 The roller lifters on the 3800 engine are retained by guides bolted to the sides of the lifter valley - remove the four bolts to take off the guides and remove the lifters

19 Tighten the bolts as directed in this Chapter's specifications in the sequence shown (see illustration).
20 The remaining installation steps are the reverse of removal.
21 Change the oil and filter (see Chapter 1).

10 Valve lifters - removal, inspection and installation

Refer to illustration 10.1
   This procedure is essentially the same as that for the 3.1L V6 engine. Refer to Part A and follow the procedure outlined there. Refer to **illustration 10.1** for details of the roller lifter retainer plates on the 3800 engine.

11 Crankshaft front oil seal - replacement

Refer to illustrations 11.7a, 11.7b and 11.14
Caution: *The crankshaft balancer is serviced as an assembly. Do not attempt to separate the pulley from the balancer hub.*
1   Disconnect the negative cable from the battery. **Caution:** *On models equipped with the Theftlock audio system, be sure the lockout feature is turned off before performing any procedure which requires disconnecting the battery.*
2   Loosen the lug nuts on the right front wheel.
3   Raise the vehicle and support it securely on jackstands.
4   Remove the right front wheel.
5   Remove the right front fender inner splash shield.
6   Remove the serpentine drivebelt (see Chapter 1).
7   Remove the lower bellhousing cover plate and hold the crankshaft with a special tool designed for this purpose (available at auto parts stores). If this tool is unavailable, position a large screwdriver in the ring gear teeth to keep the crankshaft from turning while an assistant removes the crankshaft balancer bolt (see illustrations). The bolt is normally quite tight, so use a large breaker

11.7a Wedge a large screwdriver in the teeth of the ring gear (flywheel) to keep it from turning while an assistant removes the balancer bolt

bar and a six-point socket.
8   The crankshaft balancer should pull off the crankshaft by hand. Leave the Woodruff key in place in the end of the crankshaft.
9   If there's a groove worn into the seal contact surface on the crankshaft balancer, sleeves are available that fit over the groove, restoring the contact surface to like-new condition. These sleeves are sometimes included with the seal kit. Check with your parts supplier for details.
10 Pry the old oil seal out with a seal removal tool or a screwdriver (see Chapter 2 Part A). Be very careful not to nick or otherwise damage the crankshaft in the process.
11 Apply a thin coat of RTV sealant to the outer edge of the new seal. Lubricate the seal lip with moly-base grease or clean engine oil.
12 Place the seal squarely in position in the bore and press it into place with a special seal installer (available at auto parts stores). Make sure the seal enters the bore squarely and seats completely.
13 If the special tool is unavailable, carefully drive the seal into place with a hammer and large socket or section of pipe (see Part A of this Chapter). The outer diameter of the socket or pipe

11.7b Remove the bolt in the center of the hub (arrow)

should be the same size as the seal outer diameter.
14 Installation is the reverse of removal. Align the keyway with the key (see illustration) and avoid bending the metal tabs. Be sure to apply moly-base grease to the seal contact surface on the back side of the crankshaft balancer (if it isn't lubricated, the seal lip could be damaged and oil leakage would result).

11.14 Be sure to align the keyway (arrow) with the key in the crankshaft

12.11 Timing chain cover bolt locations (arrows)

12.13 Remove all traces of old gasket material

15   Apply sealant to the threads and tighten the crankshaft bolt in two steps to the torque listed in this Chapter's Specifications.
16   Reinstall the remaining parts in the reverse order of removal.
17   Start the engine and check for oil leaks at the seal.

12   Timing chain cover, chain and sprockets - removal and installation

Removal

Refer to illustrations 12.11, 12.13, 12.14, 12.16, 12.17 and 12.19
1   Disconnect the negative battery cable from the battery. **Caution:** *On models equipped with the Theftlock audio system, be sure the lockout feature is turned off before performing any procedure which requires disconnecting the battery.*
2   Set the parking brake and put the transmission in Park. Raise the front of the vehicle and support it securely on jackstands. Remove the splash shield from the right inner fender.

3   Drain the oil and coolant (see Chapter 1). Remove the oil filter.
4   Remove the coolant hoses from the timing chain cover and water pump, and loosen the water pump pulley (see Chapter 3).
5   Remove the serpentine drivebelt (see Chapter 1) and the drivebelt tensioner assembly (see Section 9). Remove the water pump pulley. On later models, remove the power steering pump and set it aside without disconnecting the lines.
6   Remove the crankshaft balancer (see Section 11).
7   Remove the large (8 mm) water pump-to-block bolts, leaving the smaller (6 mm) diameter bolts in place.
8   Unplug the connectors from the oil pressure, camshaft and crankshaft sensors (see Chapter 6). Remove the shield over the front of the crankshaft sensor.
9   Remove the oil pan bolts which attach to the front cover, then loosen the rest of the oil pan bolts (see Section 14).
10   Remove the engine oil cooler pipes (if equipped) from the oil filter adapter housing.
11   Remove the timing chain cover-to-engine block bolts **(see illustration)**. Note that two of the bolts also secure the

crankshaft sensor. Lift the sensor off when removing these bolts.
12   Separate the cover from the front of the engine, removing it with the water pump and oil filter adapter still attached.
13   Use a gasket scraper to remove all traces of old gasket material and sealant from the cover and engine block **(see illustration)**. The cover is made of aluminum, so be careful not to nick or gouge it. Clean the gasket sealing surfaces with lacquer thinner or acetone.
14   Check the camshaft thrust surface in the cover for excessive wear **(see illustration)**. If it's worn, a new cover will be required.
15   The timing chain should be replaced with a new one if the total free play midway between the sprockets exceeds one inch. Failure to replace the timing chain may result in erratic engine performance, loss of power and lowered fuel mileage.
16   Temporarily install the crankshaft balancer bolt and turn the crankshaft clockwise to align the timing marks on the crankshaft and camshaft sprockets directly opposite each other **(see illustration)**.
17   Detach the spring (if applicable), then remove the bolt and separate the timing chain damper from the block **(see illustration)**.

12.14 The camshaft thrust surface on this cover is worn away (arrow) which means that a new cover must be installed

12.16 The marks on the crankshaft and camshaft sprockets (arrows) must be aligned adjacent to each other as shown

12.17 Remove the timing chain damper

12.19 Remove the camshaft sprocket, timing chain and crankshaft sprocket as an assembly

12.24 The balance shaft drive gear (A) must align with the balance shaft driven gear (B) before installing the timing chain and sprockets - note the dots on both gears are aligned

13.4 Remove the pressure regulator valve and spring, then check the valve for wear and damage

18 Remove the camshaft sprocket bolt. Try not to turn the camshaft in the process (if you do, realign the timing marks after the bolts are loosened).

19 Alternately pull the camshaft sprocket and then the crankshaft sprocket forward and remove the sprockets and timing chain as an assembly **(see illustration)**.

20 Remove the camshaft gear.

21 Clean the timing chain components with solvent and dry them with compressed air (if available). **Warning:** *Wear eye protection.*

22 Inspect the components for wear and damage. Look for teeth that are deformed, chipped, pitted, polished or discolored.

Installation

Refer to illustration 12.24

23 If the crankshaft has been disturbed, install the crankshaft sprocket temporarily and turn the crankshaft until the mark on the sprocket is exactly at the top. If the camshaft was disturbed, install the camshaft sprocket temporarily and turn the camshaft until the timing mark is at the bottom, opposite the mark on the crankshaft sprocket **(see illustration 12.16)**.

24 Assemble the timing chain on the sprockets, then slide the sprocket and chain assembly onto the shafts with the timing marks aligned as shown in **illustration 12.16**. **Note:** *If it was removed for any reason, be sure to install the balance shaft drive gear, which is behind the camshaft sprocket. It drives the gear on the balance shaft and the two gears must be aligned before installing the timing chain with camshaft sprocket* **(see illustration)**.

25 Install the camshaft sprocket bolt and tighten to the torque listed in this Chapter's Specifications.

26 Attach the timing chain damper assembly to the block and install the spring (if applicable).

27 Lubricate the chain and sprocket with clean engine oil.

28 Before the cover is installed, the oil pump cover must be removed and the cavity packed with petroleum jelly as described in Section 13.

29 Apply a thin layer of RTV sealant to both sides of the new gasket, then position the gasket on the engine block (the dowel pins should keep it in place). Attach the cover to the engine, making sure that the oil pump drive engages with the crankshaft.

30 Apply Teflon thread sealant to the bolt threads, then install them finger tight. Follow a criss-cross pattern when tightening the bolts and work up to the torque listed in this Chapter's Specifications in three steps to avoid warping the cover.

31 The remainder of installation is the reverse of removal.

32 Add oil and coolant, start the engine and check for leaks.

13 Oil pump - removal, inspection and installation

Removal

Refer to illustrations 13.4 and 13.5

1 Remove the oil filter (see Chapter 1).

2 Remove the timing chain cover (see Section 12).

3 Remove the four bolts holding the oil filter adapter to the timing chain cover. The cover is spring loaded, so remove the bolts while keeping pressure on the cover, then release the spring pressure carefully.

4 Remove the pressure regulator valve and spring **(see illustration)**. Use a gasket scraper to remove all traces of the old gasket.

5 Remove the oil pump cover-to-timing chain cover bolts **(see illustration)**.

6 Lift out the cover and oil pump gears as an assembly.

Inspection

Refer to illustrations 13.10 and 13.11

7 Clean the parts with solvent and dry

them with compressed air (if available). **Warning:** *Wear eye protection!*

8 Inspect all components for wear and score marks. Replace any worn out or damaged parts.

9 Reinstall the gears in the timing chain cover.

10 Measure the outer gear-to-housing clearance with a feeler gauge **(see illustration)**.

11 Measure the inner gear-to-outer gear clearance at several points **(see illustration)**.

12 Use a depth micrometer or a straight-edge and feeler gauge to measure the gear end clearance (distance from the gear to the gasket surface of the cover).

13 Check for pump cover warpage by laying a precision straightedge across the cover and trying to slip a feeler gauge between the cover and straightedge.

14 Compare the measurements to this Chapter's Specifications. Replace all worn or damaged components with new ones.

Installation

15 Remove the gears and pack the pump cavity with petroleum jelly.

13.5 The oil pump cover is attached to the inside of the timing chain cover - a T-30 Torx driver is required for removal of the screws

13.10 Measuring the outer gear-to-housing clearance with a feeler gauge

13.11 Measuring the inner gear tip-to-outer gear tip clearance with a feeler gauge

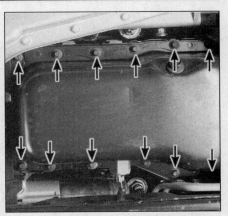

14.10 The oil pan bolts (arrows indicate most in this view from below) are located around the perimeter of the oil pan

16   Install the gears - make sure petroleum jelly is forced into every cavity. Failure to do so could cause the pump to lose its prime when the engine is started, causing damage from lack of oil pressure.

17   Install the pump cover, using a new gasket - make sure you have the correct gasket, its thickness is critical for maintaining the correct clearance.

18   Install the pressure regulator spring and valve and the oil filter adapter (with a new gasket).

19   Install the timing chain cover. Be sure to use a new gasket.

20   Install the oil filter and check the oil level. Start and run the engine and check for correct oil pressure, then look carefully for oil leaks at the timing chain cover.

21   Run the engine and check for oil leaks.

14   Oil pan - removal and installation

Removal

Refer to illustration 14.10

1   Disconnect the cable from the negative battery terminal. **Caution:** *On models equipped with the Theftlock audio system, be sure the lockout feature is turned off before performing any procedure which requires disconnecting the battery.* Remove the air cleaner intake duct.

2   Raise the vehicle and place it securely on jackstands. Drain the engine oil and replace the oil filter (refer to Chapter 1 if necessary).

3   Remove the driveplate inspection cover and starter, if necessary for access (refer to Chapter 5). Disconnect the electrical connector from the oil lever sensor, then remove the oil level sensor from the pan.

4   Disconnect the engine torque struts (see Section 17).

5   Disconnect the exhaust pipe and catalytic converter from the engine.

6   Disconnect the pipes leading from the engine oil cooler, if equipped (see Chapter 3).

7   Refer to Section 17 and remove the frame-side nuts from the engine mount at the timing-chain-end of the engine.

8   Use a transmission jack or a floorjack with a block of wood to raise the engine/transaxle by raising under the transaxle, not the engine, to allow removal of the engine mount from the engine (see Section 17).

9   On 1999 models, remove the air conditioner compressor mounting bolt and move the compressor out of the way (see Chapter 3). Disconnect the power steering oil cooler pipe brackets from the frame.

10   Remove the oil pan mounting bolts **(see illustration)** and carefully lower the oil pan from the block. Don't pry between the block and the pan or damage to the sealing surfaces may result and oil leaks may develop. Instead, tap the pan with a soft-face hammer to break the gasket seal.

11   When the pan has been lowered enough, unbolt the oil pump pickup tube and screen assembly and let it drop down and come out with the pan.

Installation

12   Clean the screen and housing assembly with solvent and dry it with compressed air, if available. **Warning:** *Wear eye protection.*

13   If the oil screen is damaged or has metal chips in it, replace it. An abundance of metal chips indicates a major engine problem which must be corrected.

14   Make sure the mating surfaces of the pipe flange and the engine block are clean and free of nicks.

15   Clean the pan with solvent and remove all old sealant and gasket material from the block and pan mating surfaces. Clean the mating surfaces with lacquer thinner or acetone and make sure the bolt holes in the block are clear. Check the oil pan flange for distortion, particularly around the bolt holes. If necessary, place the pan on a block of wood and use a hammer to flatten and restore the gasket surface.

16   Always use a new gasket whenever the oil pan is installed. The one-piece gasket is not reusable. When installing the new gasket, apply a small amount of RTV sealant to the two tabs that fit next to the rear main cap

(where the cap meets the block).

17   Place the oil pan in position under the block with the pump pickup tube and screen in the pan. When the pan is close enough, reach in and bolt the pickup tube (with a new gasket) to the block and put the pan up the rest of the way. Start all of the oil pan bolts finger-tight.

18   After the bolts are installed, tighten them to the torque listed in this Chapter's Specifications. Starting at the center, follow a criss-cross pattern and work up to the final torque in three steps. Do not overtighten the bolts or you may damage the pan and cause an oil leak.

19   The remaining steps are the reverse of the removal procedure.

20   Refill the engine with oil. Run the engine until normal operating temperature is reached and check for leaks.

15   Driveplate - removal and installation

This procedure is essentially the same as for the 3.1L engine. Refer to Section 15 in Part A of this Chapter. Refer to this Chapter's Specifications for driveplate bolt torque for the 3.8L engine.

16   Rear main oil seal - replacement

This procedure is essentially the same as for the 3.1L V6 engine. Refer to Part A and follow the procedure outlined there. However, use the bolt torque listed in this Chapter's Specifications.

17   Engine mounts - check and replacement

Refer to illustrations 17.9 and 17.11
Note: *See Chapter 7 for transaxle mount information.*

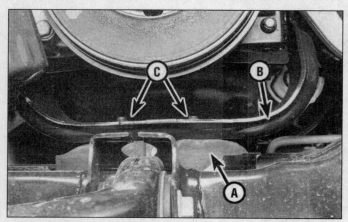

17.9 The front engine mount (A) is located between the front subframe and the engine front mount cradle (B) - remove the two nuts (C) at the cradle and two nuts below the subframe to remove the mount

17.11 Remove the through-bolts (A) and the engine torque struts (B) for replacement

Warning: *A special engine support fixture should be used to support the engine during repair operations. Similar fixtures are available from rental yards. Improper lifting methods or devices are hazardous and could result in severe injury or death. DO NOT place any part of your body under the engine/transaxle when it's supported only by a jack. Failure of the lifting device could result in serious injury or death.*

1   Engine mounts seldom require attention, but broken or deteriorated mounts should be replaced immediately or the added strain placed on the driveline components may cause damage or wear. The 3800 engine has a transaxle mount (see Chapter 7), two engine torque struts and a mount at the front (timing belt end) of the engine that attaches to a "cradle" type bracket under the front of the oil pan.

Check

2   During the check, the engine must be raised slightly to remove the weight from the mounts.

3   Raise the vehicle and support it securely on jackstands, then position a jack under the engine oil pan. Place a large block of wood between the jack head and the oil pan, then carefully raise the engine just enough to take the weight off the mounts. **Warning:** *DO NOT place any part of your body under the engine when it's supported only by a jack!*

4   Check the mounts to see if the rubber is cracked, hardened or separated from the metal plates. Sometimes the rubber will split right down the center.

5   Check for relative movement between the mount plates and the engine or frame (use a large screwdriver or prybar to attempt to move the mounts). If movement is noted, lower the engine and tighten the mount fasteners.

6   Rubber preservative may be applied to the mounts to slow deterioration.

Replacement

7   Disconnect the negative battery cable from the battery, then raise the vehicle and support it securely on jackstands (if not already done). **Caution:** *On models equipped with the Theftlock audio system, be sure the lockout feature is turned off before performing any procedure which requires disconnecting the battery.*

8   Remove the right front wheel and loosen the inner fender splash panel.

9   Raise the engine slightly with a jack or hoist. Install an engine support as described in the **Warning** above. Remove the fasteners and detach the mount from the frame bracket **(see illustration)**.

10   Remove the mount-to-block bracket bolts/nuts and detach the mount.

11   The engine torque struts mount between the engine and the upper radiator support on the body **(see illustration)**. They can be replaced without jacking up the engine, by removing the through-bolts and the bolts attaching the struts to the mounts on the radiator support. **Note:** *When reinstalling the mounts, you may have to use a prybar to rotate the engine toward or away from the radiator to align the through-bolts.*

12   Installation is the reverse of removal. Use thread locking compound on the threads and be sure to tighten everything securely.

Chapter 2 Part D
General engine overhaul procedures

Contents

Specifications

General

VIN code	
3.1L OHV	M
3.4L OHV	E
3.4L DOHC	X
3800	K
Displacement	
3.1L OHV	192 cubic inches (3.1 liters)
3.4L OHV and DOHC	204 cubic inches (3.4 liters)
3800	231 cubic inches (3.8 liters)
Cylinder compression pressure	100 psi minimum
Maximum variation between cylinders	30-percent
Firing order	
3.1L and 3.4L OHV and 3.4L DOHC	1-2-3-4-5-6
3800	1-6-5-4-3-2
Oil pressure	15 psi at 1100 rpm

Cylinder head

Warpage limit	0.003 inch (0.07 mm)* per 6 inches

If more than 0.010 inch (0.25 mm) must be removed, replace the head

Engine block

Cylinder bore	
Diameter	
3.1L OHV	3.5046 to 3.5053 inches (89.016 to 89.034 mm)
3.4L OHV and DOHC	3.6228 to 3.6235 inches (92.020 to 92.038 mm)
3800	3.8 inches (96.5 mm)
Out-of-round limit	
3.1L and 3.4L OHV	
Production	0.0005 inch (0.014 mm)
Service	0.001 inch (0.025 mm)
3.4L DOHC	0.0004 inch (0.010 mm)
3800	0.001 inch (0.0254 mm)
Taper limit (thrust side)	
3.1L and 3.4L OHV	
Production	0.0008 inch (0.020 mm)
Service	0.001 inch (0.025 mm)
3.4L DOHC	0.00051 inch (0.013 mm)
3800	0.001 inch (0.0254 mm)
Block deck warpage limit	If more than 0.010 inch (0.25 mm) must be removed, replace the block

Valves and related components

Valve margin width, minimum
    3.1L and 3.4L OHV
        Intake .... 0.083 inch (2.10 mm)
        Exhaust .... 0.106 inch (2.70 mm)
    3.4L DOHC .... 0.029 inch (0.75 mm)
    3800 .... 0.025 inch (0.635 mm)
Valve stem-to-guide clearance
    3.1L and 3.4L OHV .... 0.0010 to 0.0027 inch (0.026 to 0.068 mm)
    3.4L DOHC
        Intake .... 0.0011 to 0.0026 inch (0.028 to 0.066 mm)
        Exhaust .... 0.0018 to 0.0033 inch (0.046 to 0.084 mm)
    3800
        1995 through 2001.. 0.0015 to 0.0032 inch (0.038 to 0.081 mm)
        2002 and later
            Intake .... 0.0012 to 0.0028 inch (0.031 to 0.071 mm)
            Exhaust.. 0.0014 to 0.0029 inch (0.036 to 0.074 mm)
Valve spring free length (intake and exhaust)
    3.1L and 3.4L OHV .... 1.89 inches (48.5 mm)
    3.4L DOHC .... 1.6551 inches (42.04 mm)
    3800
        1995 and 1996 .... 1.981 inches (50.32 mm)
        1998 on .... 1.960 inches (49.78 mm)
Installed height
    3.1L and 3.4L OHV .... 1.701 inches (43 mm)
    3.4L DOHC .... 1.400 inches (35.56 mm)
    3800 .... 1.690 to 1.750 inches (42.93 to 44.45 mm)

Crankshaft and connecting rods

Connecting rod journal
    Diameter
        3.1L and 3.4L OHV and 3.4L DOHC .... 1.9987 to 1.9994 inches (50.768 to 50.784 mm)
        3800 .... 2.2487 to 2.2499 inches (57.117 to 57.147 mm)
    Bearing oil clearance
        3.1L and 3.4L OHV .... 0.0007 to 0.0024 inch (0.018 to 0.062 mm)
        3.4L DOHC.. 0.0011 to 0.0032 inch (0.028 to 0.082 mm)
        3800 .... 0.0005 to 0.0026 inch (0.0127 to 0.0660 mm)
Connecting rod side clearance (endplay)
    3.1L and 3.4L OHV and 3.4L DOHC
        1995 through 2002.. 0.007 to 0.017 inch (0.18 to 0.44 mm)
        2003 and later .... 0.010 to 0.015 inch (0.25 to 0.37 mm)
    3800 .... 0.004 to 0.020 inch (0.102 to 0.508 mm)
Main bearing journal
    Diameter
        3.1L and 3.4L OHV .... 2.6473 to 2.6483 inches (67.239 to 67.257 mm)
        3.4L DOHC.. 2.6472 to 2.6479 inches (67.239 to 67.257 mm)
        3800 .... 2.4988 to 2.4998 inches (63.470 to 63.495 mm)
    Bearing oil clearance
        3.1L and 3.4L OHV
            All except #3 .... 0.0008 to 0.0025 inch (0.019 to 0.064 mm)
            #3 (thrust bearing) .... 0.0012 to 0.0030 inch (0.032 to 0.077 mm)
        3.4L DOHC.. 0.0008 to 0.0025 inch (0.019 to 0.064 mm)
        3800 .... 0.0008 to 0.0022 inch (0.020 to 0.055 mm)
    Taper limit
        3.1L and 3.4L OHV and 3.4L DOHC .... 0.0002 inch (0.005 mm)
        3800 .... 0.00035 inch (0.00889 mm)
    Out-of-round limit
        3.1L and 3.4L OHV and 3.4L DOHC .... 0.0002 inch (0.005 mm)
        3800 .... 0.00025 inch (0.00635 mm)
Crankshaft endplay (at thrust bearing)
    3.1L and 3.4L OHV and 3.4L DOHC .... 0.0024 to 0.0083 inch (0.06 to 0.21 mm)
    3800 .... 0.003 to 0.011 inch (0.076 to 0.279 mm)

Camshaft

Bearing journal diameter
    3.1L and 3.4L OHV .... 1.868 to 1.869 inches (47.45 to 47.48 mm)
    3.4L DOHC... 2.1643 to 2.1654 inches (54.973 to 55.001 mm)
    3800 .... 1.8462 to 1.8448 inches (47.655 to 46.858 mm)

Bearing oil clearance
3.1L and 3.4L OHV .... 0.001 to 0.0039 inch (0.026 to 0.101 mm)
3.4L DOHC .... 0.0019 to 0.0040 inch (0.049 to 0.102 mm)
3800 .... 0.0016 to 0.0047 inch (0.041 to 0.119 mm)
Lobe lift
3.1L and 3.4L OHV .... 0.2727 inch (6.9263 mm)
3.4L DOHC
Intake .... 0.370 inch (9.398 mm)
Exhaust .... 0.370 inch (9.398 mm)
3800
Intake .... 0.258 inch (6.55 mm)
Exhaust
1995 through 2001 .... 0.255 inch (6.48 mm)
2002 and later .... 0.258 inch (6.55 mm)

Pistons and rings

Piston-to-bore clearance
3.1L and 3.4L OHV
1995 through 2001 .... 0.0013 to 0.0027 inch (0.032 to 0.068 mm)
2002
Non-coated
Production .... 0.0006 to 0.0020 inch (0.016 to 0.052 mm)
Service limit .... 0.0019 to 0.0033 inch (0.048 to 0.083 mm)
Grafal coated
Production .... 0.0003 to 0.0019 inch (0.008 to 0.048 mm)
Service limit .... 0.0013 to 0.0035 inch (0.033 to 0.089 mm)
2003 and later
Production
1–4 .... 0.0006 to 0.0020 inch (0.016 to 0.051 mm)
5–6 .... 0.0003 to 0.0018 inch (0.008 to 0.046 mm)
Service limit .... 0.0036 inch (0.09 mm)
3.4L DOHC .... 0.0008 to 0.0020 inch (0.020 to 0.052 mm)
3800
New piston (1.6 inches from top) .... 0.0004 to 0.0020 inch (0.010 to 0.051 mm)
Used piston (1.6 inches from top) .... 0.0020 to 0.0036 inch (0.50 to 0.91 mm)
Piston ring end gap
First compression ring
3.1L and 3.4L OHV
All except 2002 .... 0.006 to 0.014 inch (0.15 to 0.36 mm)
2002 .... 0.008 to 0.019 inch (0.21 to 0.48 mm)
3.4L DOHC .... 0.008 to 0.018 inch (0.20 to 0.45 mm)
3800
1995 through 1998 .... 0.012 to 0.022 inch (0.305 to 0.559 mm)
1999 and later .... 0.010 to 0.018 inch (0.25 to 0.46 mm)
Second compression ring
3.1L and 3.4L OHV
1995 through 2001 .... 0.0197 to 0.0280 inch (0.5 to 0.71 mm)
2002 .... 0.0213 to 0.0339 inch (0.54 to 0.86 mm)
2003 and later .... 0.0188 to 0.0291 inch (0.48 to 0.74 mm)
3.4L DOHC .... 0.022 to 0.032 inch (0.56 to 0.81 mm)
3800
1995 through 1998 .... 0.030 to 0.040 inch (0.762 to 1.016 mm)
1999 and later .... 0.023 to 0.033 inch (0.58 to 0.84 mm)
Oil control ring
3.1L and 3.4L OHV and 3.4L DOHC .... 0.0098 to 0.0299 inch (0.25 to 0.76 mm)
3800 .... 0.010 to 0.030 inch (0.254 to 0.762 mm)
Piston ring side clearance
First and second compression rings
3.1L and 3.4L OHV .... 0.002 to 0.003 inch (0.05 to 0.085 mm)
3.4L DOHC and 3800 .... 0.0013 to 0.0031 inch (0.033 to 0.079 mm)
Oil control ring
3.1L and 3.4L OHV
1995 through 2001 .... 0.008 to 0.0019 inch (0.20 to 0.048 mm)
2002 .... 0.0018 to 0.0079 inch (0.046 to 0.20 mm)
2003 and later .... 0.0028 to 0.0037 inch (0.07 to 0.095 mm)
3.4L DOHC .... 0.0011 to 0.0081 inch (0.028 to 0.206 mm)
3800
1995 through 1999 .... 0.0011 to 0.0081 inch (0.028 to 0.206 mm)
2000 and later .... 0.0009 to 0.0079 inch (0.023 to 0.201 mm)

Balance shaft (3800 only)

Endplay	0.0 to 0.0067 inch (0.0 to 0.171 mm)
Drive gear backlash	0.002 to 0.005 inch (0.050 to 0.127 mm)
Rear journal diameter	
1995 through 2002	1.4994 to 1.5002 inch (38.085 to 38.105 mm)
2003 and later	1.4989 to 1.5002 inch (38.072 to 38.105 mm)
Rear bearing oil clearance	
1995 through 2002	0.0005 to 0.0043 inch (0.0127 to 0.109 mm)
2003 and later	0.0005 to 0.0048 inch (0.0127 to 0.1219 mm)

Torque specifications***

Ft-lbs (unless otherwise indicated)

Main bearing caps, bolts/studs	
3.1L and 3.4L OHV	
Step 1	37
Step 2	Tighten an additional 77 degrees
3.4L DOHC	
Step 1	37
Step 2	Tighten an additional 75 degrees
3800 (see procedure)	
Step 1	30
Step 2	Tighten an additional 110 degrees
Side bolts	
Step 1	11
Step 2	Tighten an additional 45 degrees
Connecting rod caps	
3.1L and 3.4L OHV and 3.4L DOHC	
Step 1	15
Step 2	Tighten an additional 75 degrees
3800	
Step 1	20
Step 2	Tighten an additional 50 degrees
Camshaft retainer bolts	
3.1L and 3.4L OHV	89 in-lbs
3800	11
Intermediate shaft retainer bolts (3.4L DOHC)	89 in-lbs
Balance shaft retainer bolts	22
Balance shaft driven gear bolt	
Step 1	16
Step 2	Tighten an additional 70 degrees

***Note:** *Refer to Parts A, B or C for additional torque specifications.*

1   General information - engine overhaul

Included in this portion of Chapter 2 are the general overhaul procedures for the cylinder head and internal engine components.

The information ranges from advice concerning preparation for an overhaul and the purchase of replacement parts to detailed, step-by-step procedures covering removal and installation of internal engine components and the inspection of parts.

The following Sections have been written based on the assumption that the engine has been removed from the vehicle. For information concerning in-vehicle engine repair, as well as removal and installation of the external components necessary for the overhaul, see Chapter 2A (3.1L and 3.4L OHV), 2B (3.4L DOHC), or 2C (3800) and Section 8 of this Chapter.

The Specifications included in this Part are only those necessary for the inspection and overhaul procedures which follow. Refer to Chapter 2, Part A, Part B or Part C for additional Specifications.

It's not always easy to determine when, or if, an engine should be completely overhauled, as a number of factors must be considered.

High mileage is not necessarily an indication that an overhaul is needed, while low mileage doesn't preclude the need for an overhaul. Frequency of servicing is probably the most important consideration. An engine that's had regular and frequent oil and filter changes, as well as other required maintenance, will most likely give many thousands of miles of reliable service. Conversely, a neglected engine may require an overhaul very early in its life.

Excessive oil consumption is an indication that piston rings, valve seals and/or valve guides are in need of attention. Make sure that oil leaks aren't responsible before deciding that the rings and/or guides are bad. Perform a cylinder compression check to determine the extent of the work required (see Section 3). Also check the vacuum readings under various conditions (see Section 4).

Loss of power, rough running, knocking or metallic engine noises, excessive valve train noise and high fuel consumption rates may also point to the need for an overhaul,

especially if they're all present at the same time. If a complete tune-up doesn't remedy the situation, major mechanical work is the only solution.

An engine overhaul involves restoring the internal parts to the specifications of a new engine. During an overhaul, the piston rings are replaced and the cylinder walls are reconditioned (re-bored and/or honed). If a

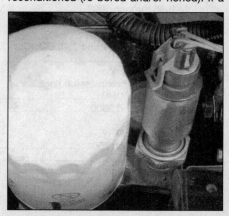

2.2 The oil pressure sending unit is located near the oil filter

re-bore is done by an automotive machine shop, new oversize pistons will also be installed. The main bearings, connecting rod bearings and camshaft bearings are generally replaced with new ones and, if necessary, the crankshaft may be reground to restore the journals. Generally, the valves are serviced as well, since they're usually in less-than-perfect condition at this point. While the engine is being overhauled, other components, such as the distributor, starter and alternator, can be rebuilt as well. The end result should be a like new engine that will give many trouble free miles. **Note:** *Critical cooling system components such as the hoses, drivebelts, thermostat and water pump should be replaced with new parts when an engine is overhauled. The radiator should be checked carefully to ensure that it isn't clogged or leaking (see Chapter 3). If you purchase a rebuilt engine or short block, some rebuilders will not warranty their engines unless the radiator has been professionally flushed. Also, we don't recommend overhauling the oil pump - always install a new one when an engine is rebuilt.*

Before beginning the engine overhaul, read through the entire procedure to familiarize yourself with the scope and requirements of the job. Overhauling an engine isn't difficult, but it is time-consuming. Plan on the vehicle being tied up for a minimum of two weeks, especially if parts must be taken to an automotive machine shop for repair or reconditioning. Check on availability of parts and make sure that any necessary special tools and equipment are obtained in advance. Most work can be done with typical hand tools, although a number of precision measuring tools are required for inspecting parts to determine if they must be replaced. Often an automotive machine shop will handle the inspection of parts and offer advice concerning reconditioning and replacement. **Note:** *Always wait until the engine has been completely disassembled and all components, especially the engine block, have been inspected before deciding what service and repair operations must be performed by an automotive machine shop.* Since the block's condition will be the major factor to consider when determining whether to overhaul the original engine or buy a rebuilt one, never purchase parts or have machine work done on other components until the block has been thoroughly inspected. As a general rule, time is the primary cost of an overhaul, so it doesn't pay to install worn or substandard parts.

As a final note, to ensure maximum life and minimum trouble from a rebuilt engine, everything must be assembled with care in a spotlessly-clean environment.

2 Oil pressure check

Refer to illustration 2.2

1   Low engine oil pressure can be a sign of an engine in need of rebuilding. A "low oil pressure" indicator (often called an "idiot light")

is not a test of the oiling system. Such indicators only come on when the oil pressure is dangerously low. Even a factory oil pressure gauge in the instrument panel is only a relative indication, although much better for driver information than a warning light. A better test is with a mechanical (not electrical) oil pressure gauge. When used in conjunction with an accurate tachometer, an engine's oil pressure performance can be compared to the manufacturers specifications.

2   Find the oil pressure indicator sending unit **(see illustration)**.

3   Remove the oil pressure sending unit and install a fitting which will allow you to directly connect your hand-held, mechanical oil pressure gauge. Use Teflon tape or sealant on the threads of the adapter and the fitting on the end of your gauge's hose.

4   Connect an accurate tachometer to the engine, according to the tachometer manufacturer's instructions.

5   Check the oil pressure with the engine running (full operating temperature) at the specified engine speed, and compare it to this Chapter's Specifications. If it's extremely low, the bearings and/or oil pump are probably worn out.

3 Cylinder compression check

Refer to illustration 3.6

1   A compression check will tell you what mechanical condition the upper end (pistons, rings, valves, head gaskets) of the engine is in. Specifically, it can tell you if the compression is down due to leakage caused by worn piston rings, defective valves and seats or a blown head gasket. **Note:** *The engine must be at normal operating temperature and the battery must be fully charged for this check.*

2   Begin by cleaning the area around the spark plugs before you remove them. Compressed air should be used, if available, otherwise a small brush or even a bicycle tire pump will work. The idea is to prevent dirt from getting into the cylinders as the compression check is being done.

3   Remove all of the spark plugs from the engine (see Chapter 1).

4   Block the throttle wide open.

5   Disable the fuel and ignition systems by removing the PCM IGN fuse from the instrument panel fuse block and the IGNITION fuse from the underhood fuse block (1995 models), the PCM BATT fuse from the instrument panel fuse block and the IGNITION fuse from the underhood fuse block (1996 through 1999 models) or the PCM/BCM/CLSTR fuse from the instrument panel fuse block (driver's side) and the IGN fuse from the lower underhood fuse block (2000 and later models).

6   Install the compression gauge in the number one spark plug hole **(see illustration)**.

7   Crank the engine over at least seven compression strokes and watch the gauge. The compression should build up quickly in a healthy engine. Low compression on the first

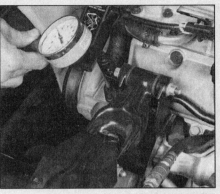

3.6 A compression gauge with a threaded fitting for the spark plug hole is preferred over the type that requires hand pressure to maintain the seal - be sure to open the throttle valve as far as possible during the compression check

stroke, followed by gradually increasing pressure on successive strokes, indicates worn piston rings. A low compression reading on the first stroke, which doesn't build up during successive strokes, indicates leaking valves or a blown head gasket (a cracked head could also be the cause). Deposits on the undersides of the valve heads can also cause low compression. Record the highest gauge reading obtained.

8   Repeat the procedure for the remaining cylinders, turning the engine over for the same length of time for each cylinder, and compare the results to this Chapter's Specifications.

9   If the readings are below normal, add some engine oil (about three squirts from a plunger-type oil can) to each cylinder, through the spark plug hole, and repeat the test.

10   If the compression increases after the oil is added, the piston rings are definitely worn. If the compression doesn't increase significantly, the leakage is occurring at the valves or head gasket. Leakage past the valves may be caused by burned valve seats and/or faces or warped, cracked or bent valves.

11   If two adjacent cylinders have equally low compression, there's a strong possibility the head gasket between them is blown. The appearance of coolant in the combustion chambers or the crankcase would verify this condition.

12   If one cylinder is about 20-percent lower than the others, and the engine has a slightly rough idle, a worn exhaust lobe on the camshaft could be the cause.

13   If the compression is unusually high, the combustion chambers are probably coated with carbon deposits. If that's the case, the cylinder heads should be removed and decarbonized.

14   If compression is way down or varies greatly between cylinders, it would be a good idea to have a leak-down test performed by an automotive repair shop. This test will pinpoint exactly where the leakage is occurring and how severe it is.

15   Install the fuses and drive the vehicle to restore the "block learn" memory.

4 Vacuum gauge diagnostic checks

A vacuum gauge provides valuable information about what is going on in the engine at a low cost. You can check for worn rings or cylinder walls, leaking head or intake manifold gaskets, incorrect carburetor adjustments, restricted exhaust, stuck or burned valves, weak valve springs, improper ignition or valve timing and ignition problems.

Unfortunately, vacuum gauge readings are easy to misinterpret, so they should be used in conjunction with other tests to confirm the diagnosis.

Both the gauge readings and the rate of needle movement are important for accurate interpretation. Most gauges measure vacuum in inches of mercury (in-Hg). As vacuum increases (or atmospheric pressure decreases), the reading will increase. Also, for every 1,000-foot increase in elevation above sea level, the gauge readings will decrease about one inch of mercury.

Connect the vacuum gauge directly to intake manifold vacuum, not to ported (carburetor) vacuum. Be sure no hoses are left disconnected during the test or false readings will result.

Before you begin the test, allow the engine to warm up completely. Block the wheels and set the parking brake. With the transmission in Park, start the engine and allow it to run at normal idle speed.

Read the vacuum gauge; an average, healthy engine should normally produce about 17 to 22 inches of vacuum with a fairly steady needle. Refer to the following vacuum gauge readings and what they indicate about the engine's condition:

1   A low, steady reading usually indicates a leaking gasket between the intake manifold and carburetor or throttle body, a leaky vacuum hose, late ignition timing or incorrect camshaft timing. Eliminate all other possible causes, utilizing the tests provided in this Chapter before you remove the timing chain cover to check the timing marks.

2   If the reading is three to eight inches below normal and it fluctuates at that low reading, suspect an intake manifold gasket leak at an intake port.

3   If the needle has regular drops of about two to four inches at a steady rate, the valves are probably leaking. Perform a compression or leak-down test to confirm this.

4   An irregular drop or down-flick of the needle can be caused by a sticking valve or an ignition misfire. Perform a compression or leak-down test and read the spark plugs.

5   A rapid vibration of about four inches-Hg vibration at idle combined with exhaust smoke indicates worn valve guides. Perform a leak-down test to confirm this. If the rapid vibration occurs with an increase in engine speed, check for a leaking intake manifold gasket or head gasket, weak valve springs, burned valves or ignition misfire.

6   A slight fluctuation, say one inch up and down, may mean ignition problems. Check all the usual tune-up items and, if necessary, run the engine on an ignition analyzer.

7   If there is a large fluctuation, perform a compression or leak-down test to look for a weak or dead cylinder or a blown head gasket.

8   If the needle moves slowly through a wide range, check for a clogged PCV system, incorrect idle fuel mixture, throttle body or intake manifold gasket leaks.

9   Check for a slow return after revving the engine by quickly snapping the throttle open until the engine reaches about 2,500 rpm and let it shut. Normally the reading should drop to near zero, rise above normal idle reading (about 5 in-Hg over) and then return to the previous idle reading. If the vacuum returns slowly and doesn't peak when the throttle is snapped shut, the rings may be worn. If there is a long delay, look for a restricted exhaust system (often the muffler or catalytic converter). An easy way to check this is to temporarily disconnect the exhaust ahead of the suspected part and re-test.

5 Engine removal - methods and precautions

If you've decided the engine must be removed for overhaul or major repair work, several preliminary steps should be taken. Locating a suitable place to work is extremely important. Adequate work space, along with storage space for the vehicle, will be needed.

Cleaning the engine compartment and engine before beginning the Removal procedure will help keep tools clean and organized. An engine hoist will also be necessary. Safety is of primary importance, considering the potential hazards involved in removing the engine from this vehicle.

If the engine is being removed by a novice, a helper should be available. Advice and aid from someone more experienced would also be helpful. There are many instances when one person cannot simultaneously perform all of the operations required when lifting the engine out of the vehicle.

Plan the operation ahead of time. Arrange for or obtain all of the tools and equipment you'll need prior to beginning the job. Some of the equipment necessary to perform engine removal and installation safely and with relative ease in addition to a hydraulic jack, jack stands and an engine hoist) are a complete sets of wrenches and sockets as described in the front of this manual, wooden blocks and plenty of rags and cleaning solvent for mopping up spilled oil, coolant and gasoline.

Plan for the vehicle to be out of use for quite a while. A machine shop will be required to perform some of the work which the do-it-yourselfer can't accomplish without special equipment. These shops often have a busy schedule, so it would be a good idea to consult them before removing the engine in order to accurately estimate the amount of time required to rebuild or repair components that may need work.

Always be extremely careful when removing and installing the engine. Serious injury can result from careless actions. Plan ahead, take your time and a job of this nature, although major, can be accomplished successfully. **Note:** *Because it may be some time before you reinstall the engine, it is very helpful to make sketches or take photos of various accessory mountings and wiring hookups before removing the engine.*

6 Engine - removal and installation

Warning 1: *The models covered by this manual are equipped with airbags. Always disable the airbag system before working in the vicinity of the impact sensors, steering column or instrument panel to avoid the possibility of accidental deployment of the airbag(s), which could cause personal injury (see Chapter 12). The yellow wires and connectors routed through the instrument panel and, on 1995 and earlier models, to the front of the vehicle, are for this system. Do not use electrical test equipment on these yellow wires or tamper with them in any way.*
Warning 2: *Gasoline is extremely flammable, so take extra precautions when you work on any part of the fuel system. Don't smoke or allow open flames or bare light bulbs near the work area, and don't work in a garage where a gas-type appliance (such as a water heater or a clothes dryer) is present. Since gasoline is carcinogenic, wear latex gloves when there's a possibility of being exposed to fuel, and, if you spill any fuel on your skin, rinse it off immediately with soap and water. Mop up any spills immediately and do not store fuel-soaked rags where they could ignite. The fuel system is under constant pressure, so, if any fuel lines are to be disconnected, the fuel pressure in the system must be relieved first. When you perform any kind of work on the fuel system, wear safety glasses and have a Class B type fire extinguisher on hand.*
Warning 3: *The air conditioning system is under high pressure - have a dealer service department or service station evacuate the system and recapture the refrigerant before disconnecting any of the hoses or fittings.*

Removal

Refer to illustrations 6.4, 6.8, 6.12 and 6.21
Note 1: *The procedure outlined below illustrates the necessary steps to remove the engine traditionally, i.e. from above with an engine hoist.*
Note 2: *On 1999 models, always replace the accelerator cable whenever the engine is removed from the vehicle. Move the cruise control cable out of the way to avoid any damage. If the cruise control cable is kinked during engine removal, replace the cable.*

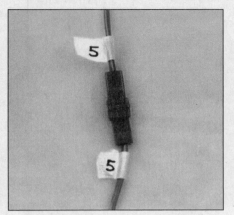

6.4 Label each wire before unplugging the connector

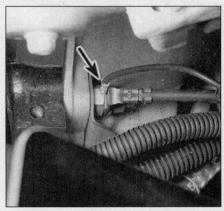

6.8 While the vehicle is raised, disconnect any wiring harnesses attached to the block

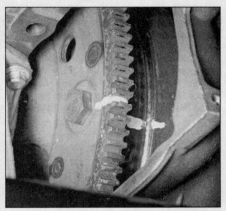

6.12 Paint or scribe alignment marks on the driveplate and the torque converter to ensure that the two components are still in balance when they're reassembled

1   Relieve the fuel system pressure (see Chapter 4), then disconnect the negative cable from the battery. **Caution:** *On models equipped with a Delco Theftlock audio system, be sure the lockout feature is turned off before performing any procedure which requires disconnecting the battery.*

2   Cover the fenders and cowl. Special pads are available to protect the fenders, but an old bedspread or blanket will also work. Remove the hood (see Chapter 11).

3   Remove the air intake duct assembly (see Chapter 4).

4   To ensure correct reassembly, label each vacuum line, emission system hose, electrical connector, ground strap and fuel line. Pieces of masking tape with numbers or letters written on them prevent confusion at assembly time **(see illustration)**. Or sketch the engine compartment routing of lines, hoses and wires.

5   Drain the cooling system (see Chapter 1) and label and detach all coolant hoses from the engine. Remove the coolant recovery tank (see Chapter 3).

6   Disconnect the throttle and cruise control cables (see Chapter 4) and TV cable (see Chapter 7).

7   Detach the air conditioning compressor from its mounting bracket and tie it out of the way, with the hoses still attached.

8   Raise the vehicle and suitably support it on jackstands. While raised, perform the disassembly procedures that can be done only from underneath, such as disconnecting the exhaust, disconnecting the transmission cooler lines where they are held by a clip to one of the oil pan bolts and disconnecting wiring harnesses attached to the block **(see illustration)**.

9   Refer to the last section ("Engine mounts") in Part A, B or C to remove the frame-side nuts from the engine mount (do not disconnect the transaxle mount). Support the transaxle with a suitable jack and block of wood, and remove the brace between the engine and transaxle.

10   Drain the engine oil and remove the filter (see Chapter 1). On 3.8L engines, remove the oil filter adapter housing, which is attached to

the timing chain cover with four bolts. The cover is spring loaded, so remove the bolts while keeping pressure on the cover, then release the spring pressure carefully.

11   Remove the starter (see Chapter 5). Remove the driveplate access cover.

12   Make an alignment mark between the driveplate and the torque converter **(see illustration)**, then rotate the crankshaft and remove the converter bolts.

13   Remove the lower bellhousing to-engine bolt/stud.

14   Remove the transmission jack, lower the vehicle and replace the floor jack under the transaxle, then support the engine with an engine hoist from above.

15   Remove the heater hoses, radiator hoses, cooling fans and radiator (see Chapter 3).

16   Unbolt the power steering pump and bracket and tie them out of the way.

17   Remove the intake manifold plenum (see Chapter 4).

18   Raise the engine enough to take the weight off the engine mounts and remove the engine torque struts (see Part A, B or C of this Chapter).

19   Working at the back of the engine, remove the remaining bellhousing bolts/stud.

20   Raise the engine and pull it forward to free it from the torque converter.

21   Tie the wiring harnesses out of the way, raise the engine with the hoist, and with a

combination of tilting, twisting and raising, move the engine around any obstructions and pull it out of the vehicle, raising it high enough to clear the front of the body **(see illustration)**.

22   Remove the driveplate or flywheel (see Part A) while the engine is out of the vehicle but still on the hoist, and mount the engine on an engine stand.

Installation

23   While the engine is out, check the engine mounts and the transmission mount (see Chapter 7). If they're worn or damaged, replace them.

24   Carefully lower the engine, twisting it to clear any harnesses or obstructions, until the converter snout lines up and the bellhousing-to-engine bolts can be inserted. **Caution:** *DO NOT use the transmission-to-engine bolts to force the transmission and engine together. Take great care when mating the torque converter to the driveplate, following the procedure outlined in Chapter 7. Make sure the alignment marks you made on the driveplate and the torque converter during removal are lined up.*

25   Install the driveplate-to-torque converter bolts and tighten them to the torque listed in Chapter 7 Specifications.

26   Reinstall the remaining components in

6.21 With the accessories tied out of the way and the engine mount through-bolts removed, raise the engine with the hoist

the reverse order of removal. Double-check to make sure everything is hooked up right, using the sketches or photos taken earlier to go by.

27   Add coolant, oil, power steering and transmission fluid as needed.

28   Run the engine and check for leaks and proper operation of all accessories, then install the hood and test drive the vehicle.

7   Engine rebuilding alternatives

The home mechanic is faced with a number of options when performing an engine overhaul. The decision to replace the engine block, piston/connecting rod assemblies and crankshaft depends on a number of factors, with the number one consideration being the condition of the block. Other considerations are cost, access to machine shop facilities, parts availability, time required to complete the project and the extent of prior mechanical experience.

Some of the rebuilding alternatives include:

Individual parts - If the inspection procedures reveal the engine block and most engine components are in reusable condition, purchasing individual parts may be the most economical alternative. The block, crankshaft and piston/connecting rod assemblies should all be inspected carefully. Even if the block shows little wear, the cylinder bores should be surface-honed.

Short-block - A short-block consists of an engine block with a crankshaft and piston/connecting rod assemblies already installed. All new bearings are incorporated and all clearances will be correct. The existing camshaft, valve train components, cylinder heads and external parts can be bolted to the short block with little or no machine shop work necessary. Some rebuilding companies include a new timing chain, camshaft and lifters with their short-block assemblies.

Long-block - A long-block consists of a short block plus an oil pump, oil pan, cylinder heads, rocker arm covers, camshaft and valve train components, timing sprockets and chain and timing chain cover. All components are installed with new bearings, seals and gaskets incorporated throughout. The installation of manifolds and external parts is all that's necessary. Give careful thought to which alternative is best for you and discuss the situation with local automotive machine shops, auto parts dealers and experienced rebuilders before ordering or purchasing replacement parts.

8   Engine overhaul - disassembly sequence

1   It's much easier to disassemble and work on the engine if it's mounted on a portable engine stand. A stand can often be rented quite cheaply from an equipment rental yard. Before it's mounted on a stand,

9.2 A small plastic bag, with an appropriate label, can be used to store the valve train components so they can be kept together and reinstalled in the original positions

the flywheel/driveplate should be removed from the engine.

2   If a stand isn't available, it's possible to disassemble the engine with it blocked up on the floor. Be extra careful not to tip or drop the engine when working without a stand.

3   If you're going to obtain a rebuilt engine, all external components must come off first, to be transferred to the replacement engine, just as they will if you're doing a complete engine overhaul yourself. These include:

Alternator and brackets
Emissions control components
Ignition coil/module assembly, spark
   plug wires and spark plugs
Thermostat and housing cover
Water pump
Engine front cover
Fuel injection components
Intake/exhaust manifolds
Oil filter
Engine mounts
Flywheel/driveplate

Note: When removing the external components from the engine, pay close attention to details that may be helpful or important during installation. Note the installed position of gaskets, seals, spacers, pins, brackets, washers, bolts and other small items.

4   If you're obtaining a short-block, then the cylinder heads, oil pan and oil pump will have to be removed as well. See Engine rebuilding alternatives for additional information regarding the different possibilities to be considered.

5   If you're planning a complete overhaul, the engine must be disassembled and the internal components removed in the following general order:

Intake and exhaust manifolds
Valve covers
Rocker arms and pushrods
Valve lifters
Cylinder heads
Timing chain cover and oil pump
Timing chain and sprockets
Camshaft

9.3 Use a valve spring compressor to compress the spring, then remove the keepers from the valve stem

Balance shaft (3800 engine only)
Oil pan
Piston/connecting rod assemblies
Crankshaft and main bearings

6   Before beginning the disassembly and overhaul procedures, make sure the following items are available. Also, refer to Engine overhaul - reassembly sequence for a list of tools and materials needed for engine reassembly.

Common hand tools
Small cardboard boxes or plastic bags
   for storing parts
Gasket scraper
Ridge reamer
Engine balancer puller
Micrometers
Telescoping gauges
Dial indicator set
Valve spring compressor
Cylinder surfacing hone
Piston ring groove-cleaning tool
Electric drill motor
Tap and die set
Wire brushes
Oil gallery brushes
Cleaning solvent

9   Cylinder head - disassembly

Refer to illustrations 9.2, 9.3 and 9.4
Note: New and rebuilt cylinder heads are commonly available for most engines at dealerships and auto parts stores. Due to the fact that some specialized tools are necessary for the disassembly and inspection procedures, and replacement parts aren't always readily available, it may be more practical and economical for the home mechanic to purchase replacement heads rather than taking the time to disassemble, inspect and recondition the originals.

1   Cylinder head disassembly involves removal of the intake and exhaust valves and related components. Remove the rocker arm bolts, pivots and rocker arms from the cylinder heads. Label the parts or store them

separately so they can be reinstalled in their original locations.

2   Before the valves are removed, arrange to label and store them, along with their related components, so they can be kept separate and reinstalled in their original locations **(see illustration)**.

3   Compress the springs on the first valve with a spring compressor and remove the keepers **(see illustration)**. Carefully release the valve spring compressor and remove the retainer, the spring and the spring seat (if used).

4   Pull the valve out of the head, then remove the oil seal from the guide. If the valve binds in the guide (won't pull through), push it back into the head and deburr the area around the keeper groove with a fine file or whetstone **(see illustration)**.

5   Repeat the procedure for the remaining valves. Remember to keep all the parts for each valve together so they can be reinstalled in the same locations.

6   Once the valves and related components have been removed and stored in an organized manner, the heads should be thoroughly cleaned and inspected. If a complete engine overhaul is being done, finish the engine disassembly procedures before beginning the cylinder head cleaning and inspection process.

10   Cylinder head - cleaning and inspection

1   Thorough cleaning of the cylinder heads and related valve train components, followed by a detailed inspection, will enable you to decide how much valve service work must be done during the engine overhaul. **Note:** *If the engine was severely overheated, the cylinder head is probably warped* (see Step 12).

Cleaning

2   Scrape all traces of old gasket material and sealant off the head gasket, intake manifold and exhaust manifold mating surfaces. Be very careful not to gouge the cylinder head. Special gasket-removal solvents that soften gaskets and make removal much easier are available at auto parts stores.

3   Remove all built-up scale from the coolant passages.

4   Run a stiff wire brush through the various holes to remove deposits that may have formed in them.

5   Run an appropriate-size tap into each of the threaded holes to remove corrosion and thread sealant that may be present. If compressed air is available, use it to clear the holes of debris produced by this operation. **Warning:** *Wear eye protection when using compressed air!*

6   Clean the rocker arm pivot stud or bolt threads with a wire brush.

7   Clean the cylinder head with solvent and dry it thoroughly. Compressed air will speed the drying process and ensure that all holes

9.4 If the valve won't pull through the guide, deburr the edge of the stem end and the area around the top of the keeper groove with a file or whetstone

and recessed areas are clean. **Note:** *Decarbonizing chemicals are available and may prove very useful when cleaning cylinder heads and valve train components. They're very caustic and should be used with caution. Be sure to follow the instructions on the container.*

8   Clean the rocker arms, pivots, bolts and pushrods with solvent and dry them thoroughly (don't mix them up during the cleaning process). Compressed air will speed the drying process and can be used to clean out the oil passages.

9   Clean all the valve springs, keepers and retainers with solvent and dry them thoroughly. Do the components from one valve at a time to avoid mixing up the parts.

10   Scrape off any heavy deposits that may have formed on the valves, then use a motorized wire brush to remove deposits from the valve heads and stems. Again, make sure the valves don't get mixed up.

Inspection

Note: *Be sure to perform all of the following inspection procedures before concluding machine shop work is required. Make a list of the items that need attention.*

Cylinder head

Refer to illustrations 10.12 and 10.14

11   Inspect the head very carefully for cracks, evidence of coolant leakage and other damage. If cracks are found, check with an automotive machine shop concerning repair. If repair isn't possible, a new cylinder head must be obtained.

12   Using a straightedge and feeler gauge, check the head gasket mating surface for warpage **(see illustration)**. If the warpage exceeds the limit in this Chapter's Specifications, it can be resurfaced at an automotive machine shop. **Note:** *If the heads are resurfaced, the intake manifold flanges will also require machining.*

13   Examine the valve seats in each of the combustion chambers. If they're pitted, cracked or burned, the head will require valve

10.12 Check the cylinder head gasket surface for warpage by trying to slip a feeler gauge under the straightedge (see this Chapter's Specifications for the maximum warpage allowed and use a feeler gauge of that thickness)

service that's beyond the scope of the home mechanic.

14   Check the valve stem-to-guide clearance by measuring the lateral movement of the valve stem with a dial indicator attached securely to the head **(see illustration)**. The valve must be in the guide and approximately 1/16-inch off the seat. The total valve stem movement indicated by the gauge needle must be divided by two to obtain the actual clearance. After this is done, if there's still some doubt regarding the condition of the valve guides, they should be checked by an automotive machine shop (the cost should be minimal).

Valves

Refer to illustrations 10.15 and 10.16

15   Carefully inspect each valve face for uneven wear, deformation, cracks, pits and burned areas. Check the valve stem for scuffing and galling and the neck for cracks. Rotate the valve and check for any obvious

10.14 A dial indicator can be used to determine the valve stem-to-guide clearance (move the valve stem as indicated by the arrows)

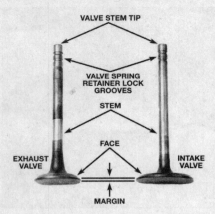

10.15 Check for valve wear at the points shown here

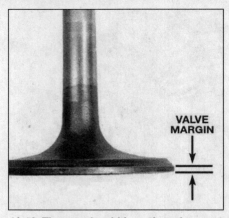

10.16 The margin width on the valve must be as specified (if no margin exists, the valve cannot be re-used)

10.17 Measure the free length of each valve spring with a dial or vernier caliper

indication that it's bent. Look for pits and excessive wear on the end of the stem. The presence of any of these conditions **(see illustration)** indicates the need for valve service by an automotive machine shop.

16   Measure the margin width on each valve **(see illustration)**. Any valve with a margin narrower than specified in this Chapter will have to be replaced with a new one.

Valve components

Refer to illustrations 10.17 and 10.18

17   Check each valve spring for wear (on the ends) and pits. Measure the free length and compare it to this Chapter's Specifications **(see illustration)**. Any springs that are shorter than specified have sagged and shouldn't be re-used. The tension of all springs should be checked with a special fixture before deciding they're suitable for use in a rebuilt engine (take the springs to an automotive machine shop for this check).

18   Stand each spring on a flat surface and check it for squareness **(see illustration)**. If any of the springs are distorted or sagged, replace all of them with new parts.

19   Check the spring retainers and keepers for obvious wear and cracks. Any questionable parts should be replaced with new ones, as extensive damage will occur if they fail during engine operation.

10.18 Check each valve spring for squareness

Rocker arm components

20   Check the rocker arm faces (the areas that contact the pushrod ends and valve stems) for pits, wear, galling, score marks and rough spots. Check the rocker arm pivot contact areas and pivots as well. Look for cracks in each rocker arm and bolt.

21   Inspect the pushrod ends for scuffing and excessive wear. Roll each pushrod on a flat surface, like a piece of plate glass, to determine if it's bent.

22   Check the rocker arm bolt holes in the cylinder heads for damaged threads.

23   Any damaged or excessively worn parts must be replaced with new ones.

All components

24   If the inspection process indicates the valve components are in generally poor condition and worn beyond the limits specified, which is usually the case in an engine that's being overhauled, reassemble the valves in the cylinder head (see Section 11 for valve servicing recommendations).

11   Valves - servicing

1   Because of the complex nature of the job and the special tools and equipment needed, servicing of the valves, the valve seats and the valve guides, commonly known as a valve job, should be done by a professional.

2   The home mechanic can remove and disassemble the head, do the initial cleaning and inspection, then reassemble and deliver it to a dealer service department or an automotive machine shop for the actual service work. Doing the inspection will enable you to see what condition the head and valvetrain components are in and will ensure that you know what work and new parts are required when dealing with an automotive machine shop.

3   The dealer service department, or

automotive machine shop, will remove the valves and springs, recondition or replace the valves and valve seats, recondition the valve guides, check and replace the valve springs, spring retainers and keepers (as necessary), replace the valve seals with new ones, reassemble the valve components and make sure the installed spring height is correct. The cylinder head gasket surface will also be resurfaced if it's warped.

4   After the valve job has been performed by a professional, the head will be in like new condition. When the head is returned, be sure to clean it again before installation on the engine to remove any metal particles and abrasive grit that may still be present from the valve service or head resurfacing operations. Use compressed air, if available, to blow out all the oil holes and passages.

12   Cylinder head - reassembly

Refer to illustrations 12.6 and 12.7

1   Regardless of whether or not the head was sent to an automotive repair shop for valve servicing, make sure it's clean before beginning reassembly.

2   If the head was sent out for valve servicing, the valves and related components will already be in place. Begin the reassembly procedure with Step 8.

3   Beginning at one end of the head, lubricate and install the first valve. Apply moly-base grease or clean engine oil to the valve stem.

4   Install the shims, if originally installed, before the valve seals.

5   Install new seals on each of the valve guides. Gently tap each seal into place until it's completely seated on the guide. Many seal sets come with a plastic installer, but use hand pressure. Do not hammer on the seals or they could be driven down too far and subsequently leak. Don't twist or cock the seals during installation or they won't seal properly on the valve stems.

6   The V6 components may be installed in

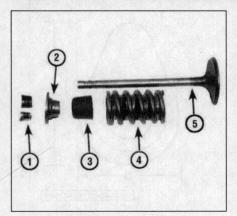

12.6 Typical valve components

1	Keepers	4	Spring
2	Retainer	5	Valve
3	Oil seal		

12.7 Apply a small dab of grease to each keeper as shown here before Installation - it'll hold them in place on the valve stem as the spring is released

13.1 Remove the bolt (arrow) and pull out the oil pump drive

the following order **(see illustration)**:

    Shims
    Seals (intake only)
    Valves, followed by the stem O-rings
    Spring dampers
    Springs
    Oil shedder shields (exhaust only)
    Retainers
    Keepers

7   Compress the springs with a valve spring compressor and carefully install the keepers in the groove, then slowly release the compressor and make sure the keepers seat properly. Apply a small dab of grease to each keeper to hold it in place if necessary **(see illustration)**. Tap the valve stem tips with a plastic hammer to seat the keepers, if necessary.

8   Repeat the procedure for the remaining valves. Be sure to return the components to their original locations - don't mix them up!

9   Check the installed valve spring height with a ruler graduated in 1/32-inch increments or a dial caliper. If the head was sent out for service work, the installed height should be correct (but don't automatically assume it is). The measurement is taken from the top of each spring seat or top shim to the

bottom of the retainer. If the height is greater than specified in this Chapter, shims can be added under the springs to correct it. **Caution:** *Do not, under any circumstances, shim the springs to the point where the installed height is less than specified.*

10   Apply moly-base grease to the rocker arm faces and the pivots, then install the rocker arms and pivots on the cylinder heads. Tighten the bolts/nuts finger-tight.

13 Camshaft (3.1L/3.4L OHV and 3800), intermediate shaft (3.4L DOHC) and balance shaft (3800) - removal and inspection

Removal

Camshaft (3.1L/3.4L OHV and 3800) and intermediate shaft (3.4L DOHC)

Refer to illustrations 13.1 and 13.3
Note: *The intermediate shaft on 3.4L DOHC engines is removed and installed much like a conventional camshaft, although it does not operate the lifters or valves.*

1   Remove the bolt and clamp holding the oil pump drive and pull the oil pump drive straight up and out of the block **(see illustration)**. Remove the camshaft position sensor (see Chapter 6).

2   Refer to Chapter 2 Part A or Part B and remove the timing chain and sprockets (lifters should already be removed and stored in a marked container).

3   Remove the bolts holding the camshaft (or intermediate shaft) thrust plate to the block **(see illustration)** and remove the thrust plate.

4   Slide the camshaft or intermediate shaft straight out of the engine, using a long bolt (with the same thread as the camshaft sprocket bolt) screwed into the front of the camshaft as a "handle." Support the shaft near the block and be careful not to scrape or nick the bearings.

Balance shaft (3800 only)
Refer to illustrations 13.8 and 13.9

5   Refer to Chapter 2 Part C and remove the timing chain and sprockets (lifters should already be removed and stored in marked plastic bags).

6   Check the gear backlash between the balance shaft drive gear (behind the camshaft sprocket) and the balance shaft driven gear. Set up a dial indicator against the top teeth of the balance shaft driven gear (the one on the front of the balance shaft) and rock the gear by hand. Compare the backlash to this Chapter's Specifications. The gears will have to be replaced if the backlash is greater than specified.

7   Remove the balance shaft drive gear (behind the camshaft sprocket). Set up a dial indicator on the nose of the balance shaft and zero it. Reaching inside the lifter valley, grab the balance shaft and move it forward and back in the block while watching the dial indicator. Compare this endplay measurement with this Chapter's Specifications. If it is incorrect, a new balance shaft thrust plate will have to be installed.

8   Remove the two balance shaft thrust plate bolts and take off the thrust plate **(see illustration)**.

13.3 Remove the retaining bolts and the camshaft thrust plate

13.8 Remove the retaining bolts and the balance shaft thrust plate

13.9 A slide hammer must be threaded into the front of the balance shaft to pull the balance shaft front bearing out of the block

13.11a Measure the camshaft bearing journals with a micrometer

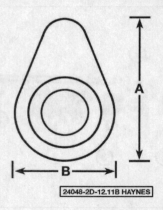

13.11b Measure the camshaft lobe maximum diameter (A) and the minimum (B) - subtract (B) from (A), the difference is the lobe lift

9   The balance shaft's front bearing fits tightly into the front of the block, and a slide hammer must be used to remove the shaft and its bearing **(see illustration)**. Once the bearing is free of the block, withdraw the balance shaft straight out by hand, being careful to not cock it against its rear bearing.

Inspection

Refer to illustrations 13.11a and 13.11b

10   After the camshaft, intermediate shaft or balance shaft has been removed, clean it with solvent and dry it, then inspect the bearing journals for uneven wear, pitting and evidence of seizure. If the journals are damaged, the bearing inserts in the block are probably damaged as well. Both the shaft and bearings will have to be replaced.

11   Measure the bearing journals with a micrometer **(see illustration)** to determine whether they are excessively worn or out-of-round. Measure the camshaft lobes also to check for wear. Measure the camshaft lobes at their highest point, then subtract the measurement of the lobe at its smallest diameter - the difference is the lobe lift **(see illustration)**.

12   Inspect the camshaft lobes for heat discoloration, score marks, chipped areas,

pitting and uneven wear. If the lobes are in good condition and if the lobe lift measurements are as specified, you can reuse the camshaft.

13   Check the camshaft bearings in the block for wear and damage. Look for galling, pitting and discolored areas.

14   The inside diameter of each bearing can be determined with a small hole gauge and outside micrometer or an inside micrometer. Subtract the camshaft bearing journal diameter(s) from the corresponding bearing inside diameter(s) to obtain the bearing oil clearance. If it's excessive, new bearings will be required regardless of the condition of the originals.

15   Balance shaft and camshaft bearing replacement requires special tools and expertise that place it outside the scope of the home mechanic. Take the block to an automotive machine shop to ensure the job is done correctly.

14   Pistons and connecting rods - removal

Refer to illustrations 14.1, 14.3, 14.4 and 14.6
Note: *Prior to removing the piston/connecting rod assemblies, remove the cylinder heads,*

14.1 A ridge reamer is required to remove the ridge from the top of each cylinder - do this before removing the pistons!

14.3 Check the connecting rod side clearance with a feeler gauge as shown

the oil pan and the oil pump by referring to the appropriate Sections in chapter 2 Part A, B or C.

1   Use your fingernail to feel if a ridge has formed at the upper limit of ring travel (about 1/4-inch down from the top of each cylinder). If carbon deposits or cylinder wear have produced ridges, they must be completely removed with a special tool **(see illustration)**. Follow the manufacturer's instructions provided with the tool. Failure to remove the ridges before attempting to remove the piston/connecting rod assemblies may result in piston breakage.

2   After the cylinder ridges have been removed, turn the engine upside-down so the crankshaft is facing up. On 3.1L and 3.4L engines, remove the oil baffle plate bolted to the main caps.

3   Before the connecting rods are removed, check the endplay with feeler gauges. Slide them between the first connecting rod and the crankshaft throw until the play is removed **(see illustration)**. The endplay is equal to the thickness of the feeler gauge(s). If the endplay exceeds the service limit, new connecting rods will be required. If new rods (or a new crankshaft) are installed, the endplay may fall under the minimum specified in this Chapter (if it does, the rods will have to be machined to restore it - consult an automotive machine shop for advice if necessary). Repeat the procedure for the remaining connecting rods.

4   Check the connecting rods and caps for identification marks. If they aren't plainly marked, use a small center-punch **(see illustration)** to make the appropriate number of indentations on each rod and cap (1, 2, 3, etc., depending on the cylinder they're associated with).

5   Loosen each of the connecting rod cap nuts 1/2-turn at a time until they can be removed by hand. Remove the number one connecting rod cap and bearing insert. Don't drop the bearing insert out of the cap.

6   Slip a short length of plastic or rubber hose over each connecting rod cap bolt to

14.4 Mark the rod bearing caps in order from the front of the engine to the rear (one mark for the front cap, two for the second one and so on)

14.6 To prevent damage to the crankshaft journals and cylinder walls, slip sections of rubber or plastic hose over the rod bolts before removing the pistons/rods

15.3 Checking crankshaft endplay with a feeler gauge

15.4 The arrow on the main bearing cap indicates the front of the engine

protect the crankshaft journal and cylinder wall as the piston is removed **(see illustration)**.

7   Remove the bearing insert and push the connecting rod/piston assembly out through the top of the engine. Use a wooden or plastic hammer handle to push on the upper bearing surface in the connecting rod. If resistance is felt, double-check to make sure all of the ridge was removed from the cylinder.

8   Repeat the procedure for the remaining cylinders.

9   After removal, reassemble the connecting rod caps and bearing inserts in their respective connecting rods and install the cap nuts finger tight. Leaving the old bearing inserts in place until reassembly will help prevent the connecting rod bearing surfaces from being accidentally nicked or gouged.

10   Don't separate the pistons from the connecting rods.

15 Crankshaft - removal

Refer to illustrations 15.3 and 15.4
Note: *The crankshaft can be removed only after the engine has been removed from the vehicle. It's assumed the flywheel/driveplate, timing chain, oil pan, oil pump and piston/connecting rod assemblies have already been removed. Also remove the 7X crankshaft position sensor from the side of the block (see Chapter 6).The rear main oil seal retainer must also be removed first.*

1   Before the crankshaft is removed, check the endplay. Mount a dial indicator with the stem in line with the crankshaft and touching one of the crank throws.

2   Push the crankshaft all the way to the rear and zero the dial indicator. Next, pry the crankshaft to the front as far as possible and check the reading on the dial indicator. The distance it moves is the endplay. If it's

greater than listed in this Chapter's Specifications, check the crankshaft thrust surfaces for wear. If no wear is evident, new main bearings should correct the endplay.

3   If a dial indicator isn't available, feeler gauges can be used. Gently pry or push the crankshaft all the way to the front of the engine. Slip feeler gauges between the crankshaft and the front face of the thrust main bearing to determine the clearance **(see illustration)**. **Note:** *The thrust bearing is located at the number three main bearing cap on 3.1L and 3.4L engines, and on the number two cap on 3800 engines.*

4   Check the main bearing caps to see if they're marked to indicate their locations. They should be numbered consecutively from the front of the engine to the rear. If they aren't, mark them with number stamping dies or a center-punch. Main bearing caps generally have a cast-in arrow, which points to the front of the engine **(see illustration)**. Loosen the main bearing cap bolts 1/4-turn at a time each, until they can be removed by hand. Note if any stud bolts are used and make sure they're returned to their original locations when the crankshaft is reinstalled.

5   Gently tap the caps with a soft-face hammer, then separate them from the engine block. If necessary, use the bolts as levers to remove the caps. Try not to drop the bearing inserts if they come out with the caps. **Note:** *Main bearing caps on 3.8L engines are press fit and should be removed with a slide hammer and a special tool available from the manufacturer that fits into the main bearing cap holes and works with the slide hammer. The factory cautions that failure to follow this procedure may result in damage to the caps, bearings and engine. Also, the three front main bearing caps on 3.8L engines have a horizontal bolt on each end of the cap, in addition to the usual two main bearing cap bolts, that must not be overlooked.*

6   Carefully lift the crankshaft straight out of the engine. It may be a good idea to have an assistant available, since the crankshaft is

quite heavy. With the bearing inserts in place in the engine block and main bearing caps, return the caps to their respective locations on the engine block and tighten the bolts finger tight.

16 Engine block - cleaning

Refer to illustrations 16.4a, 16.4b, 16.8 and 16.10

1   Remove the main bearing caps and separate the bearing inserts from the caps and the engine block. Tag the bearings, indicating which cylinder they were removed from and whether they were in the cap or the block, then set them aside.

2   Using a gasket scraper, remove all traces of gasket material from the engine block. Be very careful not to nick or gouge the gasket sealing surfaces.

3   Remove all of the covers and threaded oil gallery plugs from the block. The plugs are usually very tight - they may have to be drilled out and the holes retapped. Use new plugs when the engine is reassembled.

4   Remove the core plugs from the engine block. To do this, knock one side of the plugs

16.4a A hammer and large punch can be used to knock the core plugs sideways in their bores

16.4b Pull the core plugs from the block with pliers

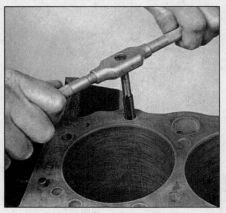

16.8 All bolt holes in the block - particularly the main bearing cap and head bolt holes - should be cleaned and restored with a tap (be sure to remove debris from the holes after this is done)

into the block with a hammer and punch, then grasp them with large pliers and pull them out **(see illustrations)**.

5   If the engine is extremely dirty, it should be taken to an automotive machine shop to be cleaned. **Note:** *If the block is cleaned in a caustic-solution hot tank, this will ruin any camshaft bearings left in the block. If the engine is being rebuilt, these bearings should be replaced anyway.*

6   After the block is returned, clean all oil holes and oil galleries one more time. Brushes specifically designed for this purpose are available at most auto parts stores. Flush the passages with warm water until the water runs clear, dry the block thoroughly and wipe all machined surfaces with a light, rust preventive oil. If you have access to compressed air, use it to speed the drying process and blow out all the oil holes and galleries. **Warning:** *Wear eye protection when using compressed air!*

7   If the block isn't extremely dirty or sludged up, you can do an adequate cleaning job with hot soapy water and a stiff brush. Take plenty of time and do a thorough job. Regardless of the cleaning method used, be sure to clean all oil holes and galleries very

16.10 A large socket on an extension can be used to drive the new core plugs into the bores

thoroughly, dry the block completely and coat all machined surfaces with light oil.

8   The threaded holes in the block must be clean to ensure accurate torque readings during reassembly. Run the proper size tap into each of the holes to remove rust, corrosion, thread sealant or sludge and restore damaged threads **(see illustration)**. If possible, use compressed air to clear the holes of debris produced by this operation. Now is a good time to clean the threads on the head bolts and the main bearing cap bolts as well.

9   Reinstall the main bearing caps and tighten the bolts finger tight.

10   After coating the sealing surfaces of the new core plugs with a non-hardening sealant (such as Permatex no. 2), install them in the engine block **(see illustration)**. Make sure they're driven in straight and seated properly or leakage could result. Special tools are available for this purpose, but a large socket, with an outside diameter that will just slip into the core plug, a 1/2-inch drive extension and a hammer will work just as well.

11   Apply non-hardening sealant (such as Permatex no. 2 or Teflon pipe sealant) to the new oil gallery plugs and thread them into the holes in the block. Make sure they're tightened securely.

12   If the engine isn't going to be reassembled right away, cover it with a large plastic trash bag to keep it clean.

17 Engine block - inspection

Refer to illustrations 17.4a, 17.4b and 17.4c

Note: *The manufacturer recommends checking the block deck for warpage and the main bearing bore concentricity and alignment. Since special measuring tools are needed, the checks should be done by an automotive machine shop.*

1   Before the block is inspected, it should be cleaned as described in Section 16.

2   Visually check the block for cracks, rust and corrosion. Look for stripped threads in the threaded holes. It's also a good idea to have the block checked for hidden cracks by

an automotive machine shop that has the special equipment to do this type of work. If defects are found, have the block repaired, if possible, or replaced.

3   Check the cylinder bores for scuffing and scoring.

4   Check the cylinders for taper and out-of-round conditions as follows **(see illustrations)**:

5   Measure the diameter of each cylinder at the top (just under the ridge area), center and bottom of the cylinder bore, parallel to the crankshaft axis.

6   Next, measure each cylinder's diameter at the same three locations perpendicular to the crankshaft axis.

7   The taper of each cylinder is the difference between the bore diameter at the top of the cylinder and the diameter at the bottom. The out-of-round specification of the

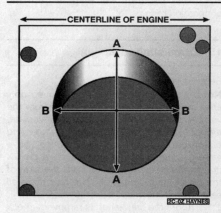

17.4a Measure the diameter of each cylinder at a right angle to the engine centerline (A), and parallel to the engine centerline (B) - out-of-round is the difference between A and B; taper is the difference between the diameter at the top of the cylinder and the diameter at the bottom of the cylinder

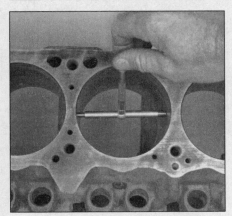

17.4b The ability to "feel" when the telescoping gauge is at the correct point will be developed over time, so work slowly and repeat the check until you're satisfied the bore measurement is accurate

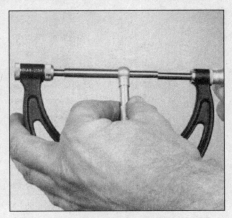

17.4c The gauge is then measured with a micrometer to determine the bore size

18.3a A "bottle brush" hone will produce better results if you've never honed cylinders before

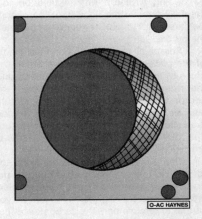

18.3b The cylinder hone should leave a smooth, crosshatch pattern with the lines intersecting at approximately a 60-degree angle

cylinder bore is the difference between the parallel and perpendicular readings. Compare your results to this Chapter's Specifications.

8   If the cylinder walls are badly scuffed or scored, or if they're out-of-round or tapered beyond the limits given in this Chapter's Specifications, have the engine block rebored and honed at an automotive machine shop.

9   If a rebore is done, oversize pistons and rings will be required.

10   Using a precision straightedge and feeler gauge, check the block deck (the surface the cylinder heads mate with) for distortion as you did with the cylinder heads (see Section 10). If it's distorted beyond the specified limit, the block decks can be resurfaced by an automotive machine shop.

11   If the cylinders are in reasonably good condition and not worn to the outside of the limits, and if the piston-to-cylinder clearances can be maintained properly, they don't have to be rebored. Honing is all that's necessary (see Section 18).

18   Cylinder honing

Refer to illustrations 18.3a and 18.3b

1   Prior to engine reassembly, the cylinder bores must be honed so the new piston rings will seat correctly and provide the best possible combustion chamber seal. **Note:** *If you don't have the tools or don't want to tackle the honing operation, most automotive machine shops will do it for a reasonable fee.*

2   Before honing the cylinders, install the main bearing caps and tighten the bolts to the torque listed in this Chapter's Specifications.

3   Two types of cylinder hones are commonly available - the flex hone or "bottle brush" type and the more traditional surfacing hone with spring-loaded stones.

Both will do the job, but for the less experienced mechanic the "bottle brush" hone will probably be easier to use. You'll also need some honing oil (kerosene will work if honing oil isn't available), rags and an electric drill motor. Proceed as follows:

a) *Mount the hone in the drill motor, compress the stones and slip it into the first cylinder* **(see illustration)**. *Be sure to wear safety goggles or a face shield!*

b) *Lubricate the cylinder with plenty of honing oil, turn on the drill and move the hone up-and-down in the cylinder at a pace that will produce a fine crosshatch pattern on the cylinder walls, and with the drill square and centered with the bore. Ideally, the crosshatch lines should intersect at approximately a 45-60-degree angle* **(see illustration)**. *Be sure to use plenty of lubricant and don't take off any more material than is absolutely necessary to produce the desired finish.* **Note:** *Piston ring manufacturers may specify a different crosshatch angle - read and follow any instructions included with the new rings.*

c) *Don't withdraw the hone from the cylinder while it's running. Instead, shut off the drill and continue moving the hone up-and-down in the cylinder until it comes to a complete stop, then compress the stones and withdraw the hone. If you're using a "bottle brush" type hone, stop the drill motor, then turn the chuck in the normal direction of rotation while withdrawing the hone from the cylinder.*

d) *Wipe the oil out of the cylinder and repeat the procedure for the remaining cylinders.*

4   After the honing job is complete, chamfer the top edges of the cylinder bores with a small file so the rings won't catch when the pistons are installed. Be very careful not to nick the cylinder walls with the end of the file.

5   The entire engine block must be washed again very thoroughly with warm, soapy water to remove all traces of the abrasive grit produced during the honing operation. **Note:**

The bores can be considered clean when a lint-free white cloth - dampened with clean engine oil - used to wipe them out doesn't pick up any more honing residue, which will show up as gray areas on the cloth. Be sure to run a brush through all oil holes and galleries and flush them with running water.

6   After rinsing, dry the block and apply a coat of light rust preventive oil to all machined surfaces. Wrap the block in a plastic trash bag to keep it clean and set it aside until reassembly.

19   Pistons and connecting rods - inspection

Refer to illustrations 19.4a, 19.4b, 19.10 and 19.11

1   Before the inspection process can be carried out, the piston/connecting rod assemblies must be cleaned and the original piston rings removed from the pistons. **Note:** *Always use new piston rings when the engine is reassembled.*

19.4a The piston ring grooves can be cleaned with a special tool, as shown here . . .

19.4b . . . or a section of broken ring

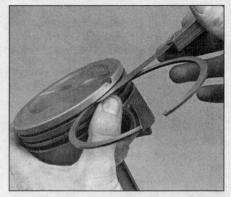

19.10 Check the ring side clearance with a feeler gauge at several points around the groove

2   Using a piston ring installation tool, carefully remove the rings from the pistons. Be careful not to nick or gouge the pistons in the process.

3   Scrape all traces of carbon from the top of the piston. A hand-held wire brush or a piece of fine emery cloth can be used once the majority of the deposits have been scraped away. Do not, under any circumstances, use a wire brush mounted in a drill motor to remove deposits from the pistons. The piston material is soft and may be eroded away by the wire brush.

4   Use a piston ring groove-cleaning tool to remove carbon deposits from the ring grooves. If a tool isn't available, a piece broken off the old ring will do the job. Be very careful to remove only the carbon deposits - don't remove any metal and do not nick or scratch the sides of the ring grooves **(see illustrations)**.

5   Once the deposits have been removed, clean the piston/rod assemblies with solvent and dry them with compressed air (if available). **Warning:** *Wear eye protection. Make sure the oil return holes in the back sides of the ring grooves are clear.*

6   If the pistons and cylinder walls aren't damaged or worn excessively, and if the engine block isn't rebored, new pistons won't be necessary. Normal piston wear appears as even vertical wear on the piston thrust surfaces and slight looseness of the top ring in its groove. New piston rings, however, should always be used when an engine is rebuilt.

7   Carefully inspect each piston for cracks around the skirt, at the pin bosses and at the ring lands.

8   Look for scoring and scuffing on the thrust faces of the skirt, holes in the piston crown and burned areas at the edge of the crown. If the skirt is scored or scuffed, the engine may have been suffering from overheating and/or abnormal combustion, which caused excessively high operating temperatures. The cooling and lubrication systems should be checked thoroughly. A hole in the piston crown is an indication that abnormal combustion (preignition) was

occurring. Burned areas at the edge of the piston crown are usually evidence of spark knock (detonation). If any of the above problems exist, the causes must be corrected or the damage will occur again. The causes may include intake air leaks, incorrect fuel/air mixture, low octane fuel, ignition timing and EGR system malfunctions.

9   Corrosion of the piston, in the form of small pits, indicates coolant is leaking into the combustion chamber and/or the crankcase. Again, the cause must be corrected or the problem may persist in the rebuilt engine.

10   Measure the piston ring side clearance by laying a new piston ring in each ring groove and slipping a feeler gauge in beside it **(see illustration)**. Check the clearance at three or four locations around each groove. Be sure to use the correct ring for each groove - they are different. If the side clearance is greater than specified in this Chapter, new pistons will have to be used.

11   Check the piston-to-bore clearance by measuring the bore (see Section 16) and the piston diameter. Make sure the pistons and bores are correctly matched. Measure the piston across the skirt, at a 90-degree angle to the piston pin **(see illustration)**. The measurement must be taken at a specific point to be accurate: The pistons are measured 0.45-inch from the bottom of the skirt, at right angles to the piston pin. Measure the cylinder bore 2.5-inches from the top for comparison with the piston measurement.

12   Subtract the piston diameter from the bore diameter to obtain the clearance. If it's greater than specified, the block will have to be rebored and new pistons and rings installed.

13   Check the piston-to-rod clearance by twisting the piston and rod in opposite directions. Any noticeable play indicates excessive wear, which must be corrected. The piston/connecting rod assemblies should be taken to an automotive machine shop to have the pistons and rods re-sized and new pins installed.

14   If the pistons must be removed from the connecting rods for any reason, they should be taken to an automotive machine shop. While they are there, have the connecting rods checked for bend and twist, since automotive

machine shops have special equipment for this purpose. **Note:** *Unless new pistons and/or connecting rods must be installed, do not disassemble the pistons and connecting rods.*

15   Check the connecting rods for cracks and other damage. Temporarily remove the rod caps, lift out the old bearing inserts, wipe the rod and cap bearing surfaces clean and inspect them for nicks, gouges and scratches. After checking the rods, replace the old bearings, slip the caps into place and tighten the nuts finger tight. **Note:** *If the engine is being rebuilt because of a connecting rod knock, be sure to install new rods.*

20   Crankshaft - inspection

Refer to illustrations 20.1, 20.2, 20.5 and 20.7

1   Remove all burrs from the crankshaft oil holes with a stone, file or scraper **(see illustration)**.

2   Clean the crankshaft with solvent and dry it with compressed air (if available). **Warning:** *Wear eye protection when using compressed air.* Be sure to clean the oil holes with a stiff brush **(see illustration)** and flush them with solvent.

3   Check the main and connecting rod bearing journals for uneven wear, scoring, pits and cracks.

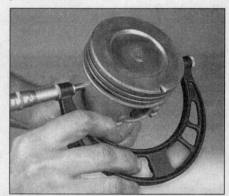

19.11 Measure the piston diameter at a 90-degree angle to the piston pin and in line with it

20.1 The oil holes should be chamfered so sharp edges don't gouge or scratch the new bearings

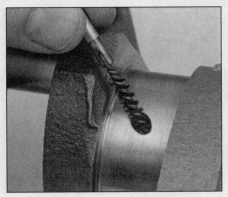

20.2 Use a wire or stiff plastic bristle brush to clean the oil passages in the crankshaft

20.5 Measure the diameter of each crankshaft journal at several points to detect taper and out-of-round conditions

4   Check the rest of the crankshaft for cracks and other damage. It should be Magnafluxed to reveal hidden cracks - an automotive machine shop will handle the procedure.

5   Using a micrometer, measure the diameter of the main and connecting rod journals and compare the results to this Chapter's Specifications **(see illustration)**. By measuring the diameter at a number of points around each journal's circumference, you'll be able to determine whether or not the journal is out-of-round. Take the measurement at each end of the journal, near the crank throws, to determine if the journal is tapered.

6   If the crankshaft journals are damaged, tapered, out-of-round or worn beyond the limits given in the Specifications, have the crankshaft reground by an automotive machine shop. Be sure to use the correct-size bearing inserts if the crankshaft is reconditioned.

7   Check the oil seal journals at each end of the crankshaft for wear and damage. If the seal has worn a groove in the journal, or if it's nicked or scratched **(see illustration)**, the new seal may leak when the engine is reassembled. In some cases, an automotive machine shop may be able to repair the journal by pressing on a thin sleeve. If repair

isn't feasible, a new or different crankshaft should be installed.

8   Examine the main and rod bearing inserts (see Section 21).

21   Main and connecting rod bearings - inspection

Refer to illustration 21.1

1   Even though the main and connecting rod bearings should be replaced with new ones during the engine overhaul, the old bearings should be retained for close examination, as they may reveal valuable information about the condition of the engine **(see illustration)**.

2   Bearing failure occurs because of lack of lubrication, the presence of dirt or other foreign particles, overloading the engine and corrosion. Regardless of the cause of bearing failure, it must be corrected before the engine is reassembled to prevent it from happening again.

3   When examining the bearings, remove them from the engine block, the main bearing caps, the connecting rods and the rod caps and lay them out on a clean surface in the same general position as their location in the engine. This will enable you to match any bearing problems with the corresponding crankshaft journal.

4   Dirt and other foreign particles get into the engine in a variety of ways. It may be left in the engine during assembly, or it may pass

20.7 If the seals have worn grooves in the crankshaft journals, or if the seal contact surfaces are nicked or scratched, the new seals will leak

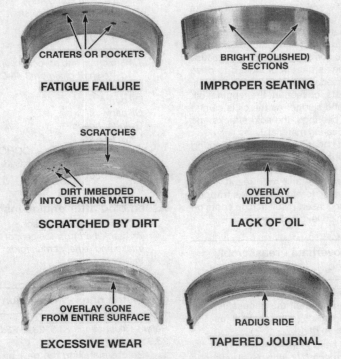

21.1 Typical bearing failures

CRATERS OR POCKETS

FATIGUE FAILURE

BRIGHT (POLISHED) SECTIONS

IMPROPER SEATING

SCRATCHES

DIRT IMBEDDED INTO BEARING MATERIAL

SCRATCHED BY DIRT

OVERLAY WIPED OUT

LACK OF OIL

OVERLAY GONE FROM ENTIRE SURFACE

EXCESSIVE WEAR

RADIUS RIDE

TAPERED JOURNAL

through filters or the PCV system. It may get into the oil, and from there into the bearings. Metal chips from machining operations and normal engine wear are often present. Abrasives are sometimes left in engine components after reconditioning, especially when parts aren't thoroughly cleaned using the proper cleaning methods. Whatever the source, these foreign objects often end up embedded in the soft bearing material and are easily recognized. Large particles won't embed in the bearing and will score or gouge the bearing and journal. The best prevention for this cause of bearing failure is to clean all parts thoroughly and keep everything spotlessly clean during engine assembly. Frequent and regular engine oil and filter changes are also recommended.

5   Lack of lubrication (or lubrication breakdown) has a number of interrelated causes. Excessive heat (which thins the oil), overloading (which squeezes the oil from the bearing face) and oil leakage or throw off (from excessive bearing clearances, worn oil pump or high engine speeds) all contribute to lubrication breakdown. Blocked oil passages, which usually are the result of misaligned oil holes in a bearing shell, will also oil starve a bearing and destroy it. When lack of lubrication is the cause of bearing failure, the bearing material is wiped or extruded from the steel backing of the bearing. Temperatures may increase to the point where the steel backing turns blue from overheating.

6   Driving habits can have a definite effect on bearing life. Low speed operation in too high a gear (lugging the engine) puts very high loads on bearings, which tends to squeeze out the oil film. These loads cause the bearings to flex, which produces fine cracks in the bearing face (fatigue failure). Eventually the bearing material will loosen in pieces and tear away from the steel backing. Short trip driving leads to corrosion of bearings because insufficient engine heat is produced to drive off the condensed water and corrosive gases. These products collect in the engine oil, forming acid and sludge. As the oil is carried to the engine bearings, the acid attacks and corrodes the bearing material.

7   Incorrect bearing installation during engine assembly will lead to bearing failure as well. Tight-fitting bearings leave insufficient oil clearance and will result in oil starvation. Dirt or foreign particles trapped behind a bearing insert result in high spots on the bearing which lead to failure.

22   Engine overhaul - reassembly sequence

1   Before beginning engine reassembly, make sure you have all the necessary new parts, gaskets and seals as well as the following items on hand:

Common hand tools
Torque wrench (1/2-inch drive) with
*   angle-torque gauge*
Piston ring Installation tool

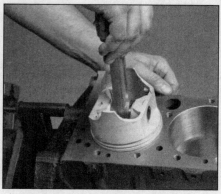

23.3 When checking piston ring end gap, the ring must be square in the cylinder bore (this is done by pushing the ring down with the top of a piston as shown)

Piston ring compressor
Crankshaft balancer Installation tool
Short lengths of rubber or plastic hose
*   to fit over connecting rod bolts*
Plastigage
Feeler gauges
Fine-tooth file
New engine oil
Engine assembly lube or moly-base
*   grease*
Gasket sealant
Thread locking compound

2   In order to save time and avoid problems, engine reassembly must be done in the following general order:

Crankshaft and main bearings
Piston/connecting rod assemblies
Balance shaft (3800 only)
Camshaft (intermediate shaft on 3.4L
*   DOHC)*
Oil pump drive assembly
Rear main oil seal
Timing chain and sprockets (interme-
*   diate shaft chain on 3.4L DOHC)*
Timing chain cover
Oil pump
Oil pan
Cylinder heads
Valve lifters
Camshaft carriers (3.4L DOHC)
Rocker arms and pushrods (3.1L/3.4L
*   and 3800 OHV)*
Driveplate

Assembled after engine installation

Camshaft position sensor
7X crankshaft position sensor
Intake and exhaust manifolds
Valve covers

23   Piston rings - installation

Refer to illustrations 23.3, 23.4, 23.5, 23.9a, 23.9b and 23.12

1   Before installing the new piston rings, the ring end gaps must be checked. It's assumed the piston ring side clearance has

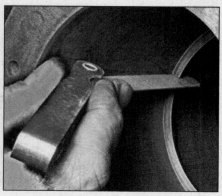

23.4 With the ring square in the cylinder, measure the end gap with a feeler gauge

been checked and verified correct (see Section 19).

2   Lay out the piston/connecting rod assemblies and the new ring sets so the ring sets will be matched with the same piston and cylinder during the end gap measurement and engine assembly.

3   Insert the top (number one) ring into the first cylinder and square it up with the cylinder walls by pushing it in with the top of the piston **(see illustration)**. The ring should be near the bottom of the cylinder, at the lower limit of ring travel.

4   To measure the end gap, slip feeler gauges between the ends of the ring until a gauge equal to the gap width is found **(see illustration)**. The feeler gauge should slide between the ring ends with a slight amount of drag. Compare the measurement to this Chapter's Specifications. If the gap is larger or smaller than specified, double-check to make sure you have the correct rings before proceeding.

5   If the gap is too small, it must be enlarged or the ring ends may come in contact with each other during engine operation, which can cause serious engine damage. The end gap can be increased by filing the ring ends very carefully with a fine file. Mount the file in a vise equipped with soft jaws, slip the ring over the file with the ends contacting the file teeth and slowly move the ring to remove material from the ends. When performing this operation, file only from the outside in **(see illustration)**. **Note:** *When you have the end gap correct, remove any burrs from the filed ends of the rings with a whetstone.*

6   Excess end gap isn't critical unless it's greater than 0.040-inch. Again, double-check to make sure you have the correct rings for the engine. If the engine block has been bored oversize, necessitating oversize pistons, matching oversize rings are required.

7   Repeat the procedure for each ring that will be installed in the first cylinder and for each ring in the remaining cylinders. Remember to keep rings, pistons and cylinders matched up.

8   Once the ring end gaps have been checked/corrected, the rings can be installed on the pistons.

23.5 If the end gap is too small, clamp a file in a vise and file the ring ends (from the outside in only) to enlarge the gap slightly

23.9a Installing the spacer/expander in the oil control ring groove

23.9b DO NOT use a piston ring installation tool when installing the oil ring side rails

9   The oil control ring (lowest one on the piston) is usually installed first. It's composed of three separate components. Slip the spacer/expander into the groove **(see illustration)**. If an anti-rotation tang is used, make sure it's inserted into the drilled hole in the ring groove. Next, install the lower side rail. Don't use a piston ring installation tool on the oil ring side rails, as they may be damaged. Instead, place one end of the side rail into the groove between the spacer/expander and the ring land, hold it firmly in place and slide a finger around the piston while pushing the rail into the groove **(see illustration)**. Next, install the upper side rail in the same manner.

10   After the three oil ring components have been installed, check to make sure both the upper and lower side rails can be turned smoothly in the ring groove.

11   The number two (middle) ring is installed next. It's usually stamped with a mark, which must face up, toward the top of the piston. **Note:** *Always follow the instructions printed on the ring package or box - different manufacturers may require different approaches. Don't mix up the top and middle rings, as they have different cross-sections.*

12   Use a piston ring installation tool and make sure the identification mark is facing the top of the piston, then slip the ring into the middle groove on the piston **(see illustration)**. Don't expand the ring any more than necessary to slide it over the piston.

13   Install the number one (top) ring in the same manner. Make sure the mark is facing up. Be careful not to confuse the number one and number two rings.

14   Repeat the procedure for the remaining pistons and rings.

24   Crankshaft - installation and main bearing oil clearance check

1   Crankshaft installation is the first step in engine reassembly. It's assumed at this point that the engine block and crankshaft have been cleaned, inspected and repaired or reconditioned.

2   Position the engine with the bottom facing up.

3   Remove the main bearing cap bolts and lift out the caps. Lay them out in the proper order to ensure correct installation.

4   If they're still in place, remove the original bearing inserts from the block and the main bearing caps. Wipe the bearing surfaces of the block and caps with a clean, lint-free cloth. They must be kept spotlessly clean.

Main bearing oil clearance check

Refer to illustrations 24.11 and 24.15
Note: *Don't touch the faces of the new bearing inserts with your fingers. Oil and acids from your skin can etch the bearings.*

5   Clean the back sides of the new main bearing inserts and lay one in each main bearing saddle in the block. If one of the bearing inserts from each set has a large groove in it, make sure the grooved insert is installed in the block. Lay the other bearing from each set in the corresponding main bearing cap. Make sure the tab on the bearing insert fits into the recess in the block or cap, neither higher than the cap's edge nor lower. **Note:** *On some engines, the inserts will project slightly and should project an equal distance on both sides.* **Caution:** *The oil holes in the block must line up with the oil holes in the bearing inserts. Do not hammer the bearing into place and don't nick or gouge the bearing faces. No lubrication should be used at this time.*

6   The flanged thrust bearing must be installed in the last main cap. **Caution:** *Some engines have a 0.008-inch oversize rear main bearing. Check your crankshaft for a marking on the last counterweight, and check the backside of the old bearing insert for a similar marking. If they are marked oversize, an oversize rear bearing will be required.*

7   Clean the faces of the bearings in the block and the crankshaft main bearing journals with a clean, lint-free cloth.

8   Check or clean the oil holes in the crankshaft, as any dirt here can go only one way - straight through the new bearings.

9   Once you're certain the crankshaft is

23.12 Installing the compression rings with a ring expander - the mark (arrow) must face up

clean, carefully lay it in position in the main bearings.

10   Before the crankshaft can be permanently installed, the main bearing oil clearance must be checked.

11   Cut several pieces of the appropriate size Plastigage (they should be slightly shorter than the width of the main bearings) and place one piece on each crankshaft main bearing journal, parallel with the journal axis **(see illustration)**.

24.11 Lay the Plastigage strips (arrow) on the main bearing journals, parallel to the crankshaft centerline

12   Clean the faces of the bearings in the caps and install the caps in their original locations (don't mix them up) with the arrows pointing toward the front of the engine. Don't disturb the Plastigage.

13   Starting with the center main and working out toward the ends, tighten the main bearing cap bolts to the torque listed in this Chapter's Specifications in three steps. Don't rotate the crankshaft at any time during this operation, and do not tighten one cap completely - tighten all caps equally. Before tightening, the main caps should be seated using light taps with a brass or plastic mallet.

14   Remove the bolts/studs and carefully lift off the main bearing caps. Keep them in order. Don't disturb the Plastigage or rotate the crankshaft. If any of the main bearing caps are difficult to remove, tap them gently from side-to-side with a soft-face hammer to loosen them. **Note:** *Main bearing caps on 3.8L engines are press fit and should be removed with a slide hammer and a special tool available from the manufacturer that fits into the main bearing cap holes and works with the slide hammer. The factory cautions that failure to follow this procedure may result in damage to the caps, bearings and engine. Also, the three front main bearing caps on 3.8L engines have a horizontal bolt on each end of the cap, in addition to the usual two main bearing cap bolts, that must not be overlooked.*

15   Compare the width of the crushed Plastigage on each journal to the scale printed on the Plastigage envelope to obtain the main bearing oil clearance **(see illustration)**. Check the Specifications to make sure it's correct.

16   If the clearance is not as specified, the bearing inserts may be the wrong size (which means different ones will be required). Before deciding different inserts are needed, make sure no dirt or oil was between the bearing inserts and the caps or block when the clearance was measured. If the Plastigage was wider at one end than the other, the journal may be tapered (see Section 20).

17   Carefully scrape all traces of the Plastigage material off the main bearing journals and/or the bearing faces. Use your fingernail or the edge of a credit card - don't nick or scratch the bearing faces.

Final crankshaft installation

18   Carefully lift the crankshaft out of the engine.

19   Clean the bearing faces in the block, then apply a thin, uniform layer of moly-base grease or engine assembly lube to each of the bearing surfaces. Be sure to coat the thrust faces as well as the journal face of the thrust bearing.

20   Make sure the crankshaft journals are clean, then lay the crankshaft back in place in the block.

21   Clean the faces of the bearings in caps, then apply lubricant to them.

22   Install the caps in their original locations

24.15 Measuring the width of the crushed Plastigage to determine the main bearing oil clearance (be sure to use the correct scale - standard and metric ones are included)

with the arrows pointing toward the front of the engine. Tap them into place using a lead or brass hammer. Don't use the bolts to pull them into place. The bottom of each cap should be parallel to the mating surface of the block. **Note 1:** *On earlier 3800 engines, two side seals must be placed in the side grooves of the rear main cap as it is installed. It wasn't necessary during the Plastigage check, but insert them now. They should be part of your engine overhaul gasket set.* **Note 2:** *Apply a thin coat of anaerobic sealant to the cap-to-block mating surfaces of the rear cap.*

23   Lubricate the bolts with clean engine oil before installing them. With all caps in place and bolts just started, tap the ends of the crankshaft forward and backward with a lead or brass hammer to line up the main bearing and crankshaft thrust surfaces.

24   Following the procedures outlined in Step 13, retighten all main bearing cap bolts to the torque listed in this Chapter's Specifications, starting with the center main and working out toward the ends. Tighten each bolt in a pair alternately and equally, to be sure the cap stays parallel to the mating surface. Don't forget the horizontal side bolts on 3.8L engines. **Note:** *On 3.8L engines, the manufacturer recommends the following procedure:*

a) *Tighten the main bearing cap bolts to 52 ft-lbs to seat them, then loosen them one full turn (360-degrees).*

b) *Tighten them in two equal stages to the value shown in Step 1 of this Chapter's Specifications.*

c) *Tighten them in three equal stages to the additional rotation shown in Step 2 of this Chapter's Specifications.*

25   Rotate the crankshaft a number of times by hand to check for any obvious binding.

26   The final step is to check the crankshaft endplay with feeler gauges or a dial indicator as described in Section 15. The endplay should be correct if the crankshaft thrust faces aren't worn or damaged and new bearings have been installed.

25.1 Coat the camshaft lobes and journals with assembly lube before installation

25   Camshaft (3.1L/3.4L OHV and 3800), intermediate shaft (3.4L DOHC) and balance shaft (3800) - installation

Camshaft (3.1/3.4L OHV and 3800) and intermediate shaft (3.4L DOHC)

Refer to illustration 25.1

1   Lubricate the camshaft bearing journals and cam lobes with a special camshaft installation lubricant **(see illustration)**.

2   Slide the camshaft into the engine, using a long bolt (the same thread as the camshaft sprocket bolt) screwed into the front of the camshaft as a "handle." Support the cam near the block and be careful not to scrape or nick the bearings. Install the camshaft retainer plate (3.1L and 3.4L OHV) or intermediate shaft plate (3.4L DOHC) and tighten the bolts to the torque listed in this Chapter's Specifications.

3   On 3.1L and 3.4L OHV and 3.4L DOHC engines, dip the gear portion of the oil pump drive in engine oil and insert it into the block. It should be flush with its mounting boss before inserting the retaining bolt. **Note:** *Position a new O-ring on the oil pump drive-shaft before installation.*

4   Complete the installation of the timing chain and sprockets (3.1L and 3.4L OHV engine: see Part A; 3.4L DOHC engine: see Part B; 3800 engine, Part C). On 3800 engines, perform the following procedure for balance shaft installation before installing the timing chain and sprockets.

Balance shaft (3800 only)

Refer to illustrations 25.5, 25.8 and 25.9

5   Lubricate the front bearing and rear journal of the balance shaft with engine oil and insert the balance shaft carefully into the block. When the front bearing approaches the insert in the front of the block, use a hammer and an appropriate-size socket to drive the front bearing into its insert. Drive it

25.5 Drive the front balance shaft bearing in (it's attached to the balance shaft) just until the retainer plate can be installed

25.8 The balance shaft gear mark (arrow) should point straight down

25.9 Align the marks (arrows) on both balance shaft gears as shown

in just enough to allow installation of the balance shaft bearing retainer **(see illustration)**. Tighten the balance shaft retainer bolts to the torque listed in this Chapter's Specifications.

6   Install the balance shaft driven gear and its bolt.

7   Turn the camshaft so that with the camshaft sprocket temporarily installed, the timing mark is straight down.

8   With the camshaft sprocket and the camshaft gear removed, turn the balance shaft so the timing mark on the gear points straight down **(see illustration)**.

9   Install the camshaft gear (that drives the balance shaft) onto the cam, aligning it with the keyway and align the marks on the balance shaft gear and the camshaft gear **(see illustration)** by turning the balance shaft.

10   After the camshaft sprocket, crankshaft sprocket and timing chain have been installed (see Chapter 2 part C), tighten the balance shaft driven gear bolt to the torque listed in this Chapter's Specifications.

26   Rear main oil seal - replacement

Refer to part A of this Chapter for the rear main seal replacement procedure.

27   Pistons and connecting rods - installation and rod bearing oil clearance check

1   Before installing the piston/connecting rod assemblies, the cylinder walls must be perfectly clean, the top edge of each cylinder must be chamfered, and the crankshaft must be in place.

2   Remove the cap from the end of the number one connecting rod (check the marks made during removal). Remove the original bearing inserts and wipe the bearing surfaces of the connecting rod and cap with a clean, lint-free cloth. They must be kept spotlessly clean.

Piston installation and rod bearing oil clearance check

Refer to illustrations 27.5, 27.11, 27.13 and 27.17

Note: *Don't touch the faces of the new bearing inserts with your fingers. Oil and acids from your skin can etch the bearings.*

3   Clean the back side of the new upper bearing insert, then lay it in place in the connecting rod. Make sure the tab on the bearing fits into the recess in the rod. Don't hammer the bearing insert into place and be very careful not to nick or gouge the bearing face. Don't lubricate the bearing at this time.

4   Clean the back side of the other bearing insert and install it in the rod cap. Again, make sure the tab on the bearing fits into the recess in the cap, and don't apply any lubricant. It's critically important that the mating surfaces of the bearing and connecting rod are perfectly clean and oil free when they're assembled.

5   Stagger the piston ring gaps around the piston **(see illustration)**.

6   Slip a section of plastic or rubber hose over each connecting rod cap bolt.

7   Lubricate the piston and rings with clean engine oil and attach a piston ring compressor to the piston. Leave the skirt protruding about 1/4-inch to guide the piston into the cylinder. The rings must be compressed until they're flush with the piston.

8   Rotate the crankshaft until the number one connecting rod journal is at BDC (bottom dead center) and apply a coat of engine oil to the cylinder walls.

9   With the mark or notch on top of the piston facing the front of the engine, gently insert the piston/connecting rod assembly into the number one cylinder bore and rest the bottom edge of the ring compressor on the engine block.

10   Tap the top edge of the ring compressor to make sure it's contacting the block around its entire circumference.

11   Gently tap on the top of the piston with the end of a wooden or plastic hammer handle **(see illustration)** while guiding the end of the connecting rod into place on the

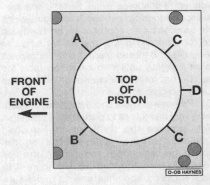

27.5 Ring end gap positions - align the oil ring spacer gap at D, the oil ring side rails at C (one inch either side of the pin centerline), and the compression rings at A and B, one inch either side of the pin centerline

crankshaft journal. The piston rings may try to pop out of the ring compressor just before entering the cylinder bore, so keep some pressure down on the ring compressor. Work slowly, and if any resistance is felt as the piston enters the cylinder, stop immediately. Find out what's hanging up and fix it before proceeding. Do not, for any reason, force the piston into the cylinder - you might break a ring and/or the piston.

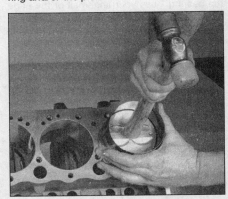

27.11 Drive the piston into the cylinder bore with the end of a wooden or plastic hammer handle

12   Once the piston/connecting rod assembly is installed, the connecting rod bearing oil clearance must be checked before the rod cap is permanently bolted in place.

13   Cut a piece of the appropriate size Plastigage slightly shorter than the width of the connecting rod bearing and lay it in place on the number one connecting rod journal, parallel with the journal axis **(see illustration)**.

14   Clean the connecting rod cap bearing face, remove the protective hoses from the connecting rod bolts and install the rod cap. Make sure the mating mark on the cap is on the same side as the mark on the connecting rod.

15   Install the nuts and tighten them to the torque listed in this Chapter's Specifications. Work up to it in three steps. **Note:** *Use a thin-wall socket to avoid erroneous torque readings that can result if the socket is wedged between the rod cap and nut. If the socket tends to wedge itself between the nut and the cap, lift up on it slightly until it no longer contacts the cap. Do not rotate the crankshaft at any time during this operation.*

16   Remove the nuts and detach the rod cap, being very careful not to disturb the Plastigage.

17   Compare the width of the crushed Plastigage to the scale printed on the Plastigage envelope to obtain the oil clearance **(see illustration)**. Compare it to this Chapter's Specifications to make sure the clearance is correct.

18   If the clearance is not as specified, the bearing inserts may be the wrong size (which means different ones will be required). Before deciding different inserts are needed, make sure no dirt or oil was between the bearing inserts and the connecting rod or cap when the clearance was measured. Also, recheck the journal diameter. If the Plastigage was wider at one end than the other, the journal may be tapered (see Section 20).

Final connecting rod installation

19   Carefully scrape all traces of the Plastigage material off the rod journal and/or bearing face. Be very careful not to scratch the bearing - use your fingernail or the edge of a credit card.

20   Make sure the bearing faces are perfectly clean, then apply a uniform layer of clean moly-base grease or engine assembly lube to both of them. You'll have to push the piston into the cylinder to expose the face of the bearing insert in the connecting rod - be sure to slip the protective hoses over the rod bolts first.

21   Slide the connecting rod back into place on the journal, remove the protective hoses from the rod cap bolts, install the rod cap and tighten the nuts to the torque listed in this Chapter's Specifications. Again, work up to the torque in three steps.

22   Repeat the entire procedure for the

27.13 Lay the Plastigage strips on each rod bearing journal, parallel to the crankshaft centerline

remaining pistons/connecting rods.

23   The important points to remember are:

a)   *Keep the back sides of the bearing inserts and the insides of the connecting rods and caps perfectly clean when assembling them.*

b)   *Make sure you have the correct piston/rod assembly for each cylinder.*

c)   *The arrow or mark on the piston must face the front of the engine.*

d)   *Lubricate the cylinder walls with clean oil.*

e)   *Lubricate the bearing faces when installing the rod caps after the oil clearance has been checked.*

24   After all the piston/connecting rod assemblies have been properly installed, rotate the crankshaft a number of times by hand to check for any obvious binding.

25   As a final step, the connecting rod endplay must be checked (see Section 14).

26   Compare the measured endplay to this Chapter's Specifications to make sure it's correct. If it was correct before disassembly and the original crankshaft and rods were reinstalled, it should still be right. If new rods or a new crankshaft were installed, the endplay may be inadequate. If so, the rods will have to be removed and taken to an automotive machine shop for re-sizing.

---

28   Initial start-up and break-in after overhaul

Warning: *Have a fire extinguisher handy when starting the engine for the first time.*

1   Once the engine has been installed in the vehicle, double-check the oil and coolant levels.

2   With the spark plugs out of the engine, remove the PCM IGN fuse from the instrument panel fuse block and the IGNITION fuse from the underhood fuse

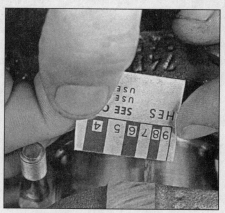

27.17 Measuring the width of the crushed Plastigage to determine the rod bearing oil clearance (be sure to use the correct scale - standard and metric ones are included)

block (1995 models), the PCM BATT fuse from the instrument panel fuse block and the IGNITION fuse from the underhood fuse block (1996 through 1999 models) or the PCM/BCM/CLSTR fuse from the instrument panel fuse block (driver's side) and the IGN fuse from the lower underhood fuse block (2000 and later models). Crank the engine until oil pressure registers on the gauge or the light goes out.

3   Install the spark plugs, hook up the plug wires and install the fuses.

4   Start the engine. It may take a few moments for the fuel system to build up pressure, but the engine should start without a great deal of effort. **Note:** *If the engine keeps backfiring, recheck the valve timing and spark plug wire routing.*

5   After the engine starts, it should be allowed to warm up to normal operating temperature. While the engine is warming up, make a thorough check for fuel, oil and coolant leaks.

6   Shut the engine off and recheck the engine oil and coolant levels.

7   Drive the vehicle to an area with no traffic, accelerate from 30 to 50 mph, then allow the vehicle to slow to 30 mph with the throttle closed. Repeat the procedure 10 or 12 times. This will load the piston rings and cause them to seat properly against the cylinder walls. Check again for oil and coolant leaks.

8   Drive the vehicle gently for the first 500 miles (no sustained high speeds) and keep a constant check on the oil level. It isn't unusual for an engine to use oil during the break-in period.

9   At approximately 500 to 600 miles, change the oil and filter.

10   For the next few hundred miles, drive the vehicle normally. Don't pamper it or abuse it.

11   After 2000 miles, change the oil and filter again and consider the engine broken in.

Chapter 3
Cooling, heating and air conditioning systems

Contents

Specifications

General

Coolant capacity	See Chapter 1
Radiator pressure cap rating	15 psi
Thermostat opening temperature	188-degrees F
Refrigerant type	R-134a
Refrigerant capacity	
1995 and 1996	2.0 lbs
1997 through 1999	1.88 lbs
2000 through 2003	2.2 lbs
2004 and later	2.3 lbs

Torque specifications

Ft-lbs (unless otherwise indicated)

Thermostat housing bolts/stud	
3.1L and 3.4L	18
3800	20
Water pump attaching bolts	
3.1L and 3.4L	89 in-lbs
3800	
1995 through 2001	
Short bolts	
Step 1	132 in-lbs
Step 2	Tighten an additional 80-degrees
Long bolts	
Step 1	15
Step 2	Tighten an additional 40-degrees
2002 and later	
Short bolts	16
Long bolts	25
Water pump pulley bolts	
3.1L and 3.4L	18
3800	115 in-lbs

1 General information

Engine cooling system

All vehicles covered by this manual employ a pressurized engine cooling system with thermostatically controlled coolant circulation. An impeller type water pump mounted on the engine block pumps coolant through the engine and radiator. The coolant flows around each cylinder and back to the radiator. Cast-in coolant passages direct coolant around the intake and exhaust ports, near the spark plug areas and the exhaust valve guides.

A wax-pellet type thermostat is located in a housing connected to the upper radiator hose. During warm up the closed thermostat prevents coolant from circulating through the radiator. As the engine nears normal operating temperature, the thermostat opens and allows hot coolant to travel through the radiator, where it's cooled before returning to the engine.

The cooling system is sealed by a pressure-type radiator cap, which raises the boiling point of the coolant and increases the cooling efficiency of the radiator. If the system pressure exceeds the cap pressure relief value, the excess pressure in the system forces the spring-loaded valve inside the cap off its seat and allows the coolant to escape through a hose into a coolant reservoir. When the system cools, the excess coolant is automatically drawn from the reservoir back into the radiator.

The coolant reservoir serves as both the point at which fresh coolant is added to the cooling system to maintain the proper level and as a holding tank for expelled coolant.

This type of cooling system is known as a closed design because coolant that escapes past the pressure cap is saved and reused.

Heating system

The heating system consists of a blower fan and heater core located under the instrument panel, the hoses connecting the heater core to the engine cooling system and the heater/air conditioning control assembly. Hot engine coolant is circulated through the heater core. When the heater mode is activated, a trap door opens to expose the heater box to the passenger compartment. A fan switch on the control head activates the blower motor, which forces air through the core, heating the air.

Air conditioning system

The air conditioning system consists of a condenser mounted in front of the radiator, an evaporator mounted adjacent to the heater core, a compressor mounted on the engine, a filter-drier (accumulator), which contains a high-pressure relief valve, and the hoses and lines connecting all of the above components.

A blower fan forces the warmer air of the passenger compartment through the evaporator core (sort of a radiator-in-reverse), transferring the heat from the air to the refrigerant. The liquid refrigerant boils off into low pressure vapor, taking the heat with it when it leaves the evaporator.

2   Antifreeze - general information

Refer to illustration 2.4

Warning: *Do not allow antifreeze to come in contact with your skin or painted surfaces of the vehicle. Rinse off spills immediately with plenty of water. Antifreeze is highly toxic if ingested. Never leave antifreeze lying around in an open container or in puddles on the floor; children and pets are attracted by its sweet smell and may drink it. Check with local authorities about disposing of used antifreeze. Many communities have collection centers which will see that antifreeze is disposed of safely. Never dump used antifreeze on the ground or pour it into drains.*
Note: *Non-toxic antifreeze is now available at most auto parts stores, but even these types should be disposed of properly.*

The cooling system should be filled with a water/ethylene glycol-based antifreeze solution which will prevent freezing down to at least -20-degrees F (even lower in cold climates). It also provides protection against corrosion and increases the coolant boiling point.

The cooling system should be drained, flushed and refilled at least every other year

(see Chapter 1). The use of antifreeze solutions for periods of longer than two years is likely to cause damage and encourage the formation of rust and scale in the system. However, 1996 and later models are filled with a new, long-life coolant called "DEX-COOL," with a manufacturer recommended maintenance interval of five years.

Before adding antifreeze to the system, check all hose connections. Antifreeze can leak through very minute openings.

The exact mixture of antifreeze to water which you should use depends on the relative weather conditions. The mixture should contain at least 50-percent antifreeze, but should never contain more than 70-percent antifreeze. Consult the mixture ratio chart on the antifreeze container before adding coolant. Hydrometers are available at most auto parts stores to test the coolant **(see illustration).** Use antifreeze which meets the vehicle manufacturer's specifications.

3   Thermostat - check and replacement

Warning: *The engine must be completely cool when this procedure is performed.*
Caution: *Don't drive the vehicle without a thermostat! The computer may stay in open loop mode and emissions and fuel economy will suffer.*

Check

1   Before assuming the thermostat is to blame for a cooling system problem, check the coolant level, drivebelt tension (see Chapter 1) and temperature gauge (or light) operation.

2   If the engine seems to be taking a long time to warm up (based on heater output or temperature gauge operation), the thermostat is probably stuck open. Replace the thermostat with a new one.

3   If the engine runs hot, use your hand to check the temperature of the upper radiator hose. If the hose isn't hot, but the engine is, the thermostat is probably stuck closed, preventing the coolant inside the engine from escaping to the radiator. Replace the thermostat.

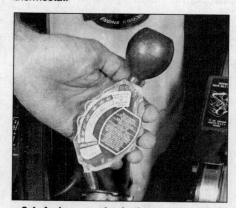

2.4 An inexpensive hydrometer can be used to test the condition of your coolant

4   If the upper radiator hose is hot, it means the coolant is flowing and the thermostat is open. Consult the *Troubleshooting* Section at the front of this manual for cooling system diagnosis.

Replacement

Refer to illustrations 3.8, 3.11a, 3.11b, 3.12a and 3.12b

5   Disconnect the negative battery cable from the battery and partially drain the cooling system (see Chapter 1). **Caution:** *On models equipped with a Theftlock audio system, be sure the lockout feature is turned off before performing any procedure which requires disconnecting the battery.* If the coolant is relatively new or in good condition, save it and reuse it. If it is to be replaced, see Section 2 for cautions about proper handling of used antifreeze.

6   Remove the air cleaner and duct (see Chapter 4).

7   On the 3800 engine, remove the fuel injection system trim cover (see Chapter 4).

8   Follow the upper radiator hose to the engine to locate the thermostat cover **(see illustration).** On all models, the thermostat is located at the top-center of the engine at the transaxle end. On the 3800 engine it is just ahead of the throttle body.

9   Loosen the hose clamp, then detach the hose from the thermostat cover. If the hose sticks, grasp it near the end with a pair of adjustable pliers and twist it to break the seal, then pull it off. If the hose is old or deteriorated, cut it off and install a new one.

10   If the outer surface of the large fitting that mates with the hose is deteriorated (corroded, pitted, etc.) it may be damaged further by hose removal. If it is, the thermostat cover will have to be replaced.

11   Remove the bolts/nuts and detach the thermostat cover **(see illustrations).** If the cover is stuck, tap it with a soft-face hammer to jar it loose. Be prepared for some coolant to spill as the gasket seal is broken.

12   Note how it's installed (which end is facing up), then remove the thermostat **(see illustrations).**

13   Remove all traces of old gasket material and sealant from the housing and cover with a gasket scraper. Clean the gasket mating surfaces with lacquer thinner or acetone.

14   Install the new thermostat in the housing. Make sure the correct end faces up - the spring end is normally directed into the engine. A new rubber seal should be in place on the thermostat before installation.

15   Install the cover and bolts/nuts, using RTV sealant around the bolt threads. Tighten the bolts to the torque listed in this Chapter's Specifications.

16   The remaining steps are the reverse of removal.

17   Refill the cooling system (see Chapter 1). **Note:** *Be sure to bleed the system of air.*

18   Start the engine and allow it to reach normal operating temperature, then check for leaks and proper thermostat operation (as described in Steps 2 through 4).

3.8 Upper radiator hose clamp at the thermostat cover - 3.1L engine shown

A   Radiator hose clamp
B   Coolant bleed screw

3.11a Thermostat cover bolts (arrows) - 3.1L engine

3.11b Thermostat cover bolts (arrows) - 3800 engine

4   Engine cooling fans and circuit - check and fan/shroud replacement

Warning: *Keep hands, tools and clothing away from the fan, even if the engine is not running. To avoid injury or damage DO NOT operate the engine with a damaged fan. Do not attempt to repair fan blades - replace a damaged fan with a new one.*

Check

Refer to illustrations 4.1 and 4.2

1   To test a fan motor, unplug the electrical connector at the motor and use fused jumper wires to connect the fan directly to the battery **(see illustration)**. If the fan still doesn't work, replace the motor.

2   If the motor tests OK, check the cooling fan relays, located in the underhood fuse/relay panel **(see illustration)**. There are three fan relays. On earlier models, number 1 and 2 are in the electrical box at the front of the right fenderwell, and number 3 is in the electrical box at the front of the left fenderwell. On later models, both fuse/relay panels are on the front of the right fenderwell, and all three cooling fan relays are in the lower panel.

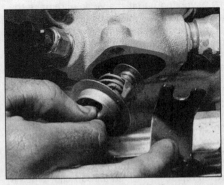

3.12a Note how it's installed, then remove the thermostat (the spring end points toward the engine)

3   Test the relays (see Chapter 12).

4   If the relays and the fan motor are good, check the wiring from the relays to the PCM (computer) for open or short circuits.

5   If the circuit checks OK but the fan(s) still don't come on, check the engine coolant temperature sensor (see Chapter 6).

Replacement

1995 through 2000 models

Refer to illustrations 4.8, 4.10 and 4.12
Note: *This procedure applies to either fan.*

6   Disconnect the cable from the negative

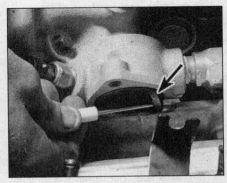

3.12b If the thermostat comes out without its rubber seal (arrow), pry it out of the housing with a small screwdriver

terminal of the battery. **Caution:** *On models equipped with a Theftlock audio system, be sure the lockout feature is turned off before performing any procedure which requires disconnecting the battery.*

7   Remove the air intake duct and air cleaner (see Chapter 4).

8   Remove the bolts and swing the engine torque strut(s) away from the radiator to allow room for fan removal **(see illustration)**. Loosen the through-bolts in the strut mounts first to avoid damage to the rubber bushings.

9   Disconnect the electrical connectors

4.1 Disconnect the electrical connector from the fan and apply fused battery power and ground to the terminals (arrows) - fan shown removed from vehicle for clarity

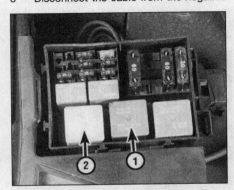

4.2 The cooling fan relays are easily identifiable by viewing the decal on the inside of the underhood fuse/relay box cover - relays no. 1 and no. 2 (shown) are in the electrical box on the right fenderwell

4.8 Unbolt the torque strut brackets (upper arrows) from the radiator support

4.10 Detach the bolts (arrows) securing the tops of the two fans (center arrows) and the sides - the bottom legs of the fan assemblies (not shown here) simply slip over tangs on the bottom of the radiator support

4.12 Remove the nut (arrow) to remove the fan blade from the motor

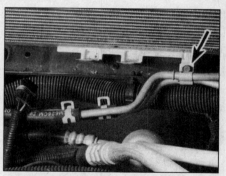

5.6 Remove the bolt (arrow) retaining the transmission lines to the radiator

from the fan(s). Unclip any wiring harnesses from the fan shroud.

10   Detach the fan retaining bolts **(see illustration)**. **Note:** *It is extremely important to mark the installed position of each fan (left side or right side) because each fan motor has a different wattage rating and insufficient cooling could occur if they are not installed in their original positions.*

11   Pull the fan assembly up slightly to dislodge its tabs from the radiator, then guide the fan assembly out from the engine compartment, making sure that all wiring clips are disconnected. Be careful not to contact the radiator cooling fins.

12   If a fan is damaged, remove the nut holding the fan blade to the motor **(see illustration)**. **Note:** *On some models, the fan motor can be separated from the plastic mount for replacement, on others it is sold only as an assembly.*

13   Installation is the reverse of removal.

2001 and later models

Note: *These models incorporate a one-piece fan shroud that fastens to the radiator and the radiator support and holds both fans.*

14   Remove the left diagonal brace (between the driver's-side front fender and the radiator support).

15   If necessary to facilitate fan shroud removal, partially drain the cooling system

and remove the radiator inlet hose.

16   Working under the vehicle, remove the transmission oil cooler lines from the retainer at the bottom of the fan shroud, and remove the pushpin fastener on the driver's side.

17   Remove the cooling fan heat shields, if equipped.

18   Remove the three bolts holding the fan shroud to the radiator.

19   Unfasten the fan shroud clip at the top of the radiator.

20   Remove the upper support brackets from the radiator and the fan shroud and remove the fan shroud.

21   Installation is the reverse of removal. When replacing the fan shroud clip, press it until it engages.

5   Radiator and coolant reservoir - removal and installation

Warning: *The engine must be completely cool when this procedure is performed.*

Radiator

Removal
Refer to illustrations 5.6, 5.7, 5.8 and 5.9

1   Disconnect the negative battery cable from the battery. On 2001 and later models, remove the battery. This may require removing the left diagonal brace (between the passenger-side front fender and the radiator support). **Caution:** *On models equipped with a Theftlock audio system, be*

sure the lockout feature is turned off before performing any procedure which requires disconnecting the battery.

2   Drain the cooling system (see Chapter 1). If the coolant is relatively new or in good condition, save it and reuse it. Refer to the coolant **Warning** in Section 2.

3   On most models, it will be necessary to remove the air cleaner assembly (see Chapter 4). On 2001 and later models, remove the lower air deflector (bolted to the bottom of the front bumper), if necessary.

4   Unbolt and swing away the engine torque strut mounts from the upper radiator support **(see illustration 4.8)**. Loosen the through-bolts in the strut mounts first to avoid damage to the rubber bushings.

5   Refer to Section 4 and remove the engine cooling fans (and fan shroud, on later models). On 1995 through 2002 models, disconnect the electrical connector from the low-coolant sensor in the right radiator tank **(see illustration 5.14)**.

6   Remove the bolt holding the transmission cooler lines to the bottom of the radiator **(see illustration)**.

7   Disconnect the cooler lines from the radiator **(see illustration)**, then cap the ends to prevent excessive fluid loss and contamination. Use a drip pan to catch spilled fluid. To remove the quick-connect fittings, first pull back the plastic cap. Then use a tool with a bent tip to pull one of the open ends of the spring clip. Rotate it to disengage the projections from the slots. This will enable you to pull the transmission cooler pipe straight out

5.7 Disconnect the transmission cooler lines (arrows) from the right side of the radiator

5.8 On the left side, disconnect the upper radiator hose (arrow) - lower radiator hose is at the bottom right of the radiator

5.9 Remove the upper radiator support bolts (A indicates right-side mount) and disconnect the coolant overflow hose (B)

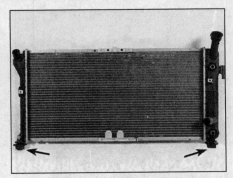

5.13 The rubber insulators (arrows) must be in place before installing the radiator

5.14 Remove the low coolant warning sensor (arrow) by prying back the two spring clips - use a new O-ring when reinstalling the sensor

5.19 Remove the screw (A), the nut (B) and the plastic retainer pin (C), then remove the coolant recovery tank

of the fitting. When reconnecting the fitting, use a new spring clip and don't push it onto the fitting, which will bend it. Place one end of the clip into a slot in the fitting. Rotate the clip until all three projections have snapped into the slots. Insert the cooler pipe, which should seat with a definite click. Pull on it to confirm that it has seated. Slide the plastic cap up and onto the fitting, making sure that it seats without a gap between it and the fitting. The yellow identification band on the tube should be hidden inside the fitting.

8   Loosen the hose clamps, then detach the radiator hoses from the fittings **(see illustration)**. If they're stuck, grasp each hose near the end with a pair of adjustable pliers and twist it to break the seal, then pull it off - be careful not to distort the radiator fittings. If the hoses are old or deteriorated, cut them off and install new ones.

9   Disconnect the reservoir hose from the radiator neck. On 1995 through 2000 models, remove the bolts from the upper radiator mounting bracket fittings **(see illustration)**.

10   Tilt the radiator back toward the engine and lift it out of the engine compartment, making sure not to hit the delicate aluminum core on any engine or body parts.

11   With the radiator removed, it can be inspected for leaks and damage. If it needs repair, have a radiator shop or dealer service department perform the work, as special techniques are required.

12   Bugs and dirt can be removed from the radiator with compressed air and a soft brush. Don't bend the cooling fins as this is done.

Installation

Refer to illustrations 5.13 and 5.14

13   Installation is the reverse of the removal procedure. Be sure that the radiator mounting insulators are in place and in good condition before installing the radiator **(see illustration)**.

14   If the radiator is to be replaced, on 1995 through 2002 models, remove the low-coolant sensor from the old radiator and attach it with the clips to the new radiator, using a new O-ring lubricated with clean coolant **(see illustration)**.

15   After installation, fill the cooling system with the proper mixture of antifreeze and water. Be sure to bleed the system of air (see Chapter 1).

16   Start the engine and check for leaks. Allow the engine to reach normal operating temperature, indicated by the upper radiator hose becoming hot. Recheck the coolant level and add more if required.

17   Check and add automatic transmission fluid as needed.

Coolant reservoir

Refer to illustration 5.19

18   Disconnect the radiator overflow hose from the top of the radiator **(see illustration 5.8)**.

19   Remove the mounting fasteners from the right shock tower. On later models, remove the cross-vehicle brace (see Chapter 11). Lift the coolant reservoir from the vehicle **(see illustration)**.

20   Prior to installation make sure the reservoir is clean and free of debris which could be drawn into the radiator (wash it with soapy water and a brush if necessary, then rinse thoroughly).

21   Installation is the reverse of removal.

---

6   Water pump - check

Refer to illustration 6.4

1   A failure in the water pump can cause serious engine damage due to overheating.

2   There are three ways to check the operation of the water pump while it's installed on the engine. If the pump is defective, it should be replaced with a new or rebuilt unit.

3   With the engine running at normal operating temperature, squeeze the upper radiator hose. If the water pump is working properly, a pressure surge should be felt as the hose is released. **Warning:** *Keep your hands away from the fan blades!*

4   Water pumps are equipped with weep or vent holes. If a failure occurs in the pump seal,

6.4 The weep hole (arrow) is located on the top of the water pump (pump removed for clarity, 3.1L shown)

coolant will leak from the hole **(see illustration)**. In most cases you'll need a flashlight and mirror to find the hole on the under side of the water pump to check for leaks.

5   If the water pump shaft bearings fail there may be a howling sound coming from the drivebelt area while the engine is running. Shaft wear can be felt if the water pump pulley is rocked up-and-down. Don't mistake drivebelt slippage, which causes a squealing sound, for water pump bearing failure.

---

7   Water pump - removal and installation

Warning: *Wait until the engine is completely cool before beginning this procedure.*

Removal

Refer to illustrations 7.3, 7.5a and 7.5b

1   Disconnect the negative battery cable from the battery. **Caution:** *On models equipped with a Theftlock audio system, be sure the lockout feature is turned off before performing any procedure which requires disconnecting the battery.*

2   Drain the cooling system (see Chapter 1). If the coolant is relatively new or in good condition, save it and reuse it. Refer to Section 5 and remove the coolant recovery tank.

7.3 Use a prybar or long screwdriver to hold the pump pulley from turning while loosening the bolts

7.5a Unscrew the water pump retaining bolts and remove the water pump (3.1L shown, 3.4L similar)

7.5b Water pump mounting bolts - 3800 engine

3   Loosen the bolts on the water pump pulley, using belt tension and a prybar to hold it **(see illustration)**.

4   Remove the serpentine belt (see Chapter 1). On 3.1L/3.4L OHV engines, remove the small belt guard just above the water pump. On 2001 and later 3.8L models, remove the power steering pump (see Chapter 10).

5   Remove the bolts/nuts and detach the water pump from the engine **(see illustrations)**. **Note:** *Most 3.1L and 3.4L models have a locating mark at the top of the pump. If yours doesn't have one, make a mark yourself for help in orienting the pump during reassembly (if the same pump is to be reinstalled).*

Installation

Refer to illustration 7.7

6   Clean the fastener threads and any threaded holes in the engine to remove corrosion and sealant.

7   Compare the new pump to the old one to make sure they're identical. If using the existing pump, inspect the back of the pump for a broken or corroded impeller **(see illustration)**.

8   Remove all traces of old gasket material from the engine with a gasket scraper.

9   Clean the engine and water pump mating surfaces with lacquer thinner or acetone.

10   Carefully attach the pump and new gasket to the engine and start the bolts/nuts finger tight. Make sure the alignment mark (3.1L and 3.4L models) is at the top.

11   Tighten the fasteners in 1/4-turn increments to the torque figure listed in this Chapter's Specifications. Don't overtighten them or the pump may be distorted.

12   Reinstall all parts removed for access to the pump.

13   Refill and bleed the cooling system (see Chapter 1). Run the engine and check for leaks.

8   Coolant temperature gauge sending unit - check and replacement

Warning: *Wait until the engine is completely cool before beginning this procedure.*

Note: *Later models do not have a coolant temperature sending unit. The PCM signals the dashboard warning light based on input from the engine coolant temperature (ECT) sensor.*

Check

Refer to illustrations 8.1a and 8.1b

1   The coolant temperature indicator system is composed of a temperature gauge or warning light mounted in the dash and a

coolant temperature sending unit mounted on the engine **(see illustrations)**. On 3.4L engines, the sending unit is a single-wire sender mounted on the left cylinder head, below the hose connection on the thermostat cover.

2   If an overheating indication occurs, check the coolant level in the system and then make sure the wiring between the gauge and the sending unit is secure and all fuses are intact.

3   To check the circuit and gauge operation, disconnect the electrical connector to the sending unit and using a jumper wire, connect the dark green wire terminal in the harness connector to ground. Turn the ignition to On (engine NOT running). If the gauge deflects full scale, the circuit and gauge are OK. The problem lies in the sending unit.

4   To confirm the sending unit is defective, check the resistance of the unit when the engine is cool. Resistance should be high - approximately 1365 ohms at 100-degrees F. Next, run the engine until it is fully warmed up and check the resistance of the sending unit again. The resistance should now be low - approximately 44 ohms at 280-degrees F. If it doesn't respond, replace the sending unit.

Replacement

5   **Warning:** *Make sure the engine is cool before removing the defective sending unit. There will be some coolant loss as the unit is removed, so be prepared to catch it. Refer to*

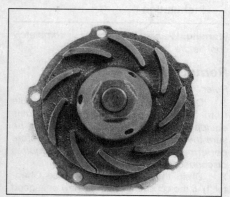

7.7 Inspect the impeller for damage or corrosion

8.1a Coolant temperature gauge sending unit (arrow) - 3.1L engine

8.1b Coolant temperature gauge sending unit (arrow) - 3800 engine

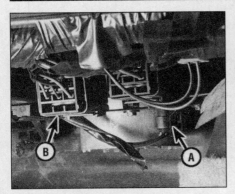

10.3 Blower motor connector location (A), and blower relay (B)

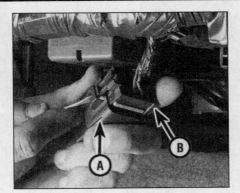

10.6 Use a small screwdriver to release the blower relay (A) from the harness connector (B)

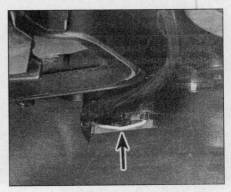

10.7 Blower motor resistor location (arrow)

the coolant **Warning** in Section 2.

6   Prepare the new sending unit by lightly coating the threads with sealant. Disconnect the electrical connector and unscrew the sensor. Install the new sensor as quickly as possible to minimize coolant loss.

7   Check the coolant level after the replacement unit has been installed and fill up the system, if necessary (see Chapter 1). Check now for proper operation of the gauge and sending unit.

9   Engine oil cooler - general information and replacement

General information

1   On earlier 3.1L and 3.4L engines, an engine oil cooler is sandwiched between the oil filter and the engine. Coolant flows through the cooler from two hoses connected to pipes. On later 3.8L engines, a radiator-type engine oil cooler is mounted at the front of the vehicle, behind the radiator grille – hoses and pipes route oil from the engine, through the cooler, and back to the engine.

Replacement

3.1L and 3.4L engines

2   Drain the engine coolant and remove the oil filter (see Chapter 1).

3   If necessary, disconnect the electrical connector from the oil pressure sending unit.

4   Disconnect the knock sensor electrical connector (see Chapter 6).

5   Disconnect the hose clamps and two coolant hoses from the oil cooler.

6   Use a deep socket to remove the threaded adapter holding the oil cooler housing to the oil filter boss on the engine. Pull the oil cooler from the block.

7   Installation is the reverse of removal. Make sure the block mounting surface is clean before installation and that the seal on the engine-side of the cooler is intact and lightly oiled.

3.8L engines

8   Remove the pushpin retainers from the upper radiator air baffle (between the radiator

support and the grille). Tilt the back of the baffle up slightly, then pull it toward the rear to unsnap the clips at the front. Remove the baffle and the upper mounting bolt for the auxiliary cooler. Working under the vehicle, remove the two lower mounting bolts and withdraw the cooler from below the bumper. Remove the line block connector and the cooler lines.

9   Installation is the reverse of removal.

10   Blower motor and circuit - check

Refer to illustrations 10.3, 10.6, 10.7, 10.9 and 10.11

Warning: *The models covered by this manual are equipped with airbags. Always disable the airbag system before working in the vicinity of the impact sensors, steering column or instrument panel to avoid the possibility of accidental deployment of the airbag(s), which could cause personal injury (see Chapter 12). The yellow wires and connectors routed through the instrument panel are for this system. Do not use electrical test equipment on these yellow wires or tamper with them in any way while working under the instrument panel.*

1   Check the fuses and all connections in the circuit for looseness and corrosion. Make sure the battery is fully charged. Refer to the heating and air conditioning system wiring diagrams at the end of Chapter 12 when performing the following checks.

2   Remove the lower right dash insulator panel (below the glove box) for access to the blower motor.

3   Disconnect the electrical connector to the blower motor and connect a voltmeter or test light to the purple wire terminal in the harness connector **(see illustration)**.

4   Turn the ignition to On and place the blower switch on High, battery voltage should be indicated. Using an ohmmeter or self-powered continuity tester, check for continuity to chassis ground on the black wire terminal.

5   If voltage is present and the ground continuity is good, but the blower motor does not operate when connected, the blower

motor is faulty.

6   If no voltage was present at the High speed, place the blower switch on Medium and/or Low and check for voltage at the blower motor connector, the voltage will be lower due to the resistors. If voltage is indicated on Medium and/or Low but not on High, the blower relay or related circuit is faulty (don't forget to check the fuses). Remove the blower relay **(see illustration)** for further testing (see Chapter 12).

7   If no voltage is present at the Medium and/or Low positions, disconnect the electrical connector from the blower motor resistor **(see illustration)**.

8   Using an ohmmeter, check for continuity between the terminal on the resistor corresponding to the dark blue wire terminal in the harness connector and each of the other terminals. Continuity should be indicated across each terminal, although the actual resistance values will vary. If any resistor indicates an open circuit, replace the resistor assembly.

9   To replace the blower resistor, remove the mounting screws and withdraw the resistor assembly from the housing. Inspect the resistor coils for an open circuit condition **(see illustration)**.

10   If the resistors are good, check the blower switch. Turn the ignition to On and check for battery voltage at the yellow, tan and light blue wire terminals in the blower resistor harness connector as the blower speed switch is moved to the different positions.

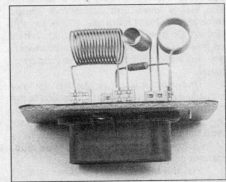

10.9 Inspect the backside of the blower resistor for burned or damaged coils

10.11 Check the terminals on the back of the blower speed switch for continuity

11.2 Remove the three screws (arrows) retaining the blower motor to the housing

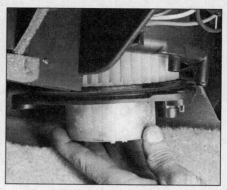

11.3 Lower the blower motor and fan assembly straight down to remove it from the vehicle

11   If voltage was not indicated on one or more of the terminals, the blower speed switch could have a fault at one or more of its switch positions. Remove the heater and air conditioning control assembly (see Section 13) and check for continuity between the terminal corresponding to the brown wire in the harness connector and each of the other terminals as the switch is moved to the different speed positions **(see illustration)**. If continuity is not indicated, replace the switch assembly.

12   If the switch is good, check for battery voltage at the brown wire terminal of the harness connector with the ignition On. If voltage is not present, check the circuit from the control panel harness connector to the fuse box. Also check the circuits from the control panel to the resistor and from the resistor to the blower relay, if necessary.

11 Blower motor - removal and installation

Refer to illustrations 11.2, 11.3 and 11.4
Warning: *The models covered by this manual are equipped with airbags. Always disable the airbag system before working in the vicinity of the impact sensors, steering column or instrument panel to avoid the possibility of accidental deployment of the airbag(s), which could cause personal injury (see Chapter 12). The yellow wires and connectors routed through the instrument panel are for this system. Do not use electrical test equipment on these yellow wires or tamper with them in any way while working under the instrument panel.*
1   Remove the lower right dash insulator panel (below the glove box) for access to the blower motor (see Chapter 11).
2   Disconnect the electrical connector from the blower motor and remove the three screws from the blower housing **(see illustration)**.
3   Pull the blower motor and fan straight down **(see illustration)**.
4   If the fan is damaged, it can be removed from the blower motor in several ways, as the

fan is not simply retained by a nut or clip. The plastic is formed around the motor's shaft **(see illustration)**. The plastic in this area can be cut with a hot knife or a soldering iron. Then support the fan with wood or metal supports placed between the fan and the motor plate, and use a drill press or arbor press to push down on the motor shaft until it is released from the plastic. **Caution:** *Do not use a hammer or the motor shaft could be damaged.* The new fan can be pressed in place, but it should have 0.30-inch clearance between it and the motor plate.
5   Blower motor installation is the reverse of the removal procedure.

12 Heater core - removal and installation

Warning: *The models covered by this manual are equipped with airbags. Always disable the airbag system before working in the vicinity of the impact sensors, steering column or instrument panel to avoid the possibility of accidental deployment of the airbag(s), which could cause personal injury (see Chapter 12). The yellow wires and connectors routed through the instrument panel are for this system. Do not use electrical test equipment on these yellow wires or tamper with them in any way while working under the instrument panel.*

11.4 The center (arrow) of the blower fan must be cut to remove a damaged fan

Removal

Refer to illustrations 12.4, 12.5a, 12.5b, 12.5c, 12.6, 12.7, 12.8a and 12.8b
1   Disconnect the battery cable at the negative battery terminal. **Caution:** *On models equipped with a Theftlock audio system, be sure the lockout feature is turned off before performing any procedure which requires disconnecting the battery.*
2   If necessary, remove the fuel injector trim cover. Drain the cooling system (see Chapter 1).
3   From the inside of the car, remove the lower left and right dash insulator panels (below the steering column and glove box, see Chapter 11).
4   Remove the two screws holding the rear floor duct adapter and remove the duct **(see illustration)**.
5   The heater core is located under the instrument panel behind a large plastic cover. Remove the screws around the perimeter of the cover and carefully work the cover off **(see illustrations)**. Later models may have plastic heat stakes next to the screws. Remove the heat stakes with a small chisel. Before reinstalling the heater core, drill the dimples next to the heat stakes with a 7/32-inch drill bit.
6   Remove the screws retaining the two coolant pipe clamps **(see illustration)**
7   Remove the metal clips where the heater core pipes enter the core, then twist

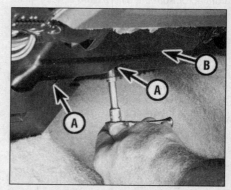

12.4 Remove the screws (A) and the rear floor duct adapter (B)

12.5a Heater core cover screw locations (arrows) (cover removed for clarity)

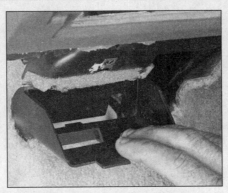

12.5b When you are ready to pull down the cover, fold this duct connector at the floor down against the carpet for clearance

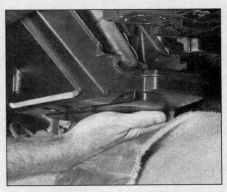

12.5c With all screws out, gently twist and pull the cover from the heater core housing

and pull the two pipes out of the core **(see illustration)**.

8 Remove the screw and the clamp at the bottom center of the heater core and pull the core down and out **(see illustrations)**. **Caution:** *Have plenty of old towels on the floor to protect the carpet from spilled coolant.*

Installation

Refer to illustration 12.9

9 Installation is the reverse of removal. **Note:** *When reinstalling the heater core, make sure new O-rings are in place where the heater core pipes enter the core* **(see illustration)**.

10 Refill and bleed the cooling system (see Chapter 1).

11 Start the engine and check for leaks and proper heater operation.

---

13 Heater and air conditioning control assembly - removal and installation

Refer to illustrations 13.3a, 13.3b and 13.3c
Warning: *The models covered by this manual are equipped with airbags. Always disable the airbag system before working in the vicinity of*

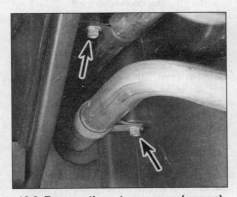

12.6 Remove these two screws (arrows) retaining the heater core pipe clamps near the firewall

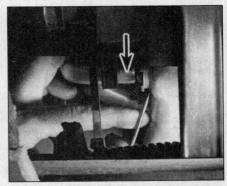

12.7 Use a small screwdriver to pry off the clips holding the pipes (arrow indicates one) to the heater core

the impact sensors, steering column or instrument panel to avoid the possibility of accidental deployment of the airbag(s), which could cause personal injury (see Chapter 12). The yellow wires and connectors routed through the instrument panel are for this system. Do not use electrical test equipment on these yellow wires or tamper with them in any way while working under the instrument panel.

1 Disconnect the battery cable from the negative battery terminal. **Caution:** *On*

models equipped with a Theftlock audio system, be sure the lockout feature is turned off before performing any procedure which requires disconnecting the battery.

2 Remove the main instrument panel bezel to allow access to the heater/air conditioning control mounting screw(s) (see Chapter 11).

3 Remove the control assembly retaining screw and pull the unit out and to your left to guide its tabs out of a slot-mount on the right

12.8a Remove the screw and take off the heater core retaining bracket (arrow)

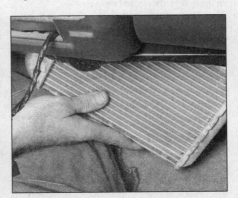

12.8b Since the pipe connections are on the left of the core, lower the core from the right first, to spill as little coolant as possible

12.9 Replace the seals where the pipes enter the heater core (arrows)

13.3a Remove the screw (arrow) on the left, then slide the panel out of its slot-mount on the right side. Later models have two screws and no slot-mount

13.3b Pull the bezel forward, then detach the two electrical connectors by squeezing the tabs together and pulling the connectors off

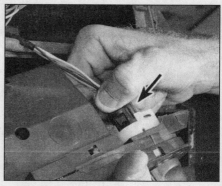

13.3c On some models, the blower speed switch connector (arrow) pulls straight out; this model has a tab that must be depressed while pulling

side **(see illustration)**. Pull it out just far enough to allow disconnecting the electrical connectors from the control head **(see illustrations)**. Later models also have two vacuum connectors.

4   To install the control assembly, reverse the removal procedure.

14   Air conditioning and heating system - check and maintenance

Warning: *The air conditioning system is under high pressure. DO NOT loosen any fittings or remove any components until after the system has been discharged. Air conditioning refrigerant should be properly discharged into an EPA-approved recovery container at a dealership service department or an automotive air conditioning repair facility. Always wear eye protection when disconnecting air conditioning system fittings.*

1   The following maintenance steps should be performed on a regular basis to ensure that the air conditioner continues to operate at peak efficiency:

a) *Check the drivebelt (see Chapter 1).*
b) *Check the condition of the hoses. Look for cracks, hardening and deterioration. Look at potential leak areas (hoses and fittings) for signs of refrigerant oil leaking out.* **Warning:** *Do not replace air conditioning hoses until the system has been discharged by a dealership or air conditioning repair facility.*
c) *Check the fins of the condenser for leaves, bugs and other foreign material. A soft brush and compressed air can be used to remove them.*
d) *Check the wire harness for correct routing, broken wires, damaged insulation, etc. Make sure the electrical connectors are clean and tight.*
e) *Maintain the correct refrigerant charge.*

2   The system should be run for about 10 minutes at least once a month. This is particularly important during the winter months because long-term non-use can cause hardening of the internal seals.

3   Because of the complexity of the air conditioning system and the special equipment required to effectively work on it, accurate troubleshooting of the system should be left to a certified air conditioning technician.

4   If the air conditioning system doesn't operate at all, check the fuse panel. Check the HVAC fuse and the air conditioning compressor relay.

5   Watch the air conditioning compressor while the system is on. The clutch at the front of the compressor should be engaged and turning. If it is not, connect a jumper wire with battery voltage to the clutch electrical connector. If it still doesn't operate, connect another jumper wire from the ground side of the clutch's electrical connector to an engine ground. If it still fails to engage, the clutch needs repair or replacement, both of which should be handled by a dealer service department or air conditioning repair shop.

6   If the compressor clutch did operate when the voltage was applied, check the low-pressure cycling switch (not on all models), located in the low-pressure line near or on the accumulator. Pull the electrical connector off and insert a short jumper wire (a paper clip formed into a U-shape will work) to connect both terminals. If the compressor clutch now engages, the refrigerant is probably low, see recharging procedure below.

7   The most common cause of poor cooling is simply a low system refrigerant charge. If a noticeable drop in cool air output occurs, the following quick check will help you determine if the refrigerant level is low. For more complete information on the air conditioning system, refer to the *Haynes Automotive Heating and Air Conditioning Manual.*

Checking the refrigerant charge

Refer to illustration 14.11

8   Warm the engine up to normal operating temperature.

9   Place the air conditioning temperature selector at the coldest setting and the blower at the highest setting. Open the doors (to make sure the air conditioning system doesn't cycle off as soon as it cools the

passenger compartment).

10   With the compressor engaged - the clutch will make an audible click and the center of the clutch will rotate - feel the surface of the accumulator and the evaporator inlet pipe. **Note:** *The 3800 V6 uses a type of compressor that does not cycle; it changes its stroke to match system demand. If the smaller diameter line feels warm and the receiver/drier feels cool, the system is properly charged. On 3800 V6 models, feel the pipe on either side of the expansion tube - there should be a noticeable difference in temperature.*

11   Place a thermometer in the dashboard vent nearest the evaporator and add refrigerant to the system until the indicated temperature is around 40 to 45-degrees F **(see illustration)**. If the ambient (outside) air temperature is very high, say 110-degrees F, the duct air temperature will probably be higher, but generally the air conditioning is 30 to 40-degrees F cooler than the ambient air. **Note:** *Humidity of the ambient air also affects the cooling capacity of the system. Higher ambient humidity lowers the effectiveness of the air conditioning system.*

Adding refrigerant

Refer to illustrations 14.12 and 14.15
Note: *There are two types of refrigerant; R-12, used on earlier models, and the more*

14.11 Use a thermometer in the center dash vent while the air conditioning is ON to check for cooling efficiency

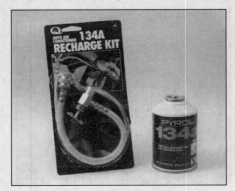

14.12 A basic charging kit for R-134a systems is available at most auto parts stores

14.15 Add refrigerant to the low-side port only (arrow) - the procedure is easier if you wrap the can with a warm, wet towel to prevent icing

14.25 Check that the evaporator drain tube (arrow) on the firewall is not plugged

environmentally friendly R-134a used on all models covered by this book. These two refrigerants (and their appropriate refrigerant oils) are not compatible and must never be mixed or components will be damaged. Use only R-134a refrigerant and compatible oils when servicing your system.

12   Buy an R-134a automotive charging kit at an auto parts store. A charging kit includes a tap valve and a short section of hose that can be attached between the tap valve and the system low side service valve **(see illustration)**. One can of refrigerant should be enough to bring the system charge up to a sufficient level. Because of the possibility of a leak in the system it is a good idea to buy a can with a colored refrigerant dye. If the system is leaking, the colored dye will leak out with the refrigerant and help you pinpoint the location of the leak.

13   Hook up the charging kit by following the manufacturer's instructions. **Warning:** DO NOT hook the charging kit hose to the system high side! The fittings on the charging kit are designed to fit **only** on the low side of the system.

14   Back off the valve handle on the charging kit and screw the kit onto the refrigerant can, making sure first that the O-ring or rubber seal inside the threaded portion of the kit is in place. **Warning:** Wear protective eye wear when dealing with pressurized refrigerant cans.

15   Remove the dust cap from the low-side charging connection and attach the quick-connect fitting on the kit hose **(see illustration)**.

16   Warm up the engine and turn on the air conditioner. Keep the charging kit hose away from the fan and other moving parts. **Note:** The charging process requires the compressor to be running. Your compressor may cycle off if the pressure is low due to a low charge. If the clutch cycles off, you can pull the low-pressure cycling switch plug from the evaporator inlet line and attach a jumper wire across the terminals. This will keep the compressor ON.

17   Turn the valve handle on the kit until the stem pierces the can, then back the handle out to release the refrigerant. You should be

able to hear the rush of gas. Add refrigerant to the low side of the system until both the accumulator surface and the evaporator inlet pipe feel about the same temperature. Allow stabilization time between each addition.

18   If you have an accurate thermometer, you can place it in the center air conditioning duct inside the vehicle and keep track of the "conditioned" air temperature. A charged system that is working properly should put out air that is 40-degrees F. If the ambient (outside) air temperature is very high, say 110-degrees F, the duct air temperature will probably be higher, but generally the air conditioning is 30 to 40-degrees-F cooler than the ambient air.

19   When the can is empty, turn the valve handle to the closed position and release the connection from the low-side port. Replace the dust cap. **Warning:** Never add more than one can of refrigerant to the system (if more than one can is required, the system should be evacuated and leak tested).

20   Remove the charging kit from the can and store the kit for future use with the piercing valve in the UP position, to prevent inadvertently piercing the can on the next use.

Heating systems

21   If the carpet under the heater core is damp, or if antifreeze vapor or steam is coming through the vents, the heater core is leaking. Remove it (see Section 12) and install a new unit (most radiator shops will not repair a leaking heater core).

22   If the air coming out of the heater vents isn't hot, the problem could stem from any of the following causes:

a) The thermostat is stuck open, preventing the engine coolant from warming up enough to carry heat to the heater core. Replace the thermostat (see Section 3).

b) A heater hose is blocked, preventing the flow of coolant through the heater core. Feel both heater hoses at the firewall. They should be hot. If one of them is cold, there is an obstruction in one of the hoses or in the heater core, or the heater control valve is shut. Detach the hoses and back flush the heater core

with a water hose. If the heater core is clear but circulation is impeded, remove the two hoses and flush them out with a water hose.

c) If flushing fails to remove the blockage from the heater core, the core must be replaced (see Section 12).

23   If the blower motor speed does not correspond to the setting selected on the blower switch, the problem could be a bad fuse, circuit, control panel or blower resistor (see Section 10).

24   If there isn't any air coming out of the vents:

a) Turn the ignition ON and activate the fan control. Place your ear at the heating/air conditioning register (vent) and listen. Most motors are audible. Can you hear the motor running?

b) If you can't (and have already verified that the blower switch and the blower motor resistor are good), the blower motor itself is probably bad (see Section 11).

25   Inspect the drain hose from the heater/evaporator assembly at the right-center of the firewall, make sure it is not clogged **(see illustration)**. If there is a humid mist coming from the system ducts, this hose may be plugged with leaves or road debris.

Eliminating air conditioning odors

26   Unpleasant odors that often develop in air conditioning systems are caused by the growth of a fungus, usually on the surface of the evaporator core. The warm, humid environment there is a perfect breeding ground for mildew to develop.

27   The evaporator core on most vehicles is difficult to access, and factory dealerships have a lengthy, expensive process for eliminating the fungus by opening up the evaporator case and using a powerful disinfectant and rinse on the core until the fungus is gone. You can service your own system at home, but it takes something much stronger than basic household germ-killers or deodorizers.

28   Aerosol disinfectants for automotive air conditioning systems are available in most auto parts stores, but remember when shopping for them that the most effective

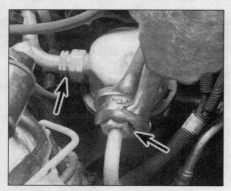

15.2 Disconnect the inlet and outlet lines (arrows) using a backup wrench so the line doesn't get twisted

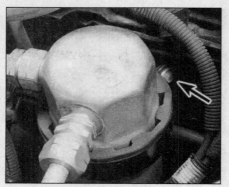

15.3 Remove the accumulator clamp bolt (arrow)

16.8 Disconnect the electrical connector (A) from the air conditioning compressor - on the 3.1L and later 3.4L OHV models there are three mounting bolts (B)

treatments are also the most expensive. The basic procedure for using these sprays is to start by running the system in the RECIRC mode for ten minutes with the blower on its highest speed. Use the highest heat mode to dry out the system and keep the compressor from engaging by disconnecting the wiring connector at the compressor (see Section 16).

29 The disinfectant can usually comes with a long spray hose. Remove the blower motor resistor (see Section 11), point the nozzle inside the hole and spray, according to the manufacturer's recommendations. Try to cover the whole surface of the evaporator core, by aiming the spray up, down and sideways. Follow the manufacturer's recommendations for the length of spray and waiting time between applications.

30 Once the evaporator has been cleaned, the best way to prevent the mildew from coming back again is to make sure your evaporator housing drain tube is clear **(see illustration 14.25)**.

---

15 Air conditioning accumulator/drier - removal and installation

Warning: *The air conditioning system is under high pressure. DO NOT loosen any fittings or remove any components until after the system has been discharged. Air conditioning refrigerant should be properly discharged into an EPA-approved container at a dealership service department or an automotive air conditioning repair facility. Always wear eye protection when disconnecting air conditioning system fittings.*

Removal

Refer to illustrations 15.2 and 15.3

1   Have the air conditioning system discharged (see **Warning** above). Disconnect the cable from the negative terminal of the battery. **Caution:** *On models equipped with a Theftlock audio system, be sure the lockout feature is turned off before performing any procedure which requires disconnecting the battery.*

2   If necessary, remove the air cleaner

assembly. Disconnect the refrigerant inlet and outlet lines **(see illustration)**, using a back-up wrench. Cap or plug the open lines immediately to prevent the entry of dirt or moisture.

3   Loosen the clamp bolt on the mounting bracket and slide the accumulator/drier assembly up and out of the bracket **(see illustration)**.

Installation

4   If you are replacing the accumulator/drier with a new one, drain the old oil out of the old drier into a measuring container. Add that amount of new oil, plus one ounce, to the new unit (oil must be R-134a compatible).

5   Place the new accumulator/drier into position in the bracket.

6   Install the inlet and outlet lines, using clean refrigerant oil on the new O-rings. Tighten the mounting bolt securely.

7   Connect the cable to the negative terminal of the battery.

8   Have the system evacuated, recharged and leak tested by a dealership service department or an automotive air conditioning repair facility.

---

16 Air conditioning compressor - removal and installation

Warning: *The air conditioning system is under high pressure. DO NOT loosen any fittings or remove any components until after the system has been discharged. Air conditioning refrigerant should be properly discharged into an EPA-approved container at a dealership service department or an automotive air conditioning repair facility. Always wear eye protection when disconnecting air conditioning system fittings.*

Note: *The accumulator/drier (see Section 15) and the expansion (orifice) tube (see Section 19) should be replaced whenever the compressor is replaced.*

Removal

Refer to illustrations 16.8 and 16.9

1   Have the air conditioning system

discharged (see **Warning** above). Disconnect the cable from the negative terminal of the battery. **Caution:** *On models equipped with Theftlock audio system, be sure the lockout feature is turned off before performing any procedure which requires disconnecting the battery.*

2   Clean the compressor thoroughly around the refrigerant line fittings.

3   Remove the serpentine drivebelt (see Chapter 1).

4   On 1995 through 2000 models, refer to Section 4 and remove the right-side electric cooling fan. On later models, remove the lower air deflector (bolted to the bottom of the front bumper).

5   If necessary, on earlier 3.1L and 3800 engines, refer to Chapter 2 Part A or Part C and remove the right-side engine strut mount bracket.

6   On most models, a plastic splash shield must be removed from underneath for access to the compressor mounts.

7   Raise the vehicle and support it securely on jackstands.

8   Disconnect the electrical connector from the air conditioning compressor **(see illustration)**.

9   Disconnect the suction and discharge lines from the compressor. Both lines are mounted to the back of the compressor with a plate secured by one bolt **(see illustration)**. Plug the open fittings to prevent the entry of dirt and moisture, and discard the seals between the plate and compressor.

10   On 3.1L and later 3.4L OHV models, remove the three bolts **(see illustration 16.8)** and remove the compressor. On 3800 and earlier 3.4L engines, unbolt and remove the rear compressor mount.

11   On 3.4L and 2003 and earlier 3800 models, remove the compressor-to-front-bracket bolts (3.4L) or nuts (3800) and remove the compressor from the engine compartment. On 2004 and later 3800 models, remove the nut and bolts. **Note:** *On 2003 and earlier 3800 models, the compressor must be pulled forward off the*

16.9 Remove the retaining bolt (arrow) securing the refrigerant lines to back of the compressor

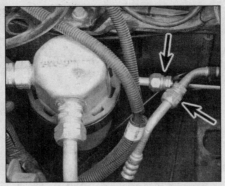

17.2 The condenser lines (arrows) are located just to the left of the radiator

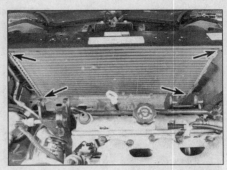

17.4 Pull the condenser core carefully until it is free of the rubber insulators (arrows)

three studs on its front mount. If there isn't room, the front engine mount may have to be removed (refer to Chapter 2, Part C).

Installation

12   If a new compressor is being installed, drain the new compressor of oil. Drain the oil from the old compressor into a graduated container. If less than one ounce was drained, add two ounces of new oil to the new compressor. If more than one ounce was drained from the old compressor, add that exact amount of new oil to the new compressor. Also follow any directions included with the new compressor. **Note:** Some replacement compressors come with refrigerant oil in them. Follow the directions with the compressor regarding the draining of excess oil prior to installation. **Caution:** The oil used must be labeled as compatible with R-134a systems.
13   Installation is the reverse of the disassembly. When installing the line fitting bolt to the compressor, use new seals lubricated with clean refrigerant oil, and tighten the bolt securely.
14   Reconnect the battery cable to the negative battery terminal.
15   Have the system evacuated, recharged and leak tested by a dealership service department or an automotive air conditioning repair facility.

17   Air conditioning condenser - removal and installation

Warning: The air conditioning system is under high pressure. DO NOT loosen any fittings or remove any components until after the system has been discharged. Air conditioning refrigerant should be properly discharged into an EPA-approved container at a dealership service department or an automotive air conditioning repair facility. Always wear eye protection when disconnecting air conditioning system fittings.

Removal

Refer to illustrations 17.2 and 17.4
1   Have the air conditioning system

discharged and recovered (see **Warning** above). Disconnect the cable from the negative terminal of the battery. **Caution:** On models equipped with a Theftlock audio system, be sure the lockout feature is turned off before performing any procedure which requires disconnecting the battery.
2   Disconnect the refrigerant line fittings from the condenser and cap the open fittings to prevent the entry of dirt and moisture. **(see illustration)**.
3   Remove the cooling fans (see Section 4) and the radiator (see Section 5).
4   Pull the condenser toward the engine, wiggling it until it is free of the upper and lower rubber insulators, then withdraw it carefully from the vehicle **(see illustration)**. **Caution:** The condenser is made of aluminum - be careful not to damage it during removal.

Installation

5   Installation is the reverse of removal. Be sure to use new, compatible O-rings on the refrigerant line fittings lubricated the O-rings with clean refrigerant oil. If a new condenser is installed, add 1 ounce of new refrigerant oil to the system (R-134a compatible).
6   Have the system evacuated, recharged and leak tested by a dealership service department or an automotive air conditioning repair facility.

18   Air conditioning evaporator - removal and installation (models through 2000)

Warning 1: The models covered by this manual are equipped with airbags. Always disable the airbag system before working in the vicinity of the impact sensors, steering column or instrument panel to avoid the possibility of accidental deployment of the airbag(s), which could cause personal injury (see Chapter 12). The yellow wires and connectors routed through the instrument panel are for this system. Do not use electrical test equipment on these yellow wires or tamper with them in any way while

working under the instrument panel.
Warning 2: The air conditioning system is under high pressure. DO NOT loosen any fittings or remove any components until after the system has been discharged. Air conditioning refrigerant should be properly discharged into an EPA-approved container at a dealership service department or an automotive air conditioning repair facility. Always wear eye protection when disconnecting air conditioning system fittings.
Note: On 2001 and later models, removal of the evaporator core requires removal of the instrument panel, steering column and cross-vehicle brace. This procedure is beyond the scope of the home mechanic.

Removal

Refer to illustrations 18.3, 18.5a and 18.5b
1   Have the air conditioning system discharged and the refrigerant recovered (see **Warning** above). Disconnect the cable from the negative terminal of the battery. **Caution:** On models equipped with a Theftlock audio system, be sure the lockout feature is turned off before performing any procedure which requires disconnecting the battery.
2   Drain the cooling system (see Chapter 1).
3   Disconnect the air conditioning lines at the passenger side of the firewall **(see illustration)**.

18.3 Remove the clamp bolt (arrow) and disconnect the two refrigerant lines at the firewall

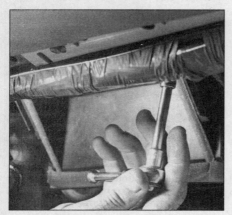

18.5a Remove the screws and the evaporator core cover . . .

18.5b . . . then pull the evaporator core (arrow) down and out to remove it

19.3 Disconnect the high pressure line at this fitting (arrow) to replace the expansion (orifice) tube

4   Follow the procedures in Section 12 for removing the heater core.

5   Remove the evaporator core cover, then slide the evaporator core out carefully **(see illustrations)**.

6   Check the core over carefully for signs of leaks.

7   If a new evaporator core is to be installed, save all of the sealing gaskets from the original unit and transfer them.

Installation

8   Installation is the reverse of the removal procedure. Lubricate all O-rings with clean refrigerant oil.

9   If a new evaporator has been installed, add 3 ounces of new refrigerant oil (oil must be R-134a compatible). Have the system evacuated, recharged and leak tested by a dealership service department or an automotive air conditioning repair facility.

19 Air conditioning expansion (orifice) tube - removal and installation

Refer to illustrations 19.3 and 19.4

Warning: *The air conditioning system is under high pressure. DO NOT loosen any fittings or remove any components until after the system has been discharged. Air conditioning refrigerant should be properly discharged into an EPA-approved container at a dealership service department or an automotive air conditioning repair facility. Always wear eye protection when discon-*

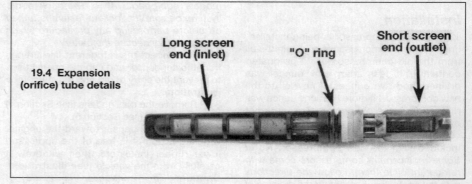

19.4 Expansion (orifice) tube details

Long screen end (inlet)   "O" ring   Short screen end (outlet)

necting air conditioning system fittings.

Note: *Whenever the expansion tube is replaced, the accumulator-drier should also be replaced* (see Section 15).

1   Have the air conditioning system discharged and the refrigerant recovered (see **Warning** above). Disconnect the cable from the negative terminal of the battery. **Caution:** *On models equipped with a Theftlock audio system, be sure the lockout feature is turned off before performing any procedure which requires disconnecting the battery.*

2   Remove the air cleaner and duct (see Chapter 4).

3   Disconnect the refrigerant high-pressure line at the fitting right over the transaxle, about ten inches behind the accumulator/drier **(see illustration)**.

4   The expansion *(orifice)* tube is a tube with a fixed-diameter orifice and a mesh filter at each end **(see illustration)**. When you separate the pipe at the fitting you will see

one end of the orifice tube inside the pipe leading to the evaporator. Use needle-nose pliers to remove the orifice tube.

5   The orifice tube acts to meter the refrigerant, changing it from high-pressure liquid to low-pressure liquid. It is possible to reuse the orifice tube if:

a) *The screens aren't plugged with grit or foreign material*

b) *Neither screen is torn*

c) *The plastic housing over the screens is intact*

d) *The brass orifice inside the plastic housing is unrestricted*

6   Installation is the reverse of removal. Be sure to insert the expansion tube with the shorter end in first, toward the evaporator. **Caution:** *Always use a new O-ring when installing the expansion tube.*

7   Retighten the fitting and refrigerant line, then have the system evacuated, recharged and leak-tested by the shop that discharged it.

Chapter 4 Fuel and exhaust systems

Contents

Specifications

General

Fuel pressure (key On, engine not running)
1995	41 to 47 psi
1996	48 to 55 psi
1997	41 to 47 psi
1998	
3.1L	41 to 47 psi
3.8L	48 to 55 psi
1999 through 2000	
3.1L and 3.4L	52 to 59 psi
3.8L	48 to 58 psi
2001 and later	
3.4L	52 to 59 psi
3.8L	53 to 59 psi

Fuel pressure at idle (with vacuum to fuel pressure regulator)
1995	31 to 44 psi
1996	38 to 52 psi
1997	31 to 44 psi
1998	
3.1L	31 to 44 psi
3.8L	38 to 52 psi
1999 through 2000	
3.1 and 3.4L	52 to 59 psi
3.8L	38 to 52 psi
2001 and later	Pressure should decrease by 3 to 10 psi from the values given above under "Fuel pressure (key On, engine not running)"
Injector resistance	11 to 14 ohms (approximate)

Torque specifications

Ft-lbs (unless otherwise indicated)

Exhaust pipe-to-manifold nuts	15 to 24
Fuel pressure regulator mounting screw	80 in-lbs
Fuel pressure regulator to fuel pipe nut	156 in-lbs
Fuel rail mounting bolts/nuts	89 in-lbs
IAC valve screws	27 in-lbs
Throttle body bolts/nuts	
3.1L and 3.4L OHV and 3.4L DOHC	18 to 21
3.8L	89 in-lbs
Throttle body support bracket bolts	89 in-lbs

1 General information

All models covered by this manual are equipped with a sequential Multiport Fuel Injection (MFI) system. This system uses timed impulses to sequentially inject the fuel directly into the intake ports of each cylinder. The Powertrain Control Module (PCM) controls the injectors. The PCM monitors various engine parameters and delivers the exact amount of fuel, in the correct sequence, into the intake ports.

All models are equipped with an electric fuel pump, mounted in the fuel tank. It is necessary to remove the fuel tank for access to the fuel pump. The fuel level sending unit is an integral component of the fuel pump module and it must be removed from the fuel tank in the same manner.

The exhaust system consists of exhaust manifolds, a catalytic converter, an exhaust pipe and a muffler. Each of these components is replaceable. For further information regarding the catalytic converter, refer to Chapter 6.

2   Fuel pressure relief procedure

Refer to illustrations 2.3a and 2.3b

Warning: *Gasoline is extremely flammable, so take extra precautions when you work on any part of the fuel system. Don't smoke or allow open flames or bare light bulbs near the work area, and don't work in a garage where a gas-type appliance (such as a water heater or a clothes dryer) is present. Since gasoline is carcinogenic, wear latex gloves when there's a possibility of being exposed to fuel, and, if you spill any fuel on your skin, rinse it off immediately with soap and water. Mop up any spills immediately and do not store fuel-soaked rags where they could ignite. The fuel system is under constant pressure, so, if any fuel lines are to be disconnected, the fuel pressure in the system must be relieved first. When you perform any kind of work on the fuel system, wear safety glasses and have a Class B type fire extinguisher on hand.*

Note: *After the fuel pressure has been relieved, it's a good idea to lay a shop towel over any fuel connection to be disassembled, to absorb the residual fuel that may leak out when servicing the fuel system.*

1   Before servicing any fuel system component, you must relieve the fuel pressure to minimize the risk of fire or personal injury.

2   Remove the fuel filler cap - this will relieve any pressure built up in the tank.

3   Locate the test port on the fuel rail and connect a fuel pressure gauge, equipped with a bleed-off valve and drain tube, to the test port. On all 3.1L/3.4L OHV engines, the fuel pressure test port is located at the front (passenger side) of the engine on the end of the right (rear) fuel rail. On 1995 3.4L DOHC engines, the fuel pressure test port is located at the front (passenger side) of the engine in the crossover pipe between the fuel rails. On 1996 through 1997 3.4L DOHC engines, the fuel pressure test port is located on the left (front) fuel rail which requires removing the injector trim cover to access the test port (see Section 13). On 1998 and later 3.8L engines, the fuel pressure test port is located at the fuel

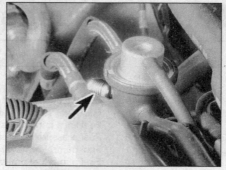

2.3a On 3.8L engines, the fuel pressure test port (arrow) is located on the fuel pressure regulator - unscrew the cap and install a fuel pump pressure gauge

pressure regulator **(see illustration)** which also requires removing the injector trim cover to access the test port (see Section 13). Relieve the fuel pressure by bleeding the fuel through the bleed-off valve and into an approved container **(see illustration)**.

4   Place shop towels around the fuel fitting to be disconnected to absorb any residual fuel that may spill out.

3   Fuel pump/fuel pressure - check

Warning: *Gasoline is extremely flammable, so take extra precautions when you work on any part of the fuel system. See the* **Warning** *in Section 2.*

Note: *In order to perform the fuel pressure test, you will need a fuel pressure gauge capable of measuring high fuel pressure. The fuel gauge must be equipped with the proper fittings or adapters required to attach it to the fuel line or fuel rail.*

Preliminary checks

1   Check that there is adequate fuel in the fuel tank.

2   Verify the fuel pump actually runs. Have an assistant turn the ignition switch to ON - you should hear a brief whirring noise (approximately two seconds) as the pump comes on

2.3b Attach a fuel pressure gauge to the test port (arrow) and open the valve to drain the excess fuel out of the drain tube (arrow) and into an approved fuel container (3.1L engine shown)

and pressurizes the system. **Note:** *The fuel pump is easily heard through the gas tank filler neck.* If there is no response from the fuel pump (makes no sound) proceed to Step 9 and check the fuel pump electrical circuit.

Fuel pump output and pressure check

Refer to illustrations 3.6 and 3.7

3   Connect a fuel pressure gauge to the fuel pressure test port (see Section 2 for test port location).

4   Turn the ignition switch ON (engine not running) with the air conditioning off. The fuel pump should run for about two seconds - note the reading on the gauge. After the pump stops running the pressure should hold steady. It should be within the range listed in this Chapter's Specifications.

5   Start the engine and let it idle at normal operating temperature. The pressure should be lower by 3 to 10 psi. If all the pressure readings are within the limits listed in this Chapter's Specifications, the system is operating properly.

6   If the pressure did not drop by 3 to 10 psi after starting the engine, apply 12 to 14 inches of vacuum to the pressure regulator, using a hand-held vacuum pump **(see illustration)**. If the pressure drops, repair the vacuum source to the regulator. If the pressure does not drop, replace the regulator.

7   If the fuel pressure is not within specifications, check the following:

  a) *If the pressure is higher than specified, check for vacuum to the fuel pressure regulator* **(see illustration)**. *Vacuum must fluctuate with the increase or decrease in the engine rpm. If vacuum is present, check for a pinched or clogged fuel return hose or pipe. If the return line is OK, replace the regulator.*

  b) *If the pressure is lower than specified, change the fuel filter to rule out the possibility of a clogged filter. If the pressure is still low, install a fuel line shut-off adapter between the pressure regulator and the return line (this can be fabricated from fuel line, a shut off valve and the necessary fittings to mate with*

3.6 Connect a vacuum pump to the fuel pressure regulator, apply vacuum to the fuel pressure regulator and check the fuel pressure - the fuel pressure should decrease as the vacuum increases

3.7 Disconnect the vacuum hose from the fuel pressure regulator (arrow) and check for vacuum - vacuum must fluctuate with the increase or decrease in engine rpm

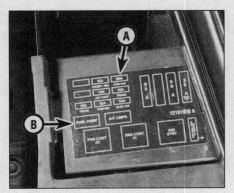

3.9 The ECM or PCM BAT (or just PCM on later models) fuse (A) and the fuel pump relay (F/PMP RLY on later models) (B) locations are clearly marked on the cover of the passenger side fuse/relay control box in the engine compartment

the pressure regulator and the return line, or, instead of a shut-off valve, use fuel hose that can be pinched with a pair of pliers). With the valve open (or the hose not pinched), start the engine (if possible) and slowly close the valve or pinch the hose (only pinch the hose on the adapter you fabricated). If the pressure rises above 47 psi, replace the regulator (see Section 13). *Warning: Don't allow the fuel pressure to exceed 60 psi. Also, don't attempt to restrict the vehicle's return line by pinching it, as the nylon fuel line will be damaged.*

c) If the pressure is still low with the fuel return line restricted, an injector (or injectors) may be leaking (see Section 13) or the in-tank fuel pump may be faulty.

8   After the testing is done, relieve the fuel pressure (see Section 2) and remove the fuel pressure gauge.

Fuel pump electrical circuit check

Refer to illustrations 3.9 and 3.10

Note: *Refer to Chapter 12 for additional wiring schematics that detail the fuel pump relay and circuit.*

9   If the pump does not turn on (makes no sound) with the ignition switch in the ON position, check the ECM or PCM BAT (fuel pump) fuse **(see illustration)**. If the fuse is blown, replace the fuse and see if the pump works. If the pump now works, check for a short in the circuit between the fuel pump relay and the fuel pump.

10   If the pump still does not work, check the fuel pump relay circuit. With the help of an assistant cycle the ignition key ON and OFF (engine not running), while checking for battery voltage at the relay connector **(see illustration)**. If battery voltage does not exist, check the circuit from the PCM to the relay.

Note 1: *If oil pressure drops below the specified pressure level, the oil pressure switch will act as a fuel pressure cut-off device. Be sure to check the oil pressure switch and circuit in the event of a difficult*

3.10 Remove the fuel pump relay and check for voltage at the electrical connector (arrow) while the ignition key is cycled ON and OFF - one terminal should have battery voltage at all times with the ignition key ON, and another terminal should have voltage for about two seconds with the ignition key ON

problem diagnosing the fuel pump circuit (refer to the wiring diagrams at the end of Chapter 12).

Note 2: *The theft deterrent system (if equipped) is equipped with a fuel enable circuit. If this system is malfunctioning it will not allow the PCM to signal the fuel pump relay or the engine to crank over. Be sure to check the theft deterrent system and circuit in the event of a difficult problem diagnosing the fuel pump circuit.*

11   If battery voltage exists, check the relay (see Chapter 12) or replace the relay with a known good relay and retest. If necessary, have the relay checked by a qualified automotive electrical specialist.

12   If the fuel pump does not activate, check for power to the fuel pump at the fuel tank. Access to the fuel pump is difficult, but it is possible to check for battery voltage at the electrical connector near the tank. If voltage is present at the fuel pump connector, replace the fuel pump.

---

4   Fuel lines and fittings - repair and replacement

Warning: *Gasoline is extremely flammable, so take extra precautions when you work on any part of the fuel system. See the **Warning** in Section 2.*

1   Always relieve the fuel pressure before servicing fuel lines or fittings on fuel-injected vehicles (see Section 2).

2   The fuel feed, return and vapor lines extend from the fuel tank to the engine compartment. The lines are secured to the underbody with clip and screw assemblies. These lines must be occasionally inspected for leaks, kinks and dents.

3   If evidence of dirt is found in the system or fuel filter during disassembly, the line should be disconnected and blown out. Check the fuel strainer on the fuel level sending unit (see Section 8) for damage and deterioration.

Steel and nylon tubing

4   Because fuel lines used on fuel-injected vehicles are under high pressure, they require special consideration.

5   If replacement of a metal fuel line or emission line is called for, use welded steel tubing meeting original equipment specifications. Don't use copper or aluminum tubing to replace steel tubing. These materials cannot withstand normal vehicle vibration.

6   If is becomes necessary to replace a section of nylon fuel line, replace it only with the correct part number - don't use any substitutes.

7   Some fuel lines have threaded fittings with O-rings. Any time the fittings are loosened to service or replace components:

a) *Use a back-up wrench while loosening and tightening the fittings.*

b) *Check all O-rings for cuts, cracks and deterioration. Replace any that appear worn or damaged.*

c) *If the lines are replaced, always use original equipment parts, or parts that meet the GM standards specified in this Section.*

d) *Use specialty fuel line disconnect tools to release the spring-lock mechanisms inside the quick-disconnect fuel line fittings particular to many of the components (fuel filter, fuel rail, fuel pressure regulator, etc.).*

Rubber hose

Warning: *These models are equipped with electronic fuel injection - use only original equipment replacement hoses or their equivalent. Others may fail from the high pressures of this system.*

8   When rubber hose is used to replace a metal line, use reinforced, fuel resistant hose. Hose other than this could fail prematurely and could fail to meet Federal emission standards. Hose inside diameter must match line outside diameter. **Warning:** *Don't substitute rubber hose for metal line on high-pressure systems. Use only genuine factory replacement lines or lines meeting factory specifications.*

9   Don't use rubber hose within four inches of any part of the exhaust system or within ten inches of the catalytic converter. Metal lines and rubber hoses must never be allowed to chafe against the frame. A minimum of 1/4-inch clearance must be maintained around a line or hose to prevent contact with the frame.

Removal and installation

Refer to illustrations 4.10, 4.12a, 4.12b and 4.13

Note: *The following procedure and accompanying illustrations are typical for vehicles covered by this manual. On quick-disconnect (non-threaded) fittings, clean off the fittings before disconnection to prevent dirt from getting in the fittings. After disconnection, clean the fittings with compressed air and apply a few drops of oil.*

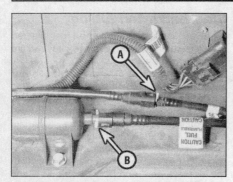

4.10 Some models are equipped with fuel lines that can be disconnected by pinching the tabs and separating each connector

A Fuel return line   B Fuel feed line

10   Relieve the fuel pressure (see Section 2) and disconnect the fuel feed, return or vapor line at the fuel tank **(see illustration)**. **Note:** *Some fuel line connections may be threaded. Be sure to use a back-up wrench when separating the connections.*
11   Remove all fasteners attaching the lines to the vehicle body.
12   Detach the fitting(s) that attach the fuel hoses to the engine compartment metal lines **(see illustrations)**. Twisting them back and forth will allow them to separate more easily.
13   Installation is the reverse of removal. Be sure to use new O-rings at the threaded fittings, if equipped **(see illustration)**.

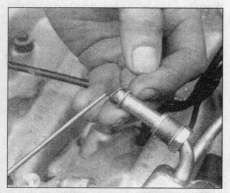

4.13 Always replace the fuel line O-rings (if equipped)

5.6 Loosen the clamps and remove the fuel filler and the vapor return hoses (arrows)

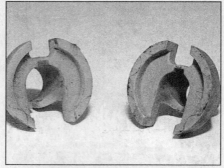

4.12a 3/8 and 5/16-inch fuel line disconnect tools

5   Fuel tank - removal and installation

Refer to illustrations 5.6, 5.7 and 5.9
Warning: *Gasoline is extremely flammable, so take extra precautions when you work on any part of the fuel system. See the **Warning** in Section 2.*
Note: *Don't begin this procedure until the fuel gauge indicates the tank is empty or nearly empty. If the tank must be removed when it isn't empty (for example, if the fuel pump malfunctions), siphon any remaining fuel from the tank prior to removal.*
1   Unless the vehicle has been driven far enough to completely empty the tank, it's a good idea to siphon the residual fuel out before removing the tank from the vehicle. **Warning:** *DO NOT start the siphoning action by mouth! Use a siphoning kit, available at most auto parts stores.*
2   Relieve the fuel system pressure (see Section 2).
3   Detach the cable from the negative terminal of the battery. **Caution:** *On models equipped with a Theftlock audio system, be sure the lockout feature is turned off before performing any procedure which requires disconnecting the battery.*
4   Raise the vehicle and support it securely on jackstands.
5   Disconnect the exhaust rubber hangers and allow the rear portion of the exhaust system to rest on the rear axle, then remove the exhaust pipe heat shields.

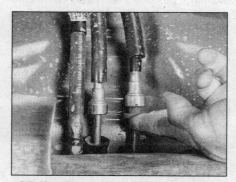

5.7 Use the special fuel line disconnect tools to disengage the fuel lines at the front of the fuel tank

4.12b On quick-connect fuel lines, use the special fuel line disconnect tools and push them into the connector (arrows) to separate the fuel lines

6   Disconnect the fuel filler hose and vapor lines from the fuel tank **(see illustration)**.
7   Disconnect the fuel feed and return lines and the vapor return line from the fuel pump **(see illustration)**. **Note:** *Use special fuel line disconnect tools* (see Section 4) *to separate the fuel lines from the harness assembly near the fuel tank supports.*
8   Support the fuel tank with a floor jack.
9   Disconnect both fuel tank retaining straps **(see illustration)**.
10   Lower the tank enough to disconnect the electrical connectors from the fuel pump/fuel level sending unit.
11   Remove the tank from the vehicle.
12   Installation is the reverse of removal.

6   Fuel tank cleaning and repair - general information

1   All repairs to the fuel tank or filler neck should be carried out by a professional who has experience in this critical and potentially dangerous work. Even after cleaning and flushing of the fuel system, explosive fumes can remain and ignite during repair of the tank.
2   If the fuel tank is removed from the vehicle, it should not be placed in an area where sparks or open flames could ignite the fumes coming out of the tank. Be especially careful inside garages where a natural gas-type appliance is located, because the pilot light could cause an explosion.

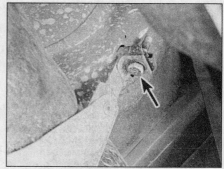

5.9 Support the fuel tank with a jack and remove the fuel tank strap bolts (arrow)

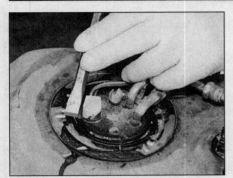

7.5 On early models, carefully tap the lock ring counterclockwise until the locking tabs align with the slots in the fuel tank

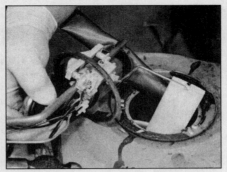

7.6 Lift the fuel pump assembly from the fuel tank and make sure the float and the strainer are not damaged by carefully angling the assembly out of the fuel tank opening

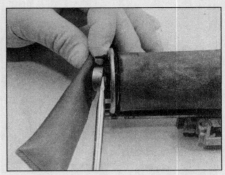

7.8 Pry on the collar to detach the strainer (filter) from the fuel pump

7 Fuel pump - removal and installation

Warning: *Gasoline is extremely flammable, so take extra precautions when you work on any part of the fuel system. See the* **Warning** *in Section 2.*

1 Relieve the fuel system pressure (see Section 2).

2 Disconnect the cable from the negative battery terminal. **Caution:** *On models equipped with a Delco Loc II or Theftlock audio system, be sure the lockout feature is turned off before performing any procedure which requires disconnecting the battery.*

3 The fuel pump/sending unit assembly is located inside the fuel tank on all models covered by this manual. Remove the fuel tank from the vehicle (see Section 5). **Note:** *On later models, the fuel pump can be removed through a small access panel in the floor behind the rear seat, but it involves removing the rear seat, rear seat trim panel, and trunk liner, and does not necessarily take less time than simply removing the fuel tank.*

1995 and 1996 models
Refer to illustrations 7.5, 7.6, 7.8, 7.9 and 7.10

4 The fuel pump/sending unit assembly on these models is held in place by a cam lock ring mechanism consisting of an inner ring with three locking cams and a fixed outer ring with three retaining tangs.

5 To unlock the fuel pump/sending unit assembly, turn the inner ring counterclockwise until the locking cams are free of the retaining tangs **(see illustration)**.

6 Lift the fuel pump/sending unit assembly out of the tank **(see illustration)**. **Caution:** *The fuel level float and sending unit are delicate. Don't bump them during removal or the accuracy of the sending unit may be affected.*

7 Inspect the condition of the O-ring around the opening of the tank. If it is dried, cracked or deteriorated, replace it.

8 Remove the strainer from the lower end of the fuel pump **(see illustration)**. If it's dirty, remove it, clean it with solvent and blow it out with compressed air. If it's too dirty to be cleaned, replace it.

9 Disconnect the electrical connector from the fuel pump **(see illustration)**.

10 Separate the fuel pump from the bracket **(see illustration)**.

11 Installation of a new fuel pump is the reverse of removal.

12 Position a new rubber O-ring around the opening in the fuel tank and guide the fuel pump/sending unit assembly into the tank.

13 Turn the inner lock ring clockwise until the locking cams are fully engaged by the retaining tangs. **Note:** *Since you've installed a new O-ring, it may be necessary to push down on the inner lock ring until the locking cams slide under the retaining tangs.*

14 Install the fuel tank (see Section 5).

1997 and later models
Refer to illustrations 7.15, 7.16, 7.18a, 7.18b and 7.21

15 The fuel pump/sending unit assembly on these models is held in place by a snapring. Using a pair of snap-ring pliers, expand the retaining collar and remove it from the top of the fuel pump assembly **(see illustration)**.

16 Lift the fuel pump/sending unit assembly from the fuel tank **(see illustration)**. **Caution:** *The fuel level float and sending unit are delicate. Do not bump them against the tank during removal or the accuracy of the sending unit may be affected.*

17 Inspect the condition of the O-ring around the opening of the tank. If it is dried, cracked or deteriorated, replace it.

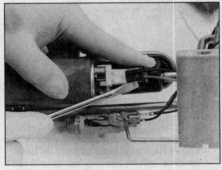

7.9 Lift the tab to release the electrical connector from the fuel pump

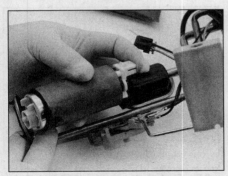

7.10 Remove the fuel pump from the bracket

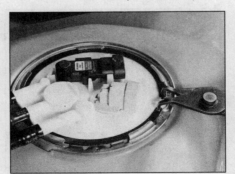

7.15 On later models, use a pair of snapring pliers to remove the retaining collar from the fuel pump assembly

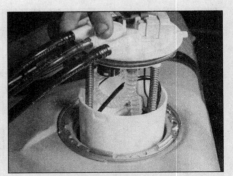

7.16 Lift the fuel pump/sending unit assembly from the fuel tank

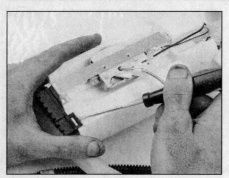

7.18a Pry on the plastic tab to remove the protective shield from the foot of the assembly

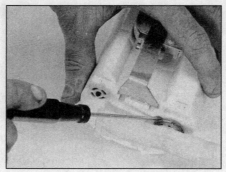

7.18b Carefully pry the fuel strainer from the inlet pipe

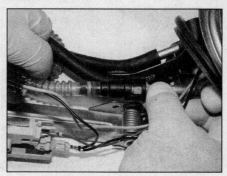

7.21 Squeeze the tabs to release the fuel line from the collar

18   Remove the strainer from the lower end of the fuel pump **(see illustrations)**. If it is dirty, clean it with a suitable solvent and blow it out with compressed air. If it is too dirty to be cleaned, replace it.

19   Remove the fuel pressure sensor mounting bolts and separate the sensor from the top of the fuel pump assembly.

20   If it is necessary to separate the fuel pump and sending unit, disconnect the electrical connectors at the pump, noting their position. Follow the procedure in Section 8.

21   Disconnect the fuel line from the pump **(see illustration)**.

22   Installation is the reverse of removal. Reassemble the fuel pump to the sending unit bracket and insert the assembly into the fuel tank.

23   Install the fuel tank (see Section 5).

---

8   Fuel level sending unit - check and replacement

Warning: *Gasoline is extremely flammable, so take extra precautions when you work on any part of the fuel system. See the* **Warning** *in Section 2.*

Check

Refer to illustration 8.3

1   Raise the vehicle and secure it on jackstands.

2   The fuel sending unit electrical connector is not accessible with the fuel tank in the vehicle. Remove the fuel tank (see Section 5) and the sending unit (see Section 8) from the fuel tank for testing.

3   Position the probes of an ohmmeter on the sending unit electrical connector terminals - purple and black or black/white **(see illustration)**. Check for resistance with the float at the top (full). The resistance of the sending unit should be about 90 ohms on 1995 through 2000 models and 250 ohms on 2001 and later models. Then check for resistance with the float at the bottom (empty). The resistance should be about 2 ohms on

1995 through 2000 models and 40 ohms on 2001 and later models.

4   If the readings are incorrect or there is very little change in resistance as the float travels from full to empty, replace the fuel level sending unit assembly.

Replacement

Refer to illustration 8.6, 8.8a and 8.8b

5   Remove the fuel tank (see Section 5) and the fuel pump/sending unit (see Section 7) from the vehicle.

6   Disconnect the sending unit electrical connector from the assembly **(see illustration)**.

7   On 1995 and 1996 models, remove the screws securing the sending unit to the return tube.

8   On 1997 and later models, carefully separate the sending unit bracket from the base of the fuel pump assembly **(see illustrations)**.

9   Installation is the reverse of removal.

---

9   Air cleaner assembly - removal and installation

Refer to illustrations 9.3 and 9.5

1   Detach the cable from the negative terminal of the battery. **Caution:** *On models equipped with a Delco Loc II or Theftlock audio system, be sure the lockout feature is*

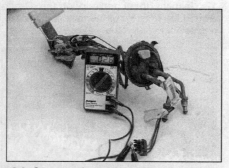

8.3 Connect the probes of an ohmmeter to the fuel level sending unit harness and check the resistance of the fuel level sending unit by moving the float from EMPTY (down) to FULL (up) and comparing the change in resistance

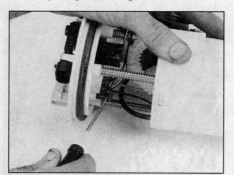

8.6 Detach the fuel level electrical connector from the fuel pump (1997 and 1998 model shown)

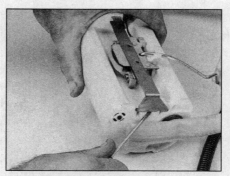

8.8a On 1997 and 1998 models, pry the bracket from the base of the fuel pump

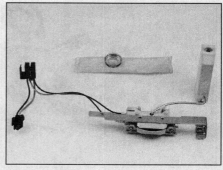

8.8b Exploded view of a 1997 and 1998 fuel level sending unit and related parts

9.3 Disconnect the electrical connectors (arrows), then loosen the clamps from the air intake duct and detach the air intake duct from the air cleaner assembly

9.5 Remove the screws (arrows) and lift out the air cleaner assembly

10.2 Slide the accelerator cable through the slot in the pedal arm

turned off before performing any procedure which requires disconnecting the battery. On later models, remove the left diagonal brace.

2   Disconnect the electrical connector to the Mass Air Flow (MAF) sensor on 3.1L and 3.4L engines and the Air Intake Temperature (IAT) sensor connector on all engines.

3   Loosen the clamps and remove the air intake duct located between the throttle body and the air cleaner assembly **(see illustration)**.

4   Unsnap the clips or remove the retaining screws from the air cleaner cover, then lift the air filter element and the air cleaner cover from the air cleaner housing (see Chapter 1).

5   If necessary, remove the PCM and wiring harness from the lower air cleaner housing, without disconnecting the PCM wiring harness. Remove the retaining screws and lift the lower housing from the engine compartment **(see illustration)**.

6   Installation is the reverse of removal.

10 Accelerator cable - removal and installation

Refer to illustrations 10.2, 10.6, 10.7 and 10.8

Removal

1   Detach the screws and the clip retaining

the lower instrument panel trim and lower the trim (if necessary) (see Chapter 11).

2   Detach the accelerator cable from the accelerator pedal **(see illustration)**.

3   Squeeze the accelerator cable cover tangs and push the cable through the firewall into the engine compartment.

4   On 3.8L engines, remove the fuel injector trim cover from the top of the engine.

5   Remove the screws to the accelerator control splash shield (if equipped).

6   Detach any accelerator cable retaining clips **(see illustration)**.

7   Squeeze the accelerator cable retaining tangs and push the cable through the accelerator cable bracket **(see illustration)**.

8   Rotate the throttle lever and pass the cable through the slot in the lever **(see illustration)**.

9   Pull the cable through the firewall and into the engine compartment.

Installation

10   Installation is the reverse of removal.
Note: *To prevent possible interference, flexible components (hoses, wires, etc.) must not be routed within two inches of moving parts, unless routing is controlled.*

11   Operate the accelerator pedal and check for any binding condition by completely opening and closing the throttle.

12   Apply sealant around the accelerator cable at the engine compartment side of the firewall.

11 Fuel injection system - general information

Refer to illustrations 11.3a and 11.3b

1   These models are equipped with the Multiport Fuel Injection (MFI) system. These modern fuel injection systems are equipped with the updated OBD II self-diagnosis system, except 1995 3.1L, engines which are equipped with the OBD I self-diagnosis system (see Chapter 6).

2   The fuel system consists of a fuel tank, an electric fuel pump and fuel pump relay, an air cleaner assembly and an electronic fuel injection system.

Multiport Fuel Injection (MFI) system

3   Multiport Fuel Injection (MFI) consists of an air intake manifold, the throttle body, the injectors, the fuel rail assembly, an electric fuel pump and associated plumbing **(see illustrations)**.

4   Air is drawn through the air cleaner and throttle body. A Mass Air Flow (MAF) sensor informs the PCM of volume and pressure variations.

10.6 Using a screwdriver detach the retaining clips securing the accelerator and the cruise control cables to the inner fenderwell

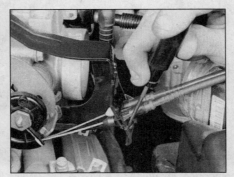

10.7 Release the locking tabs to separate the cable from the bracket

10.8 Pass the cable end through the slot in the throttle lever

11.3a Fuel injection component locations on a 3.1L engine (3.4L similar)

1	Fuel pump relay	4	Idle Air Control valve	7	Mass Air Flow sensor
2	Powertrain Control Module (PCM)	5	Throttle Position Sensor	8	Fuel pressure regulator
3	Upper intake manifold (plenum)	6	Intake Air Temperature sensor	9	Fuel rail (left bank)

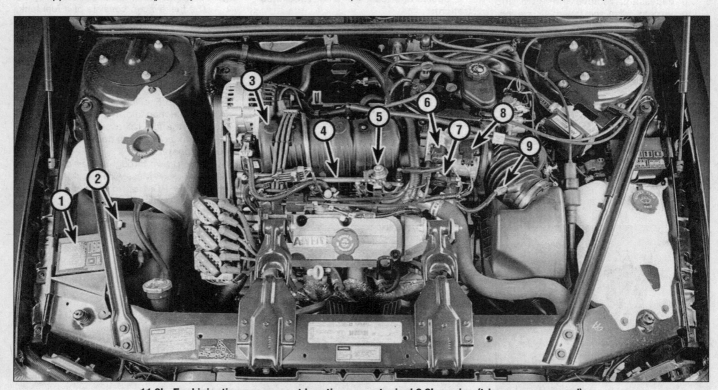

11.3b Fuel injection component locations on a typical 3.8L engine (trim cover removed)

1	Fuel pump relay	4	Fuel rail (left bank)	7	Throttle Position Sensor
2	Powertrain Control Module (PCM)	5	Fuel pressure regulator	8	Mass Air Flow sensor
3	Upper intake manifold (plenum)	6	Idle Air Control valve	9	Intake Air Temperature sensor

12.8 Use a stethoscope or screwdriver to listen and determine if the injectors are working properly - they should make a steady clicking sound that rises and falls with engine speed changes

12.9 Check the resistance of each injector and compare the readings to the Specifications

12.10 Install the "noid" light into each injector electrical connector and confirm that it blinks when the engine is cranking or running

5   While the engine is running, the fuel constantly circulates through the fuel rail, which removes vapors and keeps the fuel cool while maintaining sufficient pressure to the injectors under all running conditions.

6   Operation of the MFI system is controlled by the PCM so that it works in conjunction with the rest of the vehicle functions to provide optimum driveability and emissions control.

7   Because the MFI system meters fuel and air precisely, it is important to the proper operation of the vehicle that the fuel and air filters be changed at the specified intervals.

12 Fuel injection system - check

Refer to illustrations 12.8, 12.9 and 12.10
Warning: *Gasoline is extremely flammable, so take extra precautions when you work on any part of the fuel system. See the* **Warning** *in Section 2.*
Note: *The following procedure is based on the assumption that the fuel pump is working and the fuel pressure is adequate (see Section 3).*

1   Check to see that the battery is fully charged, as the control unit and sensors depend on an accurate supply voltage in order to properly meter the fuel.

2   Check the air filter element - a dirty or partially blocked filter will severely impede performance and economy (see Chapter 1).

3   Check the fuel filter and replace it if necessary (see Chapter 1).

4   Check the ground wire connections on the intake manifold for tightness. Check all electrical connectors that are related to the system. Loose connectors and poor grounds can cause many problems that resemble more serious malfunctions.

5   If a blown fuse is found, replace it and see if it blows again. If it does, search for a grounded wire in the harness.

6   Check the air intake duct to the intake manifold for leaks, which will result in an excessively lean mixture. Also check the condition of all vacuum hoses connected to the intake manifold.

7   Remove the air intake duct from the throttle body and check for dirt, carbon or other residue build-up. If it's dirty, clean it with aerosol carburetor cleaner and a rag.

8   With the engine running, place an automotive stethoscope against each injector, one at a time, and listen for a clicking sound, indicating operation **(see illustration)**. If you don't have a stethoscope, place the tip of a screwdriver against the injector and listen through the handle.

9   Unplug the injector electrical connector(s) and test the resistance of each injector. Compare the values to the Specifications listed in this Chapter **(see illustration)**.

10   Install an injector test light ("noid" light) into each injector electrical connector, one at a time **(see illustration)**. Crank the engine over. Confirm that the light flashes evenly on each connector. This will test for voltage to the injectors.

11   The remainder of the system checks can be found in the following Sections.

13 Fuel injection system - component check and replacement

Warning: *Gasoline is extremely flammable, so take extra precautions when you work on any part of the fuel system. See the* **Warning** *in Section 2.*

Throttle body

Check
Refer to illustration 13.2

1   Detach the air intake duct from the throttle body and move the duct out of the way.

2   Have an assistant depress the throttle pedal while you watch the throttle valve. Check that the throttle valve moves smoothly when the throttle is moved from closed (idle position) to fully open (wide open throttle). **Note:** *Spray carburetor cleaner into the throttle body, especially around the shaft area* **(see illustration)** *to free-up any binding caused by the accumulation of carbon deposits or sludge buildup.*

3   Wiggle the throttle lever while watching the throttle shaft inside the bore. If it appears worn (loose), replace the throttle body unit.

Replacement
Refer to illustrations 13.9 and 13.11
Warning: *Wait until the engine is completely cool before beginning this procedure.*
Note: *1995 3.4L engines are equipped with a one-piece intake plenum/throttle body assembly. See Chapter 2B, Section 4 for the removal procedures.*

4   Disconnect the cable from the negative terminal of the battery. **Caution:** *On models equipped with a Theftlock audio system, be sure the lockout feature is turned off before performing any procedure which requires disconnecting the battery. On 3.4L and 3.8L engines, drain the engine coolant (see Chapter 1).*

5   Detach the air intake duct (see Section 9).

6   On 3.8L engines, remove the fuel injector trim cover from the top of the engine.

7   Unplug the Idle Air Control (IAC) valve and the Throttle Position Sensor (TPS) electrical connectors (see Chapter 6). Unplug the Mass Air Flow sensor (MAF) electrical connector on 3.8L engines.

8   Mark and disconnect any vacuum hoses connected to the throttle body. Also detach

13.2 Spray carburetor cleaner into the throttle body to break away any carbon deposits or sludge that may have collected around the throttle plate

13.9 On 3.1L and 3.4L engines, remove the accelerator cable bracket bolts (arrows) (3.1L engine shown)

13.11 Throttle body mounting details (3.1L engine)

1   *Throttle body mounting bolt*
2   *Coolant bypass hose*
3   *Throttle Position Sensor*
4   *Idle Air Control valve*

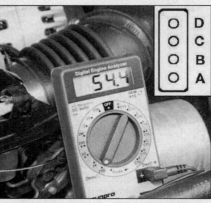

13.16 Measure the resistance across terminals D and C, then across terminals A and B

the breather hose, if equipped.

9   Disconnect the accelerator cable and the cruise control cable (see Section 10) from the throttle lever, then detach the cable retaining bracket on 3.1L and 3.4L engines **(see illustration)**.

10   On 3.1L/3.4L OHV engines, loosen and detach the coolant bypass hoses from the intake manifold. Plug the hoses and fittings to prevent coolant loss. On 3.8L engines, detach the lower throttle body support bracket.

11   Remove the throttle body nuts and bolts and detach the throttle body **(see illustration)**.

12   Clean off all traces of old gasket material from the throttle body and the plenum.

13   Install the throttle body and a new gasket and tighten the bolts to the torque listed in this Chapter's Specifications.

14   The rest of the procedure is the reverse of removal. Be sure to check the coolant level (see Chapter 1) and add, if necessary.

Idle Air Control (IAC) valve

Check

Refer to illustration 13.16

15   The Idle Air Control valve (IAC) controls the engine idle speed. This output actuator is mounted on the throttle body and is controlled by voltage pulses sent from the PCM (computer). The IAC valve pintle moves in or out, allowing more or less intake air into the system according to the engine conditions. To increase idle speed, the PCM retracts the IAC valve pintle away from the seat and allows more air to bypass the throttle bore. To decrease idle speed, the PCM extends the IAC valve pintle towards the seat, reducing the air flow.

16   To check the IAC valve, unplug the electrical connector and, using an ohmmeter, measure the resistance across terminals A and B, then terminals C and D. Each resistance check should indicate 40 to 80 ohms **(see illustration)**. If not, replace the IAC valve.

17   There is an alternate method for testing the IAC valve. Various SCAN tools are

available from auto parts stores and specialty tool companies that can be plugged into the DLC (diagnostic connector) for the purpose of monitoring the sensors. Connect the SCAN tool and switch to the Idle Air Motor Position mode and monitor the steps (motor winding position). The SCAN tool should indicate between 10 to 200 steps depending upon the rpm range. Allow the engine to idle for several minutes and while observing the count reading, snap the throttle to achieve high rpm (under 3,500). Repeat the procedure several times and observe the SCAN tool steps (counts) when the engine goes back to idle. The readings should be within 5 to 10 steps each time. If the readings fluctuate greatly, replace the IAC valve. The PCM will set codes P0506 or P0507 in the event of IAC failure. **Note:** *When the IAC valve electrical connector is disconnected for testing, the PCM will have to "relearn" its idle mode. In other words, it will take a certain amount of time before the idle motor resets for the correct idle speed. Make sure the idle is smooth and not misfiring before plugging in the SCAN tool. Refer to Chapter 6 for additional information concerning SCAN tools.*

18   Next, remove the valve (see Step 19) and inspect it:

a) *Check the pintle for excessive carbon deposits. If necessary, clean it with aerosol carburetor cleaner. Also clean the IAC valve housing to remove any deposits.*

b) *Check the IAC valve electrical connections. Make sure the pins are not bent and make good contact with the connector terminals.*

Replacement

Refer to illustration 13.20

19   Unplug the electrical connector from the Idle Air Control (IAC) valve.

20   Unscrew the valve or remove the two IAC valve attaching screws and withdraw the valve **(see illustration)**.

21   Check the condition of the rubber O-ring. If it's hardened or deteriorated, replace it. On models equipped with a gasket, remove the gasket.

22   Clean the sealing surface and the bore of the idle air/vacuum signal housing assembly to ensure a good seal. **Caution:** *The IAC valve itself is an electrical component and must not be soaked in any liquid cleaner, as damage may result.*

23   Before installing the IAC valve, the position of the pintle must be checked. If the pintle is extended too far, damage to the assembly may occur.

24   If installing a new valve, measure the distance from the flange or gasket mounting surface of the IAC valve to the tip of the pintle. If the distance is greater than 1-1/8 inch, reduce the distance by applying firm pressure onto the pintle to retract it. Try some side-to-side motion in the event the pintle binds. **Caution:** *Do not attempt to press the pintle in on a used IAC valve. The force required to move a pintle shaft with carbon buildup may damage the valve.*

25   Position the new O-ring or gasket on the IAC valve. Lubricate the O-ring with a light film of engine oil. Install the IAC valve and tighten the valve or the mounting screws securely.

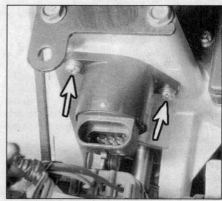

13.20 Remove the IAC valve screws (arrows) and separate the IAC from the throttle body

13.31 Use a special fuel line disconnect tool to release the fuel line couplers (arrows) from the fuel rail (3.1L engine shown)

13.34 Remove the fuel rail mounting bolts (arrows) (3.1L engine shown)

13.35 It may be necessary to gently pry the fuel rail up to remove it

26   Plug in the electrical connector at the IAC valve assembly. **Note:** *No adjustment is made to the IAC assembly after reinstallation. The IAC resetting is controlled by the PCM when the engine is started.*

Throttle Position Sensor (TPS)
Check
27   Check for stored trouble codes in the PCM using the On Board Diagnosis system (see Chapter 6).
28   For the checking and replacement procedures for the TPS, refer to *Information sensors* in Chapter 6.

Fuel rail and injectors
Refer to illustrations 13.31, 13.34, 13.35, 13.36 and 13.37
Warning: *Before any work is performed on the fuel lines, fuel rail or injectors, the fuel system pressure must be relieved (see Section 2).* **Note:** *Refer to Section 12 for the injector checking procedure.*
29   Detach the cable from the negative terminal of the battery. **Caution:** *On models equipped with a Theftlock audio system, be sure the lockout feature is turned off before performing any procedure which requires disconnecting the battery.*

30   On 3.1L and 3.4L engines, remove the upper half of the intake manifold and the throttle body assembly as a unit (see Chapter 2). On 3.8L engines, remove the fuel injector trim cover.
31   Using a special fuel line removal tool, detach the fuel lines from the fuel rail **(see illustrations 4.12a, 4.12b and the accompanying illustration)**.
32   Detach the vacuum line at the fuel pressure regulator.
33   Label and unplug the injector electrical connectors.
34   Remove the fuel rail retaining bolts/nuts **(see illustration)**.
35   Carefully remove the fuel rail with the injectors **(see illustration)**. **Caution:** *Use care when handling the fuel rail assembly to avoid damaging the injectors.*
36   To remove the fuel injectors, spread the injector retaining clip and pull the injector from the fuel rail **(see illustration)**.
37   Remove the injector O-ring seals **(see illustration)**.
38   Install the new O-ring seal(s), as required, on the injector(s) and lubricate them with a light film of engine oil. **Note:** *It is recommended that all of the O-rings be replaced whenever the fuel rail is removed.*
39   Install the injectors on the fuel rail.

40   Secure the injectors with the retaining clips.
41   Installation is the reverse of the removal procedure.

Fuel pressure regulator
Check
42   Refer to Section 3 for the fuel pressure regulator checking procedure.

Replacement
Refer to illustrations 13.46 and 13.47
43   Relieve the fuel system pressure (see Section 2).
44   Disconnect the cable from the negative terminal of the battery. **Caution:** *On models equipped with a Theftlock audio system, be sure the lockout feature is turned off before performing any procedure which requires disconnecting the battery.*
45   Remove the fuel rail following the procedure described earlier in this Section.
46   On all 3.1L and 3.4L OHV engines, remove the fuel return pipe from the bottom of the regulator, then remove the pressure regulator mounting screw **(see illustration)** and separate the fuel pressure regulator assembly from the fuel rail while noting the installed position of the filter screen.

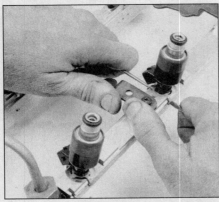

13.36 To remove an injector from the fuel rail, spread the retaining clip with a small screwdriver, then pull the injector from the fuel rail

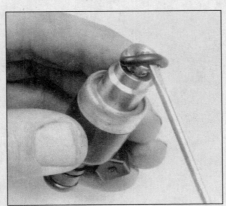

13.37 Carefully pry the seals off the injectors and replace them with new ones

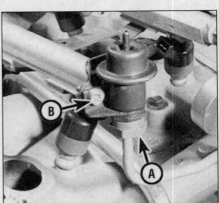

13.46 On 3.1L and 3.4L OHV engines, remove the return line (A) and the mounting screw (B) from the fuel pressure regulator

13.47 On 3.4L DOHC engines and all 3.8L engines, remove the snap-ring (arrow) from the top of the pressure regulator

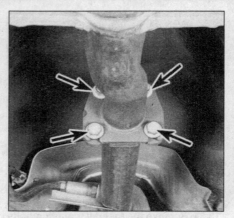

14.1a Be sure to spray penetrating lubricant onto the flange bolts (arrows) before removing them

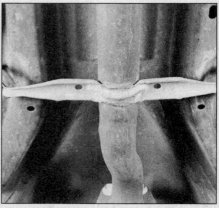

14.1b Make sure all exhaust pipe brackets are not cracked or damaged

47   On 3.4L DOHC and 3.8L engines, compress the snap-ring with snap-ring pliers and lift the ring from the regulator **(see illustration)**. Lift the regulator while simultaneously twisting it and remove it from the housing. Remove the filter screen from the regulator housing and clean it with compressed air. Install new O-rings and lubricate them with a light coat of oil.

48   Reassembly is the reverse of disassembly. Be sure to replace all gaskets and seals, otherwise a dangerous fuel leak may develop. When installing the seals, lubricate them with a light film of engine oil.

---

14   Exhaust system servicing - general information

Refer to illustrations 14.1a, 14.1b, and 14.1c
Warning: *The vehicle's exhaust system*

generates very high temperatures and must be allowed to cool down completely before any of the components are touched. Be especially careful around the catalytic converter, where the highest temperatures are generated.

Replacement of exhaust system components is basically a matter of removing the heat shields, disconnecting the component and installing a new one **(see illustrations)**. The heat shields and exhaust system hangers must be reinstalled in the original locations or damage could result. Due to the high temperatures and exposed locations of the exhaust system components, rust and corrosion can seize parts together. Penetrating oils are available to help loosen frozen fasteners. However, in some cases it may be necessary to cut the pieces apart with a hacksaw or cutting torch. The latter method should be employed only by persons experienced in this work.

14.1c Check the rubber hangers (arrows) for deterioration or cracks that may cause the exhaust system to drop

Chapter 5 Engine electrical systems

Contents

Specifications

General

Ignition coil resistance (approximate for all engines)	
Primary resistance	0.3 to 0.7 ohms
Secondary resistance	5,000 to 8,000 ohms
Spark plug wire resistance	Less than 30,000 ohms
Cylinder numbers	See Chapter 2
Firing order	See Chapter 2

Charging system

Alternator charging output	13 to 14.5 volts

1 General information and precautions

General information

The engine electrical systems include all ignition, charging and starting components. Because of their engine-related functions, these components are discussed separately from body electrical devices such as the lights, the instruments, etc. (which is included in Chapter 12).

Precautions

Always observe the following precautions when working on the electrical system:

a) Be extremely careful when servicing engine electrical components. They are easily damaged if checked, connected or handled improperly.

b) Never leave the ignition switched on for long periods of time when the engine is not running.

c) Never disconnect the battery cables while the engine is running.

d) Maintain correct polarity when connecting battery cables from another vehicle during jump starting - see the "Booster battery (jump) starting" Section at the front of this manual.

e) Always disconnect the negative battery cable before working on the electrical system.

It's also a good idea to review the safety-related information regarding the engine electrical systems located in the "Safety first!" Section at the front of this manual, before beginning any operation included in this Chapter.

Battery disconnection

Caution: *On models equipped with the Theftlock audio system, be sure the lockout feature is turned off before performing any procedure which requires disconnecting the battery (see the front of this manual).*

Several systems on the vehicle require battery power to be available at all times, either to ensure their continued operation (such as the clock) or to maintain control unit memories (such as that in the engine management system's Powertrain Control Module [PCM]) which would be wiped out if the battery were to be disconnected. Therefore, whenever the battery is to be disconnected, first note the following to ensure that there are no unforeseen consequences of this action:

a) First, on any vehicle with power door locks, it is a wise precaution to remove the key from the ignition and to keep it with you, so that it does not get locked inside if the power door locks should engage accidentally when the battery is reconnected!

b) The engine management system's PCM will lose the information stored in its memory when the battery is disconnected. This includes idling and operating values, and any fault codes detected (see Chapter 6). Whenever the battery is disconnected, the information relating to idle speed control and other operating values will have to be reprogrammed into the unit's memory. The PCM does this by itself, but until then, there may be surging, hesitation, erratic idle and a generally inferior level of performance. To allow the PCM to relearn these values, start the engine and run it as close to idle speed as possible until it reaches its normal operating temperature, then run it for approximately two minutes at 1200 rpm. Next, drive the vehicle as far as necessary - approximately 5 miles of varied driving conditions is usually sufficient - to complete the relearning process.

Devices known as "memory-savers" can be used to avoid some of the above problems. Precise details vary according to the device used. Typically, it is plugged into the cigarette lighter, and is connected by its own wires to a spare battery. The vehicle's own battery is then disconnected from the electrical system, leaving the "memory-saver" to pass sufficient current to maintain audio unit security codes and PCM memory values, and also to run permanently live circuits such as the clock. This isolates the battery in case a short-circuit occurs while work is carried out. **Warning:** *Some of these devices allow a considerable amount of current to pass, which can mean that many of the vehicle's systems are still operational when the main battery is disconnected. If a "memory-saver" is used, ensure that the circuit concerned is actually "dead" before carrying out any work on it!*

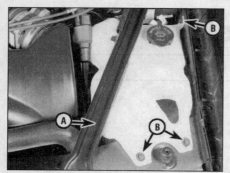

3.2a Remove the engine compartment support brace (A) and the windshield washer reservoir retaining bolts (B)

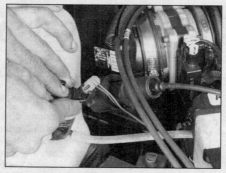

3.2b Turn the windshield washer reservoir over and disconnect the electrical connector and the washer hose - insert a vacuum plug over the reservoir outlet to avoid excessive spillage from the washer reservoir

3.4 Remove the battery hold-down bolts (arrows) from the battery carrier

2 Battery - emergency jump starting

Refer to the *Booster battery (jump) starting* procedure at the front of this manual.

3 Battery - removal and installation

Warning: *Hydrogen gas is produced by the battery, so keep open flames and lighted cigarettes away from it at all times. Always wear eye protection when working around a battery. Rinse off spilled electrolyte immediately with large amounts of water.*

Removal

Refer to illustrations 3.2a, 3.2b and 3.4

1   The battery is located at the left front corner of the engine compartment on earlier models and at the right front corner on later models.

2   Remove the appropriate engine compartment diagonal brace and, on earlier models, the windshield washer fluid reservoir **(see illustrations)**.

3   Detach the cables from the negative and positive terminals of the battery. **Warning:** *To prevent arcing, disconnect the negative (-) cable first, then remove the positive (+) cable.* **Caution:** *On models equipped with a Theftlock audio system, be sure the lockout feature is turned off before performing any procedure which requires disconnecting the battery.*

4   Remove the hold-down clamp bolts and the clamp from the battery carrier **(see illustration)**

5   Carefully lift the battery from the carrier. If equipped, remove the insulating shield from the battery. **Warning:** *Always keep the battery in an upright position to reduce the likelihood of electrolyte spillage. If you spill electrolyte on your skin, rinse it off immediately with large amounts of water.*

Installation

Note: *The battery carrier and hold-down clamp should be clean and free from corrosion before installing the battery. Make certain that there are no parts in the carrier*

before installing the battery.

6   Set the battery in position in its carrier. Don't tilt it.

7   Install the hold-down clamp and bolts. The bolt should be snug, but overtightening it may damage the battery case.

8   Install both battery cables, positive first, then the negative. **Note:** *The battery terminals and cable ends should be cleaned prior to connection* (see Chapter 1).

4 Battery cables - check and replacement

1   Periodically inspect the entire length of each battery cable for damage, cracked or burned insulation and corrosion. Poor battery cable connections can cause starting problems and decreased engine performance.

2   Check the cable-to-terminal connections at the ends of the cables for cracks, loose wire strands and corrosion. The presence of white, fluffy deposits under the insulation at the cable terminal connection is a sign the cable is corroded and should be replaced. Check the terminals for distortion, missing mounting bolts or nuts and corrosion.

3   When removing the cables, always disconnect the negative cable first and hook it up last or the battery may be shorted by the tool used to loosen the cable clamps. Even if only the positive cable is being replaced, be sure to disconnect the negative cable from the battery first. **Caution:** *On models equipped with a Theftlock audio system, be sure the lockout feature is turned off before performing any procedure which requires disconnecting the battery.*

4   Disconnect the old cables from the battery, then trace each of them to their opposite ends and detach them from the starter solenoid and ground terminals. Note the routing of each cable to ensure correct installation.

5   If you're replacing either or both cables, take the old ones with you when buying the new ones - the replacements must be identical. Cables have characteristics that

make them easy to identify: Positive cables are normally red, larger in diameter and have a larger-diameter battery post and clamp; ground cables are normally black, smaller in diameter and have a slightly smaller battery post and clamp.

6   Clean the threads of the solenoid or ground connection with a wire brush to remove rust and corrosion. Apply a light coat of petroleum jelly to the threads to prevent future corrosion.

7   Attach the cable to the solenoid or ground connection and tighten the mounting nut/bolt securely.

8   Before connecting a new cable to the battery, make sure it reaches the battery post without having to be stretched.

9   Connect the positive cable first, followed by the negative cable. Tighten the nuts and apply a thin coat of petroleum jelly to the terminal and cable connection.

5 Ignition system - general information

The engines covered in this manual are equipped with a distributorless Direct Ignition System (DIS) which is controlled by the PCM. This system offers no moving parts, less maintenance, more coil cool down time between spark plug firing and the elimination of mechanical timing adjustments.

DIS (Direct Ignition System)

The DIS ignition systems use a "waste spark" method of spark distribution. Each cylinder is paired with its opposing cylinder in the firing order (1-4, 2-5, 3-6) so one cylinder under compression fires simultaneously with its opposing cylinder, where the piston is on the exhaust stroke. Since the cylinder on the exhaust stroke requires very little of the available voltage to fire its plug, most of the voltage is used to fire the plug of the cylinder on the compression stroke.

The DIS system includes three coil packs, an ignition module, two crankshaft position sensors - except 1998 3.8L engines which use a single (dual Hall effect) sensor - an engine crankshaft balancer with crankshaft sensor interrupter rings, a camshaft position sensor, spark plugs, spark

6.3a To use a calibrated ignition tester (available at most auto parts stores), simply disconnect a spark plug wire, attach the wire to the tester, clip the tester to a convenient ground and operate the starter - if there's enough power to fire the plug, sparks will be visible between the electrode tip and the tester body

6.3b Using an ohmmeter, check the resistance of each spark plug wire

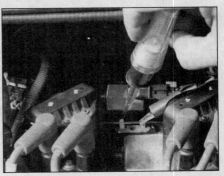

6.6 Remove the coil pack from the module assembly and check for a trigger signal on the module terminals with a test light while an assistant cranks the engine over

plug wires and the Powertrain Control Module (PCM).

Conventional ignition coils have one end of the secondary winding connected to the engine ground. On DIS, neither end of the secondary winding is grounded - instead, one end of the coil's secondary winding is directly attached to the spark plug, and the other end is attached to the spark plug of the companion cylinder.

The crankshaft reluctor ring disrupts signal voltage from the crankshaft position sensors to indicate crankshaft position and crankshaft speed. These signals are used by the Ignition Control Module (ICM) during startup and passed on to the Powertrain Control Module (PCM) to adjust ignition timing.

The DIS system is also integrated with the Knock Sensor (KS) system, which uses knock sensors in connection with the Powertrain Control Module (PCM) to control spark timing. The KS system allows the engine to have maximum spark advance without spark knock, which also improves driveability and fuel economy.

Secondary (spark plug) wiring

The secondary (spark plug) wires are a carbon-impregnated cord conductor encased in an 8 mm (5/16-inch) diameter rubber jacket with an outer silicone covering. This type of wire will withstand very high temperatures and provides an excellent insulator for the high secondary ignition voltage. Silicone spark plug boots form a tight seal on the plug. The boot should be twisted 1/2-turn before removing (for more information on spark plug wiring refer to Chapter 1).

6   Ignition system - check

Warning: *Because of the very high voltage generated by the ignition system, extreme care should be taken whenever an operation is performed involving ignition components. This not only includes the coils, control module and spark plug wires, but related*

items connected to the system as well, such as the electrical connections, tachometer and any test equipment.
Note: *All ignition system information sensors such as the crankshaft position sensor, camshaft position sensor and the knock sensors are covered in Chapter 6.*

General checks

Refer to illustrations 6.3a and 6.3b
1   Check all ignition wiring connections for tightness, cuts, corrosion or any other signs of a bad connection. A faulty or poor connection at a spark plug could also result in a misfire. Also check for carbon deposits inside the spark plug boots. Remove the spark plugs, if necessary, and check for fouling (see Chapter 1).
2   Check for ignition and battery supply to the PCM. Check the ignition fuses (see Chapter 12).
3   Use a calibrated ignition tester to verify adequate available secondary voltage (25,000 volts) at the spark plug **(see illustration)**. Using an ohmmeter, check the resistance of the spark plug wires **(see illustration)**. Each wire should measure less than 30,000 ohms.
4   Check to see if the fuel pump and relay are operating properly (see Chapter 4). The fuel pump should activate for two seconds when the ignition key is cycled ON.

Ignition module

Refer to illustration 6.6
5   Disconnect the ignition module harness connector and check for battery voltage to the pink wire (terminal L on earlier models and terminal B of the two-terminal connector on later models) from the 15 amp IGN fuse with the ignition key ON (engine not running). If no battery voltage is present, replace the fuse and check again. Repair the circuit to the ignition system if necessary.
6   Next, check for a trigger signal from the ignition module. Remove the coil pack from the ignition module to expose the module terminals. Connect a test light between each of the module terminals and have an assistant crank the engine over **(see illustration)**. This test checks the triggering circuit in the ignition module. A blinking test

light indicates the module is triggering. The test light should blink quickly and constantly as each coil pack is triggered to fire by the switching signal from the ignition module.
7   If there is no blinking light, the ignition module is most likely the problem, but not always. The PCM should also relay reference signals to fire the fuel injectors if all the information is being received from the camshaft and crankshaft sensors. It is best to install a scan tool and monitor the PCM activity to differentiate the ignition system problems (see Chapter 6).
8   A slowly blinking light, at this point, indicates the PCM is not seeing a crank sensor signal (see Chapter 6). At this point, the problem is in the camshaft or crankshaft sensor(s), sensor circuits or the ignition module. **Note:** *Refer to Chapter 6 for additional information and testing procedures for the camshaft sensor and the crankshaft sensors. It will be necessary to verify that the crankshaft sensors and camshaft sensor are operating correctly before changing the ignition module. A defective ignition module can only be diagnosed by process of elimination.*

Ignition coil packs

Refer to illustrations 6.10 and 6.11
9   Refer to Steps 6 through 8 to determine if the coils are receiving the correct trigger signal from the ignition module.

6.10 Check the coil secondary resistance by connecting the ohmmeter leads to the towers of each coil pack

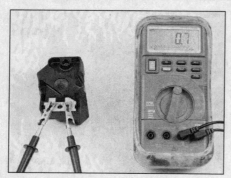

6.11 With the coil pack removed from the module assembly, check the coil primary resistance with an ohmmeter

7.2 Disconnect the electrical connectors (arrows) from the ignition module (3.1L engine shown, others similar)

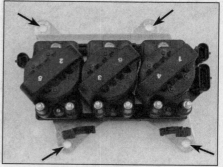

7.4 Remove the ignition module/coil pack bracket bolts (arrows) (3.1L engine shown, others similar) - module/coil pack removed for clarity

10   Use an ohmmeter and check the secondary resistance for each coil pack **(see illustration)**. Refer to the Specifications listed at the beginning of this Chapter for the correct amount of resistance.

11   Next, remove each coil pack (see Section 7) and check the primary resistance for each individual coil pack **(see illustration)**. Refer to the Specifications listed at the beginning of this Chapter for the correct amount of resistance.

12   If the indicated resistance is less than the resistance listed in this Chapter's Specifications, replace the coil pack.

7   Ignition coils and module - removal and installation

Refer to illustrations 7.2, 7.4, 7.5a and 7.5b

1   Detach the cable from the negative terminal of the battery. **Caution:** *On models equipped with a Theftlock audio system, be sure the lockout feature is turned off before performing any procedure which requires disconnecting the battery.*

2   Unplug the electrical connectors from the module **(see illustration)**.

3   If the plug wires are not numbered, label them and detach the plug wires at the coil assembly.

4   Remove the module/coil assembly mounting bolts and lift the assembly from the vehicle **(see illustration)**.

5   To remove the coils from the ignition module, simply remove the mounting screws and unplug the coil from the ignition module terminals **(see illustrations)**.

6   Installation is the reverse of removal. **Note:** *When installing the coils, make sure they are properly seated on the ignition module.*

8   Charging system - general information and precautions

Caution: *On models equipped with a Theftlock audio system, be sure the lockout feature is turned off before performing any procedure which requires disconnecting the battery.*

The charging system consists of a belt-driven alternator with an integral voltage regulator and the battery. These components work together to supply electrical power for the ignition system, the lights and all accessories.

1995 through 1997 models are equipped with the CS-130 (100 amp) alternator. 1998 through 1999 models are equipped with either the CS-130 or the CS-144 (124 amp) alternator. 2000 through 2002 models are equipped with either the Delphi CS130D (102

amp) on 3.4L/3.8L vehicles or Bosch NCB1 (125 amp) on 3.8L vehicles. 2003 and later models may have a Delphi AD230 (105 amp) alternator instead of a CS130D. All types use a conventional pulley and fan. The CS-130 alternators should be considered non-serviceable and, if found to be faulty, should be exchanged as cores for new or rebuilt units. CS-144 alternators can be rebuilt, but it is recommended that the home mechanic exchange the alternator for a rebuilt unit. Because of the expense and the limited availability of parts, no alternator overhaul information is included in this manual.

The purpose of the voltage regulator is to limit the alternator's output voltage to a preset value. This prevents power surges, circuit overloads, etc., during peak voltage output. On all models with which this manual is concerned, the voltage regulator is contained within the alternator housing.

The charging system does not ordinarily require periodic maintenance. The drivebelt, electrical wiring and connections should, however, be inspected at the intervals suggested in Chapter 1.

Take extreme care when making circuit connections to a vehicle equipped with an alternator and note the following. When making connections to the alternator from a battery, always match correct polarity. Before using arc welding equipment to repair any part of the vehicle, disconnect the wires from the alternator and the battery terminals. Never start the engine with a battery charger connected. Always disconnect both battery leads before using a battery charger.

The charging indicator light on the dash lights up when the ignition switch is turned on and goes out when the engine starts. If the light stays on or comes on once the engine is running, a charging system problem has occurred.

7.5a To detach the coil packs from the ignition module, remove the screws (arrows) ...

7.5b ... and pull straight up - when installing a coil pack, line up the blade terminals and press downward - make sure it's fully seated before tightening the retaining screws

9   Charging system - check

1   If a malfunction occurs in the charging circuit, do not immediately assume that the alternator is causing the problem.

2   First, check the following items:

a) *Make sure the battery cable connections at the battery are clean and tight.*

b) *The battery electrolyte specific gravity (if possible). If it is low, charge the battery.*

c) *Check the external alternator wiring and connections. They must be in good condition.*

d) *Check the drivebelt condition and tension (see Chapter 1).*

e) *Make sure the alternator mounting bolts are tight.*

f) *Run the engine and check the alternator for abnormal noise (may be caused by a loose drive pulley, loose mounting bolts, worn or dirty bearings, defective diode or defective stator).*

3   Check the charge light bulb and circuit. With the ignition key ON and the engine not running, the lamp should be ON. If not, detach the wiring harness at the alternator.

a) *Install a fused jumper wire (5 amp) to ground and connect the other end to the lead that was removed from the L terminal on the alternator.*

b) *If the charging lamp on the dash comes ON, the alternator is defective. Replace the alternator.*

c) *If the charging lamp on the dash remains OFF, locate the open circuit between the alternator and the bulb on the dash. First check the bulb to make sure it is not blown.*

d) *With the ignition key ON and the engine running, the lamp should be OFF. If it remains ON while running, stop the engine and remove the lead from the L terminal on the alternator.*

e) *If the lamp on the dash goes OFF, the alternator is defective.*

f) *If the lamp on the dash remains ON, there is a grounded L terminal in the wiring harness.*

4   Using a voltmeter, check the battery voltage with the engine off. It should be approximately 12 volts.

5   Start the engine and check the battery voltage again. It should now be approximately 14 to 15 volts.

10 Alternator - removal and installation

Removal

1   Detach the cable from the negative terminal of the battery. **Caution:** *On models equipped with a Theftlock audio system, be sure the lockout feature is turned off before performing any procedure which requires disconnecting the battery.*

2   Remove the drivebelt (see Chapter 1).

3.1L/3.4L and 3.8L OHV engines

Refer to illustrations 10.3 and 10.4

3   Label and detach the wires from the backside of the alternator **(see illustration)**. If necessary for access on later 3.4L models, remove the cross-vehicle brace (see Chap-

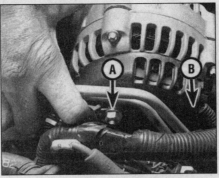

10.3 Disconnect the BAT terminal (A) and the voltage regulator connector (B) from the back of the alternator (3.1L engine shown)

ter 11) and the coolant reservoir (see Chapter 3).

4   Remove the mounting bolts and separate the alternator from the engine **(see illustration)**. **Note:** *It may be necessary to loosen or remove the front and rear alternator support brackets/brace.*

3.4L DOHC engine

Note: *This procedure requires the removal of many parts and lowering of the engine to access the alternator.*

5   Detach the ignition coils/module from the engine and position them aside (see Section 7 if necessary).

6   Raise the vehicle, support it securely on jackstands and remove the right front wheel.

7   Remove the right inner fenderwell splash shield as described in the fender removal Section of Chapter 11.

8   Remove the exhaust pipe, exhaust pipe heat shield and the catalytic converter from the rear exhaust manifold.

9   Detach the steering (intermediate) shaft from the steering gear (see Chapter 10).

10   Place a floor jack under the engine crossmember and remove the rear crossmember mounting bolts, then lower the crossmember no more than four inches to access the alternator.

11   Detach the alternator cooling duct, then label and detach the wires from the backside of the alternator.

12   Remove the alternator mounting bolts and support brackets, then separate the alternator from the engine. **Note:** *It may be necessary to remove the power steering gear inlet hose to allow alternator to be removed.*

Installation

13   If you're replacing the alternator, take the old one with you when purchasing the new one. Make sure the new/rebuilt unit is identical to the old alternator. Look at the terminals - they should be the same in number, size and location as the terminals on the old alternator. Finally, look at the identification numbers - they'll be stamped into the housing or printed on a tag attached to the housing. Make sure the numbers are the same on both alternators.

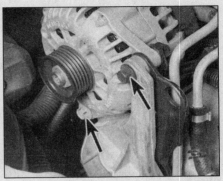

10.4 Remove the alternator mounting bolts (arrows) (3.1L engine shown)

14   Many new/rebuilt alternators DO NOT have a pulley installed, so you may have to switch the pulley from the old one to the new/rebuilt one.

15   Installation is the reverse of removal.

16   Check the charging voltage to verify proper operation of the alternator (see Section 8).

11 Starting system - general information and precautions

The function of the starting system is to crank the engine quickly enough to allow it to start. The starting system is composed of a starter motor, solenoid, ignition switch and battery. The battery supplies the electrical energy to the solenoid, which then completes the circuit to the starting motor, which does the actual work of cranking the engine.

The solenoid and starter motor are mounted together at the lower front side of the engine. No periodic lubrication or maintenance is required.

The electrical circuitry of the vehicle is arranged so that the starter motor can only be operated when the transmission selector lever is in Park or Neutral.

There are two types of starters used in these models. 1995 models and 1996 models with 3.1L engines are equipped with SD 205 series starters which have serviceable starter solenoids. All 1996 models with 3.4L engines and 1997 and later models are equipped with PG-260 series starters, which are not serviceable and in the event of failure must be replaced as a complete unit.

Always observe the following precautions when working on the starting system:

a) *Excessive cranking of the starter motor can overheat it and cause serious damage. Never operate the starter motor for more than 15 seconds at a time without pausing to allow it to cool for at least two minutes.*

b) *The starter is connected directly to the battery and could arc or cause a fire if mishandled, overloaded or shorted out.*

c) *Always detach the cable from the negative terminal of the battery before working on the starting system.*

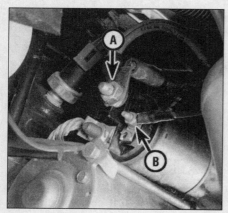

13.4 Disconnect the battery terminal (A) and the switch terminal (B) from the starter solenoid

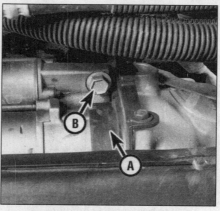

13.6 Remove the torque converter cover (A) and the starter motor bolts (one shown, B) to detach the starter from the engine block

14.3 Disconnect the starter field strap (A) from the solenoid, then remove the solenoid mounting screws (B)

12 Starter motor - testing in vehicle

Note: *Before diagnosing starter problems, make sure the battery is fully charged.*

1   If the starter motor does not turn at all when the switch is operated, make sure that the shift lever is in Neutral or Park.

2   Make sure that the battery is charged and that all cables, both at the battery and starter solenoid terminals, are secure.

3   If the starter motor spins but the engine is not cranking, the overrunning clutch in the starter motor is slipping and the motor must be removed from the engine for replacement.

4   If, when the switch is actuated, the starter motor does not operate at all but the solenoid clicks, then the problem lies with either the battery, the main solenoid contacts or the starter motor itself.

5   If the solenoid plunger cannot be heard when the switch is actuated, the solenoid itself is defective or the solenoid circuit is open.

6   To check the solenoid, connect a jumper lead between the battery (+) and the "S" terminal on the solenoid. If the starter motor now operates, the solenoid is OK and the problem is in the ignition switch, neutral start switch or in the wiring.

7   If the starter motor still does not operate, remove the starter/solenoid assembly for disassembly, testing and repair.

8   If the starter motor cranks the engine at an abnormally slow speed, first make sure that the battery is charged and that all terminal connections are clean and tight. If the engine is partially seized, or has the wrong viscosity oil in it, it will crank slowly.

9   Run the engine until normal operating temperature is reached, then stop the engine, disconnect the electrical connectors from the ignition module/coil pack assembly.

10   Connect a voltmeter positive lead to the starter motor terminal of the solenoid and then connect the negative lead to ground.

11   Crank the engine and take the voltmeter readings as soon as a steady figure is indicated. Do not allow the starter motor to turn for more than 15 seconds at a time. A reading of 9 volts or more, with the starter motor turning at normal cranking speed, is normal. If the reading is 9 volts or more but the cranking speed is slow, the motor is faulty. If the reading is less than 9 volts and the cranking speed is slow, the solenoid contacts are probably burned.

13 Starter motor - removal and installation

Refer to illustrations 13.4 and 13.6

Note: *On some vehicles, it may be necessary to remove the exhaust pipe(s) or frame cross-member to gain access to the starter motor. In extreme cases it may even be necessary to unbolt the mounts and raise the engine slightly to get the starter out.*

1   Detach the cable from the negative terminal of the battery. **Caution:** *On models equipped with a Theftlock audio system, be sure the lockout feature is turned off before performing any procedure which requires disconnecting the battery.*

2   Raise the front of the vehicle and support it securely on jackstands. Apply the parking brake and block the rear wheels to keep the vehicle from rolling off the jackstands.

3   On 3.1L engines, remove the air cleaner housing (if necessary). On later models, remove the lower air deflector (bolted to the bottom of the front bumper).

4   Working under the vehicle, clearly label, then disconnect the wires from the terminals on the starter solenoid **(see illustration)**.

5   Remove the torque converter lower cover(s).

6   Remove the mounting bolts and detach the starter. Note the locations of the spacer shims (if used) - they must be reinstalled in the same positions **(see illustration)**.

7   Installation is the reverse of removal.

14 Starter solenoid - removal and installation

Refer to illustrations 14.3 and 14.5

Note: *This procedure applies to all 1995 models and 1996 models equipped with 3.1L engines only. All 1996 models with 3.4L engines and 1997 and later models are equipped with non-serviceable starters and in the event of failure must be replaced as a complete unit.*

1   Detach the cable from the negative terminal of the battery. **Caution:** *On models equipped with a Theftlock audio system, be sure the lockout feature is turned off before performing any procedure which requires disconnecting the battery.*

2   Remove the starter motor (Section 13).

3   Disconnect the strap from the solenoid to the starter motor terminal **(see illustration)**.

4   Remove the screws that secure the solenoid to the starter motor **(see illustration 14.3)**.

5   Twist the solenoid in a clockwise direction to disengage the flange from the starter body **(see illustration)**.

6   Installation is the reverse of removal.

14.5 Rotate the solenoid 1/4-turn clockwise and disengage it from the starter motor

Chapter 6
Emissions and engine control systems

Contents

1   General information

Refer to illustrations 1.1a, 1.1b and 1.6

To prevent pollution of the atmosphere from incompletely burned and evaporating gases, and to maintain good driveability and fuel economy, a number of emission control systems are incorporated **(see illustrations)**.

They include the:

Electronic engine control system
Crankcase ventilation system
Exhaust gas recirculation system
Evaporative emissions control system
Secondary air injection system (some 1999 and later models)
Catalytic converter

All of these systems are linked, directly or indirectly, to the emission control system.

The Sections in this Chapter include general descriptions, checking procedures within the scope of the home mechanic and component replacement procedures (when possible) for each of the systems listed above.

Before assuming that an emissions control system is malfunctioning, check the fuel

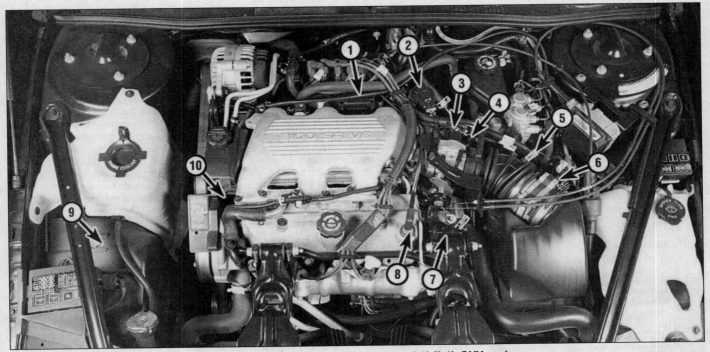

1.1a Typical engine control components - 3.1L/3.4L OHV engine

1   Manifold Absolute Pressure sensor
2   Digital EGR valve
3   Idle Air Control valve
4   Throttle Position Sensor (not visible)
5   Intake Air Temperature sensor
6   Mass Air Flow sensor
7   Engine Coolant Temperature sensor (not visible)
8   PCV valve
9   Powertrain Control Module
10 Camshaft position sensor (not visible)

1.1b Typical engine control components - 3800 engine

1   Digital EGR valve
2   Idle Air Control valve
3   Mass Air Flow sensor
4   Intake Air Temperature sensor

5   Throttle Position Sensor
6   Engine Coolant Temperature sensor (not visible)
7   Powertrain Control Module

8   PCV valve (underneath MAP sensor)
9   Manifold Absolute Pressure sensor

and ignition systems carefully. The diagnosis of some emission control devices requires specialized tools, equipment and training. If checking and servicing become too difficult or if a procedure is beyond your ability, consult a dealer service department or other properly equipped repair facility. Remember, the most frequent cause of emissions problems is simply a loose or broken vacuum hose or wire, so always check the hose and wiring connections first.

This doesn't mean, however, that emission control systems are particularly difficult to maintain and repair. You can quickly and easily perform many checks and do most of

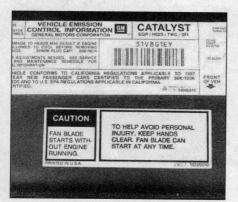

1.6 The Vehicle Emission Control Information (VECI) label is located in the engine compartment and contains information on the emission devices on your vehicle, vacuum-line routing, etc.

the regular maintenance at home with common tune-up and hand tools. **Note:** *Because of a federally mandated warranty which covers the emission control system components, check with your dealer about warranty coverage before working on any emissions-related systems. Once the warranty has expired, you may wish to perform some of the component checks and/or replacement procedures in this Chapter to save money.*

Pay close attention to any special precautions outlined in this Chapter. It should be noted that the illustrations of the various systems might not exactly match the system installed on the vehicle you're working on because of changes made by the manufacturer during production or from year-to-year.

The number of emissions control system components on later model fuel-injected vehicles has actually decreased due to the high efficiency of the new fuel injection and ignition systems. These models are equipped with a three-way catalytic converter containing beads, which are coated with a catalyst material containing platinum, palladium and rhodium to reduce the level of nitrogen oxides.

A Vehicle Emissions Control Information (VECI) label is located in the engine compartment **(see illustration)**. This label contains important emissions specifications and adjustment information, as well as a vacuum hose schematic with emissions components identified. When servicing the engine or emissions systems, the VECI label in your particular vehicle should always be checked for up-to-date information.

2   On-Board Diagnostic system and trouble codes

Diagnostic tool information

Refer to illustrations 2.1 and 2.2

1   A digital multimeter is necessary for checking fuel injection and emission related components **(see illustration)**. A digital volt-ohmmeter is preferred over the older style analog multimeter for several reasons. The analog multimeter cannot display the volts-ohms or amps measurement in hundredths and thousandths increments. When working with electronic circuits that are often very low voltage, this accurate reading is most important. Another good reason for the digital multimeter is its high impedance circuit. The digital multimeter is equipped with a high resistance internal circuitry (10 million ohms). Because a voltmeter is hooked up in parallel with the circuit when testing, it is vital that none of the voltage being measured should be allowed to travel the parallel path set up by the meter itself. This dilemma does not show itself when measuring larger amounts of voltage (9 to 12 volt circuits), but if you are measuring a low voltage circuit such as the oxygen sensor signal voltage, a fraction of a volt may be a significant amount when diagnosing a problem. However, there are several exceptions where using an analog voltmeter may be necessary to test certain sensors. **Note:** *All drawings of connectors in this Chapter show the front of the harness side, not the sensor side - as if you had removed*

the connector from the sensor and were looking into the connector on the harness side. Backprobing these connectors (see Chapter 12) would mean reversing the terminal designations given in the captions, from left to right.

2   Hand-held scanners are the most powerful and versatile tools for analyzing engine management systems used on later model vehicles **(see illustration)**. Each brand scan tool must be examined carefully to match the year, make and model of the vehicle you are working on. Often, interchangeable cartridges are available to access the particular manufacturer (Ford, GM, Chrysler, etc.). Some manufacturers will specify by continent (Asia, Europe, USA, etc.).

3   With arrival of the federally mandated emission control system (OBD-II), a specially designed scanner has been developed. Several tool manufacturers have released OBD-II scan tools for the home mechanic. Ask the parts salesman at a local auto parts store for additional information concerning availability and cost.

On-Board Diagnostic system general description

4   1995 3.1L models are equipped with the OBD-I self diagnosis system. All later models described in this manual are equipped with the second generation On-Board Diagnostic (OBD-II) system. The systems consist of an onboard computer, known as the Powertrain Control Module (PCM), information sensors and output actuators.

5   Information sensors monitor various functions of the engine and send data to the PCM. Based on the data and the information programmed into the computer's memory, the PCM generates output signals to control various engine functions via control relays, solenoids and other output actuators. The PCM is specifically calibrated to optimize the emissions, fuel economy and driveability of the vehicle.

6   Any owner-induced damage to the PCM, the sensors and/or the control devices may void the federally mandated warranty that covers the emissions system components, so it isn't a good idea to attempt diagnosis or replacement of the PCM at home while the vehicle is under warranty. If there is a PCM or system component malfunction take the vehicle to a dealer service department.

Information sensors

7   **Camshaft position sensor** - The camshaft position sensor provides information on camshaft position. The PCM uses this information, along with the crankshaft position sensor information, to control fuel injection synchronization.

8   **Crankshaft position sensor** - The crankshaft position sensor senses crankshaft position (TDC) during each engine revolution. The PCM uses this information to control ignition timing and fuel injection synchronization.

9   **Engine coolant temperature sensor** -

2.1 Digital multimeters can be used for testing all types of circuits; because of their high impedance, they are much more accurate than analog meters for measuring low-voltage computer circuits

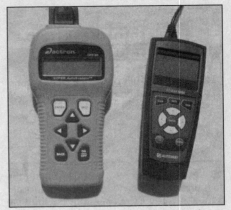

2.2 Scanners like these from Actron and AutoXray are powerful diagnostic aids - they can tell you just about anything you want to know about your engine management system

The engine coolant temperature sensor senses engine coolant temperature. The PCM uses this information to control fuel injection duration and ignition timing.

10   **Intake air temperature sensor** - The intake air temperature senses the temperature of the air entering the intake manifold. The PCM uses this information to control fuel injection duration.

11   **Knock sensor** - The knock sensor is a piezoelectric element that detects the sound of engine detonation, or "pinging". The PCM uses the input signal from the knock sensor to recognize detonation and retard spark advance to avoid engine damage.

12   **Manifold absolute pressure sensor** - The manifold absolute pressure monitors intake manifold pressure and ambient barometric pressure. The PCM uses this input signal to determine engine load and adjusts fuel injection duration accordingly.

13   **Mass airflow sensor** - The mass airflow sensor measures the amount of air passing through the sensor body and ultimately entering the engine. The PCM uses this information to control fuel delivery.

14   **Oxygen sensor** - The oxygen sensors generate a voltage signal that varies with the difference between the oxygen content of the exhaust and the oxygen in the surrounding air. The PCM uses this information to determine if the fuel system is running rich or lean.

15   **Throttle position sensor** - The throttle position sensor senses throttle movement and position. This signal enables the PCM to determine when the throttle is closed, in a cruise position, or wide open. The PCM uses this information to control fuel delivery and ignition timing.

16   **Vehicle speed sensor** - The vehicle speed sensor provides information to the PCM to indicate vehicle speed.

17   **Miscellaneous PCM inputs** - In addition to the various sensors, the PCM monitors various switches and circuits to determine vehicle operating conditions. The

switches and circuits include:
a) *Air conditioning system*
b) *Battery voltage*
c) *Brake On/Off switch*
d) *Cruise control system*
e) *EGR valve position*
f) *Engine oil level and pressure*
g) *EVAP system*
h) *Fuel level and fuel tank pressure*
i) *Ignition switch*
j) *Park/neutral position switch*
k) *Sensor signal and ground circuits*
l) *Transaxle controls*

Output actuators

18   **Air conditioning clutch relay** - The PCM controls the operation of the air conditioning compressor clutch with the air conditioning clutch relay.

19   **Check Engine light** - The PCM will illuminate the Check Engine light if a malfunction in the electronic engine control system occurs.

20   **Cruise control module** - The cruise control system operation is controlled by the PCM.

21   **Engine cooling fan relay** - The engine cooling fan is controlled by the PCM according to information received from the engine coolant temperature sensor.

22   **EGR valve** - The electronic EGR valve is controlled by the PCM. Ideal EGR flow is determined by the PCM and the EGR valve pintle position is adjusted accordingly.

23   **EVAP canister purge and vent valve solenoids** - The evaporative emission canister purge and vent valve solenoids are operated by the PCM to purge the fuel vapor canister and route fuel vapor to the intake manifold for combustion.

24   **Secondary air injection pump and vacuum valve/solenoid (some 1999 and 2000 models** - The PCM operates the secondary air injection pump and opens the vacuum valve to inject fresh air into the exhaust stream, lower emission levels under certain operating conditions.

2.30a The 12-pin Data Link Connector (DLC) found on models equipped with OBD-1

A   *Ground*
B   *Diagnostic test terminal (not on all models)*

25   **Fuel injectors** - The PCM opens the fuel injectors individually in firing order sequence. The PCM also controls the time the injector is held open (pulse width). The pulse width of the injector (measured in milliseconds) determines the amount of fuel delivered. For more information on the fuel delivery system and the fuel injectors, including injector replacement, refer to Chapter 4.

26   **Fuel pump relay** - The fuel pump relay is activated by the PCM with the ignition switch in the Start or Run position. When the ignition switch is turned on, the relay is activated to supply initial line pressure to the system. For more information on fuel pump check and replacement, refer to Chapter 4.

27   **Idle air control valve** - The idle air control valve controls the amount of air allowed to bypass the throttle plate when the throttle valve is closed or at idle position. The more air that can bypass the throttle plate, the higher the idle speed. The idle air control valve opening and the resulting idle speed is controlled by the PCM.

28   **Ignition control module** - The PCM controls ignition timing through the ignition control module depending on engine operation conditions. Refer to Chapter 5 for more information on the ignition control module.

Obtaining diagnostic trouble codes

Refer to illustrations 2.30a and 2.30b
Caution: *Don't crank or start the engine when terminals A and B are connected by the jumper wire.* **Note 1:** *On some 1995 OBD I models with a 12-pin Data Link Connector, trouble codes can be access by connecting terminal B to terminal A with a jumper wire*

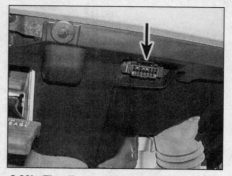

2.30b The diagnostic connector on OBD-II models is typically located under the instrument panel

with the ignition key in the ON position, and the codes can be read by watching the flashes of the SERVICE ENGINE SOON light on the instrument panel (for example, one flash, pause, followed by four flashes would indicate a code 14). It should be noted, however, that some models with a 12-pin diagnostic connector do not have a terminal B present in the connector. On these models a scan tool is required to access trouble codes. **Note 2:** *The diagnostic trouble codes on all other models can only be extracted from the Powertrain Control Module (PCM) using a specialized scan tool. Have the vehicle diagnosed by a dealer service department or other qualified automotive repair facility if the proper scan tool is not available.*

29   The PCM will illuminate the SERVICE ENGINE SOON or CHECK ENGINE light (also known as the Malfunction Indicator Lamp) on the dash if it recognizes a fault in the system. The light will remain illuminated until the problem is repaired and the code is cleared or the PCM does not detect any malfunction for several consecutive drive cycles.

30   On all later models, the diagnostic codes for the On-Board Diagnostic (OBD) system can only be extracted from the PCM using a scan tool. The scan tool is programmed to interface with the OBD system by plugging into the diagnostic connector **(see illustrations)**. When used, the scan tool has the ability to diagnose in-depth driveability problems and it allows freeze frame data to be retrieved from the PCM stored memory.

Freeze frame data is an OBD II PCM feature that records all related sensor and actuator activity on the PCM data stream whenever an engine control or emissions fault is detected and a trouble code is set. This ability to look at the circuit conditions and values when the malfunction occurs provides a valuable tool when trying to diagnose intermittent driveability problems. If the tool is not available and intermittent driveability problems exist, have the vehicle checked at a dealer service department or other qualified repair shop.

Clearing diagnostic trouble codes

31   After the system has been repaired, the codes must be cleared from the PCM memory. The preferred method is with a scan tool, but the codes can be cleared by disconnecting battery power from the PCM for a minimum of thirty seconds. Battery power can be disconnected from the PCM by removing the PCM fuse, disconnecting the PCM power connector near the positive battery terminal (if equipped) or by disconnecting the negative battery cable from the battery. **Caution:** *On models equipped with the Theftlock audio system, be sure the lockout feature is turned off before performing any procedure which requires disconnecting the battery (see the front of this manual).*

32   Always clear the codes from the PCM before starting the engine after a new electronic emission control component is installed onto the engine. The PCM stores the operating parameters of each sensor. The PCM may set a trouble code if a new sensor is allowed to operate before the parameters from the old sensor have been erased.

Diagnostic trouble code identification

33   The accompanying list of diagnostic trouble codes is a compilation of all the codes that may be encountered using a generic scan tool. Additional trouble codes may be available with the use of the manufacturer specific scan tool. Not all codes pertain to all models and not all codes will illuminate the Check Engine light when set. All models require a scan tool to access the diagnostic trouble codes.

OBD I Trouble Codes

Trouble Code	Circuit or system	Probable cause
13	Oxygen sensor circuit Replace oxygen sensor.*	Check the wiring and connectors from the oxygen sensor.
14	Coolant sensor circuit	If the engine is experiencing overheating problems, the problem must be rectified (high temperature indicated) before continuing (see Chapters 1 and 3). Check all wiring and connectors associated with the sensor. Replace the coolant sensor.*
15	Coolant sensor circuit	See above. Also, check the thermostat for proper operation (low temperature indicated).
16	System voltage low	Check the alternator and or voltage regulator and ignition feed circuit to PCM
17	Camshaft sensor circuit	Check the wiring and connectors from the camshaft position sensor. Replace camshaft position sensor.*
21	TPS circuit	Check for sticking or misadjusted TPS. Check all wiring and connections at the TPS and at (signal voltage high) the PCM. Replace the TPS* (see Section 4).

Trouble Code	Circuit or system	Probable cause
22	TPS circuit	See above. (signal voltage low)
23	Intake Air Temperature	Low temperature indicated. (IAT) sensor
24	Vehicle Speed Sensor	A fault in this circuit should be indicated only while the vehicle is in motion. (VSS) Disregard code 24 if set when drive wheels are not turning. Check connections at the PCM. Check the TPS setting.
25	Intake Air Temperature	High temperature indicated. Check the resistance of the IAT sensor. (IAT) sensor Check the wiring and connections to the sensor. Replace the (IAT) sensor.*
28	Transmission Range (TR)	TR pressure switch in the valve body indicates a fault in the shift detection pressure switch system between the 5 pressure switches and the TFT sensor. Have the vehicle diagnosed by a dealer service department or other qualified repair shop.
33	Manifold Absolute Pressure	Check vacuum hose(s) from MAP sensor. Check electrical sensor or circuit (MAP) signal voltage high connections at the PCM. Replace MAP sensor.*
34	Manifold Absolute Pressure	Check vacuum hose(s) from MAP sensor. Check electrical sensor or circuit (MAP) signal voltage low connections at the PCM. Replace MAP sensor.*
35	Idle Speed Error	Check the resistance of the IAC valve. Check the wiring and connections to the sensor.
36	24X signal Error	Check the wiring and connectors from the 24X crankshaft position sensor. Replace 24X crankshaft position sensor).*
37	Brake switch stuck "ON"	TCC brake switch indicates an open or short circuit. Have the TCC brake switch checked by a dealer service department or other qualified repair shop.
41	Ignition Control circuit	Timing circuit error. Check the wiring and connectors between the ignition module and the PCM. Check the ignition module (see Chapter 5). Replace the PCM.*
42	Ignition Control Circuit	Bypass error. Check the wiring and connectors between the ignition module and the PCM. Check the ignition module (see Chapter 5). Replace the PCM.*
43	Knock Sensor (KS) circuit	Check the PCM for an open or short to ground; if necessary, reroute the harness away from other wires such as spark plugs, etc. Replace the knock sensor (see Section 4).*
44	Lean exhaust	Check the wiring and connectors from the oxygen sensor to the PCM. Check the PCM ground terminal. Check the fuel pressure (Chapter 4). Replace the oxygen sensor.*
45	Rich exhaust	Check the evaporative charcoal canister and its components for the presence of fuel. Check for fuel or contaminated oil. Check the fuel pressure regulator. Check for a leaking fuel injector. Check for a sticking EGR valve. Replace the oxygen sensor (see Section 4).*
46	PASS-Key circuit	If engine will not start, have theft deterrent system diagnosed by a dealership service department or other qualified repair shop.
51	PROM Error	Faulty or incorrect PROM. Diagnosis should be performed by a dealer service department or other qualified repair shop
53	System voltage high	Code 53 will set if the voltage at the PCM is greater than 17.1-volts. Check the charging system (see Chapter 5).
54	Fuel pump relay low voltage	Check the fuel pump relay and circuit for shorts or damage (see Chapter 4).
58	Transmission Fluid Temperature (TFT) sensor	The TFT sensor located in the valve body indicates a low fluid temperature. Have the transmission diagnosed by a dealer service department or other qualified repair shop.
59	Transmission Fluid Temperature (TFT) sensor	The TFT sensor located in the valve body indicates a high fluid temperature. Have the transmission diagnosed by a dealer service department or other qualified repair shop.
66	A/C refrigerant pressure sensor circuit	Low pressure. signal voltage from the pressure sensor to the PCM is below .1 volt See Chapter 3.
70	A/C refrigerant pressure sensor circuit	High pressure. signal voltage from the pressure sensor to the PCM is above 4.9 volts See Chapter 3.
72	Vehicle speed sensor loss	Output speed remains undetected or inconsistent. Check the VSS.
75	Digital EGR valve	No #1 solenoid faulty or EGR passage obstructed. Have the EGR valve diagnosed by a dealer service department or other qualified repair shop.
76	Digital EGR valve	No #2 solenoid faulty or EGR passage obstructed. Have the EGR valve diagnosed by a dealer service department or other qualified repair shop.
77	Digital EGR valve	No #3 solenoids faulty or EGR passage obstructed. Have the EGR valve diagnosed by a dealer service department or other qualified repair shop.
79	Transmission fluid temperature sensor circuit	PCM detects high transmission temperature. Have the transmission fluid temp sensor and circuit diagnosed by a dealer service department or other qualified repair shop.
80	Transmission Component Error	Torque Converter Clutch (TCC) slippage above 150 RPM Have the transmission diagnosed by a dealer service department or other qualified repair shop.

OBD I Trouble Codes (continued)

Trouble Code	Circuit or system	Probable cause
82	3X signal Error	Check the wiring and connectors from the 3X crankshaft position sensor. Replace 3X crankshaft position sensor (see Section 4).*
85	PROM Error	Check connector at PCM. If OK, reprogram the PCM. Service should be performed by a dealer service department or other qualified repair shop.
86	Analog/Digital Error	Check for a short to B+ in all circuits leading to the A/D multiplexer in the PCM. Have the system diagnosed by a dealer service department or other qualified repair shop.
87	EEPROM Error	Check connector at PCM. If OK, reprogram the PCM. Service should be performed by a dealer service department or other qualified repair shop.
90	TCC solenoid circuit	PCM detects incorrect voltage values at the TCC solenoid. Have the TCC system diagnosed by a dealer service department or other qualified repair shop.
96	Transmission circuit	Low voltage. Check the charging system. Have the transmission circuit diagnosed by a dealer service department or other qualified repair shop.
98	PCM program	Invalid. reprogram the PCM. Service should be performed by a dealer service department or other qualified repair shop.
99	PCM program	Invalid. reprogram the PCM. Service should be performed by a dealer service department or other qualified repair shop.

Component replacement may not cure the problem in all cases. For this reason, you may want to seek professional advice before purchasing replacement parts.

OBD II Trouble Codes

Code	Code Identification
P0016	Incorrect timing between crankshaft and camshaft
P0030	Oxygen sensor heater circuit high current (upstream sensor)
P0036	Oxygen sensor heater control circuit malfunction (downstream sensor)
P0101	Mass air flow sensor circuit, range or performance problem
P0102	Mass air flow sensor circuit, low input
P0103	Mass air flow sensor circuit, high input
P0105	Manifold absolute pressure sensor or throttle position sensor circuit malfunction
P0106	Manifold absolute pressure sensor circuit, range or performance problem
P0107	Manifold absolute pressure sensor circuit, low input
P0108	Manifold absolute pressure sensor circuit, high input
P0112	Intake air temperature circuit, low input
P0113	Intake air temperature circuit, high input
P0116	Engine coolant temperature and intake air temperature difference range problem
P0117	Engine coolant temperature circuit, low input
P0118	Engine coolant temperature circuit, high input
P0121	Throttle position sensor circuit, range or performance problem
P0122	Throttle position sensor circuit, low input
P0123	Throttle position sensor circuit, high input
P0125	Insufficient coolant temperature for closed loop fuel control
P0128	Engine coolant temperature circuit malfunction
P0130	Oxygen sensor circuit, low voltage (upstream sensor)
P0131	Oxygen sensor circuit, low voltage (upstream sensor)
P0132	Oxygen sensor circuit, high voltage (upstream sensor)
P0133	Oxygen sensor circuit, slow response (upstream sensor)
P0134	Oxygen sensor circuit - no activity detected (upstream sensor)
P0135	Oxygen sensor heater circuit range problem (upstream sensor)
P0137	Oxygen sensor circuit, low voltage (downstream sensor)
P0138	Oxygen sensor circuit, high voltage (downstream sensor)
P0140	Oxygen sensor circuit - no activity detected (downstream sensor)
P0141	Oxygen sensor heater circuit malfunction (downstream sensor)
P0171	System too lean
P0172	System too rich
P0200	Injector circuit malfunction
P0201	Injector circuit malfunction - cylinder no. 1
P0202	Injector circuit malfunction - cylinder no. 2
P0203	Injector circuit malfunction - cylinder no. 3
P0204	Injector circuit malfunction - cylinder no. 4
P0205	Injector circuit malfunction - cylinder no. 5
P0206	Injector circuit malfunction - cylinder no. 6
P0218	Transaxle fluid over temperature
P0230	Fuel pump primary circuit malfunction
P0300	Random/multiple cylinder misfire detected
P0301	Cylinder no. 1 misfire detected
P0302	Cylinder no. 2 misfire detected
P0303	Cylinder no. 3 misfire detected
P0304	Cylinder no. 4 misfire detected
P0305	Cylinder no. 5 misfire detected
P0306	Cylinder no. 6 misfire detected
P0315	Crankshaft position sensor system variation values not learned
P0325	Knock sensor circuit malfunction
P0327	Knock sensor circuit, range or performance problem, bank 1 (front)
P0332	Knock sensor circuit, range or performance problem, bank 2 (rear)
P0335	Crankshaft position sensor circuit malfunction
P0336	Crankshaft position sensor circuit, range or performance problem

OBD II Trouble Codes

Code	Code Identification
P0340	Camshaft position sensor circuit no signal
P0341	Camshaft position sensor circuit, range or performance problem
P0342	Camshaft position sensor circuit, low input
P0350	Ignition timing control circuit performance
P0385	3X low resolution engine speed signal circuit no signal
P0386	3X low resolution engine speed signal circuit performance
P0401	Exhaust gas recirculation, insufficient flow detected
P0403	Exhaust gas recirculation circuit malfunction
P0404	Exhaust gas recirculation circuit, range or performance problem
P0405	Exhaust gas recirculation sensor circuit low
P0406	EGR valve pintle position sensor circuit high voltage
P0410	Secondary air injection system
P0412	Secondary air injection solenoid control circuit
P0418	Secondary air injection pump relay control circuit
P0420	Catalyst system efficiency below threshold
P0440	Evaporative emission control system malfunction
P0442	Evaporative emission control system, small leak detected
P0443	Evaporative emission control system, purge control circuit malfunction
P0446	Evaporative emission control system, vent system performance
P0449	Evaporative emission control system, vent control circuit malfunction
P0452	Evaporative emission control system, fuel tank pressure sensor low input
P0453	Evaporative emission control system, fuel tank pressure sensor high input
P0455	Evaporative emission control system large leak diagnostic insufficient vacuum
P0460	Fuel level sensor circuit malfunction
P0461	Fuel level sensor circuit, range or performance problem
P0462	Fuel level sensor circuit, low input
P0463	Fuel level sensor circuit, high input
P0480	Cooling fan control circuit malfunction
P0481	Cooling fan control circuit malfunction
P0496	Evaporative emission control system flow during non-purge
P0502	Vehicle speed sensor circuit low output
P0503	Vehicle speed sensor signal intermittent
P0506	Idle air control system, rpm lower than expected
P0507	Idle air control system, rpm higher than expected
P0530	Air conditioning refrigerant pressure sensor, circuit malfunction
P0560	System voltage malfunction
P0562	System voltage low
P0563	System voltage high
P0601	Internal microprocessor control error within PCM
P0602	PCM, programming error
P0620	Charging system performance
P0641	5-volt reference circuit to MAP, TP, FTP sensors or EGR valve, range problem
P0650	Malfunction Indicator Light (MIL) control circuit

Code	Code Identification
P0651	5-volt reference circuit to air conditioning refrigerant pressure sensor, range problem
P0654	Tachometer control circuit
P0705	Transmission range sensor, circuit malfunction (PRNDL input)
P0706	Transaxle range switch performance
P0711	Fluid temperature sensor circuit out-of-range
P0712	Fluid temperature sensor circuit low input
P0713	Fluid temperature sensor circuit high input
P0716	Input speed sensor circuit out-of-range
P0717	Input speed sensor circuit no signal
P0719	Torque converter clutch brake switch circuit low
P0724	Torque converter clutch brake switch circuit high
P0730	Incorrect gear ratio
P0741	Torque converter clutch system stuck off
P0742	Torque converter clutch system stuck on
P0748	Pressure control solenoid valve circuit
P0751	1-2 shift solenoid performance (2-2-3-3 shift pattern)
P0752	1-2 shift solenoid performance (1-1-4-4 shift pattern)
P0753	1-2 shift solenoid circuit malfunction
P0756	2-3 shift solenoid performance (4-3-3-4 shift pattern)
P0757	2-3 shift solenoid performance (1-2-2-1 shift pattern)
P0758	2-3 shift solenoid circuit malfunction
P1106	Manifold absolute pressure sensor circuit intermittent high voltage
P1107	Manifold absolute pressure sensor circuit intermittent low voltage
P1111	Intake air temperature sensor circuit intermittent high voltage
P1112	Intake air temperature sensor circuit intermittent low voltage
P1114	Engine coolant temperature sensor circuit intermittent low voltage
P1115	Engine coolant temperature sensor circuit intermittent high voltage
P1121	Throttle position sensor circuit intermittent high voltage
P1122	Throttle position sensor circuit intermittent low voltage
P1133	Oxygen sensor insufficient switching (upstream sensor)
P1134	Oxygen sensor transition time ratio (upstream sensor)
P1171	Fuel system lean during acceleration
P1189	Oil pressure switch circuit malfunction
P1200	Fuel injector control circuit
P1336	Crankshaft position sensor system variation not learned
P1350	By-pass line monitor
P1351	Ignition timing control circuit open
P1352	Ignition timing signal circuit open
P1361	Ignition timing control circuit not switching to PCM
P1362	Ignition timing signal circuit shorted
P1374	Crankshaft position sensor 3X reference circuit
P1380	Electronic brake control module rough road sensing error
P1381	No serial data from electronic brake control module
P1404	EGR valve pintle position open
P1406	EGR valve pintle position circuit
P1441	EVAP system flow during non-purge

OBD II Trouble Codes (continued)

Code	Code Identification
P1546	Air conditioning compressor clutch relay primary circuit malfunction
P1554	Cruise control engaged signal circuit malfunction
P1571	Electronic brake control module torque signal request, range or performance problem
P1573	Serial data communication failure with electronic brake and traction control module
P1585	Cruise control inhibit signal circuit malfunction
P1600	Internal microprocessor control error within PCM
P1601	Serial communication malfunction
P1602	Serial data communication failure with electronic brake control module
P1610	Serial data communication failure with body function controller
P1621	Internal microprocessor control error within PCM
P1626	Serial data communication failure with vehicle theft deterent controller (no password)
P1627	Internal microprocessor control error within PCM
P1630	Theft deterent PCM in learn mode
P1631	Theft deterent password incorrect
P1632	Theft deterent fuel disabled
P1635	5-volt reference circuit to MAP, TP, FTP sensors or EGR valve, range problem
P1639	5-volt reference circuit to air conditioning refrigerant pressure sensor, range problem
P1640	Output driver module 1 circuit malfunction
P1641	Malfunction indicator light control circuit
P1644	Delivered torque signal voltage problem
P1650	Output driver module 2 circuit malfunction
P1651	Electric cooling fan relay control circuit
P1652	Electric cooling fan relay control circuit
P1654	Air conditioning relay control circuit
P1655	Evaporative emission control system, purge valve solenoid control circuit

Code	Code Identification
P1660	Output driver module 3 circuit malfunction
P1662	Cruise control inhibit control circuit
P1665	Evaporative emission control system, vent valve solenoid control circuit
P1670	Output driver module 4 circuit malfunction
P1671	Malfunction indicator light control circuit
P1675	Evaporative emission control system, vent solenoid control circuit
P1676	Evaporative emission control system, purge valve solenoid control circuit
P1680	Internal microprocessor control error within PCM
P1681	Internal microprocessor control error within PCM
P1683	Internal microprocessor control error within PCM
P1689	Delivered torque signal voltage problem
P1810	Pressure switch assembly malfunction
P1811	Long shift time
P1814	Torque converter clutch high slip speed with high throttle angle and low vehicle speed
P1819	Transmission range switch signal error at engine start
P1820	Transmission range switch signal A low
P1822	Transmission range switch signal B high
P1823	Transmission range switch signal P low
P1825	Transmission range switch signal error, engine running
P1826	Transmission range switch signal C high
P1860	Torque converter clutch pulse width modulator solenoid circuit
P1887	Torque converter clutch release switch malfunction
P2610	Internal microprocessor control error within PCM
P2A00	Oxygen sensor circuit performance problem (upstream sensor)
P2A01	Oxygen sensor circuit, range or performance problem (downstream sensor)
UXXXX	Codes beginning with "U" indicate that the PCM is unable to communicate with another module

---

3   Powertrain Control Module PCM) - removal and installation

Refer to illustration 3.4

Caution: *Avoid static electricity damage to the Powertrain Control Module (PCM) by grounding yourself to the body of the vehicle before touching the PCM and using a special anti-static pad to store the PCM on, once it is removed.*

Note 1: *Anytime the PCM is replaced with a new unit the PCM must be reprogrammed by a dealership service department with special equipment. A crankshaft position sensor variation relearn procedure and a vehicle anti-theft system password relearn procedure must be performed, as well. The following procedure pertains to removal and installation of the original PCM only. If the PCM must be replaced with a new unit, take the vehicle to a dealership service department.*

Note 2: *Anytime the battery is disconnected stored operating parameters may be lost from the PCM causing the engine to run rough for sometime while the PCM relearns the information.*

1   Disconnect the cable from the negative battery terminal. **Caution:** *On models equipped with the Theftlock audio system, be sure the lockout feature is turned off before performing any procedure which requires disconnecting the battery (see the front of this manual).*

1995 through 1999 models

2   The PCM on these models is located in the right front corner of the engine compartment.

3   Remove the engine coolant reservoir (see Chapter 3).

4   Remove the PCM housing cover **(see illustration)**.

2000 and later models

5   The PCM on these models is located in the left front corner of the engine compartment, in the air cleaner housing.

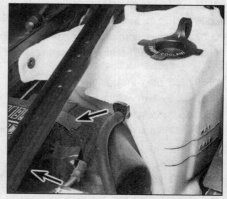

3.4 Detach the clips (arrows) from the PCM housing cover

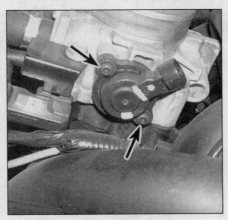

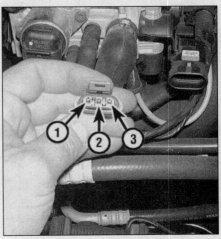

4.1 The TPS (arrow) is located on the side of the throttle body

4.3 Remove the TPS mounting screws (arrows)

5.3 Disconnect the electrical connector from the MAP sensor and check the voltage supply and ground circuits from the PCM at the harness connector

1 Sensor ground
2 MAP sensor signal
3 5-volt supply

6   Remove the left diagonal brace (between the driver's side front fender and the radiator support).

7   Remove the air cleaner duct (see Chapter 4) and the cover of the air cleaner housing.

8   Carefully lift the PCM from the engine compartment without damaging the electrical connectors and wiring harness to the computer.

9   Unplug the electrical connectors from the PCM. Each connector is color coded to fit its respective receptacle in the PCM.

10   Installation is the reverse of removal.

4   Throttle Position Sensor (TPS) - replacement

Refer to illustration 4.1

1   The Throttle Position Sensor (TPS) **(see illustration)** is a variable potentiometer connected to the end of the throttle shaft on the throttle body. By monitoring the output voltage from the TPS, the PCM can determine fuel delivery based on throttle valve angle (driver demand). A broken or loose TPS can cause intermittent bursts of fuel from the injectors and an unstable idle because the PCM thinks the throttle is moving.

Replacement

Refer to illustration 4.3

2   Disconnect the electrical connector from the TPS.

3   Remove the TPS mounting screws and remove the TPS from the throttle body **(see illustration)**.

4   Install a new O-ring on the TPS. With the throttle in the closed position, align the TPS with the throttle shaft and install the TPS. Apply a drop of thread sealing compound to the mounting screw threads. Tighten the screws securely.

5   The remainder of installation is the reverse of removal.

5   Manifold Absolute Pressure (MAP) sensor - check and replacement

1   The Manifold Absolute Pressure (MAP) sensor monitors the intake manifold pressure changes resulting from changes in engine load and speed and converts the information into a voltage output. The PCM receives information as a varying voltage signal from closed throttle (high vacuum) to wide-open throttle (low vacuum). The PCM uses the MAP sensor to control fuel delivery and ignition timing.

Check

Refer to illustrations 5.3 and 5.4

Note: *Performing the following test will set a diagnostic trouble code and illuminate the Check Engine light. Clear the diagnostic trouble code after performing the tests and making the necessary repairs* (see Section 2).

2   The MAP sensor on most models is located on the firewall side of the upper intake manifold plenum. On later 3.8L models, the MAP sensor is on the PCV valve cover, above the ignition coil pack. Check the terminals in the connector and the wires leading to the sensor for looseness and breaks. Repair as required.

3   Before checking the MAP sensor, check the vacuum supply line. Make sure full manifold vacuum is present with the engine running. Check the voltage supply and ground circuits from the PCM. Disconnect the electrical connector from the MAP sensor and connect the positive lead of a voltmeter to the brown or gray wire terminal and the negative lead to the black or orange/black wire terminal at the harness connector **(see illustration)**. Turn the ignition key On - the voltage should read approximately 5.0 volts. If the voltage is incorrect, check the wiring from the MAP sensor to the PCM. If the circuits are good, have the PCM checked at a dealer service department or other properly equipped repair facility.

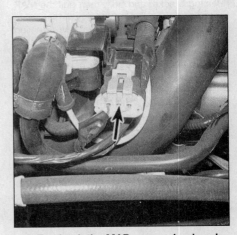

5.4 To check the MAP sensor, backprobe the light green wire terminal of the MAP sensor connector with a voltmeter

4   To check the MAP sensor operation, reconnect the connector to the MAP sensor and using a suitable probe, backprobe the light green wire terminal of the MAP sensor connector **(see illustration)** (see Chapter 12 for additional information on how to backprobe a connector). Connect the positive lead of a voltmeter to the probe and the negative lead to a good engine ground point. Turn the ignition key On - with the engine not running the voltage should read 4.0 to 5.0 volts. Start the engine and allow it to idle - the voltage should decrease to approximately 0.5 to 2.0 volts. If the test results are incorrect, replace the MAP sensor.

Replacement

Refer to illustrations 5.6a and 5.6b

5   Disconnect the electrical connector and vacuum hose from the MAP sensor.

5.6a Remove the MAP sensor mounting screws (arrows) (3.1L/3.4L OHV engine)

5.6b On 3800 engines, squeeze the clips and disengage the MAP sensor from the PCV valve housing

6.2 The mass airflow sensor on 3.1L/3.4L engines is located in the air intake duct

6   On 3.1L/3.4L OHV engines, remove the screws that retain the MAP sensor to the upper intake manifold plenum bracket **(see illustration)**. On 3.4L DOHC engines unplug the electrical connector, remove the sensor retaining bracket and bolt, then pull the MAP sensor straight out. On 3800 engines, unplug the electrical connector, detach the retaining clips (if equipped) and remove the MAP sensor **(see illustration)**.

7   Installation is the reverse of removal.

6   Mass Airflow (MAF) sensor - check and replacement

1   A Mass Airflow sensor (MAF) measures the amount of air passing through the sensor body and ultimately entering the engine through the throttle body. The PCM uses this information to control fuel delivery - the more air entering the engine (acceleration), the more fuel required.

6.3 Disconnect the electrical connector from the MAF sensor and check the voltage supply and ground circuits at the harness connector

     1   *MAF sensor signal*
     2   *Sensor ground*
     3   *12-volt supply*

Check

Refer to illustrations 6.2 and 6.3

2   The Mass Airflow Sensor (MAF) on 3.1L/3.4L engines is located in the air intake duct **(see illustration)**. On 3.8L models, the MAF sensor is on top of the throttle body. A scan tool is necessary to check the output of the MAF sensor (see Section 2). The scan tool displays the sensor output in grams per second. With the engine idling at normal operating temperature, the display should read approximately 4.0 to 6.0 grams per second. When the engine is accelerated the values should rise quickly and remain steady at a steady engine speed.

3   Before checking the MAF sensor operation, check the voltage supply and ground circuits. Disconnect the electrical connector from the MAF sensor and connect the positive lead of a voltmeter to the pink wire terminal and the negative lead to the black/white wire terminal at the harness connector **(see illustration)**. Turn the ignition key On - the voltage should read approximately 12.0 volts. If the voltage is incorrect, check the circuits

6.5 Loosen the hose clamps (arrows) and remove the mass airflow sensor

from the MAP sensor to the power distribution center and engine ground point (don't forget to check the fuses first). If the power and ground circuits are good, check the MAF sensor operation with a scan tool. If the MAF sensor does not respond as described in Step 2, replace the MAF sensor.

Replacement

Refer to illustrations 6.5 and 6.6

4   Disconnect the electrical connector from the MAF sensor.

5   On 3.1L/3.4L models, disconnect the electrical connector from the intake air temperature sensor. Loosen the hose clamp securing the air intake duct to the MAF sensor and remove the duct. Loosen the hose clamp retaining the MAF sensor to the air filter cover and remove the sensor **(see illustration)**.

6   On 3.8L models, remove the fuel injection system trim cover, then remove the screws securing the MAF sensor to the throttle body and remove the sensor **(see illustration)**.

7   Installation is the reverse of removal.

6.6 On the 3800 engine, remove the screws (arrows) securing the MAF sensor to the throttle body

7.2 Intake air temperature sensor location (typical)

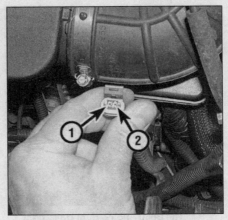

7.3 Disconnect the electrical connector from the intake air temperature sensor and check the voltage supply and ground circuits from the PCM at the harness connector

1 Intake air temperature sensor signal
2 Sensor ground

Temperature (degrees-F)	Resistance (ohms)
212	176
194	240
176	332
158	467
140	668
122	972
112	1182
104	1458
95	1800
86	2238
76	2795
68	3520
58	4450
50	5670
40	7280
32	9420

7.4 Intake air temperature sensor and engine coolant temperature sensor approximate temperature vs. resistance values

7 Intake Air Temperature (IAT) sensor - check and replacement

1   The intake air temperature sensor is a thermistor (a resistor which varies the value of its resistance in accordance with temperature changes). The change in the resistance values will directly affect the voltage signal from the sensor to the PCM. As the sensor temperature INCREASES, the resistance values will DECREASE. As the sensor temperature DECREASES, the resistance values will INCREASE.

Check

Refer to illustrations 7.2, 7.3 and 7.4
Note: *Performing the following test will set a diagnostic trouble code and illuminate the Check Engine light. Clear the diagnostic trouble code after performing the tests and making the necessary repairs* (see Section 2).
2   The intake air temperature sensor is located in the top or side of the air intake duct between the air filter housing and the throttle body **(see illustration)**. Check the terminals in the connector and the wires leading to the sensor for looseness and breaks. Repair as required.
3   Before checking the intake air temperature sensor, check the voltage supply and ground circuits from the PCM. Disconnect the electrical connector from the intake air temperature sensor and connect the positive lead a voltmeter to the tan wire terminal and the negative lead to the black or gray wire terminal at the harness connector **(see illustration)**. Turn the ignition key On - the voltage should read approximately 5.0 volts. If the voltage is incorrect, check the wiring from the sensor to the PCM. If the circuits are good, have the PCM checked at a dealer service department or other properly equipped repair facility.
4   With the ignition switch OFF, disconnect the electrical connector from the intake air

temperature sensor. Using an ohmmeter, measure the resistance between the two intake air temperature sensor terminals on the sensor while it is completely cold (50 to 80-degrees F). Reconnect the electrical connector to the sensor, start the engine and warm it up until it reaches operating temperature (180 to 200-degrees F), disconnect the connector and check the resistance again. Compare your measurements to the resistance chart **(see illustration)**. If the sensor resistance test results are incorrect, replace the intake air temperature sensor. **Note:** *A more accurate check may be performed by removing the sensor and suspending the tip of the sensor in a container of water. Heat the water on the stove while you monitor the resistance of the sensor.*

Replacement

5   Disconnect the electrical connector from the sensor.
6   Carefully remove the sensor from the air intake duct.
7   Installation is the reverse of removal.

8 Engine coolant temperature sensor - check and replacement

1   The engine coolant temperature sensor is a thermistor (a resistor which varies the value of its resistance in accordance with temperature changes). The change in the resistance values will directly affect the voltage signal from the sensor to the PCM. As the sensor temperature INCREASES, the resistance values will DECREASE. As the sensor temperature DECREASES, the resistance values will INCREASE.

8.2 Engine coolant temperature sensor location (3.1L/3.4L engines)

Check

Refer to illustrations 8.2 and 8.3
Note: *Performing the following test will set a diagnostic trouble code and illuminate the Check Engine light. Clear the diagnostic trouble code after performing the tests and making the necessary repairs* (see Section 2).
2   The engine coolant temperature sensor threads into a coolant passage near the coolant outlet **(see illustration)**. On 3.1L/3.4L engines, it's behind the thermostat housing; on 3.8L engines, it's below the housing. Check the terminals in the connector and the wires leading to the sensor for looseness and breaks. Repair as required.
3   Before checking the engine coolant temperature sensor, check the voltage supply and ground circuits from the PCM. Disconnect the electrical connector from the engine coolant temperature sensor and con-

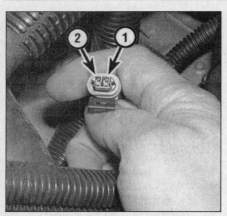

8.3 Disconnect the electrical connector from the engine coolant temperature sensor and check the voltage supply and ground circuits from the PCM at the harness connector

1 Engine coolant temperature sensor signal
2 Sensor ground

9.1 The 3800 engine dual Hall effect crankshaft sensor (arrow) is mounted behind the crankshaft balancer

9.2 7X crankshaft position sensor location (3.1L and 3.4L engines - viewed from below)

nect a voltmeter to the two terminals of the harness connector **(see illustration)**. Turn the ignition key On - the voltage should read approximately 5.0 volts. If the voltage is incorrect, check the wiring from the engine coolant temperature sensor to the PCM. If the circuits are good, have the PCM checked at a dealer service department or other properly equipped repair facility.

4   With the ignition switch OFF, disconnect the electrical connector from the engine coolant temperature sensor. Using an ohmmeter, measure the resistance between the two terminals on the sensor while it is completely cold (50 to 80-degrees F). Reconnect the electrical connector to the sensor, start the engine and warm it up until it reaches operating temperature (180 to 200-degrees F), disconnect the connector and check the resistance again. Compare your measurements to the resistance chart **(see illustration 7.4)**. If the sensor resistance test results are incorrect, replace the engine coolant temperature sensor. **Note:** *A more accurate check may be performed by removing the sensor and suspending the tip of the sensor in a container of water. Heat the water on the stove while you monitor the resistance of the sensor.*

Replacement

Warning: *Wait until the engine is completely cool before beginning this procedure.*

5   Partially drain the cooling system (see Chapter 1).

6   Disconnect the electrical connector from the sensor and carefully unscrew the sensor. **Caution:** *Handle the coolant sensor with care. Damage to this sensor will affect the operation of the entire fuel injection system.*

7   Before installing the new sensor, wrap the threads with Teflon sealing tape to prevent leakage and thread corrosion.

8   Installation is the reverse of removal.

9   Crankshaft position sensor - check and replacement

Refer to illustration 9.1

1   The crankshaft position sensor provides the ignition module and PCM with a crankshaft position signal. The ignition module uses the signal to determine the spark sequence (firing order) for each cylinder. The PCM uses the signal to precisely control ignition timing and calculate engine speed (RPM). The signal is also used by the Onboard Diagnostic system for misfire detection. Later model 3.1L and 3.4L engines are equipped with two crankshaft position sensors; a 7X crankshaft position sensor and a 24X crankshaft position sensor. The 7X crankshaft position sensor is a magnetic inductive sensor triggered by seven slots cut into a reluctor ring on the crankshaft. The sensor tip is positioned approximately 0.050 inch from the reluctor ring. As the notches pass the sensor the magnetic field is altered, producing a pulsating voltage signal seven times per crankshaft revolution. The 24X crankshaft position sensor is a Hall effect device triggered by an interrupter ring behind the crankshaft pulley. The 24X crankshaft position sensor produces on-off pulses as the 24 blades and windows of the interrupter

pass through the sensor's magnetic field. The ignition system will not operate if the PCM does not receive a 7X crankshaft position sensor input. 3800 models are equipped with a dual (18X and 3X) crankshaft position sensor which is mounted at the front of the engine behind the crankshaft balancer **(see illustration)**. This sensor is a dual Hall effect type sensor that can produce two signal patterns (outputs) at the same time. The 18X portion of the switch will produce 18 ON/OFF signals per crankshaft revolution while the 3X portion of the switch will produce 3 ON/OFF signals per crankshaft revolution.

Check

Note: *Performing the following test will set a diagnostic trouble code and illuminate the Check Engine light. Clear the diagnostic trouble code after performing the tests and making the necessary repairs (see Section 2).*

7X crankshaft position sensor

Refer to illustration 9.2

2   The 7X crankshaft position sensor is located on the rear (firewall) side of the

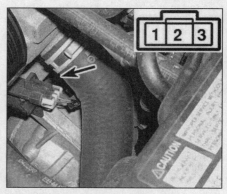

9.5 Disconnect the 24X crankshaft position sensor electrical connector (arrow) and check the voltage supply and ground circuits at the harness side of the connector (3.1L and 3.4L engines)

1 Sensor ground   3 12-volt supply
2 Sensor signal

9.4 24X crankshaft position sensor location (3.1L and 3.4L engines)

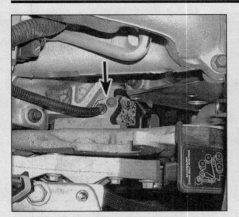

10.2a Camshaft position sensor location (3.1L and 3.4L engines) - viewed from above

10.2b On the 3800 engine, the camshaft sensor (arrow) is located on the front cover (viewed from below)

10.3 Disconnect the electrical connector from the camshaft position sensor and check the voltage supply and ground circuits at the harness connector

1 *12-volt supply (3.1L/3.4L); camshaft position sensor signal (3.8L)*
2 *Camshaft position sensor signal (3.1L/3.4L); sensor ground (3.8L)*
3 *Sensor ground (3.1L/3.4L); 12-volt supply (3.8L)*

engine block **(see illustration)**. Check the terminals in the connector and the wires leading to the sensor for looseness and breaks. Repair as required.

3 Disconnect the electrical connector from the 7X crankshaft position sensor. Connect a voltmeter to the two terminals of the sensor and set the meter to read AC volts. **Note:** *The test connection can be made at the ignition control module electrical connector purple and yellow wire terminals, if desired.* Crank the engine and note the voltage. The 7X crankshaft position sensor should produce a minimum of 200 millivolts with the engine cranking. If a crankshaft position sensor signal is not present, replace the 7X crankshaft position sensor.

24X (3.1L/3.4L) and 18X/3X (3.8L) crankshaft position sensor

Refer to illustrations 9.4 and 9.5

4 The 24X or 18X/3X crankshaft position sensor is located on the front of the engine behind the crankshaft pulley **(see Illustration)**. Check the terminals in the connector and the wires leading to the sensor for looseness and breaks. Repair as required.

5 Before checking the crankshaft position sensor, check the voltage supply and ground circuits from the PCM. Disconnect the electrical connector and connect the positive lead of a voltmeter to the red, red/white or light green wire terminal and the negative lead to the black or yellow/black wire terminal at the harness connector **(see illustration)** on 3.1L/3.4L engines. On 3.8L engines, connect the positive lead to the white/black wire terminal and the negative lead to the black/white wire terminal. Turn the ignition key On - the voltage should read approximately 12.0 volts on 3.1L/3.4L engines and 10.0 volts on 3.8L engines. If the voltage is incorrect, check the wiring from the crankshaft position sensor to the PCM. If the circuits are good, have the PCM checked at a dealer service department or other properly equipped repair facility.

6 To check the 24X crankshaft position sensor operation, reconnect the connector to

the crankshaft position sensor and using a suitable probe, backprobe the light blue/black wire terminal of the crankshaft position sensor connector (see Chapter 12 for additional information on how to backprobe a connector). Connect the positive lead of a voltmeter to the probe and the negative lead to a good engine ground point. Turn the ignition key On. The meter should indicate approximately 10.0 volts. Rotate the engine slowly with a breaker bar and socket attached to the crankshaft pulley center bolt while watching the meter. The voltage should fluctuate between 10.0 volts and zero as the blades and windows in the interrupter pass the sensor. If the test results are incorrect, replace the 24X crankshaft position sensor. **Note:** *Rotate the engine slowly. Removing the spark plugs from the engine will make the crankshaft much easier to turn.*

Replacement

Note: *Anytime a crankshaft position sensor is disturbed, A Crankshaft Position Sensor Variation Learning Procedure should be performed or a false misfire diagnostic trouble code may be set. If after replacing the sensor, a false diagnostic trouble codes is set, take the vehicle to a dealership service department for the procedure.*

7X crankshaft position sensor

7 Disconnect the 7X crankshaft position sensor wiring harness connector.
8 Remove the 7X crankshaft position sensor mounting bolt and withdraw the sensor from the engine block.
9 Replace the O-ring and lightly lubricate it with clean engine oil.
10 Installation is the reverse of removal.

24X (3.1L/3.4L) and 18X/3X (3.8L) crankshaft position sensor

11 Remove the drivebelt (see Chapter 1).
12 Raise the vehicle and support it securely on jackstands. Remove the crankshaft pulley (see Chapter 2). On 3800 engines, carefully pry off the sensor cover.
13 Remove the bolt and the sensor wiring harness retaining bracket.

14 Remove the sensor mounting bolts. Remove the sensor and withdraw the wiring harness, noting the harness routing for installation.
15 Installation is the reverse of removal.

10 Camshaft position sensor - check and replacement

1 The camshaft position sensor, in conjunction with the crankshaft position sensor, determines the timing for the fuel injection on each cylinder. The camshaft position sensor is a Hall effect device triggered by a magnet on the camshaft.

Check

Refer to illustrations 10.2, 10.2b, 10.3 and 10.4

Note: *Performing the following test will set a diagnostic trouble code and illuminate the Check Engine light. Clear the diagnostic trouble code after performing the tests and making the necessary repairs (see Section 2).*

2 The camshaft position sensor is located on the passenger side of the engine, between the upper intake manifold and the power steering pump on 3.1L/3.4L engines **(see illustration)** and above the crankshaft pulley (on the upper left, facing it) on 3.8L engines. Check the terminals in the connector and the wires leading to the sensor for looseness and breaks. Repair as required.

3 Before checking the camshaft position sensor, check the voltage supply and ground circuits from the PCM. Disconnect the electrical connector from the camshaft position sensor and connect the positive lead of a voltmeter to the red/white wire terminal and the negative lead to the black wire terminal at the harness connector **(see illustration)** on 3.1L/3.4L engines. On 3.8L engines, connect the positive lead to the white/black wire termi-

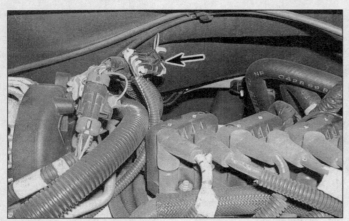

10.4 The camshaft position sensor connector is located behind the alternator - backprobe the brown/white wire terminal of the sensor connector (harness-side) with a voltmeter (3.1L/3.4L engine)

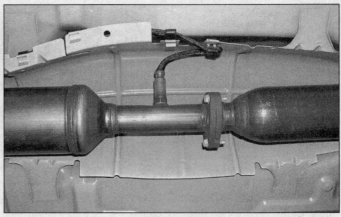

11.2 The downstream oxygen sensor is located in the exhaust pipe after the catalytic converter

nal and the negative lead to the black/white wire terminal. Turn the ignition key On - the voltage should read approximately 12.0 volts. If the voltage is incorrect, check the wiring from the camshaft position sensor to the PCM. If the circuits are good, have the PCM checked at a dealer service department or other properly equipped repair facility.

4   To check the camshaft position sensor operation, reconnect the connector to the camshaft position sensor and using a suitable probe, backprobe the brown/white wire terminal of the camshaft position sensor connector. Connect the positive lead of a voltmeter to the probe and the negative lead to a good engine ground point. Turn the ignition key On. The meter should indicate approximately 10.0 volts. Rotate the engine slowly with a breaker bar and socket attached to the crankshaft pulley center bolt while watching the meter. The voltage should remain a steady 10.0 volts then quickly drop to zero and back to 10.0 volts as the magnet passes the sensor **(see illustration)**. If the test results are incorrect, replace the camshaft position sensor. **Note:** *Rotate the engine slowly through at least two complete revolutions. Removing the spark plugs from the engine will make the crankshaft much easier to turn.*

Replacement

5   Remove the drivebelt (see Chapter 1).
6   On 3.1L/3.4L engines, remove the power steering pump and position it aside without disconnecting the hoses (see Chapter 10). On 3.8L engines, remove the coolant reservoir (see Chapter 3).
7   Disconnect the electrical connector from the sensor harness, noting the harness routing for installation.
8   Remove the camshaft position sensor mounting bolt and the sensor from the engine block (3.1L/3.4L) or the engine front cover (3.8L).
9   Installation is the reverse of removal.

11   Oxygen sensor - check and replacement

Refer to illustrations 11.2, 11.6a and 11.6b
Note: *All models are equipped with an oxygen sensor and later models have two oxygen sensors; one upstream oxygen sensor and one downstream oxygen sensor.*
1   The oxygen in the exhaust reacts with the elements inside the oxygen sensor to produce a voltage output that varies from 0.1 volt (high oxygen, lean mixture) to 0.9 volt (low oxygen, rich mixture). The upstream oxygen sensor (mounted in the exhaust system before the catalytic converter) provides a feedback signal to the PCM that indicates the amount of leftover oxygen in the exhaust. The PCM monitors this variable voltage continuously to determine the required fuel injector pulse width and to control the engine air/fuel ratio. A mixture ratio of 14.7 parts air to 1 part fuel is the ideal ratio for minimum exhaust emissions, as well as the best combination of fuel economy and engine performance. Based on oxygen sensor signals, the PCM tries to maintain this air/fuel ratio of 14.7:1 at all times.
2   The downstream oxygen sensor (mounted in the exhaust system after the catalytic converter) **(see illustration)** has no effect on PCM control of the air/fuel ratio. However, the downstream sensor is identical to the upstream sensor and operates in the same way. The PCM uses the downstream signal to monitor the efficiency of the catalytic converter. A downstream oxygen sensor will produce a slower fluctuating voltage signal that reflects the lower oxygen content in the post-catalyst exhaust.
3   An oxygen sensor produces no voltage when it is below its normal operating temperature of about 600-degrees F. During this warm-up period, the PCM operates in an open-loop fuel control mode. It does not use the oxygen sensor signal as a feedback indi-

cation of residual oxygen in the exhaust. Instead, the PCM controls fuel metering based on the inputs of other sensors and its own programs.
4   Proper operation of an oxygen sensor depends on four conditions:
 a) **Electrical** - *The low voltages generated by the sensor require good, clean connections which should be checked whenever a sensor problem is suspected or indicated.*
 b) **Outside air supply** - *The sensor needs air circulation to the internal portion of the sensor. Whenever the sensor is installed, make sure the air passages are not restricted.*
 c) **Proper operating temperature** - *The PCM will not react to the sensor signal until the sensor reaches approximately 600-degrees F. This factor must be considered when evaluating the performance of the sensor.*
 d) **Unleaded fuel** - *Unleaded fuel is essential for proper operation of the sensor.*

5   The PCM can detect several different oxygen sensor problems and set diagnostic trouble codes to indicate the specific fault (see Section 2). When an oxygen sensor fault occurs, the PCM will disregard the oxygen sensor signal voltage and revert to open-loop fuel control as described previously.

Check

Refer to illustrations 11.6a and 11.6b
Caution: *The oxygen sensor is very sensitive to excessive circuit loads and circuit damage of any kind. For safest testing, disconnect the oxygen sensor connector, install jumper wires to the two connectors and connect your voltmeter to the jumper wires. If jumper wires aren't available, carefully backprobe the wires in the connector shell with suitable probes (such as T-pins). Do not puncture the oxygen sensor wires or try to backprobe the sensor itself. Use only a digital voltmeter to test an oxygen sensor.*

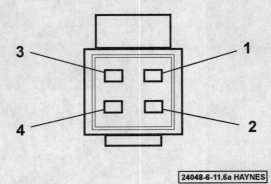

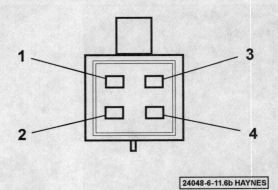

24048-6-11.6a HAYNES   24048-6-11.6b HAYNES

11.6a Upstream heated oxygen sensor connector   **11.6b Downstream heated oxygen sensor connector**

    1   *Reference low*
    2   *Signal high*
    3   *Heater control low*
    4   *12-volt supply*

    1   *Signal low (2004 and earlier); reference low (2005 and later)*
    2   *Signal high*
    3   *Ground (2004 and earlier); heater control low (2005 and later)*
    4   *12-volt supply*

Note: *Performing the following test will set a diagnostic trouble code and illuminate the Check Engine light. Clear the diagnostic trouble code after performing the tests and making the necessary repairs (see Section 2).*

6   Connect your voltmeter positive (+) lead to terminal no. 2 and connect the negative (-) lead to terminal no.1 at the oxygen sensor connector **(see illustrations)**. If testing a single-wire oxygen sensor, connect the negative lead to a good chassis ground. Turn the ignition ON but do not start the engine. The meter should read approximately 400 to 450 millivolts (0.40 to 0.45 volt). If it doesn't, trace and repair the circuit from the sensor to the PCM.

7   Start the engine and let it warm up to normal operating temperature; again check the oxygen sensor signal voltage.

    a) *Voltage from an upstream sensor should range from 100 to 900 millivolts (0.1 to 0.9 volt) and switch actively between high and low readings.*

    b) *Voltage from a downstream sensor should also read between 100 to 900 millivolts (0.1 to 0.9 volt) but it should not switch actively. The downstream oxygen sensor voltage may stay toward the center of its range (about 400 millivolts) or stay for relatively longer periods of time at the upper or lower limits of the range.*

8   Check the battery voltage supply and ground circuits to the oxygen sensor heater. Disconnect the electrical connector and connect the voltmeter negative (-) lead to terminal no. 3 and the positive (+) lead to terminal no. 4 of the sensor connector. Turn the ignition ON. The meter should read approximately 12 volts. If battery voltage is not present, check the power and ground circuits to the sensor (don't forget to check the fuses first).

9   Allow the oxygen sensor to cool and check the resistance of the oxygen sensor

heater. With the connector disconnected. Connect an ohmmeter to the two oxygen sensor heater terminals of the connector (oxygen sensor side). The oxygen sensor pigtail is generally not color coded, but the heater wires are usually the white wires. The oxygen sensor heater resistance should be 3.0 to 10.0 ohms. If an open circuit or excessive resistance is indicated, replace the oxygen sensor. **Note:** *If the tests indicate that a sensor is good, and not the cause of a driveability problem or diagnostic trouble code, check the wiring harness and connectors between the sensor and the PCM for an open or short circuit. If no problems are found, have the vehicle checked by a dealer service department or other qualified repair shop.*

Replacement

Refer to illustration 11.13

10   The exhaust pipe contracts when cool, and the oxygen sensor may be hard to loosen when the engine is cold. To make sensor removal easier, start and run the engine for a minute or two; then shut it off. Be careful not to burn yourself during the following procedure. Also observe these guidelines when replacing an oxygen sensor.

    a) *The sensor has a permanently attached pigtail and electrical connector which should not be removed from the sensor. Damage or removal of the pigtail or electrical connector can harm operation of the sensor.*

    b) *Keep grease, dirt and other contaminants away from the electrical connector and the louvered end of the sensor.*

    c) *Do not use cleaning solvents of any kind on the oxygen sensor.*

    d) *Do not drop or roughly handle the sensor.*

11   If replacing the downstream oxygen sensor, raise the vehicle and place it securely on jackstands.

12   Disconnect the electrical connector from the sensor.

13   Using a suitable wrench or specialized oxygen sensor socket, unscrew the sensor from the exhaust manifold **(see illustration)**.

14   Anti-seize compound must be used on the threads of the sensor to aid future removal. The threads of most new sensors will be coated with this compound. If not, be sure to apply anti-seize compound before installing the sensor.

15   Install the sensor and tighten it securely.

16   Reconnect the electrical connector to the sensor and lower the vehicle.

12   Knock sensor(s) - check and replacement

1   The knock sensor(s) detects abnormal vibration (spark knock or pinging) in the engine. The knock control system is designed to reduce spark knock during peri-

11.13 A special slotted socket, allowing clearance for the wiring harness, may be required for oxygen sensor removal (the tool is available at most auto parts stores)

12.2 Knock sensor location (arrow) (3.1L/3.4L engine)

13.2 Vehicle speed sensor location (arrow)

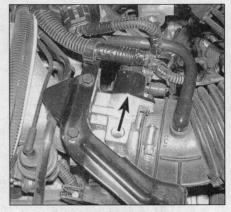

14.2 IAC valve location

ods of heavy detonation. This allows the engine to use maximum spark advance to improve driveability. Knock sensors produce AC output voltage which increases with the severity of the knock. The signal is fed into the PCM and the timing is retarded to compensate for the severe detonation.

Check

Refer to illustration 12.2

2   The knock sensor on 3.1L/3.4L engines is located on the front (radiator) side of the engine block above the oil filter **(see illustration)**. 3.8L engines have two knock sensors, one on the front (radiator) side and one on the back, about midway, below the exhaust manifolds.

3   Disconnect the electrical connector from the knock sensor. Using an ohmmeter, measure the resistance between the two terminals of the sensor connector (harness side - not the sensor side) on earlier models or between the single terminal of the sensor connector and ground on later models. The resistance should be approximately 90 to 110 K-ohms. If the resistance is not as specified, check the wiring harness from the sensor connector to the PCM, including the PCM connector for looseness or damage. If the harness and connections are good, replace the PCM.

4   To check the sensor operation, reconnect the connector to the sensor. Backprobe both terminals, if applicable. Connect the positive lead to the dark blue wire and the negative lead to the gray wire (or to ground on later models). Set the voltmeter on the AC volts scale. Start the engine and check for an AC voltage signal from the knock sensor. The AC voltage should increase as the engine speed increases. If a voltage signal is not present, replace the knock sensor.

Replacement

Warning: *The engine must be completely cool before beginning this procedure.*

5   Drain the cooling system (see Chapter 1).

6   Raise the vehicle and support it securely on jackstands.
7   Disconnect the electrical connector from the knock sensor.
8   Remove the sensor from the engine block.
9   Installation is the reverse of removal.
10   Refill the cooling system (see Chapter 1).

---

13   Vehicle Speed Sensor (VSS) - check and replacement

---

1   The Vehicle Speed Sensor (VSS) is a permanent magnet generator mounted on the transaxle. A toothed rotor on the transaxle output shaft triggers the sensor. As the output shaft rotates, the sensor produces an AC voltage, the frequency of which is proportional to vehicle speed. The PCM uses the sensor input signal for several different engine and transmission control functions. The VSS signal also drives the speedometer on the instrument panel. A defective VSS can cause various driveability and transaxle problems.

Check

Refer to illustration 13.2

2   Raise the vehicle and support it securely on jackstands. Locate the vehicle speed sensor **(see illustration)**. Check the terminals in the connector and the wires leading to the sensor for looseness and breaks. Repair as required.

3   To check the VSS operation, backprobe the two wire terminals of the VSS connector using suitable probes (see Chapter 12 for additional information on how to backprobe a connector). Connect a voltmeter to the probes and set the meter on the AC volts scale. Turn the ignition key On. Rotate the right front tire by hand while watching the voltmeter. The sensor should produce a minimum of 0.5 volts and the voltage should increase as the transaxle output shaft rotates faster.

4   Turn the ignition key Off and disconnect the electrical connector from the sensor. Using an ohmmeter, measure the resistance across the two terminals of the sensor. The sensor resistance should be between 1500 and 1650 ohms at 68-degrees F. If the test results are incorrect, have the VSS checked by a dealer service department.

Replacement

5   Raise the vehicle and support it securely on jackstands.
6   Disconnect the electrical connector from the VSS.
7   Remove the mounting bolt and withdraw the VSS from the transaxle case.
8   Replace the sensor O-ring.
9   Installation is the reverse of removal.

---

14   Idle Air Control (IAC) valve - check and replacement

---

1   The idle speed is controlled by the Idle Air Control (IAC) valve. The IAC valve regulates the air bypassing the throttle plate by moving the pintle in or out of the air passage. The IAC valve is controlled by the PCM, adjusting the idle speed depending upon the running conditions of the engine (air conditioning system, power steering, cold and warm running etc.). The engine idle speed is not adjustable on these models.

Check

Refer to illustration 14.2

Note: *Performing the following test will set a diagnostic trouble code and illuminate the Check Engine light. Clear the diagnostic trouble code after performing the tests and making the necessary repairs (see Section 2).*

2   The Idle Air Control (IAC) valve is located on the throttle body **(see illustration)**. A scan tool is required for complete testing of the IAC valve and circuits. However, there are several tests the home mechanic can perform on the IAC system to

14.9 Before installing a new Idle Air Control valve, measure the distance from the tip of the pintle to the mounting flange - press the pintle in until the distance is less than 1-1/8 inch

15.2 PCV valve location on 3.1L/3.4L models

16.4 EGR valve harness connector terminal identification

1   EGR valve control ground
2   Pintle position sensor ground
3   Pintle position sensor signal
4   Pintle position sensor 5-volt supply
5   12-volt supply

verify operation but they are limited and are useful only in the case of definite IAC valve failure.

3   When the engine is started cold, the IAC valve should vary the idle as the engine begins to warm-up. Allow the engine to warm-up, then place a load on the engine by placing the transaxle in gear (automatic), turning the air conditioning on and/or operating the power steering. **Warning:** *While performing this check, stay in the vehicle, depress the brake pedal firmly and make sure nobody is in front of or behind the vehicle.* The idle should remain steady or increase slightly. If the engine stumbles or stalls, or if there are obvious signs that the IAC valve is not working, stop the engine and continue testing.

4   Disconnect the electrical connector from the IAC valve. Using an ohmmeter, measure the resistance across terminals 1 and 2 of the IAC valve, then measure the resistance across terminals 3 and 4 (the IAC valve terminals are numbered 1, 2, 3, 4, left-to-right) - the resistance should be about the same on both sets. If one or both checks indicate an open circuit, replace the IAC valve.

5   If the IAC valve is good, have the PCM diagnosed by a dealer service department or other qualified repair shop.

Replacement

Refer to illustration 14.9

6   Disconnect the electrical connector from the IAC valve.

7   Remove the two mounting screws from the valve and withdraw it from the throttle body.

8   Inspect the IAC valve pintle and the air passage and valve seat in the throttle body for heavy carbon deposits. Clean the IAC valve with aerosol carburetor cleaner, a shop towel and a soft brush, if necessary. Do not submerge the IAC valve in any liquid cleaner. If the air passage requires further cleaning, remove the throttle body and clean it thoroughly.

9   If installing a new IAC valve, measure the distance from the tip of the IAC valve pintle to the mounting flange **(see illustration)**. If the distance is greater than 1-1/8 inch, press the pintle in by hand, as necessary. **Caution:** *Do not attempt to press the pintle in on a used IAC valve. The force required to move a pintle shaft with carbon build-up may damage the valve.*

10   Install a new O-ring and lubricate it with clean engine oil.

11   Install the IAC valve and tighten the screws securely. Connect the electrical connector.

12   Cycle the ignition key On for ten seconds, then Off for ten seconds to reset the valve. Start the engine, allow it to reach operating temperature and check the idle operation.

15 Positive Crankcase Ventilation (PCV) system

Refer to illustration 15.2

1   When the engine is running, a certain amount of the gasses produced during combustion escapes past the piston rings into the crankcase as blow-by gasses. The Positive Crankcase Ventilation (PCV) system is designed to reduce the resulting hydrocarbon emissions (HC) by routing the gasses and vapors from the crankcase into the intake manifold and combustion chambers, where they are consumed during engine operation.

2   The main component of the Positive Crankcase Ventilation (PCV) system is the PCV valve **(see illustration)**. Fresh air flows from the air intake duct through a vent tube into the engine. Crankcase vapors are drawn from the crankcase by the PCV valve. To maintain idle quality and good driveability, the PCV valve restricts the flow when the intake manifold vacuum is high. When intake manifold vacuum is lower, maximum vapor flow is allowed through the valve.

3   Checking and replacement of the PCV valve is covered in Chapter 1.

16 Exhaust Gas Recirculation (EGR) system

1   The Exhaust Gas Recirculation (EGR) system is used to lower NOx (oxides of nitrogen) emission levels caused by high combustion temperatures. The EGR valve recirculates a small amount of exhaust gases into the intake manifold. The additional mixture lowers the temperature of combustion thereby reducing the formation of NOx compounds.

2   The EGR system consists of an electronic EGR valve and the PCM. The PCM controls the EGR flow rate by energizing the EGR valve solenoid coil, opening or closing the EGR passage in small increments. The PCM monitors the EGR valve pintle position with an EGR position sensor that is built into the EGR valve. This system allows for precise control of EGR flow, achieving optimum EGR flow depending on engine operating conditions.

Check

Refer to illustration 16.4

3   The EGR valve is located at the rear of the upper intake manifold, on the driver's side. A scan tool is required for complete testing of the EGR valve, control system and circuits. However, there are a couple of tests the home mechanic can perform on the system to verify operation but they are limited and are useful only in the case of definite system failure.

4   Disconnect the electrical connector from the EGR valve. Connect the negative lead of a voltmeter to a good engine ground point and probe terminal no. 1 of the EGR valve electrical connector (harness side) with the positive lead **(see illustration)**. Turn the ignition key On - the battery voltage should

16.7 Remove the EGR valve mounting bolts (arrows) - 3.1L/3.4L OHV engine

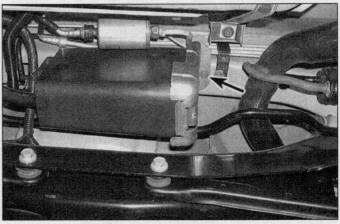

17.10 Remove the EVAP canister bracket mounting bolt (arrow)

be indicated on the meter. If battery voltage is not indicated, check the circuits from the PCM to the EGR valve. If the circuits are good, have the PCM diagnosed by a dealer service department or other qualified repair shop.

5   Check the voltage supply and ground circuits to the EGR valve position sensor. Disconnect the electrical connector from the EGR valve. Connect the positive lead of a voltmeter to terminal no. 4 of the EGR valve electrical connector (harness side). Connect the negative lead to terminal no. 2. Turn the ignition key On - approximately 5.0 volts should be indicated on the meter. If the 5.0 volt supply voltage is not present, check the circuits from the PCM to the EGR valve. If the circuits are good, have the PCM diagnosed by a dealer service department or other qualified repair shop.

EGR valve replacement

Refer to illustration 16.7

6   Disconnect the electrical connector from the EGR valve.

7   Remove the EGR valve mounting bolts **(see illustration)**. Some 3.8L models have a small EGR valve heat shield that must also be removed. Remove the EGR valve and gaskets. Discard the gaskets.

8   Using a gasket scraper, clean the EGR valve gasket surfaces.

9   Installation is the reverse of removal.

---

17 Evaporative emissions control system

---

1   The fuel evaporative emissions control (EVAP) system absorbs fuel vapors from the fuel tank and, during engine operation, releases them into the engine intake system where they mix with the incoming air/fuel mixture. The main components of the evaporative emissions system are the canister (filled with activated charcoal to absorb fuel vapors), the purge valve, the vent valve, the

fuel pressure sensor, the fuel tank and the vapor and purge lines.

2   After passing through a check valve, fuel tank vapor is carried through the vapor hose to the charcoal canister. The activated charcoal in the canister absorbs and stores the vapors. When a programmed set of conditions are met (engine running, warmed to a pre-set temperature, etc.), the PCM opens the purge valve and the vent valve. Fuel vapors from the canister are then drawn through the purge hose by intake manifold vacuum into the intake manifold and combustion chamber where they are consumed during normal engine operation.

3   The PCM regulates the rate of vapor flow from the canister to the intake manifold by controlling the duty cycle of the EVAP purge valve control solenoid. During cold running conditions and hot start time delay, the PCM does not energize the solenoid. After the engine has warmed up to the correct operating temperature, the PCM purges the vapors into the intake manifold according to the running conditions of the engine. The PCM will cycle (ON then OFF) the purge valve control solenoid about 5 to 10 times per second. The flow rate will be controlled by the pulse width, or length of time, the solenoid is allowed to be energized.

4   The system performs a self-diagnostic check when the engine is started cold. When the programmed conditions are met, the PCM opens the EVAP canister purge valve, leaving the vent valve closed. This action allows engine vacuum to draw a vacuum on the entire EVAP system. Once the proper vacuum level is reached, the PCM closes the purge valve, sealing the system. The PCM then monitors the fuel tank pressure sensor and sets a diagnostic code if a leak is detected.

Check

Note: *The evaporative control system, like all emission control systems, is protected by a federally-mandated warranty (5 years or*

50,000 miles at the time this manual was written). The EVAP system probably won't fail during the service life of the vehicle; however, if it does, the hoses or charcoal canister are usually to blame.

5   Always check the hoses first. A disconnected, damaged or missing hose is the most likely cause of a malfunctioning EVAP system. Refer to the vacuum hose routing diagram (attached to the radiator support) to determine whether the hoses are correctly routed and attached. Repair any damaged hoses or replace any missing hoses as necessary.

6   Check the related fuses and wiring to the purge and vent valves. Refer to the wiring diagrams at the end of Chapter 12, if necessary. The purge and vent valves are normally closed - no vapors will pass through the ports. When the PCM energizes the solenoid (by completing the circuit to ground), the valve opens and vapors flow through.

7   A scan tool is required to thoroughly check the system. If the above checks fail to identify the problem area, have the system diagnosed by a dealer service department or other qualified repair shop.

Component replacement

Refer to illustrations 17.10, 17.12 and 17.16

EVAP canister

8   The EVAP canister is attached to a bracket near the fuel tank.

9   Raise the vehicle and support it securely on jackstands.

10   Label and remove the hoses from the canister. Remove the bracket mounting bolt and remove the canister **(see illustration)**.

11   Installation is the reverse of removal.

Purge valve

12   The purge valve is attached to the rear (firewall side) cylinder head below the ignition coils **(see illustration)** on earlier models. On later models, it's near the throttle body, between the EGR valve and the IAC valve.

17.12 EVAP purge valve/control solenoid location on earlier 3.1L/3.4L OHV models

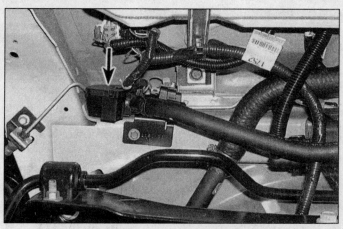

17.16 Typical EVAP vent valve/control solenoid location

13   Disconnect the electrical connector. Label and remove the hoses from the purge valve.
14   Using a small screwdriver, depress the locking tab and remove the purge valve from the bracket.
15   Installation is the reverse of removal.

Vent valve

16   The vent valve is mounted on a bracket near the fuel tank (see Illustration).
17   Raise the vehicle and support it securely on jackstands.
18   Disconnect the electrical connector. Remove the hose from the vent valve.
19   Remove the bracket mounting bolt and remove the vent valve. Depress the locking tab and remove the vent valve from the bracket.
20   Installation is the reverse of removal.

Fuel tank pressure sensor

21   The fuel tank pressure sensor is located on the fuel pump module.
22   Remove the fuel tank (see Chapter 4).
23   Disconnect the electrical connector from the fuel tank pressure sensor.
24   Release the retaining clip and remove the sensor from the top of the fuel pump module.
25   Installation is the reverse of removal.

18   Secondary air injection system

1   Some 1999 and later models are equipped with a secondary air injection (AIR) system. The secondary air injection system is used to reduce tailpipe emissions on initial engine start-up. The system uses an electric motor/pump assembly, vacuum valve/solenoid, check valve and tubing to inject fresh air directly into the exhaust manifolds. The fresh air (oxygen) reacts with the exhaust gas in the catalytic converter to reduce HC and CO levels. The air pump and solenoid are controlled by the PCM. During initial start-up,

when the coolant temperature is between 50-degrees F and 176-degrees F, the PCM will energize the vacuum valve/solenoid, opening the check valve and operate the air pump for approximate one minute. During normal operation, the check valve is closed to prevent exhaust backflow into the system.

Check

Refer to illustration 18.2
2   On earlier models, the pump is at the right front of the engine compartment, attached to the fenderwell, and the valve and solenoid are in front of the front valve cover. On later models, the pump is outside the left frame rail, behind the front bumper, and the valve and solenoid are mounted on the fuel injection system trim cover bracket, behind the rear valve cover. Check the air pump hoses and the vacuum hoses (see Illustration). Repair any damaged hoses or replace any missing hoses as necessary. Check the vacuum source to the vacuum valve/solenoid. Intake manifold vacuum should be present with the engine running.
3   Check the related fuses and wiring to the air pump and vacuum valve/solenoid. Refer to the wiring diagrams at the end of Chapter 12, if necessary. The vacuum valve/solenoid is normally closed - no vac-

uum is applied to the check valve. When the PCM energizes the solenoid (by completing the circuit to ground), the valve opens, vacuum is applied to the check valve, the check valve opens and air flows through the tube into the exhaust pipe.
4   A scan tool is required to thoroughly check the system. If the above checks fail to identify the problem area, have the system diagnosed by a dealer service department or other qualified repair shop.

Component replacement

Refer to illustration 18.11

Air pump

5   Disconnect the electrical connector and remove the hose from the air pump.
6   Remove the splash shield bolts and move the splash shield aside to access the air pump mounting bolts.
7   Remove the mounting bolts and remove the air pump assembly.
8   Installation is the reverse of removal.

Vacuum valve/solenoid

9   Disconnect the electrical connector from the valve/solenoid.
10   Label and disconnect the vacuum hoses from the valve/solenoid.

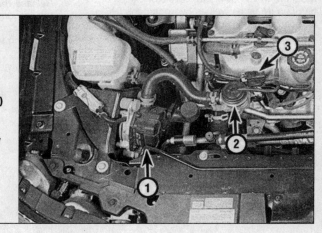

18.2 Secondary air injection component locations (earlier models)

1   *Air pump*
2   *Check valve*
3   *Vacuum valve/solenoid*

18.11 Remove the mounting nut (arrow) from the vacuum valve/solenoid

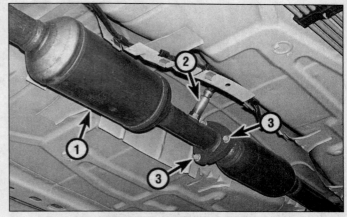

19.7 Catalytic converter and related components

1	Catalytic converter	3	Flange bolts
2	Downstream oxygen sensor		

11   Remove the mounting nut and remove the vacuum valve/solenoid **(see Illustration)**.

12   Installation is the reverse of removal.

Check valve

13   Remove the vacuum valve/solenoid.

14   Remove the air hose from the check valve.

15   Disconnect the air tube from the exhaust pipe.

16   Remove the mounting bolts and remove the check valve and tube.

17   Installation is the reverse of removal.

19   Catalytic converter

Note: *Because of a federally mandated warranty which covers emissions-related components such as the catalytic converter, check with a dealer service department before replacing the converter at your own expense.*

1   The catalytic converter is an emission control device added to the exhaust system to reduce pollutants from the exhaust gas stream. A three-way (reduction) catalyst design is used. The catalytic coating on the three-way catalyst contains platinum and rhodium, which lowers the levels of oxides of nitrogen (NOx) as well as hydrocarbons (HC) and carbon monoxide (CO).

2   The test equipment for a catalytic con-

verter is expensive and highly sophisticated. If you suspect that the converter on your vehicle is malfunctioning, take it to a dealer or authorized emissions inspection facility for diagnosis and repair.

Check

3   Whenever the vehicle is raised for servicing of underbody components, check the converter for leaks, corrosion, dents and other damage. Check the welds/flange bolts that attach the front and rear ends of the converter to the exhaust system. If damage is discovered, the converter should be replaced.

4   A catalytic converter may become plugged. The easiest way to check for a restricted converter is to use a vacuum gauge to diagnose the effect of a blocked exhaust on intake vacuum.

a) *Connect a vacuum gauge to an intake manifold vacuum source.*

b) *Warm the engine to operating temperature, place the transmission in Park and apply the parking brake.*

c) *Note and record the vacuum reading at idle.*

d) *Open the throttle until the engine speed is about 2000 rpm.*

e) *Release the throttle quickly and record the vacuum reading.*

f) *Perform the test three more times, recording the reading after each test.*

g) *If the reading after the fourth test is more than one in-Hg lower than the reading recorded at idle, the catalytic converter, muffler or exhaust pipes may be plugged or restricted.*

Replacement

Refer to illustration 19.7

Note: *Refer to the exhaust system servicing section in Chapter 4 for additional information.*

5   Raise the vehicle and support it securely on jackstands.

6   Disconnect the electrical connector from the downstream oxygen sensor.

7   Remove the catalytic converter-to-exhaust pipe flange bolts and separate the exhaust pipe from the catalytic converter **(see Illustration)**. Support the exhaust pipe. **Caution:** *On later models, the rear of the converter has a flexible coupling. To prevent internal damage to the coupling when installing a new converter (or reinstalling the old one), limit vertical movement at the back of the converter to 6 degrees.*

8   Remove the bolts and detach the catalytic converter header pipe from the exhaust manifold (see Chapter 2A, 2B, 2C or 2D). Remove the catalytic converter and pipe assembly.

9   Clean the carbon deposits from the mounting flanges and install new gaskets.

10   Installation is the reverse of removal.

Chapter 7 Automatic transaxle

Contents

Specifications

General

Fluid type and capacity	See Chapter 1

Torque specifications
Ft-lbs (unless otherwise indicated)

PNP switch-to-case bolts	18
Shift lever retaining screw (column-mounted)	13 in-lbs
Shift control assembly nuts (floor mounted)	18
Shift cable bracket bolts (at transaxle)	18 to 22
Vehicle speed sensor bolt	71 to 124 in-lbs
Transaxle-to-engine bolts	55
Torque converter-to-driveplate bolts	46
Torque converter cover bolts	
1995 through 1999	60 in-lbs
2000 and later	89 in-lbs
TV cable-to-transaxle case bolt	72 in-lbs
Rear engine mount	
Bracket-to-transaxle bolts	70
Mount-to-bracket nuts	35
Mount-to-chassis nuts	46
Engine/transaxle brace	
Brace-to-engine bolts	46
Brace-to-transaxle bolts	32

1 General information

Refer to illustration 1.1

The vehicles covered by this manual are equipped with either a three or four-speed Hydra-Matic automatic transaxle. Three models of Hydra-Matic automatic transaxles are used on these vehicles: the 3T40 three-speed, and the 4T60E and 4T65E electronic four-speeds.

Due to the complexity of the clutches and the hydraulic control system, and because of the special tools and expertise required to perform an automatic transaxle overhaul, it should not be undertaken by the home mechanic. Therefore, the procedures in this Chapter are limited to general diagnosis, routine maintenance, adjustment and transaxle removal and installation.

If the transaxle requires major repair work, it should be left to a dealer service department or an automotive or transmission repair shop. You can, however, remove and install the transaxle yourself and save the expense, even if the repair work is done by a transmission shop (but be sure a proper diagnosis has been made before removing the transaxle).

Replacement and adjustment procedures the home mechanic can perform include those involving the throttle valve (TV) cable and the shift linkage. **Caution 1:** *On models equipped with a Theftlock audio system, be sure the lockout feature is turned off before performing any procedure which requires disconnecting the battery.* **Caution 2:** *Never tow a disabled vehicle with an automatic transaxle at speeds greater than 35 mph or for distances over 50 miles if the front wheels are on the ground.*

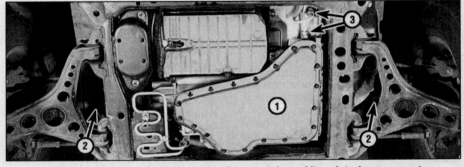

1.1 An underside view of an automatic transaxle and its related components
1 Transaxle fluid pan   2 Driveaxles   3 Transaxle cooler lines

2   Diagnosis - general

Note: *Automatic transmission malfunctions may be caused by five general conditions: poor engine performance, improper adjustments, hydraulic malfunctions, mechanical malfunctions or malfunctions in the computer or its signal network. Diagnosis of these problems should always begin with a check of the easily repaired items: fluid level and condition (see Chapter 1) and shift linkage adjustment. Next, perform a road test to determine if the problem has been corrected or if more diagnosis is necessary. If the problem persists after the preliminary tests and corrections are completed, additional diagnosis should be done by a dealer service department or transmission repair shop. Refer to the Troubleshooting Section at the front of this manual for information on symptoms of transmission problems.*

Preliminary checks

1   Drive the vehicle to warm the transaxle to normal operating temperature.
2   Check the fluid level as described in Chapter 1:
   a) If the fluid level is unusually low, add enough fluid to bring the level within the designated area of the dipstick, then check for external leaks (see below).
   b) If the fluid level is abnormally high, drain off the excess, then check the drained fluid for contamination by coolant. The presence of engine coolant in the automatic transmission fluid indicates that a failure has occurred in the internal radiator walls that separate the coolant from the transmission fluid (see Chapter 3).
   c) If the fluid is foaming, drain it and refill the transaxle, then check for coolant in the fluid or a high fluid level.
3   Check the engine idle speed. **Note:** *If the engine is malfunctioning, do not proceed with the preliminary checks until it has been repaired and runs normally.*
4   Check the shift linkage or cable (see Section 6 or 7). Make sure it's properly adjusted and operates smoothly.
5   On models equipped with a 3T40 transaxle (some 1995 and 1996 models), check the throttle valve (TV) cable (see Section 6). Make sure it's properly adjusted and operates smoothly. On models equipped with a four-speed transaxle, check the vacuum modulator and its base for leaks (see Section 5).

Fluid leak diagnosis

6   Most fluid leaks are easy to locate visually. Repair usually consists of replacing a seal or gasket. If a leak is difficult to find, the following procedure may help.
7   Identify the fluid. Make sure it's transmission fluid and not engine oil or brake fluid (automatic transmission fluid is a deep red color).
8   Try to pinpoint the source of the leak. Drive the vehicle several miles, then park it

over a large sheet of cardboard. After a minute or two, you should be able to locate the leak by determining the source of the fluid dripping onto the cardboard.
9   Make a careful visual inspection of the suspected component and the area immediately around it. Pay particular attention to gasket mating surfaces. A mirror is often helpful for finding leaks in areas that are hard to see.
10   If the leak still cannot be found, clean the suspected area thoroughly with a degreaser or solvent, then dry it.
11   Drive the vehicle for several miles at normal operating temperature and varying speeds. After driving the vehicle, visually inspect the suspected component again.
12   Once the leak has been located, the cause must be determined before it can be properly repaired. If a gasket is replaced but the sealing flange is bent, the new gasket will not stop the leak. The bent flange must be straightened.
13   Before attempting to repair a leak, check to make sure that the following conditions are corrected or they may cause another leak. **Note:** *Some of the following conditions cannot be fixed without highly specialized tools and expertise. Such problems must be referred to a transmission repair shop or a dealer service department.*

Gasket leaks

14   Check the pan periodically. Make sure the bolts are tight, no bolts are missing, the gasket is in good condition and the pan is flat (dents in the pan may indicate damage to the valve body inside).
15   If the pan gasket is leaking, the fluid level or the fluid pressure may be too high, the vent may be plugged, the pan bolts may be too tight, the pan sealing flange may be warped, the sealing surface of the transaxle housing may be damaged, the gasket may be damaged or the transaxle casting may be cracked or porous. If sealant instead of gasket material has been used to form a seal between the pan and the transaxle housing, it may be the wrong type of sealant.

Seal leaks

16   If a transaxle seal is leaking, the fluid level or pressure may be too high, the vent may be plugged, the seal bore may be damaged, the seal itself may be damaged or improperly installed, the surface of the shaft protruding through the seal may be damaged or a loose bearing may be causing excessive shaft movement.
17   Make sure the dipstick tube seal is in good condition and the tube is properly seated. Periodically check the area around the speedometer gear or sensor for leakage. If transmission fluid is evident, check the O-ring for damage.

Case leaks

18   If the case itself appears to be leaking, the casting is porous and will have to be repaired or replaced.

3.3 Dislodge the differential seal by working around the outer edge with a hammer and chisel

19   Make sure the oil cooler hose fittings are tight and in good condition.

Fluid comes out vent pipe or fill tube

20   If this condition occurs, the transaxle is overfilled, there is coolant in the fluid, the case is porous, the dipstick is incorrect, the vent is plugged or the drain-back holes are plugged.

3   Driveaxle oil seals - replacement

Refer to illustration 3.3
1   Raise the vehicle and support it securely on jackstands.
2   Remove the driveaxle(s) (see Chapter 8).
3   Use a hammer and chisel to pry up the outer lip of the seal to dislodge it so it can be pried out of the housing **(see illustration)**. **Note:** *The manufacturer recommends using a slide hammer to remove the metal-type seal.*
4   Compare the new seal to the old one to make sure they're the same.
5   Coat the lips of the new seal with transmission fluid.
6   Place the new seal in position and tap it into the bore with a hammer and a large socket or a piece of pipe that's the same diameter as the outside edge of the seal.
7   Reinstall the various components in the reverse order of removal.

4   Vehicle Speed Sensor (VSS) - removal and installation

Refer to illustrations 4.2 and 4.4
Note: *Any time the speed sensor is removed, you MUST install a new O-ring.*
1   The speed sensor is located on the right (passenger) side of the extension housing. To determine if the O-ring is leaking, look for transmission fluid around the sensor.
2   Unplug the sensor electrical connector **(see illustration)**.
3   Remove the sensor hold-down bolt and remove the sensor.
4   Remove the old O-ring **(see illustration)** and install a new O-ring on the sensor.
5   Installation is the reverse of removal. Tighten the sensor hold-down bolt securely.

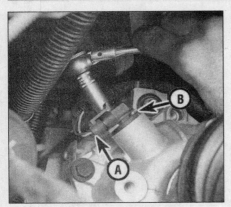

4.2 Disconnect the electrical connector (A) from the speed sensor (B), then remove the hold-down bolt and sensor (the socket here is on the bolt)

4.4 Before reinstalling the speed sensor, replace the O-ring with a new one

5.2 Vacuum modulator assembly
1 Vacuum connection   2 Plunger

5 Vacuum modulator (earlier four-speed transaxles) - check and replacement

Note: *Later models do not have a vacuum modulator. The PCM handles this function electronically.*

Check

Refer to illustration 5.2

1   The vacuum modulator is connected to engine manifold vacuum to rapidly respond to changes in engine loading, and has an important effect on shift quality. If your vehicle exhibits shifting problems such as slipping or shifts that are either too soft or too harsh, check the vacuum supply to the modulator. With the engine running, connect a vacuum gauge to the modulator's vacuum line (at the modulator). Anything less than normal engine vacuum here of 13 to 17 inches (idling hot in Drive with the brakes applied) could cause shifting problems. If vacuum is too low, find the engine problem, hose kink or hose leak that is causing the low vacuum signal.

2   Connect a hand-held vacuum pump to the vacuum connection on the modulator (removed from vehicle) and apply 15 to 20 inches of vacuum while watching the plunger

(see illustration). If the plunger isn't drawn in as vacuum is applied, the modulator should be replaced. The modulator should be able to hold this vacuum for at least half a minute.

3   When the modulator is withdrawn from the transaxle, turn it so the vacuum pipe is down. If any oil, water or other fluid drips out, the modulator should be replaced. **Note:** *A vehicle with a modulator whose diaphragm has a leak may exhibit excessive smoking at the tailpipe, due to transaxle fluid being drawn into the engine and burned.*

4   The body of the modulator can be checked for leaks by coating the outside with soapy water and blowing (by mouth, no more than 6 psi) into the vacuum connector, using a short length of vacuum hose. Bubbles on the outside of the modulator or along the seam indicate a leak.

Replacement

Refer to illustrations 5.6, 5.7 and 5.8

5   The modulator is located on the front (radiator) side of the transaxle, below the exhaust crossover pipe.

6   Disconnect the vacuum line, and remove the mounting bolt or stud, then withdraw the modulator **(see illustration).**

7   Remove the O-ring from the modulator cavity, using a small screwdriver or hook **(see illustration).**

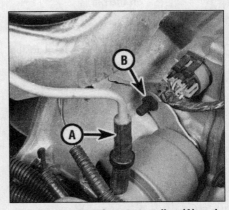

5.6 Disconnect the vacuum line (A) and remove the mounting bolt (B)

8   Use a small magnet to remove the modulator valve from the transaxle **(see illustration).** Inspect the valve for signs of abnormal wear or scoring.

9   Installation is the reverse of the removal procedure. Always use a new O-ring and make sure the modulator valve is installed the same way it came out.

6 Throttle valve (TV) cable (three-speed transaxles) - replacement and adjustment

Replacement

Refer to illustration 6.5

1   Disconnect the TV cable from the throttle by rotating the throttle until the cable eye can be pulled out of the throttle notch with needle-nose pliers.

2   Disconnect the TV cable housing from the throttle bracket by compressing the tangs and pushing the cable housing back through the bracket

3   Disconnect any clips or straps retaining the cable to the transaxle. Refer to Chapter 4 for removal of the air cleaner and duct.

4   Remove the bolt retaining the cable to the transaxle.

5   Pull up on the cover until the end of the cable can be seen, then disconnect it from

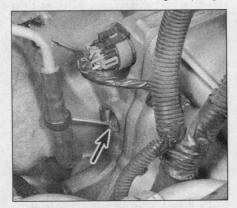

5.7 Remove the O-ring (arrow) from the transaxle case

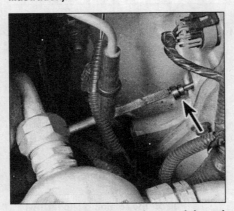

5.8 A magnet can be used to reach in and extract the modulator valve (arrow)

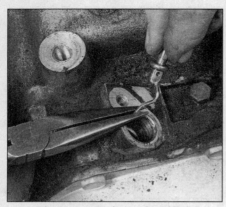

6.5 Hold the transaxle TV link with needle-nose pliers and slide the cable link off the pin

7.3 Pry up on the cable end (arrow) until it releases from the stud on the transaxle lever

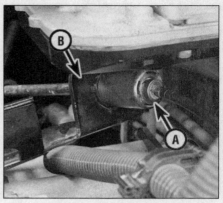

7.4 Squeeze the sides of the cable housing grommet (A) to release it from the bracket (B)

the transaxle TV link **(see illustration)**. Remove the cable from the vehicle.

6   To install the cable, connect it to the transaxle TV link and push the cover securely over the cable. Route the cable to the top of the engine, push the housing through the throttle bracket until it clicks into place, place the connector over the throttle lever pin and pull back to lock it. Secure the cable with any retaining clips or straps.

Adjustment

7   The engine MUST NOT be running during this adjustment.

8   Depress the re-adjust button (located at the throttle lever end of the cable) and push the slider through the fitting (away from the throttle lever) as far as it will go.

9   Release the re-adjust button.

10   Manually turn the throttle lever to the "wide open throttle" position until the re-adjust tab makes audible clicks, then release the throttle lever. The cable is now adjusted.

Note: *Don't use excessive force at the throttle lever to adjust the TV cable. If great effort is required to adjust the cable, disconnect the cable at the transaxle end and check for free operation. If it's still difficult, replace the cable. If it's now free, suspect a bent TV link in the transaxle or a problem with the throttle lever.*

7   Shift cable - replacement and adjustment

Warning: *The models covered by this manual are equipped with airbags. Always disable the airbag system before working in the vicinity of the impact sensors, steering column or instrument panel to avoid the possibility of accidental deployment of the airbag(s), which could cause personal injury (see Chapter 12). The yellow wires and connectors routed through the console are for this system. Do not use electrical test equipment on these yellow wires or tamper with them in any way while working around the console.*

Floor shift models

Refer to illustrations 7.3, 7.4, 7.6, 7.7a and 7.7b

1   Disconnect the cable from the negative battery terminal. **Caution:** *On models equipped with a Theftlock audio system, be sure the lockout feature is turned off before performing any procedure which requires disconnecting the battery.*

2   Refer to Chapter 4 and remove the air cleaner and duct.

3   Disconnect the shift cable from the shift lever on the transaxle **(see illustration)**.

4   To detach the shift cable from the

transaxle bracket, remove the U-clip retainer (if used), then squeeze the tangs on the cable housing grommet and pull the cable and grommet through the bracket **(see illustration)**.

5   Pull the retaining clip from the front of the shift handle, just below the grip, slip the grip off, then remove the center console (see Chapter 11).

6   Disconnect the shift cable from the shift lever **(see illustration)**.

7   Remove the clip at the cable housing end, then pry out the grommet **(see illustrations)** from the front of the shift lever assembly and pull out the shift cable through the hole in the mount. You may have to pull back the carpeting to expose the cable. **Note:** *There may be one or two cable-ties holding the cable to the vehicle's wiring harness in the engine compartment. Cut the ties off to release the cable.*

8   Guide the new cable through the hole in the floor and install the grommet.

9   Connect the shift cable to the shift lever.

10   Install the center console trim panel (see Chapter 11).

11   Place the shift control lever (inside the vehicle) in Neutral. Make sure it remains in the Neutral position until the shift cable is installed.

12   Attach the shift cable to the transaxle bracket.

7.6 Pry the shift cable end (arrow) from the stud on the shifter

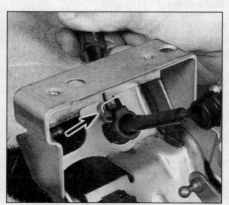

7.7a Pull off the retaining clip (arrow) from the shift cable

7.7b Squeeze the grommet (arrow) and pull the cable forward through the hole in the bracket

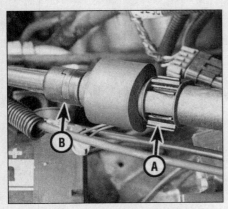

7.20 The shift cable is in two halves, retained by an adjuster clip (A) and a horse-shoe clip (B) - do not remove either clip!

13   Place the shift lever on the transaxle in the Neutral position by rotating it counterclockwise from Park through Reverse into Neutral.
14   Connect the shift cable end to the shift lever on the transaxle, and install new cable-ties where needed.
15   Reconnect the cable to the negative battery terminal.

Column shift models

16   Perform Steps 1 through 4.
17   Refer to Chapter 11 and remove the lower sound insulator panel and the lower steering column cover.
18   Disconnect the cable end from the shift control lever, and pry the cable grommet from the U-shaped mount on the steering column.
19   Pull the cable through the hole in the firewall to the engine side. Installation is the reverse of removal.

Adjustment

Refer to illustration 7.20
20   The shift control cable is in two sections, joined by a coupler retained by a metal spring clip **(see illustration)**. Do not remove this clip! If either section of the cable is damaged, replace the whole assembly as a unit. **Note:** *A new cable may come as two pieces, with instructions for the proper engagement of the two sections.*
21   Install the two sections of new cable to their respective end mountings at the transaxle and shift control. Push the adjuster clip into its first "notch" on the end of the shift control side of the coupling.
22   With both the transaxle and shift control set in the Neutral position, connect the two halves until you feel them lock together, then push the clip onto its last position. There is a smaller clip in the transaxle end of the coupler, and when fully assembled, this clip should be flush with the coupler (not sticking out at all). Pull the two halves of the cable away from each other to test that the connection is secure. Once engaged, do not remove the adjuster clip or another new cable set will have to be purchased.

8   Shift lever assembly - removal and installation

Refer to illustration 8.10
1   Disconnect the negative cable from the battery. **Caution:** *On models equipped with a Theftlock audio system, be sure the lockout feature is turned off before performing any procedure which requires disconnecting the battery.*

Column-shift models

2   Remove the steering column upper cover (see Chapter 11).
3   Pull the shift lever boot up to the angle in the lever. Disconnect the shift lever electrical connector.
4   Remove the lever retaining screw and the lever.
5   Installation is the reverse of removal.
6   Reconnect the negative battery cable.

Floor-shift models

7   Remove the console (see Chapter 11).
8   Disconnect the shift cable from the gear shift lever (see Section 7).
9   Disconnect the interlock cable from the gear shift lever (see Section 10), then disconnect the shift indicator cable (see Section 9).
10   Remove the retaining nuts and lift the floor shift control assembly out of the vehicle **(see illustration)**.
11   Place the floor shift control assembly in position on the mounting studs and install the nuts. Tighten the nuts to the specified torque.
12   Connect the shift cables.
13   Install the console.
14   Reconnect the negative battery cable.

9   Shift indicator cable (column shift) - replacement and adjustment

Warning: *The models covered by this manual are equipped with airbags. Always disable the airbag system before working in the vicinity of the impact sensors, steering column or instrument panel to avoid the possibility of accidental deployment of the airbag(s), which could cause personal injury (see Chapter 12). The yellow wires and connectors routed through the console are for this system. Do not use electrical test equipment on these yellow wires or tamper with them in any way while working around the console.*
Note: *Later models do not have a shift indicator cable. The transaxle range indicator is electronic.*

Replacement

1   Refer to Chapter 10 and lower the steering column from the dashboard.
2   Remove the steering column covers (see Chapter 11).
3   The shift indicator cable attaches to the shift control lever on the top side of the steering column.

4   Disconnect the shift indicator cable on the column by pulling the end out of its square hole.
5   Follow the cable to the instrument panel, removing any retaining clips along the way, and disconnect the upper end from the shift indicator in the instrument panel.
6   Replacement is the reverse of the removal process.

Adjustment

7   Where the steering column meets the bottom of the instrument panel, remove the small filler panel that covers the shift indicator.
8   With the engine Off and the parking brake applied, put the shift lever in Neutral. **Note:** *Go by feel of the detents, rather than the shift indicator.*
9   By hand, move the indicator's pointer until the orange portion of the indicator completely fills the slot under the letter N on the indicator panel. Once adjusted, the shift indicator should show all of the gear positions correctly throughout the shift range.

10   Brake/transmission shift interlock system - description, check and component replacement

Warning: *The models covered by this manual are equipped with airbags. Always disable the airbag system before working in the vicinity of the impact sensors, steering column or instrument panel to avoid the possibility of accidental deployment of the airbag(s), which could cause personal injury (see Chapter 12). The yellow wires and connectors routed through the console are for this system. Do not use electrical test equipment on these yellow wires or tamper with them in any way while working around the console.*

Description

1   The brake transmission interlock system prevents the (column or floor-mounted) shift lever from being moved out of Park unless the brake pedal is depressed simultaneously. When the car is started, a solenoid is energized, locking the shift lever in Park; when the brake pedal is depressed, the solenoid is de-energized, unlocking the shift lever so that it can be moved out of Park. **Note:** *Before making the following checks, refer to Chapter 9 and verify that the brake light switch is functioning properly because it is part of the interlock circuit.*

Check

Refer to illustration 10.3
2   On column-shift models, remove the trim panel under the dash, in front of the steering column and the metal plate above it. Using a flashlight, locate the brake/transmission shift interlock solenoid - it's mounted to the left of the column, just ahead of the column mount.
3   On console-shift models, remove the

8.10 Shift lever assembly mounting nuts (arrows)

10.3 On console-shift models, the solenoid (arrow) is mounted in the shift assembly in the console

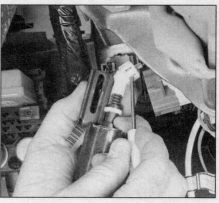

10.11 To disengage the column-shift solenoid from the actuator rod, pry the fingers loose and pull the solenoid half of the actuator rod connector from the other half of the connector

center console (see Chapter 11) and locate the brake/transmission shift interlock solenoid, in front of the shift lever **(see illustration)**. **Note:** *For solenoid testing, reattach the wiring connector to the interlock solenoid.*

4   Verify that the brake/transmission shift interlock solenoid operates as follows:

  a) *When the ignition key is in the Lock position, the solenoid plunger should be in and you should not be able to move the shift lever, even with the brake pedal applied.*

  b) *When the ignition key is turned to the Off position, the solenoid plunger should be popped out and you should be able to move the shift lever to any gear position without applying the brake pedal.*

  c) *When the ignition key is turned to the Run position, the solenoid should go back into the solenoid and you should not be able to move the shift lever; except with the brake pedal applied, the solenoid plunger should be released (pop out) and you should be able to move the shift lever out of Park into any gear.*

  d) *Place the key in the Lock position, then turn the key to the Acc (accessory) position. The solenoid plunger should go in a little further than it does when the key is turned to Lock, and you should*

not be able to move the shift lever (even with the brake applied).

5   Column-mounted solenoids may require adjustment, as follows: pull out the locking tab, press in on the actuator block, then slide the actuator block out as far as possible and push in the locking tab.

6   If the solenoid doesn't operate as described in Step 4, unplug the electrical connector from the solenoid, apply battery voltage to the solenoid and verify that it "clicks" on, then open the circuit and verify that the solenoid clicks off.

  a) *If the solenoid doesn't operate as described, replace it.*

  b) *If the solenoid is operating properly, troubleshoot the circuit between the battery and the solenoid, and between the solenoid and ground.*

  c) *If the solenoid circuit is okay, take the vehicle to a dealer service department.*

Component replacement
Solenoid

7   Disconnect the cable from the negative battery terminal. **Caution:** *On models equipped with a Theftlock audio system, be sure the lockout feature is turned off before performing any procedure which requires disconnecting the battery.*

Column-shift models
Refer to illustration 10.12

8   Disable the airbag system (see Chapter 12).

9   Remove the trim panel under the left side of the dash (see Chapter 11) and the metal plate above it.

10   If necessary, lower the steering column (see Chapter 10).

11   Unplug the electrical connector from the solenoid, and remove the solenoid mounting screw (if equipped).

12   Disengage the solenoid from the actuator rod **(see illustration)**. Remove the solenoid assembly, spring and solenoid-half of the actuator rod connector.

13   Remove the solenoid-half of the actuator rod connector and spring and install them on the new solenoid.

14   Connect the new solenoid assembly to the actuator rod. Installation is otherwise the reverse of removal.

Floor-shift models
Refer to illustration 10.17

15   Remove the center console (see Chapter 11).

16   Unplug the electrical connector from the solenoid.

17   Pry the end of the solenoid rod from its pin on the shift lever assembly, and detach the solenoid from the shift control base **(see illustration)**.

18   Installation is the reverse of removal.

---

11   Park/lock cable - replacement and adjustment

Warning: *The models covered by this manual are equipped with airbags. Always disable the airbag system before working in the vicinity of the impact sensors, steering column or instrument panel to avoid the possibility of accidental deployment of the airbag(s), which could cause personal injury (see Chapter 12). The yellow wires and connectors routed*

10.17 Pry the solenoid's rod-end (arrow) from the shifter

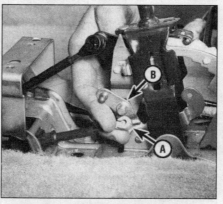

11.4 Pull rearward on the shift cable end (A) until it comes off the pin (B) on the shifter

11.5a Remove the clip (arrow) from the cable housing end . . .

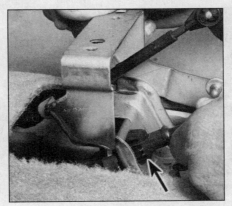

11.5b . . . then use pliers to squeeze the grommet (arrow) until the cable can be worked forward through the hole in the floor

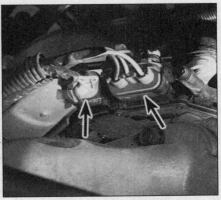

12.6 Electrical connectors (arrows) on the side of the PNP switch

through the console are for this system. Do not use electrical test equipment on these yellow wires or tamper with them in any way while working around the console.

1   The park/lock interlock serves a dual purpose: it prevents the shift lever from being moved out of Park when the ignition switch is in the Off/Lock position, and it prevents the ignition switch from being turned to the Off/Lock position unless the shift lever is in Park. On floor-shift models, the interlock consists of a cable that runs between the console and the ignition switch. Later column-shift models use a linear shift assembly switch on the steering column with a cable to the ignition switch. (Column-shift models also have the brake/transmission interlock solenoid assembly on the steering column, as described in Section 10.)

2   Disconnect the cable from the negative battery terminal. **Caution:** *On models equipped with the Theftlock audio system, be sure the lockout feature is turned off before performing any procedure which requires disconnecting the battery.*

Floor-shift models (park/lock cable)

Refer to illustrations 11.4, 11.5a and 11.5b

3   Remove the center console, the left lower dash trim panel, the knee bolster and the knee bolster deflector (see Chapter 11).

4   Move the shifter to the Park position and detach the Park/lock cable from the shift lever **(see illustration)**. **Note:** *Pull rearward on the cable end to disengage it from the pin on the shifter assembly.*

5   Detach the Park/lock cable from the bracket on the shift lever assembly **(see illustrations)**.

6   If necessary, Refer to Chapter 10 and lower the steering column from the dashboard. **Warning:** *The airbag system must be disabled* (see Chapter 12).

7   Remove the covers from the lower steering column to expose the back of the ignition switch.

8   Turn the ignition key to the Run position. Insert a small screwdriver into the back of the

ignition switch to depress the plastic latch and withdraw the cable from the ignition switch.

9   Remove the Park/lock cable.

10   Installation is the reverse of removal with the following additions:

a) *When installing the cable into the shifter, the cable lock button should be up, and the shift lever should be in Park. Install the cable connector into the shifter base without installing the cable end onto the pin.*

b) *Install the cable into the ignition housing, making sure the ignition switch is in the On position.*

c) *Turn the ignition switch to Off/Lock and install the cable end onto the shifter pin.*

d) *Push the cable nose forward to remove the slack, then push the cable lock button down without applying pressure to the cable sleeve.*

11   If the cable is correctly installed, you should not be able to move the shift lever out of Park when the ignition switch is in the Off/Lock position, and you should not be able to turn the ignition switch to Off/Lock unless the shift lever is in Park.

12   Check for proper operation of the interlock. If necessary, pull the cable lock button up and repeat Step 10 d). If you are unable to remove the key when the shift lever is in Park, pull the cable lock button up and move the cable nose toward the rear until you can remove the key. Then push the cable lock button down.

Column-shift models (linear shift assembly)

13   Remove the shift lever (see Section 8).

14   Remove the steering column covers and the knee bolster (see Chapter 11).

15   Disconnect the electrical connector from the brake/transmission interlock solenoid assembly (see Section 10) and remove the assembly.

16   Turn the ignition switch to Off/Lock.

17   Disconnect the linear shift assembly cable from the ignition switch.

18   Remove the four linear shift assembly

retaining screws and remove the assembly from the steering column.

19   Installation is the reverse of removal.

20   Check for proper operation of the interlock. With the shift lever in Park and the ignition switch in the Off position, you should be able to remove the key easily. If necessary for proper operation, the cable length can be adjusted as follows:

a) *Move the white adjustment tab outward from the adjuster in the middle of the cable.*

b) *Move the shift lever from Park to Reverse and back to Park.*

c) *Turn the ignition key to Off/Lock.*

d) *Press the white adjustment tab to lock the adjuster in place.*

12 Park Neutral Position (PNP) switch - check and replacement

Refer to illustrations 12.6, 12.7 and 12.9

1   The park/neutral position switch on the transmission prevents the engine from being started except when the shift lever is in Park or Neutral. 2003 and later models do not have a park/neutral position switch; instead, this function (and others) is provided by an Internal Mode Switch (IMS), which is part of the manual (shift) shaft and is mounted inside the transaxle case.

2   Disconnect the negative cable from the battery. **Caution:** *On models equipped with a Theftlock audio system, be sure the lockout feature is turned off before performing any procedure which requires disconnecting the battery.*

3   Shift the transaxle into Neutral.

4   Refer to Chapter 4 and remove the air cleaner and the duct to the throttle body.

5   Refer to Section 7 and remove the shift cable from the shift lever and the cable bracket. Make a paint or scribe mark on the transaxle shift lever, relative to its position on the splined shaft from the transaxle when in Neutral, then remove the nut and take off the shift lever.

6   Disconnect the electrical connectors from the PNP (or Range Selector) switch **(see illustration)**.

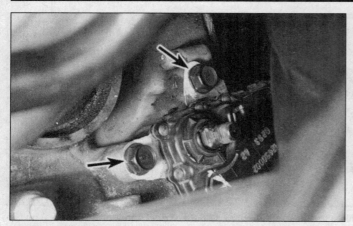

12.7 Remove the two mounting bolts (arrows) and take off the PNP switch

12.9 Align your old switch on reinstallation by positioning the scratched circles (arrows) exactly under the bolts

7   Remove the bolts and detach the switch **(see illustration)**.

8   To install the switch (transmission shaft still in its Neutral position), line up the flats on the switch with the flats in the shaft and lower the switch onto the shaft.

9   Install the bolts. The alignment of the switch is made by moving the switch slightly when tightening the two mounting bolts. A factory tool makes this easier, but the tool isn't absolutely necessary. If you are reinstalling your original switch, the bolts will have made a scratched circle on the mounting bosses **(see illustration)**. If you bolt it down with the bolts aligned exactly over these circles, the switch be positioned correctly. If you are installing a new switch, the replacement switch comes with a plastic pin inside that locks it into the Neutral position. Just bolt it down. When you attach the shift lever and cable and move the selector through its range, the plastic pin will shear off inside and the PNP switch will be perfectly adjusted.

10   The remainder of installation is the reverse of removal.

11   Connect the negative battery cable and verify that the engine will start only in Neutral or Park.

13 Auxiliary transaxle oil cooler - removal and installation

1   On some models, an auxiliary oil cooler is provided for the automatic transaxle fluid. The cooler looks like a small radiator and is mounted in front of the engine radiator and air-conditioning condenser, just behind the grille. Transaxle fluid flow comes from the transaxle to the auxiliary cooler through the transaxle fluid output line, and then from the auxiliary cooler to the standard cooler in the right-hand tank of the engine radiator.

2   If necessary, remove the upper radiator air baffle (between the radiator support and the grille). Place a suitable drain pan under the cooler to catch the fluid and use backup wrenches to remove the lower fluid line from the cooler.

3   When no more fluid comes out, remove the fitting on the upper fluid line.

4   Remove the screws (one or two into the upper radiator support, two into the lower radiator support) and remove the cooler. **Caution:** *If transaxle fluid spills on painted body surfaces, clean it off immediately to avoid damaging the finish.*

5   Installation is the reverse of the removal

procedure. **Caution:** *Do not tighten the mounting bolts until you are sure the cooling lines are properly threaded into the cooler, with no cross-threading.*

14 Transaxle mount - check and replacement

Refer to illustrations 14.1, 14.3 and 14.5

1   Insert a large screwdriver or prybar into the space between the transaxle bracket and the mount and try to pry the transaxle up slightly **(see illustration)**. The transaxle bracket should not move away from the insulator much at all.

2   To replace the mount, raise and suitably support the front of the vehicle on jackstands.

3   Remove the left front wheel and the inner splash shield **(see illustration)**.

4   Support the engine with a floorjack and a block of wood, and raise the engine/transaxle enough to take some tension off the transaxle mount.

5   Remove the nuts attaching the insulator to the crossmember and the nuts attaching the insulator to the transaxle **(see illustration)**.

6   Raise the engine/transaxle slightly with

14.1 Pry on the transaxle mount to check for a broken insulator

14.3 Remove the two screws (arrows) and take off the left inner splash shield for access to the transaxle mount

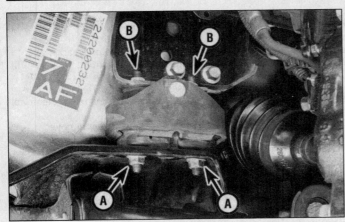

14.5 Remove the mount-to-chassis nuts (A), then the mount-to-transaxle-bracket nuts (B)

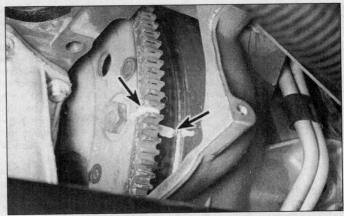

15.5 Make alignment marks (arrows) on the flywheel and torque converter so they can be reinstalled in the same relative positions

the jack and remove the insulator, noting which holes are used in the support for proper alignment during installation.

7   Installation is the reverse of the removal procedure. Tighten the nuts/bolts to the torque listed in this Chapter's Specifications.

15   Automatic transaxle - removal and installation

Refer to illustrations 15.5, 15.18a and 15.18b
Warning: *This is a difficult procedure for the home mechanic, requiring the use of several specialized tools, including a transmission jack and a three-bar engine support fixture. Such tools can be rented, but the job is still difficult to do without a hydraulic lift. Safely raising the vehicle enough for the transaxle and subframe to be pulled out from underneath is a problem without a hoist.*

Removal

1   Disconnect the negative cable from the battery. **Caution:** *On models equipped with a Theftlock audio system, be sure the lockout feature is turned off before performing any procedure which requires disconnecting the battery.*
2   Raise the vehicle and support it securely on jackstands.
3   Drain the transaxle fluid (Chapter 1).
4   Remove the torque converter cover.
5   Mark the torque converter-to-driveplate relationship so they can be installed in the same position **(see illustration)**.
6   Remove the torque converter-to-drive-plate bolts. Turn the crankshaft pulley bolt for access to each bolt.
7   Remove the air cleaner duct and the starter motor (see Chapter 5).
8   Remove the driveaxles (see Chapter 8).
9   Disconnect the speed sensor (see Section 4).
10   Disconnect the electrical connectors from the transaxle.
11   On models so equipped, disconnect the vacuum hose(s).
12   Remove any exhaust components which will interfere with transaxle removal (see Chapter 4).
13   If equipped, disconnect the TV cable from the transaxle (see Section 6).
14   Disconnect the shift linkage from the

transaxle (see Section 7).
15   Support the engine using a three-bar support fixture to retain the engine in the body.
16   Support the transaxle with a jack - preferably a special jack made for this purpose. Safety chains will help steady the transaxle on the jack.
17   Remove the brace between the engine and transaxle (attached to the oil pan on the right side) and the bolts securing the transaxle to the flywheel end of the engine.
18   Lower the transaxle slightly and disconnect and plug the transaxle cooler lines **(see illustrations)**. Make sure all of the fluid has drained out into a suitable container.
19   Remove the dipstick tube. Refer to Chapter 8 and remove the driveaxles.
20   Refer to Chapter 10 and disconnect the tie rod ends, then unbolt the steering rack and hold it to the body with heavy wire, away from the chassis.
21   Refer to Chapter 2 and disconnect the engine mount nuts at the chassis, then support the front subframe assembly with a jack and remove the four bolts holding the subframe to the vehicle. **Warning:** *Never put any part of your body under the front*

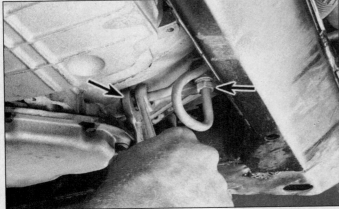

15.18a Use a flare nut wrench on the tube nut and an open end wrench on the fitting adapter when detaching the transaxle cooler lines (arrows) from the transaxle

15.18b Remove the bolt (arrow) retaining the transaxle cooler lines to the side of the transaxle

subframe while it is unbolted from the vehicle.

22   Move the transaxle back to disengage it from the engine block dowel pins and make sure the torque converter is detached from the driveplate. Secure the torque converter to the transaxle so it will not fall out during removal. Lower the front subframe and transaxle from the vehicle. Remove the transaxle mount from the subframe and separate the transaxle.

Installation

23   Prior to installation, make sure the torque converter is fully engaged in the transmission. To do this, rotate the converter while pushing it toward the transaxle. If it wasn't already fully in place, you'll feel it "clunk" into position as it engages with the input shaft and front pump. It may even "clunk" more than once. Lubricate the torque converter hub with multi-purpose grease.

24   With the transaxle and subframe secured to the jack, raise it evenly into position. Be sure to keep it level so the torque converter does not slide out. **Warning:** *Do not place any part of your body under the subframe until the four subframe bolts are back in place.*

25   Turn the torque converter to line up the bolt holes with the holes in the driveplate. The mark on the torque converter and the driveplate made in Step 5 must line up.

26   Move the transaxle forward carefully until the dowel pins and the torque converter are engaged.

27   Install the transaxle housing-to-engine bolts. Tighten them securely.

28   Install the torque converter-to-driveplate bolts. Tighten the bolts to the specified torque.

29   Install the suspension and chassis components which were removed. Tighten the bolts and nuts to the specified torque.

30   Remove the jacks supporting the transaxle and the engine.

31   Install the dipstick tube.

32   Install the starter motor (Chapter 5).

33   Connect the vacuum hose(s) (if equipped).

34   Connect the shift and TV linkage.

35   Plug in the transaxle electrical connectors.

36   Install the torque converter cover.

37   Install the driveaxles (Chapter 8).

38   Connect the speedometer/speed sensor cable.

39   Adjust the shift linkage (Section 7).

40   Install any exhaust system components that were removed or disconnected.

41   Lower the vehicle.

42   Fill the transaxle (Chapter 1), run the vehicle and check for fluid leaks.

Chapter 8   Driveaxles

Contents

Specifications

Torque specifications

	Ft-lbs
Driveaxle hub nut	159
Hub/bearing assembly-to-steering knuckle bolts	
1995	60
1996 through 1999	52
2000 and later	96
Wheel lug nuts	See Chapter 1

1   Driveaxles - general information and inspection

Power is transmitted from the transaxle to the front wheels by two driveaxles, which consist of splined solid axles with constant velocity (CV) joints at each end.

There are two types of CV joints used. The outer joint is a double-offset design using ball bearings with an inner and outer race is used to allow angular movement. The inner CV joint is a tripot design, with a spider bearing assembly and tripot housing to allow angular movement and permit the driveaxle to slide in and out.

The CV joints are protected by rubber boots, which are retained by clamps so the joints are protected from water and dirt. The boots should be inspected periodically (see Chapter 1). Damaged CV joint boots must be replaced immediately or the joints can be damaged. Boot replacement involves removing the driveaxles (Section 2). It's a good idea to disassemble, clean, inspect and repack the CV joint whenever replacing a CV joint boot to make sure the joint isn't contaminated with moisture or dirt, which would cause premature failure of the CV joint (see Section 3).

The most common symptom of worn or damaged CV joints, besides lubricant leaks, are a clicking noise in turns, a clunk when accelerating from a coasting condition or vibration at highway speeds.

Some specialized tools and procedures are required to disassemble and overhaul the CV joints in a driveaxle. Once removed from the vehicle, a spindle removal tool or hydraulic press is required to separate the hub and bearing assembly from the outer end of the driveaxle. Because rebuilt driveaxles are commonly available at auto parts stores, we recommend that the home mechanic not rebuild the axles, but instead bring them to a shop for hub/bearing removal and replacement with a fully-rebuilt, guaranteed unit.

Warning: *Since many of the procedures covered in this Chapter involve working under the vehicle, make sure it's securely supported on sturdy jackstands or on a hoist where the vehicle can easily be raised and lowered.*

2   Driveaxles - removal and installation

Lumina and 1999 and earlier Monte Carlo models

Removal

Refer to illustrations 2.1, 2.5a, 2.5b, 2.6, 2.7a and 2.7b

1   Remove the wheel cover and loosen the hub nut **(see illustration)**. **Note:** *This isn't necessary if you are only removing the driveaxle for access to other components.*

Loosen the wheel lug nuts, raise the front of the vehicle and support it securely on jackstands. Apply the parking brake and block the rear wheels to keep the vehicle from rolling off the jackstands. Remove the front wheel.

2   Remove the driveaxle hub nut (again, this is only necessary if you plan to separate the hub/bearing assembly from the driveaxle). To prevent the hub from turning, insert a screwdriver through the caliper and into a disc cooling vane, then remove the nut.

3   Remove the brake caliper, disc and caliper mounting bracket (see Chapter 9). **Note:** *Support the caliper out of the way with a piece of wire.*

2.1 Before raising the vehicle, remove the wheel center cap and use a breaker bar and socket to loosen the hub nut

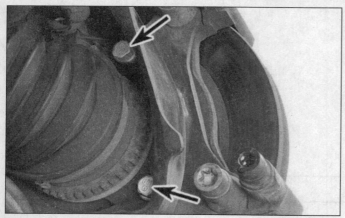

2.5a Remove the caliper bracket bolts and disc, then remove the two bolts (arrows) at the rear of the hub/ bearing assembly

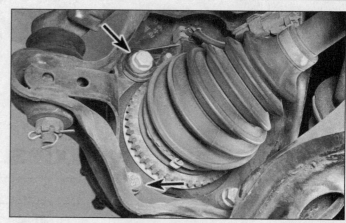

2.5b Remove the remaining two front bolts (arrows) from the hub/ bearing assembly

2.6 A large prybar (arrow) can be used to pry the inner joint of the driveaxle outward from the transaxle

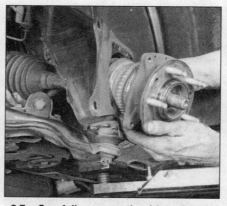

2.7a Carefully remove the driveaxle and hub/bearing assembly through the opening in the steering knuckle

2.7b Take care to avoid nicking the teeth of the ABS exciter ring (arrow) on the outer driveaxle ends

4   Refer to Chapter 9 and disconnect the electrical connector from the ABS wheel sensor, then remove the wheel sensor.

5   Remove the four bolts securing the hub/bearing assembly to the steering knuckle **(see illustrations)**.

6   Using a large screwdriver or prybar, carefully pry the driveaxle out of the transaxle **(see illustration). Caution:** *Do not tear the inner joint's boot with the prybar.*

7   Support the CV joints and carefully remove the driveaxle through the opening in the steering knuckle **(see illustrations). Caution:** *Do not tear the inner or outer boots on any sharp components as you withdraw the axle. Do not nick the ABS exciter ring on the outer joint of each driveaxle.*

Installation

Refer to illustration 2.9

8   Lubricate the differential seal with multi-purpose grease. Install the driveaxle through the opening in the steering knuckle. While supporting the CV joints, insert the splined end of the inner CV joint into the differential side gear.

9   Seat the shaft in the side gear by positioning the end of a screwdriver in the groove in the CV joint and tapping it into position with a hammer **(see illustration)**.

10   Grasp the inner CV joint housing (not the driveaxle) and pull out to make sure the axle has seated securely.

11   Install the hub/bearing assembly onto the steering knuckle. Tighten the mounting bolts to the torque listed in this Chapter's Specifications.

12   If removed, install a NEW driveaxle hub nut and tighten it securely.

13   Install the brake disc, caliper mount and caliper (see Chapter 9).

14   Install the wheel and lower the vehicle. Tighten the driveaxle hub nut to the torque listed in this Chapter's Specifications.

15   Install the wheel cover.

2000 and later Monte Carlo and Impala models

Removal

Refer to illustrations 2.17, 2.19 and 2.20

16   Remove the wheel cover and loosen the driveaxle hub nut. Loosen the wheel lug nuts, raise the front of the vehicle and support it securely on jackstands. Apply the parking brake and block the rear wheels to keep the vehicle from rolling off the jackstands. Remove the front wheel. Place a drain pan under the transaxle.

2.9 Use a large screwdriver (fitted into the ledge or groove on the inner joint) to seat the inner CV joint in the transaxle

2.17 A screwdriver inserted through the caliper and into a disc cooling vane will hold the hub stationary while unscrewing the hub nut

2.19 A two-jaw puller works well for pushing the axle out of the hub

2.20 Remove the right-side driveaxle from the transaxle using a slide hammer and adapter

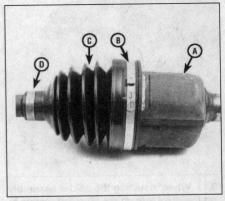

3.3 Inner tripot joint components

A	Tripot housing	C	Boot
B	Inner clamp	D	Outer clamp

17   Remove the driveaxle hub nut. To prevent the hub from turning, insert a screwdriver through the caliper and into a rotor cooling vane, then remove the nut **(see illustration)**.

18   Remove the control arm-to-steering knuckle balljoint stud nut and separate the lower arm from the steering knuckle (see Chapter 10 if necessary). On models equipped with anti-lock brakes (ABS), remove the ABS wheel speed sensor and place it to one side.

19   Separate the driveaxle from the hub. If it sticks, remove the brake caliper and disc (see Chapter 9), push the driveaxle out of the hub with a puller **(see illustration)**, then support the outer end of the driveaxle with a piece of wire to prevent damage to the inner CV joint.

20   If you're removing the right-side driveaxle, use a slide hammer and adapter to separate the driveaxle from the transaxle **(see illustration)**.

21   If you're removing the left-side driveaxle, carefully pry the driveaxle out of the transaxle with a large prybar positioned between the inner CV joint and the transaxle case. Use the subframe as the leverage point.

22   On all models, support the CV joints and carefully remove the driveaxle from the vehicle.

Installation

23   Lubricate the differential seal with multi-purpose grease, raise the driveaxle into position while supporting the CV joints and insert the splined end of the inner CV joint into the differential side gear. Seat the shaft in the side gear by positioning the end of a screwdriver in the groove in the CV joint and tapping it into position with a hammer **(see illustration 2.9)**.

24   Grasp the inner CV joint housing (not the driveaxle) and pull out to make sure the axle has seated securely.

25   Apply a light coat of multi-purpose grease to the outer CV joint splines, pull out on the strut/steering knuckle assembly and install the stub axle in the hub.

26   Insert the control arm balljoint stud into the steering knuckle and tighten the nut to the torque listed in the Chapter 10 Specifications. Be sure to use a new cotter pin (refer to Chapter 10). If equipped with ABS, install the ABS wheel speed sensor.

27   Install the brake disc and caliper, if they were removed (see Chapter 9).

28   Install a **new** driveaxle hub nut. Lock the disc so it can't turn, using a screwdriver or punch inserted through the caliper into a disc cooling vane, and tighten the hub nut securely (it will be tightened to the proper torque after the vehicle has been lowered).

29   Check the transaxle lubricant level and add some, if necessary, to bring it to the appropriate level (see Chapter 1).

30   Install the wheel and lower the vehicle, tightening the lug nuts to the torque listed in the Chapter 1 Specifications. Tighten the driveaxle hub nut to the torque listed in this Chapter's Specifications, then install the wheel cover.

3   Driveaxle boot - replacement

Note: *If the inner or outer joints exhibit wear indicating the need for an overhaul (usually due to torn boots), explore all options before beginning the job. Complete rebuilt driveaxles are available on an exchange basis, which eliminates a lot of time and work. Whatever is decided, check on the cost and availability of parts before disassembling the vehicle.*

1   Remove the driveaxle (see Section 2).

2   Place the driveaxle in a vise lined with rags to avoid damage to the shaft.

Inner tripot joint

Refer to illustrations 3.3, 3.4, 3.10 and 3.11

3   Cut off the boot retaining clamps and slide the boot towards the center of the driveaxle **(see illustration)**. Mark the tripot housing and driveaxle so they can be

3.4 Snap-ring pliers should be used to remove both the inner and outer retaining rings

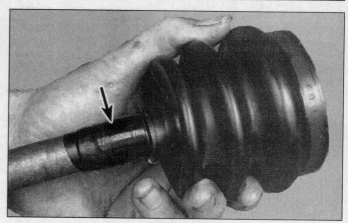

3.10 Before installing the boot, wrap the axle splines with electrical tape (arrow) to prevent damage to the boot

3.11 When installing the spider assembly on the driveaxle, make sure the recess in the counterbore (arrow) is facing the end of the driveaxle

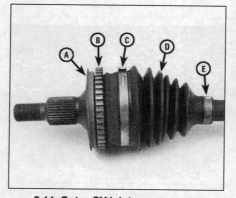

3.14 Outer CV joint components

A   *Outer deflector ring*
B   *ABS exciter ring*
C   *Outer boot clamp*
D   *Boot*
E   *Inner boot clamp*

3.15 Use snap-ring pliers to spread the inner retaining ring, then pull the CV joint off the axleshaft

reinstalled in the same relative positions, then slide the housing off the spider assembly.

4   Remove the spider assembly from the axle by first removing the inner retaining ring and sliding the spider assembly back to expose the outer retaining ring. Remove the outer retaining ring and slide the joint off the driveaxle **(see illustration)**.

5   Use tape or a cloth wrapped around the spider bearing assembly to retain the bearings during removal and installation.

6   Remove the spider assembly from the axle, followed by the inner retaining ring.

7   Slide the boot off the axle.

8   Clean all of the old grease out of the housing and spider assembly. Carefully disassemble each section of the spider assembly, one at a time, and clean the needle bearings with solvent. Inspect the rollers, spider cross, bearings and housing for scoring, pitting and other signs of abnormal wear. Apply a coat of CV joint grease to the inner bearing surfaces to hold the needle bearings in place when reassembling the spider assembly.

9   Pack the housing with half of the grease furnished with the new boot and place the remainder in the boot.

10   Wrap the driveaxle splines with tape to

avoid damaging the boot, then slide the new inner clamp and boot onto the axle **(see illustration)**. Remove the tape and install the inner retaining ring, sliding it past its groove.

11   Install the spider bearing with the recess in the counterbore facing the end of the

3.18 Gently tap the inner race with a brass punch to tilt it enough to allow ball bearing removal

driveaxle **(see illustration)**. Install the outer retaining ring, slide the spider to the end of the shaft, then seat the inner retaining ring in its groove.

12   Install the tripot housing.

13   Seat the boot in the housing and axle seal grooves, then position the joint mid-way through its (in/out) travel. Insert a small screwdriver between the boot and housing to

3.19 Using a dull screwdriver, carefully pry the balls out of the cage

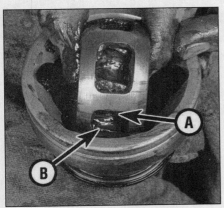

3.20 Tilt the inner race and cage 90-degrees, then align the windows in the cage (A) with the lands (B) and rotate the inner race up and out of the outer race

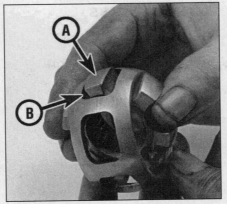

3.21 Align the inner race lands (A) with the cage windows (B) and rotate the inner race out of the cage

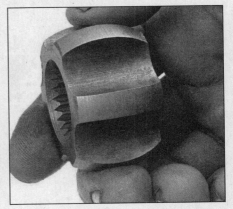

3.22a Check the inner race lands and grooves for pitting and score marks

3.22b Check the cage for cracks, pitting and score marks - shiny spots are normal and don't affect operation

equalize the pressure inside the boot, then install and tighten the retaining clamps. **Note:** *A special clamp crimping tool, available at most auto parts stores, is required to tighten the clamps.* Install the driveaxle as described in Section 2.

Outer CV joint

Refer to illustrations 3.14, 3.15, 3.18, 3.19, 3.20, 3.21, 3.22a, 3.22b, 3.25, and 3.26

14   Cut the two boot clamps with sharp side-cutter pliers and remove them, then slide the boot toward the center of the driveaxle **(see illustration)**.
15   Using snap-ring pliers, spread the retaining ring and slide the joint assembly off the axleshaft **(see illustration)**.
16   Slide the old boot off the driveaxle.
17   Place marks on the inner race and cage so they both can be installed facing out when reassembling the joint.
18   Press down on the inner race far enough to allow a ball bearing to be removed. If it's difficult to tilt, tap the inner race with a brass punch and hammer **(see illustration)**.
19   Pry the balls out of the cage, one at a time, with a blunt screwdriver or wooden tool **(see illustration)**.
20   With all of the balls removed from the cage and the cage/inner race assembly tilted 90-degrees, align the cage windows with the outer race lands and remove the assembly from the outer race **(see illustration)**.
21   Remove the inner race from the cage by turning the inner race 90-degrees in the cage, aligning the inner lands with the cage windows and rotating the inner race out of the cage **(see illustration)**.
22   Clean the components with solvent to remove all traces of grease. Inspect the cage and races for pitting, score marks, cracks and other signs of wear and damage. Shiny, polished spots are normal and won't adversely affect CV joint operation **(see illustrations)**.
23   Install the inner race in the cage by reversing the technique described in Step 21.
24   Install the inner race and cage assembly in the outer race by reversing the procedure

in Step 20. The marks that were previously applied to the inner race and cage must both be visible after the assembly is installed in the outer race.
25   Press the balls into the cage windows **(see illustration)**.
26   Pack the CV joint assembly with lubricant through the inner splined hole. Force the grease into the bearing by inserting a wooden dowel through the splined hole and pushing it to the bottom of the joint. Repeat this procedure until the bearing is completely packed **(see illustration)**.
27   Install the small clamp and the boot on the driveaxle as described in Step 10. Apply a liberal amount of grease to the inside of the axle boot. **Note:** *There are several grooves on the driveaxle at the point where the boot will be clamped. There are three large grooves. The lip on the boot should go in the large groove closest to the narrow groove.*
28   Position the CV joint assembly on the axleshaft, aligning the splines. Press the CV joint onto the axleshaft until the retaining ring is seated in the groove.
29   Seat the inner end of the boot in the seal

groove and install and tighten the retaining clamps. **Note:** *A special clamp crimping tool, available at most auto parts stores, is required to tighten the clamps.*
30   Install the driveaxle as described in Section 2.

3.25 Align the cage windows and the inner and outer race grooves, then tilt the cage and inner race to insert the balls

3.26 Apply grease through the splined hole, then insert a wooden dowel (approximately 15/16-inch diameter) through the hole and push down - the dowel will force the grease into the joint

Notes

Chapter 9   Brakes

Contents

Specifications

General
Brake fluid type .... See Chapter 1

Disc brakes
Brake pad lining minimum thickness .... See Chapter 1
Disc (front and rear)
  Minimum thickness .... Refer to the dimension stamped into the disc
  Runout (maximum) .... 0.002 inch
  Thickness variation limit .... 0.0005 inch

Drum brakes
Brake shoe lining minimum thickness .... See Chapter 1
Brake drum
  Maximum diameter .... Refer to the dimension stamped into the drum
  Runout (maximum) .... 0.006 inch

Torque Specifications Ft-lbs (unless otherwise indicated)
Bleeder valve
  Front .... 115 in-lbs
  Rear
    Caliper .... 97 in-lbs
    Wheel cylinder .... 62 in-lbs
Caliper mounting (slide) bolts (1995 through 1998)
  Front 80
  Rear 20
Caliper mounting bolts
  1999 through 2000
    Front 63
    Rear 32
  2001 and later
    Front 70
    Rear 32
Caliper mounting bracket bolts
  Front .... 133 to 148
  Rear 81
Brake hose-to-caliper bolt
  Front and rear (1995 through 1998) 32
  Front (1999 on) 40
  Rear
    1999 32
    2000 and later 40
Proportioner valve caps 20
Wheel cylinder mounting bolts 15
Wheel lug nuts .... See Chapter 1

2.2 The ABS modulator/motor pack (arrow) is mounted on the side of the master cylinder (earlier models)

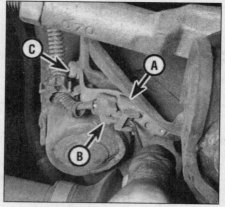

2.4a The front wheel ABS sensor (A) is mounted to the hub/bearing assembly - the electrical connector (B) snaps on and the sensor is retained by a bracket and bolt (C)

2.4b An ABS sensor (arrow) is also mounted at each rear wheel, behind the brake assembly

1   General information

General

The vehicles covered by this manual are equipped with hydraulically operated front and rear brake systems. All front brake systems are disc type, while the rear brakes are either disc or drum. All brakes are self adjusting. Front and rear disc brakes automatically compensate for pad wear. Rear drum brakes incorporate an adjusting mechanism which is activated any time the service brakes are applied.

Hydraulic system

The hydraulic system consists of two separate circuits. The master cylinder has separate reservoirs for the two circuits and in the event of a leak or failure in one hydraulic circuit, the other circuit will remain operative. A visual warning of circuit failure or air in the system is given by a warning light activated on the dash.

Proportioner valves

The proportioner valves are designed to provide better front to rear braking balance with heavy brake application. These valves allow more pressure to be applied to the front brakes (under certain braking operations) due to the fact the rear of the vehicle is lighter and does not require as much braking force.

Power brake booster

The power brake booster, utilizing engine manifold vacuum and atmospheric pressure to provide assistance to the hydraulically operated brakes, is mounted on the firewall in the engine compartment.

Parking brake

The parking brake operates the rear brakes only, through cable actuation. It's activated by a pedal mounted on the left side kick panel.

Service

After completing any operation involving disassembly of any part of the brake system, always test drive the vehicle to check for proper braking performance before resuming normal driving. When testing the brakes, perform the tests on a clean, dry flat surface. Conditions other than these can lead to inaccurate test results.

Test the brakes at various speeds with both light and heavy pedal pressure. The vehicle should stop evenly without pulling to one side or the other. Avoid locking the brakes because this slides the tires and diminishes braking efficiency and control of the vehicle.

Tires, vehicle load and front-end alignment are factors which also affect braking performance. **Caution:** *On models equipped with the "Theftlock" audio system, be sure the lockout feature is turned off before performing any procedure which requires disconnecting the battery.*

2   Anti-lock Brake System (ABS) - general information

Refer to illustrations 2.2, 2.4a and 2.4b

The Anti-lock Brake Systems (ABS) maintains vehicle maneuverability, directional stability, and optimum deceleration under severe braking conditions on most road surfaces. It does so by monitoring the rotational speed of the wheels and controlling the brake line pressure to the wheels during braking. This prevents the wheels from locking up on slippery roads or during hard braking.

Hydraulic modulator/motor pack assembly

The hydraulic modulator/motor pack assembly, also called the brake pressure modulator valve (BPMV), controls hydraulic pressure to the front calipers and rear wheel cylinders or calipers by modulating hydraulic pressure to prevent wheel lock-up **(see illustration)**.

The electronic brake control module (EBCM) monitors the ABS system and controls the anti-lock valve solenoids. It accepts and processes information received from the brake switch and wheel speed sensors to control the hydraulic line pressure and avoid wheel lock up. It also monitors the system and stores fault codes which indicate specific problems.

Each wheel sensor assembly consists of a variable reluctance sensor mounted adjacent to a "toothed ring" with an air gap between them **(see illustrations)**. A wheel speed sensor and toothed ring are mounted in the hub/bearing unit of each front wheel and each rear wheel. The air gap between the sensors and the rings is not adjustable, and the sensors themselves are not rebuildable. If a sensor malfunctions, the sensor must be replaced. If a ring malfunctions, it must be driven off the hub/bearing unit and a new one pressed on.

A wheel speed sensor measures wheel speed by monitoring the rotation of the toothed ring. As the teeth of the ring move through the magnetic field of the sensor, an AC voltage signal is generated. This signal frequency increases or decreases in proportion to the speed of the wheel. The EBCM monitors these three signals for changes in wheel speed; if it detects the sudden deceleration of a wheel, i.e. wheel lockup, the EBCM activates the ABS system. On earlier models with ABS, the hydraulic modulator/motor pack assembly is mounted on the side of the master cylinder, and the EBCM is located under the left side of the dash. On later models the EBCM mates to the BPMV, and both are mounted on a bracket attached to the left strut tower, separate from the master cylinder.

Warning lights

The ABS system has self-diagnostic capabilities. Each time the vehicle is started, the EBCM runs a self-test. There are three warning lights on the instrument panel, a red BRAKE light, an amber ABS light and a blue LOW TRAC light, each with their own functions. During starting, the red BRAKE warning light should come on briefly then go out. If the red BRAKE light stays on, it indicates a problem with the main braking system, such as low fluid level detected or the parking

3.5 Spray the caliper and disc with brake cleaner before beginning any repairs

3.6 Position a large C-clamp so that the solid end of the clamp is on the back of the caliper and the adjustable end is against the outer pad - tighten the clamp to push the pistons back

3.7 Mounting bolt locations for the front caliper (arrows)

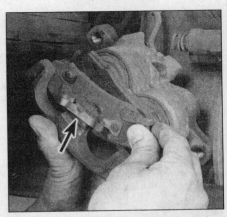

3.9 It may be necessary to pry the spring of the outer pad (arrow) away from the caliper while removing the outer pad

brake is still on. If the lights stays on after the parking brake is released, check the brake fluid level in the master cylinder reservoir (see Chapter 1).

The amber ABS light indicates a problem with the ABS system, not the main or basic brake system. If the light stays on steadily, it indicates that there is a problem with the ABS system, but the main system is still working. If you have a steady ABS light, drive to a dealer service department or other qualified repair shop for diagnosis and repair. However, if the ABS light *flashes*, there is a more serious fault in the ABS system which may have affected the regular braking system. Pull over immediately and have the vehicle towed to a dealer or other qualified repair shop for service.

Checks

Although a special electronic tester is necessary to properly diagnose the system, the home mechanic can perform a few preliminary checks before taking the vehicle to a dealer service department which is equipped with this tester:

a) *Make sure the brake calipers are in good condition.*
b) *Check the electrical connector at the controller.*
c) *Check the fuses.*
d) *Follow the wiring harness to the speed sensors and brake light switch and make sure all connections are secure and the wiring isn't damaged.*

If the above preliminary checks don't rectify the problem, the vehicle should be diagnosed by a dealer service department.

3   Disc brake pads - replacement

Warning: *Disc brake pads must be replaced on both front or rear wheels at the same time - never replace the pads on only one wheel. Also, the dust created by the brake system is harmful to your health. Never blow it out with compressed air and don't inhale any of it. An approved filtering mask should be worn when working on the brakes. Do not, under any cir-*

cumstances, use petroleum-based solvents to clean brake parts. Use brake cleaner or denatured alcohol only!

1995 through 1998 models
Front

Removal

Refer to illustrations 3.5, 3.6, 3.7, 3.9, 3.10a and 3.10b

1   Remove and discard two-thirds of the brake fluid from the master cylinder.
2   Loosen the wheel lug nuts.
3   Raise the vehicle and support it securely on jackstands.
4   Remove the wheel and reinstall two lug nuts to hold the disc in position.
5   Clean the caliper, disc and other components with brake system cleaner before beginning any brake work **(see illustration)**. This should remove traces of potentially hazardous brake dust. Collect the drippings in a plastic container.
6   Use a large C-clamp over the caliper to push the pistons back into the body of the caliper **(see illustration)**.
7   Remove the caliper mounting bolts **(see illustration)**.

8   Pull the caliper straight up and off, but do not allow it to hang by the brake hose.
9   Remove the outer pad from the caliper **(see illustration)**. If necessary, use a screwdriver to pry up on the retaining spring of the outer pad while sliding it out of the caliper.
10   Unclip the inner pad from the pistons and suspend the caliper by a wire to avoid damaging the brake hose **(see illustrations)**.

3.10a Pull the inner pad from the caliper and . . .

3.10b . . . then suspend the caliper by a wire

3.11 Apply some anti-squeal compound to the back of the pads

3.12a Snap the new inner pad into the caliper pistons . . .

3.12b . . . then install the new outer pad (caliper shown removed for clarity)

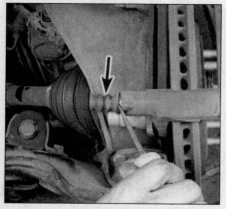

3.13 If the boots need replacing, pry them out

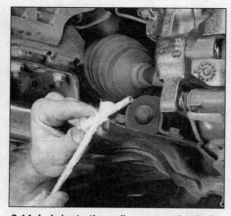

3.14 Lubricate the caliper mounting bolts before inserting and tightening them to Specifications

3.23 Use a pair of needle-nose pliers, with the tips engaged with the cutouts in the piston face, to turn the piston into the cylinder bore

Installation

Refer to illustrations 3.11, 3.12a, 3.12b, 3.13 and 3.14

11   Coat the back of the new brake pads with an anti-squeal compound **(see illustration)**.

12   Install the new inner and outer pads into the caliper **(see illustrations)**.

13   If the boots for the caliper mounting bolts need replacing, pry them out with a small screwdriver **(see illustration)**.

14   Install the caliper over the disc and align the bolt holes. The rubber boots should be between the caliper and the mounting bracket. Lubricate the entire length of the mounting bolts with a thin film of silicone grease **(see illustration)**. Be sure to tighten the caliper mounting bolts to the torque listed in this Chapter's Specifications.

15   Lower the vehicle. Fill the reservoir with the recommended fluid (see Chapter 1) and pump the brake pedal several times to bring the pads into contact with discs.

16   Road test the vehicle carefully before returning it to normal service.

Rear

Removal

17   Remove and discard two-thirds of the brake fluid from the reservoir.

18   Loosen the wheel lug nuts, raise the

vehicle and support it securely on jackstands. Remove the wheels.

19   Install two lug nuts to retain the disc when the caliper is removed.

20   Remove the bolt and washer attaching the cable support bracket to the caliper body, which allows enough cable slack to permit the caliper body to rotate enough for pad replacement. It isn't necessary to detach the cable or the brake hose.

21   Remove the lower caliper bolt, then pivot the caliper up.

22   Remove the pads and anti-rattle clips from the caliper mounting bracket.

Installation

Refer to illustrations 3.23, 3.25a, 3.25b, 3.25c and 3.25d

23   Using a two-pin spanner or a pair of needle-nose pliers, turn the piston to retract it into the caliper bore **(see illustration)**. Turn the piston as necessary so that a line drawn through the slots in the piston face would be exactly perpendicular to a line drawn through the caliper mounting bolt holes.

24   Using a small screwdriver, gently lift one edge of the piston boot to release any trapped air; the boot should lay flat.

25   Apply a coating of anti-squeal com-

pound to the backing plates of the new pads. Install the anti-rattle clips and the pads in the caliper **(see illustrations)**. **Note:** *The pad with the wear sensor is the outer pad.*

26   Pivot the caliper down over the disc and pads. Lubricate the caliper mounting bolt with high-temperature grease and install it, tightening it to the torque listed in this Chapter's Specifications.

27   The remainder of reassembly is the opposite of disassembly. **Warning:** *Before driving the vehicle, pump the brakes several times to seat the pads against the disc. Road test the vehicle carefully before returning it to normal service.*

1999 and later models (front or rear)

Refer to illustrations 3.32a through 3.32m

Warning: *Disc brake pads must be replaced on both front or both rear wheels at the same time - never replace the pads on only one wheel. Also, the dust created by the brake system is harmful to your health. Never blow it out with compressed air and don't inhale any of it. An approved filtering mask should be worn when working on the brakes. Do not,*

3.25a Install the upper anti-rattle clip . . .

3.25b . . . and the lower anti-rattle clip in the caliper mounting bracket - make sure they're both fully seated

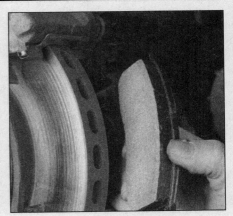

3.25c Install the inner pad . . .

3.25d . . . and the outer pad in to the caliper mounting bracket, then swing the caliper down into place. Install the caliper mounting bolt and tighten it to the torque listed in this Chapter's Specifications

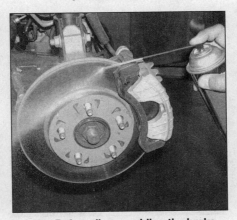

3.32a Before disassembling the brake, wash it thoroughly with brake system cleaner and allow it to dry - position a drain pan under the brake to catch the residue - DO NOT use compressed air to blow off brake dust!

3.32b To make room for the new pads, use a C-clamp to depress the piston into the caliper before removing the caliper and pads - do this a little at a time, keeping an eye on the fluid level in the master cylinder to make sure it doesn't overflow

under any circumstances, use petroleum-based solvents to clean brake parts. Use brake system cleaner only!

Note: *This procedure applies to the front* **and** *rear brake pads.*

28 Remove the cap from the brake fluid reservoir. If the fluid level is higher than the midpoint, remove and discard enough fluid to bring the level to approximately the midpoint. **Caution:** *Brake fluid will damage paint. If any fluid is spilled, wash it off immediately with plenty of clean, cold water.*

29 Loosen the front or rear wheel lug nuts, raise the front or rear of the vehicle and support it securely on jackstands. Block the wheels at the opposite end.

30 Remove the wheels. Work on one brake assembly at a time, using the assembled brake for reference, if necessary.

31 Inspect the brake disc carefully as outlined in Section 5. If machining is necessary, follow the information in that Section to remove the disc.

32 Follow the accompanying photo sequence for the actual pad replacement procedure (see illustrations 3.32a through

3.32m). Be sure to stay in order and read the caption under each illustration.

33 When reinstalling the caliper, be sure to tighten the mounting bolts to the torque listed in this Chapter's Specifications. **Caution:** *On*

2002 and later models, the two front caliper mounting bolts are not identical. The upper, or leading bolt has a bushing at the tip, whereas the bottom, or trailing bolt does not. Be sure to install each in the correct place.

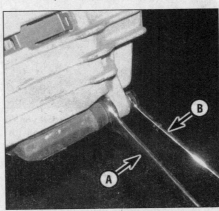

3.32c Hold the caliper slide pin with an open-end wrench (A) and loosen the lower mounting bolt with another wrench (B)

3.32d Pivot the caliper up and support it in this position for access to the brake pads

3.32e Remove the inner brake pad

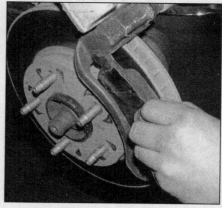

3.32f Remove the outer brake pad

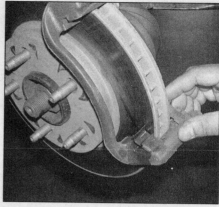

3.32g Remove the upper and lower pad retainers from the caliper mounting bracket

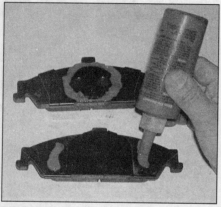

3.32h Apply anti-squeal compound to the back of both pads (let the compound "set up" a few minutes before installing them)

3.32i Install the upper and lower pad retainers

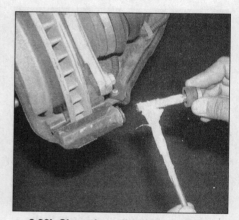

3.32j Clean the caliper slide pin and inspect it for scoring and corrosion; coat the pin with high-temperature grease

3.32k Install the inner brake pad; if you're replacing the front pads, it's the one with the wear indicator on it, which must be positioned at the top (on the rear brakes, the outer pad has the wear indicator)

Note: *The bolt boot must fit snugly into the groove at the top of each bolt. Replace any damaged boots. Tighten the wheel lug nuts to the torque listed in the Chapter 1 Specifications.*

3.32l Install the outer brake pad; if you're replacing the rear pads, it's the one with the wear indicator on it, which must be positioned at the bottom

34　After the job has been completed, firmly depress the brake pedal a few times to bring the pads into contact with the disc. Check the level of the brake fluid, adding some if necessary (see Chapter 1). Check the operation of the brakes carefully before placing the vehicle into normal service.

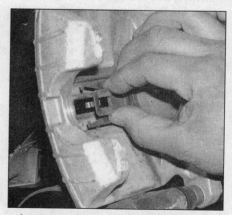

3.32m Check the condition of the anti-rattle spring in the center of the caliper, replacing it if necessary. Swing the caliper down over the pads and install the lower mounting bolt, tightening it to the torque listed in this Chapter's Specifications.
Note: *If the caliper won't fit over the pads, use a C-clamp to push the piston into the caliper a little further*

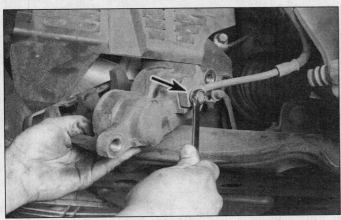

4.1 Remove the bolt (arrow) to separate the hydraulic line from the caliper

5.3 The brake pads on this vehicle were obviously neglected, as they wore down to the rivets and cut deep grooves into the disc - wear this severe will require replacement of the disc

4 Brake caliper - removal and installation

Warning: *Dust created by the brake system is harmful to your health. Never blow it out with compressed air and don't inhale any of it. An approved filtering mask should be worn when working on the brakes. Do not, under any circumstances, use petroleum-based solvents to clean brake parts. Use brake cleaner or denatured alcohol only!*

Note: *If caliper replacement is indicated (usually because of fluid leakage) explore all options before beginning the job. New and factory-rebuilt calipers are available on an exchange basis, which makes this job quite easy.*

Removal

Refer to illustration 4.1

1   The removal procedure is the same as in Section 3 with the exception of disconnecting the hydraulic line from the caliper **(see illustration)**. Instead of pivoting the caliper up, remove the upper bolt and the caliper. Install two lug nuts finger tight to retain the disc when the caliper is removed. On 1995 through 1998 rear calipers, the parking brake cable will have to be disconnected from the caliper.

Installation

2   The installation procedure is the same as in Section 3.
3   When attaching the hydraulic line to the caliper, use new copper washers at the line-to-caliper connection. Tighten the fitting bolt to the torque listed in this Chapter's Specifications. **Caution:** *On 2002 and later models, the two front caliper mounting bolts are not identical. The upper, or leading bolt has a bushing at the tip, whereas the bottom, or trailing bolt does not. Be sure to install each in the correct place.*
Note: *The bolt boot must fit snugly into the groove at the top of each bolt. Replace any damaged boots.*

5.4a Check for runout with a dial indicator - mount it with the indicator needle about 1/2-inch from the outer edge of the disc

4   Bleed the hydraulic system as described in Section 10.

5 Brake disc - inspection, removal and installation

Refer to illustrations 5.3, 5.4a, 5.4b, 5.5a, 5.5b and 5.6

Inspection

1   Loosen the wheel lug nuts, raise the vehicle and support it securely on jackstands. Apply the parking brake and block the wheels to keep the vehicle from rolling off the jackstands. Remove the wheel and install the lug nuts, flat side against the disc, to hold the disc in place. It may be necessary to install washers under the lug nuts to enable the nuts to apply pressure to the disc.
2   Remove the brake caliper as outlined in Section 3 (it's part of the pad replacement procedure). You don't have to disconnect the brake hose. After removing the caliper bolts, suspend the caliper out of the way with a piece of wire - DO NOT let it hang by the hose.
3   Visually inspect the disc surface for

5.4b If you don't have the discs machined, at the very least be sure to remove the glaze from the disc surface with sandpaper or emery cloth (use a swirling motion as shown here)

score marks and other damage. Light scratches and shallow grooves are normal and may not be detrimental to brake operation, but deep score marks - over 0.015-inch (0.38 mm) deep - require disc removal and refinishing by an automotive machine shop. Be sure to check both sides of the disc **(see illustration)**. If pulsating has been felt during application of the brakes, suspect excessive disc runout.
4   To check disc runout, mount a dial indicator with the stem resting at a point about 1/2-inch from the outer edge of the disc **(see illustration)**. Set the indicator to zero and turn the disc. The indicator reading should not exceed the specified allowable runout limit. If it does, the disc should be refinished by an automotive machine shop. **Note:** *The discs should be resurfaced, regardless of the dial indicator reading, to impart a smooth finish and ensure perfectly flat brake pad surfaces which will eliminate pedal pulsations. At the very least, if you don't have the discs resurfaced, remove the glaze with sandpaper or emery cloth using a swirling motion* **(see illustration)**.

5.5a The minimum wear (or discard) thickness is cast into the disc

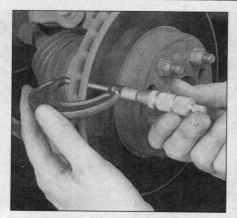

5.5b Measure the thickness of the disc at several points with a micrometer

5.6 Remove the two caliper mounting bracket bolts (arrows) - they are Torx-head bolts

5   Never machine the disc to a thickness less than the specified minimum allowable refinish thickness. The minimum wear (or discard) thickness is cast into the disc **(see illustration)**. This shouldn't be confused with the minimum refinish thickness. The disc thickness can be checked with a micrometer **(see illustration)**.

Removal

6   Remove the lug nuts that were put on to hold the disc in place. Remove the caliper mounting bracket and remove the disc from the hub **(see illustration)**. **Note:** *The mounting bracket bolts on some models require a Torx bit to remove.*

Installation

7   Install the caliper mounting bracket, using a non-hardening thread locking compound on the (cleaned) bolts and tighten them to the torque listed in this Chapter's Specifications. Place the disc in position over the threaded studs.
8   Install the caliper mounting bracket, brake pads and caliper (refer to Section 3, if necessary). Tighten the mounting bracket bolts and the caliper bolts to the torque values listed in this Chapter's Specifications.
9   Install the wheel, then lower the vehicle to the ground. Tighten the lug nuts to the torque listed in the Chapter 1 Specifications. Depress the brake pedal a few times to bring the brake pads into contact with the disc. Bleeding of the system won't be necessary unless the brake hose was disconnected from the caliper. Check the operation of the brakes carefully before driving the vehicle in traffic.

6   Drum brake shoes - replacement

Warning: *Drum brake shoes must be replaced on both rear wheels at the same time - never replace the shoes on only one wheel. Also, the dust created by the brake*

system is harmful to your health. Never blow it out with compressed air and don't inhale any of it. An approved filtering mask should be worn when working on the brakes. Do not, under any circumstances, use petroleum-based solvents to clean brake parts. Use brake cleaner or denatured alcohol only!

Removal

Refer to illustrations 6.3, 6.4, 6.5a, 6.5b, 6.5c, 6.5d and 6.5e

1   Loosen the wheel lug nuts, raise the rear of the vehicle and support it securely on jackstands. Block the front wheels to keep the vehicle from rolling off the jackstands.
2   Release the parking brake and remove the wheel. **Note:** *All four rear shoes must be replaced at the same time, but to avoid mixing up parts, work on only one brake assembly at a time.*
3   Remove the brake drum. If it's difficult to remove, back off the parking brake cable (see Section 12), remove the access hole plug from the backing plate, insert a screwdriver through the hole and turn the adjuster screw star wheel **(see illustration)**. This will allow

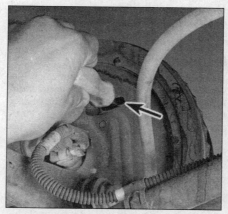

6.3 Insert a screwdriver through the hole (arrow) in the backing plate and turn the adjuster screw star wheel to retract the brake shoes

the brake shoes to retract. Use a rubber mallet to tap gently on the outer rim of the drum and/or around the inner drum diameter by the spindle. Avoid using excessive force.
4   Clean the brake assembly with brake system cleaner - DO NOT use compressed air to blow the dust out of the brake assembly **(see illustration)**.
5   Refer to the accompanying photo sequence and perform the brake shoe removal procedure **(see illustrations)**. Be sure to stay in order and to read the caption under each illustration.

Installation

Refer to illustrations 6.6a, 6.6b, 6.6c and 6.8

6   Installation of the shoes is the reverse of removal. Lubricate the components as shown **(see illustrations overleaf)**.
7   Set the preliminary shoe adjustment by turning the star wheel on the adjuster so that the drum just slips over the shoes.
8   Before reinstalling the drum, check it for cracks, score marks, deep scratches and hard spots, which will appear as blue discolored areas. If the hard spots can't be removed

6.4 Before doing any work on the rear brakes, wash down the whole assembly with brake cleaner

6.5a Drum brake components

1 *Actuator spring*
2 *Trailing shoe*
3 *Retractor spring*
4 *Leading shoe*
5 *Adjuster screw*
6 *Actuator lever*
7 *Wheel cylinder*
8 *Backing plate*

6.5b Use a pair of needle-nose pliers to remove the actuator spring

6.5c Wedge a flat-bladed screwdriver under the spring and pry it out of the leading brake shoe, then remove the shoe, adjuster screw and actuator lever

6.5d Lift the retractor spring from the trailing brake shoe and swing the shoe out from the hub area to gain access to the parking brake cable

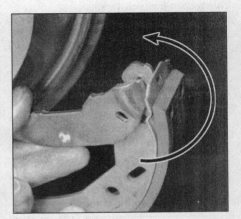

6.5e Rotate the brake shoe to release the parking brake lever from the shoe

with fine emery cloth or if any of the other conditions listed above exist, the drum must be taken to an automotive machine shop to have it turned. **Note:** *The drums should be resurfaced, regardless of the surface appearance,*

to impart a smooth finish and ensure a perfectly round drum (which will eliminate brake pedal pulsations related to out-of-round drums). At the very least, if you don't have the drums resurfaced, remove the glaze from the

surface with sandpaper or emery cloth using a swirling motion. If the drum won't "clean up" before the maximum service limit is reached in the machining operation, install a new one. The maximum wear diameter is cast into each

6.6a Lubricate the contact surfaces of the backing plate with high-temperature grease

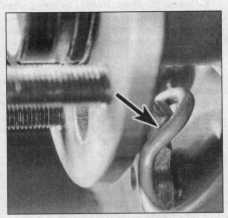

6.6b Use a screwdriver to pry the retractor spring over the alignment peg (arrow)

6.6c Lubricate the adjuster screw with high-temperature grease prior to installation

6.8 The maximum permissible diameter is cast into the drum

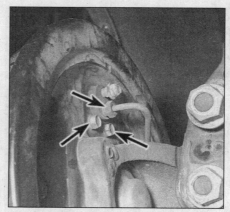

7.4 A flare-nut wrench should be used to unscrew the brake line fitting (upper arrow) - to remove the wheel cylinder, remove the two bolts (lower arrows)

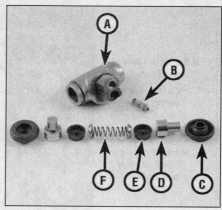

7.7 Wheel cylinder components - exploded view

A Wheel cylinder body	D Piston
	E Seal
B Bleeder screw	F Spring
C Boot	

brake drum **(see illustration)**.
9   Install the brake drum on the hub flange. Using a screwdriver inserted through the backing plate, adjust the shoes until they drag on the drum as the drum is turned, then back-off the star wheel until the shoes don't drag.
10   Mount the wheel, install the lug nuts, then lower the vehicle.
11   Apply and release the brake pedal 30 to 35 times using normal pedal force. Pause about one second between pedal applications. After adjustment, make sure that both wheels turn freely.

7   Wheel cylinder - removal, overhaul and installation

Refer to illustrations 7.4 and 7.7
Note: *If an overhaul is indicated (usually because of fluid leakage or sticking brakes) explore all options before beginning the job. New wheel cylinders are available, which makes this job quite easy. If you do rebuild the wheel cylinder, make sure rebuild kits are available before proceeding. If the vehicle has high mileage, new wheel cylinders are highly recommended.*
Warning: *Never rebuild or replace just one wheel cylinder. Replace or rebuild both rear wheel cylinders at the same time.*

Removal

1   Raise the rear of the vehicle and support it securely on jackstands. Block the front wheels to keep the vehicle from rolling off the jackstands.
2   Remove the brake shoe assembly (see Section 6).
3   Carefully clean the area around the wheel cylinder on both sides of the backing plate.
4   Unscrew the brake line fitting **(see illustration)**, but don't pull the line away from the wheel cylinder.
5   Remove the wheel cylinder retaining bolts.
6   Remove the wheel cylinder from the brake backing plate and place it on a clean workbench. Immediately plug the brake line

on the vehicle to prevent fluid loss and contamination.

Overhaul

7   Remove the bleeder valve, seals, pistons, boots and spring assembly from the wheel cylinder body **(see illustration)**. *Take note of exactly how the seals and pistons were installed, and which direction the seals face.*
8   Clean the wheel cylinder with brake fluid, denatured alcohol or brake system cleaner. **Warning:** *Do not, under any circumstances, use petroleum-based solvents to clean brake parts.*
9   Use compressed air to dry the wheel cylinder and blow out the passages.
10   Check the bore for corrosion and score marks. Crocus cloth may be used to remove light corrosion and stains, but the cylinder must be replaced with a new one if the defects can't be removed easily, or if the bore is scored.
11   Lubricate the new seals with brake fluid.
12   Install the spring in the cylinder first, making sure that the metal end caps are still attached at each end.
13   Install the seals. **Note:** *The flared sides of the seals must face the inside of the wheel cylinder, matching the flare on the metal cups at each end of the spring. The flat side of the seals must face the inner ends of the pistons.*
14   Lubricate the pistons with clean brake fluid, then install them with the larger diameter end toward the seals. Install the boots over the smaller diameter end of the pistons and seat the boots all around the groove at each end of wheel cylinder. Squeeze the two piston ends back and forth against the spring pressure to make sure neither piston is binding.

Installation

15   Place the wheel cylinder in position.
16   Connect the brake line, tightening the fitting by hand.
17   Install the wheel cylinder bolts and tighten them to the torque listed in this Chapter's Specifications.

18   Tighten the brake line fitting securely.
19   Install the brake shoes (see Section 6).
20   Bleed the brakes (see Section 10).

8   Master cylinder - removal, overhaul and installation

Warning 1: *On earlier models with ABS brakes, the master cylinder is combined with the ABS hydraulic unit/modulator and employs a set of spring-loaded, precision gears. The alignment and tensioning of these is a critical safety concern. While the master cylinder and ABS hydraulic unit may be unbolted from the vehicle (such as for replacement of the power brake booster), they must not be separated from each other. Only a technician with a factory scan tool can relieve the tension on these gears and safely separate the master cylinder from the ABS hydraulic unit/modulator assembly. The gear tensioning relief procedure must be performed with the master cylinder assembly installed in the vehicle, not removed from the vehicle. On later models, the EBCM mates to the BPMV, and both are mounted on a bracket attached to the left strut tower. The assembly can be disconnected from the master cylinder, and the EBCM can be removed from the BPMV, but the BPMV unit itself must not be disassembled.*
Warning 2: *On later models, removing only the master cylinder requires only a normal brake bleeding upon reconnection. However, removing the BPMV requires the automated ABS bleed procedure upon reconnection, which can be done only with the appropriate scan tool and is not described in this manual.*

Removal

Refer to illustrations 8.2 and 8.6
1   Detach the cable from the negative battery terminal.

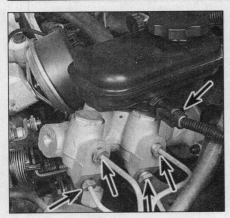

8.2 Unplug the fluid level sensor connector (upper arrow) and unscrew the brake line fittings (lower arrows) (non-ABS master cylinder)

8.6 Remove the master cylinder mounting nuts (arrows)

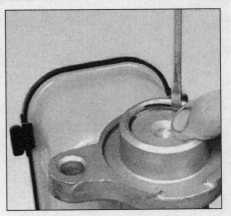

8.11 Press down on the piston and remove the primary piston lock ring

2   Unplug the electrical connector from the fluid level sensor switch **(see illustration)**. On earlier models with ABS, also disconnect the two solenoid valve electrical connectors and the ABS motor pack six-terminal electrical connector.

3   Place rags under the line fittings and prepare caps or plastic bags to cover the ends of the lines once they're disconnected. **Caution:** *Brake fluid will damage paint. Cover all painted parts and be careful not to spill fluid during this procedure.*

4   Loosen the fittings at the ends of the brake lines where they enter the master cylinder. To prevent rounding off the flats on the fittings, use a flare-nut wrench, which wraps around the hex.

5   Pull the brake lines away from the master cylinder or hydraulic unit and plug the ends to prevent contamination.

6   Remove the two mounting nuts **(see illustration)** and detach the master cylinder (or master cylinder/hydraulic unit assembly) from the vehicle.

7   Remove the reservoir cover and reservoir diaphragm, then discard any remaining fluid.

Overhaul (non-ABS models only)

Refer to illustrations 8.11, 8.12, 8.16, 8.18, 8.19a, 8.19b, 8.19c, 8.19d, 8.19e, 8.19f, 8.20 and 8.32

8   Mount the master cylinder in a vise. Clamp the master cylinder only at the flange; do not clamp the body. Remove the fluid level sensor (if equipped) by using needle-nose pliers to depress the retaining tabs and push the sensor through the reservoir.

9   The fluid reservoir is attached to the master cylinder body with two roll pins. Drive them out with a 1/8-inch punch. Pull straight up on the reservoir assembly and separate it from the master cylinder body. Remove and discard the two O-rings.

10   Remove the proportioner valve caps, which are on top of the large bosses on the left side of the master cylinder (just above where the fluid lines attached). Using needle-nose pliers, carefully remove the O-rings, the springs, the proportioner valve pistons and seals. Make sure you don't scratch or otherwise damage the piston stems or the bores. Set each proportioner valve assembly aside.

11   Remove the primary piston lock ring by depressing the piston and prying the ring out with a screwdriver **(see illustration)**.

12   Remove the primary piston assembly from the bore **(see illustration)**.

13   Remove the secondary piston assembly from the bore. It may be necessary to remove the master cylinder from the vise and invert it, carefully tapping it against a block of wood to expel the piston.

14   Clean the master cylinder body, the primary and secondary piston assemblies, the proportioner valve assemblies and the reservoir in brake cleaner or denatured alcohol and dry them off with filtered, unlubricated compressed air or a clean (lint-free) shop rag. **Warning:** *DO NOT, under any circumstances, use petroleum-based solvents to clean brake parts.*

15   Inspect the master cylinder piston bore for corrosion and score marks. If any corrosion or damage in the bore is evident, replace the master cylinder body - don't use abrasives to try to clean it up.

16   Remove the old seals from the secondary piston assembly and install the new seals with the cup lips facing out **(see illustration)**.

17   Attach the spring retainer to the secondary piston assembly.

18   Lubricate the cylinder bore with clean brake fluid and install the spring and secondary piston assembly **(see illustration)**.

8.12 Remove the primary piston assembly

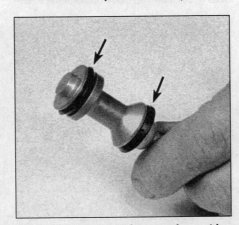

8.16 The secondary piston seals must be installed with the lips facing out as shown

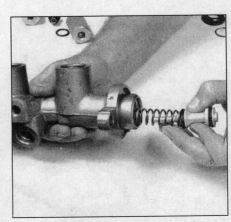

8.18 Install the secondary piston assembly

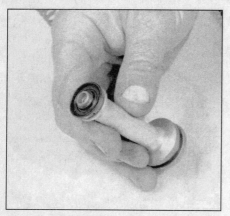

8.19a The primary piston seal must be installed with the lip facing away from the piston

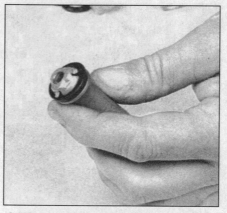

8.19b Install the seal guard over the seal

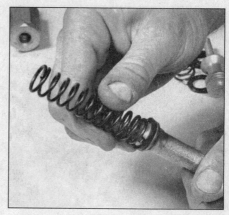

8.19c Place the primary piston spring in position

19   Disassemble the primary piston assembly, noting the locations of the parts, then lubricate the new seals with clean brake fluid and install them on the piston **(see illustrations)**.
20   Install the primary piston assembly in the cylinder bore **(see illustration)**, depress it and install the lock ring.
21   Inspect the proportioner valves for corrosion and score marks. Replace them if necessary.
22   Lubricate the new O-rings and proportioner valve seals with the silicone grease supplied with the rebuild kit. Also lubricate the stem of the proportioner valve pistons.
23   Install the new seals on the proportioner valve pistons with the seal lips facing toward the cap assembly.
24   Install the proportioner valve pistons and seals in the master cylinder body.
25   Install the springs in the master cylinder body.
26   Install the new O-rings in their respective grooves in the proportioner valve cap assemblies.
27   Install the proportioner valve caps in the master cylinder and tighten them to the torque listed in this Chapter's Specifications.
28   Inspect the reservoir for cracks and dis-

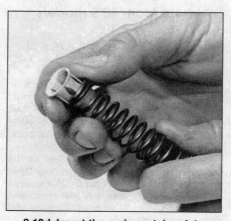

8.19d Insert the spring retainer into the spring

tortion. If any damage is evident, replace it.
29   Lubricate the new reservoir O-rings with clean brake fluid and press them into their respective grooves in the master cylinder body. Make sure they're properly seated.
30   Lubricate the reservoir fittings with clean brake fluid and install the reservoir on the master cylinder body by pressing it straight down.
31   Drive in new reservoir retaining (roll) pins. Make sure you don't damage the reser-

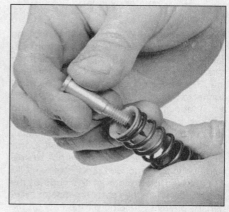

8.19e Insert the spring retaining bolt through the retainer and spring and thread it into the piston

voir or master cylinder body.
32   Inspect the reservoir diaphragm and cover for cracks and deformation. Replace any damaged parts with new ones and attach the diaphragm to the cover **(see illustration)**.
Note: *Whenever the master cylinder is removed, the complete hydraulic system must be bled (see Section 10). The time required to bleed the system can be reduced*

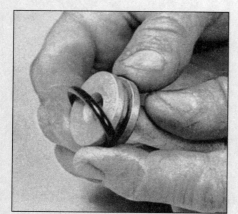

8.19f Lubricate the O-ring with clean brake fluid, then install it on the piston

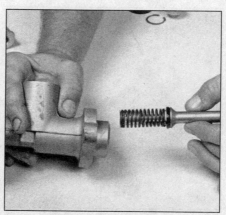

8.20 Insert the primary piston assembly into the bore

8.32 Install the reservoir diaphragm in the cover

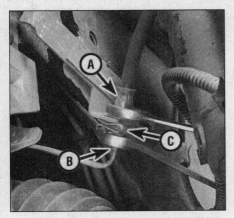

9.2 Using a back-up wrench on the flexible hose side of the fitting (A), loosen the tube nut (B) with a flare-nut wrench and remove the U-clip (C) from the hose fitting

if the master cylinder is filled with fluid and bench bled (refer to Steps 33 through 36) before it's installed on the vehicle.

33   Insert threaded plugs of the correct size into the brake line outlet holes and fill the reservoirs with brake fluid. The master cylinder should be supported so brake fluid won't spill during the bench bleeding procedure.

34   Loosen one plug at a time and push the piston assembly into the bore to force air from the master cylinder. To prevent air from being drawn back in, the appropriate plug must be replaced before allowing the piston to return to its original position.

35   Stroke the piston three or four times for each outlet to ensure that all air has been expelled.

36   Since high pressure isn't involved in the bench bleeding procedure, there is an alternative to the removal and replacement of the plugs with each stroke of the piston assembly. Before pushing in on the piston assembly, remove one of the plugs completely. Before releasing the piston, however, instead of replacing the plug, simply put your finger tightly over the hole to keep air from being drawn back into the master cylinder. Wait several seconds for the brake fluid to be drawn from the reservoir into the piston bore, then repeat the procedure. When you push down on the piston it'll force your finger off the hole, allowing the air inside to be expelled. When only brake fluid is being ejected from the hole, replace the plug and go on to the other port.

37   Refill the master cylinder reservoirs and install the diaphragm and cover assembly. **Note:** *The reservoirs should only be filled to the top of the reservoir divider to prevent overflowing when the cover is installed.*

Installation

38   Carefully install the master cylinder by reversing the removal steps, fill the reservoir with the recommended fluid (see Chapter 1), then bleed the brakes at each wheel (see Section 10).

9   Brake hoses and lines - inspection and replacement

Refer to illustration 9.2

Warning: *On ABS-equipped vehicles, do not replace any rubber brake hoses except with parts specifically designated for ABS models.*

1   About every six months, raise the vehicle and support it securely on jackstands, then check the flexible hoses that connect the steel brake lines to the front and rear brake assemblies. Look for cracks, chafing of the outer cover, leaks, blisters and other damage. The hoses are important and vulnerable parts of the brake system and the inspection should be thorough. A light and mirror will be helpful to see into restricted areas. If a hose exhibits any of the above conditions, replace it with a new one.

Front brake hose

2   Using a back-up wrench, disconnect the brake line from the hose fitting, being careful not to bend the frame bracket or twist the brake line **(see illustration)**.

3   Use pliers to remove the U-clip from the female fitting at the bracket, then remove the hose from the bracket.

4   At the caliper end of the hose, remove the bolt from the fitting block, then remove the hose and the copper washers on either side of the fitting block.

5   When installing the hose, always use new copper washers on either side of the fitting block and lubricate all bolt threads with clean brake fluid.

6   With the fitting flange engaged with the caliper locating ledge, attach the hose to the caliper.

7   Without twisting the hose, install the female fitting in the hose bracket. It'll fit the bracket in only one position.

8   Install the U-clip retaining the female fitting to the frame bracket.

9   Using a back-up wrench, attach the brake line to the hose fitting.

10   When the brake hose installation is complete, there shouldn't be any kinks in the hose. Make sure the hose doesn't contact any part of the suspension. Check it by turning the wheels to the extreme left and right positions. If the hose makes contact, remove the hose and correct the installation as necessary. Fill the master cylinder reservoir and bleed the system (refer to Section 10).

Rear brake hose

11   Using a back-up wrench, disconnect the hose at both ends, being careful not to bend the bracket or steel lines.

12   Remove the U-clip with pliers and separate the female fittings from the brackets.

13   Unbolt the hose retaining clip and remove the hose.

14   Without twisting the hose, install the female ends in the frame bracket. It'll fit the bracket in only one position.

15   Install the U-clip retaining the female

end to the bracket.

16   Using a back-up wrench, attach the steel line fittings to the female fittings. Again, be careful not to bend the bracket or steel line.

17   Make sure the hose installation didn't loosen the frame bracket. Tighten the bracket if necessary.

18   Fill the master cylinder reservoir and bleed the system (refer to Section 10).

Metal brake lines

19   When replacing brake lines, be sure to buy the correct replacement parts. Don't use copper or any other tubing for brake lines.

20   Prefabricated brake lines, with the ends already flared and fittings installed, are available at auto parts stores and dealer service departments. If necessary, carefully bend the line to the proper shape. A tubing bender must be used for this. **Caution:** *Don't crimp or damage the line.*

21   When installing the new line, make sure it's securely supported in the brackets with plenty of clearance between moving or hot components.

22   After installation, check the master cylinder fluid level and add fluid as necessary. Bleed the brake system as outlined in the next Section and test the brakes carefully before driving the vehicle in traffic.

10   Brake hydraulic system - bleeding

Refer to illustrations 10.5 and 10.13

Note: *Bleeding the brakes is necessary to remove air that manages to find its way into the system when it's been opened during removal and installation of a hose, line, caliper or master cylinder.*

Warning: *Wear eye protection when bleeding the brake system. If you get fluid in your eyes, rinse them immediately with water and seek medical attention.*

ABS-equipped models only

1   Do not touch the brake pedal at any time during this preliminary procedure, which must be performed before any bleeding operation.

2   Start the vehicle and watch the amber ABS warning light for at least ten seconds. If the warning light stays ON this long, your vehicle exhibits an ABS problem that can only be solved at a dealership or other qualified repair shop equipped with the proper scan tool.

3   If the warning light performed normally, i.e. it turned OFF after about three seconds, then turn the vehicle OFF. Repeat the procedure and if the ABS warning light turns OFF again after about three seconds, turn the vehicle OFF and you can bleed the brake system as described below for non-ABS vehicles.

4   After the bleeding process is completed, if the pedal feels soft, perform the above warning light test five times, **without** touch-

ing the brake pedal, then repeat the bleeding procedure.

5   **Warning:** *If an earlier ABS-equipped model has been allowed to run dry at the master cylinder, the hydraulic modulator assembly must be bled before bleeding the calipers/wheel cylinders.* Attach the bleeder hose to the rearmost bleeder valve on the modulator assembly **(see illustration)**. With the other end of the hose in a jar partially filled with clean brake fluid, crack the valve slowly and have an assistant depress the brake pedal. Keep the pedal down until fluid flows. Close the valve and release the brake pedal. Repeat this until no air is evident as the fluid enters the jar, then repeat the procedure for the forward bleeder valve. After bleeding the hydraulic modulator assembly, bleed the rest of the braking systems as described below. **Warning:** *On later ABS-equipped models with a BPMV/ECBM unit separate from the master cylinder, the automated ABS bleed procedure must be performed upon reconnection. This can be done only with the appropriate scan tool and is not described in this manual.*

All models

Note: *This procedure applies only to ABS models which have passed the test described in Steps 1 through 3.*

6   It'll probably be necessary to bleed the system at all four brakes if air has entered the system due to low fluid level, or if the brake lines have been disconnected at the master cylinder.

7   If a brake line was disconnected at only one wheel, then only that caliper or wheel cylinder must be bled.

8   If a brake line is disconnected at a fitting located between the master cylinder and any of the brakes, that part of the system served by the disconnected line must be bled.

9   Remove any residual vacuum from the power brake booster by applying the brake several times with the engine off.

10   Remove the master cylinder reservoir cover and fill the reservoir with brake fluid. Reinstall the cover. **Note:** *Check the fluid level often during the bleeding procedure and add fluid as necessary to prevent the level from falling low enough to allow air bubbles into the master cylinder.*

11   Have an assistant on hand, as well as a supply of new (DOT 3) brake fluid, an empty, clear plastic container, a length of inch plastic, rubber or vinyl tubing to fit over the bleeder valve and a wrench to open and close the bleeder valve.

12   Beginning at the right rear wheel, loosen the bleeder valve slightly, then tighten it to a point where it's snug but can still be loosened quickly and easily.

13   Place one end of the tubing over the bleeder valve and submerge the other end in brake fluid in the container **(see illustration)**.

14   Have your assistant depress the pedal to the floor, then hold the pedal down firmly.

15   While the pedal is held down, open the bleeder valve just enough to allow fluid to

10.5 ABS hydraulic modulator assembly bleeder valves - earlier models

A Rear bleeder   B Front bleeder

flow out of the valve. Watch for air bubbles to exit the submerged end of the tube. When the fluid slows after a couple of seconds, close the valve and have your assistant release the pedal.

16   Repeat Steps 14 and 15 until no more air is seen leaving the tube, then tighten the bleeder valve and proceed to the left front wheel, the left rear wheel and the right front wheel, in that order, and perform the same procedure. Be sure to check the fluid in the master cylinder reservoir frequently.

17   Never use old brake fluid. It contains moisture which will can boil, rendering the brakes useless.

18   Fill the master cylinder with fluid at the end of the operation.

19   Check the operation of the brakes. The pedal should feel firm when depressed. If necessary, repeat the procedure. On ABS-equipped models, see Step 4.

20   Do not operate the vehicle if you have any doubts as to the effectiveness of the brake system. Seek professional advice if you can't obtain a firm pedal.

---

11 Power brake booster - check, removal and installation

Refer to illustration 11.21

1   The power brake booster unit requires no special maintenance apart from periodic inspection of the vacuum hose and the case.

Operating check

2   Depress the brake pedal several times with the engine off and make sure there is no change in the pedal reserve distance (the minimum distance to the floor).

3   Depress the pedal and start the engine. If the pedal goes down slightly, operation is normal.

Airtightness check

4   Start the engine and turn it off after one or two minutes. Depress the pedal several times

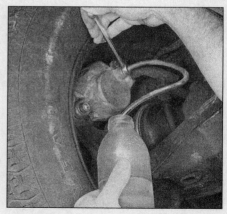

10.13 When bleeding the brakes, a hose is connected to the bleeder valve at the caliper and then submerged in brake fluid - air will be seen as bubbles in the container and in the tube (all air must be expelled before continuing to the next wheel)

slowly. If the pedal goes down farther the first time but gradually rises after the second or third depression, the booster is airtight.

5   Depress the brake pedal while the engine is running, then stop the engine with the brake pedal depressed. If there is no change in the pedal reserve travel after holding the pedal for 30 seconds, the booster is airtight.

Removal

6   Dismantling of the power unit requires special tools and is not ordinarily done by the home mechanic. If a problem develops, install a new or factory rebuilt unit.

7   If necessary, remove the left side under-dash panel (see Chapter 11). From the passenger compartment, disconnect the brake pushrod and stoplight switch electrical connector from the top of the brake pedal. **Caution:** *Keep the pedal from moving while doing this, to avoid damage to the brake switch.*

1995 through 1999 models

8   On 3.4L models, remove the upper intake manifold (see Chapter 2B). On 3.8L models, remove the fuel injection system trim cover.

2000 and later models

3.4L models

9   In the engine compartment, remove the cross-vehicle brace (see Chapter 11) and the air cleaner duct.

10   Relieve the fuel system pressure and disconnect the fuel feed and return lines (see Chapter 4).

11   Disconnect the EVAP purge valve pipe (see Chapter 6).

12   Disconnect the heater inlet and outlet hoses at the engine, and remove the heater inlet pipe.

13   Rotate the engine (see Chapter 1).

3.8L models

14   In the engine compartment, remove the cross-vehicle brace (see Chapter 11), air

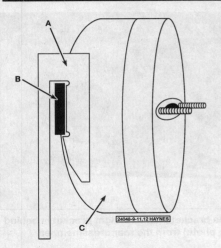

11.21 Booster "cam-lock" components

A   Firewall bracket with slot
B   Tab shown locked in bracket slot
C   Booster assembly

cleaner duct and fuel injection system trim cover.

15   Disconnect the throttle and cruise control cables from the throttle body along with the bracket and set the bracket aside.

16   Rotate the engine (see Chapter 1).

17   Remove the EGR valve heat shield and the EGR valve (see Chapter 6).

18   Remove the bracket that holds the transaxle fluid dipstick tube and set the tube aside.

All years

19   Disconnect the electrical connector from the brake fluid level sensor (if equipped). Remove the nuts attaching the master cylinder to the booster and carefully pull the master cylinder forward until it clears the mounting studs. Be careful to avoid bending or kinking the brake lines. **Warning:** *On ABS-equipped models, do not disconnect the master cylinder from the hydraulic modulator assembly* (see Section 8).

20   Disconnect the vacuum hose and check valve, if equipped, where it attaches to the power brake booster.

21   The booster is mounted to the firewall with a "cam-lock" bracket. On the right side of the bracket, use a screwdriver to pry the booster's locking tab out of the notch on the bracket **(see illustration)**. Insert the screwdriver between the tab and the notch.

22   If you do not have access to the factory tool that holds the front of the booster for removal/installation, there are two other ways to do the job. If you have a large strap wrench, wrap it around the body of the booster. You can also install two short lengths of rubber fuel hose over the master-cylinder mounting studs at the front of the booster, and use a prybar between the two studs to turn the booster as described in the next Step.

23   While holding the tab out of the notch (toward the firewall), rotate the booster coun-

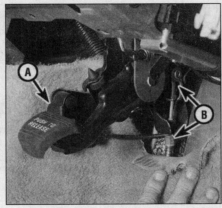

12.5 Parking brake pedal (A) and front end of parking brake cable (B)

terclockwise until it comes free of the bracket. **Caution:** *Be careful not to tear the boot (interior side of the firewall) around the booster pushrod as you remove the booster.*

Installation

24   Installation is the reverse of removal. Make sure the locking tab is completely seated in the firewall bracket slot.

25   Carefully test the operation of the brakes before driving the vehicle.

12 Parking brake - adjustment

Rear disc brakes

Refer to illustrations 12.5 and 12.7

Note: *The parking brake mechanism has no release lever. You step on the parking brake pedal to apply the parking brake, then the next time you step on the pedal, the parking brake is released.*

1   Using heavy pedal pressure, depress the parking brake pedal six times.

2   Make sure the parking brake is fully released.

3   Raise the rear of the vehicle and support it securely on jackstands.

4   Turn the ignition key to the On position.

5   If the brake warning light is on, pull down on the front parking brake cable to remove the slack from the pedal assembly **(see illustration)**.

6   At the rear caliper housings, the two parking brake levers should be against the lever stops. If they are not, check for binding in the rear cables and/or loosen the cables at the adjuster until both the left and the right levers are against the stops.

7   Tighten the parking brake cable at the equalizer **(see illustration)** until either the left or right lever just begins to move off the stop. There should be 0.020 to 0.040-inch clearance between the lever and the stop.

8   While holding down on the main (hydraulic) brake pedal, operate the parking brake several times to check for a firm pedal. Lower the vehicle.

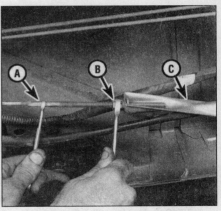

12.7 Hold the cable with a small wrench (A) while turning the adjuster nut (B) at the equalizer (C)

Rear drum brakes

9   Adjust the rear brake shoes (see Section 6).

10   Apply the parking brake 10 clicks, then release it. Repeat this five times.

11   Make sure the parking brake is fully released. Turn the ignition on. If the brake warning light is on, operate the manual brake release and pull down on the front parking brake cable to remove slack.

12   Raise the car and support it securely on jackstands.

13   Adjust the parking brake by turning the nut on the equalizer **(see illustration 12.7)** while spinning both rear wheels. When either wheel begins to drag, stop adjusting and back off the equalizer nut one full turn.

14   Apply the parking brake 4 clicks and check the rear wheel rotation. You should not be able to turn the wheel by hand in the direction of forward movement; the wheel should drag or not turn at all when spun in the direction of rearward rotation.

15   Release the parking brake and be sure the rear wheels spin freely, then lower the car.

13 Parking brake cables - replacement

Refer to illustrations 13.7 and 13.14

Front cable

1   Remove the left side underdash panel (see Chapter 11). If necessary, remove the left carpet retaining strip(s). On later Impala models, remove the lower center pillar trim panel (covering the seatbelt) by pulling it out to disengage the retainers, then sliding it down and out from under the upper trim panel.

2   Detach the front cable from the parking brake lever assembly **(see illustration 12.5)**.

3   Raise and support the vehicle.

4   Loosen the adjuster nut at the equalizer **(see illustration 12.7)**.

5   Remove the nut at the underbody bracket.

6   Detach the clip from the underbody.

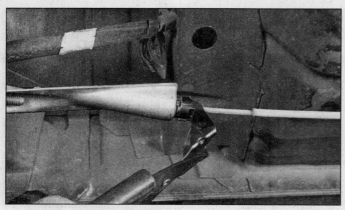

13.7 Special pliers like these can be used to release parking brake cables wherever cable retainers go through brackets (shown at equalizer) - regular pliers or a hose clamp can also be used to depress the fingers of the retainer

13.14 Detach the cable brackets (arrows, right bracket is behind exhaust pipe in photo) from the rear crossmember

7   Release the cable end from the equalizer **(see illustration)**. Special tools (available at auto parts stores) are available and make disconnecting cable retainers much easier, but an ordinary pair of pliers or a small hose clamp tightened around the fingers of the retaining clip can be used.

8   Installation is the reverse of removal.

Rear cable, left or right

9   Raise the vehicle and support it.

10   Disconnect the spring from the equalizer, if necessary.

11   Detach the equalizer from the cable.

12   On models with rear drum brakes, detach the cable from the backing plate and parking brake lever (see Section 6). On models with rear disc brakes, detach the rear cable from the front cable at the retainer.

13   On rear disc models, detach the cable and retainer from the caliper lever. Detach the cable from the caliper bracket.

14   Detach the clips holding the cable to the rear suspension crossmember **(see illustration)**.

15   Installation is the reverse of removal.

14.1 Disconnect the electrical connectors (A and B) from the brake light switch (C) - the wires at connector A are the ones to check for brake light operation

14   Brake light switch - check, replacement and adjustment

Check

Refer to illustration 14.1

1   The brake light switch **(see illustration)** is located on the brake pedal bracket, just to the right of the steering column mount. You'll need to remove the left underdash sound panel (the trim panel beneath the steering column) to get to the switch and connector (see Chapter 11).

2   With the brake pedal in the fully released position, the switch plunger is pressed into the switch housing. When the brake pedal is depressed, the plunger protrudes from the switch, which closes the circuit and sends current to the brake lights.

3   If the brake lights are inoperative, check the fuse (see Chapter 12).

4   If the fuse is okay, verify that voltage is available at the switch (orange wire, **see illustration 14.1)**.

5   If there's no voltage to the switch, use a test light to find the open circuit condition between the fuse panel and the switch. If there is voltage to the switch, close the switch (depress the brake pedal) and verify that there's voltage on the other side of the switch.

6   If there's no voltage on the other side of the switch with the brake pedal depressed, replace the switch (see Step 7). If voltage is available, check for voltage at the brake lights. If the no power is present, look for an open circuit condition between the switch and the brake lights. Also check the brake light bulbs, even though it isn't likely that both of them would fail at the same time.

Replacement

7   Remove the left under-dash sound insulator panel (see Chapter 11).

8   Unplug the electrical connector from the switch **(see illustration 14.1)**.

9   Remove the switch from the bracket.

10   The switch must be adjusted as it's installed (see below).

Adjustment

11   Depress the brake pedal, insert the switch into its bracket and push it in until it's fully seated.

12   Slowly pull the brake pedal to the rear until you no longer hear any "clicking" sounds. The switch should now be adjusted.

13   You can check your work with an ohmmeter or continuity tester by verifying that the switch contacts are open at one inch or less of brake pedal travel, and closed thereafter.

14   Installation is otherwise the reverse of removal.

15   Parking brake shoes - replacement

Note: *This procedure only applies to 1999 and later models with rear disc brakes.*

1   Loosen the rear wheel lug nuts, raise the rear of the vehicle and support it securely on jackstands. Remove the wheels.

2   Remove the brake caliper (see Section 4) and the brake disc (see Section 5).

3   Disconnect the parking brake cable from the bracket and the actuator lever.

4   Unbolt the parking brake cable bracket.

5   Remove the rear hub and bearing assembly (see Chapter 10).

6   Remove the parking brake actuator and the parking brake shoe.

7   When installing the new shoe and lining assembly, turn the adjuster screw until the shoe lining just drags on the braking surface inside the disc. Then remove the disc and back-off the adjuster screw until the shoe lining doesn't drag when the disc is installed and turned.

8   Installation is otherwise the reverse of the removal procedure. Be sure to tighten the hub and bearing assembly bolts to the torque listed in the Chapter 10 Specifications, the caliper mounting bolts and mounting bracket bolts to the torque listed in the Chapter 9 Specifications, and the wheel lug nuts to the torque listed in the Chapter 1 Specifications.

Chapter 10
Suspension and steering systems

Contents

Specifications

Torque specifications

Front suspension

Ft-lbs (unless otherwise stated)

Lumina and 1999 and earlier Monte Carlo models
Control arm pivot bolts	52
Subframe-to-body bolts	
Tighten in order: right rear, right front, left rear, left front	133
Lower balljoint nut	63
Stabilizer bar clamp nuts	35
Front hub and wheel bearing assembly bolts	See Chapter 8
Strut mount cover nuts	24
Strut damper shaft nut	59
Strut cartridge nut	82
Driveaxle hub nut	See Chapter 8

2000 and later Monte Carlo and Impala models
Lower control arm ballstud to steering knuckle nut	
2000 through 2003	15 (then tighten an additional 120 degrees)
2004 and later	22 (then tighten an additional 120 degrees)
Lower control arm-to-balljoint/ballstud nut	50
Lower control arm mounting nuts	
2000 through 2003	77 to 83
2004 and later	92
Stabilizer bar clamp bolt/nut	35
Stabilizer bar link nut	17
Front hub and wheel bearing assembly bolts	See Chapter 8
Strut-to-body mounting nuts	24
Strut damper shaft nut	
2000 through 2003	52
2004 and later	63
Strut-to-steering knuckle bolts/nuts	90
Driveaxle hub nut	See Chapter 8

Rear suspension
Rear hub and wheel bearing assembly bolts	52 to 55
Strut-to-body nuts	30 to 37
Strut-to-knuckle nut	90
Trailing arm-to-body nut/bolt	
1995 through 1998	44 (then tighten an additional 90-degrees)
1999 through 2003	70 to 77
2004 and later	37

Torque specifications

Rear suspension (continued)

Trailing arm-to-knuckle nut/bolt	
1995 through 1998	66 (then tighten an additional 75-degrees)
1999 and 2000	
With bolt size 16 x 2 x 90...	66 (then tighten an additional 75-degrees)
With bolt size 16 x 2 x 105...	52 (then tighten an additional 65-degrees)
2001 through 2003	52 (then tighten an additional 120-degrees)
2004	
Step 1...	52 (then tighten an additional 120-degrees)
Step 2...	148
2005 and later	177
Suspension crossmember-to-body bolt.................................	81 to 85
Stabilizer bar link bolt	52
Stabilizer bar link nut	
1995 through 2003	26
2004 and later	38
Stabilizer bar clamp bolt..	35 to 40
Lateral link rod	
To knuckle	
1995 through 1999..	177
2000 and later...	110
To crossmember	103 to 111

Steering system

Airbag module-to-steering wheel screws..............................	25 in-lbs
Steering gear mounting bolts	59
Tie-rod end nut	
1995 through 1999	40
2000 through 2004	22 (then tighten an additional 115 degrees)
2005 and later	34
Tie-rod jam nut	50
Intermediate shaft pinch-bolt	35
Power steering pump mounting bolts	25
Steering wheel hub nut...	30 to 33
Wheel lug nuts	See Chapter 1

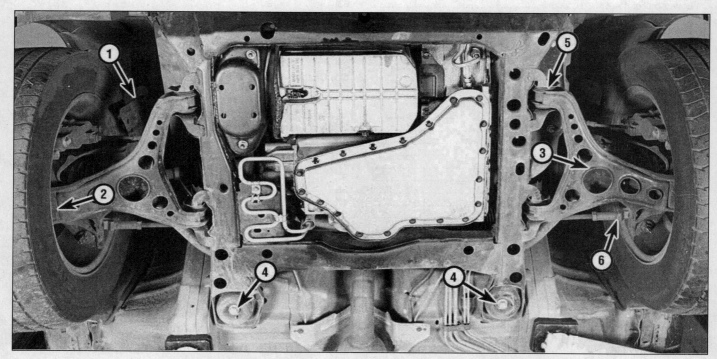

1.1a Front suspension components (Lumina and 1999 and earlier (Monte Carlo)

1	*Strut/knuckle assembly*	*3*	*Control arm*	*5*	*Control arm pivot bolt*
2	*Balljoint*	*4*	*Subframe bolts*	*6*	*Tie-rod end*

1 General information

Refer to illustrations 1.1a, 1.1b and 1.2

Warning: *Whenever any of the suspension or steering fasteners are loosened or removed, they must be inspected and, if necessary, replaced with new ones of the same part number or of original equipment quality and design. A prevailing torque type fastener can be re-used, provided that it is in good condition and offers at least 27 in-lbs of resistance when tightening (before it contacts the part it retains). Torque specifications must be followed for proper reassembly and component retention. Never attempt to heat or straighten any suspension or steering components. Instead, replace any bent or damaged part with a new one.*

The front suspension on Lumina and 1999 and earlier Monte Carlo models is a strut design that is made up of a strut welded to a knuckle and supported by a coil spring. The strut/knuckle bearing is located under the lower spring seat, with the upper spring seat attaching to the chassis. Because of the location of the bearing on the Lumina and 1999 and earlier Monte Carlo models, the strut cartridge can be removed from the engine compartment without disassembling the spring and strut/knuckle. On 2000 and later model Monte Carlo and Impala models, strut replacement requires disassembly of the spring and strut/knuckle assembly. The strut/knuckle assemblies are connected by balljoints to the lower control arms, which are mounted to the frame. The control arms are connected by a stabilizer bar, which reduces body lean during cornering **(see illustrations)**.

The rear suspension is independent, with a coil spring/strut assembly on each side bolted to knuckle assemblies that are located by trailing arms, parallel lateral links, and a stabilizer bar **(see illustration)**.

The rack-and-pinion steering gear is located behind the engine/transaxle assembly on the subframe and actuates the steering arms that connect to the steering knuckles. All vehicles are equipped with power steering. The steering column is connected to the steering gear through an insulated coupler. The steering column is designed to collapse in the event of an accident.

Note: *On models equipped with the Theftlock audio system, be sure the lockout feature is turned off before performing any procedure, which requires disconnecting the battery.*

2 Stabilizer bar and bushings (front) - removal and installation

Refer to illustrations 2.3a, 2.3b and 2.4

Removal

1 Loosen the lug nuts on both front wheels, raise the vehicle and support it securely on jackstands. Remove the front wheels.

2 Remove the steering shaft pinch bolt

1.1b Front suspension components (2000 and later Impala and Monte Carlo)

1	Strut/knuckle assembly	5	Control arm front pivot bolt
2	Balljoint	6	Control arm rear pivot bolt
3	Control arm	7	Tie-rod end
4	Subframe bolts		

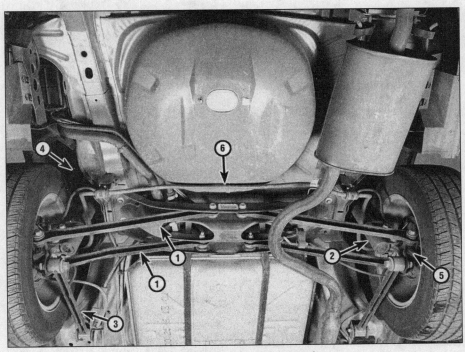

1.2 Rear suspension components

1	Lateral link rods	4	Coil spring
2	Strut	5	Knuckle
3	Trailing arm	6	Stabilizer bar

and separate the shaft from the steering gear (see Section 17). **Warning:** *The wheels should be straight ahead and the steering column locked. On airbag-equipped models,* *don't allow the steering wheel to turn after the steering shaft is disconnected from the steering gear. Pass the seat belt through the steering wheel and clip it into place.*

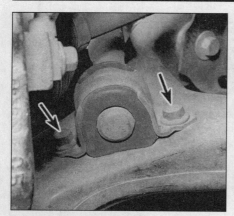

2.3a Remove the stabilizer bar bolts (arrows) on the control arm (1995 through 1999)

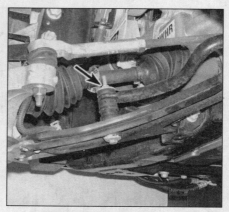

2.3b On 2000 and later models, use two wrenches to remove the link bolt/nut

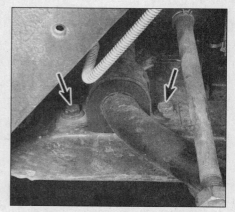

2.4 Remove the stabilizer bar bracket-to-frame bolts (arrows)

3.3a Check for movement between the balljoint and steering knuckle when prying up

3.3b With the prybar positioned between the steering knuckle boss and balljoint, pry down and check for play in the balljoint - if there is any play, replace the balljoint

3   Remove the stabilizer bar-to-control arm nuts/bolts. On 1995 through 1999 models, the stabilizer shaft bolts to the control arm with a bushing and clamp similar to those that attach it to the frame. On 2000 and later models, the bushing, or stabilizer link, is vertical, with a bolt through the center **(see illustrations)**. When disassembling the stabilizer link, be sure to note the order in which the bushings, spacers and washers are installed.

4   Remove the stabilizer bar bracket-to-frame nuts/bolts **(see illustration)**.

5   Place a jack under the rear of the subframe crossmember, then loosen the two front subframe-to-body bolts four turns. Remove the two rear subframe-to-body bolts **(see illustration 1.1)**. Slowly lower the jack and allow the rear of the subframe to drop down.

6   Pull the stabilizer bar to the rear, swing it down then remove it through the left side wheel well. **Warning:** *Do not place any part of your body under the subframe assembly when it is lowered from the vehicle, even though a jack supports it.*

7   Inspect the bushings for wear and damage and replace them if necessary. To remove them, pry the bushing clamp off with

a screwdriver and pull the bushings off the bar. To ease installation, spray the inside and outside of the bushings with a silicone-based lubricant. Do not use petroleum-based lubricants on any rubber suspension part!

Installation

8   Assemble the shaft bushings and clamps on the bar, guide the bar through the wheel well, over the frame and into position.

9   Install the clamps loosely to the frame and control arm and install all of the bolts before tightening any of them. Tighten the bolts to the torque listed in this Chapter's Specifications. **Caution:** *Do not tighten the stabilizer link nuts unless the vehicle is at normal ride height and is supported by the control arms. You can simulate ride height with a floor jack under each control arm, or wait until the wheels have been installed and the vehicle lowered, in Step 12.*

10   Raise the subframe into place while guiding the steering shaft into position in the steering gear and install the rear bolts. Tighten the subframe bolts to the torque figures listed in this Chapter's Specifications.

11   Install the pinch bolt and tighten it to the torque listed in this Chapter's Specifications.

Warning: *Make sure that the intermediate steering shaft is seated before installing the pinch bolt, otherwise the two shafts may not engage.*

12   Install the wheels and lower the vehicle. Tighten the lug nuts to the torque listed in the Chapter 1 Specifications.

3   Balljoint - check and replacement

Refer to illustrations 3.3a and 3.3b

Check

1   Raise the front of the vehicle and support it securely on jackstands. Apply the parking brake and block the rear wheels to keep the vehicle from rolling off the jackstands.

2   Inspect the rubber seal visually for damage, deterioration and leaking grease. If any of these conditions are noticed, the balljoint should be replaced.

3   Place a large prybar under the balljoint and attempt to push the balljoint up. Next, position the prybar between the steering knuckle and control arm and pry down **(see illustrations)**. If any movement is seen or felt during either of these checks, a worn out balljoint is indicated.

4   Have an assistant grasp the tire at the top and bottom and move the top of the tire in-and-out. If you see any play in the balljoint, replace it.

5   Separate the control arm from the steering knuckle (see Section 4). Using your fingers (don't use pliers), try to twist the stud in the socket. If the stud turns, replace the balljoint.

Replacement

6   Loosen the wheel lug nuts, raise the front of the vehicle and support it securely on jackstands. Apply the parking brake and block the rear wheels to keep the vehicle from rolling off the jackstands. Remove the wheel.

7   Separate the control arm from the steering knuckle (see Section 4).

8   Using a 1/8-inch drill bit, drill a pilot hole

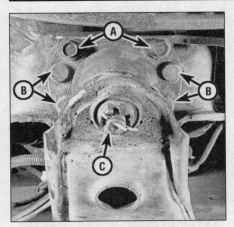

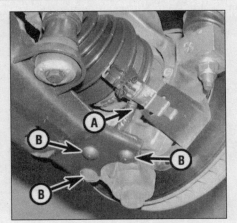

4.3a Balljoint components (Lumina and 1999 and earlier Monte Carlo)

A   Balljoint heat shield bolts (some models)
B   Balljoint rivets
C   Castellated balljoint nut and cotter pin

4.3b Balljoint components (Impala and 2000 and later Monte Carlo models)

A   Castellated balljoint nut and cotter pin
B   Balljoint rivets

4.4 Use a two-jaw puller clamped over the control arm with the center bolt of the puller pushing on the balljoint nut

into the center of each balljoint-to-steering knuckle rivet **(see illustrations 4.3a and 4.3b)**. Be careful not to damage the CV joint boot in the process.

9   Using a 1/2-inch drill bit, drill the head off each rivet. Work slowly and carefully to avoid deforming the holes in the steering knuckle.

10   Loosen (but don't remove) the stabilizer bar-to-control arm bolts. Pull the control arm down and remove the balljoint from between the control arm and steering knuckle. **Note:** *You may have to chisel between the steering knuckle and the balljoint to shear off the remains of the rivets.*

11   Position the new balljoint on the steering knuckle and install the bolts (supplied in the balljoint kit) with the heads on top and the nuts underneath. Tighten the bolts to the torque specified in the new balljoint instruction sheet.

12   Insert the balljoint into the control arm, install the castellated nut, tighten it to the torque listed in this Chapter's Specifications

and install a new cotter pin. It may be necessary to tighten the nut some to align the cotter pin hole with an opening in the nut, which is acceptable. Never loosen the castellated nut to allow cotter pin insertion.

13   Tighten the stabilizer bar-to-control arm bolts to the torque listed in this Chapter's Specifications.

14   Install the wheel, lower the vehicle and tighten the lug nuts to the torque listed in the Chapter 1 Specifications. It's a good idea to take the vehicle to a dealer service department or alignment shop to have the front wheel alignment checked and, if necessary, adjusted.

4   Control arm - removal and installation

Refer to illustrations 4.3a, 4.3b, 4.4, 4.5a and 4.5b

Removal

1   Loosen the wheel lug nuts, raise the front of the vehicle and support it securely on

jackstands. Apply the parking brake and block the rear wheels to keep the vehicle from rolling off the jackstands. Remove the wheel. Disconnect the ABS wheel speed sensor connector and harness, if equipped.

2   If only one control arm is being removed, disconnect only that end of the stabilizer bar. If both control arms are being removed, disconnect both ends (see Section 2 if necessary).

3   Remove the cotter pin and loosen the balljoint stud-to-control arm castellated nut **(see illustrations)**. **Note:** *On some early models, it will be necessary to remove the two bolts and the balljoint heat shield.*

4   Separate the balljoint from the knuckle with a two-jaw puller, with the center bolt on the nut and stud **(see illustration)**. Remove the nut once the stud is free and pry the control arm down.

5   Remove the two control arm pivot bolts and detach the control arm **(see illustration)**.

6   The control arm bushings are replaceable, but special tools and expertise are necessary to do the job. Carefully inspect the bushings for hardening, excessive wear and cracks. If they appear to be worn or

4.5a Remove the two control-arm-to-subframe bolts/nuts (arrows) (Lumina and 1999 and earlier Monte Carlo)

4.5b Remove the front (1) and rear (2) control-arm-to-subframe bolts/nuts (2000 and later Impala and Monte Carlo)

deteriorated, take the control arm to a dealer service department or other qualified repair shop.

Installation

7   Position the control arm in the subframe brackets and install the pivot bolts/nuts. Don't tighten the bolts completely yet. **Note:** *Later models use prevailing-torque nuts that should not be reused.*

8   Insert the balljoint stud into the control arm boss, install the castellated nut and tighten it to the torque listed in this Chapter's Specifications. (Installing the stud so that the cotter pin hole is parallel to the steering knuckle will make it easier to install the pin.) If necessary, tighten the nut a little more (but not more than one flat of the nut) if the cotter pin hole doesn't line up with an opening on the nut. Install a new cotter pin. **Caution:** *The ends of the cotter pin must not contact the ABS wheel speed sensors or connectors or the driveaxles.*

9   Place a floor jack under the balljoint and raise the suspension to simulate normal ride height. Tighten the control arm pivot bolts/nuts to the torque listed in this Chapter's Specifications.

10   On 1995 through 1999 models, install the stabilizer bar-to-control arm clamp over the end bushing. On 2000 and later models, install the stabilizer link. Tighten the bolts/nuts to the torque listed in this Chapter's Specifications (see Section 2).

11   Install the wheel and reconnect the ABS electrical connectors (if equipped) and lower the vehicle. Tighten the lug nuts to the torque listed in the Chapter 1 Specifications.

12   Drive the vehicle to a dealer service department or an alignment shop to have the front wheel alignment checked and, if necessary, adjusted.

---

5   Strut and spring assembly (front) - removal and installation

Lumina and 1999 and earlier Monte Carlo models

Note: *On these models the strut cartridge can be replaced with the strut and spring assembly installed in the vehicle (see Section 7). Because it isn't necessary to remove and disassemble the strut and spring assembly for strut cartridge replacement, removal of the assembly should only be required to repair damage to the spring, seats and strut/knuckle components.*

Removal

Refer to illustration 5.2

1   Loosen the wheel lug nuts, raise the front of the vehicle and support it securely on jackstands. Apply the parking brake and block the rear wheels to keep the vehicle from rolling off the jackstands. Remove the wheel.

2   Mark the position of the strut mount

5.2 Mark the position of the strut mount cover (arrow) before loosening the three nuts

cover to the strut tower **(see illustration)**.

3   Separate the tie-rod end from the steering knuckle as described in Section 15.

4   Refer to Chapter 9 and remove the brake caliper, mounting bracket and disc. Hang the caliper out of the way. On models so equipped, remove the bolt and secure the ABS sensor out of the way.

5   Remove the hub and wheel bearing bolts (see Section 8).

6   Remove the driveaxle (see Chapter 8).

7   Separate the balljoint from the lower control arm (see Section 4).

8   Support the strut and spring assembly with one hand and remove the three strut mount tower nuts **(see illustration 5.2)**. Lower the assembly and remove it from the vehicle.

Inspection

9   Check the strut body for leaking fluid, dents, cracks and other obvious damage, which would warrant repair or replacement.

10   Check the coil spring for chips and cracks in the spring coating (this will cause premature spring failure due to corrosion). Inspect the spring seats for hardening, cracks and general deterioration.

11   Inspect the knuckle/strut for corrosion, bending or twisting.

Installation

12   Slide the strut assembly up into the fenderwell and insert the three upper mounting studs through the holes in the shock tower. Once the three studs protrude from the shock tower, install the strut cover to the marked position, then the nuts so the strut won't fall back through. This may require an assistant, since the strut is quite heavy and awkward.

13   Connect the lower balljoint to the control arm and install the nut. Tighten the nut to the torque listed in this Chapter's Specifications and install a new cotter pin. If the cotter pin won't pass through, tighten the nut a little more, but just enough to align the hole in the stud with a castellation on the nut (don't loosen the nut).

14   Install the driveaxle and hub/wheel bearing assembly (see Chapter 8).

15   Install the brake components (see Chapter 9).

16   Install the tie-rod end in the steering arm and tighten the castellated nut to the torque listed in this Chapter's Specifications. Install a new cotter pin. If the cotter pin won't pass through, tighten the nut a little more, but just enough to align the hole in the stud with a castellation on the nut (don't loosen the nut).

17   Install the wheel, lower the vehicle and tighten the lug nuts to the torque listed in the Chapter 1 Specifications.

18   Tighten the three upper mounting nuts to the torque listed in this Chapter's Specification.

2000 and later Monte Carlo and Impala models

Removal

19   Loosen the wheel lug nuts, raise the front of the vehicle and support it securely on jackstands. Apply the parking brake and block the rear wheels to keep the vehicle from rolling off the jackstands. Remove the wheel.

20   Mark the strut-to-steering knuckle relationship by making a line around the strut-to-steering knuckle bolt heads. Also mark the relationship of the flange to the steering knuckle.

21   Remove the nuts from the strut-to-knuckle bolts and knock the bolts out with a brass punch and a hammer.

22   Separate the strut from the steering knuckle. Be careful not to overextend the inner CV joint or stretch the brake hose. If necessary, support the control arm with a jack.

23   Support the strut and spring assembly with one hand and remove the upper strut mounting nuts/bolt. Remove the strut and spring assembly.

Inspection

24   Check the strut body for leaking fluid, dents, cracks and other obvious damage, which would warrant repair or replacement.

25   Check the coil spring for chips and cracks in the spring coating (this will cause premature spring failure due to corrosion). Inspect the spring seat for hardening, cracks and general deterioration.

26   If wear or damage is evident, replace the strut and/or coil spring as necessary (see Section 6).

Installation

27   Guide the strut assembly up into the fenderwell and insert the upper mounting studs through the holes in the shock tower. Once the studs protrude from the shock tower, install the nuts so the strut won't fall back through. This may require an assistant, since the strut is quite heavy and awkward.

28   Slide the steering knuckle into the strut flange and insert the two bolts. Install the nuts, align the marks you made prior to disassembly and tighten the nuts to the torque listed in this Chapter's Specifications.

29   Install the wheel, lower the vehicle and

6.2 Install the spring compressor and alternately tighten each clamp to evenly compress the spring

6.4 Remove the cartridge retaining nut (arrow) with a two-pin spanner

6.5 Slide the strut cartridge out of the strut body

6.6 When installing the spring, place the end into the recessed portion of the lower seat (arrow)

7.2 Remove the strut shaft nut using this tool (arrow) with a wrench on it, and an extension with a Torx bit through the top to hold the strut shaft from turning

tighten the wheel lug nuts to the torque listed in the Chapter 1 Specifications.

30   Tighten the upper mounting nuts/bolt to the torque listed in this Chapter's Specifications.

31   Drive the vehicle to a dealer service department or an alignment shop to have the front wheel alignment checked and, if necessary, adjusted (this is only necessary if the strut has been modified for camber adjustment).

---

6   Coil spring/strut body - replacement

Warning: *Disassembling a strut is potentially dangerous and utmost attention must be directed to the job, or serious injury may result. Use only a high-quality spring compressor and carefully follow the manufacturer's instructions furnished with the tool. After removing the coil spring from the strut assembly, set it aside in a safe, isolated area.* **Note:** *If the struts exhibit the telltale signs of wear (leaking fluid, loss of damping capability, chipped, sagging or cracked coil springs) explore all options before beginning any work. Strut assemblies complete with springs may be available on an exchange basis, which eliminates much time and work. Whichever route you choose to take, check on the availability of parts before disassembling your vehicle.*

Lumina and 1999 and earlier Monte Carlo models

Refer to illustrations 6.2, 6.4, 6.5 and 6.6

1   Refer to Section 5 to remove the coil spring/strut body/steering knuckle assembly from the vehicle. Mount the assembly in a sturdy vise. **Warning:** *A compressed coil spring can be dangerous. Follow all instructions included with the spring compressor for safe operation, and if chains or safety clamps are included with the tool, use them.*

2   The strut body and the steering knuckle are serviced as an assembly (they are welded together). If either the spring or the strut/knuckle assembly must be replaced, rent or purchase a coil-spring compressor and attach it to the spring with the two clamps on opposite sides of the spring **(see illustration)**.

3   Refer to Section 7 and remove the nut from the strut cartridge, then remove the upper strut components to take the compressed spring off. **Warning:** *When releasing the compressor from the spring, release it just as evenly and slowly as you installed it.*

4   To replace the strut cartridge (out of vehicle), use a two-pin spanner to remove the cartridge nut **(see illustration)**. **Note:** *The special tool used in Section 7 isn't necessary when the spring is removed from the strut assembly.*

5   Remove the cartridge from the strut/knuckle assembly **(see illustration)**.

6   Reassembly is the reverse of the removal process. **Note:** *When installing a new spring, make sure the end of the lowest coil fits snugly into the notch on the lower spring mount and stays there during the installation process* **(see illustration)**.

2000 and later Monte Carlo and Impala models

Removal

7   Follow Steps 1 through 6 to replace the coil spring or strut body, but note that the strut cartridge is not a serviceable component of the strut body.

---

7   Strut cartridge - replacement in vehicle

Refer to illustrations 7.2, 7.3a, 7.3b, 7.4a, 7.4b and 7.5

Note: *This procedure applies to Lumina and 1999 and earlier Monte Carlo models only.*

1   Mark the position of the strut mount cover **(see illustration 5.2)** and remove the nuts and the cover. **Note:** *The vehicle should be on the ground with full weight on the suspension.*

2   Remove the strut shaft nut, using a special tool that grips the nut while allowing a Torx bit to be used to keep the shaft from turning **(see illustration)**.

3   Pry out the strut mount bushing and the upper strut bumper **(see illustrations)**. You may have to compress the strut shaft down into the cartridge using a length of pipe that just fits over the strut shaft.

4   Remove the strut cartridge nut using a special tool, which engages with the slots in the nut (available at most auto parts stores) **(see illustrations)**.

5   Grasp the strut cartridge and lift it out **(see illustration)**.

6   If the old cartridge had been leaking oil, use a suction pump to remove the damper fluid from the strut body and pour it into an approved oil container.

7   Insert the replacement strut cartridge, which is a self-contained unit, into position and install the nut. Tighten the cartridge nut to the torque listed in this Chapter's Specifications.

8   Install the bumper.

9   Temporarily install the strut shaft nut enough to grip it with locking pliers to raise the shaft if it doesn't come up by itself, then remove the nut and install the bushing.

10   Install the strut shaft nut. Tighten the nut to the torque listed in this Chapter's Specifications.

11   Install the strut mount cover and nuts. Tighten the nuts to the torque listed in this Chapter's Specifications.

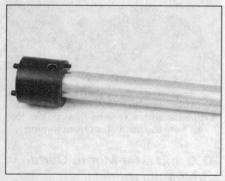

7.4a Strut cartridge nut removal tool - the lugs at the large end fit into the slots in the nut

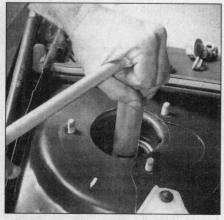

7.4b In use, the tool fits down over the strut shaft and a breaker bar can be used to turn it

7.3a Remove the strut mount bushing (arrow) . . .

---

8   Front hub and wheel bearing assembly - removal and installation

---

Note: *The front hub and wheel bearing assembly is sealed-for-life and must be replaced as a unit.*
Warning: *Dust created by the brake system is harmful to your health. Never blow it out with compressed air and don't inhale any of it. Do not, under any circumstances, use petroleum-based solvents to clean brake parts. Use brake cleaner or denatured alcohol only.*

Lumina and 1999 and earlier Monte Carlo models

1   The hub/bearing assembly is pressed onto the front driveaxle. Refer to Chapter 8 for removal of the driveaxle.

2   Take the driveaxle to a dealership, driveline shop or other automotive repair facility to have the hub/bearing assembly pressed off the driveaxle.

3   Inspect the bearing assembly and if it is to be reused, grease the axle splines with

7.5 Lift the cartridge out

7.3b . . . and the upper strut bumper (arrow)

multi-purpose grease and have the shop press it onto the driveaxle. **Note:** *Only a new driveaxle nut should be used. Do not reuse the old one.* Tighten the nut to the Specifications listed in Chapter 8.

4   Push the driveaxle and hub/bearing assembly into position and install the bolts. Tighten the bolts to the torque listed in the Chapter 8 Specifications.

5   Install the brake disc, caliper and (if equipped) the ABS sensor (see Chapter 9).

6   Install the wheel, lower the vehicle and tighten the lug nuts to the torque listed in the Chapter 1 Specifications.

2000 Monte Carlo and Impala models- removal and installation

7   Remove the wheel cover, then break the driveaxle/hub nut loose with a socket and large breaker bar. **Note:** *If the socket won't fit through the opening in the center of the wheel, remove the wheel and install the spare (the nut is very tight and is easier to loosen when the wheel is on the ground).*

8   Loosen the front wheel lug nuts, raise the vehicle and support it securely on jackstands. Remove the wheel.

9   Remove the driveaxle/hub nut and washer. To prevent the disc/hub from turning, insert a long punch into the brake disc cooling vanes and allow it to rest against the caliper mounting bracket.

10   Remove the caliper and hang it out of the way with a piece of wire, then remove the caliper mounting bracket (see Chapter 9). Pull the disc off the hub.

11   Unplug the electrical connector for the wheel speed sensor.

12   Working from the back side of the steering knuckle, remove the hub retaining bolts from the steering knuckle. Remove the disc shield.

13   Attach a puller to the hub flange and draw it off the driveaxle. The hub assembly should come right out of the steering knuckle, but if it doesn't, tap it from side-to-side to free it. Carefully guide the wiring

9.2 Disconnect the stabilizer bar mounts by removing the pivot bolts/nuts (A), allowing the insulator brackets to come out with the bar, or remove the bracket bolts (B), spread the clamp and remove the bar from the clamp (C is the rubber insulator)

9.5 Remove the two strut-to-knuckle nuts (arrows) and pull off the stabilizer bar end clamps and rubber insulators

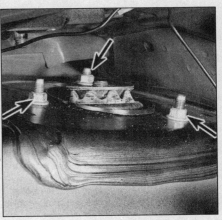

10.3 Location of the rear strut-to-body bolts (arrows)

10.9 Remove the rear strut-to-knuckle bolts (A) - B is the brake hose bracket bolt

harness and electrical connector for the wheel speed sensor through the opening between the driveaxle outer CV joint and the steering knuckle. **Caution:** *Be careful not to pull outward on the driveaxle, as this could separate the inner CV joint components.*

14   Clean the mating surfaces on the steering knuckle, bearing flange and knuckle bore.

15   Insert the hub and bearing assembly into the steering knuckle and onto the end of the driveaxle. Position the disc shield and install the three bolts, tightening them to the torque listed in this Chapter's Specifications. **Warning:** *The manufacturer states that these bolts must be replaced whenever they are removed or become loose and that failure to do so may result in loss of vehicle control and personal injury.*

16   Install the brake disc, caliper mounting bracket and caliper (see Chapter 9).

17   Install the hub nut and tighten it securely to seat the driveaxle in the hub. Prevent the axle from turning by inserting a screwdriver through the caliper and into a disc cooling vane.

18   Install the wheel, lower the vehicle and tighten the lug nuts to the torque listed in the Chapter 1 Specifications.

19   Tighten the driveaxle/hub nut to the torque listed in the Chapter 8 Specifications.

9   Stabilizer bar and bushings (rear) - removal and installation

Refer to illustrations 9.2 and 9.5

1   Raise the rear of the vehicle and support it securely on jackstands. Block the front wheels to keep the vehicle from rolling off the jackstands.

2   Remove the bolts and detach the two stabilizer shaft insulators at the chassis **(see illustration)**.

3   Mark the strut-to-knuckle position by scribing or painting around the strut bolts and nuts.

5   Support the left knuckle with a jack and remove the nuts from the strut-to-knuckle bolts **(see illustration)**. **Warning:** *Do not remove the strut-to-knuckle bolts.*

6   The strut-to-knuckle nuts retain the end clamps on the stabilizer bar. Pry the clamps and insulators from the ends of the bar.

7   Remove the stabilizer bar through the left side. **Note:** *You may need a prybar or large screwdriver to pry the bar ends past the strut.*

8   Inspect the bushings for cracks, hardening and wear. Replace them if necessary.

9   Installation is the reverse of the removal procedure. Make sure the marks made in Step 3 line up before tightening the knuckle bolts.

10   Rear strut - removal and installation

Refer to illustrations 10.3 and 10.9

1   Loosen the wheel lug nuts, raise the rear of the vehicle and support it securely on jackstands. Block the front wheels to keep the vehicle from rolling off the jackstands. Remove the wheel.

2   Support the bottom of the knuckle with a floor jack.

3   Open the trunk and loosen the three strut-to-body nuts **(see illustration)**.

4   Detach the brake hose bracket from the strut housing.

5   Remove the brake caliper and hang it out of the way on a piece of wire (see Chapter 9).

6   Mark the relationship of the strut to the knuckle and outline the knuckle bolts/nuts.

7   Detach the stabilizer bar from the knuckle (see Section 9).

8   Remove the strut-to-body nuts **(see illustration 10.3)**, and lower the strut

assembly until there is no more spring pressure on the knuckle.

9   Remove the strut-to-knuckle nuts and knock the bolts out with a brass or plastic hammer **(see illustration)**.

10   Separate the strut from the knuckle and remove the strut (with coil spring assembly in place) from the vehicle.

11   Refer to Section 6 for removal of the coil spring from the strut. If the strut is being replaced, install the coil spring and upper strut components from the old assembly to the new strut.

12   Installation is the reverse of the removal procedure. Make sure the strut-to-knuckle alignment marks made during Step 6 line up before tightening the bolts to the torque listed in this Chapter's Specifications.

11   Rear hub and wheel bearing assembly - removal and installation

Refer to illustration 11.2
Note: *The rear hub and wheel bearing assembly is sealed-for-life and must be replaced as a unit.*

Removal

1   Loosen the wheel lug nuts, raise the rear of the vehicle and support it securely on jackstands. Block the front wheels to keep the vehicle from rolling off the jackstands. Remove the wheel.
2   Remove the brake drum or the brake caliper and disc (see Chapter 9). Support the caliper with a piece of wire. If equipped, unplug the ABS electrical connector **(see illustration)**.
3   On models with rear disc brakes, remove the parking brake cable from the actuator bracket on the backing plate.
4   Remove the four hub-to-knuckle bolts.
5   Remove the hub and bearing assembly.

Installation

6   Position the hub and bearing assembly on the knuckle and align the holes. Install the bolts. After all four bolts have been installed, tighten them to the torque listed in this Chapter's Specifications.
7   Install the brake drum or the brake caliper and disc, tightening the caliper bolts to the torque listed in the Chapter 9 Specifications. Install the wheel. Lower the vehicle and tighten the wheel lug nuts to the torque listed in Chapter 1 Specifications.

---

12 Rear suspension arms - removal and installation

1   Loosen the wheel lug nuts, raise the rear of the vehicle and support it securely on jackstands. Block the front wheels to keep the vehicle from rolling off the jackstands. Remove the wheels.
2   If necessary, remove the stabilizer bar as outlined in Section 9.
3   If necessary, remove the brake drums or calipers and discs from the hubs. See Chapter 9 if difficulty is encountered. If equipped, unplug the ABS electrical connectors **(see illustration 11.2)**.

Trailing arms

Refer to illustration 12.4
4   Remove the trailing arm-to-knuckle nut and bolt and the trailing arm-to-chassis nut and bolt **(see illustration)**.
5   Detach the trailing arm and lower it from the vehicle.
6   Installation is the reverse of removal. Do not tighten the nuts and bolts to the torque listed in this Chapter's Specifications until the vehicle weight has been lowered onto the suspension (you can simulate normal ride height by raising the suspension with a floor jack). Reconnect the ABS electrical connector, if removed.

Lateral link rods

Refer to illustrations 12.7 and 12.8
7   Remove the nuts and bolts connecting the rods to the knuckle **(see illustration)**.
8   Remove the rod inner bolts at the crossmember **(see illustration)**. **Note:** *The bolts for the front rods are difficult to access. You will have to lower the rear of the fuel tank a few inches for better access* (see Chapter 4).
9   Installation is the reverse of removal. Don't tighten the bolts to the torque listed in this Chapter's Specifications until the vehicle weight has been lowered onto the suspension (you can simulate normal ride height by raising the suspension with a floor jack). After installation have the rear toe checked by a dealer service department or alignment shop.

---

13 Rear knuckle - removal and installation

1   Mark the strut-to-knuckle relationship and scribe or paint a line around the knuckle nuts.
2   Refer to Section 11 and remove the rear hub/bearing assembly.
3   On models with rear drum brakes, remove the brake shoe assembly and the

11.2 Disconnect the rear-wheel ABS electrical connector (arrow), if equipped

backing plate (see Chapter 9).
4   Remove the bolts/nuts and detach the trailing arm, lateral link rods and stabilizer bar from the knuckle (see Sections 9 and 12).
5   Remove the strut-to-knuckle nuts and knock the bolts out with a brass or plastic hammer.
7   Separate the knuckle from the strut.
8   To install the knuckle, slide it into the strut flange. Install the stabilizer bar bracket and insert the two bolts. Install the nuts finger tight. Connect the lateral link rods and trailing arm to the knuckle, but do not tighten at this time. Align the marks made in Step 1 and tighten the strut-to-knuckle bolts to the torque listed in this Chapter's Specifications. The remainder of installation is the reverse of removal.
9   Don't tighten the trailing arm or lateral link rod bolts/nuts to the torque listed in this Chapter's Specifications until the vehicle weight has been lowered onto the suspension (you can simulate normal ride height by raising the suspension with a floor jack). After installation have the rear toe checked by a dealer service department or alignment shop.

12.4 Remove the trailing arm-to-knuckle bolt and nut (A) and the trailing arm-to-chassis nut and bolt (B)

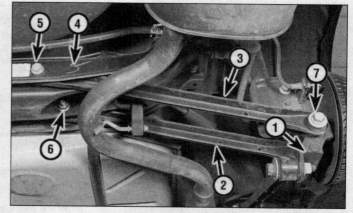

12.7 Lateral link rod details

1 Knuckle	5 Rear rod inner mounting bolt
2 Front rod	6 Front rod inner mounting bolt
3 Rear rod	7 Rear rod outer mounting bolt (front rod bolt similar)
4 Crossmember	

12.8 Locations of the inner lateral link rod bolts/nuts (arrows)

14.2a On 1995 through 1999 models, use a Torx bit to remove the two airbag module screws from behind the steering wheel

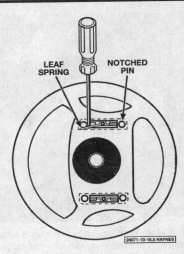

14.2b To detach the airbag module from the steering wheel on 2000 and later models, rotate the wheel 90-degrees, insert a screwdriver into each of the four holes in the backside of the steering wheel and pry each leaf spring aside to release it from its notched pin (there are four of them)

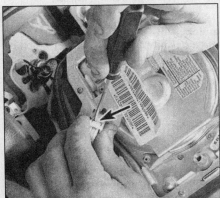

14.3a Use a small screwdriver to release the plastic locking clip (arrow) from the airbag module connector, then . . .

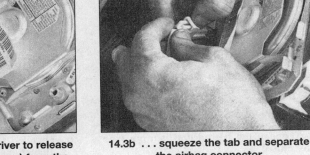

14.3b . . . squeeze the tab and separate the airbag connector

14 Steering wheel - removal and installation

Refer to illustrations 14.2a, 14.2b, 14.3a, 14.3b, 14.4, 14.5, 14.6, 14.7 and 14.8

Warning: *These models are equipped with airbags. Always turn the steering wheel to the straight ahead position, place the ignition switch in the Lock position and disable the airbag system (see Chapter 12) before working in the vicinity of the impact sensors, steering column or instrument panel to avoid the possibility of accidental deployment of the airbag, which could cause personal injury.*

1   Disconnect the negative battery cable.
Note: *On models equipped with the Theftlock audio system, be sure the lockout feature is turned off before performing any procedure which requires disconnecting the battery.*

2   On 1995 through 1999 models, use a number 30 Torx bit to remove the two screws that secure the airbag module to the steering wheel **(see illustration)**. On 2000 and later models, turn the steering wheel 90-degrees to gain access to the holes in the back side of the steering wheel (the side facing the dash).

Insert a screwdriver into the hole for each of the four spring clips and push the spring aside to release the pin **(see illustration)**. Then rotate the steering wheel so the other two openings are at the top and disengage the other two clips. There are four pins and four springs.

3   Lift the airbag module carefully away from the steering wheel and disconnect the yellow airbag electrical connector(s). This is a two-part disconnection, as there is a plastic clip that must be removed before the connector(s) can be disconnected **(see illustrations)**. If necessary, rotate the horn contact lead (in the center of the steering wheel) counterclockwise until it unlocks (approximately 1/4 turn) and remove it from the steering wheel. Note the routing of the various wires for correct reinstallation. Remove the module. **Warning:** *When carrying the airbag module, keep the driver's side of it away from your body, and when you place it on the bench, have the driver's side facing up.*

4   Remove the steering wheel nut **(see illustration)**.

5   Mark the relationship of the steering wheel to the shaft **(see illustration)**.

14.4 Remove the steering wheel nut with a deep socket

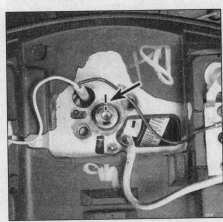

14.5 Make two paint marks (arrow) to show alignment of wheel before removal

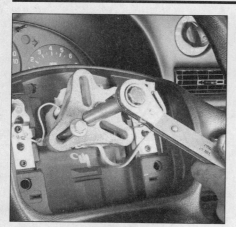

14.6 A steering wheel puller threads into two holes in the steering wheel - tightening the center bolt removes the wheel

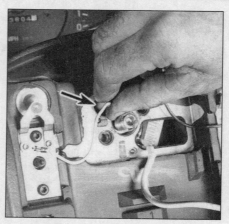

14.7 Disconnect the horn and ground wire connector

14.8 When properly aligned, the airbag coil will be centered with the marks aligned (in circle here) and the tab fitted between the projections on the top of the steering column (arrow)

6   Install a steering wheel puller (available at most auto parts stores) and turn the center bolt until the wheel is free **(see illustration)**.

7   Remove the puller and disconnect the horn and ground wire connector if not already done **(see illustration)**. Remove the steering wheel. **Warning:** *Don't allow the steering shaft to turn with the steering wheel removed. If the shaft turns, the airbag coil assembly (the mechanism which protects the airbag wiring when the steering wheel is turned) will become uncentered, which may cause the airbag harness to break when the vehicle is returned to service.*

8   Installation is the reverse of removal. Before installing the steering wheel, make sure the airbag coil assembly is centered **(see illustration)**. If it isn't, see Chapter 12, Section 8, Step 14 for the centering procedure. Connect the airbag connector to the back of the airbag module just as it was before steering wheel removal, i.e. with the plastic locking device(s) in place. Be sure to tighten the steering wheel nut and airbag screws to the torque listed in this Chapter's Specifications.

9   Refer to Chapter 12 for the procedure to enable the airbag system.

15   Tie-rod ends - removal and installation

Refer to illustrations 15.2, 15.3 and 15.4

Removal

1   Loosen the wheel lug nuts, raise the front of the vehicle and support it securely on jackstands. Apply the parking brake and block the rear wheels to keep the vehicle from rolling off the jackstands. Remove the wheel.

2   Loosen the tie-rod end jam nut **(see illustration)**.

3   Mark the relationship of the tie-rod end to the threaded portion of the tie-rod **(see illustration)**. This will ensure the toe-in setting is restored when reassembled.

4   Remove the cotter pin, loosen the nut and disconnect the tie-rod end from the steering knuckle arm with a puller **(see illus-**

tration). **Note:** *Back the tie-rod end nut off until it is flush with the stud, apply the puller's center bolt against it until it breaks free, then remove the nut and detach the tie-rod end from the knuckle arm.*

5   Unscrew the tie-rod end from the tie-rod.

Installation

6   Thread the tie-rod end onto the tie-rod to the marked position and connect the tie-rod end to the steering arm. Install the castellated nut and tighten it to the torque listed in this Chapter's Specifications. Install a new cotter pin.

7   Tighten the jam nut securely and install the wheel. Lower the vehicle and tighten the lug nuts to the torque listed in the Chapter 1 Specifications.

8   Have the front end alignment checked by a dealer service department or an alignment shop.

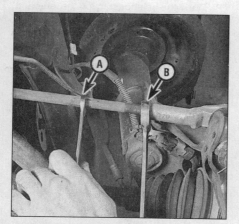

15.2 Hold the tie-rod with one wrench on the flats (A) while using another wrench to loosen the jam nut (B)

15.3 Make a paint mark (arrow) to indicate exactly how many threads were engaged in the tie-rod end (jam nut has been backed off)

15.4 Use a puller to remove the tie-rod end

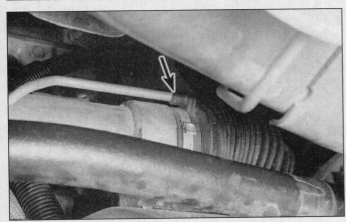

16.15 Align the connector on the boot with the breather tube (arrow)

17.6 Remove the pinch bolt (arrow) - this view is looking down on the steering gear below the brake master cylinder and booster

16 Steering gear boots - replacement

Refer to illustration 16.15

1   To replace the steering gear boots with the steering gear on the vehicle, start with Step 2. Otherwise, remove the steering gear from the vehicle (see Section 17) and start with Step 7.

2   Disconnect the cable from the negative battery terminal. **Caution:** *On models equipped with the Theftlock audio system, be sure the lockout feature is turned off be performing any procedure which requires disconnecting the battery.*

3   On models equipped with the 3.4L DOHC engine, remove the air cleaner and duct assembly.

4   Loosen the front wheel lug nuts, raise the front of the vehicle and support it securely on jackstands. Apply the parking brake and block the rear wheels to keep the vehicle from rolling off the jackstands. Remove both front wheels. **Note:** *The jackstands must be behind the front suspension subframe, not supporting the vehicle by the subframe.*

5   On models equipped with the 3.4L DOHC engine, remove the right-side engine splash shield.

6   The front wheels must point straight ahead, with the steering column in the locked position. **Warning:** *Failure to do this can result in damage to the airbag system.*

7   Roll back the boot at the bottom of the steering column to expose the flange and steering coupler assembly. Mark the relationship of the coupler and steering column shaft and remove the pinch bolt **(see illustration 17.6).**

8   Support the rear of the subframe assembly with a jack and remove the rear bolts. Loosen (but do not remove) the front bolts of the subframe and lower the rear approximately five inches (three inches on 3.4L DOHC models). **Caution:** *Lowering the subframe too far may damage engine components near the cowl.*

9   Remove the tie-rod ends from the steering gear (see Section 15).

10   Remove the jam nuts and outer boot clamps.

11   Cut off both inner boot clamps and discard them.

12   Mark the location of the breather tube (if used) in relation to the rack assembly, then remove the boots and the tube.

13   Install a new clamp on the inner end of the boot.

14   Apply multi-purpose grease to groove on the tie-rod (where the outer boot clamp will ride) and the mounting grooves on the steering gear (where the inner boot end will be clamped).

15   Line up the breather tube with the marks made during removal and slide the new boot onto the steering gear housing **(see illustration)**.

16   Make sure the boot isn't twisted, then tighten the new inner clamp.

17   Install the outer clamps and tie-rod end jam nuts.

18   Install the tie-rod ends (see Section 15) and tighten the nuts securely.

19   Install the steering gear assembly or, if it wasn't removed, start with Section 17, Step 20. Remember to use NEW subframe bolts.

17 Steering gear - removal and installation

Refer to illustrations 17.6 and 17.13

Warning: *Make sure the steering shaft is not turned while the steering gear is removed or you could damage the airbag system. To prevent the shaft from turning, place the ignition key in the LOCK position or thread the seat belt through the steering wheel and clip it into place.*

Removal

1   Disconnect the cable from the negative battery terminal. **Note:** *On models equipped with the Theftlock audio system, be sure the lockout feature is turned off before performing any procedure, which requires disconnecting the battery.*

2   On models equipped with the 3.4L DOHC engine, remove the air cleaner and duct assembly.

3   Loosen the front wheel lug nuts, raise the front of the vehicle and support it securely on jackstands. Apply the parking brake and block the rear wheels to keep the vehicle from rolling off the jackstands. Remove both front wheels. **Note:** *The jackstands must be behind the front suspension subframe, not supporting the vehicle by the subframe.*

4   On models equipped with the 3.4L DOHC engine, remove the right side engine splash shield.

5   Set the steering wheel straight ahead, check that the wide spline or "block tooth" on the upper steering shaft assembly is at the 12 o'clock position and that the ignition switch is set to "lock." **Warning:** *Failure to do this can result in damage to the airbag system's coil unit.*

6   Roll back the boot at the bottom of the steering column to expose the flange and steering coupler assembly. Mark the coupler and steering column shaft, remove the pinch bolt and separate the steering column from the power steering input shaft **(see illustration)**.

7   On models equipped with the 3.4L DOHC V6 engine, remove the exhaust pipe and catalytic converter assembly.

8   Separate the tie-rod ends from the steering arms (see Section 15).

9   Support the rear of the subframe assembly with a jack and remove the rear bolts. Loosen (but do not remove) the front bolts of the subframe and lower the rear approximately five inches (three inches on models equipped with the 3.4L DOHC V6 engine). **Caution:** *Lowering the subframe too far may damage engine components near the cowl.*

10   Remove the heat shield from the steering gear.

11   Remove the fluid pipe clip from the rack.

12   Place a drain pan or tray under the vehicle, positioned beneath the steering gear.

17.13 Steering rack mounting bolt/nut (arrow) - left-side shown, right-side similar

18.6 Disconnect the return line (A) and the pressure line (B)

Using a flare-nut wrench, disconnect the pressure and return lines from the steering gear. Plug the lines to prevent excessive fluid loss.

13 Remove the steering gear mounting bolts and nuts **(see illustration)**.

14 Lift the steering gear out of the mounts then move it forward and detach the coupler from the steering gear.

15 Support the steering gear and carefully maneuver the entire assembly out through the left side wheel opening.

Installation

16 Pass the steering gear assembly through the left wheel opening and place it in position in the mounts. Install the mounting bolts and nuts, tightening them to the torque listed in this Chapter's Specifications.

17 Attach the pressure and return lines to the steering gear. Connect the line retainer.

18 Install the heat shield.

19 Raise the subframe into position and install NEW bolts. Tighten the subframe bolts to the torque listed in this Chapter's Specifications.

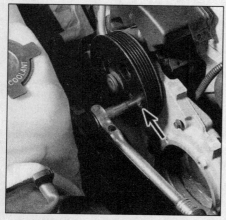

18.8 Using a socket and short extension inserted through one of the holes in the pulley (arrow), remove the three pump mounting bolts - rotate the pulley to access each bolt

20 Connect the tie-rod ends to the steering arms and tighten the nuts to the torque listed in this Chapter's Specifications. Install new cotter pins.

21 Install the exhaust system, if removed.

22 Center the steering gear and have an assistant guide the coupler onto the steering shaft, with the previously applied marks aligned. Install and tighten the pinch bolt to the torque listed in this Chapter's Specifications. **Warning:** *Be sure the shaft is seated before you install the pinch bolt or the shafts may disengage.*

23 Install the front wheels, lower the vehicle and tighten the lug nuts to the torque listed in the Chapter 1 Specifications.

24 Reconnect the negative battery cable.

25 Fill the power steering pump with the recommended fluid, bleed the system (see Section 19) and recheck the fluid level. Check for leaks.

26 Have the front end alignment checked by a dealer service department or an alignment shop.

18 Power steering pump - removal and installation

Refer to illustrations 18.6, 18.8, 18.9a and 18.9b

Removal

1 Disconnect the cable from the negative battery terminal. **Note:** *On models equipped with the Theftlock audio system, be sure the lockout feature is turned off before performing any procedure, which requires disconnecting the battery.*

2 Remove the coolant recovery reservoir, if necessary.

3 On models equipped with the 3.4L DOHC V6 engine, remove the air cleaner and duct assembly.

4 On models equipped with the 3.1L and 3.4L OHV engine, detach the ignition control wiring harness near the pump and position it aside. On 3.8L engines, remove the electrical connector from the pump.

5 Remove the drivebelt (see Chapter 1).

6 Position a drain pan under the vehicle. Remove as much fluid from the reservoir as possible with a suction pump, then remove the return line (rubber hose connection with clamp) from the rack to the reservoir **(see illustration)**.

7 Using a flare-nut wrench and a back-up wrench, disconnect the pressure hose from the pump.

8 Remove the pump mounting bolts and detach the pump from the engine, being careful not to spill the remaining fluid **(see illustration)**.

Installation

9 If a new pump is to be installed, the pulley will have to be transferred to the new pump. Use a power steering pulley puller (available at most auto parts stores) to remove the pulley and install it on the new pump **(see illustrations)**. **Note:** *Take note of how far the pulley was pressed onto the old pump's shaft before removing the pulley.*

10 If your new pump doesn't come with a reservoir, you can swap your old one to the new pump. Remove the reservoir by pulling on the two sliding clips that hold the reservoir to the pump. Install a new O-ring at the fluid connection and clip the reservoir onto the new pump.

11 Position the pump on the mounting bracket and install the bolts.

12 Connect the pressure and return lines to the pump.

13 Fill the reservoir with the recommended fluid and bleed the system, following the procedure described in the next Section.

19 Power steering system - bleeding

1 Following any operation in which the power steering fluid lines have been disconnected, the power steering system must be bled to remove air and obtain proper steering performance.

2 With the front wheels turned all the way to the left and the ignition key OFF, check the

18.9a Remove the pulley with the puller - the flanged collar (arrow) fits onto the groove on the front of the pulley

18.9b Press the pulley onto the shaft with the installation tool

power steering fluid level and, if low, add fluid until it reaches the Cold mark on the dipstick.

3   Start the engine and allow it to run at fast idle. Recheck the fluid level and add more if necessary to reach the Cold mark on the dipstick.

4   Bleed the system by turning the wheels from side-to-side, without hitting the stops. This will work the air out of the system. Don't allow the reservoir to run out of fluid.

5   When the air is worked out of the system, return the wheels to the straight ahead position and leave the engine running for several minutes before shutting it off. Recheck the fluid level.

6   Road test the vehicle to be sure the steering system is functioning normally with no noise.

7   Recheck the fluid level to be sure it's up to the Hot mark on the dipstick while the engine is at normal operating temperature. Add fluid if necessary.

20 Wheels and tires - general information

Refer to illustration 20.1

All vehicles covered by this manual are equipped with metric-size fiberglass or steel belted radial tires **(see illustration)**. The use of other size or type tires may affect the ride and handling of the vehicle. Don't mix different types of tires, such as radials and bias belted, on the same vehicle, since handling may be seriously affected. Tires should be replaced in pairs on the same axle, but if only one tire is being replaced, be sure it's the same size, structure and tread design as the other.

Because tire pressure affects handling and wear, the tire pressures should be checked at least once a month or before any extended trips (see Chapter 1).

Wheels must be replaced if they're bent, dented, leak air, have elongated bolt holes,

are heavily rusted, out of vertical symmetry or if the lug nuts won't stay tight. Wheel repairs by welding or peening aren't recommended.

Tire and wheel balance is important to the overall handling, braking and performance of the vehicle. Unbalanced wheels can adversely affect handling and ride characteristics as well as tire life. Whenever a tire is installed on a wheel, the tire and wheel should be balanced by a shop with the proper equipment.

21 Wheel alignment - general information

Refer to illustration 21.1

A wheel alignment refers to the adjustments made to the wheels so they're in proper angular relationship to the suspension and the ground. Wheels that are out of proper alignment not only affect steering control, but also increase tire wear. The adjustment most commonly required is the toe-in adjustment

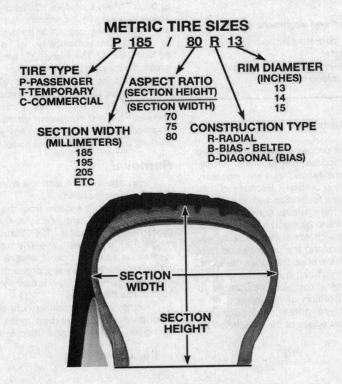

20.1 Metric size code

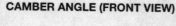

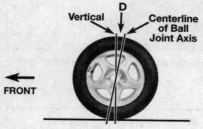

CAMBER ANGLE (FRONT VIEW)

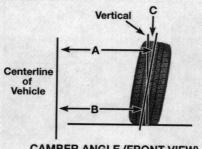

CASTER ANGLE (SIDE VIEW)

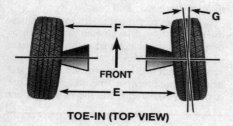

TOE-IN (TOP VIEW)

21.1 Front end alignment details

A minus B = C (degrees camber)
D = degrees caster
E minus F = toe-in (measured in inches)
G = toe-in (expressed in degrees)

but camber adjustment is also possible **(see illustration)**.

Getting the proper wheel alignment is a very exacting process, one in which complicated and expensive machines are necessary to perform the job properly. Because of this, you should have a technician with the proper equipment perform these tasks. We will, however, attempt to give you a basic idea of what's involved with wheel alignment so you can better understand the process and deal intelligently with the shop that does the work.

Toe-in is the turning in of the wheels. The purpose of a toe specification is to ensure parallel rolling of the wheels. In a vehicle with zero toe-in, the distance between the front edges of the wheels will be

the same as the distance between the rear edges of the wheels. The actual amount of toe-in is normally only a fraction of an inch. Incorrect toe-in will cause the tires to wear improperly by making them scrub against the road surface. On the front end, toe adjustment is controlled by the tie-rod end position on the tie-rod. On the rear, a special tool is required to adjust the position of the rear lateral link rod in its inner mount.

Camber is the tilting of the wheels from the vertical when viewed from the front or rear of the vehicle. When the wheels tilt out at the top, the camber is said to be positive (+). When the wheels tilt in at the top the camber is negative (-). The amount of tilt is measured in degrees from the vertical and this measurement is called the camber angle. This angle affects the amount of tire tread which contacts the road and compensates for changes in the suspension geometry when the vehicle is cornering or traveling over an undulating surface. Camber can be adjusted after the strut mounting holes have been elongated with a file. Camber adjustment, front or rear, must be done with the vehicle on the alignment rack, by an experienced technician.

Caster is not adjustable. If the caster angle is not to specification, the suspension components must be checked for damage.

22 Steering column - removal and installation

Warning: *These models are equipped with airbags. Always disable the airbag system before working in the vicinity of the impact sensors, steering column or instrument panel to avoid the possibility of accidental deployment of the airbag(s), which could cause personal injury (see Chapter 12 for the airbag disabling procedure). The yellow wires and connectors routed through the instrument panel are for this system. Do not use electrical test equipment on these yellow wires or tamper with them in any way while working under the instrument panel.*

Removal

1   Park the vehicle with the front wheels pointing straight ahead.
2   Disconnect the cable from the negative battery terminal and disable the airbag system (see Chapter 12). **Caution:** *On models equipped with the Theftlock audio system, be sure the lockout feature is turned off before performing any procedure which requires disconnecting the battery (see the front of this manual).*
3   Remove the steering wheel, multi-function switch and airbag system clock-spring (see Section 14 and Chapter 12).

4   Remove the steering column trim covers, left side knee bolster, knee bolster bracket and left instrument panel insulator (see Chapter 11).
5   On column-shift models, remove the park/lock cable, shift cable, and park/neutral position switch (if equipped).
6   Disconnect any steering column electrical connectors. Follow the airbag clockspring wiring harness along the steering column and cut any wire ties that may be securing it or other wiring harnesses to the column.
7   Pull back the steering column boot and remove the steering shaft-to-intermediate shaft pinch bolt. Insert a large screwdriver into the gap in the intermediate shaft joint and spread it apart slightly to loosen it.
8   Remove the steering column lower mounting bolts and upper mounting nuts. On later models, remove the anchor cable from the stud.
9   Remove the steering column from under the instrument panel. **Caution 1:** *Do not support the steering column by just the upper or lower support bracket, as this could damage the lower bearing adapter.* **Caution 2:** *Use care in handling the steering column after removal from the vehicle. Dropping, leaning on or hammering it could damage the plastic injections and affect the column's structural integrity and collapsibility.*

Installation

10   Installation is the reverse of the removal procedure, with the following additions:
a) *Install all of the steering column fasteners before tightening any of them, then tighten them to the torque listed in this Chapter's Specifications, in the following order.*
   1) Intermediate shaft pinch bolt. **Warning:** *Make sure that the intermediate shaft is seated before installing the pinch bolt, otherwise the two shafts may not engage.*
   2) Right lower mounting bolt; left lower mounting bolt.
   3) Left upper mounting nut; right upper mounting nut. **Warning:** *The lower steering column bolts must be tightened before the upper nuts, to avoid damage to the steering column. Do not over-torque the fasteners—this could affect the steering column's collapsibility.*
b) *Center and install the airbag system clockspring as described in Chapter 12.*
c) *Secure the clockspring wiring harness with new wire ties.*
d) *Install the steering wheel as described in Section 14.*
e) *Refer to Chapter 12 for the procedure to enable the airbag system.*

Chapter 11 Body

Contents

1 General information

Warning: *The models covered by this manual are equipped with airbags. Always disable the airbag system (see Chapter 12) before working in the vicinity of the impact sensors, steering column or instrument panel. Failure to follow these procedures may cause accidental deployment of the airbag, which could cause personal injury. The airbag circuits are easily identified by yellow insulation covering the entire wiring harness. Do not use electrical test equipment on any of these wires or tamper with them in any way.*
Caution: *On models equipped with a Theftlock audio system, be sure the lockout feature is turned off before performing any procedure which requires disconnecting the battery.*

These models feature a "unibody" construction, using a floor pan with front and rear frame side rails which support the body components, front and rear suspension systems and other mechanical components.

Certain body components are particularly vulnerable to accident damage and can be unbolted and repaired or replaced. Among these parts are the body moldings, front fenders, doors, bumpers, the hood, trunk lid and all glass.

Only general body maintenance practices and body panel repair procedures within the scope of the do-it-yourselfer are included in this Chapter.

2 Body - maintenance

1   The condition of your vehicle's body is very important, because the resale value depends a great deal on it. It's much more difficult to repair a neglected or damaged body than it is to repair mechanical components. The hidden areas of the body, such as the wheel wells, the frame and the engine compartment, are equally important, although they don't require as frequent attention as the rest of the body.

2   Once a year, or every 12,000 miles, it's a good idea to have the underside of the body steam cleaned. All traces of dirt and oil will be removed and the area can then be inspected carefully for rust, damaged brake lines, frayed electrical wires, damaged cables and other problems. The front suspension components should be greased after completion of this job.

3   At the same time, clean the engine and the engine compartment with a steam cleaner or water-soluble degreaser.

4   The wheel wells should be given close attention, since undercoating can peel away and stones and dirt thrown up by the tires can cause the paint to chip and flake, allowing rust to set in. If rust is found, clean down to the bare metal and apply an anti-rust paint.

5   The body should be washed about once a week. Wet the vehicle thoroughly to soften the dirt, then wash it down with a soft sponge and plenty of clean soapy water. If the surplus dirt is not washed off very carefully, it can wear down the paint.

6   Spots of tar or asphalt thrown up from the road should be removed with a cloth soaked in solvent.

7   Once every six months, wax the body and chrome trim. If a chrome cleaner is used to remove rust from any of the vehicle's plated parts, remember that the cleaner also removes part of the chrome, so use it sparingly.

3 Vinyl trim - maintenance

Don't clean vinyl trim with detergents, caustic soap or petroleum-based cleaners. Plain soap and water works just fine, with a soft brush to clean dirt that may be ingrained. Wash the vinyl as frequently as the rest of the vehicle. After cleaning, application of a high-quality rubber and vinyl protectant will help prevent oxidation and cracks. The protectant can also be applied to weatherstripping, vacuum lines and rubber hoses, which often fail as a result of chemical degradation, and to the tires.

4 Upholstery and carpets - maintenance

1   Every three months, remove the floormats and clean the interior of the vehicle (more frequently if necessary). Use a stiff whisk broom to brush the carpeting and loosen dirt and dust, then vacuum the upholstery and carpets thoroughly, especially along seams and crevices.

2   Dirt and stains can be removed from carpeting with basic household or automotive carpet shampoos available in spray cans. Follow the directions and vacuum again, then use a stiff brush to bring back the "nap" of the carpet.

3   Most interiors have cloth or vinyl upholstery, either of which can be cleaned and maintained with a number of material-specific cleaners or shampoos available in auto supply stores. Follow the directions on the product for usage, and always spot-test any upholstery cleaner on an inconspicuous area (bottom edge of a back seat cushion) to ensure that it doesn't cause a color shift in the material.

4   After cleaning, vinyl upholstery should be treated with a protectant. **Note:** *Make sure the protectant container indicates the product can be used on seats - some products may make a seat too slippery.* **Caution:** *Do not use protectant on vinyl-covered steering wheels.*

5   Leather upholstery requires special care. It should be cleaned regularly with saddlesoap or leather cleaner. Never use alcohol, gasoline, nail polish remover or thinner to clean leather upholstery.

6   After cleaning, regularly treat leather upholstery with a leather conditioner, rubbed in with a soft cotton cloth. Never use car wax on leather upholstery.

7   In areas where the interior of the vehicle is subject to bright sunlight, cover leather seating areas of the seats with a sheet if the vehicle is to be left out for any length of time.

5   Body repair - minor damage

Plastic body panels

The following repair procedures are for minor scratches and gouges. Repair of more serious damage should be left to a dealer service department or qualified auto body shop. Below is a list of the equipment and materials necessary to perform the following repair procedures on plastic body panels. Although a specific brand of material may be mentioned, it should be noted that equivalent products from other manufacturers may be used instead.

Wax, grease and silicone removing
   solvent
Cloth-backed body tape
Sanding discs
Drill motor with three-inch disc holder
Hand sanding block
Rubber squeegees
Sandpaper
Non-porous mixing palette
Wood paddle or putty knife
Curved tooth body file
Plastic body panel repair compound
   and material

Flexible panels (front and rear bumper fascia)

1   Remove the damaged panel, if necessary or desirable. In most cases, repairs can be carried out with the panel installed.
2   Clean the area(s) to be repaired with a wax, grease and silicone removing solvent applied with a water-dampened cloth.
3   If the damage is structural, that is, if it extends through the panel, clean the backside of the panel area to be repaired as well. Wipe dry.
4   Sand the rear surface about 1-1/2 in beyond the break.
5   Cut two pieces of fiberglass cloth large enough to overlap the break by about 1-1/2 in. Cut only to the required length.
6   Mix the adhesive from the repair kit according to the instructions included with the kit, and apply a layer of the mixture approximately 1/8-inch thick on the backside of the panel. Overlap the break by at least 1-1/2 inches.
7   Apply one piece of fiberglass cloth to the adhesive and cover the cloth with additional adhesive. Apply a second piece of fiberglass cloth to the adhesive and immediately cover the cloth with additional adhesive insufficient quantity to fill the weave.
8   Allow the repair to cure for 20 to 30 minutes at 60-degrees to 80-degrees F.
9   If necessary, trim the excess repair material at the edge.
10   Remove all of the paint film over and around the area(s) to be repaired. The repair material should not overlap the painted surface.
11   With a drill motor and a sanding disc (or a rotary file), cut a "V" along the break line approximately 1/2-inch wide. Remove all dust and loose particles from the repair area.
12   Mix and apply the repair material. Apply a light coat first over the damaged area; then continue applying material until it reaches a level slightly higher than the surrounding finish.
13   Cure the mixture for 20 to 30 minutes at 60-degrees to 80-degrees F.
14   Roughly establish the contour of the area being repaired with a body file. If low areas or pits remain, mix and apply additional adhesive.
15   Block sand the damaged area with sandpaper to establish the actual contour of the surrounding surface.
16   If desired, the repaired area can be temporarily protected with several light coats of primer. Because of the special paints and techniques required for flexible body panels, it is recommended that the vehicle be taken to a paint shop for completion of the body repair.

Steel body panels

See photo sequence

Repair of minor scratches

17   If the scratch is superficial and does not penetrate to the metal of the body, repair is very simple. Lightly rub the scratched area with a fine rubbing compound to remove loose paint and built-up wax. Rinse the area with clean water.
18   Apply touch-up paint to the scratch, using a small brush. Continue to apply thin layers of paint until the surface of the paint in the scratch is level with the surrounding paint. Allow the new paint at least two weeks to harden, then blend it into the surrounding paint by rubbing with a very fine rubbing compound. Finally, apply a coat of wax to the scratch area.
19   If the scratch has penetrated the paint and exposed the metal of the body, causing the metal to rust, a different repair technique is required. Remove all loose rust from the bottom of the scratch with a pocket knife, then apply rust inhibiting paint to prevent the formation of rust in the future. Using a rubber or nylon applicator, coat the scratched area with glaze-type filler. If required, the filler can be mixed with thinner to provide a very thin paste, which is ideal for filling narrow scratches. Before the glaze filler in the scratch hardens, wrap a piece of smooth cotton cloth around the tip of a finger. Dip the cloth in thinner and then quickly wipe it along the surface of the scratch. This will ensure that the surface of the filler is slightly hollow. The scratch can now be painted over as described earlier in this Section.

Repair of dents

20   When repairing dents, the first job is to pull the dent out until the affected area is as close as possible to its original shape. There is no point in trying to restore the original shape completely as the metal in the damaged area will have stretched on impact and cannot be restored to its original contours. It is better to bring the level of the dent up to a point which is about 1/8-inch below the level of the surrounding metal. In cases where the dent is very shallow, it is not worth trying to pull it out at all.
21   If the back side of the dent is accessible, it can be hammered out gently from behind using a soft-face hammer. While doing this, hold a block of wood firmly against the opposite side of the metal to absorb the hammer blows and prevent the metal from being stretched.
22   If the dent is in a section of the body which has double layers, or some other factor makes it inaccessible from behind, a different technique is required. Drill several small holes through the metal inside the damaged area, particularly in the deeper sections. Screw long, self-tapping screws into the holes just enough for them to get a good grip in the metal. Now the dent can be pulled out by pulling on the protruding heads of the screws with locking pliers.
23   The next stage of repair is the removal of paint from the damaged area and from an inch or so of the surrounding metal. This is done with a wire brush or sanding disk in a drill motor, although it can be done just as effectively by hand with sandpaper. To complete the preparation for filling, score the surface of the bare metal with a screwdriver or the tang of a file, or drill small holes in the affected area. This will provide a good grip for the filler material. To complete the repair, see the subsection on filling and painting later in this Section.

Repair of rust holes or gashes

24   Remove all paint from the affected area and from an inch or so of the surrounding metal using a sanding disk or wire brush mounted in a drill motor. If these are not available, a few sheets of sandpaper will do the job just as effectively.
25   With the paint removed, you will be able to determine the severity of the corrosion and decide whether to replace the whole panel, if possible, or repair the affected area. New body panels are not as expensive as most people think and it is often quicker to install a new panel than to repair large areas of rust.
26   Remove all trim pieces from the affected area except those which will act as a guide to the original shape of the damaged body, such as headlight shells, etc. Using metal snips or a hacksaw blade, remove all loose metal and any other metal that is badly affected by rust. Hammer the edges of the hole in to create a slight depression for the filler material.
27   Wire brush the affected area to remove the powdery rust from the surface of the metal. If the back of the rusted area is accessible, treat it with rust inhibiting paint.
28   Before filling is done, block the hole in some way. This can be done with sheet metal riveted or screwed into place, or by stuffing

the hole with wire mesh.

29   Once the hole is blocked off, the affected area can be filled and painted. See the following subsection on filling and painting.

Filling and painting

30   Many types of body fillers are available, but generally speaking, body repair kits which contain filler paste and a tube of resin hardener are best for this type of repair work. A wide, flexible plastic or nylon applicator will be necessary for imparting a smooth and contoured finish to the surface of the filler material. Mix up a small amount of filler on a clean piece of wood or cardboard (use the hardener sparingly). Follow the manufacturer's instructions on the package, otherwise the filler will set incorrectly.

31   Using the applicator, apply the filler paste to the prepared area. Draw the applicator across the surface of the filler to achieve the desired contour and to level the filler surface. As soon as a contour that approximates the original one is achieved, stop working the paste. If you continue, the paste will begin to stick to the applicator. Continue to add thin layers of paste at 20-minute intervals until the level of the filler is just above the surrounding metal.

32   Once the filler has hardened, the excess can be removed with a body file. From then on, progressively finer grades of sandpaper should be used, starting with a 180-grit paper and finishing with 600-grit wet-or-dry paper. Always wrap the sandpaper around a flat rubber or wooden block, otherwise the surface of the filler will not be completely flat. During the sanding of the filler surface, the wet-or-dry paper should be periodically rinsed in water. This will ensure that a very smooth finish is produced in the final stage.

33   At this point, the repair area should be surrounded by a ring of bare metal, which in turn should be encircled by the finely feathered edge of good paint. Rinse the repair area with clean water until all of the dust produced by the sanding operation is gone.

34   Spray the entire area with a light coat of primer. This will reveal any imperfections in the surface of the filler. Repair the imperfections with fresh filler paste or glaze filler and once more smooth the surface with sandpaper. Repeat this spray-and-repair procedure until you are satisfied that the surface of the filler and the feathered edge of the paint are perfect. Rinse the area with clean water and allow it to dry completely.

35   The repair area is now ready for painting. Spray painting must be carried out in a warm, dry, windless and dust free atmosphere. These conditions can be created if you have access to a large indoor work area, but if you are forced to work in the open, you will have to pick the day very carefully. If you are working indoors, dousing the floor in the work area with water will help settle the dust which would otherwise be in the air. If the repair area is confined to one body panel, mask off the surrounding panels.

9.3 Before removing the hood, draw a mark around the hinge plate

This will help minimize the effects of a slight mismatch in paint color. Trim pieces such as chrome strips, door handles, etc., will also need to be masked off or removed. Use masking tape and several thickness of newspaper for the masking operations.

36   Before spraying, shake the paint can thoroughly, then spray a test area until the spray painting technique is mastered. Cover the repair area with a thick coat of primer. The thickness should be built up using several thin layers of primer rather than one thick one. Using 600-grit wet-or-dry sandpaper, rub down the surface of the primer until it is very smooth. While doing this, the work area should be thoroughly rinsed with water and the wet-or-dry sandpaper periodically rinsed as well. Allow the primer to dry before spraying additional coats.

37   Spray on the top coat, again building up the thickness by using several thin layers of paint. Begin spraying in the center of the repair area and then, using a circular motion, work out until the whole repair area and about two inches of the surrounding original paint is covered. Remove all masking material 10 to 15 minutes after spraying on the final coat of paint. Allow the new paint at least two weeks to harden, then use a very fine rubbing compound to blend the edges of the new paint into the existing paint. Finally, apply a coat of wax.

6   Body repair - major damage

1   Major damage must be repaired by an auto body/frame repair shop with the necessary welding and hydraulic straightening equipment.

2   If the damage has been serious, it is vital that the structure be checked for proper alignment or the vehicle's handling characteristics may be adversely affected. Other problems, such as excessive tire wear and wear in the driveline and steering may occur.

3   Due to the fact that all of the major body components (hood, fenders, etc.) are separate and replaceable units, any seriously damaged components should be replaced rather than

9.4 Use a small screwdriver to pry the retaining clip out of its locking groove, then detach the end of the strut from the mounting stud

repaired. Sometimes these components can be found in a wrecking yard that specializes in used vehicle components, often at considerable savings over the cost of new parts.

7   Hinges and locks - maintenance

Once every 3000 miles, or every three months, the hinges and latch assemblies on the doors, hood and trunk should be given a few drops of light oil or lock lubricant. The door latch strikers should also be lubricated with a thin coat of grease to reduce wear and ensure free movement. Lubricate the door and trunk locks with spray-on graphite lubricant.

8   Windshield and fixed glass - replacement

Replacement of the windshield and fixed glass requires the use of special fast setting adhesive/caulk materials. These operations should be left to a dealer or a shop specializing in glass work.

9   Hood - removal, installation and adjustment

Note: *The hood is somewhat awkward to remove and install, at least two people should perform this procedure.*

Removal and installation

Refer to illustrations 9.3 and 9.4

1   Open the hood, then place blankets or pads over the fenders and cowl area of the body. This will protect the body and paint as the hood is lifted off.

2   Disconnect any cables or wires that will interfere with removal.

3   Make marks or scribe a line around the hood hinge to ensure proper alignment during installation **(see illustration)**.

4   Have an assistant support the weight of the hood and detach the support struts **(see illustration)**.

These photos illustrate a method of repairing simple dents. They are intended to supplement *Body repair - minor damage* in this Chapter and should not be used as the sole instructions for body repair on these vehicles.

1 If you can't access the backside of the body panel to hammer out the dent, pull it out with a slide-hammer-type dent puller. In the deepest portion of the dent or along the crease line, drill or punch hole(s) at least one inch apart . . .

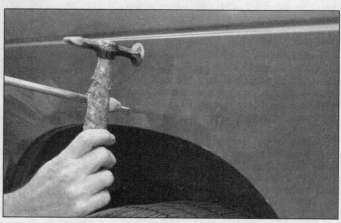

2 . . . then screw the slide-hammer into the hole and operate it. Tap with a hammer near the edge of the dent to help 'pop' the metal back to its original shape. When you're finished, the dent area should be close to its original contour and about 1/8-inch below the surface of the surrounding metal

3 Using coarse-grit sandpaper, remove the paint down to the bare metal. Hand sanding works fine, but the disc sander shown here makes the job faster. Use finer (about 320-grit) sandpaper to feather-edge the paint at least one inch around the dent area

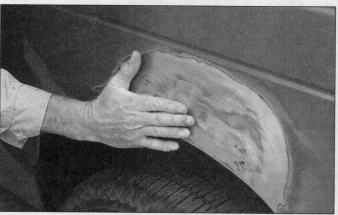

4 When the paint is removed, touch will probably be more helpful than sight for telling if the metal is straight. Hammer down the high spots or raise the low spots as necessary. Clean the repair area with wax/silicone remover

5 Following label instructions, mix up a batch of plastic filler and hardener. The ratio of filler to hardener is critical, and, if you mix it incorrectly, it will either not cure properly or cure too quickly (you won't have time to file and sand it into shape)

6 Working quickly so the filler doesn't harden, use a plastic applicator to press the body filler firmly into the metal, assuring it bonds completely. Work the filler until it matches the original contour and is slightly above the surrounding metal

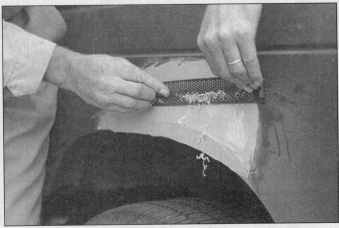

7 Let the filler harden until you can just dent it with your fingernail. Use a body file or Surform tool (shown here) to rough-shape the filler

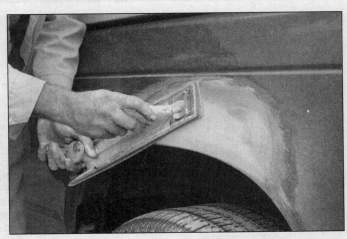

8 Use coarse-grit sandpaper and a sanding board or block to work the filler down until it's smooth and even. Work down to finer grits of sandpaper - always using a board or block - ending up with 360 or 400 grit

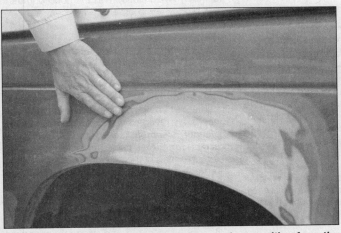

9 You shouldn't be able to feel any ridge at the transition from the filler to the bare metal or from the bare metal to the old paint. As soon as the repair is flat and uniform, remove the dust and mask off the adjacent panels or trim pieces

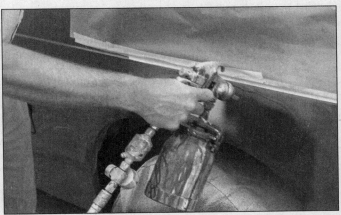

10 Apply several layers of primer to the area. Don't spray the primer on too heavy, so it sags or runs, and make sure each coat is dry before you spray on the next one. A professional-type spray gun is being used here, but aerosol spray primer is available inexpensively from auto parts stores

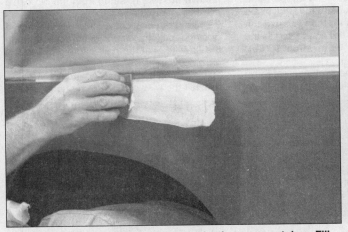

11 The primer will help reveal imperfections or scratches. Fill these with glazing compound. Follow the label instructions and sand it with 360 or 400-grit sandpaper until it's smooth. Repeat the glazing, sanding and respraying until the primer reveals a perfectly smooth surface

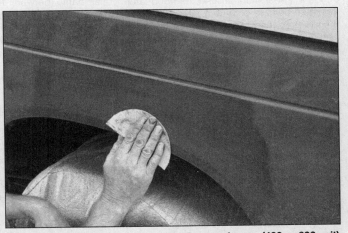

12 Finish sand the primer with very fine sandpaper (400 or 600-grit) to remove the primer overspray. Clean the area with water and allow it to dry. Use a tack rag to remove any dust, then apply the finish coat. Don't attempt to rub out or wax the repair area until the paint has dried completely (at least two weeks)

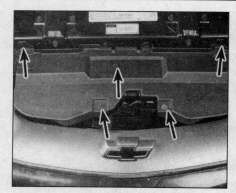

9.10a Remove the bolts and plastic retaining pins (arrows) securing the air deflector to access the hood latch assembly

9.10b Loosen the bolts (arrows) and move the hood latch to adjust the hood closed position

9.11 Screw the hood bumpers (arrow) in or out to adjust the hood flush with the fenders

5   Remove the hinge-to-hood bolts and lift off the hood.
6   Installation is the reverse of removal. Align the hinge bolts with the marks made in step 3.

Adjustment

Refer to illustrations 9.10a, 9.10b and 9.11

7   Fore-and-aft and side-to-side adjustment of the hood is done by moving the hinge plate slot after loosening the bolts or nuts.
8   Scribe a line around the entire hinge plate so you can determine the amount of movement.
9   Loosen the bolts or nuts and move the hood into correct alignment. Move it only a little at a time. Tighten the hinge bolts and carefully lower the hood to check the position.
10   If necessary after installation, the entire hood latch assembly can be adjusted up-and-down as well as from side-to-side on the radiator support so the hood closes securely and flush with the fenders. To make the adjustment, first remove the air deflector covering the hood latch **(see illustration)**. Scribe a line or mark around the hood latch mounting bolts to provide a reference point, then loosen them and reposition the latch assembly, as necessary **(see illustration)**. Following adjustment, retighten the mounting bolts.
11   Finally, adjust the hood bumpers on the radiator support so the hood, when closed, is

flush with the fenders **(see illustration)**.
12   The hood latch assembly, as well as the hinges, should be periodically lubricated with white, lithium-base grease to prevent binding and wear.

---

10   Hood latch and release cable - removal and installation

Warning: *The models covered by this manual are equipped with airbags. Always disable the airbag system (see Chapter 12) before working in the vicinity of the impact sensors, steering column or instrument panel. Failure to follow these procedures may cause accidental deployment of the airbag, which could cause personal injury. The airbag circuits are easily identified by yellow insulation covering the entire wiring harness. Do not use electrical test equipment on any of these wires or tamper with them in any way.*

Latch

Refer to illustration 10.2

1   If necessary, remove the upper radiator air baffle (between the radiator support and the grille). Scribe a line around the latch to aid alignment when installing, then remove the retaining bolts securing the hood latch to the radiator support **(see illustration 9.10b)**. Remove the latch.
2   Disconnect the hood release cable by disengaging the cable from the latch

assembly **(see illustration)**.
3   Installation is the reverse of removal.
Note: *Adjust the latch so the hood engages securely when closed and the hood bumpers are slightly compressed.*

Cable

Refer to illustrations 10.6 and 10.7

4   Disconnect the hood release cable from the latch assembly as described in step 1.
5   Attach a piece of thin wire or string to the end of the cable and unclip all remaining cable retaining clips. **Note:** *It may be necessary on some vehicles to remove the air cleaner assembly (see Chapter 4) to allow access for release cable removal.*
6   Working in the passenger compartment, remove the driver's side lower insulating panel **(see illustration)**.
7   Remove the two hood release lever mounting bolts and detach the hood release lever **(see illustration)**.
8   Pull the cable and grommet rearward into the passenger compartment until you can see the wire or string. Ensure that the new cable has a grommet attached then remove the wire or string from the old cable and fasten it to the new cable.
9   With the new cable attached to the wire or string, pull the wire or string back through the firewall until the new cable reaches the latch assembly.
10   Working in the passenger compartment, reinstall the new cable into the hood release

10.2 Pry out the cable retainer (arrow) from the backside of the hood latch assembly, then disengage the cable

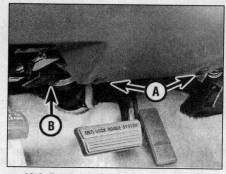

10.6 Detach the plastic clips (A) and remove the driver's side lower insulating panel (B) to access the hood release lever

10.7 Remove the hood release lever retaining screws (arrows) and pull the cable rearward into the passenger compartment

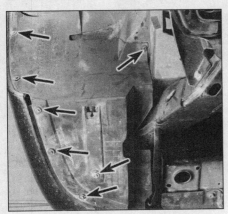

11.3 Remove the inner fenderwell extension panel screws (arrows) from inside the wheel opening and from the lower front corner(s) of the bumper cover

lever. Use pliers to crimp the retaining clip which secures the cable to the release lever.
11 The remainder of the installation is the reverse of removal. **Note:** *Push on the grommet with your fingers from the passenger compartment to seat the grommet in the firewall correctly.*

11 Bumpers - removal and installation

Warning: *The models covered by this manual are equipped with airbags. Always disable the airbag system (see Chapter 12) before working in the vicinity of the impact sensors, steering column or instrument panel. Failure to follow these procedures may cause accidental deployment of the airbag, which could cause personal injury. The airbag circuits are easily identified by yellow insulation covering the entire wiring harness. Do not use electrical test equipment on any of these wires or tamper with them in any way.*
Caution: *On models equipped with a Theftlock audio system, be sure the lockout feature is turned off before performing any procedure which requires disconnecting the battery.*

11.6 Using a ratchet, long extension and a socket, remove the front bumper retaining bolts (arrows)

11.4a Detach the lower air deflector . . .

Front bumper

Refer to illustrations 11.3, 11.4a, 11.4b, 11.5, 11.6 and 11.7
1   Open the hood and disconnect the negative battery cable.
2   Raise the front of the vehicle and support it securely on jackstands.
3   Working in the front wheel opening, detach the retaining screws securing the inner fenderwell to the bumper cover (**see illustration**). On earlier models, disconnect the side marker lamp electrical connectors. On later models, remove the inner fenderwell splash shields (see Section 12), headlights and fog lights, if equipped.
4   On earlier models, remove the lower radiator air deflector and the lower bumper cover support panel (**see illustrations**).
5   Remove the retaining screws/nuts securing the bumper cover to each fender (**see illustration**).
6   On earlier models, working under the front of the vehicle, remove the retaining nuts securing the bumper to the bumper energy absorbers (**see illustration**).
7   Remove the upper retaining pins securing the bumper cover in the hood opening (**see illustration**).
8   On earlier models, separate the bumper cover from the fenders, then pull the bumper assembly straight out and away from the vehicle to remove it.
9   To remove the bumper cover from the

11.7 Remove the the center pin to release the clips securing the bumper cover in the hood opening

11.4b . . . and the lower bumper cover support bolt (arrow)

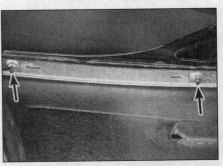

11.5 Detach the bolts (arrows) securing the bumper cover to both fenders

bumper, simply detach the plastic clips securing the upper and lower edges of the bumper cover.
10   Installation is the reverse of removal.

Rear bumper

Refer to illustrations 11.12, 11.13, 11.15a, 11.15b, 11.16 and 11.17
11   Apply the parking brake, raise the rear of the vehicle, support it securely on jackstands and remove the rear wheels.
12   Working in the rear wheel opening, detach the splash shield located at the rear of the wheel opening from each side of the vehicle (**see illustration**). To remove the rear splash shield on later models:

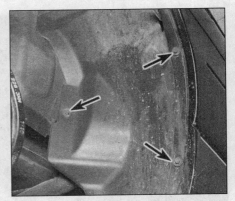

11.12 Detach the nuts, bolts and screws (arrows) and remove the rear wheel opening splash shield

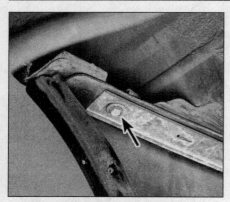

11.13 Working in the splash shield opening, remove the bolt (arrow) securing the bumper cover to the rear quarter panels

11.15a Fasteners (arrows) secure the bumper cover to the rear quarter panels. Later Monte Carlo models have two bolts (one upward, one downward) through the quarter panel and no nut at the tail light.

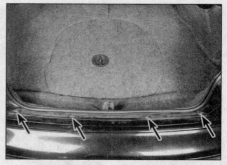

11.15b Remove the retaining clips securing the bumper in the trunk lid opening

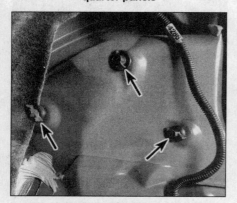

11.16 Detach the plastic retaining nuts (arrows) to release the tail light housing from the rear quarter panel

a) If equipped, drill out the plastic rivet at the bottom of the rear splash shield that attaches it to the rear bumper cover. Also remove the screw above it.

b) Remove the bolt and push-in retainer that secure the rear underside of the splash shield to the bottom of the bumper cover.

c) Remove the three nuts - one at the upper inside edge and two on the lower part of the outside edge.

11.17 Using a ratchet, long extension and a socket, remove the rear bumper retaining bolts (arrows)

d) Remove the two screws near the two lower nuts just removed.

13   Working under the vehicle, remove the retaining bolts securing the bumper cover to the rear quarter panels (see illustration).

14   Remove the license plate lamp. On earlier models, remove the rear side marker lights. On later Monte Carlo models, remove the back-up lights.

15   Working inside the trunk compartment, remove the plastic retaining nuts and clips

securing the trunk finishing panels. Peel back the trunk finishing panels and remove the remaining nuts and bolts securing the bumper cover to rear quarter panels and the trunk opening (see illustrations).

16   On earlier models, detach the rear tail light housings, disconnect the electrical connectors and remove both tail light housings from the vehicle (see illustration).

17   On earlier models, working back under the vehicle, remove the retaining nuts securing the bumper to the bumper energy absorbers (see illustration). Pull the bumper assembly straight out and away from the vehicle to remove it. To remove the bumper cover from the bumper, simply detach the plastic clips securing the upper and lower edges of the bumper cover.

18   On later models, remove the push-in retainers under the front edge of the bumper cover that secure it to the bumper. Remove the energy absorber, secured by two push-in retainers, and unbolt the bumper.

19   Installation is the reverse of removal.

12 Front fender - removal and installation

Refer to illustrations 12.4, 12.6a, 12.6b, 12.6c and 12.6d

1   Remove the hood (see Section 9). On later models, if removing the right fender, remove the windshield washer fluid reservoir.

12.4 Detach the inner fenderwell retaining bolts (arrows) and remove the inner fenderwell

12.6a Remove the retaining bolt (arrow) securing the front of the fender

2   Raise the vehicle, support it securely on jackstands and remove the front wheel.

3   Remove the rocker panel finish molding (if equipped) from the side of the vehicle that the fender is to be removed.

4   Remove the inner fenderwell splash shield **(see illustration)**, and, on later models, the front fender sound insulator. To remove the splash shield on later models:

   a) *If equipped, drill out the two plastic rivets that attach the front of the splash shield to the bumper cover and the one rivet that attaches the bottom rear to the rocker panel.*

   b) *Remove the three screws that secure the front underside of the splash shield to the bottom of the bumper cover.*

   c) *Remove the bolt that secures the front tab from the splash shield to the lower engine compartment side rail (it's in the space above the three screws just removed).*

   d) *Remove the nut from the stud on the rear inner side of the splash shield.*

   e) *Remove the five screws that secure the splash shield: three along the front outside edge, one along the rear edge, and one at the bottom rear.*

5   Remove the front bumper assembly (see Section 11).

6   Remove the remaining fender mounting bolts **(see illustrations)**.

7   Detach the fender. It's a good idea to have an assistant support the fender while it's being moved away from the vehicle to prevent damage to the surrounding body panels.

8   Installation is the reverse of removal.

---

13   Trunk lid and balance spring/strut - removal, installation and adjustment

---

Note: *The trunk lid is heavy and somewhat awkward to remove and install - at least two people should perform this procedure.*

Removal and installation

Trunk lid

Refer to illustration 13.3

1   Open the trunk lid and cover the edges of the trunk compartment with pads or cloths to protect the painted surfaces when the lid is removed.

2   Disconnect any cables or wire harness connectors attached to the trunk lid that would interfere with removal.

3   Make alignment marks around the trunk lid hinge bolts **(see illustration)**.

4   While an assistant supports the lid, remove the hinge bolts from both sides and lift the trunk lid off the vehicle.

5   Installation is the reverse of removal.

Note: *When reinstalling the trunk lid, align the hinge bolts with the marks made during removal.*

12.6b Remove the fender retaining bolt (arrow) located in the wheel opening

12.6c Remove the retaining bolts (arrows) securing the fender to the rocker panel

12.6d Detach the remaining bolts (arrows) in the hood opening, then remove the fender from the vehicle

Balance spring

Refer to illustration 13.7

6   Open the trunk lid and have an assistant support the lid.

7   Use a long piece of pipe or similar tool to pry the balance spring end up and over its retaining bracket **(see illustration)**.

8   Slide the balance spring out from the hinged end and remove it from the vehicle.

9   Installation is the reverse of removal.

Struts

10   Later models use struts (like small shock absorbers) rather than a spring to hold the trunk lid open. To replace a strut, lift the retainer at each end with a small screwdriver and pull each end out of its ball stud. Pull

only at the ends, not the middle, or you may damage the strut.

11   Installation is the reverse of removal. Each end of the strut should snap into the ball stud to seat completely.

Adjustment

Refer to illustrations 13.15 and 13.16

12   Fore-and-aft and side-to-side adjustment of the trunk lid is done by moving the hood in relation to the hinge plate after loosening the bolts or nuts.

13   Scribe a line around the hinge bolt heads as described earlier in this Section so you can judge the amount of movement.

14   Loosen the bolts or nuts and move the trunk lid into correct alignment. Move it only a

13.3 Before removing the trunk lid, draw marks around the bolt heads to aid in the reinstallation process

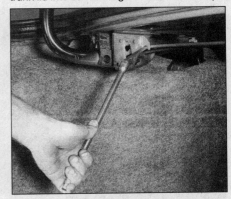

13.7 Pry the balance spring up and over the spring retaining bracket to release spring tension

13.15 Loosen the bolts (arrows) and move the latch assembly as necessary to adjust the trunk lid flush with the quarter panels in the closed position

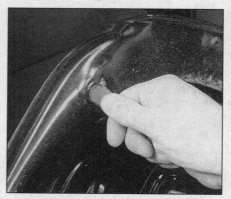

13.16 Adjust the bumpers so they're slightly compressed when the trunk lid is in the closed position

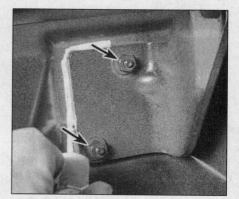

14.4 The latch striker is retained by nuts (arrows) - scribe a line around the striker before removal as a reference point

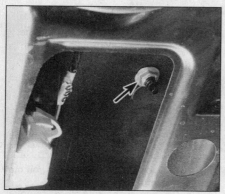

14.6a Remove the nuts (arrow) securing the center . . .

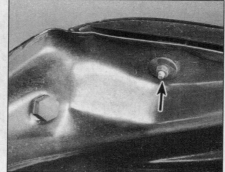

14.6b . . . and the outer edges (arrow) of the rear trim panel . . .

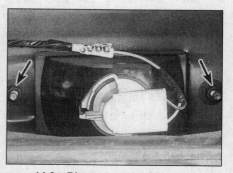

14.6c Disconnect the electrical connectors from the reverse lamps and remove the bolts (arrows), then detach the rear trim panel from the trunk lid and remove it from the vehicle

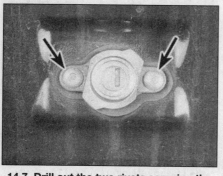

14.7 Drill out the two rivets securing the lock cylinder

little at a time. Tighten the hinge bolts or nuts and carefully lower the trunk lid to check the alignment.

15   If necessary after installation, the entire trunk lid latch assembly can be adjusted up and down as well as from side to side on the trunk lid so the lid closes securely and is flush with the rear quarter panels. To do this, scribe a line around the trunk lid latch mounting bolts to provide a reference point. Then loosen the bolts and reposition the latch assembly as necessary **(see illustration)**. Following adjustment, retighten the mounting bolts.

16   Adjust the bumpers on the trunk lid, so that the trunk lid is flush with the rear quarter panels when closed **(see illustration)**.

17   The trunk lid latch assembly, as well as the hinges, should be periodically lubricated with white lithium-base grease to prevent sticking and wear.

14   Trunk lid latch, latch striker and lock cylinder - removal and installation

Latch and latch striker

Refer to illustration 14.4

1   Unplug any electrical connectors and detach any cables from the latch assembly.

2   The trunk lid latch is retained by bolts/nuts which can readily be removed with a wrench **(see illustration 13.15)**. For adjustment procedures, see Section 13.

3   To access the striker, remove the plastic retaining nuts and clips securing the rear trunk finishing panel. Then scribe a line around the latch striker to provide a reference point.

4   Detach the striker retaining nuts/bolts and remove the striker from the vehicle **(see illustration)**. On later models, remove the license plate to expose an access hole through which the exterior striker retaining bolts can be removed.

5   Installation is the reverse of removal.

Lock cylinder

Refer to illustrations 14.6a, 14.6b, 14.6c and 14.7

6   On earlier models, remove the trunk lid rear trim panel **(see illustrations)**. On later Impala models, remove the trunk lid applique (the small panel that holds the back-up lights) by disconnecting the electrical connector and removing the wing nuts on the inside of the trunk lid.

7   On earlier models, and later Impala models, using a small drill bit, drill out the rivets securing the lock cylinder **(see illustration)**, then pull the lock cylinder out of the trunk lid and remove it from the vehicle.

8   On later Monte Carlo models, the lock cylinder is held in place by a retainer clip inside the trunk lid. Remove the clip and pull out the lock cylinder.

9   Installation is the reverse of removal.

15   Door trim panel - removal and installation

Caution: *On models equipped with a Theftlock audio system, be sure the lockout feature is turned off before performing any procedure which requires disconnecting the battery.*

15.1 Detach the retaining screw (arrow) and pull the inside handle lever to remove the bezel. On later Monte Carlo models, pry out the front and pull forward to release the rear clip.

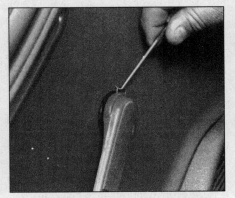

15.2 If your vehicle is equipped with manual windows, use a hooked tool like this to remove the window crank retaining clip

15.3 Use a small screwdriver to disengage the retaining clips securing the switch control plate

Removal

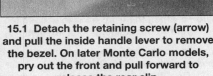

Refer to illustrations 15.1, 15.2, 15.3, 15.4, 15.5, 15.6a, 15.6b, 15.7 and 15.9

1   Disconnect the cable from the negative terminal of the battery. Remove the inside door handle trim bezel **(see illustration)**.

2   On manual window equipped models, remove the window crank, using a hooked tool to remove the retainer clip **(see illustration)**. A special tool is available for this purpose, but it's not essential. With the clip removed, pull off the handle.

3   On earlier power window equipped models, pry out the armrest switch control plate **(see illustration)** and disconnect the electrical connections. On some later models, this is part of a recessed pull cup, held by two screws, that provides a grip when closing the door. On later Impala models, also remove two screws from the pull handle bracket. If removing the front door trim panel on later Monte Carlo models, this step is unnecessary.

4   On earlier models, remove the finishing panel from above the armrest pull handle **(see illustration)**.

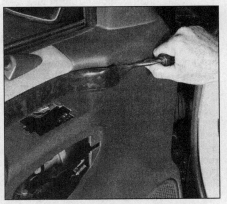

15.4 Use a small screwdriver or similar tool to pry out the armrest finishing panel

5   On earlier models, and later Monte Carlo models, detach the armrest pull handle retaining screw **(see illustration)**.

6   Remove the remaining door panel retaining screws securing the outer edge of the door panel **(see illustrations)**.

7   Insert a wide putty knife or a special trim panel removal tool between the trim panel and the head of the retaining clip to disengage the door panel retaining clips **(see illustration)**. Note: *Door trim panel retaining*

15.5 Remove the screws (arrow) securing the armrest pull handle

clips are approximately six to ten inches apart. Pry at the clip location only. Prying in between clips will result in distorted or damaged door trim panels.

8   Once all of the clips and screws are disengaged, detach the trim panel and remove the trim panel from the vehicle by gently pulling it up and out. **Note:** *On later Monte Carlo models, support the trim panel while disconnecting the power window and/or mirror switch electrical connectors.*

15.6a Remove the screws (arrow) securing the upper edge . . .

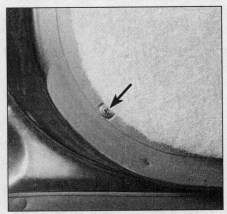

15.6b . . . and (on earlier models) lower edge (arrow) of the door trim panel

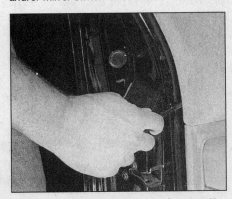

15.7 Insert a trim removal tool or a putty knife between the door and the trim panel to disengage the clips along the outer edge of the door trim panel

15.9 To access the inner door, detach the door panel support bracket retaining clip

9   For access to the inner door remove the door panel support bracket **(see illustration)**. Then peel back the watershield, taking care not to tear it.

10   To install the door panel, work through the window opening and engage the hooks on the back of the trim panel onto the door and push down until they are seated, then press the door panel retaining clips into place. When installing the lower retaining clips, be careful not to damage the speaker cones. **Note 1:** *The manufacturer advises that new retaining clips must be used when reinstalling the trim panel.* **Note 2:** *When installing door trim panel retaining clips, make sure the clips are lined up with their mating holes first, then gently tap inward with the palm of your hand.*

11   The remainder of the installation is the reverse of removal.

16   Door - removal, installation and adjustment

Caution: *On models equipped with a Theftlock audio system, be sure the lockout feature is turned off before performing any procedure which requires disconnecting the battery.*

Note: *The door is heavy and somewhat awkward to remove and install - at least two people should perform this procedure. This procedure applies to both front and rear doors.*

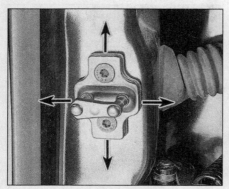

16.12 Adjust the door lock striker by loosening the mounting screws and gently tapping the striker in the desired direction

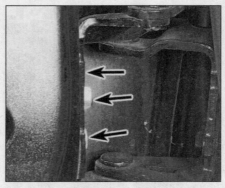

16.7a Front door retaining bolts (arrows)

Removal and installation

Refer to illustrations 16.7a and 16.7b

1   Raise the window completely and disconnect the negative cable from the battery if equipped with power windows.

2   Open the door all the way and support it on jacks or blocks covered with rags to prevent damaging the paint.

3   Remove the door trim panel and water shield (see Section 15).

4   Unplug all electrical connections, ground wires and harness retaining clips from the door. **Note:** *It is a good idea to label all connections to aid the reassembly process.*

5   Working on the door side, detach the rubber conduit between the body and the door. Pull the wiring harness through the conduit hole and remove the wiring from the door.

6   Mark around the door hinges with a pen or a scribe to facilitate realignment during reassembly.

7   Have an assistant hold the door, remove the hinge-to-door bolts **(see illustrations)** and lift the door off.

8   Installation is the reverse of removal.

Adjustment

Refer to illustration 16.12

9   Having proper door-to-body alignment is a critical part of a well functioning door assembly. First check the door hinge pins and bushings for excessive play. **Note:** *If the door can be lifted (1/16-inch or more) without*

17.2 Remove the latch retaining screws (arrows) from the end of the door, then detach the actuating rods and pull the latch assembly through the access hole

16.7b Open the front door to access the rear door retaining bolts (arrows)

the car body lifting with it the hinge pins and bushings should be replaced.

10   Door-to-body alignment adjustments are made by loosening the hinge-to-body bolts or hinge-to-door bolts and moving the door. Proper body alignment is achieved when the top of the doors are parallel with the roof section, the front door is flush with the fender, the rear door is flush with the rear quarter panel and the bottom of the doors are aligned with the lower rocker panel. If these goals can't be reached by adjusting the hinge-to-body or hinge-to-door bolts, body alignment shims may have to be purchased and inserted behind the hinges to achieve correct alignment.

11   To adjust the door closed position, first check that the door latch is contacting the center of the latch striker bolt. This can be checked by applying modeling clay or body caulk to the lock, then closing the door far enough to allow the striker to contact the clay and indicate its position. If not, remove the striker bolt and add or subtract washers to achieve correct alignment.

12   Finally, adjust the latch striker bolt as necessary (up and down or sideways) to provide positive engagement with the latch mechanism **(see illustration)** and secure the door panel flush with the center pillar or rear quarter panel.

17   Door latch, lock cylinder and handles - removal and installation

Door latch

Refer to illustration 17.2

1   Raise the window then remove the door trim panel and watershield as described in Section 15.

2   Remove the screws securing the latch to the door **(see illustration)**.

3   Working through the large access hole, position the latch as necessary to disengage the outside door handle and outside lock cylinder-to-latch rods and the inside handle-to-latch rod. On later Monte Carlo models, also remove the window channel retainer screw and the channel.

4   All door locking rods are attached by plastic clips. The plastic clips can be removed by unsnapping the portion engaging

17.9 To remove the lock cylinder, detach the plastic clip securing the lock rod, then pry off the lock cylinder retaining clip (arrow)

17.11 Lift the outside handle to access the retaining rivets (arrows)

17.15 Detach the actuating rods (A), drill out the handle retaining rivets (B), then remove the retaining bolt (C)

the connecting rod and then by pulling the rod out of its locating hole.

5   Position the latch as necessary to disengage the door lock actuator rod. Then remove the latch assembly from the door.

6   Installation is the reverse of removal.

Door lock cylinder and outside handle

Refer to illustrations 17.9 and 17.11

7   To remove the lock cylinder, raise the window and remove the door trim panel and watershield as described in Section 15. When removing the outside front door handle on later models, remove the bolt from the rear window channel - it's on the inside door panel, a little below the lock opening. Pull the lower window channel down, to disengage the retainer clip from the upper channel, and remove the channel.

8   Working through the large access hole, disengage the plastic clip that secures the lock cylinder to the latch rod.

9   Using a pair of pliers, slide the lock cylinder retaining clip out of engagement and remove the lock cylinder from the door **(see illustration)**.

10   To remove the outside handle, work through the access hole and disengage the plastic clip that secures the outside handle-to-latch rod.

11   On earlier models, drill out the rivets securing the outside handle **(see illustration)**. Later models have two bolts (heads inside the

door) instead of rivets, one covered by a hole plug. Remove the bolts. Then pull the handle out of the door and remove it from the vehicle.

12   Installation is the reverse of removal. When reinstalling the lower rear window channel, make sure the retainer clip engages with the upper channel. **Note:** *Later models have adjustable lock rods, which permits adjusting the amount of travel required (that is, the effort required to operate the handle). When installing these rods, all free play between the handle and the lock must be removed. Do not operate the handle before making this adjustment.*

Inside handle

Refer to illustration 17.15

13   Remove the door trim panel as described in Section 15 and peel away the watershield.

14   Detach the actuating rods from the handle and position them aside.

15   Drill out the rivet securing the inside handle **(see illustration)**.

16   Remove the handle retaining bolt. Then pull forward on the handle to disengage it from the inner door panel.

17   Installation is the reverse of removal.

18   Door window glass - removal and installation

Refer to illustrations 18.4 and 18.5

1   Remove the door trim panel and the plastic watershield (see Section 15).

2   Lower the window glass all the way down into the door.

3   Carefully pry out the inner and outer

weatherstripping from the door window opening. Later models have a sealing strip on the outside. To remove the strip from the front doors, remove the rearview mirror and the sealing strip retaining screw(s) on the inside of the door, then remove the strip. On rear doors, after removing the screws, pull the strip from the pinch-weld flange.

4   Loosen the front guide channel **(see illustration)** and remove the window frame weatherstripping.

5   Raise the window just enough to access the window retaining rivets (bolts on later models) through the hole in the door frame **(see illustration)**.

6   Place a rag over the glass to help prevent scratching the glass, then drill out the two glass mounting rivets or remove the bolts.

7   Remove the glass by pulling it up and out.

8   Installation is the reverse of removal. **Note 1:** *When replacing windows, install the forward regulator bolt first.* **Note 2:** *When replacing the sealing strip, both lips should not be rolled over and pointing downward, or the window will not operate correctly.*

19   Door window glass regulator - removal and installation

Refer to illustrations 19.4 and 19.5

Warning: *The regulator arms are under extreme pressure and can cause serious injury if the motor or counter-balance spring is removed without locking the sector gear. This can be done by inserting a bolt and nut through the holes in the backing plate and*

18.4 Remove the forward window guide channel retaining bolts (arrow)

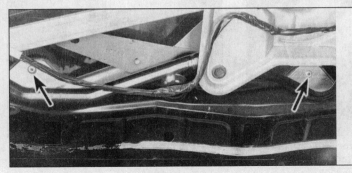

18.5 Raise the window just enough to access the glass-retaining rivets/bolts (arrow) through the hole in the door frame, then drill out the rivets or remove the bolts

19.4 Detach the window equalizer arm retaining bolt (arrow)

19.5 Remove the regulator retaining bolts (arrows) or drill out the window regulator rivets (if equipped) - earlier models

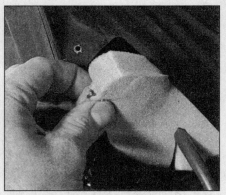

20.3 Peel out the foam insulating pad from the door window frame

sector gear to lock them together.
Caution: *On models equipped with a Theftlock audio system, be sure the lockout feature is turned off before performing any procedure which requires disconnecting the battery.*
1   Remove the door trim panel and the plastic watershield (see Section 15).
2   Remove the window glass assembly (see Section 18). It's also possible to perform this procedure with the glass in place. Leave a 1/4-inch opening at the top, and tape the glass securely to the window frame. Then drill out the rivets or remove the bolts that secure the window to the regulator.
3   On models with power windows, disconnect the electrical connector from the window regulator motor.
4   Remove the equalizer arm retaining bolt, if equipped **(see illustration)**.
5   Remove the retaining bolts or drill out the rivets that secure the window regulator to the door frame **(see illustration)**.
6   Pull the equalizer arm and regulator assemblies through the service hole in the door frame to remove it.
7   Installation is the reverse of removal.

20 Outside mirrors - removal and installation

Refer to illustrations 20.3 and 20.5
Caution: *On models equipped with a*

Theftlock audio system, be sure the lockout feature is turned off before performing any procedure which requires disconnecting the battery.
1   Disconnect the negative cable from the battery.
2   Remove the door trim panel and the plastic watershield (see Section 15).
3   Remove the foam insulating pad from the door window frame **(see illustration)**.
4   Disconnect the electrical connector from the mirror.
5   Remove the three mirror retaining nuts or bolts and detach the mirror from the vehicle **(see illustration)**.
6   Installation is the reverse of removal.

21 Center console - removal and installation

Refer to illustrations 21.3, 21.4, 21.6 and 21.7
Warning: *The models covered by this manual are equipped with airbags. Always disable the airbag system before working in the vicinity of the impact sensors, steering column or instrument panel to avoid the possibility of accidental deployment of the airbag(s), which could cause personal injury (see Chapter 12). The yellow wires and connectors routed*

through the console are for this system. Do not use electrical test equipment on these yellow wires or tamper with them in any way while working around the console.
Caution: *On models equipped with a Theftlock audio system, be sure the lockout feature is turned off before performing any procedure which requires disconnecting the battery.*
1   Disconnect the negative cable from the battery.
2   Apply the parking brake lever and place the gear selector into the neutral position (1995 through 1999 models) or second gear (2000 and later models).
3   On 1999 and earlier models, pry out the shift lever knob retaining clip and remove the knob **(see illustration)**. On 2000 and later models, open the storage compartment door. On later Monte Carlo models, remove the front bezel screw located ahead of the gear selector.
4   Pry out the gear selector trim bezel:
   a) *On 1995 through 1999 models, disengage the clips on the front edge (see illustration).*
   b) *On 2000 and later models, pry the rear of the bezel away from the console, then pull it backward to disengage it. Disconnect any accessible electrical connections. Remove the ashtray.*
5   Disconnect any remaining electrical connectors and remove the bezel from the

20.5 Outside mirror retaining nut locations (arrows)

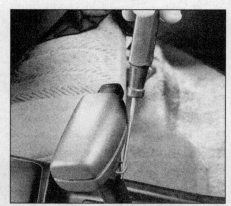

21.3 Pry out the retaining clip and remove the shift knob

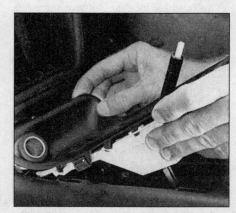

21.4 Pry out the gear selector trim bezel

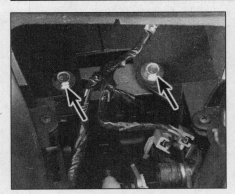

21.6 Remove the screws (arrows) located under the gear selector trim plate

21.7 Open the console glove box and remove the retaining screws (arrows), securing the rear half of the console

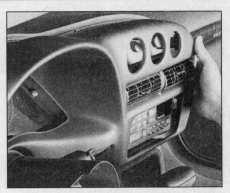

22.2 Grasp the Instrument cluster bezel and carefully pull outward to detach the retaining clips

console assembly. On 2000 and later models, rotate the bezel to allow it to pass over the shift lever knob.

6   Remove the retaining screws securing the front half of the console **(see illustration)**. Later Impala models also have a bolt near the instrument panel.

7   Working in the console glove box, remove the mat and detach the retaining screws securing the rear half of the console **(see illustration)**.

8   Lift the console up and over the shift lever. Disconnect any electrical connections and remove the console from the vehicle.

9   Installation is the reverse of removal.

22   Dashboard trim panels - removal and installation

Warning: *The models covered by this manual are equipped with airbags. Always disable the air bag system before working in the vicinity of the impact sensors, steering column or instrument panel to avoid the possibility of accidental deployment of the airbag(s), which could cause personal injury (see Chapter 12). The yellow wires and connectors routed through the instrument panel are for this system. Do not use electrical test equipment on these yellow wires or tamper with them in any way while working around the instrument panel.*

Caution: *On models equipped with a Theftlock audio system, be sure the lockout feature is turned off before performing any procedure which requires disconnecting the battery.*

Instrument cluster bezel
Refer to illustration 22.2

1   Tilt the steering wheel down to the lowest position. **Note:** *If the vehicle is equipped with a column shift lever, place the gear selector in the L1 position. On 2000 and later models:*

a)   *Move the shift lever (both column-shift and console models) to first gear. Use a small screwdriver to remove the bezel from the ignition switch cylinder. On column-shift models, leave the key in the switch.*

b)   *Remove the left underdash panel (see below) and the left fuse block access hole cover. On Impala models, also remove the right fuse block access hole cover. (The access hole covers are at either end of the dashboard.)*

c)   *Remove the bezel screws. Impala models have one in each fuse block opening and one at the steering wheel. Monte Carlo models have one in the left fuse block opening and one accessed by opening the glove box.*

2   Grasp the bezel securely and pull back sharply to detach the clips from the instrument

panel **(see illustration)**. On 2000 and later models, start at the right side. When removing the bezel on Monte Carlo models, twist the left side to clear the instrument panel.

3   Unplug any electrical connectors that interfere with removal.

4   Installation is the reverse of removal.

Left underdash panel
Refer to illustration 22.5

5   Remove the lower clips securing the left instrument panel insulator (see below) to the left underdash panel, then remove the underdash panel retaining screws **(see illustration)**.

6   Lift the lower edge of the underdash panel upward and detach the clips or fasteners on the upper edge.

7   Unplug any electrical connectors, then lower the trim panel from the instrument panel.

8   Installation is the reverse of removal.

Knee bolster
Refer to illustration 22.10

9   Remove the left underdash panel as described above.

10   Detach the knee bolster retaining screws and remove it from the vehicle **(see illustration)**.

11   Installation is the reverse of removal.

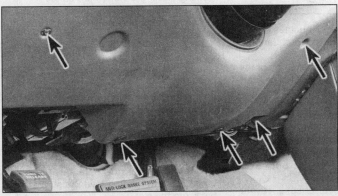

22.5 Lower steering column cover retaining screw and clip locations (arrows)

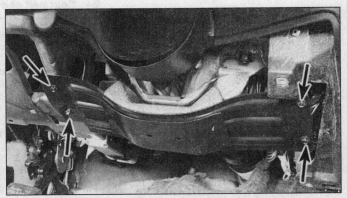

22.10 Knee bolster retaining bolt locations (arrows)

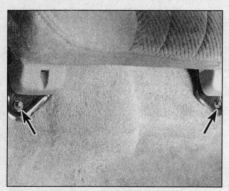

23.2 Detach the trim covers (if equipped) and remove the bolts (arrows) from the front and rear of the seat

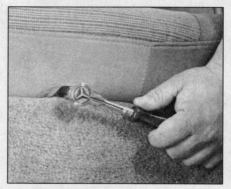

23.5 Using a socket and ratchet, remove the rear seat cushion retaining bolts

23.6 Detach the bolts securing the lower corners of the seat back, then lift upward and out to remove the seat back

Left and right instrument panel insulators

12   Detach the retainers on the insulator from the lower instrument panel trim pad and lower the insulator.
13   Twist the courtesy lamp counter-clockwise and remove it from the insulator.
14   If removing the left insulator, disengage it from the stud at the accelerator pedal.

Glove box

15   To remove the glove box, simply remove the screws from the hinge. On 2000 and later models, this will require removing the right instrument panel insulator (see above). Detach the doorstop cables (they slip into keyhole openings).
16   Squeeze the plastic sides in and lower the glove box from the instrument panel.
17   Installation is the reverse of the removal procedure.

23   Seats - removal and installation

Warning: *The models covered by this manual are equipped with airbags. Always disable the airbag system before working in the vicinity of the impact sensors, steering column or instrument panel to avoid the possibility of accidental deployment of the airbag(s), which could cause personal injury (see Chapter 12 for the airbag disabling procedure). The yellow wires and connectors routed through the instrument panel are for this system. Do not use electrical test equipment on these yellow wires or tamper with them in any way while working under the instrument panel.*

Front seat

Refer to illustration 23.2
1   Position the seat all the way forward or all the way to the rear to access the front seat retaining bolts. Refer to the **Warning** above and disable the airbag system. Disconnect the yellow airbag electrical connector, located under the seat.
2   Detach any bolt trim covers and remove the retaining bolts **(see illustration)**. On later models, remove the seatbelt nut from the door side of the seat.

3   Tilt the seat forward to access the underside, then disconnect any electrical connectors and hook attachments. Lift the seat from the vehicle.
4   Installation is the reverse of removal.

Rear seat

Refer to illustrations 23.5 and 23.6
5   On earlier models, remove the seat cushion retaining bolts **(see illustration)** (later models have no bolts). Then lift up on the front edge and remove the cushion from the vehicle. On later models, if the retainer comes out with the cushion, remove it and press it back into the floorpan.
6   Detach the retaining bolts at the lower edge of the seat back **(see illustration)**, then lift up on the lower edge of the seat back and remove it from the vehicle.
7   To remove folding seat backs, unbolt the center seatbelts. On later Monte Carlo models, also use a putty knife to detach the lower seat back trim panel clips and remove the panel.
8   Detach the retaining bolts and nut at the lower edge of the seat back.
9   Fold the seat backs down. Remove the bolts from the seat latches in the rear frame and remove the latches. Fold the seat backs up again and remove the seat back.
10   Installation is the reverse of removal.

24   Seat belt check

1   Check the seat belts, buckles, latch plates and guide loops for obvious damage and signs of wear.
2   See if the seat belt reminder light comes on when the key is turned to the Run or Start position. A chime should also sound.
3   The seat belts are designed to lock up during a sudden stop or impact, yet allow free movement during normal driving. Make sure the retractors return the belt against your chest while driving and rewind the belt fully when the buckle is unlatched.
4   If any of the above checks reveal problems with the seat belt system, replace parts as necessary.

25   Cross-vehicle brace - removal and installation

1   The cross-vehicle brace (used on later models) is at the back of the engine compartment and extends between the shock absorber towers at the two rear corners. To remove it, remove the nuts from each end of the brace. Have an assistant hold the stud plates, to keep them from falling when the brace is removed or installed. Reinstall the nuts temporarily to hold the stud plates in place.
2   Installation is the reverse of removal.

26   Steering column covers - removal and installation

Warning: *These models are equipped with airbags. Always disable the airbag system before working in the vicinity of the impact sensors, steering column or instrument panel to avoid the possibility of accidental deployment of the airbag(s), which could cause personal injury (see Chapter 12 for the airbag disabling procedure). The yellow wires and connectors routed through the instrument panel are for this system. Do not use electrical test equipment on these yellow wires or tamper with them in any way while working under the instrument panel.*
1   Disconnect the negative battery cable. On airbag-equipped models, disable the airbag system (see Chapter 12).
2   Remove the steering wheel (see Chapter 10).
3   Remove the tilt lever by pulling it straight out.
4   Remove the two lower retaining screws (if equipped) and the lower half of the steering column trim cover.
5   Remove the Torx-head screw (if equipped) and the upper half of the trim cover.
6   Installation is the reverse of removal. When replacing the tilt lever, push it straight back into the slot.

Chapter 12
Chassis electrical system

Contents

1   General information

The electrical system is a 12-volt, negative ground type. Power for the lights and all electrical accessories is supplied by a lead/acid-type battery which is charged by the alternator.

This Chapter covers repair and service procedures for the various electrical components not associated with the engine. Information on the battery, alternator, ignition system and starter motor can be found in Chapter 5. It should be noted that when portions of the electrical system are serviced, the negative battery cable should be disconnected from the battery to prevent electrical shorts and/or fires. **Caution:** *On models equipped with a Theftlock audio system, be sure the lockout feature is turned off before performing any procedure which requires disconnecting the battery.*

2   Electrical troubleshooting - general information

Refer to illustrations 2.5a, 2.5b, 2.6, 2.9 and 2.15

A typical electrical circuit consists of an electrical component, any switches, relays, motors, fuses, fusible links or circuit breakers related to that component and the wiring and connectors that link the component to both the battery and the chassis. To help you pinpoint an electrical circuit problem, wiring diagrams are included at the end of this Chapter.

Before tackling any troublesome electrical circuit, first study the appropriate wiring diagrams to get a complete understanding of what makes up that individual circuit. Trouble spots, for instance, can often be narrowed down by noting if other components related to the circuit are operating properly. If several components or circuits fail at one time, chances are the problem is in a fuse or ground connection, because several circuits are often routed through the same fuse and ground connections.

Electrical problems usually stem from simple causes, such as loose or corroded connections, a blown fuse, a melted fusible link or a failed relay. Visually inspect the condition of all fuses, wires and connections in a problem circuit before troubleshooting the circuit.

If test equipment and instruments are going to be utilized, use the diagrams to plan ahead of time where you will make the necessary connections in order to accurately pinpoint the trouble spot.

The basic tools needed for electrical troubleshooting include a circuit tester or voltmeter (a 12-volt bulb with a set of test leads can also be used), a continuity tester, which includes a bulb, battery and set of test leads, and a jumper wire, preferably with a circuit breaker incorporated, which can be used to bypass electrical components **(see illustrations)**. Before attempting to locate a problem with test instruments, use the wiring diagram(s) to decide where to make the connections.

Voltage checks

Voltage checks should be performed if a circuit is not functioning properly. Connect one lead of a circuit tester to either the negative battery terminal or a known good ground. Connect the other lead to a connector in the circuit being tested, preferably nearest to the battery or fuse **(see illustration)**. If the bulb of the tester lights, voltage is present, which means that the part of the circuit between the connector and the battery is problem free. Continue checking the rest of the circuit in the same fashion. When you reach a point at which no voltage is present, the problem lies between that point and the last test point with voltage. Most of the time the problem can be traced to a loose connection. **Note:** *Keep in mind that some circuits receive voltage only when the ignition key is in the Accessory or Run position.*

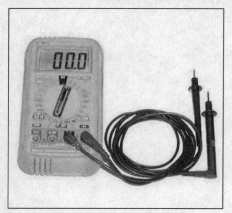

2.5a The most useful tool for electrical troubleshooting is a digital multimeter that can measure volts, amps and resistance

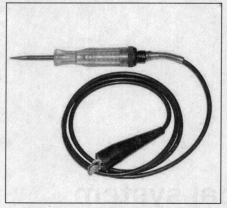

2.5b A test light is a very handy tool for checking voltage

2.6 In use, the test light lead is clipped to a known good ground, then the pointed probe can test connectors, wires or electrical sockets - if the bulb lights, the circuit being tested has battery voltage

Finding a short

One method of finding shorts in a circuit is to remove the fuse and connect a test light or voltmeter in place of the fuse terminals. There should be no voltage present in the circuit. Move the wiring harness from side-to-side while watching the test light. If the bulb goes on, there is a short to ground somewhere in that area, probably where the insulation has rubbed through. The same test can be performed on each component in the circuit, even a switch.

Ground check

Perform a ground test to check whether a component is properly grounded. Disconnect the battery and connect one lead of a continuity tester or multimeter (set to the ohms scale), to a known good ground. Connect the other lead to the wire or ground connection being tested. If the resistance is low (less than 5 ohms), the ground is good. If the bulb on a self-powered test light does not go on, the ground is not good.

Continuity check

A continuity check is done to determine if there are any breaks in a circuit - if it is passing electricity properly. With the circuit off (no power in the circuit), a self-powered continuity tester or multimeter can be used to check the circuit. Connect the test leads to both ends of the circuit (or to the "power" end and a good ground), and if the test light comes on the circuit is passing current properly **(see illustration)**. If the resistance is low (less than 5 ohms), there is continuity; if the reading is 10,000 ohms or higher, there is a break somewhere in the circuit. The same procedure can be used to test a switch, by connecting the continuity tester to the switch terminals. With the switch turned On, the test light should come on (or low resistance should be indicated on a meter).

Finding an open circuit

When diagnosing for possible open

circuits, it is often difficult to locate them by sight because the connectors hide oxidation or terminal misalignment. Merely wiggling a connector on a sensor or in the wiring harness may correct the open circuit condition. Remember this when an open circuit is indicated when troubleshooting a circuit. Intermittent problems may also be caused by oxidized or loose connections.

Electrical troubleshooting is simple if you keep in mind that all electrical circuits are basically electricity running from the battery, through the wires, switches, relays, fuses and fusible links to each electrical component (light bulb, motor, etc.) and to ground, from which it is passed back to the battery. Any electrical problem is an interruption in the flow of electricity to and from the battery.

Connectors

Most electrical connections on these vehicles are made with multiwire plastic connectors. The mating halves of many connectors are secured with locking clips molded into the plastic connector shells. The mating halves of large connectors, such as some of those under the instrument panel, are held together by a bolt through the center of the connector.

To separate a connector with locking

clips, use a small screwdriver to pry the clips apart carefully, then separate the connector halves. Pull only on the shell, never pull on the wiring harness as you may damage the individual wires and terminals inside the connectors. Look at the connector closely before trying to separate the halves. Often the locking clips are engaged in a way that is not immediately clear. Additionally, many connectors have more than one set of clips.

Each pair of connector terminals has a male half and a female half. When you look at the end view of a connector in a diagram, be sure to understand whether the view shows the harness side or the component side of the connector. Connector halves are mirror images of each other, and a terminal shown on the right side end-view of one half will be on the left side end view of the other half.

Backprobing a connector

It is often necessary to take circuit voltage measurements with a connector connected. Whenever possible, carefully insert a small straight pin (not your meter probe) into the rear of the connector shell to contact the terminal inside, then clip your meter lead to the pin. This kind of connection

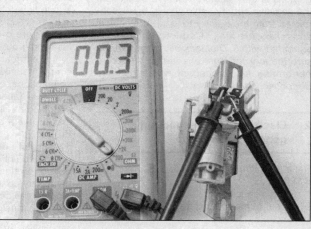

2.9 With a multimeter set to the ohms scale, resistance can be checked across two terminals - when checking for continuity, a low reading indicates continuity, a high reading indicates lack of continuity

2.15 To backprobe a connector, insert a small, sharp probe (such as a straight-pin) into the back of the connector alongside the desired wire until it contacts the metal terminal inside; connect your meter leads to the probes - this allows you to test a functioning circuit

3.1a The passenger compartment fuse block is located on the right side of the instrument panel and becomes accessible after removing the cover

3.1b There are two engine compartment fuse blocks, one located on the right side by the coolant reservoir . . .

is called "backprobing" (see illustration). When inserting a test probe into a male terminal, be careful not to distort the terminal opening. Doing so can lead to a poor connection and corrosion at that terminal later. Using the small straight pin instead of a meter probe results in less chance of deforming the terminal connector.

3   Fuses - general information

Refer to illustrations 3.1a, 3.1b, 3.1c and 3.3

1   The electrical circuits of the vehicle are protected by a combination of fuses, circuit breakers and fusible links. The fuse blocks are located under a cover on the right end of the instrument panel and in the engine compartment (see illustrations).

2   Each of the fuses is designed to protect a specific circuit, and the various circuits are identified on the fuse panel itself.

3   Miniaturized fuses are employed in the fuse block. These compact fuses, with blade terminal design, allow fingertip removal and replacement. If an electrical component fails, always check the fuse first. The easiest way to check fuses is with a test light. Check for power at the exposed terminal tips of each fuse. If power is present on one side of the fuse but not the other, the fuse is blown. A blown fuse can also be confirmed by visually inspecting it (see illustration).

4   Be sure to replace blown fuses with the correct type. Fuses of different ratings are physically interchangeable, but only fuses of the proper rating should be used. Replacing a fuse with one of a higher or lower value than specified is not recommended. Each electrical circuit needs a specific amount of protection. The amperage value of each fuse is molded into the fuse body. If the replacement fuse immediately fails, don't replace it again until the cause of the problem

3.1c . . . and another is located on the left side next to the windshield washer fluid reservoir - both fuse blocks contain fuses and relays

is isolated and corrected. In most cases, the cause will be a short circuit in the wiring caused by a broken or deteriorated wire.

4   Fusible links - general information

Some circuits are protected by fusible links. Fusible links are circuit protection devices that are part of the wiring harness itself, that are designed to melt and open the circuit when a short causes excessive current flow. Fusible links are used in circuits which are not ordinarily fused, such as the ignition circuit.

Although the fusible links appear to be a heavier gauge than the wire they are protecting, the appearance is due to the thick insulation. All fusible links are several wire gauges smaller than the wire they are designed to protect.

Fusible links cannot be repaired, but a new link of the same size wire can be put in its place. The procedure is as follows:

3.3 When a fuse blows, the element between the terminal melts - the fuse on the left is blown, the fuse on the right is good

a) *Disconnect the negative cable from the battery.*

b) *Disconnect the fusible link from the wiring harness.*

c) *Cut the damaged fusible link out of the wiring just behind the electrical connector.*

d) *Strip the insulation back approximately 1/2-inch.*

e) *Position the electrical connector on the new fusible link and crimp it into place.*

f) *Use rosin core solder at each end of the new link to obtain a good solder joint.*

g) *Use plenty of electrical tape around the soldered joint. No wires should be exposed.*

h) *Connect the battery ground cable. Test the circuit for proper operation.*

5   Circuit breakers - general information

Refer to illustrations 5.1 and 5.2

Circuit breakers protect components such as power windows, power seats and headlights. Several circuit breakers are

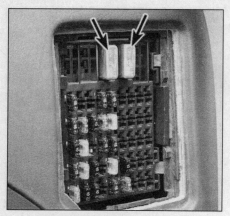

5.1 Circuit breakers for the power window and power seat circuits are located in the interior compartment fuse block

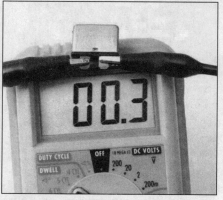

5.2 Perform a continuity test with an ohmmeter to check a circuit breaker - no reading (infinite resistance) indicates a bad circuit breaker

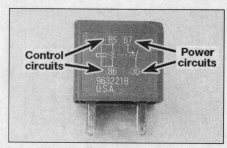

6.4 Most relays are marked on the outside to easily identify the control circuit and power circuits

located in the interior fuse box **(see illustration)**. On some models the circuit breaker resets itself automatically, so an electrical overload in the circuit will cause it to fail momentarily, then come back on. If the circuit doesn't come back on, check it immediately. Once the condition is corrected, the circuit breaker will resume its normal function. Some circuit breakers have a button on top and must be reset manually.

To test a circuit breaker, simply use an ohmmeter to check continuity between the terminals. A reading of zero to 1.0 ohms indicates a good circuit breaker. No reading on the meter indicates a bad circuit breaker **(see illustration)**.

6   Relays - general information and testing

General information

1   Several electrical accessories in the vehicle, such as the fuel injection system, horns, starter, and fog lamps use relays to transmit the electrical signal to the component. Relays use a low-current circuit (the control circuit) to open and close a high-current circuit (the power circuit). If the relay is defective, that component will not operate properly. The various relays are mounted in engine compartment **(see illustration 3.1b)** and several locations throughout the vehicle. If a faulty relay is suspected, it can be removed and tested using the procedure below or by a dealer service department or a repair shop. Defective relays must be replaced as a unit.

Testing

Refer to illustration 6.4

2   It's best to refer to the wiring diagram for the circuit to determine the proper hookups for the relay you're testing. However, if you're not able to determine the correct hook-up from the wiring diagrams, you may be able to determine the test hook-ups from the information that follows.

3   On most relays, two of the terminals are the relay's control circuit (they connect to the relay coil which, when energized, closes the large contacts to complete the circuit). The other terminals are the power circuit (they are connected together within the relay when the control-circuit coil is energized).

4   Most relays are marked as an aid to help you determine which terminals are the control circuit and which are the power circuit **(see illustration)**.

5   Connect a fused jumper wire between one of the two control circuit terminals and the positive battery terminal. Connect another jumper wire between the other control circuit terminal and ground. When the connections are made, the relay should click. On some relays, polarity may be critical, so, if the relay doesn't click, try swapping the jumper wires on the control circuit terminals.

6   With the jumper wires connected, check for continuity between the power circuit terminals as indicated by the markings on the relay.

7   If the relay fails any of the above tests, replace it.

7   Turn signal/hazard flasher - check and replacement

Refer to illustration 7.1

Warning: *The models covered by this manual are equipped with airbags. Always disable the airbag system before working in the vicinity of the impact sensors, steering column or instrument panel to avoid the possibility of accidental deployment of the airbag(s), which could cause personal injury (see Section 26). The yellow wires and connectors routed through the instrument panel are for this system. Do not use electrical test equipment on these yellow wires or tamper with them in any way while working under the instrument panel.*
Caution: *On models equipped with a Theftlock audio system, be sure the lockout feature is turned off before performing any procedure which requires disconnecting the battery.*

Check

1   Models from 1995 through 2001 use a single combination turn signal and hazard flasher. On 1995 through 2000 models, the flasher module is mounted in a junction block to the left of the steering column under the instrument panel **(see illustration)**. On 2001 models, the flasher module is part of the hazard flasher switch, on the right side of the instrument panel. On 2002 and later models, turn signal and hazard flashing is controlled electronically.

2   When the flasher unit on 2001 and earlier models is functioning properly, an audible click can be heard during its operation. If the turn signals fail on one side or the other and the flasher unit does not make its characteristic clicking sound, a faulty turn signal bulb is indicated.

3   If both turn signals fail to blink, the problem may be due to a blown fuse, a faulty flasher unit, a broken switch or a loose or open connection. If a quick check of the fuse box indicates that the turn signal fuse has blown, check the wiring for a short before installing a new fuse.

Replacement

4   On 1995 through 2000 models, remove the left instrument panel insulator (see Chapter 11). Disconnect the electrical connector and remove the flasher unit from the firewall.

5   On 1999 through 2001 models, remove the instrument panel trim bezel (see Chap-

7.1 On earlier models, the combination turn signal and hazard flasher (arrow) is mounted to the firewall just to the left of the steering column under the instrument panel

8.2 Use a small screwdriver to pry off the steering column trim cover (earlier models)

8.3a Remove the snap-ring and lift the airbag coil off

8.3b Use a special tool (available at most auto parts stores) to compress the lock plate for access to the retaining ring

ter 11). The hazard flasher switch comes off with the bezel.

6   Make sure that the replacement unit is identical to the original. Compare the old one to the new one before installing it.

7   Installation is the reverse of removal.

8   Steering column switches - removal and installation

Warning: *The models covered by this manual are equipped with airbags. Always disable the airbag system before working in the vicinity of the impact sensors, steering column or instrument panel to avoid the possibility of accidental deployment of the airbag(s), which could cause personal injury (see Section 26). The yellow wires and connectors routed through the instrument panel are for this system. Do not use electrical test equipment on these yellow wires or tamper with them in any way while working under the instrument panel.*
Caution: *On models equipped with a Theftlock audio system, be sure the lockout feature is turned off before performing any procedure which requires disconnecting the battery.*

Removal

Refer to illustrations 8.2, 8.3a, 8.3b, 8.4, 8.5, 8.6a, 8.6b, 8.6c and 8.8

1   Detach the cable from the negative

8.4 Remove the hazard warning knob (arrow)

battery terminal and disable the airbag system (see Section 26).

2   Remove the steering wheel (see Chapter 10) and the steering column trim cover **(see illustration** and Chapter 11**)**.

1995 through 1999 models

3   Remove the airbag coil retaining snap-ring and remove the coil assembly; let the coil hang by the wiring harness. Remove the wave washer. Using a lock plate removal tool, depress the lock plate for access to the retaining ring **(see illustrations)**. Use a small

8.5 Remove the cancel cam assembly

screwdriver to pry the retaining ring out of the groove in the steering shaft and remove the lock plate.

4   Use a small screwdriver to remove the hazard warning knob **(see illustration)**.

5   Remove the turn signal cancel cam **(see illustration)**.

6   Disconnect the electrical connector from the turn signal lever then pull the lever straight out to detach from the switch assembly. Detach the retaining screws securing the dimmer switch and position it to the side, then remove the turn signal switch mounting screws **(see illustrations)**.

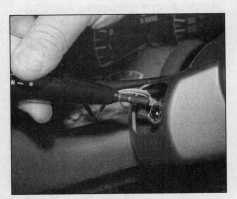

8.6a Grasp the turn signal lever securely and pull it straight out to detach it

8.6b Remove the dimmer switch retaining screws (arrows), then position it to the side

8.6c Place the switch in the right turn position to access all the switch retaining screws (arrows)

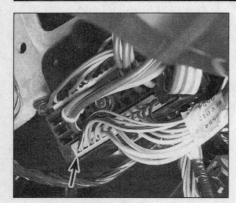

8.7 The turn signal switch electrical connector is located under the dash near the steering column

8.14 To center the airbag coil, depress the spring lock (arrow); rotate the hub in the direction of the arrow until it stops; back the hub off 2-1/2 turns and release the spring lock

8.15 When properly installed, the airbag coil will be centered with the marks aligned (circle) and the tab fitted between the projections on the top of steering column (arrow)

7   Remove the left underdash panel and the knee bolster as described in Chapter 11. Locate the turn signal switch electrical connector and unplug it **(see illustration)**. Remove the wiring protector.

8   Pull the wiring harness and electrical connector up through the steering column and remove the switch assembly.

2000 and later models

9   Unclip the wiring harness from the strap on the column, noting which connectors it retains - it must be reinstalled the same way. Slide the two side connectors (for the turn signal and multifunction switches) out of the main connector (for the airbag coil). Remove the two screws from the top and left side of the switch assembly and remove the switch.

Installation

Refer to illustrations 8.14 and 8.15

1995 through 1999 models

10   Feed the turn signal switch connector and wiring harness down through the column. Use a section of mechanics wire to pull it through, if necessary.

11   Plug in the connector and replace the wiring protector.

12   Seat the turn signal switch on the column and install the turn signal switch mounting screws and lever arm. Install the hazard knob and multi-function lever. Press the multi-function lever straight in until it snaps in place.

13   Install the cancel cam and the lock plate. Depress the lock plate and install the retaining ring.

14   If necessary, center the airbag coil as follows (it will only become uncentered if the spring lock is depressed and the hub rotated with the coil off the column) **(see illustration)**:

a) *Turn the coil over and depress the spring lock.*

b) *Rotate the hub in the direction of the arrow until it stops.*

c) *Rotate the hub in the opposite direction 2-1/2 turns and release the spring lock.*

15   Install the wave washer and the airbag

coil **(see illustration)**. Pull the slack out of the airbag coil lower wiring harness to keep it tight through the steering column, or it may be cut when the steering wheel is turned. Install the airbag coil retaining snap-ring.

16   The remainder of installation is the reverse of removal.

2000 and later models

17   Installation is the reverse of removal. **Note:** *The electrical contact on the switch assembly must rest on the turn signal cancel cam* **(see illustration 8.5)**.

---

9   Ignition switch and key lock cylinder - removal and installation

Warning: *The models covered by this manual are equipped with airbags. Always disable the airbag system before working in the vicinity of the impact sensors, steering column or instrument panel to avoid the possibility of accidental deployment of the airbag(s), which could cause personal injury (see Section 26). The yellow wires and connectors routed through the instrument panel are for this system. Do not use electrical test equipment on*

9.3 Lift off the buzzer switch and clip with needle-nose pliers or a small screwdriver

these yellow wires or tamper with them in any way while working under the instrument panel. **Caution:** *On models equipped with a Theftlock audio system, be sure the lockout feature is turned off before performing any procedure which requires disconnecting the battery.*

1995 through 1999 models

Lock cylinder

Refer to illustrations 9.3 and 9.4

1   The lock cylinder is located on the upper right-hand side of the steering column. It should be removed only in the Run position, otherwise damage to the warning buzzer switch may occur.

2   Remove the steering wheel (Chapter 10) and turn signal switch (see Section 8). **Note:** *The turn signal switch need not be fully removed provided that it is pushed to the rear far enough for it to be slipped over the end of the shaft. Do not pull the harness out of the column.*

3   Insert the key and place the lock cylinder in the Run position, then use needle-nose pliers or a small screwdriver to remove the buzzer switch **(see illustration)**.

4   Remove the lock cylinder retaining screw **(see illustration)**.

9.4 The lock cylinder is held in place by a Torx-head screw (arrow)

9.12a Remove the bolts (arrows) securing the steering column to the lower edge of the instrument panel

9.12b Detach one bolt (arrow) at the base of the steering column to help lower the column enough to access the ignition switch

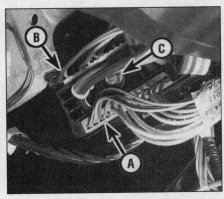

9.13a Disconnect the turn signal switch connector (A), the dimmer switch connector (B) and the ignition switch connector retaining bolt (C)

9.13b After the steering column has been lowered, remove the ignition switch retaining screws (arrows)

5   Remove the lock cylinder by turning the key to the Start position, then pulling the assembly straight out.
6   To install, rotate the lock cylinder and align the cylinder key with the keyway in the steering column housing.
7   Push the lock all the way in and install the retaining screw.
8   Install the remaining components, referring to the appropriate Sections.

Ignition switch

Refer to illustrations 9.12a, 9.12b, 9.13a and 19.13b

9   Disconnect the negative cable at the battery and disable the airbag system as described in Section 26.
10   Place the ignition switch in the Lock position. If the key lock cylinder has been removed, pull the actuating rod up until a definite stop can be felt, then move it down one detent.
11   Remove the left underdash panel from beneath the steering column.
12   Remove the bolts that secure the steering column to the dash assembly **(see illustrations)**, then carefully lower steering column down and rest the steering wheel on the seat. On column shift models, remove the shift indicator cable clip and detach the PRNDL adjuster bracket.
13   Disconnect the turn signal switch and the dimmer switch electrical connectors from the ignition switch connector at the base of the steering column, then remove the ignition switch connector **(see illustration)**. Remove the ignition switch retaining screws **(see illustration)** and lift the switch out of the steering column jacket. On floor shift models, detach the park lock cable from the ignition switch.
14   Prior to installation, make sure the ignition switch is in the Lock position.
15   Connect the actuating rod to the switch.
16   Press the switch into position and install the screws.
17   The remainder of the installation is the reverse of the removal. Raise the steering column into position and install and tighten the nuts to 20 ft-lbs. Make sure the switch is actuated when the ignition key is turned to

the Start position. If it doesn't, loosen the switch screws and adjust the position of the switch on the steering column.

2000 and later models

Ignition switch and lock cylinder

Note: *Removing the lock cylinder on these models requires removal of the ignition switch.*

18   Disconnect the negative cable at the battery and disable the airbag system as described in Section 26.
19   Remove the instrument cluster bezel, left underdash panel and knee bolster (see Chapter 11).
20   Remove the two ignition switch retaining bolts and the switch. Insert the key and turn it to the On position.
21   Remove the park/lock cable by pressing the retainer to release it, then pulling it from the switch.
22   Release the lock cylinder by pressing the detent on the bottom of the switch and removing the cylinder with the key.
23   Disconnect the electrical connectors, including the Passlock connector, if equipped. (The lock cylinder must be removed before the Passlock connector can be removed.)
24   Installation is the reverse of removal.

10   Headlight switch - removal and installation

Refer to illustrations 10.3a and 10.3b

Warning: *The models covered by this manual are equipped with airbags. Always disable the airbag system before working in the vicinity of the impact sensors, steering column or instrument panel to avoid the possibility of accidental deployment of the airbag(s), which could cause personal injury (see Section 26). The yellow wires and connectors routed through the instrument panel are for this system. Do not use electrical test equipment on these yellow wires or tamper with them in any way while working under the instrument panel.*

Caution: *On models equipped with a Theft-lock audio system, be sure the lockout feature is turned off before performing any procedure which requires disconnecting the battery.*

Note: *To remove the dimmer switch follow the steering column switch removal procedures (see Section 8).*

1   Detach the cable from the negative battery terminal and disable the airbag system (see Section 26).
2   Remove the instrument cluster bezel (see Chapter 11).
3   On earlier models, pry out the defogger

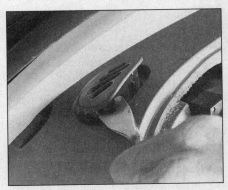

10.3a Using a small screwdriver or a trim removal tool pry out the defogger grille from the corner of the instrument panel

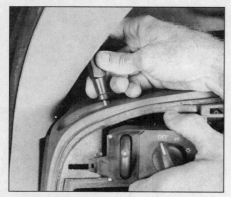

10.3b Depress the switch locking tabs and pull the switch outward to remove it

11.3a Remove the bolts (arrows) securing the radio

grille from the corner of the instrument panel **(see illustration)**. Using a small screwdriver detach the retaining clips securing the switch **(see illustration)**.

4   On later models, remove the two screws that secure the switch to the instrument panel.

5   Disconnect the electrical connector and remove the switch from the vehicle.

6   Installation is the reverse of removal.

11 Radio and speakers - removal and installation

Warning: *The models covered by this manual are equipped with airbags. Always disable the airbag system before working in the vicinity of the impact sensors, steering column or instrument panel to avoid the possibility of accidental deployment of the airbag(s), which could cause personal injury (see Section 26). The yellow wires and connectors routed through the instrument panel are for this system. Do not use electrical test equipment on these yellow wires or tamper with them in any way while working under the instrument panel.*

Caution: *On models equipped with a Theftlock audio system, be sure the lockout feature is turned off before performing any procedure which requires disconnecting the battery.*

Radio

Refer to illustrations 11.3a and 11.3b

1   Detach the cable from the negative battery terminal and disable the airbag system (see Section 26).

2   Remove the instrument cluster bezel (see Chapter 11).

3   Remove the screws, pull the radio out and disconnect the electrical connection and antenna lead **(see illustrations)**.

4   Remove the radio from the instrument panel.

5   Installation is the reverse of removal.

Note: *After installing a DE 153 series radio, perform the Radio Setup procedure, using a scan tool.*

11.3b Pull the radio out, support it and unplug the connectors

Front speakers

Refer to illustration 11.7

6   Remove the front door trim panel (see Chapter 11).

7   Remove the speaker retaining bolts. Disconnect the electrical connector and remove the speaker from the vehicle **(see illustration)**.

8   Installation is the reverse of removal.

Note: *On Impala models with two speakers in each door, the manufacturer advises replacing both speakers as a set.*

Rear speakers

9   Remove the rear seat from the vehicle (see Chapter 11). On later Impala models, remove the rear upper quarter trim panel by pulling down and out to disengage the retainer clips, then sliding the roof leg out from under the trim panel over the door. On later Monte Carlo models, remove the rear upper quarter trim panel by removing the coat hook and disengaging the push-in retainers.

10   Detach the rear seat belts through the slot in the rear parcel shelf.

11   Pry up the plastic clips securing the rear parcel shelf. Then lift up and out to remove it from the vehicle.

12   Remove the speaker retaining screws or tabs. If the speaker seal has bonded with the metal shelf, hold the tabs and pry the housing away from the metal. Disconnect the electrical connector and remove the speaker from the vehicle.

13   Installation is the reverse of removal.

11.7 Remove the screws (arrows), detach the speaker and unplug the electrical connector

12 Antenna - removal and installation

Caution: *On models equipped with a Theftlock audio system, be sure the lockout feature is turned off before performing any procedure which requires disconnecting the battery.*

Fixed antenna

Refer to illustrations 12.2, 12.3 and 12.4

1   Working in the trunk, pry out the plastic clips securing the passenger side trunk finishing panels to allow access to the backside of the antenna.

2   Disconnect the antenna lead from the

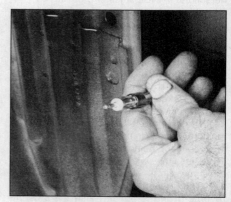

12.2 Detach the antenna lead from the antenna base by pulling the cable straight out

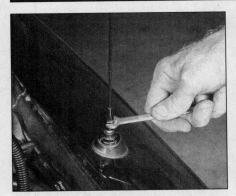

12.3 Use a small wrench to remove the antenna mast

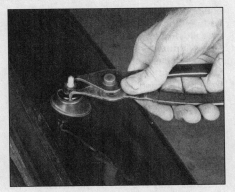

12.4 The antenna base retaining nut can be removed using a pair of snap-ring pliers or similar tool

13.5 When measuring the voltage at the rear window defogger grid, wrap a piece of aluminum foil around the positive probe of the voltmeter and press the foil against the wire with your finger

antenna base **(see illustration)**.

3   Use a small wrench and remove the antenna mast **(see illustration)**.

4   Using a pair of snap-ring pliers or similar tool, detach the antenna base retaining nut and remove the antenna base assembly from the vehicle **(see illustration)**.

5   Installation is the reverse of removal.

Power antenna mast

Note: *At least two people should perform this task.*

6   Remove the antenna mast retaining nut **(see illustration 12.4)**.

7   With one person controlling the ignition switch and the second person holding the antenna mast, turn the ignition key and the radio to the ON position. This will enable the antenna mast to unwind itself from the motor assembly.

8   When installing the antenna mast insert the antenna cable with the teeth facing the antenna motor. Then have your assistant turn the ignition key and the radio to the ON position. This will enable the antenna mast to wind itself back into the motor assembly.

9   The remainder of the installation is the reverse of removal.

Power antenna motor

10   Remove the antenna mast retaining nut **(see illustration 12.4)**.

11   Working in the trunk, pry out the plastic clips securing the passenger side trunk finishing panels to allow access to the antenna motor.

12   Detach the motor retaining bolts. Disconnect the electrical connector, antenna lead and the antenna ground strap then remove the antenna motor from the vehicle.

13   Installation is the reverse of removal.

13   Rear window defogger - check and repair

1   The rear window defogger consists of a number of horizontal elements baked onto the glass surface.

2   Small breaks in the element can be repaired without removing the rear window.

Check

Refer to illustrations 13.5 and 13.6

3   Turn the ignition switch and defogger system switches to the ON position.

4   Using a voltmeter, place the positive probe against the battery feed terminal and the negative probe against the negative (ground) bus bar. The positive terminal is located on the drivers side and the negative terminal is located on the passengers side. If battery voltage is not indicated, check the fuse, defogger switch and related wiring.

5   When measuring voltage during the next two tests, wrap a piece of aluminum foil around the tip of the voltmeter positive probe and press the foil against the heating element with your finger **(see illustration)**.

6   Place the negative lead against the negative (ground) bus bar. Check the voltage at the center of each heating element **(see illustration)**. If the voltage is 6-volts, the element is okay (there is no break). If the voltage is 10-volts or more, the element is broken somewhere between the mid-point and ground. If the voltage is 0-volts the element is broken between the mid-point and the positive side.

7   To find the break, slide the probe toward the positive side. The point at which the voltmeter deflects from zero to several volts is the point at which the heating element is broken. **Note:** *If the heating element is not broken, the voltmeter will indicate 12-volts at the positive side and gradually decrease to 0-volts as you slide the positive probe toward the ground side.*

Repair

Refer to illustration 13.13

8   Repair the break in the element using a repair kit specifically recommended for this purpose, such as Dupont paste No. 4817 (or equivalent). Included in this kit is plastic conductive epoxy.

9   Prior to repairing a break, turn off the system and allow it to cool off for a few minutes.

13.6 To determine if a heating element has broken, check the voltage at the center of each element - if the voltage is 6-volts, the element is unbroken

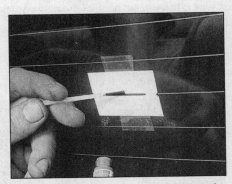

13.13 To use a defogger repair kit, apply masking tape to the inside of the window at the damaged area, then brush on the special conductive coating

10   Lightly buff the element area with fine steel wool, then clean it thoroughly with rubbing alcohol.

11   Use masking tape to mask off the area being repaired.

12   Thoroughly mix the epoxy, following the instructions provided with the repair kit.

13   Apply the epoxy material to the slit in the masking tape, overlapping the undamaged

14.3 Rotate the headlight bulb holder counterclockwise and pull the bulb socket assembly out of the housing - when installing the new bulb, don't touch the surface (clean it with rubbing alcohol if you do)

area about 3/4-inch on either end **(see illustration)**.

14   Allow the repair to cure for 24 hours before removing the tape and using the system.

14   Headlight bulb - replacement

Refer to illustration 14.3

Warning: *Halogen gas filled bulbs are under pressure and may shatter if the surface is scratched or the bulb is dropped. Wear eye protection and handle the bulbs carefully, grasping only the base whenever possible. Do not touch the surface of the bulb with your fingers because the oil from your skin could cause it to overheat and fail prematurely. If you do touch the bulb surface, clean it with rubbing alcohol.*

1   Open the hood.

2   Remove the headlight housing (see Section 15).

3   Remove the rubber access cover (if

equipped). Rotate the headlight bulb holder counterclockwise as viewed from the rear **(see illustration)**.

4   Withdraw the bulb assembly from the headlight housing.

5   Remove the bulb from the bulb holder by pulling it straight out.

6   If it's necessary to replace the bulb holder, simply unplug the electrical connector and replace it with a new one.

7   Without touching the glass with your bare fingers, insert the new bulb into the socket assembly and then lock the bulb holder into the place by aligning the tabs with the headlight housing and rotating the bulb holder clockwise until stops.

8   Reinstall the headlight housing and test the headlight operation, then close the hood.

15   Headlight housing - removal and installation

Refer to illustrations 15.1 and 15.2

Warning: *The models covered by this manual are equipped with airbags. Always disable the airbag system before working in the vicinity of the impact sensors, steering column or instrument panel to avoid the possibility of accidental deployment of the airbag(s), which could cause personal injury (see Section 26). The yellow wires and connectors routed through the instrument panel are for this system. Do not use electrical test equipment on these yellow wires or tamper with them in any way while working under the instrument panel.*

1   Remove the radiator baffle retaining clip and position the top of the baffle aside **(see illustration)**.

2   While holding the headlight housing in place, remove the thumbscrews or clips securing the housing to the housing support **(see illustration)**.

3   If necessary, pull the inboard end out

15.1 Detach the retaining clip securing the radiator air baffle

slightly, then slide the headlight housing towards the center of the vehicle to dislodge the retaining clips from the outer edge.

4   Disconnect the headlight bulbs (see Section 14) and the turn signal bulb from the headlight housing and remove the housing from the vehicle.

5   The remainder of the installation is the reverse of removal.

16   Headlights - adjustment

Refer to illustrations 16.1 and 16.3

Caution: *The headlights must be aimed correctly. If adjusted incorrectly they could blind the driver of an oncoming vehicle and cause a serious accident or seriously reduce your ability to see the road. The headlights should be checked for proper aim every 12 months and any time a new headlight is installed or front end body work is performed. It should be emphasized that the following procedure is only an interim step which will provide temporary adjustment until the headlights can be adjusted by a properly equipped shop.*

1   Headlights have two spring-loaded

15.2 Working behind the headlight housing, detach the headlight housing retaining screws (arrows)

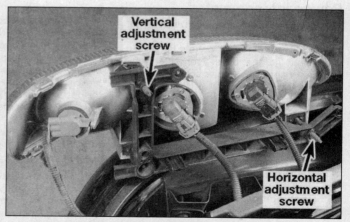

16.1 The headlight adjustment screws (arrows) can be accessed from behind the headlight housing - a Torx-head tool will be required for making headlight adjustments (headlight housing removed for clarity purposes only)

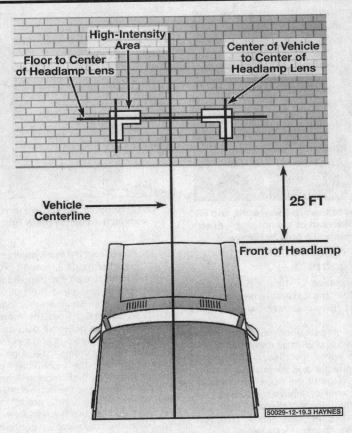

High-Intensity Area

Floor to Center of Headlamp Lens

Center of Vehicle to Center of Headlamp Lens

Vehicle Centerline

25 FT

Front of Headlamp

50029-12-19.3 HAYNES

16.3 Headlight aiming details

17.2 After the headlight housing has been removed, the front turn signal/parking light bulb can be replaced by depressing the socket retaining clip (arrow) and rotating it counterclockwise

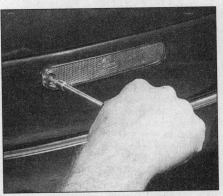

17.4 Remove the side marker/turn signal housing retaining screw (arrow) . . .

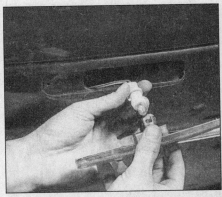

17.5 . . . then rotate the bulb socket counterclockwise to separate it from the lens

adjusting screws, one on the top controlling up-and-down movement and one on the side controlling left-and-right movement **(see illustration)**.

2   There are several methods of adjusting the headlights. The simplest method requires a blank wall 25 feet in front of the vehicle and a level floor.

3   Position masking tape vertically on the wall in reference to the vehicle centerline and the centerlines of both headlights **(see illustration)**.

4   Position a horizontal tape line in reference to the centerline of all the headlights. **Note:** *It may be easier to position the tape on the wall with the vehicle parked only a few inches away.*

5   Adjustment should be made with the vehicle sitting level, the gas tank half-full and no unusually heavy load in the vehicle.

6   Starting with the low beam adjustment, position the high intensity zone so it is two inches below the horizontal line and two inches to the right of the headlight vertical line. Adjustment is made by turning the top adjusting screw clockwise to raise the beam and counterclockwise to lower the beam. The adjusting screw on the side should be used in the same manner to move the beam left or right.

7   With the high beams on, the high intensity zone should be vertically centered with the exact center just below the horizontal line. **Note:** *It may not be possible to position the headlight aim exactly for both high and low beams. If a compromise must be made, keep in mind that the low beams are the most used and have the greatest effect on safety.*

8   Have the headlights adjusted by a dealer service department or service station at the earliest opportunity.

17   Bulb replacement

Front turn signal and parking lights

Refer to illustration 17.2

1   Remove the headlight housing as described in Section 15.

2   Depress the socket retaining clip and twist the bulb socket a quarter turn counterclockwise, then remove the bulb assembly from the housing **(see illustration)**.

3   The defective bulb can then be twisted out of the socket and replaced.

Front side marker lights

Refer to illustrations 17.4 and 17.5

Note: *Earlier models have separate side marker lights. On later models, the side marker*

lights are part of the headlight assembly.

4   Detach the side marker light retaining screw **(see illustration)**.

5   Pull the side marker light outward. Then twist the bulb socket a quarter turn counterclockwise and remove the bulb assembly from the side marker light lens **(see illustration)**.

6   The defective bulb can then be pulled straight out of the socket and replaced.

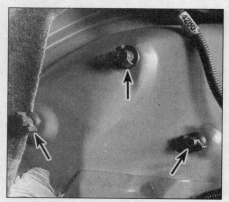

17.9 With the trunk compartment rear finishing panel removed, detach the plastic retaining nuts (arrow) securing the tail light housing

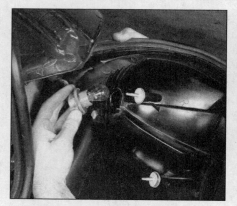

17.11 Squeeze the clip then rotate and lift the bulb holder out of the housing - push in and rotate the bulb to remove it

17.17 Remove the screws (arrows) to access the license plate light bulb

7   Installation of the lens is the reverse of removal.

Rear turn signal, brake and tail lights

Refer to illustrations 17.9 and 17.11

8   On earlier models, detach the plastic clips securing the trunk compartment rear finishing panel, then remove the panel from the vehicle. On later models, remove the upper wing nut from the tail light and pull back the trim panel.
9   Working from the inside of the trunk detach the retaining nuts securing the rear tail light housing **(see illustration)**.
10   Pull the tail light assembly outward to access the tail light bulbs.
11   Depress the socket retaining clip and twist the bulb socket a quarter turn counter-clockwise, then remove the bulb assembly from the housing **(see illustration)**.
12   The defective bulb can then be twisted out of the socket and replaced.
13   Installation of the tail light housing is the reverse of removal. On later Monte Carlo models, be sure to route the wiring correctly, to avoid damage.

Back-up lights

14   On earlier models, back-up lights are part of the tail light assembly (see above). Later models have separate back-up light assemblies.
15   On later Impala models, remove the trunk lid applique (the small panel that holds the back-up lights) by disconnecting the electrical connector and removing the wing nuts on the inside of the trunk lid. On later Monte Carlo models, remove the screws that secure the light to the rear bumper cover. The back-up light sockets can then be removed by turning them counterclockwise.
16   Installation is the reverse of removal.

License plate light

Refer to illustration 17.17

17   Detach the retaining screws which secure the lens **(see illustration)**.
18   The defective bulb can then be pulled straight out of the socket and replaced.
19   Installation of the lens is the reverse of removal.

High-mounted brake light

Refer to illustration 17.21

20   The high-mounted brake light bulb can

be accessed from the trunk compartment.
21   On earlier models, reach up under the high mounted brake light, depress the socket retaining clip and twist the bulb socket a quarter turn counterclockwise, then remove the bulb assembly from the housing **(see illustration)**. The defective bulb can then be twisted out of the socket and replaced.
22   On later models, the high-mounted brake light is in the trunk lid. Remove the screw from the high-mounted brake light bracket and remove the bracket. Remove the screws from the light, press in on the retainers and remove the light from the trunk lid. Disconnect the electrical connector.
23   Installation is the reverse of removal.

Interior light

Refer to illustration 17.24

24   Using a small screwdriver to pry up the right side, remove the lens and replace the bulb **(see illustration)**.

Instrument cluster illumination

Refer to illustration 17.25

25   To gain access to the instrument cluster illumination lights, the instrument cluster will have to be removed (see Section 19). The bulbs can then be removed and replaced from the rear of the cluster **(see illustration)**.

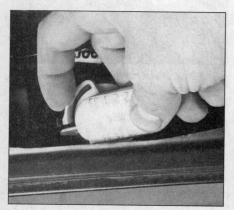

17.21 The high-mounted brake light bulb can be reached through the access hole in the trunk compartment

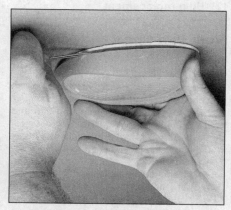

17.24 Pry off the interior light lens to access the bulb

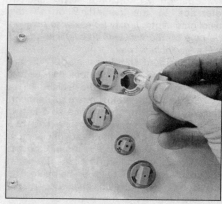

17.25 Rotate the bulb and lift it out of the cluster

19.3 Remove the instrument cluster retaining screw (arrows)

18 Daytime Running Lights (DRL) - general information

The Daytime Running Lights (DRL) system used on all Canadian and later US models illuminates the headlights whenever the engine is running. The only exception is with the engine running and the parking brake engaged. Once the parking brake is released, the lights will remain on as long as the ignition switch is on, even if the parking brake is later applied.

The DRL system supplies reduced power to the headlights so they will be bright enough for daytime visibility while prolonging headlight life.

19 Instrument cluster - removal and installation

Refer to illustration 19.3
Warning: *The models covered by this manual are equipped with airbags. Always disable the airbag system before working in the vicinity of the impact sensors, steering column or instrument panel to avoid the possibility of accidental deployment of the airbag(s), which could cause personal injury (see Section 26). The yellow wires and connectors routed through the instrument panel are for this system. Do not use electrical test equipment on these yellow wires or tamper with them in any way while working under the instrument panel.*
Caution: *On models equipped with a Theftlock audio system, be sure the lockout feature is turned off before performing any procedure which requires disconnecting the battery.*
1   Detach the cable from the negative battery terminal and disable the airbag system (see Section 26).
2   Remove the instrument cluster bezel (see Chapter 11).
3   Remove the screws securing each side of the instrument cluster **(see illustration)**.
4   Tilt the top of the instrument cluster inward towards the center of the passenger compartment, then detach the electrical connector from the back of the cluster.
5   Disengage the instrument cluster lower locating pins from the instrument panel and remove it from the vehicle
6   Installation is the reverse of removal.

20 Wiper motor - check and replacement

Check

Note: *Refer to the wiring diagrams for wire colors and locations in the following checks. Keep in mind that power wires are generally larger in diameter and brighter colors, where ground wires are usually smaller in diameter and darker colors. When checking for voltage, probe a grounded 12-volt test light to each terminal at a connector until it lights; this verifies voltage (power) at the terminal.*
1   If the wipers work slowly, make sure the battery is in good condition and has a strong charge (see Chapter 1). If the battery is in good condition, remove the wiper motor (see below) and operate the wiper arms by hand. Check for binding linkage and pivots. Lubricate or repair the linkage or pivots as necessary. Reinstall the wiper motor. If the wipers still operate slowly, check for loose or corroded connections, especially the ground connection. If all connections look OK, replace the motor.
2   If the wipers fail to operate when activated, check the fuse. If the fuse is OK, connect a jumper wire between the wiper motor and ground, then retest. If the motor works now, repair the ground connection. If the motor still doesn't work, turn the wiper switch to the HI position and check for voltage at the motor. If there's voltage at the motor, remove the motor and check it off the vehicle with fused jumper wires from the battery. If the motor now works, check for binding linkage (see Step 1 above). If the motor still doesn't work, replace it. If there's no voltage at the motor, check for voltage at the wiper control module. If there's voltage at the wiper control module and no voltage at the at the wiper motor, check the switch for continuity. If the switch is OK, the wiper control module is probably bad.
3   If the interval (delay) function is inoperative, check the continuity of all the wiring between the switch and wiper control module. If the wiring is OK, check the resistance of the delay control knob of the multifunction switch (see Section 8). If the delay control knob is within the specified resistance, replace the wiper control module.
4   If the wipers stop at the position they're in when the switch is turned off (fail to park), check for voltage at the park feed wire of the wiper motor connector when the wiper

20.7 Use a small screwdriver to pry off the wiper arm retaining nut cover, then remove the washer hose and the nut (arrow) and pull the arm straight off its splined shaft

switch is OFF but the ignition is ON. If no voltage is present, check for an open circuit between the wiper motor and the fuse panel.
5   If the wipers won't shut off unless the ignition is OFF, disconnect the wiring from the wiper control switch. If the wipers stop, replace the switch. If the wipers keep running, there's a defective limit switch in the motor; replace the motor.
6   If the wipers won't retract below the hoodline, check for mechanical obstructions in the wiper linkage or on the vehicle's body which would prevent the wipers from parking. If there are no obstructions, check the wiring between the switch and motor for continuity. If the wiring is OK, replace the wiper motor.

Replacement

Refer to illustrations 20.7, 20.8a, 20.8b, 20.8c, 20.10a, 20.10b and 20.12
7   Pry off the cover from the wiper arm retaining nuts, unscrew the nuts, detach the washer hoses and remove both wiper arms **(see illustration)**.
8   Remove the screws (push in retainers on later models), the washer hose and detach

20.8a Remove the screws (arrows) securing the outer edges of the cowl cover . . .

20.8b . . . then remove the screws (arrows) securing the center of the cowl cover

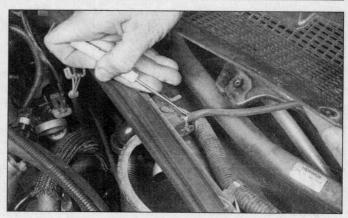

20.8c Lift the cowl cover up slightly and disconnect the washer hose

20.10a Remove the wiper motor linkage retaining bolts (arrows) from the drivers side of the cowl . . .

20.10b . . .and at the center of the cowl (arrow)

the cowl cover **(see illustrations)**. On later models, also remove the water deflector above the wiper motor, held by one push-in retainer.

9   Disconnect the electrical connectors from the wiper motor.
10   Remove the wiper linkage bracket mounting bolts **(see illustrations)**.
11   Pull the linkage assembly out from

the cowl.
12   On earlier models, turn the linkage over to access the wiper motor retaining screws. Remove the screws and the wiper motor spindle nut **(see illustration)**. Separate the components.
13   On later models, the mounting screws are on top and the wiper motor spindle has a screw under its cover. Remove the cover, screw and spindle. Then remove the wiper motor mounting screws, the shaft seal and the water shield.
14   Installation is the reverse of removal. When reinstalling the wiper motor spindle on later models, the gap between the spindle and the vertical tab on the bracket should be 3/16 to 5/16 inch.

21   Horn - check and replacement

Check

Refer to illustration 21.4
Note: *Check the fuses before beginning electrical diagnosis.*
1   Remove the plastic air deflector surrounding the hood latch assembly and disconnect the electrical connector from the horn.

2   To test the horn(s), connect battery voltage to the horn terminal with a pair of jumper wires. If the horn doesn't sound, replace it.
3   If the horn does sound, check for voltage at the terminal when the horn button is depressed. If there's voltage at the terminal, check for a bad ground at the horn.
4   If there's no voltage at the horn, check

20.12 Turn the linkage assembly over to access the spindle nut (A) and the wiper motor retaining bolts (B)

21.4 The horn relay (arrow) location is clearly marked on the engine compartment fuse block cover

22.5 The cruise control module (arrow) is located in the engine compartment on the (driver's side) inner fenderwell - check for damage to the connectors

21.9 Disconnect the electrical connector, remove the bolt(s) (arrows) and detach the horn(s)

the relay (see Section 6). Note that most horn relays are either the four-terminal or externally grounded three-terminal type. The horn relay is located in the engine compartment fuse block on the drivers side of the vehicle **(see illustration)**.

5   If the relay is OK, check for voltage to the relay power and control circuits. If either of the circuits is not receiving voltage, inspect the wiring between the relay and the fuse panel.

6   If both relay circuits are receiving voltage, depress the horn button and check the circuit from the relay to the horn button for continuity to ground. If there's no continuity, check the circuit for an open. If there's no open circuit, replace the horn button.

7   If there's continuity to ground through the horn button, check for an open or short in the circuit from the relay to the horn.

Replacement

Refer to illustration 21.9

8   To access the horns remove the plastic air deflector surrounding the hood latch assembly.

9   Disconnect the electrical connectors and remove the bracket bolts **(see illustration)**.

10   Installation is the reverse of removal.

22   Cruise control system - description and check

Refer to illustration 22.5

1   The cruise control system maintains vehicle speed with an electronic servo motor located in the engine compartment, which is connected to the throttle linkage by a cable. The system consists of the electronic control module, brake switch, control switches, a relay, the vehicle speed sensor and associated wiring. Listed below are some general procedures that may be used to locate common cruise control problems.

2   Locate and check the fuse (see Section 3).

3   Have an assistant operate the brake lights while you check their operation (voltage from the brake light switch deactivates the cruise control).

4   If the brake lights don't come on or don't shut off, correct the problem and retest the cruise control.

5   Inspect the cable linkage between the cruise control module and the throttle linkage. The cruise control module is located on the left (drivers) inner fenderwell of the engine compartment **(see illustration)**.

6   Visually inspect the wires connected to the cruise control actuator and check for damage and broken wires.

7   The cruise control system uses a speed sensing device. The speed sensor is located in the transmission. To test the speed sensor see Chapter 6.

8   Test drive the vehicle to determine if the cruise control is now working. If it isn't, take it to a dealer service department or an automotive electrical specialist for further diagnosis and repair.

23   Power window system - description and check

Refer to illustration 23.12

1   The power window system operates electric motors, mounted in the doors, which lower and raise the windows. The system consists of the control switches, the motors, regulators, glass mechanisms and associated wiring.

2   The power windows can be lowered and raised from the master control switch by the driver or by remote switches located at the individual windows. Each window has a separate motor which is reversible. The position of the control switch determines the polarity and therefore the direction of operation.

3   The circuit is protected by a fuse and a circuit breaker. Each motor is also equipped with an internal circuit breaker, this prevents one stuck window from disabling the whole system.

4   The power window system will only operate when the ignition switch is ON. In addition, many models have a window lockout switch at the master control switch

which, when activated, disables the switches at the rear windows and, sometimes, the switch at the passenger's window also. Always check these items before troubleshooting a window problem.

5   These procedures are general in nature, so if you can't find the problem using them, take the vehicle to a dealer service department or other properly equipped repair facility.

6   If the power windows won't operate, always check the fuse and circuit breaker first.

7   If only the rear windows are inoperative, or if the windows only operate from the master control switch, check the rear window lockout switch for continuity in the unlocked position. Replace it if it doesn't have continuity.

8   Check the wiring between the switches and fuse panel for continuity. Repair the wiring, if necessary.

9   If only one window is inoperative from the master control switch, try the other control switch at the window. **Note:** *This doesn't apply to the drivers door window.*

10   If the same window works from one switch, but not the other, check the switch for continuity.

11   If the switch tests OK, check for a short or open in the circuit between the affected switch and the window motor.

12   If one window is inoperative from both switches, remove the trim panel from the

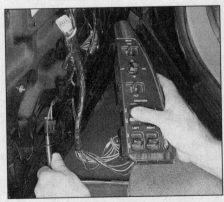

23.12 If no voltage is found at the motor with the switch depressed, check for voltage at the switch

affected door and check for voltage at the switch and at the motor while the switch is operated **(see illustration)**.

13   If voltage is reaching the motor, disconnect the glass from the regulator (see Chapter 11). Move the window up and down by hand while checking for binding and damage. Also check for binding and damage to the regulator. If the regulator is not damaged and the window moves up and down smoothly, replace the motor. If there's binding or damage, lubricate, repair or replace parts, as necessary. **Note:** *The window motor is an integral part of the window regulator assembly. See Chapter 11 for the removal procedures.*

14   If voltage isn't reaching the motor, check the wiring in the circuit for continuity between the switches and motors. You'll need to consult the wiring diagram for the vehicle. If the circuit is equipped with a relay, check that the relay is grounded properly and receiving voltage.

15   Test the windows after you are done to confirm proper repairs.

24   Power door lock system - description and check

Refer to illustration 24.6

The power door lock system operates the door lock actuators mounted in each door. The system consists of the switches, actuators, a control unit and associated wiring. Diagnosis can usually be limited to simple checks of the wiring connections and actuators for minor faults which can be easily repaired. Since this system uses an electronic control unit, in-depth diagnosis should be left to a dealership service department. The door lock control unit is located behind the instrument panel, to the right of the fuse box.

Power door lock systems are operated by bi-directional solenoids located in the doors. The lock switches have two operating positions: Lock and Unlock. When activated, the switch sends a ground signal to the door lock control unit to lock or unlock the doors. Depending on which way the switch is activated, the control unit reverses polarity to the solenoids, allowing the two sides of the circuit to be used alternately as the feed (positive) and ground side.

Some vehicles may have an anti-theft systems incorporated into the power locks. If you are unable to locate the trouble using the following general Steps, consult your a dealer service department or other qualified repair shop.

1   Always check the circuit protection first. Some vehicles use a combination of circuit breakers and fuses.

2   Operate the door lock switches in both directions (Lock and Unlock) with the engine off. Listen for the click of the solenoids operating.

3   Test the switches for continuity. Replace

24.6 Check for voltage at the lock solenoid while the switch is operated

the switch if there's not continuity in both switch positions.

4   Check the wiring between the switches, control unit and solenoids for continuity. Repair the wiring if there's no continuity.

5   Check for a bad ground at the switches or the control unit.

6   If all but one lock solenoids operate, remove the trim panel from the affected door (see Chapter 11) and check for voltage at the solenoid while the lock switch is operated One of the wires should have voltage in the Lock position; the other should have voltage in the Unlock position **(see illustration)**.

7   If the inoperative solenoid is receiving voltage, replace the solenoid.

8   If the inoperative solenoid isn't receiving voltage, check for an open or short in the wire between the lock solenoid and the control unit. **Note:** *It's common for wires to break in the portion of the harness between the body and door (opening and closing the door fatigues and eventually breaks the wires).*

25   Electric rear view mirrors - description and check

1   Electric rear view mirrors use two motors to move the glass; one for up-and-down adjustments and one for left-to-right adjustments.

2   The control switch has a selector portion which sends voltage to the left or right side mirror. With the ignition ON, engine OFF, roll down the windows and operate the mirror control switch through all functions (left-right and up-down) for both the left and right side mirrors.

3   Listen carefully for the sound of the electric motors running in the mirrors.

4   If the motors can be heard but the mirror glass doesn't move, there's probably a problem with the drive mechanism inside the mirror. Remove and disassemble the mirror to locate the problem.

5   If the mirrors don't operate and no sound comes from the mirrors, check the

fuse (see Section 3).

6   If the fuse is OK, remove the mirror control switch from its mounting without disconnecting the wires attached to it. Turn the ignition ON and check for voltage at the switch. There should be voltage at one terminal. If there's no voltage at the switch, check for an opening or short in the wiring between the fuse panel and the switch.

7   If there's voltage at the switch, disconnect it. Check the switch for continuity in all its operating positions. If the switch does not have continuity, replace it.

8   Re-connect the switch. Locate the wire going from the switch to ground. Leaving the switch connected, connect a jumper wire between this wire and ground. If the mirror works normally with this wire in place, repair the faulty ground connection.

9   If the mirror still doesn't work, remove the cover and check the wires at the mirror for voltage with a test light. Check with ignition ON and the mirror selector switch on the appropriate side. Operate the mirror switch in all its positions. There should be voltage at one of the switch-to-mirror wires in each switch position (except the neutral position).

10   If there's not voltage in each switch position, check the wiring between the mirror and control switch for opens and shorts.

11   If there's voltage, remove the mirror and test it off the vehicle with jumper wires. Replace the mirror if it fails this test (see Chapter 11).

26   Airbag - general information

Warning: *The models covered by this manual are equipped with airbags. Airbag system components are located in the steering wheel, steering column, instrument panel and under the front passenger seat. The airbag(s) could accidentally deploy if any of the system components or wiring harnesses are disturbed, so be extremely careful when working in these areas and don't disturb any airbag system components or wiring. You could be injured if an airbag accidentally deploys, or the airbag might not deploy correctly in a collision if any components or wiring in the system have been disturbed. The yellow wires and connectors routed through the instrument panel and below the passenger seat are for this system. Do not use electrical test equipment on these yellow wires or tamper with them in any way while working in their vicinity.*

Caution: *On models equipped with a Theftlock audio system, be sure the lockout feature is turned off before performing any procedure which requires disconnecting the battery.*

Description

Refer to illustration 26.2

1   The models covered by this manual are equipped with a Supplemental Inflatable Restraint (SIR) system, more commonly

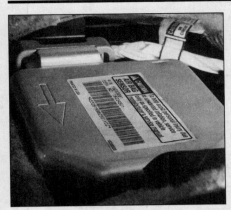

26.2 The airbag sensing and diagnostic module is located under the front passenger's seat

known as an airbag system. The SIR system is designed to protect the driver and passenger from serious injury in the event of a head-on or frontal collision.

2   The SIR system consists of a driver side airbag; located in the center of the steering wheel, a passenger side air bag located in the top of the dashboard above the glove box, an SIR coil assembly located in the steering column, an AIRBAG warning light located in the instrument cluster and a sensing and diagnostic module located under the front passenger seat **(see illustration)**.

Sensing and diagnostic module

3   The sensing and diagnostic module is designed to detect frontal crashes and deploy the air bags if a crash is severe enough to warrant air bag deployment, record system data during a frontal crash and to supply back-up power to deploy the airbags in the event battery power is lost during a collision.

4   The sensing and diagnostic module also contains an on-board microprocessor which monitors the operation of the system. It performs a diagnostic check of the system every time the vehicle is started. If the system is operating properly, the AIRBAG warning light will blink on and off seven times. If there is a fault in the system, the light will remain on and the airbag control module will store fault codes indicating the nature of the fault. If the AIRBAG warning light remains on after staring, or comes on while driving, the vehicle should be taken to your dealer immediately for service.

Operation

5   For the airbag(s) to deploy, an impact of sufficient G force must occur within 30-degrees of the vehicle centerline. When this

condition occurs, the circuit to the airbag inflator is closed and the airbag inflates. If the battery is destroyed by the impact, or is too low to power the inflators, a back-up power supply inside the diagnostic/energy reserve module supplies current to the airbags.

Self-diagnosis system

6   A self-diagnosis circuit in the module displays a light when the ignition switch is turned to the On position. If the system is operating normally, the light should go out after seven flashes. If the light doesn't come on, or doesn't go out after seven flashes, or if it comes on while you're driving the vehicle, there's a malfunction in the SIR system. Have it inspected and repaired as soon as possible. Do not attempt to troubleshoot or service the SIR system yourself. Even a small mistake could cause the SIR system to malfunction when you need it.

Servicing components near the SIR system

7   Nevertheless, there are times when you need to remove the steering wheel, radio or service other components on or near the instrument panel. At these times, you'll be working around components and wiring harnesses for the SIR system. SIR system wiring is easy to identify; they're all covered by a bright yellow conduit. Do not unplug the connectors for the SIR system wiring, except to disable the system. And do not use electrical test equipment on the SIR system wiring. **Always disable the SIR system before working near the SIR system components or related wiring.**

Disabling the SIR system

Refer to illustration 26.10

8   Turn the steering wheel to the straight ahead position, place the ignition switch in Lock and remove the key. Remove the airbag fuse from the fuse block (see Section 3). It's also a good idea to disconnect the cable from the negative terminal of the battery, although this is not actually specified by the manufacturer. **Caution:** *On models equipped with a Theftlock audio system, be sure the lockout feature is turned off before performing any procedure which requires disconnecting the battery.*

9   Remove the steering column lower trim panel and sound insulator panel below the instrument panel (see Chapter 11).

10   Unplug the yellow Connector Position Assurance (CPA) connector **(see illustration)** from the steering column harness. This step disables the driver side air bag.

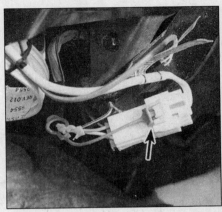

26.10 The driver's side airbag connector (arrow) is located at the base of the steering column; the passenger's side airbag connector is located behind the instrument panel glove box

11   Remove the glove box door assembly from the instrument panel (see Chapter 11).

12   Unplug the yellow Connector Position Assurance (CPA) connector located behind the instrument panel glove box. This step disables the passenger side air bag.

Enabling the SIR system

13   After you've disabled the airbags and performed the necessary service, plug in the steering column (driver's side) and passenger side CPA connectors. Reinstall the steering column lower trim panel, the sound insulator panel and the glove box.

14   Install the airbag fuse. Reconnect the negative battery cable.

27   Wiring diagrams - general information

Since it isn't possible to include all wiring diagrams for every year covered by this manual, the following diagrams are those that are typical and most commonly needed.

Prior to troubleshooting any circuit, check the fuse and circuit breakers (if equipped) to make sure they're in good condition. Make sure the battery is properly charged and check the cable connections (see Chapter 1).

When checking a circuit, make sure that all electrical connectors are clean, with no broken or loose terminals. When unplugging an electrical connector, do not pull on the wires. Pull only on the connector housings themselves.

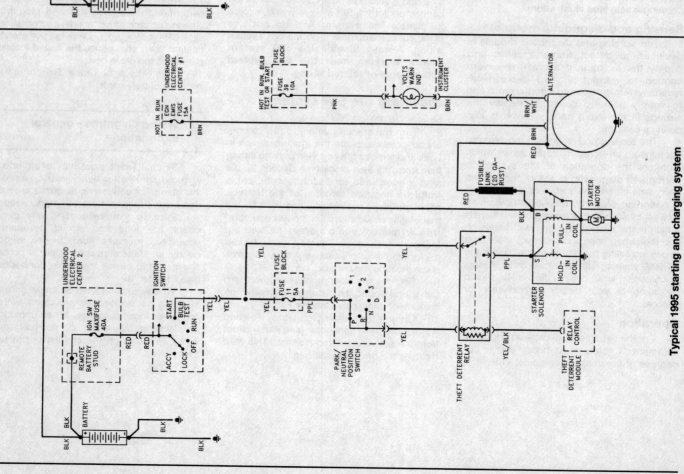

Typical 1996 and later model starting and charging system

Typical 1995 starting and charging system

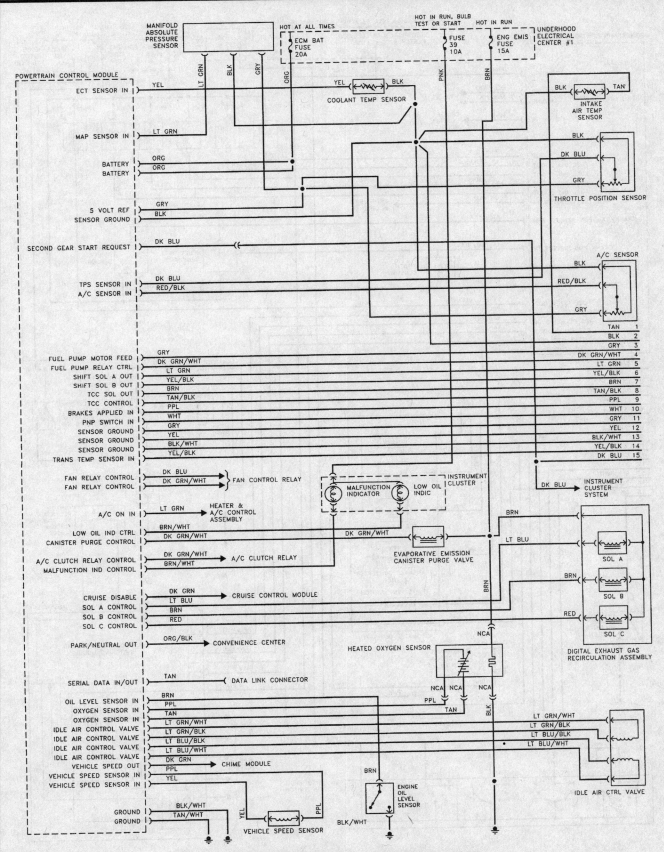

Typical 1995 3.1L engine control system system (1 of 2)

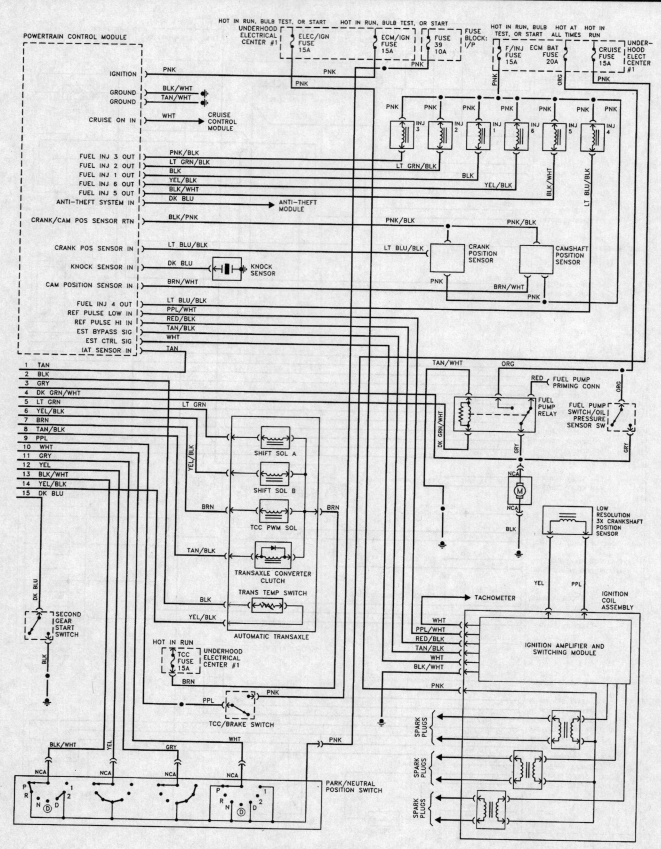

Typical 1995 3.1L engine control system system (2 of 2)

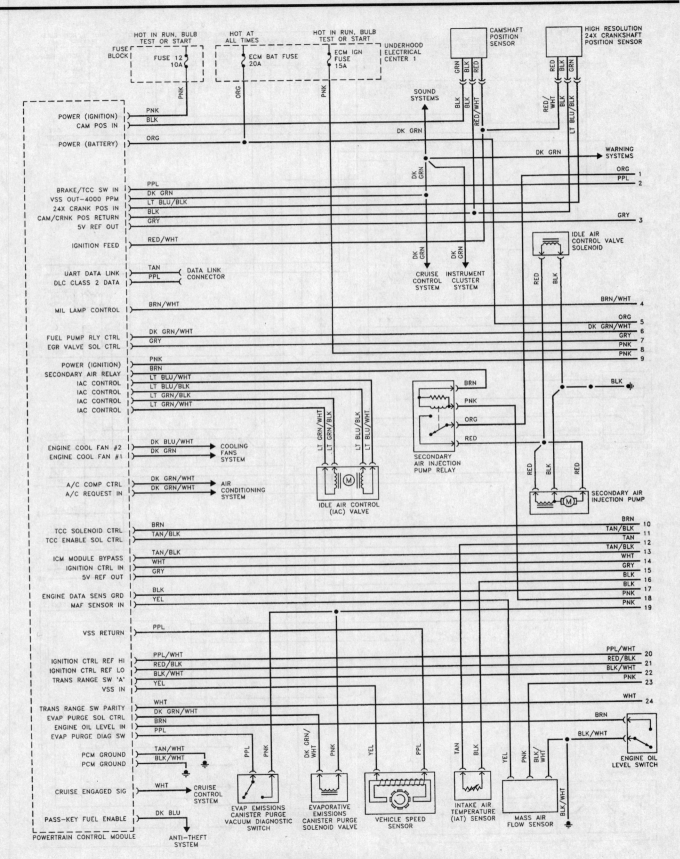

Typical 1995 3.4L DOHC engine control system system (1 of 3)

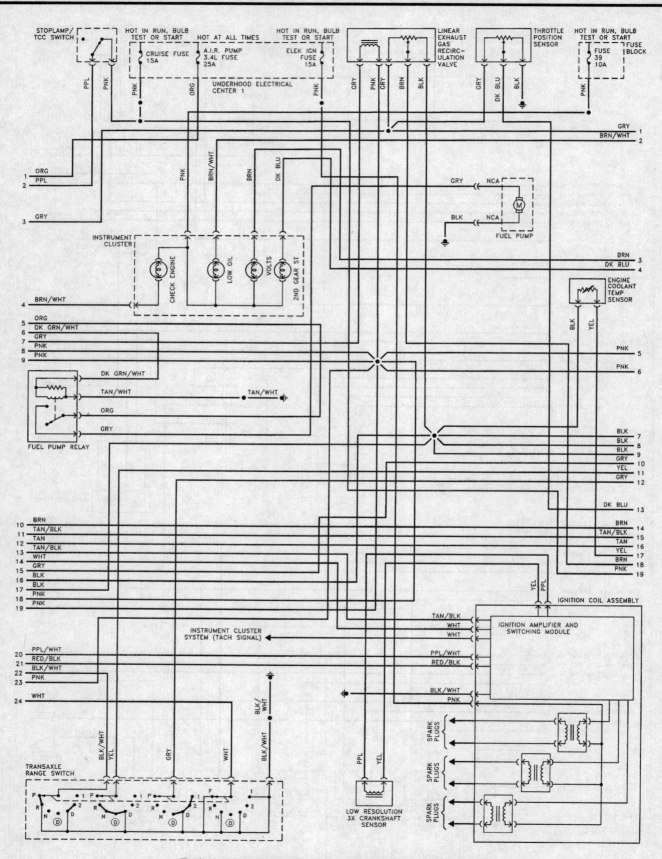

Typical 1995 3.4L DOHC engine control system system (2 of 3)

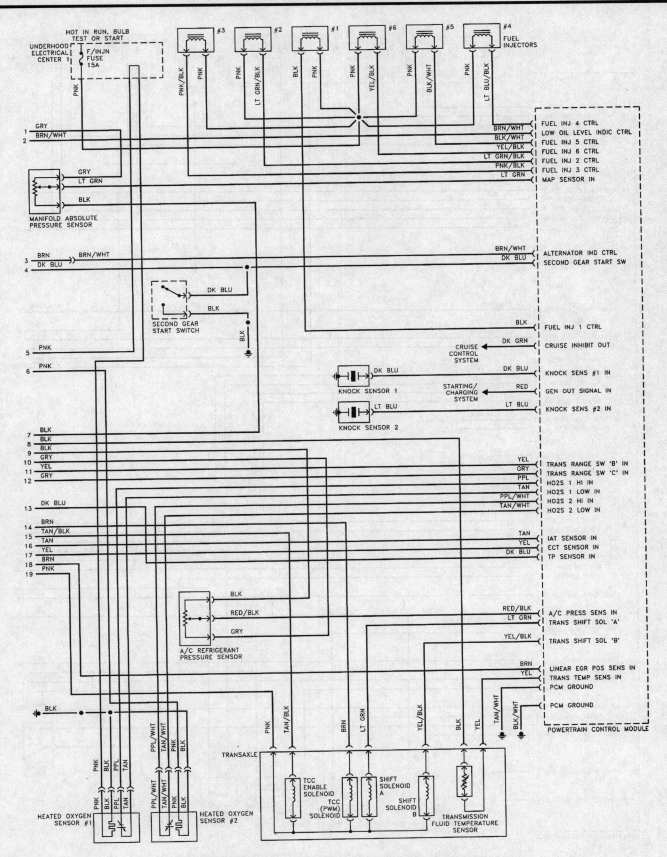

Typical 1995 3.4L DOHC engine control system system (3 of 3)

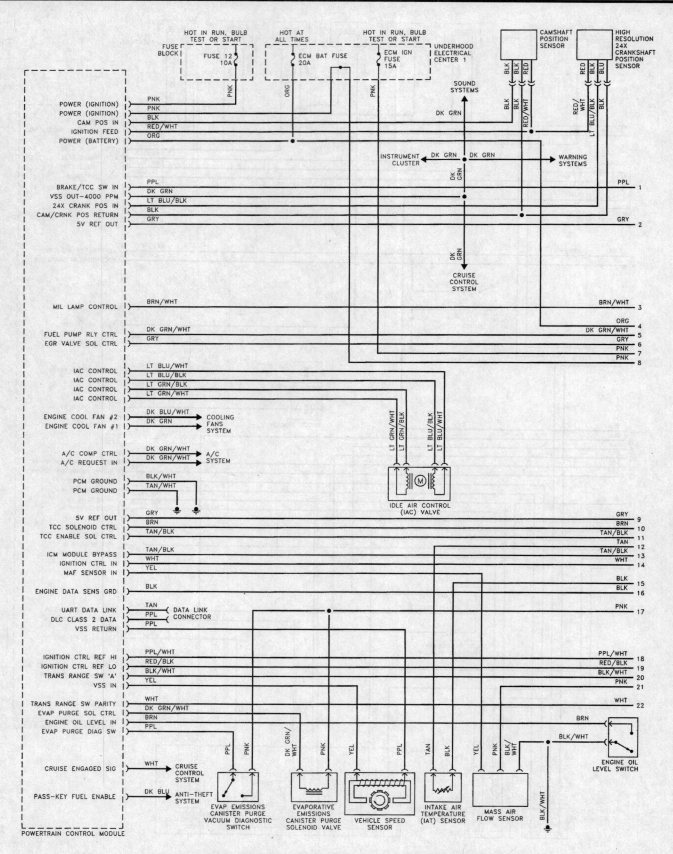

Typical 1996 3.1L engine control system system (1 of 3)

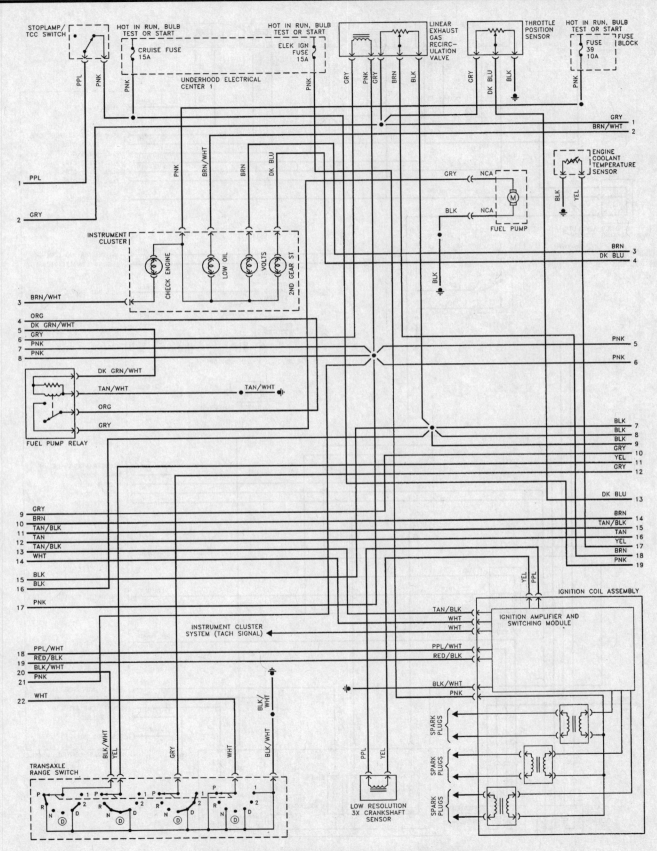

Typical 1996 3.1L engine control system system (2 of 3)

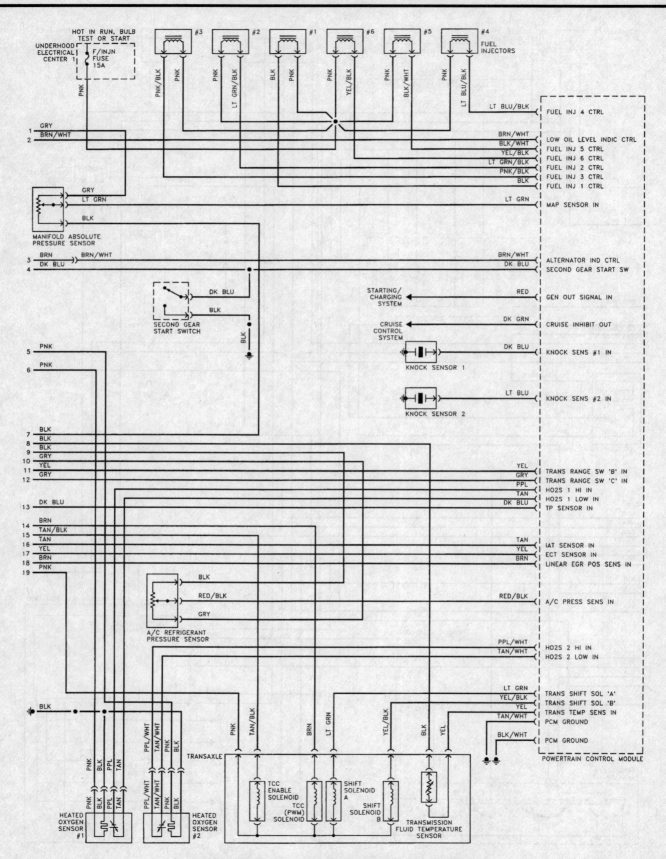

Typical 1996 3.1L engine control system system (3 of 3)

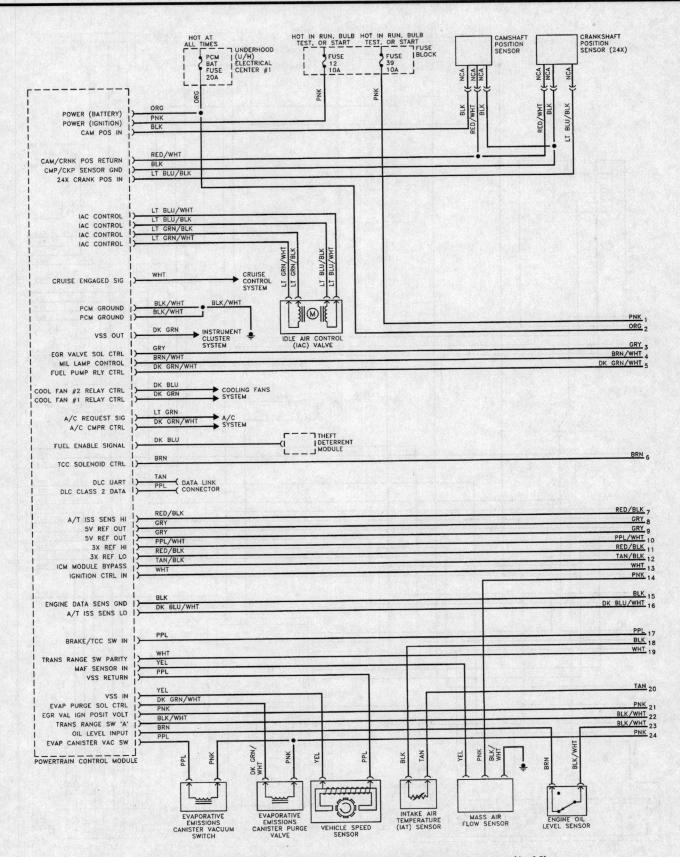

Typical 1996 and later 3.4L DOHC and 1997 3.1L engine control system (1 of 3)

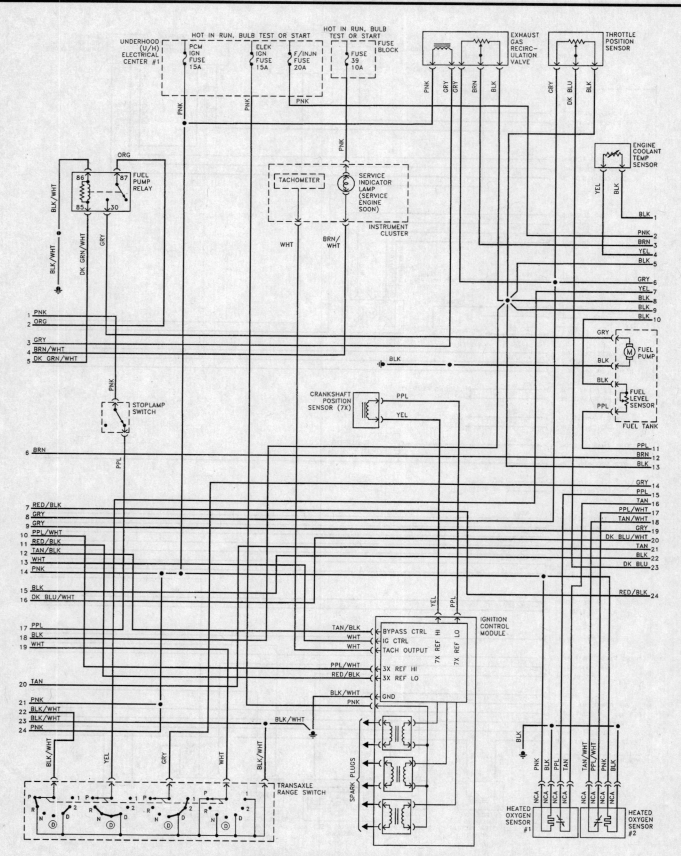

Typical 1996 and later 3.4L DOHC and 1997 and later 3.1L engine control system (2 of 3)

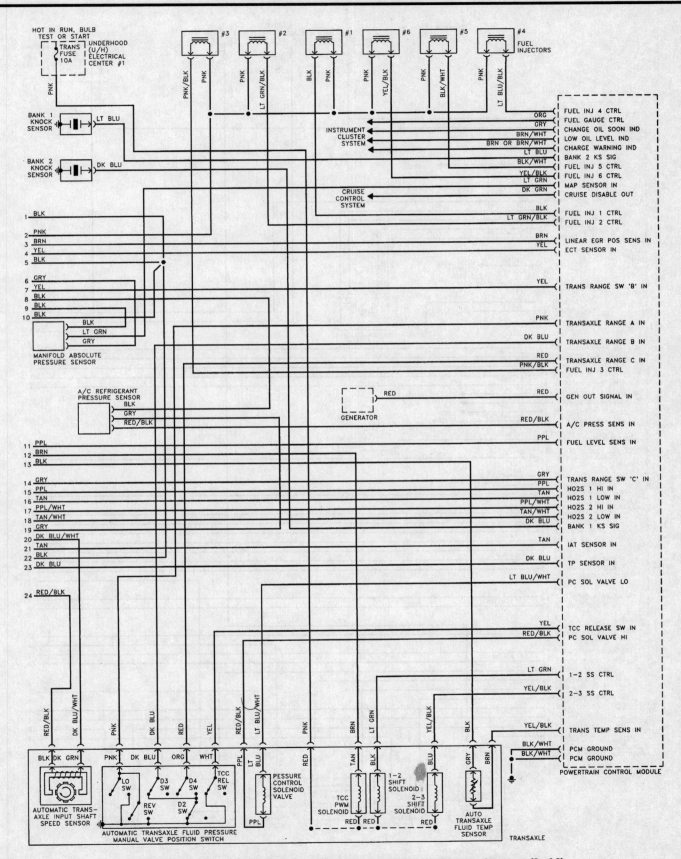

Typical 1996 and later 3.4L DOHC and 1997 and later 3.1L engine control system (3 of 3)

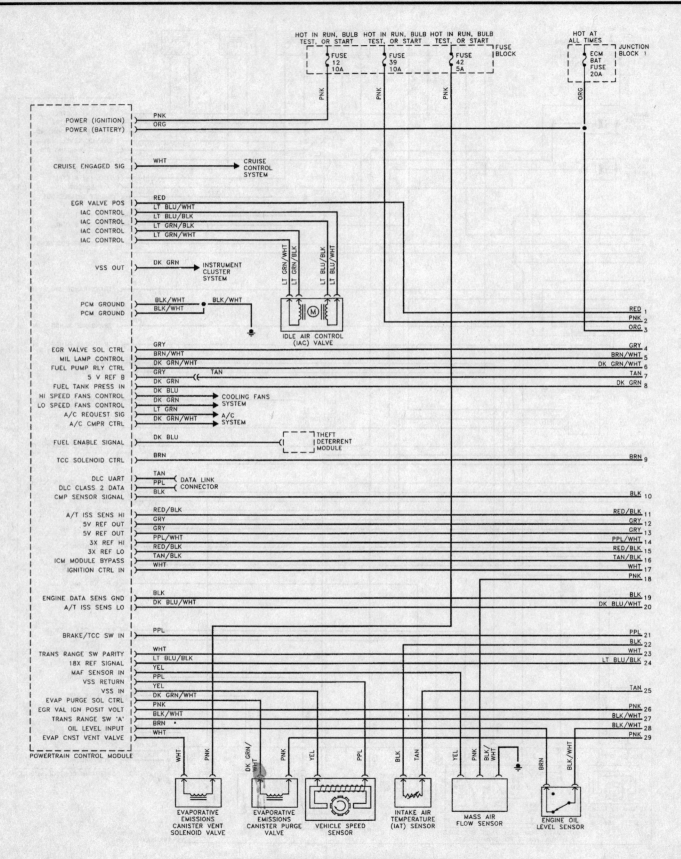

Typical 3.8L engine control system (1 of 3)

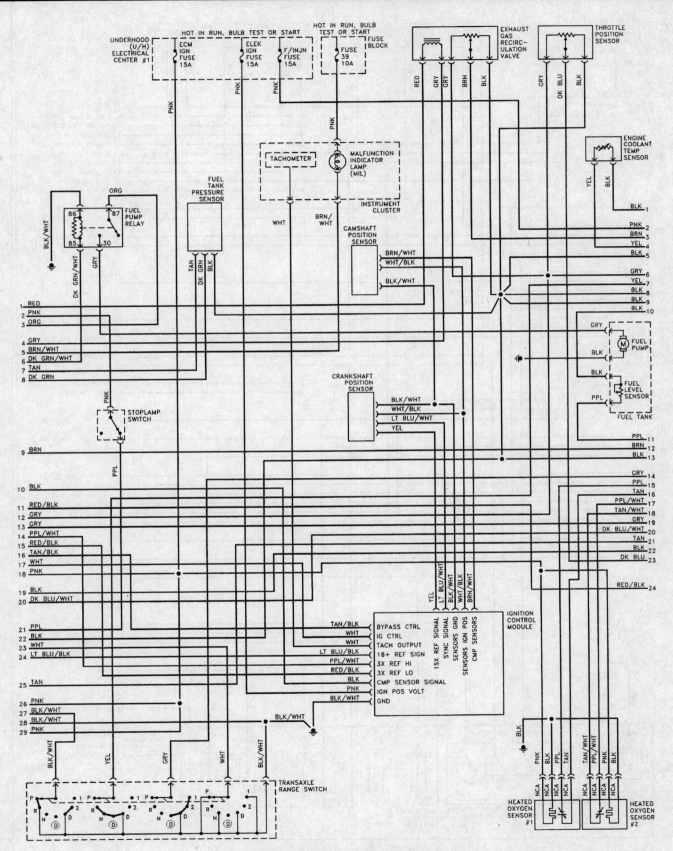

Typical 3.8L engine control system (2 of 3)

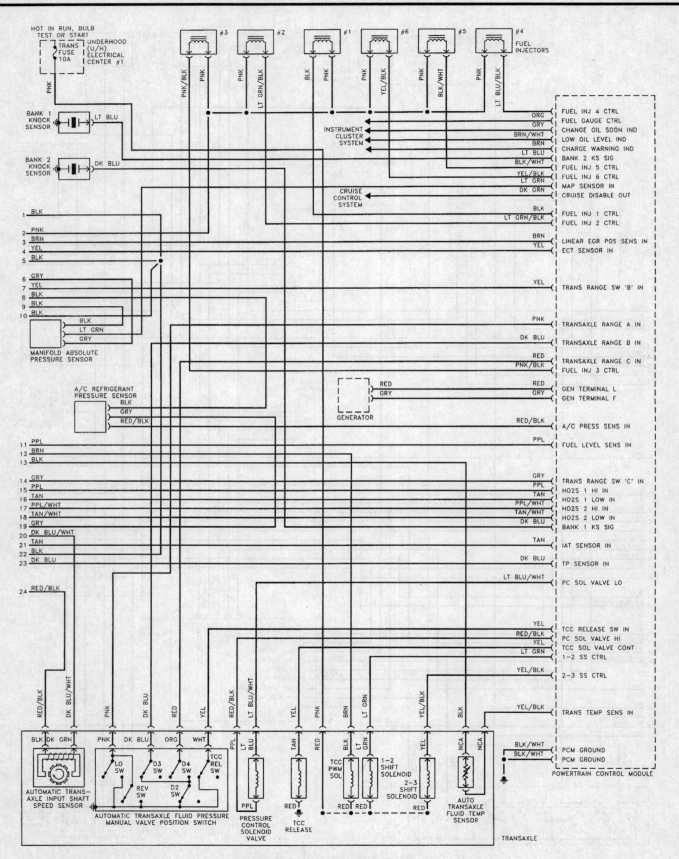

Typical 3.8L engine control system (3 of 3)

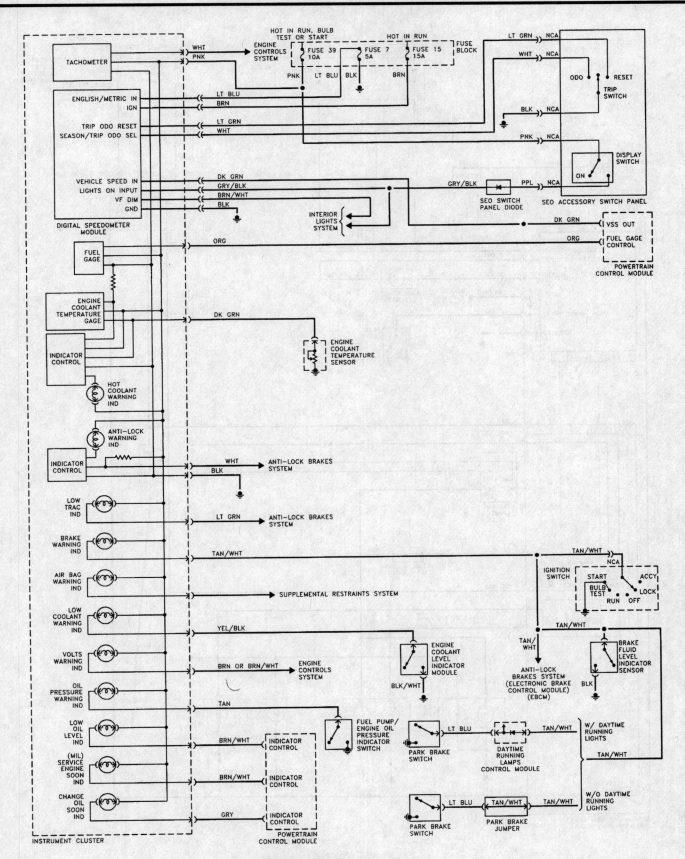

Typical engine warning system

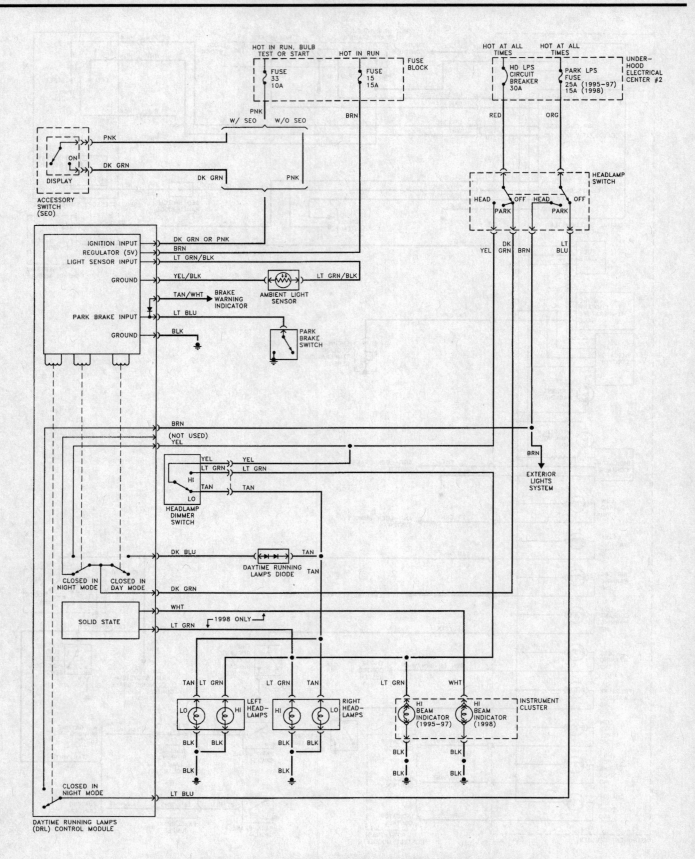

Typical Lumina and 1999 and earlier Monte Carlo headlight system

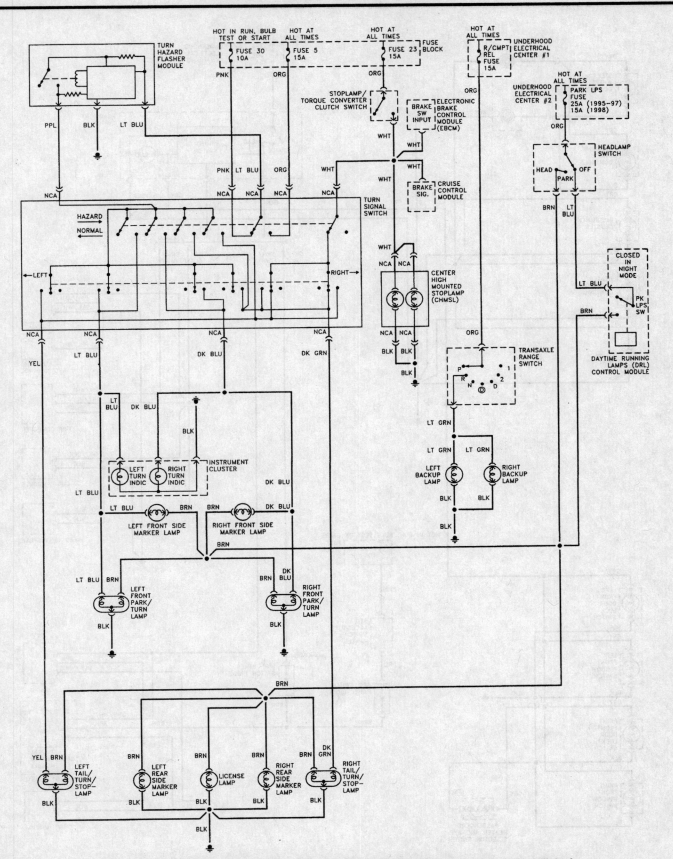

Typical Lumina and 1999 and earlier Monte Carlo exterior lighting system (except headlights)

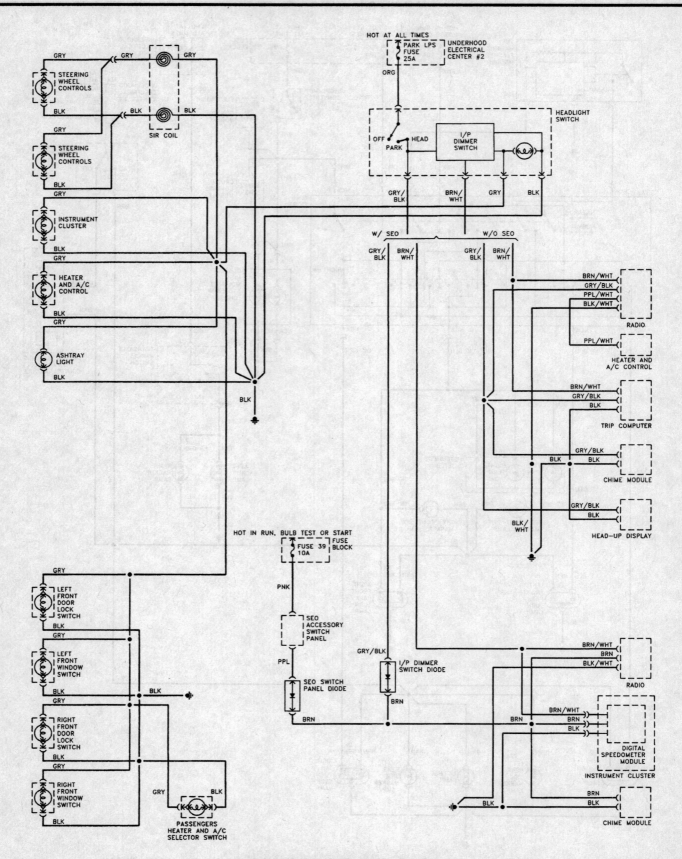

Typical 1995 interior illumination system

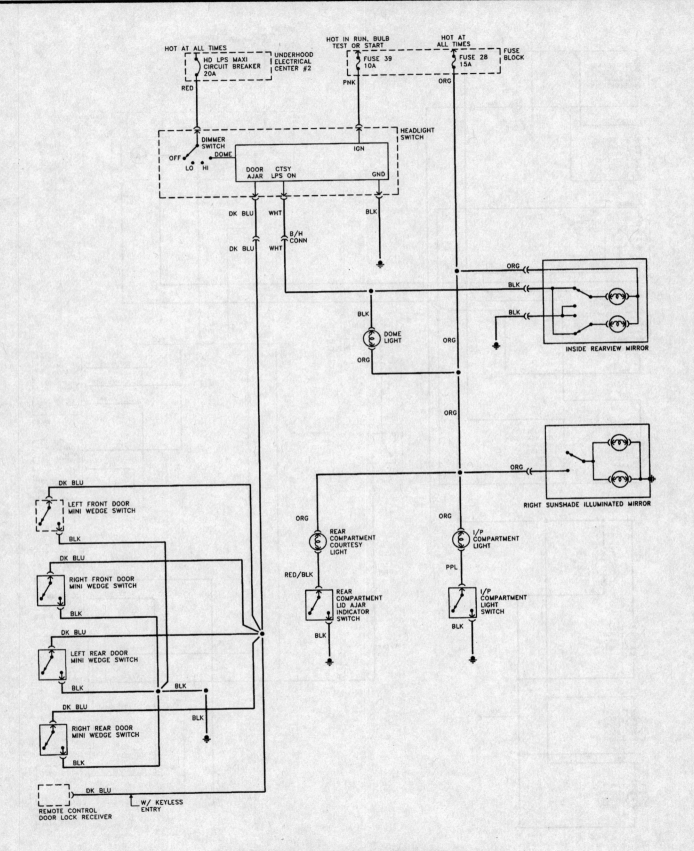

Typical 1995 interior courtesy illumination system

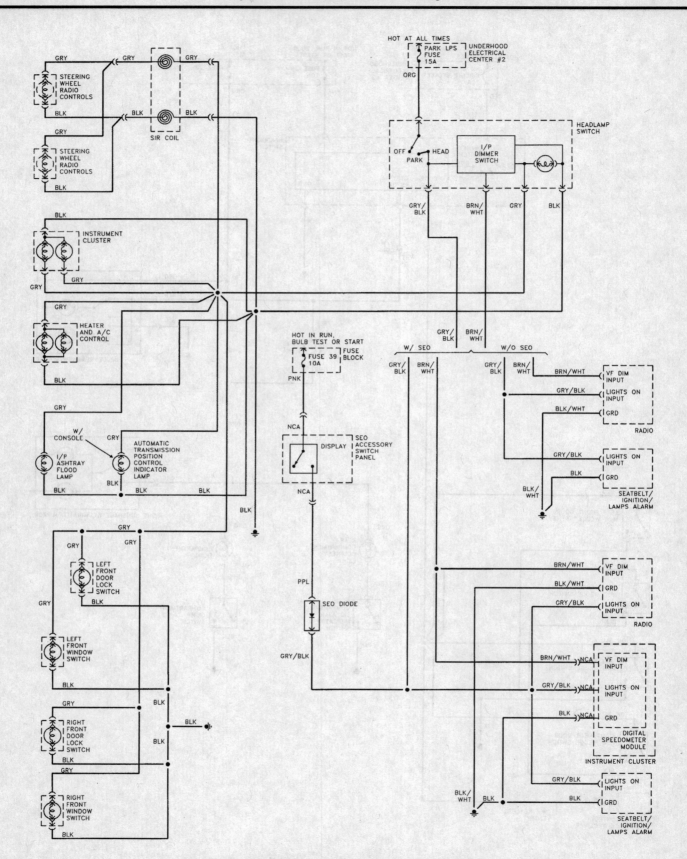

Typical Lumina and 1999 and earlier Monte Carlo interior illumination system

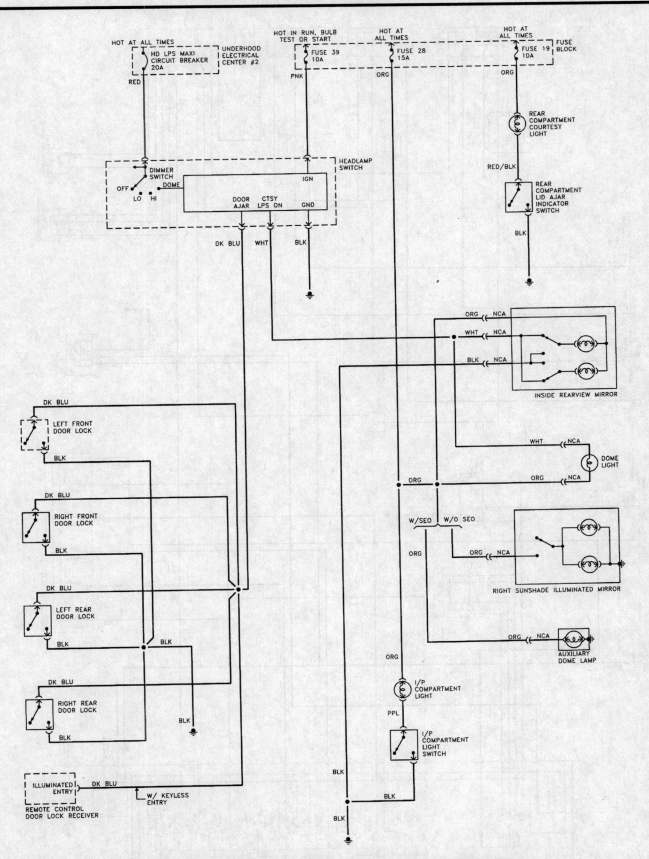

Typical Lumina and 1999 and earlier Monte Carlo interior courtesy light system

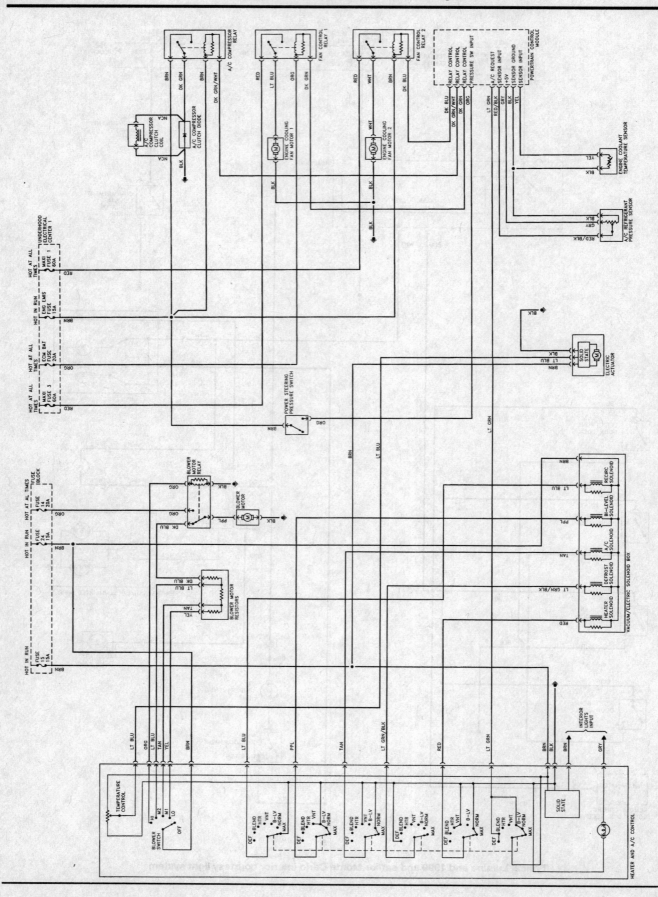

Typical 1995 heating, air conditioning and cooling system

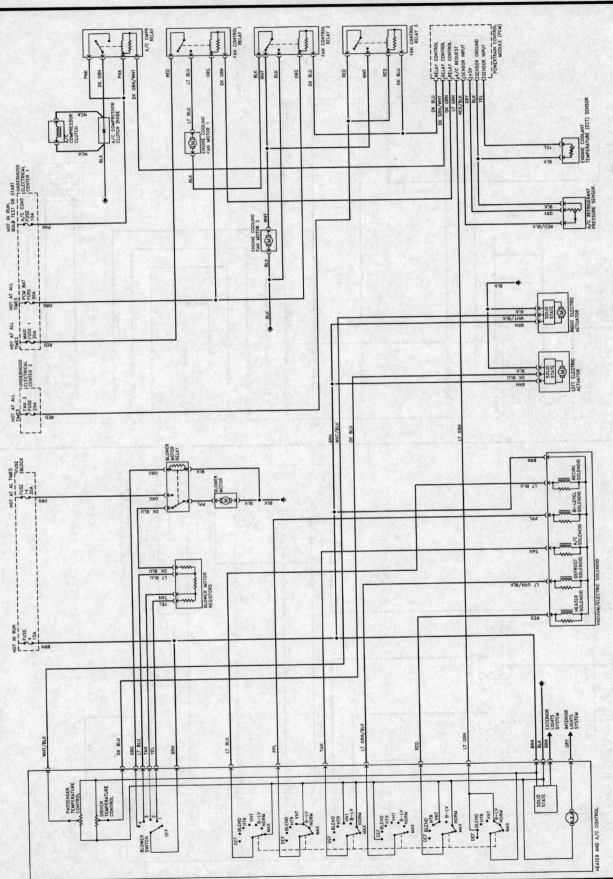

Typical Lumina and 1999 and earlier Monte Carlo heating, air conditioning and cooling system

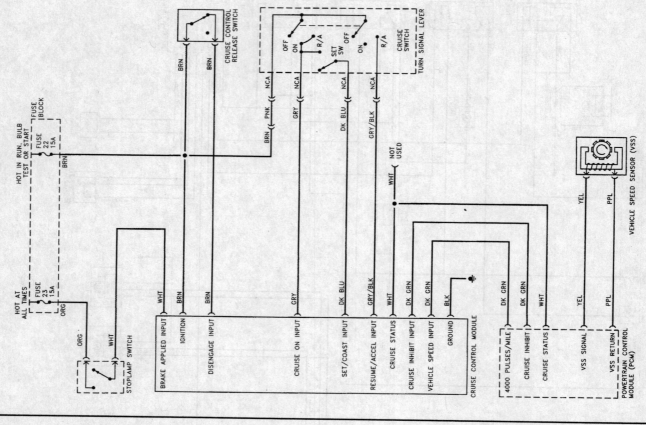

Typical Lumina and 1999 and earlier Monte Carlo cruise control system

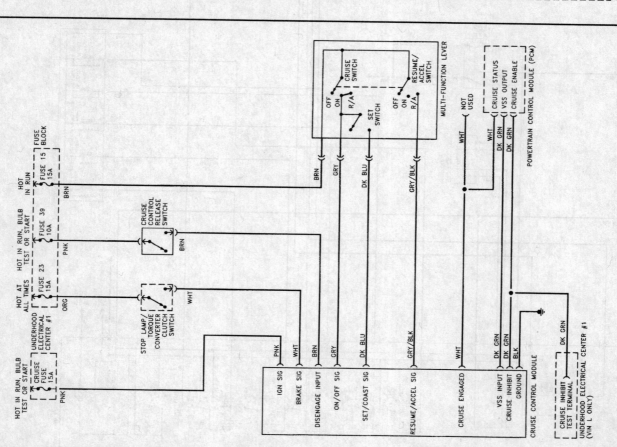

Typical 1995 cruise control system

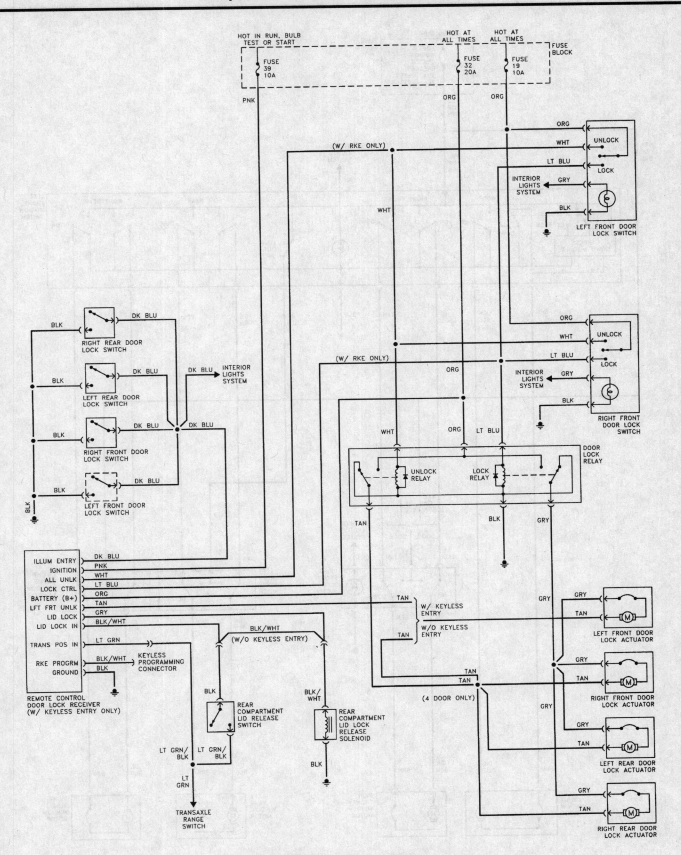

Typical power door lock system

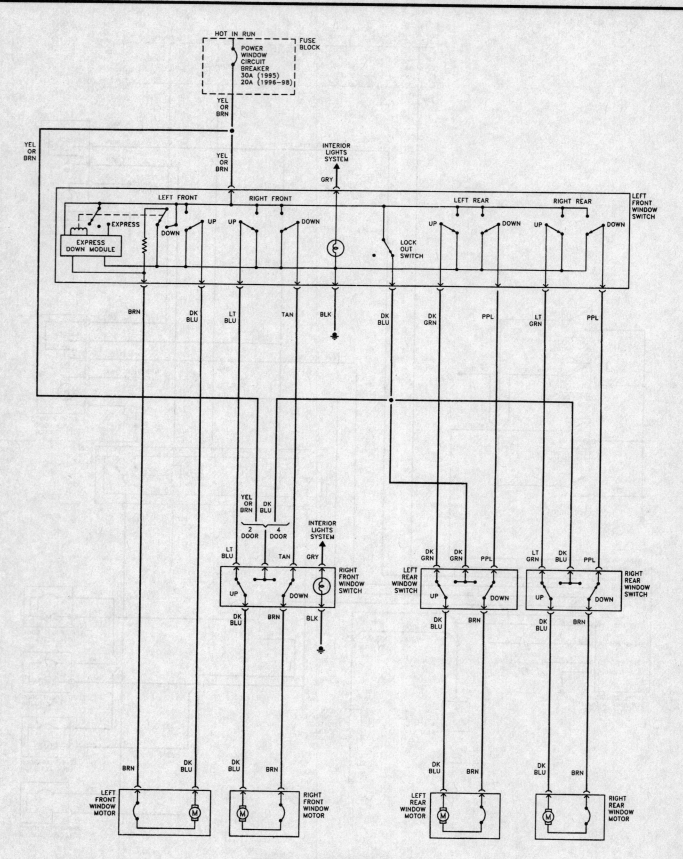

Typical power window system

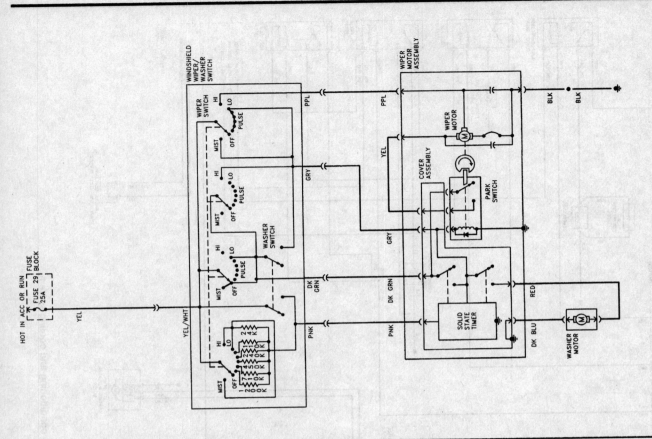

Typical Lumina and 1999 and earlier Monte Carlo windshield wiper and washer system

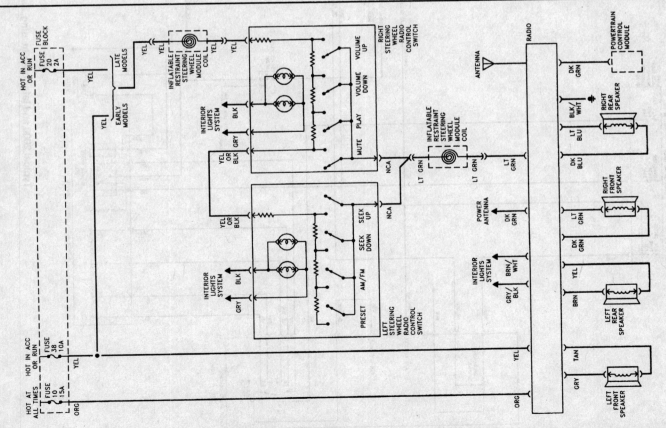

Typical audio system

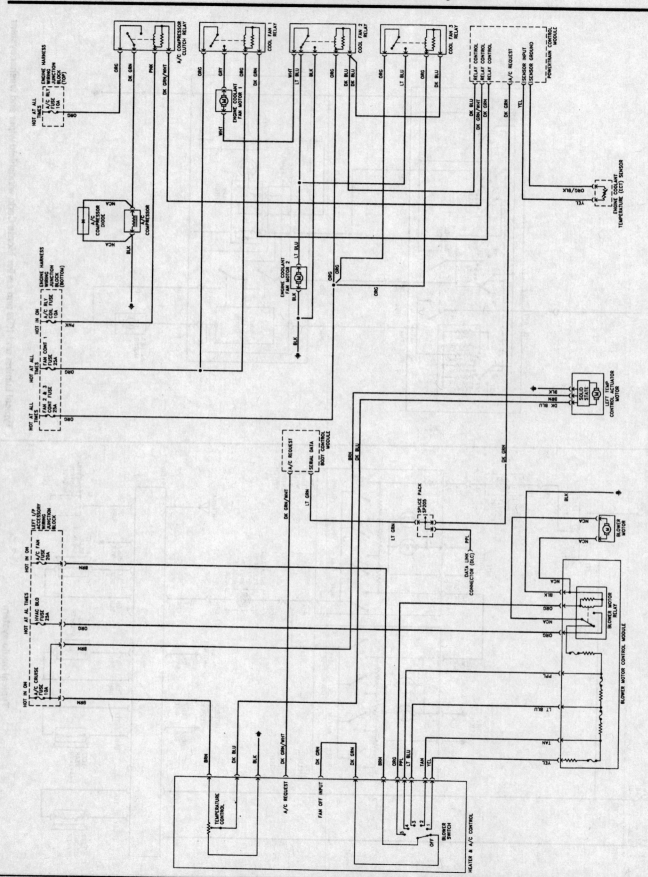

Typical 2000 and later base heating, air conditioning and cooling system

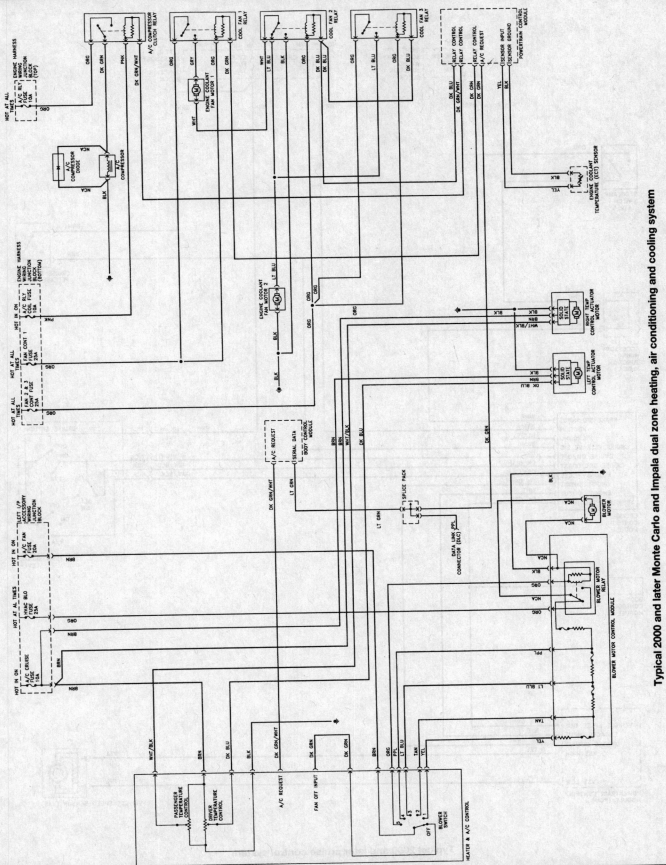

Typical 2000 and later Monte Carlo and Impala dual zone heating, air conditioning and cooling system

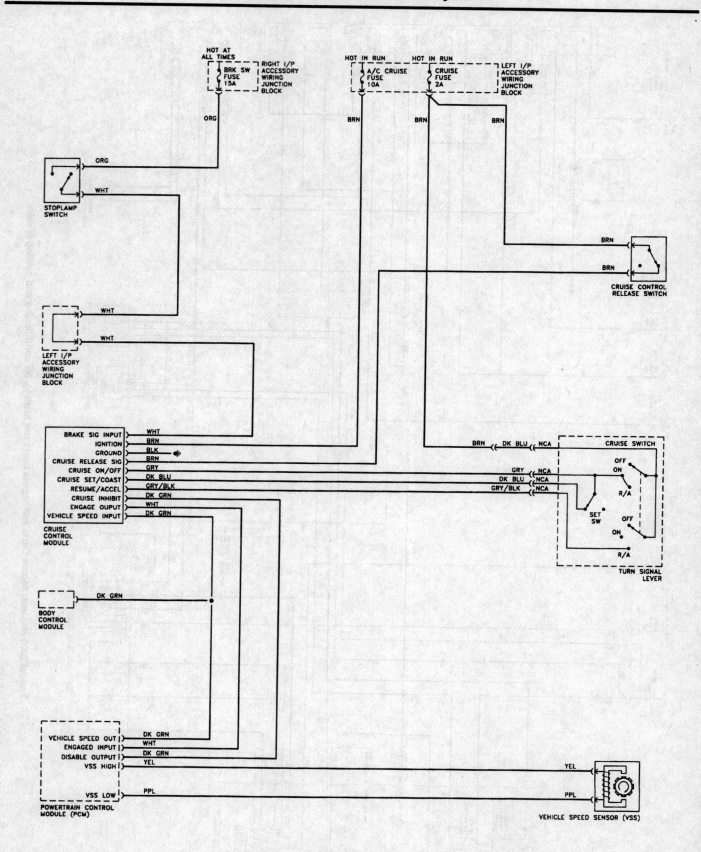

Typical 2000 and later cruise control system

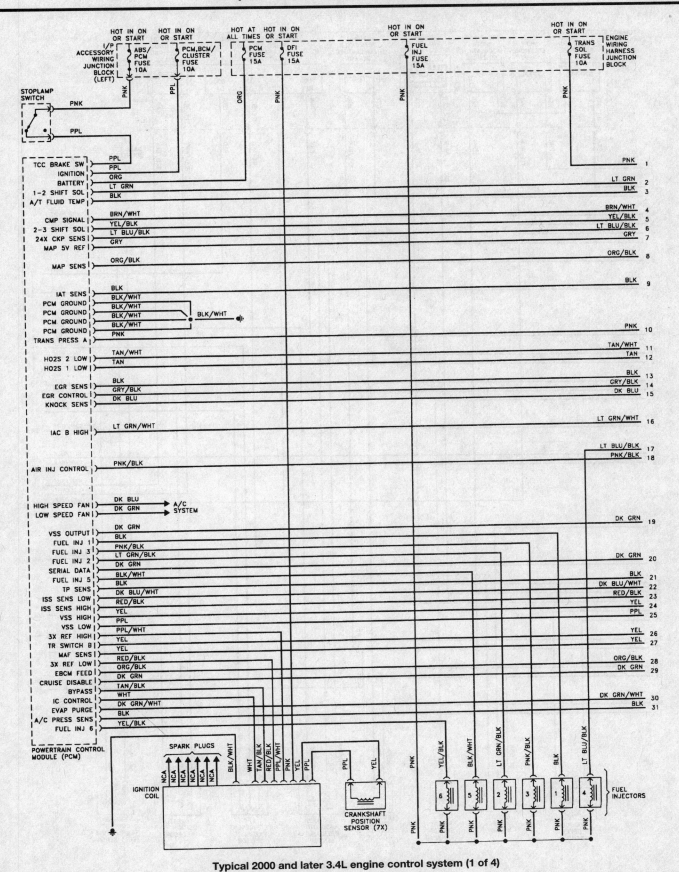

Typical 2000 and later 3.4L engine control system (1 of 4)

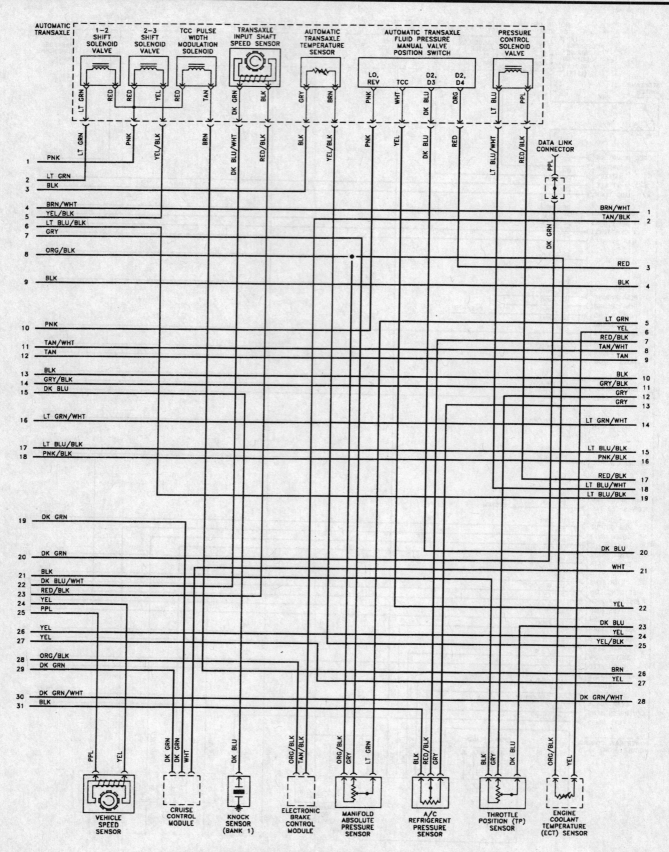

Typical 2000 and later 3.4L engine control system (2 of 4)

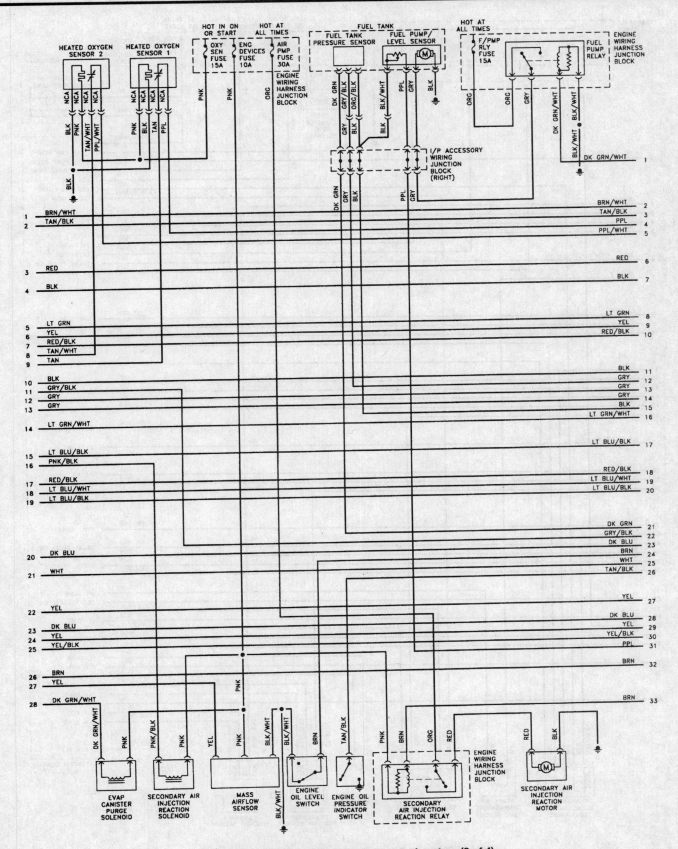

Typical 2000 and later 3.4L engine control system (3 of 4)

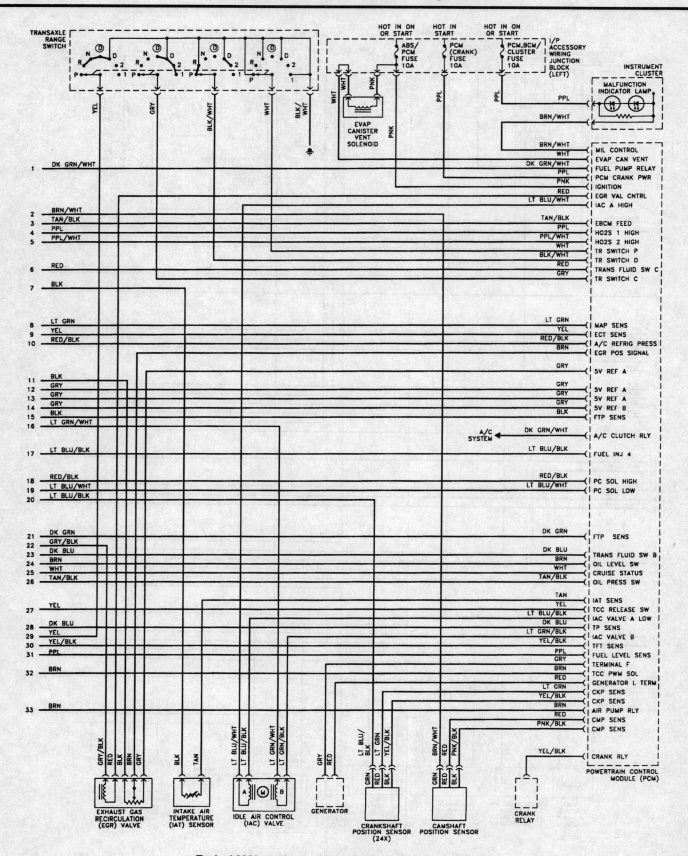

Typical 2000 and later 3.4L engine control system (4 of 4)

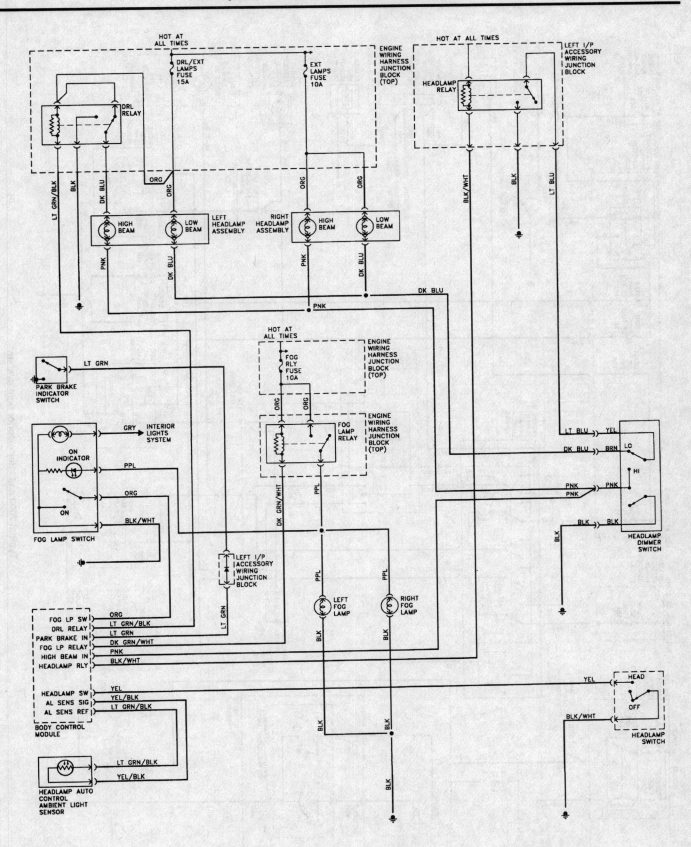

Typical 2000 and later headlight system

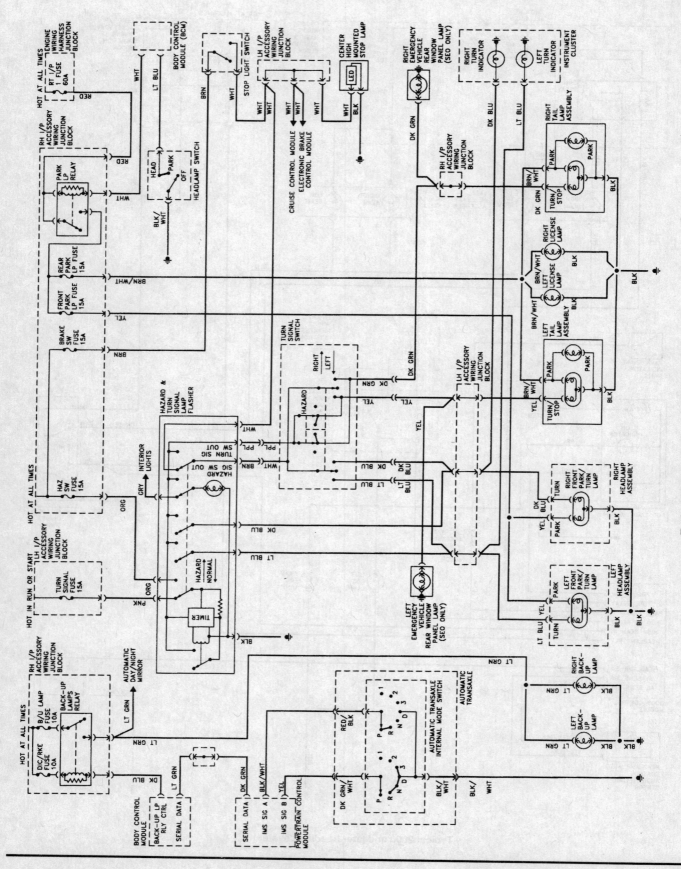

Typical 2000 and later exterior light system

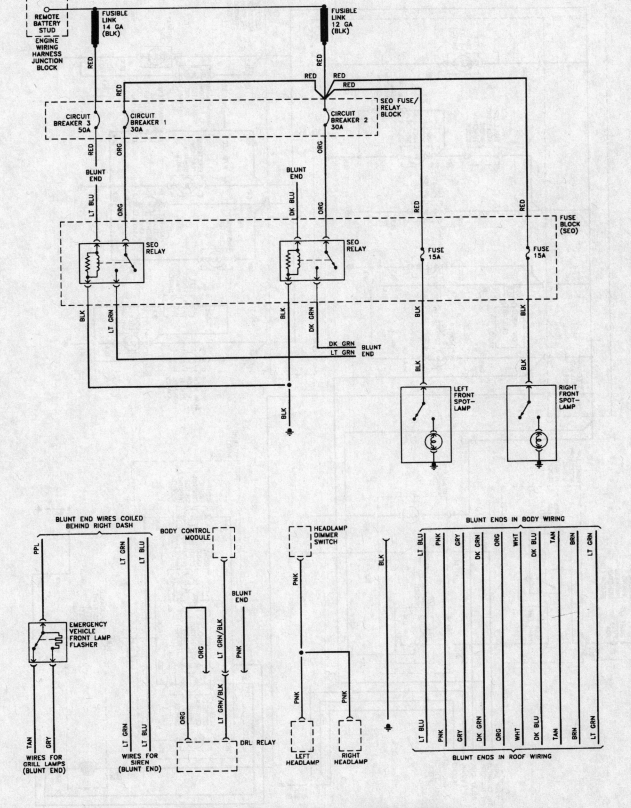

Typical 2000 and later police package exterior light system

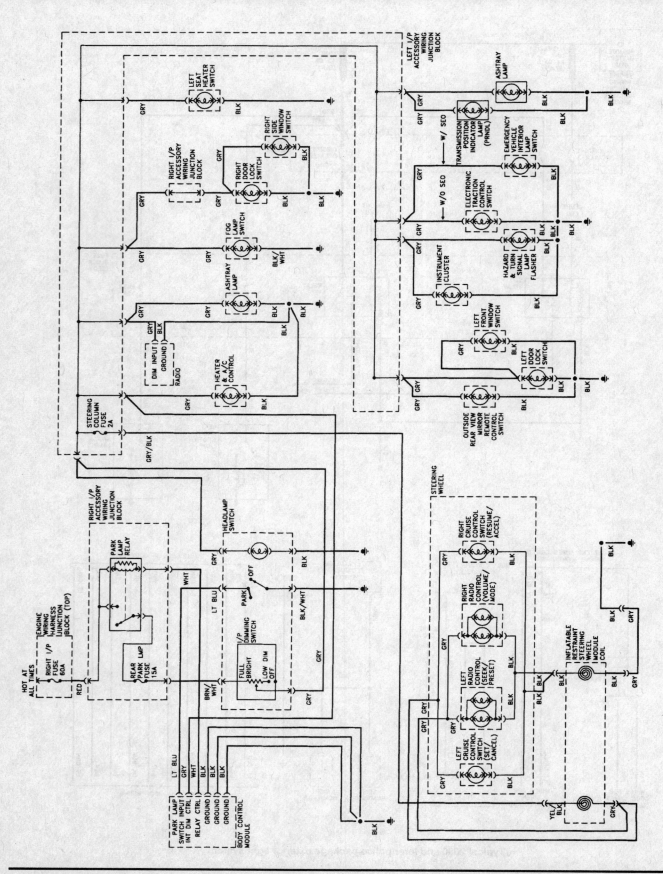

Typical 2000 and later interior and instrument light system

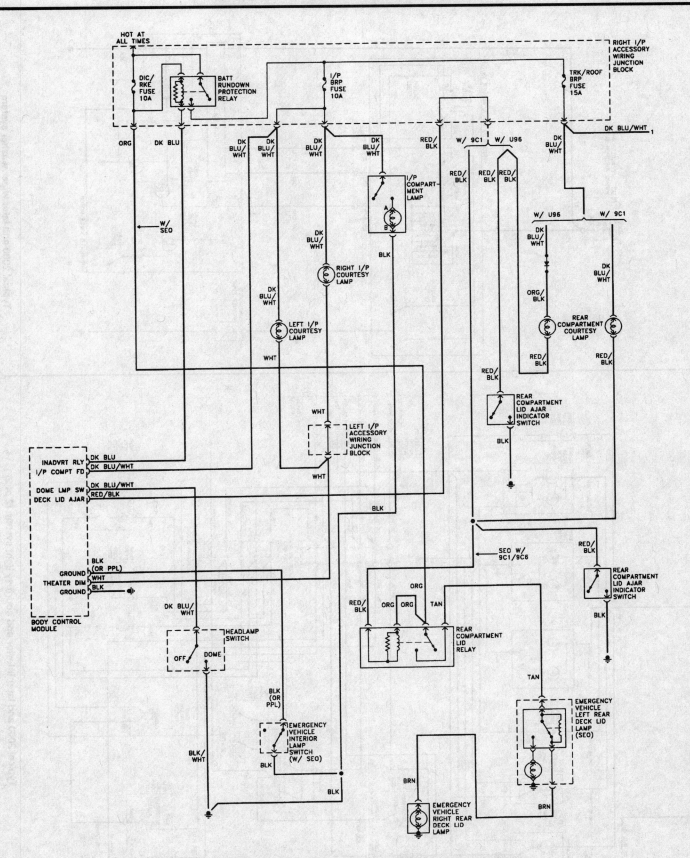

Typical 2000 and later interior and courtesy light system (1 of 2)

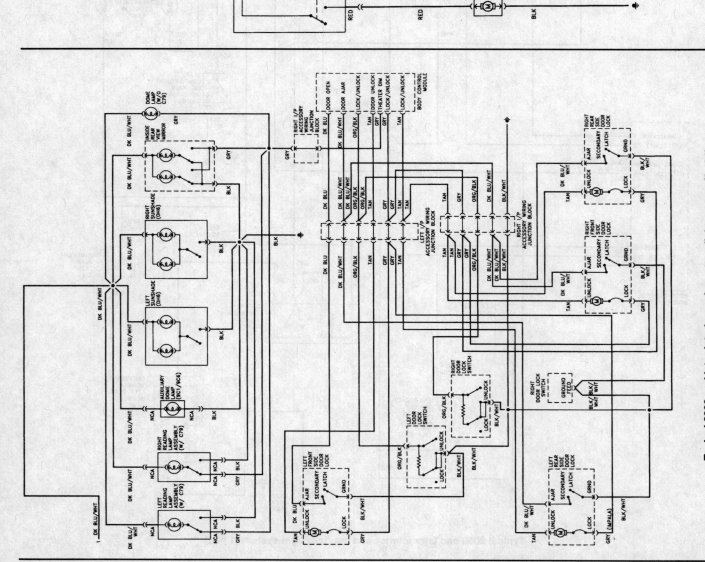

Typical 2000 and later wiper washer system

Typical 2000 and later interior and courtesy light system (2 of 2)

Index

Haynes Automotive Manuals

NOTE: If you do not see a listing for your vehicle, consult your local Haynes dealer for the latest product information.

ACURA
12020 Integra '86 thru '89 & Legend '86 thru '90
12021 Integra '90 thru '93 & Legend '91 thru '95
12050 Acura TL all models '99 thru '08

AMC
Jeep CJ - see JEEP (50020)
14020 Concord/Hornet/Gremlin/Spirit '70 thru '83
14025 (Renault) Alliance & Encore '83 thru '87

AUDI
15020 4000 all models '80 thru '87
15025 5000 all models '77 thru '83
15026 5000 all models '84 thru '88
15030 Audi A4 '02 thru '08

AUSTIN
Healey Sprite - see MG Midget (66015)

BMW
18020 3/5 Series '82 thru '92
18021 3 Series including Z3 models '92 thru '98
18022 3-Series '99 thru '05, including Z4 models
18025 320i all 4 cyl models '75 thru '83
18050 1500 thru 2002 except Turbo '59 thru '77

BUICK
19010 Buick Century '97 thru '05
Century (front-wheel drive) - see GM (38005)
19020 Buick, Oldsmobile & Pontiac Full-size
(Front wheel drive) '85 thru '05
19025 Buick, Oldsmobile & Pontiac Full-size
(Rear wheel drive) '70 thru '90
19030 Mid-size Regal & Century '74 thru '87
Regal - see GENERAL MOTORS (38010)
Skyhawk - see GM (38030)
Skylark - see GM (38020, 38025)
Somerset - see GENERAL MOTORS (38025)

CADILLAC
21030 Cadillac Rear Wheel Drive '70 thru '93
Cimarron, Eldorado & Seville - see
GM (38015, 38030, 38031)

CHEVROLET
10305 Chevrolet Engine Overhaul Manual
24010 Astro & GMC Safari Mini-vans '85 thru '05
24015 Camaro V8 all models '70 thru '81
24016 Camaro all models '82 thru '92, Cavalier -
see GM (38015), Celebrity - see GM (38005)
24017 Camaro & Firebird '93 thru '02
24020 Chevelle, Malibu, El Camino '69 thru '87
24024 Chevette & Pontiac T1000 '76 thru '87
Citation - see GENERAL MOTORS (38020)
24027 Colorado & GMC Canyon '04 thru '09
24032 Corsica/Beretta all models '87 thru '96
24040 Corvette all V8 models '68 thru '82
24041 Corvette all models '84 thru '96
24045 Full-size Sedans Caprice, Impala,
Biscayne, Bel Air & Wagons '69 thru '90
24046 Impala SS & Caprice and
Buick Roadmaster '91 thru '96
Lumina '90 thru '94 - see GM (38010)
24047 Impala & Monte Carlo all models '06 thru '08
24048 Lumina & Monte Carlo '95 thru '05
Lumina APV - see GM (38035)
24050 Luv Pick-up all 2WD & 4WD '72 thru '82
Malibu - see GM (38026)
24055 Monte Carlo all models '70 thru '88
Monte Carlo '95 thru '01 - see LUMINA
24059 Nova all V8 models '69 thru '79
24060 Nova/Geo Prizm '85 thru '92
24064 Pick-ups '67 thru '87 - Chevrolet & GMC,
all V8 & in-line 6 cyl, 2WD & 4WD '67 thru '87;
Suburbans, Blazers & Jimmys '67 thru '91
24065 Pick-ups '88 thru '98 - Chevrolet & GMC,
all full-size models '88 thru '98; C/K Classic
'99 & '00; Blazer & Jimmy '92 thru '94; Suburban
'92 thru '99; Tahoe & Yukon '95 thru '99
24066 Pick-ups '99 thru '06 - Chevrolet
Silverado & GMC Sierra '99 thru '06;
Suburban/Tahoe/Yukon/Yukon XL/Avalanche
'00 thru '06
24067 Chevrolet Silverado & GMC Sierra
'07 thru '09
24070 S-10 & GMC S-15 Pick-ups '82 thru '93
24071 S-10, Sonoma & Jimmy '94 thru '04
24072 Chevrolet TrailBlazer, GMC Envoy &
Oldsmobile Bravada '02 thru '09
24075 Sprint '85 thru '88, Geo Metro '89 thru '01
24080 Vans - Chevrolet & GMC '68 thru '96
24081 Chevrolet Express & GMC Savana
Full-size Vans '96 thru '07

CHRYSLER
10310 Chrysler Engine Overhaul Manual
25015 Chrysler Cirrus, Dodge Stratus,
Plymouth Breeze, '95 thru '00
25020 Full-size Front-Wheel Drive '88 thru '93
K-Cars - see DODGE Aries (30008)
Laser - see DODGE Daytona (30030)
25025 Chrysler LHS, Concorde & New Yorker,
Dodge Intrepid, Eagle Vision, '93 thru '97
25026 Chrysler LHS, Concorde, 300M,
Dodge Intrepid '98 thru '04
25027 Chrysler 300, Dodge Charger &
Magnum '05 thru '09
25030 Chrysler/Plym. Mid-size '82 thru '95
Rear-wheel Drive - see DODGE (30050)
25035 PT Cruiser all models '01 thru '09
25040 Chrysler Sebring/Dodge Avenger '95 thru '05,
Dodge Stratus '01 thru '05

DATSUN
28005 200SX all models '80 thru '83
28007 B-210 all models '73 thru '78
28009 210 all models '78 thru '82
28012 240Z, 260Z & 280Z Coupe '70 thru '78
28014 280ZX Coupe & 2+2 '79 thru '83
300ZX - see NISSAN (72010)
28018 510 & PL521 Pick-up '68 thru '73
28020 510 all models '78 thru '81
28022 620 Series Pick-up all models '73 thru '79
720 Series Pick-up - NISSAN (72030)
28025 810/Maxima all gas models, '77 thru '84

DODGE
400 & 600 - see CHRYSLER (25030)
30008 Aries & Plymouth Reliant '81 thru '89
30010 Caravan & Ply. Voyager '84 thru '95
30011 Caravan & Ply. Voyager '96 thru '02

30012 Challenger/Plymouth Saporro '78 thru '83
Challenger '67-'76 - see DART (30025)
30013 Caravan, Chrysler Voyager, Town &
Country '03 thru '07
30016 Colt/Plymouth Champ '78 thru '87
30020 Dakota Pick-ups all models '87 thru '96
30021 Durango '98 & '99, Dakota '97 thru '99
30022 Durango '00 thru '03, Dakota '00 thru '04
30023 Durango '04 thru '06, Dakota '05 and '06
30025 Dart, Challenger/Plymouth Barracuda
& Valiant 6 cyl models '67 thru '76
30030 Daytona & Chrysler Laser '84 thru '89
Intrepid - see Chrysler (25025, 25026)
30034 Dodge & Plymouth Neon '95 thru '99
30035 Omni & Plymouth Horizon '78 thru '90
30036 Dodge and Plymouth Neon '00 thru '05
30040 Pick-ups all full-size models '74 thru '93
30041 Pick-ups all full-size models '94 thru '01
30042 Pick-ups full-size models '02 thru '08
30045 Ram 50/D50 Pick-ups & Raider and
Plymouth Arrow Pick-ups '79 thru '93
30050 Dodge/Ply./Chrysler RWD '71 thru '89
30055 Shadow/Plymouth Sundance '87 thru '94
30060 Spirit & Plymouth Acclaim '89 thru '95
30065 Vans - Dodge & Plymouth '71 thru '03

EAGLE
Talon - see MITSUBISHI (68030, 68031)
Vision - see CHRYSLER (25025)

FIAT
34010 124 Sport Coupe & Spider '68 thru '78
34025 X1/9 all models '74 thru '80

FORD
10320 Ford Engine Overhaul Manual
10355 Ford Automatic Transmission Overhaul
36004 Aerostar Mini-vans '86 thru '97
Aspire - see FORD Festiva (36030)
36006 Contour/Mercury Mystique '95 thru '00
36008 Courier Pick-up all models '72 thru '82
36012 Crown Victoria & Mercury
Grand Marquis '88 thru '10
36016 Escort/Mercury Lynx '81 thru '90
36020 Escort/Mercury Tracer '91 thru '00
Expedition - see FORD Pick-up (36059)
36022 Escape & Mazda Tribute '01 thru '07
36024 Explorer & Mazda Navajo '91 thru '01
36025 Explorer/Mercury Mountaineer '02 thru '10
36028 Fairmont & Mercury Zephyr '78 thru '83
36030 Festiva & Aspire '88 thru '97
36032 Fiesta all models '77 thru '80
36034 Focus all models '00 thru '07
36036 Ford & Mercury Full-size '75 thru '87
36044 Ford & Mercury Mid-size '75 thru '86
36048 Mustang V8 all models '64-1/2 thru '73
36049 Mustang II 4 cyl, V6 & V8 '74 thru '78
36050 Mustang & Mercury Capri '79 thru '86
36051 Mustang all models '94 thru '04
36052 Mustang '05 thru '07
36054 Pick-ups and Bronco '73 thru '79
36058 Pick-ups and Bronco '80 thru '96
36059 F-150 & Expedition '97 thru '09, F-250
'97 thru '99 & Lincoln Navigator '98 thru '09
36060 Super Duty Pick-ups, Excursion '99 thru '10
36061 F-150 full-size '04 thru '09
36062 Pinto & Mercury Bobcat '75 thru '80
36066 Probe all models '89 thru '92
36070 Ranger/Bronco II gas models '83 thru '92
36071 Ford Ranger '93 thru '10 &
Mazda Pick-ups '94 thru '09
36074 Taurus & Mercury Sable '86 thru '95
36075 Taurus & Mercury Sable '96 thru '01
36078 Tempo & Mercury Topaz '84 thru '94
36082 Thunderbird/Mercury Cougar '83 thru '88
36086 Thunderbird/Mercury Cougar '89 thru '97
36090 Vans all V8 Econoline models '69 thru '91
36094 Vans full size '92 thru '10
36097 Windstar Mini-van '95 thru '07

GENERAL MOTORS
10360 GM Automatic Transmission Overhaul
38005 Buick Century, Chevrolet Celebrity,
Olds Cutlass Ciera & Pontiac 6000 '82 thru '96
38010 Buick Regal, Chevrolet Lumina,
Oldsmobile Cutlass Supreme & Pontiac
Grand Prix front wheel drive '88 thru '07
38015 Buick Skylark, Cadillac Cimarron,
Chevrolet Cavalier, Oldsmobile Firenza
Pontiac J-2000 & Sunbird '82 thru '94
38016 Chevrolet Cavalier/Pontiac Sunfire '95 thru '05
38017 Chevrolet Cobalt & Pontiac G5 '05 thru '09
38020 Buick Skylark, Chevrolet Citation,
Olds Omega, Pontiac Phoenix '80 thru '85
38025 Buick Skylark & Somerset, Olds Achieva,
Calais & Pontiac Grand Am '85 thru '98
38026 Chevrolet Malibu, Olds Alero & Cutlass,
Pontiac Grand Am '97 thru '03
38027 Chevrolet Malibu '04 thru '07
38030 Cadillac Eldorado & Oldsmobile
Toronado '71 thru '85, Seville '80 thru '85,
Buick Riviera '79 thru '85
38031 Cadillac Eldorado & Seville '86 thru '91,
DeVille & Buick Riviera '86 thru '93,
Fleetwood & Olds Toronado '86 thru '92
38032 DeVille '94 thru '05, Seville '92 thru '04
Cadillac DTS '06 thru '10
38035 Chevrolet Lumina APV, Oldsmobile
Silhouette & Pontiac Trans Sport '90 thru '96
38036 Chevrolet Venture, Olds Silhouette,
Pontiac Trans Sport & Montana '97 thru '05
General Motors Full-size
Rear-wheel Drive - see BUICK (19025)
38040 Chevrolet Equinox '05 thru '09
Pontiac Torrent '06 thru '09

GEO
Metro - see CHEVROLET Sprint (24075)
Prizm - see CHEVROLET (24060) or
TOYOTA (92036)
40030 Storm all models '90 thru '93
Tracker - see SUZUKI Samurai (90010)

GMC
Vans & Pick-ups - see CHEVROLET

HONDA
42010 Accord CVCC all models '76 thru '83
42011 Accord all models '84 thru '89
42012 Accord all models '90 thru '93
42013 Accord all models '94 thru '97
42014 Accord all models '98 thru '02

42015 Accord models '03 thru '07
42020 Civic 1200 all models '73 thru '79
42021 Civic 1300 & 1500 CVCC '80 thru '83
42022 Civic 1500 CVCC all models '75 thru '79
42023 Civic all models '84 thru '91
42024 Civic & del Sol '92 thru '95
42025 Civic '96 thru '00, CR-V '97 thru '01,
Acura Integra '94 thru '00
Passport - see ISUZU Rodeo (47017)
42026 Civic '01 thru '10, CR-V '02 thru '09
42035 Odyssey models '99 thru '04
42037 Honda Pilot '03 thru '07, Acura MDX '01 thru '07
42040 Prelude CVCC all models '79 thru '89

HYUNDAI
43010 Elantra all models '96 thru '06
43015 Excel & Accent all models '86 thru '09
43050 Santa Fe all models '01 thru '06
43055 Sonata all models '99 thru '08

ISUZU
Hombre - see CHEVROLET S-10 (24071)
47017 Rodeo, Amigo & Honda Passport '89 thru '02
47020 Trooper '84 thru '91, Pick-up '81 thru '93

JAGUAR
49010 XJ6 all 6 cyl models '68 thru '86
49011 XJ6 all models '88 thru '94
49015 XJ12 & XJS all 12 cyl models '72 thru '85

JEEP
50010 Cherokee, Comanche & Wagoneer
Limited all models '84 thru '01
50020 CJ all models '49 thru '86
50025 Grand Cherokee all models '93 thru '04
50026 Grand Cherokee '05 thru '09
50029 Grand Wagoneer & Pick-up '72 thru '91
50030 Wrangler all models '87 thru '08
50035 Liberty '02 thru '07

KIA
54070 Sephia '94 thru '01, Spectra '00 thru '09

LEXUS
ES 300 - see TOYOTA Camry (92007)

LINCOLN
Navigator - see FORD Pick-up (36059)
59010 Rear Wheel Drive all models '70 thru '10

MAZDA
61010 GLC (rear wheel drive) '77 thru '83
61011 GLC (front wheel drive) '81 thru '85
61015 323 & Protegé '90 thru '00
61016 MX-5 Miata '90 thru '09
61020 MPV all models '89 thru '98
Navajo - see FORD Explorer (36024)
61030 Pick-ups '72 thru '93
Pick-ups '94 on - see Ford (36071)
61035 RX-7 all models '79 thru '85
61036 RX-7 all models '86 thru '91
61040 626 (rear wheel drive) '79 thru '82
61041 626 & MX-6 (front wheel drive) '83 thru '92
61042 626 '93 thru '01, & MX-6/Ford Probe '93 thru '01

MERCEDES-BENZ
63012 123 Series Diesel '76 thru '85
63015 190 Series 4-cyl gas models, '84 thru '88
63020 230, 250 & 280 6 cyl sohc '68 thru '72
63025 280 123 Series gas models '77 thru '81
63030 350 & 450 all models '71 thru '80
63040 C-Class: C230/C240/C280/C320/C350 '01 thru '07

MERCURY
64200 Villager & Nissan Quest '93 thru '01
All other titles, see FORD listing.

MG
66010 MGB Roadster & GT Coupe '62 thru '80
66015 MG Midget & Austin Healey Sprite
Roadster '58 thru '80

MITSUBISHI
68020 Cordia, Tredia, Galant, Precis &
Mirage '83 thru '93
68030 Eclipse, Eagle Talon &
Plymouth Laser '90 thru '94
68031 Eclipse '95 thru '05, Eagle Talon '95 thru '98
68035 Galant '94 thru '03
68040 Pick-up '83 thru '96, Montero '83 thru '93

NISSAN
72010 300ZX all models incl. Turbo '84 thru '89
72011 350Z & Infiniti G35 all models '03 thru '08
72015 Altima all models '93 thru '06
72020 Maxima all models '85 thru '92
72021 Maxima all models '93 thru '01
72030 Pick-ups '80 thru '97, Pathfinder '87 thru '95
72031 Frontier Pick-up, Xterra, Pathfinder '96 thru '04
72032 Frontier & Xterra '05 thru '08
72040 Pulsar all models '83 thru '86
72050 Sentra all models '82 thru '94
72051 Sentra & 200SX all models '95 thru '06
72060 Stanza all models '82 thru '90
72070 Titan pick-ups '04 thru '09, Armada '05
thru '10

OLDSMOBILE
73015 Cutlass '74 thru '88
For other OLDSMOBILE titles, see
BUICK, CHEVROLET or GM listings.

PLYMOUTH
For PLYMOUTH titles, see DODGE.

PONTIAC
79008 Fiero all models '84 thru '88
79018 Firebird V8 models except Turbo '70 thru '81
79019 Firebird all models '82 thru '92
79025 G6 all models '05 thru '09
79040 Mid-size Rear-wheel Drive '70 thru '87
For other PONTIAC titles, see
BUICK, CHEVROLET or GM listings.

PORSCHE
80020 911 Coupe & Targa models '65 thru '89
80025 914 all 4 cyl models '69 thru '76
80030 924 all models incl. Turbo '76 thru '82
80035 944 all models incl. Turbo '83 thru '89

RENAULT
Alliance, Encore - see AMC (14020)

SAAB
84010 900 including Turbo '79 thru '88

SATURN
87010 Saturn all S-series models '91 thru '02
87011 Saturn Ion '03 thru '07
87020 Saturn all L-series models '00 thu '04
87040 Saturn VUE '02 thru '07

SUBARU
89002 1100, 1300, 1400 & 1600 '71 thru '79
89003 1600 & 1800 2WD & 4WD '80 thru '94
89100 Legacy models '90 thru '99
89101 Legacy & Forester '00 thru '06

SUZUKI
90010 Samurai/Sidekick/Geo Tracker '86 thru '01

TOYOTA
92005 Camry all models '83 thru '91
92006 Camry all models '92 thru '96
92007 Camry/Avalon/Solara/Lexus ES 300 '97 thru '01
92008 Toyota Camry, Avalon and Solara &
Lexus ES 300/330 all models '02 thru '06
92015 Celica Rear Wheel Drive '71 thru '85
92020 Celica Front Wheel Drive '86 thru '99
92025 Celica Supra all models '79 thru '92
92030 Corolla all models '75 thru '79
92032 Corolla rear wheel drive models '80 thru '87
92035 Corolla front wheel drive models '84 thru '92
92036 Corolla & Geo Prizm '93 thru '02
92037 Corolla models '03 thru '08
92040 Corolla Tercel all models '80 thru '82
92045 Corona all models '74 thru '82
92050 Cressida all models '78 thru '82
92055 Land Cruiser FJ40/43/45/55 '68 thru '82
92056 Land Cruiser FJ60/62/80/FZJ80 '80 thru '96
92060 Matrix & Pontiac Vibe '03 thru '08
92065 MR2 all models '85 thru '87
92070 Pick-up all models '69 thru '78
92075 Pick-up all models '79 thru '95
92076 Tacoma, 4Runner & T100 '93 thru '04
92077 Tacoma all models '05 thru '09
92078 Tundra '00 thru '06, Sequoia '01 thru '07
92079 4Runner all models '03 thru '09
92080 Previa all models '91 thru '95
92081 Prius '01 thru '08
92082 RAV4 all models '96 thru '05
92085 Tercel all models '87 thru '94
92090 Sienna all models '98 thru '09
92095 Highlander & Lexus RX-330 '99 thru '06

TRIUMPH
94007 Spitfire all models '62 thru '81
94010 TR7 all models '75 thru '81

VW
96008 Beetle & Karmann Ghia '54 thru '79
96009 New Beetle '98 thru '05
96016 Rabbit, Jetta, Scirocco, & Pick-up gas
models '75 thru '92 & Convertible '80 thru '92
96017 Golf, GTI & Jetta '93 thru '98, Cabrio '95 thru '02
96018 Golf, GTI & Jetta '99 thru '05
96020 Rabbit, Jetta, Pick-up diesel '77 thru '84
96023 Passat '98 thru '05, Audi A4 '96 thru '01
96030 Transporter 1600 all models '68 thru '79
96035 Transporter 1700, 1800, 2000 '72 thru '79
96040 Type 3 1500 & 1600 '63 thru '73
96045 Vanagon air-cooled models '80 thru '83

VOLVO
97010 120, 130 Series & 1800 Sports '61 thru '73
97015 140 Series all models '66 thru '74
97020 240 Series all models '76 thru '93
97040 740 & 760 Series all models '82 thru '88

TECHBOOK MANUALS
10205 Automotive Computer Codes
10206 OBD-II & Electronic Engine Management
10210 Automotive Emissions Control Manual
10215 Fuel Injection Manual, 1978 thru 1985
10220 Fuel Injection Manual, 1986 thru 1999
10225 Holley Carburetor Manual
10230 Rochester Carburetor Manual
10240 Weber/Zenith/Stromberg/SU Carburetor
10305 Chevrolet Engine Overhaul Manual
10310 Chrysler Engine Overhaul Manual
10320 Ford Engine Overhaul Manual
10330 GM and Ford Diesel Engine Repair
10333 Engine Performance Manual
10340 Small Engine Repair Manual
10345 Suspension, Steering & Driveline
10355 Automotive Transmission Overhaul
10360 GM Automatic Transmission Overhaul
10405 Automotive Body Repair & Painting
10410 Automotive Brake Manual
10415 Automotive Detailing Manual
10420 Automotive Electrical Manual
10425 Automotive Heating & Air Conditioning
10430 Automotive Reference Dictionary
10435 Automotive Tools Manual
10440 Used Car Buying Guide
10445 Welding Manual
10450 ATV Basics
10452 Scooters 50cc to 250cc

SPANISH MANUALS
98903 Reparación de Carrocería & Pintura
98904 Carburadores para los modelos Holley
& Rochester
98905 Códigos Automotrices de la Computadora
98910 Frenos Automotriz
98913 Electricidad Automotriz
98915 Inyección de Combustible 1986 al 1999
99040 Chevrolet & GMC Camionetas '67 al '87
99041 Chevrolet & GMC Camionetas '88 al '98
99042 Chevrolet Camionetas Cerradas '68 al '95
99043 Chevrolet/GMC Camionetas '94 al '04
99055 Dodge Caravan/Ply. Voyager '84 al '95
99075 Ford Camionetas y Bronco '80 al '94
99077 Ford Camionetas Cerradas '69 al '91
99088 Ford Modelos de Tamaño Mediano '75 al '86
99091 Ford Taurus & Mercury Sable '86 al '95
99095 GM Modelos de Tamaño Grande '70 al '90
99100 GM Modelos de Tamaño Mediano '70 al '88
99106 Jeep Cherokee, Wagoneer & Comanche '84 al '00
99110 Nissan Camionetas & Pathfinder '80 al '96
99118 Nissan Sentra '82 al '94
99125 Toyota Camionetas y 4-Runner '79 al '95

Over 100 Haynes
motorcycle manuals
also available

8-10

Haynes North America, Inc., 861 Lawrence Drive, Newbury Park, CA 91320 • (805) 498-6703 • http://www.haynes.com